Woodcock-Johnson Psycho-Educational Battery—Revised: Recommendations and Reports

Nancy Mather
and
Lynne Jaffe

Clinical Psychology Publishing Co., Inc.
4 Conant Square
Brandon, Vermont 05733

Library of Congress Catalog Card Number: 91-75518
ISBN: 0-88422-115-6

 4 Conant Square
Brandon, Vermont 05733

Cover Design: Michael F. Gauthier

Printed in the United States of America.

Fifth Printing, 1994

Permission to reprint all material from the *Woodcock-Johnson Psycho-Educational Battery—Revised* by R. W. Woodcock and M. B. Johnson has been generously granted by DLM. © 1979, 1989 DLM.

Acknowledgments

We are grateful to several individuals who contributed to this project. Our husbands, George and Brian, were constantly supportive and kept our lives going while we were submerged in this project. Our children, David, Benjamin, and Daniel, were a great incentive to finish this project A.S.A.P. David encouraged his Mommy to send the book far away to Africa. Our parents provided love, encouragement, and support. Ms. Jane Todorski, our production editor, sustained us with her humor, wit, and postcards. We would love to meet her—without having to write another book. Dr. Richard W. Woodcock provided helpful comments on the first draft of this manuscript. Mr. David McPhail helped prepare and typeset several charts. Ms. Mary Kord typeset and revised many figures. Dr. Anthony DeFeo, Ms. Ruth Jones, and Ms. Cindy Doyen of the University of Arizona Speech and Language Clinic provided valuable information and advice. Ms. Rose Daly-Rooney at the Arizona Center for the Law in the Public Interest helped summarize the laws governing the provision of special services to people with disabilities. Thanks to Ms. Edith Jaffe for preparation of the study guide and to Drs. Julie Reichmann and June Downing for their suggestions regarding recommendations for individuals with sensory impairments. Thanks also to Dr. Candace Bos, Ms. Connie McDonald, Ms. Melissa Moffitt, Ms. Margaret Patterson, Dr. Dan McDonnell, Ms. Kathy Anderson, Ms. Julie Aasen, and Ms. Judi Macdonald for their contributions to the diagnostic reports. We appreciate our colleagues' encouragement and requests that we *finish* this book so that they could use it. We are indebted to Drs. Samuel A. Kirk, Richard W. Woodcock, William C. Healey, and Candace S. Bos for their instruction, guidance, and support throughout our careers. The authors would like to thank each other for a friendship that is still intact.

We have referenced all published materials and methods. Many of the ideas for recommendations, however, are not original, but were gathered from our experiences working with students with special needs. We would like to thank all of the educators who developed ideas for promoting student success in educational settings and to express gratitude to the teachers who implement these ideas.

CONTENTS

CONTENTS

CONTENTS

viii

CONTENTS

LIST OF FIGURES

INTRODUCTION

This reference book is intended to serve as a resource for evaluators using the *Woodcock-Johnson Psycho-Educational Battery—Revised* (WJ-R) (Woodcock & Johnson, 1989) in educational and clinical settings. Its purpose is to assist examiners in preparing and writing psychoeducational reports for individuals of all ages. The book is divided into three sections and an Appendix.

In the first section, a wide variety of educational recommendations are provided for the cognitive factors, oral language, and the achievement areas of reading, written language, mathematics, and knowledge/content. Additional recommendations are provided for attention, behavior management, social skills/self-esteem, and for students with sensory impairments.

The second section provides a brief discussion on writing behavioral objectives. The purpose of this section is to help classroom teachers and educational therapists convert recommendations from a psychoeducational report into measurable goals and objectives that may be used to monitor student progress.

The third section presents diagnostic reports that illustrate applications of the WJ-R in educational and clinical settings. These diagnostic reports depict a variety of learning problems in individuals of different age levels. Although information obtained from other diagnostic instruments is integrated into some sample reports, the emphasis here is placed on presenting and interpreting information from the WJ-R.

The Appendix contains summaries, arranged alphabetically, of methods and techniques that were included in the recommendations or the diagnostic reports. These types of summaries may be attached to a psychoeducational report so that classroom or special education teachers, tutors, or parents may implement the recommended procedure.

PART I
RECOMMENDATIONS

1

RECOMMENDATIONS: INTRODUCTION

The following recommendations have been arranged by skill and subskill area. Although an attempt has been made not to duplicate recommendations, some of the recommendations are appropriate for more than one skill area and so the reader is directed to related sections. As examples, many of the recommendations for reading comprehension are also appropriate for written language or content area instruction, and many of the recommendations under auditory processing are also appropriate for development of word attack and spelling skills. Wherever possible, the recommendations are ordered in a developmental sequence, progressing from the more elementary to the more advanced requirements of a skill. Depending upon the severity of the problem, an older student may profit from recommendations at the readiness or beginning level of a skill. Conversely, a student advanced in an area may benefit from higher-level recommendations.

Before writing recommendations, an evaluator must consider the referral question, analyze the results of diagnostic testing, and assess the specific needs of a student within an educational setting. The goal is to select specific modifications and interventions that will enhance an individual's opportunities for success. The evaluator should also identify the person who would implement the recommendation and then adapt the wording accordingly. For example, an evaluator may make recommendations directly to a student or client, such as: "You should arrange appointments with each of your teachers at the beginning of each semester." Or, a recommendation may be made to the student's teacher, parents, or counselor, such as: "Help Mark arrange appointments with his teachers at the beginning of each semester." For some evaluation reports, the examiner may wish to organize the Recommendation section by the person responsible for implementation (e.g., teacher, parent, student).

After identifying the areas of concern, an examiner may read through a section of recommendations and select those appropriate for a particular student. In most instances, the recommendations have been written for providing individualized instruction, but they could easily be adapted to emphasize small group instruction. All of the recommendations may be modified, rewritten, or combined, as needed. Based upon assessment results and consideration of the specific circumstances, evaluators will create other recommendations. For this purpose, space is left at the end of each chapter for recording additional ideas.

Many excellent techniques and programs are available for teaching individuals with learning difficulties. This collection of recommendations is not meant to be exhaustive. The recommendations included in this handbook are ones that the authors and their colleagues have used successfully in teaching students or that the authors learned about while researching this handbook. Consequently, failure to mention a specific technique or program should not be interpreted as a lack of endorsement. Additional descriptions of a variety of remedial techniques may be found in *An Instructional Guide to the Woodcock-Johnson Psycho-Educational Battery—Revised* (Mather, 1991).

2

COGNITIVE FACTORS

Long-Term Retrieval

Review/Retention

1. When teaching the student facts, introduce only as much information as s/he is able to master in a session.

2. Before requiring automaticity or rapid recall of facts, make sure that the student understands and is able to demonstrate the underlying concepts.

3. Ensure that the student understands the concept underlying any new information or skill, as well as how each part or aspect of the new information is related to every other part.

4. When teaching the student factual information, provide as much review and repetition as needed for mastery.

5. In each teaching session, before introducing new information to the student, review previous information from the last lesson and check for mastery.

6. To promote mastery, provide the student with regular, then intermittent, reinforcement of any skills or content being learned.

7. When teaching the student new skills, provide frequent opportunities for practice and review. Provide systematic review within a few hours and for the next few days and then slowly fade review. Check retention after a week without review.

Multisensory Instruction

1. As much as possible, present all new information so that the student simultaneously hears and sees what s/he is expected to learn.

2. Provide the student with multisensory learning experiences. Use visual, auditory, tactile, and kinesthetic channels to reinforce learning whenever possible.

3. To improve retention, provide the student with multisensory activities that involve visual, auditory, tactile, and kinesthetic channels. For example, when the student is learning spelling words, have him/her trace the word as s/he pronounces it and then write the word from memory.

Strategies

1. Teach the student specific memory strategies and how to recognize which strategy may be most useful in a variety of situations. Examples include: using

verbal rehearsal, chunking, making ridiculous visual images composed of items that one has to remember, and creating mnemonics.

2. Help the student learn that any new piece of information that is clearly associated with something you already know is easier to remember (Lorayne & Lucas, 1974). Help him/her learn to form relationships, organize information, and integrate new with prior knowledge.

3. Teach the student that the memory process involves three stages: registration, retention, and retrieval. Registration requires AID (*a*ttention, *i*nterest, and *d*esire). Retention requires the intensification of meaning and may be accomplished by using the techniques of association, visualization, or organization. Retrieval is facilitated by rehearsal or a cue (i.e., anything that can trigger memory recall, such as visual imagery) (Herold, 1982).

4. To increase retention of information, teach the student to create a visual image of what s/he hears.

5. When introducing new information and skills, provide the student with pictures to look at or a way to visualize and form associations regarding what s/he is learning.

6. Use graphic organizers to teach new concepts and information. When the student can picture how the ideas are interrelated, s/he will be able to store and retrieve them more easily.

7. The student will understand and retain all types of information best if verbal information is presented in association with visual stimuli such as pictures, charts, graphs, semantic maps, and videotapes.

8. When presenting the student with tasks involving several steps, provide a list of steps on an index card to help the student recall procedural knowledge.

9. Teach the student a simple strategy to aid in recall. One example is the PAR formula, *P*icture it, *A*ssociate it, and *R*eview it. This may be combined with the USA formula guide for clear visualization: *U* = *U*nusual, unforgettable; *S* = *S*ee the picture as vividly as you can using as many senses as you can; *A* = *A*ction, see the item happening with action (Herold, 1982). Provide practice in systematic storing and retrieving of information.

10. Teach the student the technique of forming associative images to recall information. Have the student create a visual scenario that depicts strange or ridiculous interactions among the information to be remembered. Encourage the student to use as many senses as possible to create vivid pictures. Have the student practice retrieving the relevant information.

11. Use the keyword method to help the student learn new vocabulary (Mastropieri, 1988). Three steps are used: recoding, relating, and retrieving. For recoding, the student changes the new vocabulary word into a known word, the keyword, that has a similar sound and is easily pictured. For relating, the student associates the keyword with the definition of the new vocabulary word through a mental image or a sentence. For retrieving, the student thinks of the keyword, remembers the association, and then retrieves the definition.

12. Teach the student how to use a first-letter mnemonic strategy to make facts easier to remember. With this strategy, have the student learn to make up words, phrases, or sentences based on the first letter of the items to be remembered. If this information is needed for a test, teach the student to write the mnemonic at the top of the test, as soon as s/he gets a copy. This strategy is useful for improving ability to recall lists of information (Nelson & Archer, 1972).

13. Teach the student how to use a substitute word concept for memorizing abstract material. When s/he hears a word that seems abstract, have him/her think of something that sounds like or reminds him/her of the word and can be easily pictured mentally. For example, s/he may remember the state, Minnesota, as a "mini soda." Teach him/her how to form a link, or another association, with the next word or concept that s/he is trying to remember (Lorayne & Lucas, 1974).

14. Teach the student how to use a number-rhyme system when s/he has to memorize information. Each number from 1 to 12 has a rhyme associated with it. Have the student memorize the numbers and their rhymes or make up and memorize his/her own keywords: 1 - bun, 2 - glue, 3 - tree, 4 - door, 5 - dive, 6 - bricks, 7 - heaven, 8 - gate, 9 - wine, 10 - tent, 11 - elephant, 12 - shelf (Herold, 1982). Teach him/her how to incorporate and visualize the information that s/he is trying to memorize with the number rhymes. For example, if the student were

trying to memorize the 3 Cs of Arizona industry, copper, cattle, and cotton, s/he may picture a hamburger bun, made of copper, and cattle with their hooves glued to the ground, standing under a tree that produces big cotton flowers.

15. Teach the student to use a body-file system to help in remembering information. Retrieval cues for this mental filing system are body parts and locations. Have the student begin with the first six cues, body parts, from the top of the head to the tip of the toes: hair, nose, mouth, hands, pocket, foot. Have the student repeat and touch each place, until s/he can mentally visualize the six places without any touching. The next six places are spaces around the body that make an uncompleted circle: left, front, right, back, above, and below. Have the student memorize and practice the body spaces. Make sure that the student can visualize the 12 file places in the correct sequence. As s/he associates information, teach him/her to use action ideas with each of the body-file places. For example, an item s/he is trying to remember could be stuck in his/her hair or blowing his/her hair around (Herold, 1982).

Short-Term Memory

(Related Sections: Hearing Impairment, Oral Language)

Following Directions

1. Seat the student in the front row of the classroom or as close to the teacher as possible to reduce distractions and increase his/her ability to attend to oral directions.

2. Secure the student's attention before giving him/her oral instructions. Limit your instructions to two or three steps. When you are finished, ask the student: "What are you going to do?" or "How many things do you have to do?"

3. Make sure you have the student's attention before speaking to him/her. If you are giving a series of oral directions, ask the student to repeat them, or, if the directions are lengthy (such as a list of chores for the weekend or steps to accomplish in a project), ask the student to write them down.

4. Prior to giving directions, make certain that the student has secured the relevant materials. For example, when explaining the directions on a worksheet, make sure that the student is looking at the assignment.

5. When the student is not listening to directions, use a signal to cue him/her, such as placing your hand on his/her shoulder.

6. Give only one simple direction to the student at a time. Allow him/her to complete the direction before adding another step. For example, you may say: "Please take out your spelling book." Wait until the student has the spelling book out and then say: "Please turn to page 15."

7. When giving instructions to the student, use brief simple sentences that are sequenced in the order of the tasks.

8. Teach the student to count the number of tasks or instructions, tell you how many, and repeat them as s/he touches his/her fingers, one instruction to a finger. If s/he repeats the tasks correctly, provide positive feedback. Increase the number of directions as appropriate.

9. When giving directions for a task or assignment, write the steps on the board so that the student can review directions as much as needed.

10. When the student asks for directions to be repeated, repeat the directions using the same words, so that s/he will not have to process new information.

11. Encourage the student to request help when s/he does not understand directions or has missed part of the instructions.

12. When giving directions, stop at various points to ensure that the student is understanding you. When speaking to the entire class, make frequent eye contact with the student.

13. When giving the student directions, incorporate nonverbal input and visual reinforcement as much as possible. For example, use gestures, draw on the board, or model the steps of a process.

14. When giving directions for an assignment, have another student write down the steps on an index card.

15. Set up a buddy system. Seat the student next to a responsible peer who will review directions with the student and answer any questions the s/he has.

16. When giving oral directions within an activity, provide enough time for the student to accomplish the direction before going on. For example, when giving a spelling test, after you have asked the student to number his/her paper, wait until s/he is finished before beginning to read the words. When you go back over the correct spellings, provide 2–3 seconds of check-time after providing the correct spellings.

17. Prior to transitions, help the student and other students by giving clear directions. For example, all students might be required to stay seated and quiet while you present the directions in the order they are to be followed. When you have completed the directions, say: "Go ahead."

18. Teach the student specific behaviors that will help him/her follow oral directions, such as listening carefully, writing down important points, asking questions, and waiting to start a task until all directions have been completed.

19. If the student is to follow several directions, encourage him/her to visualize or form a mental picture of what s/he is going to do prior to beginning the tasks.

Strategies/Compensations

1. Discuss with the student what strategies s/he uses to help recall information. Help him/her identify and learn other strategies to enhance recall.

2. Because of difficulty with tasks requiring rote memory, provide the student with compensations as needed, such as a calculator to use in math.

3. Provide the student with as much review and repetition as needed for mastery.

4. Have the student put a colored rubber band on his/her wrist or tie a string around his/her finger as a reminder of a task that s/he is supposed to do. Have the student remove the rubber band or piece of string as soon as the task is completed.

5. To help the student recall information, provide initial instruction using concrete objects and present items grouped by categories.

6. To teach or reinforce the use of visual imagery, play memory games with the student, such as: "Grandmother went on a trip and in her suitcase she took . . ." or "Simon Says."

7. Teach the student to make a list of tasks s/he wishes to accomplish by drawing simple pictures. For example, if s/he wants to remember to get a book from the library, the student would draw a simple picture of a book.

8. Teach the student to make a list of tasks s/he wishes to accomplish. Have him/her write one keyword for each task (e.g., *bed* for "make the bed," *bath* for "take a bath").

9. Teach the student to use verbal rehearsal for instructions that s/he has to remember for only a short time. Initially, give no more than two instructions. When s/he can routinely complete all the tasks without reminders, increase the number of instructions to three.

10. Train the student to use verbal rehearsal for information that s/he has to remember for only a short time. For example, when trying to remember a phone number long enough to dial it, have the student repeat the number over and over until s/he is finished dialing.

11. Provide the student with practice in reading short, simple stories and then recalling the events in sequential order.

12. Help the student develop systematic ways to keep track of and organize materials. For example, help him/her create an assignment notebook for recording all homework and test dates.

13. Teach the student specific strategies to aid in recall. (See Long-Term Retrieval section for examples.)

14. Teach the student how to request the specific compensations s/he needs for tasks requiring short-term memory.

Listening

1. When listening to lectures, help the student learn to recognize common words for ordering a sequence of instructions, such as "first," "next," and "finally."

2. Teach the student a strategy for active listening. One example is to teach him/her to observe a speaker's verbal cues by attending to keywords that signal that important information is about to be given, such as: "first," "more important," or "in summary."

3. When the student is required to learn information for a test, direct his/her attention to the material to be remembered. For example, say: "This next information is very important and I would like you to learn it."

4. Provide the student with a copy of the notes of a student who is a particularly good note-taker. This will allow the student to give his/her complete attention to the speaker.

5. Encourage the student to tape-record class lectures. Teach him/her how to take notes as s/he listens to the tape. Have him/her hit the pause button as s/he writes notes and rewind the tape whenever clarification is needed.

Processing Speed

Adjusting Time Requirements

1. Do not require the student to work under time pressure. Place the emphasis in evaluation on accuracy rather than speed.

2. Because the student has difficulty performing tasks rapidly under pressure, provide him/her with ample time to complete work or shorten the assignments so they can be accomplished within the alloted time.

3. The student may need extra time to complete reading, math, or writing tasks. Make sure s/he is allowed this time in a way that does not bring negative attention to him/her.

4. Provide the student with activities designed to increase his/her rate of production, such as recording the starting and stopping time on an assignment or using a stopwatch or timer to increase response rate.

5. Reduce the amount of work the student is required to do during independent seatwork assignments so that s/he is likely to complete his/her work in school.

6. Allow the student to take unfinished work home to complete so that the quality of work is not compromised by his/her working rate. Monitor that the student does not consistently have to spend more time on homework than the other students.

Visual Scanning/Copying

1. Provide the student with extra visual structure on worksheets and assignments. For example, arrange problems in numbered boxes or columns.

2. When the class is doing seatwork, periodically pass the student's desk to make sure s/he has not inadvertently skipped items. If s/he has, point out the missed items.

3. Provide the student with an index card or a bookmark to help keep his/her place when reading.

4. Provide the student with an index card or marker to use during standardized tests that require shading in circles.

5. Limit near- or far-point copying activities. When copying is necessary, do not require speed or accuracy.

6. Do not require the student to copy problems from his/her math or other textbooks. Instead, provide him/her with clear worksheets that contain only a few problems and plenty of white space.

7. When the student has to copy material from the chalkboard, allow him/her to move to the front of the room.

8. Teach the student to use verbal mediation when s/he copies material from the chalkboard. Have him/her say each letter, word, or phrase as s/he copies it from the board to his/her paper.

Auditory Processing

(Related Sections: Word Attack, Spelling, Hearing Impairment)

Further Evaluation

1. Refer the student to the speech/language pathologist for a more comprehensive evaluation.

2. Based upon extreme weaknesses in auditory processing and a history of early ear infections, refer the student to the speech/language pathologist for a more comprehensive evaluation.

3. The student's weaknesses in auditory processing and reading skills may be indicators of a language disorder. A full language evaluation should be conducted by a speech/language pathologist.

Compensations

1. Provide the student with preferential seating so that s/he can easily see your face when you are speaking.

2. When you speak, face the student, enunciate clearly, and have the student watch your mouth as the sounds are made. Pause between clauses or ideas.

3. Encourage the student to tape-record all important lectures so that s/he may listen to and write down the significant points at a later date.

4. Provide the student with visual outlines and graphic organizers for tasks involving listening.

5. Because of a deficit in auditory processing, the student may have difficulty listening to lectures and taking class notes. When possible, provide him/her with visual aids and a note-taker for all listening activities.

6. Because of a deficit in auditory processing, do not require the student to take a foreign language in high school or college.

Rhyming

1. To help the student increase his/her phonological awareness, play games that focus on the sounds of words. These include rhyming games and songs, thinking of words that start with a particular sound, and counting the "beats" (syllables) of words.

2. Play rhyming games with the student. Give him/her a clue and then have him/her generate a rhyming word. For example, you might say: "I'm thinking of what you check out at a library that rhymes with the word 'took'" or "I'm thinking of an animal that rhymes with the word 'log.'"

3. Read the student pairs of words and have him/her tell you whether the words rhyme or do not rhyme.

4. Show the student an array of pictures and have him/her match the pictures whose names rhyme. Later, show him/her pictures and ask him/her to tell you a rhyming word.

5. Show the student common pictures and ask him/her to identify a word that rhymes with the picture.

6. Have the student complete familiar nursery rhymes with the appropriate rhyming words.

7. Encourage the student to play with language sounds. For example, ask him/her to name five words that rhyme with "cat" and then have him/her ask you to name five words that rhyme with another word.

8. Read predictable books aloud to the student that emphasize rhyming words, such as the Dr. Seuss books. Have the student say back or read back the rhymes.

9. Teach the student poems, emphasizing the rhyming words. Use an oral cloze procedure to practice the poem. Play a game in which you recite the poem and pause before the end of each line. Have the student supply the missing word.

Auditory Analysis Skills

1. Help the student to improve his/her auditory analysis skills. For example, teach him/her to tap out the "rhythm" of a word when counting the number of syllables. Help him/her learn to identify which sound in a word is heard first, second, etc.

2. Have the student clap hands for the number of words s/he hears in sentences. Have him/her clap hands for the number of syllables s/he hears in a word.

3. When teaching the student to analyze words into syllables, have him/her place a hand over his/her mouth to feel and count the lip movements.

4. To help the student increase his/her facility with sounds, use the *Auditory Discrimination in Depth* training program (Lindamood & Lindamood, 1975), a multisensory program designed to help students develop prerequisite auditory processing skills for reading and spelling.

5. Provide the student with many opportunities to see how language sounds relate to written language. For example, when writing words on the chalkboard, pronounce them slowly and enunciate each sound as it is recorded.

6. Using manipulatives, such as letter tiles from a Scrabble game or magnetic letters, teach the student how to build words from individual sounds, as well as how to break them apart.

7. Using manipulatives, teach the student a common cluster, such as "at." Form new words by changing the initial consonant. Have the student pronounce the new word.

8. When working with counting the number of words in sentences, or of syllables or sounds in words, use visual representations, such as colored tiles or poker chips. As an alternative activity, have

the student move a token along a sequence of squares that represents the correct number of words, syllables, or sounds. Have the student pronounce the corresponding word, syllable, or sound as s/he pushes forward the token.

9. Devise activities that reinforce the student's ability to discriminate between "real" and "silly" (nonsense) words.

10. Write a familiar word on a piece of paper. Have the student say the word. Without changing the word, alter various letters, both consonants and vowels, and ask the student how the new word would be pronounced. For example, you may write the word *sank* and ask the student what the word would be if you changed the "s" to a "t," or the "a" to an "i," or the "n" to a "c," etc. If necessary, have the student write the new word to aid in pronunciation.

11. Play games to increase phonological awareness and knowledge of sound–symbol correspondence. For example, number a paper from 1 to 10 (or any other number). Write a short, phonically regular word. Pass the paper to the student and ask him/her to form a new word by just changing one letter. Letters may be inserted, omitted, or rearranged. If the student cannot think of a word, provide as much assistance as needed. After s/he writes a word, s/he returns the paper to you. Continue until ten words are written. When finished, have the student read the list of words.

12. To remediate the mispronunciations that may be attributable to the student's auditory processing weakness, introduce all new vocabulary words visually, specifically pointing out individual sounds/letters and word parts. Emphasize their sequence. Have the student learn to write the word as well as pronounce it. Provide ample practice in saying the word without the visual cue.

13. Dictate short words with regular sound–symbol correspondence for the student to write. Pronounce words slowly so that the student can hear the separate phonemes. Have him/her pronounce each sound as s/he writes the letter or letter combinations.

14. Help the student develop the metalinguistic skills that are important to the development of early reading and spelling skills. These skills include sound blending, putting sounds together to form words, phonemic analysis, breaking words apart into their component sounds, and segmentation, breaking sentences into words and words into a sequence of syllables or sounds.

Auditory Closure/Sound Blending

1. Train the student in auditory closure, first using familiar words with sounds omitted and later using printed words with letters or syllables omitted. Finally, present partial words in printed sentences so the student may use context clues.

2. Provide the student with direct instruction in sound blending using the following steps: (a) have the student say the word, (b) present the word with prolonged sounds but no break between the sounds and ask the student to say the word, (c) present the sounds with a short break between them and ask the student to say the word, (d) present the word with a quarter-second, then half-second, then 1-second break between the sounds, with the student saying the word after each presentation (Kirk, Kirk, & Minskoff, 1985).

3. Teach the student how to blend three sounds into a syllable or word. Add sounds until s/he is able to blend a consonant-blend-vowel-consonant-blend pattern.

4. Based upon his/her facility with tasks involving phonological awareness, use a phonics approach with the student to increase his/her reading skill.

5. Provide the student with direct instruction in sound blending. If s/he cannot develop skill in sound blending, select a nonphonic approach for beginning reading instruction.

6. Teach and emphasize development of abilities in analyzing and synthesizing the sounds and syllables of words.

Visual Processing

1. Provide opportunities for the student to play with blocks, puzzles, and other manipulatives.

2. Provide the student with activities that require classification. For example, have him/her sort a variety of objects by different attributes, such as size, shape, or color.

3. Have the student trace over a variety of geometric shapes using a crayon on a plastic overlay.

4. Have the student look at objects that have a missing part. Have him/her identify and add the missing part.

5. To increase the student's attention to visual detail, play games such as Concentration. The cards are turned over and the players attempt to locate matching pairs. Directly teach the student how to look for details.

6. Encourage the student to participate in activities that have elements of visual problem solving and manual manipulation, such as chess, designing and building, and art projects.

7. Encourage the student to talk him/herself through tasks that are visually based, such as reorganizing the furniture in his/her room or drawing a map of the school playground.

8. Provide activities that will increase the student's attention to visual detail. For example, have him/her interpret and describe the elements of a picture or locate objects hidden in a background.

9. To take advantage of the student's good awareness of visual details, use visual displays in the classroom when illustrating key points.

10. Provide the student with practice in reading charts, diagrams, and graphs.

11. Provide the student with activities that will allow him/her to use his/her excellent mechanical skills.

12. Consider the student's superior visual processing skills when providing career and vocational counseling.

Comprehension/Knowledge

(See: Knowledge/Content Areas, Oral Language)

Fluid Reasoning

1. Help the student learn to use his/her excellent reasoning skills and conceptual ability to overcome difficulties with memory. Provide him/her with meaningful activities that will involve finding solutions to problems, understanding and applying rules, and predicting logical conclusions.

2. When teaching the student any new process or skill, provide slow, step-by-step instruction. Use manipulatives and concrete objects whenever possible to illustrate the concepts.

3. Do not introduce abstract concepts until you are sure the student has mastered the prerequisite skills.

4. Create opportunities for the student to teach concepts to younger students.

5. Provide reasoning problems in areas where the student possesses expertise so that s/he can draw on background knowledge to help him/her solve problems.

6. Select materials to use with the student that will promote logical thinking. Help him/her develop strategies to solve the problems. A variety of materials and computer software to promote thinking skills are available from Midwest Publishing Company, P.O. Box 448, Pacific Grove, CA 93950.

7. Use the Hilda Taba Critical Thinking Strategies to teach the student. These group-oriented, highly interactive strategies raise students' level of thinking and problem solving from dealing with concrete information to making valid and supported generalizations. An updated, organized description of these strategies may be found in *A Comprehensive Approach to Teaching Thinking* (Schiever, 1991).

8. When working with tasks that involve problem solving, provide the student with a list of steps to follow written on an index card.

9. Teach the student how to analyze tasks into their component steps and then to sequence the steps. Directly teach generalization to a variety of tasks such as writing a research paper or planning a trip.

10. Provide the student with practice in using problem-solving strategies that are generalizable to a variety of situations. Include the following steps: deciding what the problem is and what the best outcome would be; brainstorming possible solutions; considering which solutions are feasible; considering the positive and negative outcomes of each of the solutions; choosing the solution that seems best; trying it; asking if it is working; and modifying it or selecting a different solution if the strategy does not work.

11. Teach the student a specific strategy to use for solving problems, such as one that includes defining the problem, task analysis, brainstorming alternative solutions, considering possible outcomes, choosing a solution, etc. Provide practice in application of the strategy in a variety of situations.

12. Review the problem-solving strategy that the student is learning. When you are with the student, use it yourself to solve everyday problems. Say the steps aloud as you perform the task. Help the student use the strategy to solve real problems.

13. Even when the final solutions or answers are incorrect, provide the student with encouragement and praise for persistence in problem solving and attempts to discover a solution.

14. Encourage creative thinking by providing the student with a variety of different activities, such as provided on the 64 cards in the *Creative Whack Pack*. Available from: Roger von Oech, Creative Think, Box 7354, Menlo Park, CA 94026, (415) 321-6775.

15. Integrate higher-level thinking skills into daily lessons. Good resources for activities that foster self-directed thinking are *Catch Them Thinking: A Handbook of Classroom Strategies* (Bellanca & Fogarty, 1986), *Creating the Thoughtful Classroom: Strategies to Promote Student Thinking* (Udall & Daniels, 1991), and *A Comprehensive Approach to Teaching Thinking* (Schiever, 1991). These books present strategies that may be used to teach thinking skills in all classes.

16. Help the student increase his/her ability to understand verbal analogies. Have the student infer the relationships among the pairs of words. Discuss the relationships with the student.

17. Help the student select courses in high school that emphasize practical and experiential learning and do not require a high level of abstract reasoning.

Quantitative Ability

(See: Mathematics)

Additional Ideas:

3

ORAL LANGUAGE

The following recommendations focus particularly on language skills directly related to school readiness and classroom functioning. Recommendations specifically pertinent to the academic areas of reading, written language, mathematics, and knowledge are found in those sections. Recommendations for language remediation for an individual with a specific language impairment should be generated in conjunction with the speech/language pathologist. Evaluators and teachers using the following recommendations should be aware of the linguistic and metalinguistic ability levels required for the student to benefit from the selected recommendations.

Further Evaluation

1. Request a full language evaluation by a speech/language pathologist that will include the assessment of receptive and expressive language skills. Specifically request that a language sample be obtained.

2. To evaluate the severity and nature of the student's language impairment more specifically, provide diagnostic therapy with a speech/language pathologist experienced in working with (preschool, school-age) children. The therapy should focus on (specify area of concern).

3. To establish whether or not the language level of the student's textbooks is above the student's receptive language level, select a variety of passages from the textbook in question. Establish a purpose for reading, introduce the vocabulary, read the passage to the student, and ask him/her comprehension questions.

General

1. Consult a speech/language pathologist for recommendations on oral language development and effective teaching approaches for the student.

2. Provide the student language therapy with a speech/language pathologist for a minimum of ( ) hour(s) daily (weekly).

3. Provide consultation to the parent and the student's (preschool) teacher with a speech/language pathologist for specific ways to enhance language development.

4. Establish a system of communication between the school (preschool) and home whereby vocabulary and language forms the student is learning or beginning to use will be mutually encouraged and reinforced.

5. Educate the student's teacher(s) as to the nature of the student's language impairment and how it affects his/her academic, social, and general classroom functioning.

6. Educate the student's teacher(s) as to the nature of the student's learning strengths and ways to capitalize on those strengths for instruction.

7. Identify and encourage development in the student's areas of strength or his/her talents in non-linguistic areas such as mechanical skills, music, art, or sports.

8. Place the student in a classroom in which the students are given maximal opportunity to participate in small- and large-group discussions in a non-competitive environment.

9. The student's teacher and parents should provide him/her specific and nonthreatening opportunities to discuss subjects the student knows, events that s/he has experienced, books s/he has read, etc.

10. Have the student spend time with an adult who will expose him/her to wide a variety of experiences, explain what is happening, name objects and actions, and answer questions.

Compensations

1. Seat the student near the teacher and away from environmental noises.

2. When teaching or speaking to the student, face him/her, pause between phrases for processing time, limit sentence or clause length, and use simple vocabulary. Give the student an opportunity to request repetition or clarification.

3. Limit sentence length and complexity when speaking to the student.

4. Be aware of the linguistic complexity of the language you use in instructions, questions, and test items. Encourage the student to ask you to restate difficult instructions or questions using simpler vocabulary.

5. Be aware of when the student has become inattentive or looks confused. Repeat what you have said or otherwise reinforce the message.

6. Directly teach the student to request repetition or rephrasing of instructions, questions, or statements when necessary.

7. Allow the student to ask you to paraphrase test questions. Frequently the student may know the content but not understand the question.

8. If, when called on, the student does not appear to know the answer to a question, repeat it verbatim. If the student still does not appear to know the answer, rephrase the question in simpler terms.

9. Call on the student soon after posing a question. In a long wait period, the student is likely to forget the question and/or the answer s/he had wanted to give.

10. When calling on the student in class, provide him/her with as much time as necessary to organize his/her thoughts and formulate a response. S/he may know the answer but need extra time to find the words. Privately, alert the student to this plan so that s/he does not feel pressured to come up with an answer quickly.

11. As the student's word-retrieval problem interferes with the fluency of his/her oral reading, do not require the student to read aloud in the classroom. Call on the student if s/he volunteers.

12. Never assume that the student has prior knowledge or previous experience of the words or information you are using to teach new concepts.

13. Modify assignments to accommodate the student's language impairment. For example, to accommodate a weakness in formulating sentences, reduce the length of an assigned report.

14. When grading the student's papers, make allowances for the effect of his/her specific language disorder. For example, overlook grammatical errors in a paper with good conceptual content.

15. Waive foreign language requirements for the student.

Teaching Approaches

Classroom-Therapy Collaboration

1. Use a collaborative model for teaching language/academic skills. To facilitate this, the speech/language pathologist and the classroom teacher(s) should have ongoing communication for the following purposes: (a) The speech/language pathologist should share with the teacher the current focus of therapy and ways to integrate this into classroom work for reinforcement of newly developing language skills. (b) The teacher should share with the speech/language pathologist the current unit or skill being presented in class and request ideas for modifications in teaching techniques or style of presentation that will allow the student to process the information adequately.

2. Encourage the use of newly learned language skills in the classroom. Structure situations that require the student to use the skills s/he is working on in language therapy. Reinforce the student for use of new language skills by recognizing the value of the information s/he has offered or the clarity with which it was stated.

3. In coordination with the speech/language pathologist, integrate the skills the student is learning in therapy with classroom work. For example, find out how to help the student use strategies for word retrieval to help in word recognition in reading.

Teaching Principles

1. Introduce activities and tasks by explicitly stating the focus and purpose — what the student is meant to learn and why. For example, introduce a topic for discussion as "the upcoming election" rather than "current events"; explain the purpose of a worksheet as practice in deciding *when* to use regular versus irregular past tense rather than as simply practicing the use of past tense.

2. Provide ample examples of a new concept or skill that relate the new information to what is already known.

3. Help the student organize and relate new and known content area information and skills by using metacognitive strategies such as the adapted K-W-L-S Strategy (Know, Want to Find Out, Learned, Still Need to Learn). (See Appendix.)

4. Begin language remediation for the student in contextualized language (speaking about things in the immediate environment and pertaining to the current situation) and move gradually into decontextualized language.

5. Use reading and writing as models for oral language skills as well as for reinforcement.

6. Integrate oral language, reading, and writing for all language skills taught. When presenting any new skill or concept, move from pictorial stimuli to print (reading/writing) and oral language (listening/speaking). For example, when teaching cause/effect terms, use pictures that clearly depict the relationship, then offer printed sentences that denote the relationship. Move into oral comprehension, oral expression, and writing.

7. When teaching any new process or skill, provide slow, step-by-step instruction.

8. When introducing a new concept, skill, or language pattern, use simple sentence structures and familiar, concrete vocabulary so that the focus of attention is on the new information.

9. Draw the student's attention to new concepts, words, or constructs by placing vocal stress on them when speaking.

10. When initially introducing a new concept, present the information more slowly than you would when speaking about a familiar concept.

11. Provide redundancy and repetition in teaching any new concept. Repeat important statements verbatim and explain the concept in a variety of ways.

12. Teach new concepts and skills within thematic units so that all new learning is interrelated conceptually. The thematic unit provides a consistent framework and familiar context to facilitate the introduction of new concepts and skills.

13. Within thematic units, use many contexts to highlight the concept or skill you are introducing. For example, if teaching temporal relationships in social studies, you might read about how ancient people used interesting rock formations and discuss the sequence of events in the story. For science, you might do experiments with different types of rocks, using the specific temporal terms you are teaching in your instructions as well as in class discussion after the experiment.

14. Encourage reading in the classroom. Use incentives for the student if necessary. Reading will help the student improve his/her vocabulary and syntactical knowledge.

15. Do not exclusively use reading materials that are highly dependent on word families and specific phonic elements (e.g., "The dog hopped on the log in the bog"). The necessity of maintaining particular word forms restricts the use of meaningful, familiar language, making it difficult for the student with a language impairment to predict upcoming words and syntactic forms.

Multimodality Instruction

1. Present all types of verbal information accompanied by visual stimuli that clearly illustrate the concept being taught. Examples are pictures, charts, graphs, semantic maps, and videotapes. Simultaneous visual-verbal presentation is necessary for the student's comprehension and retention of the information.

2. Teach the student to create a visual image of what s/he hears and reads so that s/he can provide him/herself with visual input to supplement verbal information.

3. If the student is unable to take in auditory and visual information simultaneously, direct the student to look at the complete visual display, then direct him/her to the portion of it about which you will be speaking. When s/he has had adequate time to look at the illustration, give a brief oral explanation. Then, direct the student to look at the visual again.

4. When possible, involve the student in concept or skill learning tactile-kinesthetically or experientially.

5. Be aware that the student's ability to benefit from any activity that is purely auditory, such as round-robin reading, is extremely limited.

Lectures

1. When lecturing, present ideas in an organized and logical sequence. Keep the points as simple as possible and group related information.

2. When presenting lectures, use an overhead projector to highlight the important points.

3. Prior to beginning a lecture, write on the board the important points to be covered and review the major points at the end of the lecture. This will help the student recognize and retain the critical information.

4. Provide the student with an outline of questions to follow during a lecture. Go over the questions before beginning the lecture and guide a discussion of the answers after the lecture.

5. For increased comprehension of lectures, provide the student with a study guide that identifies the critical information. Encourage the student to complete the study guide and then use it to study for exams.

Instructions

Giving Instructions

(See: Short-Term Memory, Attention)

Following Instructions

1. Evaluate further the student's ability to follow complex oral and written instructions in the classroom setting.

2. Use barrier games to develop the awareness that careful listening is necessary for following instructions. Using the barrier, the student may be asked to give or receive instructions for building objects, drawing designs, or writing information. Tape-record the instructions given by the teacher and the student. In the case of a disagreement about the wording of instructions given, the tape may be played back.

3. Teach the student to monitor his/her understanding of instructions so that s/he recognizes when s/he needs to ask for clarification. Some techniques for this purpose are barrier games and giving instructions that have ambiguous or nonsense statements in them.

4. In order to teach the student when to recognize the need for clarification of instructions, present instructions in which information is either missing, unclear, or incompatible with another statement. Teach the student how to ask specific questions for clarification.

5. Teach the student to comprehend the sequence of instructions, the terms used to denote sequence, and a strategy to remember more than two steps.

6. Use barrier games to practice following directions using spatial terms, such as *right top*, *below*, and *center*. Tape-record the instructions given by the teacher and the student. In the case of a disagreement about the wording of instructions given, the tape may be played back.

7. Once the student has learned basic spatial terms, teach him/her to follow spatial directions on a map. Start with maps of familiar areas, such as the student's house.

8. Teach the student to write lists of things s/he has to do or remember.

Vocabulary

General

1. Evaluate further the level of the student's vocabulary knowledge and the level of concrete to abstract concepts s/he can comprehend.

2. At the preschool, arrange some activities around certain themes with which the children are familiar, such as medical offices, plants, transportation, or various ethnic groups within the class. Teach and reinforce vocabulary for each of the themes.

3. To increase vocabulary, emphasize building general knowledge.

4. Directly work on vocabulary development in reading, writing, and oral discussion. Ensure that oral vocabulary continues to develop and that new words are pronounced and used correctly.

5. Correct mispronunciations by teaching the student the correct spelling of a word. For example, show the student that the word s/he is pronouncing as "dethascope" is spelled *stethoscope*.

6. Expose the student to multiple repetitions of new words in many different contexts and settings.

7. When teaching vocabulary, do not use passive learning activities such as looking words up in the dictionary and memorizing their definitions.

8. When teaching vocabulary, activate the student's awareness of his/her familiarity or lack of familiarity with the words. (See Appendix, Vocabulary: Activating Awareness.)

9. Teach all new vocabulary by association with known concepts. (See Appendix, Vocabulary: Exclusive Brainstorming, Semantic Feature Analysis: Vocabulary.)

10. Focus on building receptive and expressive vocabulary skills through vocabulary games based on any unfamiliar words the student finds in his/her reading or hears during the day.

11. Introduce new vocabulary by expanding the student's statements. For example, if the student says, "The house is old and ugly," the teacher might say, "Yes, that house looks *dilapidated*."

12. Use interesting pictures to foster and reinforce vocabulary development. The book *Animalia* (Base, 1986) presents numerous objects and activities in detailed pictures. Each page represents a letter; all of the pictures on the page begin with that letter.

13. Read stories to the student that are on or *slightly* above his/her language level. Discuss any unknown words using pictures or known synonyms. Provide ample practice in using the new words.

14. Directly teach the student that words can have more than one meaning. Teach multiple meanings (e.g., *prompt* can mean *on time* or a *cue*) and provide practice in using them.

15. Teach the student to use a thesaurus for writing. It may be either a book or a pocket-sized, computerized thesaurus.

Concepts

1. Using tests such as the Boehm Test of Basic Concepts—Revised (Boehm, 1986) or the Brigance Inventory of Early Development (Brigance, 1991), evaluate further the student's comprehension of words denoting basic concepts.

2. Play games that focus on word meanings. These include thinking of words that go together, making collages of pictures that go together, and discussing how the words or pictures are related. Later, incorporate the concept of opposites.

3. Play games with the student while driving in the car or when taking a walk that will require him/her to categorize words. For example, you may say, "Tell me everything you see that looks like a circle" or, "Tell me everything you see that is a machine."

4. Play games in which the student tells how two or more objects or groups of objects are similar

(e.g., a kitten and a puppy are baby animals) or different (e.g., toys and cooking utensils).

5. Teach the student the meanings of question words (e.g., "what," "when," "where," "why," and "how"). During play activities, ask questions using these words and guide the student to the appropriate answer. Later, use the question words in less experiential settings, such as before, during, or after a story is read (e.g., "Look at the picture. What is happening? Why do you think the boy is doing that?").

6. Devise activities to develop the idea of sequence in daily events, in the different parts of one event, and in the events within a story. Use sequence words (e.g., "first," "second," "finally") to describe the events and set up situations in which the student demonstrates comprehension of these words (e.g., "What did we do second?").

7. Plan experiences with the student in which s/he helps to decide the necessary sequence of activities (e.g., in building a sand castle, s/he might decide to get the bucket, shovel, and water, make a pile of sand, shape it, and jump on it). Within these situations, teach comprehension and expression of temporal and sequence words (e.g., "first," "before," "later," "last").

8. Teach/reinforce positional (e.g., first/last), directional (e.g., right/left), and quantitative (e.g., more, fewer) concepts by using them in a variety of experiential contexts. For example, when the students line up to go for a walk, count them from the first child in line, then assign each a cardinal number (e.g., "Jimmy, you're first. Alicia, you're second. Tina is last today, but she might be first tomorrow.").

9. Directly teach the concepts of antonyms and synonyms and provide many activities for practice in finding antonyms and synonyms for given words.

10. Use all possible situations to teach the student words for feelings. Ask what s/he is feeling during or after specific activities and conflicts. Supply more precise words for the student. For example, if the student says, "I'm sad," the teacher may say, "I understand; and are you also feeling a little bit ashamed of hitting your friend? Ashamed means sorry and knowing that it wasn't the right thing to do."

11. Teach the student to comprehend the linguistic relationships signaled by temporal, spatial, cause/ effect, analogous, exceptional, and comparative terms. Teach the student a variety of specific terms for each of these concepts. (See, also, Cohesive Devices.)

Word Retrieval

1. Through informal testing or diagnostic teaching, determine whether or not the student's dysfluency is due, at least in part, to a word-retrieval deficit.

2. Ensure that all new words presented are well integrated into a conceptual framework and firmly understood.

3. Provide activities to reinforce integration of recently learned and familiar words within a strong conceptual framework. Strong associations with known words and concepts might help to prevent word-retrieval problems. (See Appendix, Semantic Feature Analysis: Vocabulary and Concepts, Vocabulary: Exclusive Brainstorming, Semantic Mapping for Evaluating/Activating Prior Knowledge.)

4. Teach the student to recognize when s/he is having difficulty retrieving a word so that s/he may use a retrieval strategy.

5. Teach the student to visualize the object or the spelling of the word to prompt recall of the verbal label.

6. Teach the student to think of a category for the target word and mentally list associated objects to try and prompt recall. For example, if the student is trying to retrieve the word "thief," s/he could list "crook," "robber," and "bad guy."

7. Teach the student to visualize a different context for the word and mentally describe it with a sentence. Example: For "blocks," the student would think, "Children build with _____."

8. To facilitate word retrieval, encourage the student to try to recall and say the first sound of the word.

9. To facilitate word retrieval, teach the student to "talk around the word," describing its appearance, function, and/or category.

10. If the student cannot recall a word, encourage him/her to use a synonym.

Organizational Structure (Macrostructure)

Narrative and Expository Structures

1. Through diagnostic teaching or informal testing, evaluate further the student's ability to comprehend the structure of expository discourse and text compared to his/her ability to comprehend narrative discourse or story grammar.

2. Through diagnostic teaching or informal testing, evaluate further the student's ability to comprehend different expository discourse/text structures.

3. Teach the student to use a story grammar for following, retelling, and generating narratives. For example, the student might use the STORE the Story strategy. (See Appendix.)

4. Until the student becomes more familiar with expository structure, present informational material in narrative structure.

5. Select reading and listening materials with clear organizational structures. For example, it may be easier for a student to understand and recall a story containing all the elements of a story grammar (i.e.,

style and another written in expository style, but with similar information. Discuss with the student the stylistic differences.

8. Directly teach the student to understand the organizational structure of expository material. Examples of expository paragraph structures include: sequence (main idea and details which must be given in a specific order), enumerative (topic sentence and supportive examples), cause/effect (topic sentence and details telling why), descriptive (topic sentence and description of attributes), problem solving (statement of problem followed by description, causes, solutions), comparison/contrast (statements of differences and similarities).

9. Teach the student different ways information might be organized and draw a visual pattern to illustrate that type of organization. For example, contrast might be depicted as a divided square with two subheadings and blocks down the side for categories (see Figure 3-1a); description might be depicted as a tree with smaller branches coming off each major limb (see Figure 3-1b); and cause/effect might be depicted as a circle or

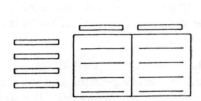  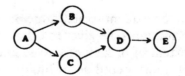

Figure 3–1a. Contrast.   Figure 3–1b. Description.   Figure 3–1c. Cause-Effect.

setting, problem, internal response, attempt at resolution, consequence, ending) than to infer those elements from a story written in repeated language such as "The House that Jack Built."

6. Teach the student to recognize the structure of the type of discourse and text you are using in the classroom. For example, if working with stories in a narrative structure, teach the student to recognize the elements of a story grammar. For expository discourse or text, teach structures such as comparison/contrast and enumeration.

7. Teach the student the differences between narrative and expository styles. As a basis for discussion, give the student a paragraph written in narrative

number of circles with an arrow leading from one circle to another (see Figure 3-1c); chronological sequence might be depicted as a timeline. Subsequently, teach the student to recognize these patterns in reading material and orally presented information and to use these patterns to organize information for writing.

10. Use simple semantic mapping to help the student organize information for a short oral report. First the student can base the report on notes written from the semantic map; later s/he should learn to organize thoughts into a mental semantic map to guide expression of ideas. (See Appendix, Semantic Maps: Designing.)

11. Ensure that any strategy the student learns for oral comprehension is generalized to speaking and writing.

Generation of Ideas

1. Further evaluate the student's ability to generate ideas in a variety of circumstances, such as making conversation, retelling a movie or book, telling about a familiar topic, creating a story from a picture stimulus, or creating a story with no visual stimulus.

2. Facilitate the student's ability to generate ideas by using a variety of techniques including: (a) story starters, (b) expansion of one sentence by using reporter questions (i.e., "who," "what," "when," "where," "why," "how"), (c) story structures with specific questions to facilitate each element, and (d) brainstorming with retention of only those sentences that can be related to each other, adding details or story elements as needed.

3. Use story or movie retellings to facilitate generation of ideas for speaking or writing.

4. To facilitate generation of ideas, provide the student with an outline of a story or report on a familiar topic. Have the student fill in missing information. Gradually decrease the amount of information given in the outline.

5. Teach the student to elaborate on explanations and information s/he gives to others by recognizing the extent of or lack of shared knowledge and providing more detail accordingly.

Semantic–Syntactic Relationships (Microstructure)

Sentence Structure

1. Through diagnostic teaching, determine the level of complexity of the sentence structures that the student can comprehend and use for expression.

2. Provide visual cues for teaching morphological markers. For example, to highlight the concept of plural *s*, you could use a picture of two cats with an *s* after the second cat. To illustrate the concept of *er*, use a picture of a can of paint with *er* written after it followed by an equal sign and a picture of a person painting a house.

3. When correcting the student's syntactic errors and modeling correct word order, speak slowly and change as little as necessary to make the sentence correct. Write the sentence and have him/her read it or say the sentence correctly and ask him/her to repeat it.

4. Use pictures to accompany activities in oral sentence comprehension.

5. Use written sentences or phrases to accompany activities in oral sentence comprehension.

6. Repeatedly expose the student to complex sentence structures in stories before introducing these sentence structures out of context for remediation activities.

7. Teach the student strategies for interpreting the following complex sentence structures: (fill in types of sentence structures). (See Appendix, Sentence Comprehension: Analysis of Sentence Forms.)

8. Specifically teach the student the meaning of transition words and how they signal the relationship between dominant and subordinate clauses. Teach the student to write complex sentences and then to use them in his/her expressive language.

9. When teaching the meanings of and providing practice in the use of specific connecting words, maintain awareness of the difficulty of complex sentence structures, probable versus nonprobable event sequences, and the level of vocabulary and concepts.

10. Provide a variety of activities in which the student combines given phrases and selected transition words into complex sentences. (See Appendix, Sentence Comprehension: Order of Events.)

11. Provide extensive oral practice with sentence-combining exercises. Present the student with several clauses or short sentences and have him/her generate as many sentence patterns as s/he can by using a variety of connecting words. As an alternative activity, provide the student with a specific word or words to use in joining several clauses or sentences.

12. Once the student is proficient with a basic level of complex sentences, teach him/her to understand and use sentences containing relative clauses (i.e., clauses embedded in a sentence that begin with words such as "who," "what," "where," "that").

13. Teach the student to comprehend passive voice by constructing active sentences out of word cards.

Show the student how to resequence them, adding cards for *was* and *by* to create passive sentences or omitting *was* and *by* to create active sentences.

14. Due to the student's dependence on using an "order of mention" strategy to interpret sentences, teach the student that word order does not necessarily imply sentence meaning. Provide training to move the student from semantically oriented comprehension to syntactically oriented comprehension. (See Appendix, Sentence Comprehension: Analysis of Sentence Forms.)

15. Teach the student to interpret sentences in which the order of mention does not match the order of events. (See Appendix, Sentence Comprehension: Order of Events.)

Sentence Formulation

1. Using diagnostic teaching, further evaluate the extent to which problems in word retrieval and/or complex sentence structure interfere with the student's ability to formulate well-constructed sentences.

2. Focus remediation on sentence formulation, the ability to manipulate components of a sentence mentally so that their combination conveys the intended message.

3. Teach the student how to sequence his/her ideas mentally so that s/he can state them in an organized fashion. For example, before speaking, s/he should ask, "What is the beginning of what I want to say? The middle? The end?"

4. Use elaboration to model how the student might add details and information to his/her statements.

Inference

1. Evaluate further the student's ability to use prior knowledge and experience to interpret given oral or textual information. Attend to the types of cohesive devices the student can interpret and his/her ability to infer information within as well as across sentences. (See Appendix, Cohesive Devices: Types.)

2. Guide the student to infer the feelings of classmates and characters in stories and movies.

3. Give the student practice in determining what materials, tools, or pieces of information are missing in given situations. First, use actual situations. Later, have the student consider situations that are familiar

but are not actually happening. Finally, use situations that are less familiar, requiring more generalization from what s/he already knows.

4. Use pictures and devise activities to give the student practice in interpolative thinking—inferring the middle event when told the first and last event (e.g., Show a picture of a boy in his swimsuit about to dive into a swimming pool and a picture of the boy drying off with a towel. Ask, "What happened in between?").

5. Teach the student to infer information that is not given in instructions and stories. For example, the teacher might tell a story about Curious George eating a piece of a puzzle and getting a stomachache. Then, s/he would help the student to infer that it was the piece of wood in George's stomach that made it hurt.

6. While reading stories, watching videotapes, and conducting simple science experiments, encourage the student to predict the outcome. Afterwards, ask him/her to evaluate the prediction.

7. Provide activities to help the student develop an "inferential mind set," the understanding that inferences based on prior knowledge are necessary for understanding of reading/listening material. These activities are often best done in a small group. (See Appendix, Inferencing: Getting the Idea.)

8. Use techniques to activate prior knowledge before introducing new concepts, reading material, or oral information. Directly teach the student the necessity of using his/her own prior knowledge and experience to help understand the information. (See Appendix, PReP, Semantic Feature Analysis: Concepts, Semantic Mapping.)

9. Use predicting strategies in listening and reading activities to increase the student's comprehension and retention of implied information. (See Appendix, Directed Reading-Thinking Activity.)

10. Teach the student how to recognize when information is missing from discourse or text and the type of information that needs to be inferred. (See Appendix, Inference: Types, Inference: Deciding the Type of Inference Needed.)

11. Teach the student how to make inferences within sentences before teaching inferencing across sentences.

Cohesive Devices

1. Through diagnostic teaching or informal testing, evaluate the student's comprehension of the transition words, appropriate for his/her age level, that signal linguistic-conceptual ties between clauses and sentences.

2. Through diagnostic teaching or informal testing, determine which types of cohesive devices the student can interpret, such as reference, lexical, conjunction, substitution, and ellipsis, as well as any difficulties within these categories. (See Appendix, Cohesive Devices: Types.)

3. Teach the student to interpret and use cohesive devices in oral and written language. Cohesive devices include the categories of referential, lexical, conjunction, substitution, and ellipsis. (See Appendix, Cohesive Devices: Types, Cohesive Devices: Activities.)

4. Teach the student to use cohesive devices to help the listener follow the organization of his/her narrative.

5. Demonstrate how terms denoting linguistic relationships in text and in oral language help to clarify relationships among events, objects, people. Use examples from social studies, science, and literature.

6. Teach the student to interpret cohesive devices in language that is explicitly directed at the listener/reader followed by cohesive devices in language between characters, such as dialogue.

7. Review reading/listening material and modify as necessary so that cohesive devices in the text and in comprehension questions do not require inferences that are above the student's current language level. If necessary, rewrite material to make implied information explicit.

Verbal Reasoning

1. Ask the student to provide a rationale for statements or opinions s/he offers in the classroom (e.g., "And what do you think is the reason that happened?"). Provide as much prompting and guidance as needed.

2. To improve verbal reasoning, use the ReQuest Procedure when reading stories or textbooks. You may also use this strategy with short portions of taped stories or textbooks. (See Appendix.)

3. Use the Directed Reading-Thinking Activity as an oral activity to help the student increase his/her understanding of content area textbooks. Read aloud to the student and stop at certain points to have him/her predict what might happen next. Read on to confirm the predictions. (See Appendix.)

4. Use the Directed Reading-Thinking Activity as an oral activity to increase the student's ability to listen actively to a story or explanation of an event. Tell the student a portion of the story and ask him/her to use information from the story and his/her own experience to guess what will happen. Make sure that s/he can support his/her prediction. (See Appendix.)

Figurative Language

1. Through diagnostic teaching or formal testing with a test such as the Test of Language Competence—Expanded (Wiig & Secord, 1988), evaluate the student's ability to understand figurative language and ambiguous statements.

2. Teach the student to understand and use figurative language such as metaphors (e.g., "The teacher watched him with an eagle eye"), similes (e.g., "The teacher watched him like a hawk"), idioms (e.g., "He threw away a wonderful opportunity"), and proverbs (e.g., "Necessity is the mother of invention").

3. Teach the student to understand humor such as jokes and riddles. Use direct explanation, many examples, and pictures, where appropriate.

4. Teach the student to recognize the humor in intentional ambiguity (e.g., "Won't you join me in a cup of tea?").

5. Teach the student to recognize ambiguity in his/her own sentences and provide clarification, or, in someone else's sentences, ask for clarification. (See Appendix, Cohesive Devices: Activities.)

Style: Oral versus Literate

1. Teach the student to write in a more literate style. Use practice in literate writing as a basis for practicing a literate style of speaking.

2. To facilitate writing and speaking in a more literate style, teach the student to differentiate between oral and literate language. A sequence of

activities requiring increasing skill may include: (a) dividing pairs of sentences into categories of style (oral and literate), (b) labeling a given sentence as oral or literate in style, (c) rewriting sentences from oral to literate style based on previous practice in complex sentence structures and cohesive devices, and (d) rewriting passages in a variety of styles (e.g., letter to a close friend, news article) (Wallach & Miller, 1988). As much as possible, include practice using the student's language.

Example:

Oral: This one guy goes scraping salt on-onto the road everyday and he's been scared of him—then he met him in the church—he was nice and everything.

Literate: The boy's been scared of a man who scraped salt onto the street every day, but when they met in church, the man was nice.

Pragmatics

General

1. Informally evaluate the student's abilities in the following areas of pragmatic language skills (fill in specific areas).

2. Provide situations in which pretend play and role playing are encouraged.

3. To teach pragmatic language skills, use a combination of modeling, direct teaching, and videotaping.

4. Teach the student how to take the existence or lack of a shared context into account when speaking to someone else.

5. Develop an awareness in the student of the need to provide the listener with sufficient information when introducing and discussing experiences.

6. Teach the student to be aware of what information the listener could be expected to have. Teach him/her to explain people and places s/he discusses in narratives.

7. Teach the student to be sure that the referent for each pronoun and deictic term s/he uses (e.g., "here," "there," "this," "that") is clear.

Social

1. Teach the student how to change his/her manner of speech depending upon to whom s/he is speaking (e.g., a teacher versus a friend).

2. Teach the student to interpret the social language of his/her peers and how to use social language in a variety of situations.

3. Teach the student how to take turns in a game, discussion, or conversation.

4. Teach the student how to maintain the topic in a conversation.

Additional Ideas:

4

GENERAL: EDUCATION AND TRANSITION

Further Evaluation

1. Schedule a full psychoeducational evaluation to include a thorough assessment of cognitive abilities, including receptive/expressive language abilities and achievement areas.

2. Schedule an evaluation of the student that includes cognitive abilities, oral language skills, academic achievement, adaptive behavior skills, and vocational aptitude and interest.

Conferences

1. Have a conference with the student's teacher(s) and school counselor at the beginning of the school year to discuss the findings of this assessment.

2. At the beginning of the school year, establish a later conference date for the parents, school personnel, and the student, if appropriate, to discuss the student's progress and suggest changes in his/her educational plan, if necessary.

Compensations

1. Match all of the student's classroom assignments to his/her present academic performance level. Ensure that classroom expectations are realistic and grade accordingly.

2. If possible, select instructors for the student who are organized in class structure and lecture style.

3. Help the student select a college program that will provide the necessary compensations and accommodations the student requires to succeed.

Self-Advocacy

1. Help the student become a self-advocate. Help him/her understand what compensations s/he needs in a classroom and how to request them.

2. Ensure that the student understands clearly the nature of his/her difficulties. Teach ways in which s/he may use his/her strengths to compensate for weaknesses.

3. Teach the student how to explain his/her learning difficulties to another person, such as a teacher or employer, as well as how to request modifications

that will help him/her succeed in the particular situation. For example, the student may ask an employer to give a set of instructions slowly enough so that s/he can write them down.

4. Help the student set up appointments to meet with teachers individually at the beginning of each semester to introduce him/herself and explain his/her special needs. Encourage the student to meet with each teacher during office hours at least every 2 weeks to check on progress.

Instruction

1. If the student was not an active participant in making up his/her Individualized Educational Plan (IEP), share with him/her the long-term goals and short-term objectives. Help the student to understand the instructional plan so that s/he can recognize his/her own progress toward specific goals.

2. Periodically review with the student what s/he has accomplished and how these accomplishments relate to his/her long-term goals and short-term objectives.

3. Using charts and graphs, document the student's proficiency in a skill before and during instruction so that s/he may see progress. Periodically review samples of previous work.

4. When teaching any new skill or information to the student, insure that s/he understands what s/he is supposed to do *before* starting to work.

5. Use drill and practice activities only after the student understands newly presented concepts and their application.

6. In any task that the student is expected to do, make sure that s/he knows: (a) what to do, (b) why s/he is doing it, (c) how to do every step of the process, (d) when s/he is finished, and (e) what to do next.

7. After practicing the basics of any new skill, provide the student with supervised practice in application of the skill. For example, the student may apply syllabication skills to unfamiliar words while reading an interesting magazine, use math facts to figure out a budget for his/her allowance, or incorporate new spelling words into a composition.

Tutoring/Educational Therapy

1. Use diagnostic teaching to evaluate further the student's proficiency and needs in the targeted area.

Obtain a measure of baseline performance prior to instruction. Establish objective criteria to measure each aspect of the targeted skill.

2. Use diagnostic teaching to determine the most effective technique for teaching the targeted skill or content area information. Obtain a measure of baseline performance prior to instruction. Establish objective criteria to evaluate the efficacy of each technique.

3. Provide the student with individual tutoring or small group instruction in the following areas: (specify areas of need).

4. Coordinate instruction with the student's classroom teacher(s) so that you reinforce each other's efforts.

5. The student needs intensive tutoring to help him/her improve academic skills. Encourage the student to reduce his/her class load by one course in order to devote his/her attention to learning the skills that will help with future courses.

6. To help the student move smoothly into school next year, obtain a list of academic and behavioral skills expected of the average student entering (   ) grade. Use these to create teaching objectives.

7. Find out what courses the student will be required to take during the next year. Help him/her learn reading, writing, note-taking, study, and learning strategies that are directly applicable to these courses. If possible, obtain a syllabus prior to the beginning of class and use the course material to teach study strategies.

8. Based on the class syllabus, introduce new concepts and skills slightly ahead of the teacher. Plan sufficient time to teach the concepts and to build in reinforcement of the classroom skills that the student is learning.

9. Provide the student with specific instruction in study skills to help him/her become a more independent learner. A good resource designed for teaching study skills is the *Landmark Study Skills Guide*. This book provides suggestions for helping students who have difficulty organizing themselves, taking notes, using textbooks, or studying efficiently. Available from: Landmark Outreach Program, Box 79, Prides Crossing, MA 01965, (508) 927-4440.

Homework

General

1. Make sure that all homework assignments are at the student's independent level of performance. The student should understand what to do and how to perform the task.

2. Use homework to provide practice and reinforcement of skills that the student already understands.

3. Do not penalize the student for errors made on homework. Instead, confer with him/her regarding the errors in an attempt to determine why they were made. Use this information to design appropriate instruction and/or to revise the homework assignments.

Recording Assignments

Daily Assignments

1. Encourage the student to write down all homework assignments as they are given. If s/he is confused about an assignment, have him/her meet with the teacher after class or during office hours.

2. The student should have an assignment book in which to write his/her homework for each class. The teacher should check it for legibility and accuracy and sign it. If there is no homework, the student should write "none" and have it signed. At homework time, the parent should check the child's assignment book, help him/her prioritize the assignments, check the completed homework, and sign his/her book for each completed assignment.

3. Before the student goes home, check his/her assignment book to ensure that all homework assignments are legible, accurate, and complete.

4. Make sure that the student has an assignment book that s/he brings home from school every day. Try to enlist the aid of a teacher or responsible peer in checking the assignment book and in helping the student make sure s/he has the needed materials.

Tests

1. Teach the student to record information concerning upcoming tests on a special Test Information page immediately following his/her regular assignment calendar sheet. Or, the student may designate a special section in the assignment book for Test Information.

2. Teach the student how to record information regarding tests as follows: (a) the date of the test (on the Test Information page and in his/her regular calendar), (b) the chapters to be covered, (c) the dates of lecture notes to be included, (d) additional information such as field trips or movies, (e) the type of questions to be asked (e.g., essay, multiple-choice), and (f) the point value of the test. The student should also note any information that the teacher states will *not* be on the test.

Organizing/Managing Time

General

1. Teach the student specific organizational skills to use with homework. These may include: (a) learning how to keep an assignment book, (b) learning how to task-analyze assignments, (c) allocating appropriate amounts of time to complete assignments, (d) identifying and locating required materials and information, and (e) planning the steps leading to completion of extended assignments, such as term papers.

2. Help the student develop a notebook for organizing class notes and assignments. Use a binder notebook that is divided into several sections and has pockets that may be used for completed assignments.

Long-Term Assignments/Tests

1. Teach the student how to plan for long-term assignments. For example, s/he could establish intermediate, sequential deadlines on each assignment within a unit of work and place each completed piece in a special folder on the "due date." The next-to-last date would be the due date for the last assignment and the final date would be when the entire contract is due. The intervening time would be used for final proofreading and editing. Alternatively, record progressive due dates on the assignments within the contract and have the student hand in each assignment as s/he completes it.

2. Notify the student's parents as far in advance as possible of any major project that the student will need to work on at home. Examples include research reports, book reports, map drawings, timelines, science fair projects, and upcoming tests. Provide written instructions to the parents that include all of the requirements for the project and the grading criteria.

3. Whenever the parent is notified of a long-term project, s/he should help the student break it into stages and write deadlines for the completion of each stage on a large wall calendar. A certain amount of time should be set aside nightly or weekly to work on the project.

4. Teach the student to ask his/her teachers periodically about upcoming test dates. Some teachers announce tests only a few days ahead of time. As the student needs additional time to prepare for tests, s/he should learn to take an active role in obtaining this information.

5. Teach the student to include on his/her assignment book or calendar specific days and times to study for upcoming tests. S/he should also note what information to study in each session and the method s/he is going to use. An example is:

Sunday	Monday	Tuesday	Wednesday	Thursday	Friday
10-10:30	none	7-8:00	6:30-7:30	7-8:00	Test
List dates		Outline	List events	Map	
& events		chapter	Write dates	Outline	

6. Maintain and post on the wall a master list of in-class assignments, homework assignments, and tests. This will help the student self-monitor what assignments are currently due and which are not yet completed.

Completing Assignments

1. Request that the student's parents help him/her create a clean, quiet, organized space for nightly homework.

2. Request that the student's parents set aside a regular period of time each day for homework and that one parent be available during that time to provide help, as needed.

3. Before the student begins each night's homework, make sure that s/he understands what is required and then encourage him/her to complete the homework independently.

4. Before beginning nightly homework, help the student review all assignments, estimate the time each will take, prioritize them, and then list them in order on an index card. As the student finishes an assignment, have him/her cross it off the list.

5. Set a specific amount of time for the student to work on homework and include short breaks.

6. Encourage the student to estimate how long a task will take and then record the time actually needed to complete the task. Trying to meet his/her estimated time will help the student sustain attention and increase his/her accuracy in estimating the necessary time.

Test Taking

Modifications

1. Allow the student to take exams in a quiet room without other students present.

2. Allow the student to take untimed exams.

3. Allow the student to take open-book exams.

4. Reduce the number of questions that the student will be required to answer on a test.

5. Sequence the questions on the exam from easy to difficult. Either assign the student a certain number of questions to complete or just the questions at his/her present performance level.

6. Review exams and identify the questions appropriate for the student. On the exams, circle each question you would like him/her to complete. Inform the student to start with the circled questions and then to complete any other questions if s/he has enough time.

7. When assessing the student's knowledge of content areas, keep writing requirements to a minimum. On tests, provide him/her with multiple choice, matching, true-false, or sentence completion questions, rather than essay questions.

8. In content area classes, allow the student to take oral examinations so that you can accurately assess what s/he has learned rather than what s/he is able to read or write.

9. On timed examinations, only evaluate the items that the student was able to complete.

Strategies

1. Teach the student specific test-taking strategies, such as reading over the entire test before starting, outlining the answers to essay questions, and reading all multiple-choice answers with the stem sentence before selecting a response.

2. Teach the student to preview a test before starting to write and to circle any items with which s/he

will have difficulty. Then the student should take the test, answering all of the items for which s/he knows the answer. If the student skips a question, s/he should write its number down after the last question to remind him/herself to go back to answer it.

3. Teach the student how to employ prewriting strategies, such as brainstorming, writing down thoughts, and then organizing the key ideas before answering an essay question.

4. Teach the student how to estimate the amount of time s/he will need to complete specific questions on exams composed of several short essay questions.

5. Teach the student to overprepare for tests so that his/her stress and anxiety will be reduced.

Transition

Further Evaluation

1. Have a vocational specialist evaluate the student's interests and aptitude for suggestions as to possible vocational directions. Begin this process as soon as possible.

2. Using an adaptive behavior scale, assess the student's ability to function independently in non-academic areas, such as personal living skills, community orientation, work-related skills, social communication skills, and motor skills. Identify specific goals and objectives that will help him/her develop independent living skills.

3. Assess the student's functioning levels related to transition. Areas for assessment should include work behaviors, as well as social, independent living, and vocational skills.

4. Assess the student's ability to function independently and age-appropriately in the following aspects of adult living: current vocational skills, vocational training, independent living or residential placement, transportation, finances, recreation/leisure, social relationships, and sexual awareness.

Planning for Transition

1. As the student begins middle school, consult a vocational specialist to design and involve the student in a structured program of career exploration. As the student moves toward one broad vocational path, select high school courses that will provide the prerequisite skills.

2. As part of the student's IEP, write an Individualized Transition Plan (ITP) for the transition into adult life. Begin this process 4 years prior to the student's proposed graduation. Update the ITP annually.

3. Work with the student's parents in prioritizing transition goals. Some considerations include current therapy, opportunities for mainstreaming in school, community-based instruction, and technical training.

4. To facilitate the transition from school to independent living, obtain information from the parent regarding the child's medical history and needs, family history, independent living skills, and social/emotional development.

5. Request that the student's parents complete a questionnaire regarding their plans and expectations for their son/daughter after graduation, the level of involvement they expect to maintain, and areas in which they foresee him/her needing assistance.

6. Assist the student in acquiring the skills needed for transition, including appropriate work behaviors, as well as social, independent living, and vocational skills.

7. Assist the student's parents in developing a plan for encouraging and training independent responsibility in their son/daughter over the next ( ) years. Particular areas of focus include helping the student: (a) do financial planning, (b) obtain a social security number, (c) make a will, (d) apply for Supplemental Security Income, (e) set realistic goals, and (f) develop self-advocacy skills. Other areas include: (a) monitoring good grooming habits, (b) encouraging and facilitating social activities with peers, (c) providing sex education, (d) reinforcing good work habits, (e) encouraging and supporting the student in a job in the community, (f) teaching daily living skills such as cooking, cleaning, and doing laundry, (g) teaching and monitoring money management such as budgeting and saving, and (h) helping him/her develop leisure time skills, such as participating in sports, daily exercise, or hobbies, or acquiring computer skills.

8. Provide consultation from a Vocational Transition Specialist regarding equipment modifications that may be necessary on the job.

9. Many excellent recommendations for designing transition programs can be found in *A Road Map to Transition for Young Adults with Severe Disabilities* (1990).

Accessing Services

1. Provide the student and his/her parents with information regarding community services available to adults with handicapping conditions.

2. Obtain information from agencies and services for adults with handicaps regarding eligibility requirements and help the student apply to the appropriate services.

3. Educate the student and his/her parents about the procedures within the school system and community service agencies for accessing services.

Coordinating Services

1. Train the student's parents in advocacy and case management so that they can effectively secure services for their son/daughter and coordinate the services and information from professionals working with him/her.

2. Provide consultation from a Vocational Transition Specialist to coordinate school services, related services, and adult services in the community.

Vocational Training

1. Educate the student and his/her parents about options for future vocational placements and the requirements for entering and being successful in those placements.

2. Suggest vocational training to the student as an alternative to college. S/he may be more willing to devote energy to learning skills that have more immediate and practical applications.

3. Assist the student in exploring vocational training programs at the community college and local technical schools.

Additional Ideas:

5

READING

Further Evaluation

1. Administer an informal reading inventory to the student to evaluate further his/her reading skill.

2. Further evaluate the student's reading performance using the classroom reading series. Identify an appropriate level for instruction.

3. Establish the readability level of the student's texts by checking the level of a variety of samples throughout the text.

Support

1. Based on the student's present level of reading achievement, s/he would benefit from individual or small group instruction from a qualified tutor, reading specialist, or learning disability specialist.

2. Provide the student with as much individualized instruction as possible. Elicit the help of volunteer, peer, or cross-age tutors.

3. To help in transfer of any newly learned skill or strategy, secure agreement from the regular classroom teacher to remind the student to use the

skill/strategy when appropriate. Devise a method for monitoring the frequency and accuracy of his/her use of the skill.

4. Directly teach the student to generalize each new reading skill s/he learns to functional reading in other areas of the curriculum. Write a behavioral objective for generalization of skills.

Modifications

Instructional Level

1. Make sure that the student is not given reading materials that are frustrating to him/her. Classroom instructional materials should not be above the ( )-grade level.

2. Place the student in reading materials at the ( )-grade level. Use a reading text other than the classroom series.

3. Depending on the level of assistance provided, match the readability of all classroom materials to the student's independent or instructional reading level.

Assignments

1. Reduce the length of the student's reading assignments so that s/he can complete them in the allotted time.

2. When assigning reading to the student, base the number of pages on his/her reading rate and skill.

3. Assign the student short passages at his/her reading level so that s/he can complete his/her reading without difficulty.

4. As an alternative to assigning the student a specific number of pages to read in class or for homework, specify a certain amount of time for the student to read. Have the student keep a record of the number of pages completed within the time period.

5. Teach the student to see his/her reading assignments in smaller, more manageable units of text (e.g., one chapter, sections within a chapter, or paragraphs within a section).

Color Coding

1. Before the student reads a textbook, color-code with a yellow highlighter the sections that are most important for him/her to read.

2. Using a yellow highlighter, underline the main ideas and concepts in the text so that the student will know what is important.

3. Using a dark felt-tip pen, delete all materials from the text that are not considered critical for the student to read.

4. Using different color markers, highlight specific types of information in the text that the student should know. For example, highlight important vocabulary words in pink, important concepts in yellow, and important names and dates in green.

Taped Books

1. If a reading selection is too difficult for the student to read independently, have a peer read it with him/her or have the student listen to a tape of the book as s/he follows along with the print.

2. Since his/her listening comprehension is at approximately the (higher) grade level, but his/her reading comprehension is at approximately the (lower) grade level, allow the student to listen to taped content area textbooks and to take oral examinations.

3. Give the student a study guide or a cloze passage to complete as s/he listens to the text. Have him/her hit the pause button or turn off the tape recorder whenever s/he needs to write in information. Encourage him/her to rewind the tape as needed.

4. Have the student tape-record all lectures in classes. Use these tapes to help him/her learn to listen for the major points.

Interest/Motivation

School

1. For independent reading activities, provide the student with a selection of high-interest, low-vocabulary readers so that s/he will discover that reading is enjoyable.

2. Read and discuss high-interest material with the student to increase his/her willingness to spend time reading.

3. Select or have the student choose materials to read that are directly related to his/her interests.

4. Encourage the student to discuss with others the materials that s/he has read. Provide structured

activities for these types of discussions within the classroom.

5. Have the student share with the class or a small group something interesting that s/he has learned from a book.

6. Set aside a certain amount of time each day for recreational reading.

7. Do not ask the student to read aloud in class unless s/he volunteers.

8. Inform the student of the passage that s/he will be asked to read aloud in class. Have the student practice the material several times, before s/he is asked to read to the group.

9. Encourage and reinforce independent reading. For example, let the student select an activity that s/he would enjoy after reading for a specified amount of time.

10. Discuss with the student how daily silent reading will help him/her improve reading skill. Discuss with him/her the benefits of being a good reader for scholastic and/or occupational success.

11. Establish a system using reinforcers to increase the amount of time the student spends in daily reading. For example, provide the student with a sticker for every ( ) pages s/he reads or a poster for each book that s/he completes.

12. Establish a contract with the student that identifies the minimum number of pages s/he will read in a day. Let the student trade the number of pages for points that may be exchanged for a specified reward when the contract has been completed. Make sure the student's reading selections are at his/her independent reading level.

13. Increase the student's exposure to literature and nonfiction books. Read with the student and discuss the stories or information with him/her.

14. Use a variety of reading materials in the classroom to help the student recognize the need for reading in daily life. Examples include: cookbooks, board games, magazines, newspapers, menus, directions on food and medicine packages, game instructions, catalogues, the Yellow pages, a TV schedule, or a driver's manual.

15. Provide the student with reading materials directly related to his/her career or vocational goals.

Home

1. Read with your son/daughter for about 15 minutes every night. Enlist the help of the children's librarian at the public library to select interesting books that are at the instructional reading level (slightly above the child's present level of linguistic development).

2. As a pleasurable activity, select a high-interest book or magazine at your child's independent reading level and read with him/her in the evenings. Stop at certain points and encourage your child to discuss the pictures and ideas presented in the story. Ask your child questions that will enhance his/her interest and understanding of the story.

3. Schedule weekly trips to the library so that your child can select books for recreational reading. Request help from the children's librarian in selecting books and magazines that are related to your child's interests.

4. Watch "Reading Rainbow" (Public Broadcasting System) with your child and obtain the books that s/he finds interesting from the library.

5. To increase his/her interest in reading, encourage your son/daughter to read simple stories to his/her younger siblings. Books using repetitive language would be appropriate. These types of books may be found in the children's literature section of the public library.

6. When reading with your son/daughter at home, provide as much assistance as needed. Alternate reading sentences, paragraphs, or pages. Initially, you may need to read a larger portion of the text. For example, you read three sentences and your child reads one.

7. When reading with your son/daughter at home, tell him/her any word that s/he has difficulty identifying. Too much time spent trying to figure out unknown words may detract from comprehension, as well as from the enjoyment of reading.

8. In order for your child to see that reading can be functionally enjoyable, play games at home that require simple reading.

9. To increase interest in reading activities, play computer games that require reading to progress from one stage to another.

10. If you own a computer, buy enjoyable reading programs appropriate for your child's instructional reading level.

11. Help your son/daughter select and order one or two magazines of interest with a readability level at or below his/her instructional reading level.

12. Encourage discussions in the home about any books or magazines that your son/daughter is reading independently.

13. Provide opportunities in the home for functional reading, such as reading recipes, directions, catalogues, or television guides.

Basic Skills

Further Evaluation

1. Listen to the student read several short passages from his/her textbook aloud. Record and analyze the types of errors that s/he makes. Plan appropriate instruction to assist the student with word identification skill.

2. Use a phonic checklist to evaluate further the student's word attack skills. Attempt to identify which phonic elements the student knows and which ones s/he needs to be taught. (See Appendix, Phonics Check-Off Chart.)

3. Before beginning the instructional program, tape-record the student reading several graded passages from an informal reading inventory. Keep the taped readings and the error analysis to use to document progress.

General

1. Before and as you teach the student any skill, build in an understanding of *why* the skill is important (e.g., how punctuation may change the meaning of a sentence, how a sequence of letters changes how a word is pronounced) and *how* the skill is applied.

2. Help the student learn common reading terminology, such as: letter name, letter sound, word, syllable, sentence, and paragraph.

3. Discuss with the student how improvement in basic reading skills will make reading easier and more enjoyable. Obtain a commitment from the student that s/he wishes to improve his/her basic reading skills.

4. Until the student's basic reading skills improve, do not require him/her to read aloud in class.

5. Until the student's sight vocabulary and word attack skills improve, do not try to eliminate his/her subvocalization. S/he appears to need the auditory input to help identify and remember words.

6. Provide ample practice with basic reading skills in context. Directly teach the student to recognize *when* and how to apply the skills s/he is mastering.

7. Provide the student with systematic instruction in basic skills, as well as extensive opportunities to read meaningful texts.

8. Provide the student with the opportunity to teach any reading skill that is close to mastery to a peer or younger student who needs that skill.

Letter Identification

1. When teaching the student the alphabet, begin with the letters in his/her first name, and then his/her last name. Using these letters, help him/her create and write simple words.

2. Simultaneously teach recognizing, naming, and writing of letters.

3. Teach the student the alphabet song.

4. Have the student memorize the letters of the alphabet in sequence. For example, have him/her point to each letter as s/he sings the alphabet song.

5. When teaching the student the alphabet, introduce a few letters at a time. Once s/he has mastered these letters, introduce a few more.

6. Have the student practice creating letter forms out of clay by copying a printed letter.

7. In a shallow pan of pudding, lightly trace a letter with a skewer or chopstick. Have the student name and trace the letter with his/her finger. When the letter is formed correctly, s/he may lick that finger.

8. Use gross motor movements to help the student visualize and remember letter forms. For example, have him/her stand up straight and stick both arms out to form the letter "T."

9. Use visual imagery to help the student remember letter forms or their spatial orientation. For example,

teach the student that a "b" looks like a bat and a ball, but the bat comes first.

10. Help the student make sandpaper or colored dry gelatin letters to use in tracing. Write a letter on an index card, outline it in glue, and then sprinkle fine sand or dry colored gelatin over the glue.

11. Help the student make raised letters to use in tracing. Write a letter with a colored marker on an index card and have the student write over it with Elmer's glue. Once the card has dried, have the student trace over the letter with his/her index finger. As letters are mastered, create new cards.

12. When teaching the student a letter of the alphabet, place it on an index card. Have the student trace the letter over and over while saying the letter name (or sound). After repeated tracings, have him/her turn over the card and attempt to write the letter from memory. With guidance, have him/her check the letter against the model for accuracy.

13. Using an erasable slate, write a letter and tell the student its name. Have the student look at the letter, then erase the letter, and attempt to reproduce it on the slate from memory.

14. Using letters on cards or puzzles, have the student match upper- and lowercase letters.

15. Teach discrimination between upper- and lowercase letters by making a game out of circling all of the uppercase letters on a page of text.

16. Do not teach the student upper- and lowercase letters simultaneously. Introduce the other letter form after one form is mastered.

17. When introducing the letters of the alphabet, begin with uppercase letters as they are easier for the young child to discriminate.

18. When introducing the letters of the alphabet, begin with lowercase letters as they are used more frequently in reading and writing.

19. Provide ample exposure to uppercase letters using games and puzzles. Later, use games and puzzles to match upper- and lowercase letters.

20. Use a simple electronic speller so that the student can key in a letter and hear the letter name. Alternatively, s/he can choose a key, guess the name, and check him/herself.

21. As the student learns new letters, have him/her teach these letters to a younger child.

Sight Word Identification

General

1. Discuss with the student that some words are not consistent in sound–symbol correspondence and that these irregular words must be memorized or learned as sight words.

2. Teach sight words from one of the lists of words most frequently used in reading materials, such as the 220 words of the Dolch Basic Sight Word List (Dolch, 1939) or 1,000 Instant Words (Fry, Polk, & Fountoukidis, 1991).

3. Teach the student to recognize the 300 Instant Words (Fry, 1980) that make up 65% of written material. (See Appendix.)

4. Use diagnostic teaching to determine the most effective method for helping the student to learn sight words.

Configuration

1. Teach the student how to analyze word configurations to discriminate among sight words with similar appearances, such as *where* and *were*, or *where* and *there*.

2. Have the student write a sight word and then draw a heavy or colored outline around it to aid in noticing the general visual configuration of the word. Have the student match a list of sight words to their corresponding shapes. Have the student write the sight words into the correct configuration boxes.

Word Box/Index Cards

1. Have the student develop a word box. S/he may use a recipe box with letter tabs or a shoe box with envelopes to file the words alphabetically. Have the student add only words that s/he knows to the box.

2. Have the student write the words that s/he is learning on index cards. On the other side, have him/her put a picture or a phrase that will help him/her remember the word. Have him/her file the words in a word box.

3. Provide the student with many and varied opportunities for review of the sight words in his/her

word box. For example, have the student teach his/her words to another student, write a story using the words, or sort them into categories.

4. Teach the student sight words in semantic categories. For example, teach several color or number words at one time and have him/her file the words in the word box.

5. Have the student classify words from his/her sight word box into a variety of categories, such as grouping all the words that relate to action, all the words that are used to describe, or all the words for animals or colors.

6. Create modified cloze exercises. Have the student fill in the blanks in sentences using the words from his/her word box.

Strategies

1. Use the spelling study strategy Look-Spell-See-Write to teach the student sight words. (See Appendix.)

2. Use the Sight Word Association Procedure (SWAP) (Bos & Vaughn, 1991) for teaching sight words. (See Appendix.)

3. Teach the student sight words using the Fernald method (Fernald, 1943). Have the student trace the word on an index card, turn over the card, and then attempt to write the word from memory. (See Appendix.)

4. Use a modified letter cloze procedure to help the student with word identification. Write the whole word on the front of an index card and then rewrite the word on the back of card, deleting all the vowels. After showing the student both sides twice, have him/her identify the word and the missing vowels.

5. Review sight vocabulary words every few days with the student to ensure retention. Drop words from the review list only after s/he identifies them easily in context.

6. Introduce and practice unknown words with the student prior to reading a story.

7. Use patterned language books that repeat words and phrases to increase the student's word recognition. If the student does not retain the words introduced in these books, provide additional practice with flash cards. If the student does not retain

the words using flash cards, add a tracing component.

8. Use a modified language experience approach (Bos & Vaughn, 1991) to help the student establish a positive attitude toward reading and increase his/her sight vocabulary. (See Appendix.)

9. Using magnetic letters or letter tiles, show the student a word, say the word, scramble the letters, and ask the student to rebuild and pronounce the word.

10. Provide rapid exposure to sight words. This may be done with index cards, a simple tachistoscope, or a computer. Expose the word for progressively decreasing periods of time.

11. To help the student generalize sight word recognition to text, have him/her scan printed material and name and cross out target sight words s/he recognizes. *Word Tracking: High Frequency Words* (Kratoville, 1989), a book of tracking worksheets using the Francis-Kucera list of the 1,092 most frequently used words in English, is appropriate for this type of activity (Kucera & Francis, 1967).

Survival Sight Vocabulary

1. Teach the student survival sight words, such as *exit*, *entrance*, *danger*, *men*, *women*, and *yield*.

2. Provide the student with practice reading informational signs in the environment.

3. For independent reading, provide the student with an electronic speaking dictionary, such as the dictionaries developed by Franklin Learning Resources, 122 Burrs Road, Mt. Holly, NJ 08060, (800) 525-9673.

4. Select words to teach the student that will be used in his/her particular vocation or avocation.

Word Attack

(Related sections: Auditory Processing, Spelling)

Letter-Sound Associations

1. Help the student understand the reason for learning letter-sound associations and how these skills are applied in beginning reading to determine unfamiliar words.

2. When introducing letter-sound instruction, use pictures that will help the student remember the letter

shape and sound. For example, present the letter "o" as a drawing of an octopus, the letter "m" as two mountains, the letter "e" as an egg, and the letter "s" as a snake.

3. Play games with the student to help him/her activate, organize, and develop his/her knowledge of the relationship between letters and words. For example, play the game, "My family owns a . . ." You may say: "My family owns a pet store and they sell something that begins with the letter *C*." With the student's help, brainstorm as many words as you can generate. Continue the game with another letter.

4. Teach the student that letters are like animals in that they have both names and sounds. For example, show the student a picture of a lion and say: "His name is lion, but his sound is /roar/." When s/he understands this concept, teach about letter names and sounds.

5. When the student is familiar with many of the consonants and vowels, point out to him/her how the letters are put together to make up words and how the words go together to make sentences. Build in the concept that letters and words are the building blocks of written language.

6. When teaching the student the sound of each letter of the alphabet, think up a word that s/he knows that begins with the letter. This may help the student recall the letter through association with a word.

7. Have the student create his/her own set of alphabet cards. On each card have him/her write a letter and then draw a picture of a word that begins with that letter.

8. When practicing with alphabet cards, have the student say the letter name and then identify the sound and associated word.

9. Use language clues for teaching the sounds of frequently confused letters, such as *m* and *n*. For example, a short verbal cue could be: *M* has *m*any *m*ountains and *N* does *n*ot.

10. If the student has difficulty retaining new phonic elements, add a tactile component, such as tracing the new letter–sound combinations as they are learned. Reinforce the element by having him/her say the sound while s/he writes the letter(s) from memory.

11. Provide daily drill and review of the common phonic elements that the student is learning by selecting a list of words from his/her reading material.

12. Ask the student to find and attempt to pronounce words in his/her reading materials that include one or two of the phonics elements s/he is learning.

13. Use letter tiles to teach the concept of sound sequencing and blending. Arrange a given set of tiles and have the student attempt to pronounce real or nonsense words. Resequence, omit, add, or substitute one letter at a time and have the student pronounce the new word. For a change of activity, pronounce a word and have the student arrange the letters to match the sequence of sounds. Modify the pronunciation slightly and have the student rearrange the letter tiles.

14. Since the student has a tendency to overrely on picture clues, use high-interest books with few pictures so that s/he will pay more attention to graphophonic clues.

15. To help the student improve his/her ability to use graphophonic information, discourage reliance on pictures as aids for word recognition.

16. Since the student tends to overrely on the use of context clues for word recognition, directly teach him/her to use graphophonic information.

17. Praise the student for any attempts s/he makes at pronouncing unknown words when reading aloud. Encourage him/her to try and identify the word rather than guessing or skipping over the word.

18. When the student is reading independently, do not encourage him/her to skip words. Instead, teach the student to examine the word carefully and then reread the sentence in which the word appears. Discuss with the student how attempting to pronounce unknown words, when s/he is reading independently, will improve his/her word attack skills.

19. Provide the student with practice in word attack skills using high interest reading materials. When the student comes to a word that s/he does not know, provide phonic clues to help him/her identify the word.

20. When teaching the student phonic skills, be sure to focus also on time for activities involving language and reading comprehension.

Methods

1. Teach phonics through a highly structured, sequential program that will help the student form a strong association between letter patterns and their corresponding sounds.

2. Teach the student phonics skills using a highly structured program that incorporates a strong tactile-kinesthetic component, such as the Slingerland method (Slingerland, 1971) or the Orton-Gillingham approach (Gillingham & Stillman, 1973).

3. Use an adaptation of the Orton-Gillingham or Slingerland approaches such as *Rescue the Students Now!*, which simultaneously teaches reading, spelling, and penmanship and provides 98 multisensory lessons, or *Words*, which presents 50 lessons based on word structure, and the *Tutor* series, which includes 40 lessons in each of three books. The *Rescue* program is available from: D & R Enterprises, 6406 Scenic Drive, Yakima, WA 98908. The *Words* and *Tutor* series are available from LEX PRESS, P.O. Box 859, Los Gatos, CA 95031.

4. Teach the student phonic skills by using a highly structured program. Examples include the *Phonic Remedial Reading Drills* (Kirk, Kirk, & Minskoff, 1985), the *Spalding* method (Spalding & Spalding, 1986), *Angling for Words* (Bowen, 1972), *Reading Mastery* (Engelmann et al., 1983-1984), and *Corrective Reading* (Engelmann et al., 1988).

5. Use a program with the student such as Visual Phonics, a system of 46 hand signs and written symbols that suggest how a sound is made. This program can be used in conjunction with any reading, literacy, speech, or ESL program. More information is available from: International Communication Learning Institute (ICLI), 7108 Bristol Blvd., Edina, MN 55435, (612) 929-9381.

6. Use a program such as the Stevenson Language Program, a language skills program that teaches students language rules by connecting them to images that can be readily visualized. This sequential system provides lessons in reading, vocabulary building, spelling, penmanship, grammar, comprehension, and typing. At the beginning level, decoding and spelling are emphasized. Materials are available from: Stevenson Learning Skills, Inc., 85 Upland Road, Attleboro, MA 02703 or through the Guide Line: (800)-343-1211.

Phonics/Linguistics

1. Combine phonics instruction with a linguistic reading program. Select reading materials where the majority of the words have regular sound–symbol correspondence. This will allow the student to learn to apply his/her newly acquired skills successfully.

2. Teach the student new words in families. Select common word patterns, such as *at* or *am*, and then identify and practice common words in the family. Help the student learn to identify the patterns rapidly and automatically.

3. When teaching the student linguistic patterns, use known sight words as a basis for introducing common patterns. Provide practice in generalizing those patterns to new words with the same pattern (e.g., *boat*, *coat*, *float*.)

4. Use a linguistic (patterned) reading program to teach the student phonic skills. Make sure s/he automatically recognizes the word pattern and can use it to pronounce unfamiliar words in other types of reading material.

5. Use the words in the student's sight vocabulary as a basis for building phonic skills. For example, start with a word that s/he automatically recognizes, such as "run," and then show him/her how that pattern can help him/her identify a new word, such as "fun." Help promote generalization of common patterns by frequently pointing out similarities in words.

6. As the student learns sight words, place them in a word box and create word families around them. A variety of activities may be created to help the student associate words within a family. (See Appendix, Word Bank Activities.)

7. Do not teach the student phonic rules or generalizations. Instead, encourage the student to recognize sound patterns automatically.

8. Teach phonics, syllabication, and structural analysis through a highly structured and sequential program that highlights the visual aspect of the word parts and reinforces a strong association with their corresponding sounds. One such method is the Glass-Analysis Method for Decoding Only (Glass, 1973, 1976). (See Appendix.)

Structural Analysis

1. Make sure that the student understands how improved ability to pronounce multisyllabic words will enhance his/her reading skill.

2. Teach structural analysis by cutting apart words into common clusters. Keep the letters of the words you are working with large. Combine the word parts in a variety of ways to make nonsense or real words to pronounce. Let the student then scramble the letters to make new words for you to pronounce.

3. When pronouncing multisyllabic words, have the student slide his/her index finger slowly under the word parts as s/he pronounces them.

4. Emphasize the visual aspect of reading/spelling words to compensate for slow visual processing of symbols or difficulty with visual recall of symbol sequences. For example, have the student color-code or highlight the common word parts or affixes that you are teaching.

5. When you are working with the student on one particular morpheme, such as *ing* or *ed*, color code it each time it appears in the text prior to reading the passage.

6. Use a method such as Glass-Analysis for Decoding Only (Glass, 1973, 1976) to teach the student how to recognize and pronounce common visual and auditory clusters. (See Appendix.)

7. Teach the student how to use structural analysis to decode multisyllabic words. Ensure that s/he overlearns these skills so that s/he begins to see unfamiliar words as a sequence of recognizable word parts. Teach him/her to identify both meaning parts (prefixes, suffixes, and root words) and pronunciation parts (common clusters and syllables).

8. To familiarize the student visually with affixes, introduce him/her to a short list of prefixes and suffixes with their most common meanings. Provide practice pronouncing these affixes with a variety of root words.

9. Write the most common prefixes, suffixes, and root words on index cards. Have the student build and then pronounce both real and nonsense words by rearranging the cards.

10. Make a chart with several suffixes listed down the side, such as *ing*, *er*, and *ed*. Write root words across the top. Have the student determine which endings can be added to form new words. When s/he has completed the chart, have him/her read all the words.

11. To teach immediate visual recognition of common affixes, have the student scan for them in his/her school texts or the newspaper.

12. Teach the student only the most common syllabication rules (e.g., vc/cv, v/cv, vc/v).

13. Prior to having the student read a passage, underline any multisyllabic words that s/he may have difficulty pronouncing. Review pronunciation of the words. Have the student then practice reading the words fluently in context.

14. Use high-interest materials, such as magazines or newspaper articles, to reinforce pronunciation of multisyllabic words. Before reading, have the student scan the passage, underline, and attempt to pronounce words containing three or more syllables.

15. Teach the student a learning strategy such as DISSECT (Lenz, Schumaker, Deshler, & Beals, 1984) to use when s/he encounters unknown words.

16. Teach the student how to use a dictionary and its pronunciation symbols to pronounce unfamiliar words.

Fluency

Further Evaluation

1. Tape-record the student reading several graded passages. Record the number of words in the passage and the amount of time that it took the student to read it. Keep the taped readings and the record of rate to use to document progress.

2. Use a series of graded textbooks or an informal reading inventory to establish the reading level at which the student is able to read fluently. Note both rate and expression.

Visual Tracking

1. Because the student loses his/her place frequently when reading, encourage him/her to track lines of print with his/her finger.

2. Provide an index card for the student to hold under the line s/he is reading.

3. To improve rapid scanning of text, tracking, and visual discrimination, use *Letter Tracking* (1975), a book of tracking worksheets designed to give a student practice in scanning for upper- and lower-case letters.

4. To help the student develop automatic recognition of common word parts and letter clusters in text, provide practice in worksheets, such as those provided in *Cues and Signals* (Wehrli, 1971).

5. To improve the student's visual tracking skill, make a game out of alternate reading. Either reader may stop after reading aloud at least one complete sentence (or more, as specified); the other must know where to resume reading.

Methods

1. Use a fluency method with the student to increase his/her ability to decode unfamiliar words quickly.

2. Use the Presenting Technique (Heckelman, 1986) as a prereading method to increase the student's oral language skills. (See Appendix.)

3. Have the student practice reading a short predictable story or book (repeated words and phrases) until s/he is able to read it with ease. Have him/her read the book to someone else. Tape his/her first and final readings to document progress and so that the student can hear him/herself read in a fluent manner.

4. Use an assisted reading method to help the student increase his/her reading readiness or fluency. Read the student a phrase or sentence and then have the student read it back. Move your finger along the line of print to help the student focus on the word. Reread the passage several times. Have the student read independently when s/he recognizes words. Provide assistance with words that s/he does not know (Hoskisson, 1975).

5. When reading with the student at home, take turns reading, alternating paragraphs or pages. To help the student keep his/her place, point to the words with your finger or hold an index card under the line being read.

6. Use paired reading with the student in the classroom (or home) to help him/her increase fluency. In the classroom, select a peer with whom the student enjoys working. Use the following steps:

(a) the student and tutor read aloud together; (b) when the student wants to read independently, s/he taps the tutor to stop reading; (c) the student reads aloud independently until s/he does not know a word or makes an error; (d) the tutor provides the word, the student pronounces the word, and the pair resumes choral reading. Use the procedure five times a week for a minimum of 5 minutes for a period of 6 to 8 weeks (Topping, 1987).

7. Use a method with the student that is designed to improve reading rate. For example, read a paragraph to the student while s/he watches and then have him/her reread the same passage.

8. Use the Repeated Readings Procedure (Samuels, 1979) to help the student improve his/her reading speed. (See Appendix.) Tape the student's first and final reading of the passage to document progress and so that s/he can hear him/herself read in a fluent manner.

9. Use the Neurological Impress Method (Heckelman, 1966, 1986) with the student for 10 minutes daily. (See Appendix.) You may use a volunteer, a peer, or a cross-age tutor to work with the student.

10. Teach the student's parents how to do the Neurological Impress Method (Heckelman, 1966, 1986). (See Appendix.) Ask them to use this method for 10 to 15 minutes each night, reading material that their son/daughter has selected.

Taped Books

1. Have the student listen to a taped passage or a short book over and over as s/he reads along with the tape. When s/he has mastered the passage or book, have him/her read it to someone else.

2. Have the student listen to taped books as s/he reads along with a copy of the book.

3. Provide the student with taped copies of all his/her textbooks.

4. Have him/her listen to his/her tapes with headsets as s/he reads along during all independent reading time.

5. Provide the student with information on how to obtain taped books. (See Appendix.) Many public libraries also have a selection of taped books for loan.

Altering Rate

1. Teach the student how to alter his/her reading rate depending upon the purpose for reading. For example, s/he may want to scan for specific information, skim to see if an article is appropriate for a report, read a technical manual or history text slowly, or read at a fast pace for pleasure.

2. Teach the student how to slow down his/her reading when s/he encounters difficult material. Teach him/her to reread passages when the meaning is unclear.

3. Teach the student how to skim a passage to obtain the general idea. This skill is necessary in selecting appropriate reading materials for reports and for pleasure reading.

4. Teach the student how to scan a passage for specific information, such as answering questions in a text, taking an open-book test, or looking for information on a specific topic for a report.

Fluency/Comprehension

1. Combine a fluency method with a method for increasing comprehension. For example, read aloud several paragraphs with the student and then stop to discuss the story. Before resuming choral reading, have the student predict what s/he thinks will happen next.

2. Use choral repeated reading with the student to increase both fluency and comprehension. Select a high-interest book one or two levels above the student's instructional level. Establish a purpose for reading by skimming the book. Encourage the student to make predictions about the content. Read the book using this three-step process: (a) read a short passage from the book as the student watches, running your finger smoothly under the text; (b) read the same section together with the student as many times as needed so that s/he feels comfortable reading independently; (c) have the student read the passage independently. After each section, discuss how the content related to your predictions and set new purposes for reading (Bos & Vaughn, 1991).

3. Have the student use the *Timed Readings in Literature* series by Jamestown Publishers (Spargo, 1989) to increase reading speed and comprehension. Each book contains short passages followed by questions. The student should practice reading at a slightly faster-than-normal speed and then answer questions about what s/he read.

Comprehension

(Related sections: Oral Language, Knowledge/Content Areas)

Further Evaluation

1. Further evaluate the student's reading comprehension using the student's classroom texts. Have him/her read several passages silently and then retell the major points.

2. Further evaluate the student's reading comprehension by conducting a structured retelling. Have him/her read a passage or story and then ask him/her several questions to assess comprehension.

General

1. When providing instruction in reading comprehension, make sure that the student's instructional materials are at the independent reading level in word recognition. Materials at the independent level will allow the student to devote attention to the comprehension activities.

2. Place a student in a reading group based on his/her present performance level in language and reading comprehension, rather than his/her performance in word identification skills.

3. Praise the student for independently using any new skills and strategies in his/her reading.

4. Present purposeful reading assignments. For example, within text have the student locate and take notes on information that s/he will use to lead a discussion or provide information to his/her cooperative learning group.

5. Ensure that any selected comprehension strategies for the student involve active participation. This will help the student pay attention and, subsequently, increase understanding of the material.

6. Before the student reads a chapter or a book, let him/her know that you will have a conference after s/he is finished to discuss his/her reaction to the material.

7. Use the language experience approach to reading instruction with the student and place an emphasis

on comprehension activities, such as forming questions, paraphrasing the story, or using context clues to identify words.

8. Teach the student the importance of punctuation for understanding the meaning of a passage.

9. Teach the student critical reading skills such as recognition of fact vs. opinion, objective vs. persuasive language, supported vs. unsupported generalizations, and valid vs. invalid arguments.

10. Help the student improve his/her reading comprehension skills using texts that will be required or similar to the types required in his/her college courses.

11. A variety of strategies for teaching reading comprehension may be found in *Reading Strategies and Practices: A Compendium* (Tierney, Readence, & Dishner, 1985) or *Teaching Reading Comprehension: From Theory to Practice* (Devine, 1986).

Prereading Activities

Background Knowledge

1. Before assigning a reading selection to the student, find out what s/he already knows about the topic. If s/he lacks the knowledge necessary to understand the selection, preteach the necessary background information.

2. Before assigning independent reading, make sure that the student has the necessary vocabulary and background knowledge to understand the story or chapter. Help the student relate any new information to his/her own experiences.

3. When teaching the student new concepts, attempt to relate them to ideas that s/he already understands by using analogies from his/her own experience.

4. Prior to or after reading with the student, try to relate an event or character in the story to your own lives.

5. Teach the student to read actively for meaning, attempting to associate the meaning of the passage with his/her own knowledge or experience.

6. Help the student understand the meaning of concepts in his/her texts with which s/he has not had direct experience.

7. Read a selection with the student before asking him/her to read it independently. Make sure that s/he understands all new concepts and vocabulary.

8. Before assigning independent reading, provide a preview of all new concepts and vocabulary in the assignment. List them on the board and provide ample opportunities for discussion.

9. Use a K-W-L-S strategy sheet (Ogle, 1986) to help the student organize his/her knowledge of a topic both before and after reading a passage. (See Appendix.)

10. When eliciting background knowledge from the student, try to organize the information in a semantic map (Pearson & Johnson, 1978). The final diagram should visually present the information in such a way that the relationships are evident. Seeing his/her own information organized in this way will help him/her create a framework to accommodate new information.

11. As a prereading activity to set a purpose for content area reading, create a Semantic Feature Analysis chart (Anders & Bos, 1986; Bos, Anders, Filip, & Jaffe, 1989; Johnson & Pearson, 1984) for the student. (See Appendix.) This chart will help the student activate prior knowledge about the topic, note key vocabulary and concepts, and think about the relationships among them. Have the student fill out as much of the chart as s/he can prior to reading the selection and then correct or confirm his/her predictions after reading the selection. This procedure is particularly effective in a group setting as students discuss their reasons for choices both before and after reading.

12. Follow these guidelines to help the student develop prior knowledge: (a) build upon what the student already knows, (b) provide much of the background information through discussion, (c) provide real-life experiences, (d) explain parts of the passage before the student reads it, (e) help the student develop expand his/her knowledge, and (f) encourage wide reading (Devine, 1986).

Vocabulary

1. Do not teach vocabulary from lists unrelated to classroom context. Select new vocabulary directly from the student's reading, your lecture, or classroom projects. Ensure his/her ability to understand and

use these words in context before presenting new words.

2. Teach new vocabulary in the student's reading selections by using synonyms or short phrases. Simplify dictionary definitions.

3. Help the student relate new vocabulary words and their meanings to his/her own experiences. Elicit from the student any associated words that s/he knows. This will aid in retention and alert you to misinterpretations of word meaning.

4. Use Semantic Feature Analysis (Johnson & Pearson, 1984) to help the student relate new concepts or vocabulary to his/her prior knowledge. (See Appendix.)

5. Use the Directed Vocabulary Thinking Activity (Cunningham, 1979) to help the student learn how to infer the meaning of unknown words from context. (See Appendix.)

6. Teach the student the meaning of the most common prefixes and suffixes. Provide a root word, attach affixes to create real or nonsense words, and have the student determine a possible meaning. For example, the nonsense word "circumcessable" could mean "able to go around."

7. Provide the student with lists of common prefixes and suffixes. Have him/her locate examples of words using these affixes in his/her reading.

Context Clues

General

1. Teach the student additional ways to use his/her good reasoning and language skills to identify unfamiliar words. One suggestion is to have him/her look at the first few letters or any part of the word that s/he recognizes, read to the end of the sentence for clues about what word makes sense, and then go back and identify the unknown word.

2. In reading, encourage the student to use context clues and directly teach a variety of ways to do so (e.g., reading to the end of a sentence, recognizing definitions, monitoring whether or not what s/he is reading makes sense).

3. Teach the student how to monitor his/her reading for meaning, as well as how to use specific strategies when what s/he has read did not make sense (e.g., use context clues, reread, ask someone).

4. Teach the student how to recognize and use a variety of context clues within the text. Examples include: direct explanation (within an appositive, signaled by "that is," or explained later in the paragraph); explanation through example; synonym or restatement; summary; comparison or contrast; words in a series; and inference (Thomas & Robinson, 1972). (See Appendix.)

Cloze Procedure

1. Use the cloze procedure to increase the student's ability to use syntactic and semantic information. Systematically delete keywords that can be identified using the context.

2. When training the student in the use of the cloze procedure, progress from single sentences to paragraphs and from teacher-directed activities to individual work.

3. When introducing the cloze procedure to the student, begin by providing a list of the deleted words at the bottom of the page. As skill increases, add several distractors to the list. As a final step, phase out all clues.

4. To increase attention to context clues, construct a cloze passage from the student's language experience stories. Have him/her try to reconstruct the story.

5. Use a modified cloze procedure to help the student increase his/her ability to use syntactic and semantic clues. Initially, delete words at the end of the sentence and then, as his/her skill increases, delete words randomly.

6. To increase the student's attention to certain categories of words, such as nouns or verbs, use the cloze procedure with specific deletions. (See Appendix.)

Strategies

Predicting/Making Inferences

1. When reading a story to the student, stop at specific points and ask him/her questions about the story events. Ask him/her to predict what s/he thinks will happen next.

2. Develop the student's thinking skills within the context of reading. Teach him/her to predict events based on a limited amount of information and then judge the accuracy of his/her predictions.

3. Help the student incorporate his/her past experiences and knowledge to make predictions about the story events. Have him/her read to verify his/her predictions and to revise them as necessary.

4. Prior to reading, provide the student with a list of prediction questions or possible outcomes. Have the student discuss these questions with a peer or in a small group and then read to find the answers.

5. When reading with the student, make a prediction map on the board or on a piece of paper. Stop at appropriate points and have the student predict what s/he thinks will happen next. Record the prediction on the map and then read to find out if it is correct. If the answer is incorrect, revise the map.

6. Have the student read short stories with the endings deleted. Have him/her develop a logical conclusion either orally or in writing.

7. To develop critical and active reading, involve the student in an individualized or group Directed Reading-Thinking Lesson (DRTL) (Stauffer, 1969; Tierney, Readence, & Dishner, 1985).

Retelling/Paraphrasing

1. After reading the student a story, ask him/her to retell the main idea and the sequence of events.

2. After the student reads a story, have him/her describe the main characters, the problem they encounter, and how the problem is solved.

3. While the student is reading, teach him/her to pause and paraphrase the main ideas of the passage as a way to monitor understanding. Teach the student then to use verbal rehearsal to review the sections of text s/he has just learned from a textbook.

4. Teach the student to check/reinforce his/her own comprehension at the paragraph level by paraphrasing the main idea and at least two supporting details orally or in writing. Teach the student to include a clear statement of the relationship among ideas.

5. Help the student learn to monitor understanding of what s/he reads and then to use a specific strategy, such as rereading a passage, when the meaning is unclear. When initially learning to monitor comprehension, have him/her start with one or two sentences at a time. As skill improves, increase the number of sentences between self-checks.

6. Teach the student to attempt to visualize or make a "mental movie" of what s/he reads. As s/he reads each passage, have him/her describe in detail the images that s/he created. Initially, ask the student detail and inferential questions about the images and passages. As skill increases, allow his/her description of images to progress without interruption.

7. Teach the student to summarize text as s/he reads according to the following five rules: (a) delete unimportant information, (b) delete redundant information, (c) superordinate lists (e.g., write "steel products" rather than listing each product), (d) select the topic sentence, and (e) construct a topic sentence when one is not obvious in the text (Brown & Day, 1983).

8. Teach the student strategies for monitoring his/her comprehension of nonfiction text that have been demonstrated to be effective, such as paraphrasing the main idea of a paragraph after reading it (Schumaker, Denton, & Deshler, 1984) or answering questions about the main idea of a passage (Nolan, Alley, & Clark, 1980; Wong & Jones, 1982).

9. Teach the student how to take notes in the margin to summarize information while s/he is reading to enhance his/her comprehension. Have him/her place question marks by any sections in the text that s/he does not understand and ask a parent, teacher, or friend to explain it.

10. In nonfiction materials, teach the student to use paraphrasing of the main idea and supporting details to help him/her draw a semantic map of the structure and content of the material.

Questioning

1. Help the student set a purpose for reading by presenting him/her with a picture, title, segment of text, or a combination of these. Have him/her generate as many different questions as possible, then read to find the answers.

2. When reading stories or content area textbooks, teach the student to read the questions at the end of the chapter first so that s/he knows what information is important.

3. When introducing a new chapter, have the student write the questions from the chapter on an index card and refer to the card while s/he is reading the

chapter. Have him/her check off each question when s/he locates the answer.

4. Teach the student a self-questioning strategy to use while reading content area information. Teach the student to:

   a. Ask yourself: Why am I studying this passage?
   b. Locate the main idea in the paragraph and underline it.
   c. Think of a question about the main idea.
   d. Read to learn the answer.
   e. Look back at the question and answer for each paragraph to determine a relationship. (Wong & Jones, 1982)

As a modification of this technique, the student may write down the answer to his/her main idea question in a complete sentence (Wong & Jones, 1982). Teach the student how to create a structured overview of a selection based on his/her written answers to main idea questions generated by use of the self-questioning strategy.

5. Teach the student how to set a purpose for reading by turning chapter subheadings into questions and then reading to find the answer.

6. Teach reading study skills, such as surveying a chapter in a textbook prior to reading it, to establish a framework for understanding the information.

7. Teach the student how to create and answer the reporter questions for each subsection of content area reading material (i.e., *when, where, who, what, why,* and *how*).

8. Teach the student to recognize when a question cannot be answered based solely on the information given in the reading selection. Teach him/her to use prior knowledge as well as the information given in the text to make inferences.

9. For all reading selections, prepare inference-level questions to give to the student as a guide for reading.

10. In reading for key ideas and critical details, ask the student to underline or note elements that s/he would expect to be covered on a test.

11. After the student learns how to recognize key ideas and critical details, reinforce this skill by having him/her make up test questions for the teacher or other students on a literature or content area selection.

12. Teach the student how to apply SQ3R (Survey, Question, Read, Recite, Review; Robinson, 1970). This technique is used to help the student create a framework for the context to be read, set a purpose for reading, and learn to monitor comprehension. (See Appendix.)

13. Teach the student how to use a modification of SQ3R, such as PQ4R (Preview, Question, Read, Reflect, Recite, Review; Thomas & Robinson, 1972) or PQ5R (Preview, Question, Read, Record, Recite, Review, Reflect) (Graham & Robinson, 1984). In the PQ5R strategy, the student writes down the critical information for review.

14. Use the ReQuest procedure (Manzo, 1969) to increase the student's ability to ask questions actively when reading. Read a story together with the student. Take turns asking questions of each other. When first learning the procedure, ask questions about factual material. As soon as possible, ask questions that will promote higher-level comprehension skills. (See Appendix.)

15. Use a modified ReQuest procedure with the student (Alley & Hori, 1981) to develop verbal reasoning and active reading. (See Appendix.)

16. With any questioning strategy that the student learns, provide him/her with many opportunities to practice and apply the selected technique in school reading assignments.

Study Guides

1. To encourage interaction with the text, provide the student with study guides in a variety of formats for his/her reading assignments. (See Appendix.)

2. Teach the student how to summarize important information from a chapter on a one-page or two-page study guide that s/he can then use to prepare for tests.

3. Provide the student with a structured study guide that provides specific questions and the page number and paragraph in the text where the information is located. As skill in locating information increases, eliminate these prompts.

4. After the student recognizes or is guided to recognize, the passage structure, provide an outline, based on the passage, in which s/he can record content. These summarizations will aid retention and

then may be used as study notes. Ensure that the student has prior knowledge of the concept of main idea and adequate summarization skills (Slater, Graves, & Piche, 1984). A sample guide follows:

a. Cause: _____
   Support: _____
   Support: _____
   Support: _____
b. Related Topic: _____
   Support: _____
   Support: _____
   Support: _____
c. Effect: _____
   Support: _____
   Support: _____
   Support: _____

5. Insert questions into the text for the student to answer while s/he is reading. To minimize writing in the textbook, make a study guide with numbered questions pertaining to specific information in the text. Record the question number in pencil in the margin next to the related information.

6. Before the student reads an assignment, provide him/her with questions that highlight the most important points. Have the student answer the questions as s/he locates the answers in the text. After reading, discuss the same questions with the student.

7. To set a purpose for reading and help the student understand the structure of information in the text, provide him/her with a study guide that will direct him/her to the key ideas, most critical details, and/or the organization of the information.

8. Provide the student with questions to answer while s/he is reading. After s/he has answered the questions, have him/her write a brief summary that includes the main ideas and important details.

9. Prior to reading, provide the student with a set of questions to answer. Create some questions that require factual recall to be answered and others that may be answered using prior knowledge. Before the student reads the material, have him/her attempt to answer as many questions as s/he can.

Organization

Stories

1. Teach the student how to recognize the sequence of events, ideas, steps, times, and places in stories and literature selections.

2. Teach the student a simple story grammar to use when reading and discussing stories, such as that all stories have a beginning, middle, and end. As proficiency develops, introduce a more complex story grammar.

3. Teach the student a simple story grammar that includes these four questions:
   a. Who is the story about?
   b. What is s/he trying to do?
   c. What happens when s/he tries to do it?
   d. What happens in the end? (Carnine & Kinder, 1985)

4. Teach the student a story grammar, the underlying structure of stories, so that s/he has a framework for understanding new stories that s/he reads. Elements of a story grammar include: setting (time, place, situation), major characters, problem (and problems within the problem), resolution of the problem, and an ending (Thomas, Englert, & Morsink, 1984).

5. Teach the student a specific mnemonic strategy to use when s/he is reading and identifying the various elements of stories, such as STORE the Story (Schlegel & Bos, 1986). (See Appendix.)

6. Help the student develop higher-level inferential skills, such as determining the theme or moral of a story, the motivation for a character's action, or the interaction of the events.

7. When reading short stories, teach the student to: (a) identify the main problem or conflict, (b) draw inferences from the text about the personalities and motivations of the main characters, (c) identify how the main problem is solved, and (d) determine the theme or what the author was trying to say (Gurney, Gersten, Dimino, & Carnine, 1990).

Text

1. To help the student increase his/her understanding of how ideas are organized, separate the paragraphs in a report or article. Have him/her read the paragraphs, and then reassemble them into a logical sequence.

2. Teach the student that the main idea is the sentence that holds the paragraph together. When the main idea sentence is deleted or covered, the paragraph loses its meaning. The student can check his/her choice of a main idea by reading the paragraph without that sentence to see if it does, in fact, diminish the paragraph's meaning (Wong, 1985).

3. Teach the student how to tell the difference among main ideas, supporting details, and tangential information in both fiction and nonfiction material.

4. Teach the student to recognize sentences that signal a transition from one subtopic to the next and keywords that signal transition (e.g., *then, but, however, yet, meanwhile, consequently*.) Later, teach the student to recognize transition paragraphs (Robinson, Andresen, Hittleman, Patterson, & Paulsen, 1978).

5. Help the student increase his/her awareness of terms denoting linguistic relationships (such as temporal, spatial, cause/effect, analogous, exceptions, comparison/contrast) in text to help clarify relationships among events, objects, people. Use specific illustrations of these words and phrases from social studies, science, and literature textbooks.

6. Teach the student to recognize different patterns for the organization of information within a paragraph or within a longer selection. Examples include: sequential, comparison/contrast, or cause/effect.

7. Directly teach the student different ways that information in textbooks can be organized (e.g., listing, sequential, comparison/contrast, hierarchical, main idea and details, description, cause/effect).

8. Teach the student how to read the introduction of an article or a content area textbook chapter to find the general topic, what the author wants to say about the topic, the key points of the selection, and how the key points will be related to each other and the central idea (Robinson et al., 1978).

9. Teach the student how to read the conclusion of content area text to find a restatement of the central idea, the key points, and the organizational pattern of the chapter (Robinson et al., 1978).

10. Teach the student how to organize the content of fiction and nonfiction materials through the use of semantic mapping or webbing. This technique visually displays the relationships among the major concepts. (See Appendix.)

11. Teach the student to categorize information from a reading selection to aid recall. Examples include: Major battles fought in Europe during World War II or the effects of the lack of light on cave-dwelling animals.

12. Teach the student to use semantic mapping to clarify the key ideas and supporting details in a selection and the structure by which they are interrelated. After the student reads the selection, s/he might: (a) brainstorm everything that s/he can remember, categorize this information, and depict the organization of this information in a semantic map, or (b) use the headings and subheadings in the chapter to create a preliminary map and fill in the critical details from the text. (See Appendix.)

13. Teach the student to recognize the organizational structure in a passage. Examples are a position/opinion statement with supportive information, list of causes and effects concerning a particular situation with information on each, and a statement of a problem with solutions given in succeeding paragraphs (Slater, Graves, & Piche, 1984).

14. Teach the student how to sequence ideas and events using a timeline drawn on paper.

15. When working with text ordered chronologically/sequentially, such as history or literature, teach the student to place events on a timeline to help visualize the temporal and possibly the cause/effect relationships. Emphasize that a temporal relationship does not imply cause/effect.

Additional Ideas:

6

WRITTEN LANGUAGE

Handwriting

Further Evaluation

1. Based upon the severity of fine-motor problems, refer the student to an occupational therapist who is skilled at dealing with visual-motor and handwriting problems.

Compensations

1. Because of his/her extreme difficulty with handwriting, have the student dictate responses to a peer or into a tape recorder whenever writing is required. Encourage the student to develop handwriting skill, but only in noncompetitive situations.

2. Do not penalize or grade the student in handwriting. Instead, provide many ungraded opportunities for skill to develop.

3. As long as the student's handwriting is legible, do not penalize him/her.

4. When working with the student on visual-motor activities or handwriting, provide ample positive

reinforcement for effort rather than just for improvement or quality of his/her product.

5. Because of extreme difficulty with handwriting, teach the student how to type.

6. Encourage the student to take a typing course as one of his/her electives.

7. Teach the student how to use a word processor and allow him/her to use it for all writing assignments.

Readiness

1. To develop finger coordination and strength, provide the student with activities that require use of hands and fingers. Examples include playing with clothespins or squeezing rubber balls.

2. Give the student lots of practice using utensils in activities that will give him/her the opportunity to plan and execute a movement using the small muscles of his/her hand. If necessary, directly teach the student how to visualize where the pencil, marker, or scissors should be at the end of each stroke or cut.

3. Provide the student with opportunities to participate in fine-motor activities, such as cutting, pasting, finger painting, and drawing.

4. Provide activities throughout the summer that will help the student improve his/her visual-motor skills, such as drawing, painting, and coloring.

5. Provide the student with many opportunities for use of fine-motor skills in activities consistent with his/her current ability level. Such activities may include: simple paper folding; cutting paper across a bold line; cutting out large simple shapes with bold borders and tracing them; and copying large, simple shapes on the chalkboard. A variety of fun and interesting mediums should be used, such as fingerpaints, watercolors, pudding (to lick off his/her finger after making a shape), and glitter on glue designs. Also provide many activities in which the goal is not recognizable figures, but simply free-form designs.

6. Use activities such as tracing, using templates, and coloring within simple, bold-line drawings, before moving on to copying forms and drawing pictures.

7. Use art activities to improve visual-motor integration. Provide the student with simple designs and pictures with bold outlines. Encourage him/her to attempt to color within the boundaries.

8. When providing practice with copying or tracing shapes, gradually decrease the size of the shapes as the student's performance improves and the tasks become easier. Do not increase the task difficulty until s/he has mastered the current task.

9. Use finger painting with the student to let him/her practice forming straight lines, curved lines, and circles. Play around with formation of a variety of shapes. When simple shapes are mastered, begin to teach uppercase letters. After letters are mastered with finger paint, provide practice with a pencil or a felt-tip pen.

10. Using chalk, have the student draw large shapes or letters on the playground.

11. Keep fine-motor activity periods short and intersperse them with activities that are fun, interesting, or active, such as listening to a story, dancing, and playing on the playground.

12. Encourage the student to participate in pencil-and-paper activities, such as completing dot-to-dot drawings or solving mazes.

13. Since the student is highly motivated to write, explain to him/her how spending time in fine-motor activities will make handwriting easier.

Materials

1. Teach the student to write on primary paper that has a dotted middle line.

2. The student needs a tactile reinforcer to enhance his/her awareness of the line on which s/he is supposed to write. Draw with white glue over the bottom line (if using paper with guidelines) on the paper. When the glue dries, it will leave a clear, raised line.

3. To help the student keep his/her letters on the line, underline the bottom line with a red felt-tip pen.

4. Provide the student with paper with a dotted middle line to use for both handwriting practice and/or compositions.

5. When practicing handwriting, have the student use a black felt-tip pen on lined paper.

6. Let the student sample a variety of writing implements and select the one that s/he likes best for handwriting practice.

7. If assignments must be written in ink, permit the student to use an erasable ballpoint pen.

Grip

1. Teach the student how to hold a pencil. Have him/her hold the pencil between the index finger and thumb, resting the pencil on the middle finger. The pencil is then slanted at a forty-five degree angle.

2. Use modeling clay around the pencil to help the student develop a more relaxed grip.

3. Have the student use a triangular rubber grip to aid in developing a more efficient pencil grip.

4. Place a rubber band right above the shaved area of the pencil to help the student remember where to hold the pencil.

5. Teach the student an alternative grip, such as the D'Nealian grip (Thurber, 1988), that does not require much fingertip pressure to hold the writing instrument. Have the student hold the pencil between the index and middle fingers with about a 25-degree slant.

Practice/Evaluation

1. Recognize the student's effort in trying to write neatly. Provide only words of encouragement as s/he develops handwriting skill.

2. Provide the student with daily handwriting practice that incorporates immediate feedback into the activity.

3. Provide guided handwriting practice until the student's motor patterns are firmly established.

4. Date all handwriting samples so that the student can see concrete evidence of his/her progress.

5. Help the student become self-motivated to improve his/her handwriting. Discuss practical reasons for improving legibility.

6. Identify the specific illegibilities in the student's handwriting and provide corrective work.

7. Have the student work on handwriting daily for short lessons. Have the student apply the skills that s/he is learning in context.

8. When the student is concentrating on handwriting instruction, provide exercises that require little thinking so that s/he can devote his/her attention to legibility. As s/he develops mastery, increase the conceptual level of the task.

9. Teach the student how to evaluate his/her own handwriting in relation to letter formation, spacing, alignment, slant, and line quality.

10. After handwriting practice, have the student evaluate his/her own writing. Have him/her circle and rewrite the specific letters that need correction or improvement.

11. Have the student concentrate on neat handwriting only when s/he is preparing the final drafts of papers.

12. Have the student concentrate on improving the legibility of his/her writing. When s/he is writing final drafts of papers, have him/her make legibility a priority.

13. Help the student understand how performance in handwriting may affect how someone evaluates his/her school papers or his/her job applications.

Reversals

1. Because the student has become anxious about his/her letter reversals in writing, do not bring attention to them. Treat reversals as spelling errors that will be corrected during the editing stage of writing.

2. Provide the student with cards that include keywords containing frequently reversed letters, such as *dog* for *d*, that s/he may keep at his/her desk and refer to when writing.

3. Use visual clues for teaching the student the forms of frequently confused letters. For example, show the student that the letter *b* can be formed with the fingers of the left hand and *d* with the right. Teach him/her that since the alphabet is written from left to right and *b* comes first in the alphabet, *b* is the letter made with the left hand. Since the letter *d* comes after *b*, it is made with the right hand.

4. Help the student recall the orientation of letters by using language clues. For example, remind the student that a lowercase *b* is just a capital *B* that lost the top.

5. Use linguistic clues for teaching the student the forms of frequently confused letters. For example, draw an association between the letter *b* and the word *baseball*. Tell the student a story about the girl who wanted to play baseball. She could play catch with just a ball, but for *baseball*, the bat comes first.

6. Teach the student how to form the letter *b* using a forward circle (clockwise) and the letter *d* using a backward circle (counterclockwise).

7. Teach the student that the letter *d* starts like an *a* and the letter *b* starts like an *l*.

8. Have the student complete worksheets that provide additional practice with frequently reversed letters. For example, the student could circle all of the *d*s on a page and write the letter several times.

9. Show the student how to check his/her papers for *b/d* reversals. By turning the paper to the right, a correctly formed *b* will look like the start of a pair of glasses.

10. After identifying the letters that the student reverses, have him/her practice one letter daily in different applications. For example, have the student trace the letter and write it from memory, write several keywords that contain the letter, and circle as many of the letter that s/he can find in a magazine or newspaper article. At the end of the week, provide discrimination practice among the letters that s/he has been practicing.

11. Provide the student with practice of letters that s/he frequently reverses. Present a model of the correctly formed letter, followed by the letter formed several times with a series of dots. Gradually fade out the dots so that the student is required to form the letter independently.

12. To reduce reversals in writing, have the student state aloud the movement pattern s/he should make when writing a frequently reversed letter. For example, when forming the letter *b*, s/he may say: "start high, line down, back up and around."

13. Based upon his/her frequent letter reversals, teach the student cursive writing.

Paper Position

1. Teach the student how to position his/her paper correctly. For a right-handed writer, the bottom left-hand corner should point at the child's navel. The position is the reverse for a left-handed writer. Show the student how the paper runs parallel to the writing arm like a railroad track.

2. Show the student how to hold his/her paper steady with the nonwriting hand.

3. Provide the student with a clipboard to use in writing activities. This will make writing easier for him/her by keeping his/her paper in a consistent position.

Format

1. Glue stars on the paper to show the student where to start and stop writing.

2. Show the student how to use margins and indentations when formatting a paper.

3. Place a dot about 1 inch in from the margin to remind the student to indent paragraphs. Have him/her make a dot before starting each new paragraph.

4. To help the student learn to use margins, fold the paper along the side to make a crease to remind him/her where to stop writing.

5. To help the student remember to use margins, have him/her use a ruler and felt-tip pens to "format" a stock of blank composition paper. Use green pen to draw in the left margin and red pen to draw the right.

6. To help the student remember to use margins, place a piece of scotch tape along the right side to remind him/her to go to the next line.

7. To help the student visualize the format of a well-organized piece of writing, provide him/her with some samples of page formats. For example, the paper in Figure 6–1 is formatted with name, date, title, three indented paragraphs, and equal margins.

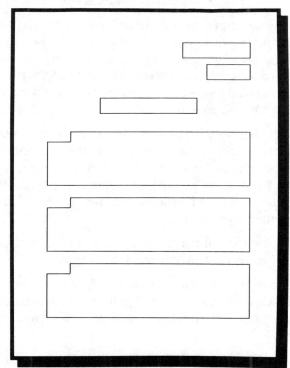

Figure 6–1.

Spacing

1. Show the student how to reduce the spacing between his/her words and letters to improve legibility. Explain to him/her that letters are written next to each other and a small space about the size of his/her letter *o* is left between words.

2. To provide additional practice with spacing between letters, have the student practice writing words on graph paper with one letter in each box. The sets of lines will help him/her with spacing, size, and alignment.

Slant

1. Since regularity of slant is affecting legibility, use lightly drawn slant indicators (//////) on the paper to remind the student to form letters consistently.

2. Show the student how altering his/her paper position can make it easier to produce letters with a consistent slant.

3. Provide opportunities for the student to evaluate the regularity of slant in his/her writing. Model forming letters with a consistent slant and provide practice for mastery.

Letter Formation/Manuscript

1. Demonstrate proper letter formation to the student. Provide systematic practice with one letter before introducing another. Reinforce the student for properly formed letters. For example, let the student select a sticker whenever s/he carefully completes an assignment.

2. Use the following progression to teach the student letter formation. Have him/her: (a) trace the letter, (b) complete a dot-to-dot pattern of the letter, (c) copy from an index card, (d) write the letter after seeing it briefly on a flash card, and (e) reproduce the letter from memory.

3. Show the student a letter on a card and have him/her trace it in wet sand or cornmeal.

4. Have the student make raised letters with glue sprinkled with dry colored gelatin, cornmeal, or sand. Have him/her trace the letter before writing it.

5. Introduce letter shapes to the student with manipulatives, such as plastic letters. Before beginning paper-and-pencil tasks, have the student practice forming letters out of clay.

6. Roll out a slab of clay and have the student practice forming letters with a pencil or wooden stylus. Initially, provide a light etching for the student to trace more deeply.

7. Because of the student's fine-motor difficulties, introduce uppercase letters first; they require less motor coordination.

8. When practicing letter formation have the student use his/her whole arm, making large letters in the air while naming the letter out loud.

9. Show the student a letter on a card and have him/her trace it with his/her finger as s/he says the letter name. Have him/her then trace the letter with a crayon or felt-tip pen and then with a pencil. When the student is able to trace the letter accurately, have him/her copy the letter while looking at a model.

10. Have the student trace a letter with a crayon on a plastic sheet placed over the printed model. Have him/her place the plastic sheet over lined paper and write the letter. Then, have him/her place the letter over the printed model to see how closely they match.

11. When teaching the student how to write letters, first guide his/her hand to show proper formation. Keep practicing until the student feels that s/he can imitate the pattern independently.

12. When teaching the student how to form letters, provide a verbal description of the sequence of the strokes. When the student is forming the letters, have him/her verbalize the sequence of strokes while s/he writes the letter. Some handwriting programs, such as D'Nealian (Thurber, 1984), provide specific audio directions.

13. Use audio directions to teach the student the formation of each letter. Trace the letter on his/her hand, back, arm, or finger as you say the directions. This will help the student associate the oral directions with the kinesthetic/tactile formation of letters.

14. Have the student verbalize his/her movements as s/he forms large letters on the chalkboard. For example, to form the letter *n*, s/he would say: "down, up, make a hump, and back down." Encourage the student to make the letter as large as s/he can.

15. Help the student learn the proper heights of letters by teaching him/her the following story: "All letters start out living on the ground. Some, the short letters, stay there. Other letters stick their heads up into the sky, and still others hang their bottoms into the ocean. If letters who don't belong in the sky stick their heads up there, they'll blow away. If letters who don't belong in the ocean hang their bottoms in the ocean, they'll drown." At first, you may color-code the ocean, ground, and sky.

16. Use colors, arrows, and dots as cues to help the student remember the proper direction of strokes in letter formation.

17. To help him/her recall letter forms, place an alphabet strip at the top of the student's desk.

18. Obtain worksheets from the teacher that will allow the parent or tutor to help the student practice letter formation.

19. Teach the student how to form letters using the Spalding approach (Spalding & Spalding, 1986). The following rules are used for letter formation: (a) the letters must always sit on the line; (b) the letters come in only two sizes, tall and short (two-thirds of the space between the lines is for tall letters and one-third of the space is for short letters); and (c) the hands of the clock and straight lines are the two primary shapes used to form letters. (The clock is used as a model for placement of lines.)

20. Teach the student D'Nealian letter formation, a continuous stroke method which helps to prevent reversals and facilitates the transition to cursive writing (Thurber, 1984).

21. Do not require cursive writing, since the student's manuscript is legible and easier for him/her to produce than cursive.

Cursive

1. Do not require the student to learn cursive writing. Instead, help him/her focus efforts on improving legibility of his/her printing.

2. Have the student concentrate on improving the legibility of his/her cursive writing.

3. Teach the student cursive writing. Cursive writing minimizes spatial and directional confusion of letter forms. D'Nealian is one of the easier forms of cursive writing to learn and to use (Thurber, 1984). The student will need specific instruction in the formation as well as the direction of each stroke.

4. When introducing cursive writing, provide the student with as much practice as s/he needs with one letter before introducing another. As you teach him/her to join letters together, use real words to improve simultaneously his/her reading and spelling skills.

5. When introducing new letter forms to the student, follow a developmental sequence based on the similarity of motor patterns used to form each letter. For example, introduce formation of the lowercase cursive letter e with letters that are formed with a similar stroke, such as l, f, and k.

6. Use the following sequence for teaching the student lowercase cursive letters: The e family (e, l, h, f, b, k); the c family (c, a, d, o, g); the "hump" family (n, m, v, y, x); tails tied in the back (f, q); tails tied in the front (g, p, y, and z); the r and s (Hanover, 1983).

7. Check formation and joining of all cursive letters in writing. Provide practice in the correct formation of those that cause the student difficulty.

8. Give the student additional practice with letters that require a bridge or handle when joined to other letters: b, o, v, and w.

Rate

1. Do not penalize the student for his/her slow handwriting rate. Provide the student with ample time to complete writing assignments.

2. Discuss with the student how his/her slow rate of handwriting is affecting classroom performance. Design a program to increase writing speed.

3. To build handwriting speed, have the student do timed writings. Count the number of letters or words that s/he is able to copy from a book in a 1- to 3-minute period. Chart performance daily so that s/he is able to see his/her progress.

Basic Skills

Punctuation and Capitalization

1. Teach the student punctuation and capitalization rules sequentially, one rule at a time, with practice in a variety of situations (e.g., worksheets,

finding the use of the rule in reading, writing sentences and paragraphs, and editing one's own work or a peer's).

2. Introduce punctuation and capitalization rules to the student as s/he needs them for writing. Do not teach a new skill, such as the use of quotation marks, until s/he is ready to incorporate it into writing.

3. Make sure that the student masters one punctuation or capitalization rule before introducing another. For example, teach the student how to use a period at the end of a sentence. When this rule is mastered, introduce the use of a question mark.

4. Choose one error made by the student in writing and discuss it. Illustrate correct usage of the skill. Have the student practice using this skill correctly until it is mastered.

5. Teach the student how to recognize sentence boundaries for writing complete sentences and including the appropriate ending punctuation marks.

6. Teach the student the punctuation rules for the use of periods and commas and provide practice in applying these skills.

7. Review with the student the major uses of a comma, such as in a series, in a direct quotation, and after subordinate clauses.

8. Teach the student how to use quotation marks when s/he is writing dialogue. Have him/her examine the punctuation of dialogue in stories.

9. Have the student keep a list of the punctuation and capitalization rules that s/he is learning on an index card as a reference when editing writing.

Proofreading

Further Evaluation

1. Further evaluate the student's proofreading skill by having him/her edit several of his/her rough drafts. Ask the student to mark and attempt to correct all errors. Perform an error analysis to see the types of mistakes that the student is able to correct.

2. Provide the student with papers to proofread that list the number of errors to be located on the top of the paper, or in the margin by each line, if necessary. Perform an error analysis to identify how many and what types of errors the student was able to identify and correct.

Feedback

1. Use a consistent set of proofreading symbols when editing the student's work. Make sure that s/he understands the meaning of all the symbols.

2. When editing the student's paper, do not mark every error. Instead, select a few errors for him/her to correct.

3. After the student has proofread a paper, reinforce him/her for both identifying and correcting any errors.

4. Discuss with the student the types of errors that s/he makes frequently in writing, such as omitting endings from words. Remind him/her always to check word endings carefully when proofreading a paper.

Assistance

1. Make sure that the student receives additional help from someone (teacher, parent, peer) in proofreading papers before s/he turns in a final draft. You may set up a buddy system for peer editing in class.

2. When the student is proofreading a paper, have him/her circle any mistakes and then go to a peer proofreader for help in making corrections and finding other mistakes.

3. Encourage the student to ask a parent to help him/her edit written homework assignments.

4. Prior to having the student edit a paper, underline all misspelled words so that s/he can correct the spelling.

5. Have the student proofread his/her paper for spelling errors, underlining all words s/he thinks may be spelled incorrectly. Teach him/her how to use a pocket-sized, computerized spelling checker to make the needed changes.

6. Provide opportunities for the student to help younger students proofread and correct their papers. In addition to building his/her self-esteem, s/he will gain additional practice with editing.

7. Give the student practice in proofreading by having him/her review other students' papers.

Strategies

1. Teach the student a specific strategy for proof-reading and editing his/her papers. One strategy is the Error Monitoring strategy that uses the mnemonic COPS: Capitalization (C), Overall appearance including sentence structure (O), Punctuation (P), and Spelling (S) (Schumaker, Deshler, Nolan, Clark, Alley, & Warner, 1981). (See Appendix.)

2. Teach the student a modification of the Error Monitoring strategy (Schumaker et al., 1981), using the mnemonic SH! COPS! — Spelling (S), Hand-writing (H), Capitalization (C), Overall appearance (O) including visual format (e.g., margins, indentations, poor erasures), Punctuation (P), and Sentences (S) (structure, sentence boundaries). (See Appendix.)

3. Provide the student with daily opportunities for improving proofreading skill. For example, write sentences on the chalkboard that contain common mistakes, such as misspelled words and missing endings. Ask the student to identify the errors and make the necessary corrections.

4. When proofreading for spelling errors, have the student read his/her paper backwards, looking carefully at the spelling of each word.

5. Encourage the student to read his/her paper aloud when proofreading. This will help him/her hear sentences that can be improved.

6. Have the student read his/her rough draft into a tape recorder. Have him/her play back the tape and listen to the material before rewriting sections.

Checklists

1. Give the student a checklist to use when s/he proofreads his/her paper. Make sure that the student understands how to use all of the rules on the list.

2. Make a list of the student's most frequent writing errors. Have him/her use this list when s/he proof-reads his/her papers.

3. Before the student proofreads his/her paper, give him/her a list that contains the numbers of errors in spelling, punctuation, capitalization, and usage.

4. Instead of marking the specific errors in the student's paper, put a check in the margin by any line that contains an error. If there are two mistakes in the line, place two checks. Have the student try to find and correct the errors in each line.

Revising

Feedback/Conferences

1. Help the student improve his/her attitude toward writing by increasing the amount of attention and positive feedback s/he receives on assignments.

2. In helping the student with his/her writing, always stress meaning first; then teach any skills that s/he needs in the context of meaning.

3. When evaluating the student's papers, emphasize the clarity of thought and the meaning of the message over basic writing skills so that his/her interest and willingness to write are not diminished. Remind yourself that the ideas the student writes are more important than how s/he writes them.

4. Provide individualized peer or teacher feedback to the student on his/her writing assignments. Focus on the paper's strengths and present constructive suggestions for improvement.

5. Make sure that the student receives positive and corrective feedback on his/her writing assignments. You do not have to evaluate every piece of written work. Let the student know exactly which papers you will evaluate and when you will read them.

6. Have a brief revision conference with the student before s/he attempts to revise a paper. Discuss specific ideas that will help the student improve the paper.

7. After reading the student's paper with him/her, discuss in detail any parts that do not make sense. Ask the student to come up with ideas for improvement.

8. Meet with the student and provide him/her with constructive feedback regarding the organization of his/her paper. Identify problems and have him/her generate solutions.

9. Have the student work with a peer who will help him/her organize and revise his/her papers.

Strategies

1. Show the student how to use a cut-and-paste revision process. Have him/her locate the best passages in his/her writing and cut them out. Have

him/her arrange them in different orders. Have him/her reassemble the pieces in the best order and then write the necessary transitions.

2. Show the student various editing techniques that are used for revision, such as cutting up parts of a paper with scissors to reorganize sections or circling blocks of text and drawing an arrow to show where they should be inserted.

3. Help the student improve his/her editing skills by providing assistance in revising assignments that s/he has written on a computer. Teach the student how to delete and insert words and sentences and how to move blocks of text.

4. Teach the student how to evaluate the organization of his/her paper. Teach him/her to review the style and point of view, the sequence of the ideas, the relevance of the details to the stated purpose, the clarity of the message, and the consistency between the discussion and conclusions (Polloway, Patton, & Cohen, 1981).

5. Help the student understand that when s/he is revising and organizing ideas, s/he should not simultaneously attempt to edit for spelling, punctuation, and sentence structure.

6. Teach the student how to use a thesaurus. Provide opportunities for practice with this reference book during writing. For example, in a rough draft, have the student cross out certain words and locate and select synonyms from the thesaurus.

Spelling

Further Evaluation

1. Conduct a careful error analysis of the student's spelling to aid in selecting an appropriate remedial strategy. Evaluate several writing samples to determine any patterns of spelling errors.

2. Use diagnostic teaching to ascertain an effective spelling study strategy for the student.

3. Determine exactly which words the student knows and does not know how to spell from a high-frequency word list, such as Instant Words (Fry, 1980). Establish a program to help the student master the spellings of these words. (See Appendix.)

4. Dictate to the student a paragraph from a story in his/her reading series. Analyze the frequency and types of spelling errors. Save the sample to use to evaluate progress.

5. Dictate to the student a paragraph such as provided by Peters (1979). Analyze and classify the types of errors to assist in developing a remedial spelling program.

Invented Spelling

1. As writing skill develops, encourage the student to use invented spelling. This will help him/her increase understanding of the relationships between spoken and written words.

2. Deemphasize the need for correct spelling. Encourage the use of invented spelling by immersing the student in frequent, purposeful writing activities. As skill develops, provide formal spelling instruction.

3. Discuss with the student the difference between invented and conventional spelling. Explain to the student how learning to spell words correctly will help him/her increase knowledge of English spelling patterns.

General/Compensations

1. Ensure the student understands that the purpose for learning to spell correctly is to enhance his/her ability to communicate thoughts in writing.

2. Have the student spend 10 to 15 minutes daily studying and practicing his/her spelling words. Make sure that the study method s/he is using is effective for him/her.

3. Praise the student for systematic and logical attempts to spell words even when the words are spelled incorrectly.

4. Do not penalize the student for misspellings in his/her written work. Provide assistance as needed with correcting spelling for the final draft.

5. Do not discuss spelling errors with the student until s/he is ready to edit the final drafts of his/her papers.

6. Use a variety of spelling games and exercises to build interest and to reinforce correct spelling and the acquisition of spelling generalizations.

7. Provide opportunities for the student to use any of the words that s/he is learning to spell in context. For example, have the student write "spelling stories" using his/her words. (See Appendix.)

8. Give the student practice using his/her spelling words in written compositions and letters.

9. Designate a peer tutor to assist the student with mastery of spelling words. Provide the pair with high-interest activities designed to increase spelling accuracy.

10. Emphasize the functional use of spelling. Demonstrate the importance of correct spelling in practical and social situations.

11. Have the student enter any words that s/he has difficulty spelling alphabetically in a pocket note-book. Encourage him/her to use this personalized dictionary to edit his/her writing.

12. Provide the student with a poor spellers' dictionary. This is a book with words listed according to many of their possible misspellings with the correct spelling after each listing.

13. Provide the student with a pocket-sized, com-puterized spelling checker and teach him/her how to use it.

14. Help the student learn to use a spell checker on a word processing program to edit his/her work.

Word Lists

1. Individualize the student's lists. Do not use the basal spelling program. Instead, have the student create his/her own spelling list, selecting words that are frequently misspelled in his/her writing. Alter-natively, you choose words that s/he frequently misspells in writing.

2. Do not assign the student any spelling words that s/he cannot read easily, does not know the mean-ing of, or does not use in his/her writing.

3. Use a spelling flow list to help the student master the spelling of commonly used words. Teach only a few spelling words at a time. Provide daily review and practice until the words are mastered. Review the words weekly to ensure retention. (See Appendix.)

4. Present the student with just three or four new spelling words at a time at three intervals throughout the week rather than 10 or 15 words all at one time. Provide study time when the new words are pre-sented.

5. Select specific spelling words for the student to master, such as words with phonically regular spell-ing patterns.

6. Have the student select words that are misspelled in his/her stories for extra credit spelling words.

7. Have the student develop his/her own spelling dictionary that includes words that s/he frequently misspells in his/her writing. Use these words as the basis of his/her spelling program.

8. Select spelling words from "Instant Words" (Fry, 1980), a list of the 300 most common words used in writing. (See Appendix.) Have the student keep a chart that displays the words s/he has mastered.

9. Select words from "Instant Words—The 1000 Most Used Words in the English Language" and "Frequently Misspelled Words" (separate lists for elementary and high school students) as the basis of the student's spelling lists. Pretest before assigning words (Fry, Polk, & Fountoukidis, 1985).

Tests

1. When assigning the student a list of words to study, be sure to give him/her a pretest to identify the words that s/he does not know. Make sure that s/he is not being assigned too many words.

2. Have a peer test the student on his/her individualized spelling list.

3. Dictate to the student words with regular spellings, one at a time. Pronounce the sounds of the word separately and slowly in sequence. Remind him/her to write each letter sound as s/he hears it.

4. When dictating spelling words to the student, say each word slowly and pause between syllables. Repeat the word several times so that the student has time to listen to, write, and check the word.

5. Provide corrective feedback to the student immediately after completion of a spelling test. Have the student touch each letter of the word with his/her pencil as you spell the word out loud. Have the student correct each word that has an error.

Rules

1. Teach the student only the most common spelling rules (e.g., when a word ending in *y* is made plural, drop the *y* and add *ies*; *u* always follows *q*; when adding an ending starting with a vowel, double the final consonant to maintain the short vowel sound). Reinforce generalization to words in his/her classroom writing.

2. Teach the student that each syllable within a word must contain at least one vowel. Reinforce the student for including a vowel in every syllable.

3. Help the student with spelling using a highly structured program based on spelling rules and structural analysis, such as *Corrective Spelling Through Morphographs* (Dixon & Engelmann, 1979).

4. Help the student improve his/her spelling by using the *Childs Spelling System* (Childs & Childs, 1973). This program reviews and provides practice with the basic rules for English spelling, including the formation of plurals, the use of apostrophes, and the addition of suffixes and prefixes.

5. Use a daily dictation to help the student master the spelling rules that s/he is learning. An example of a manual that provides dictations that review spelling rules, word building, and word patterns is *The Spell of Words* (Rak, 1984).

Study Strategies: General

1. Discuss with the student the strategy that s/he is presently using to study his/her spelling words. If the present technique is ineffective, teach the student a new strategy to try.

2. Teach the student how to use a specific spelling study strategy. A variety of techniques can be found in many texts on teaching students with learning difficulties such as *Strategies for Teaching Students with Learning and Behavior Problems* (Bos & Vaughn, 1991) or *An Instructional Guide to the Woodcock-Johnson Psycho-Educational Battery— Revised* (Mather, 1991). Make sure that any spelling strategy selected includes multiple writings of the word without copying from a model.

3. Teach spelling through direct instruction, rather than expecting the student to learn how to spell words through reading or looking up difficult words in a dictionary. Provide opportunities for the student to practice the procedure independently.

4. Regardless of the selected spelling strategy, provide opportunities for the student to write the word correctly without a model and to self-check his/her accuracy.

5. Have the student use a spelling method that involves visual, auditory, and kinesthetic imagery and places an emphasis on recall.

6. Teach the student how to use the Fernald method (Fernald, 1943) for studying his/her spelling words. (See Appendix.)

7. Teach spelling and reading patterns simultaneously so that they are mutually reinforcing (e.g., teach the cvc reading pattern along with spelling words with this pattern).

8. Provide opportunities for the student to practice his/her spelling words on the computer.

9. Incorporate additional practice of spelling words into high-interest writing activities. One example of a game activity is a Spelling Story. (See Appendix.)

10. Use high-interest activities to help the student build his/her spelling skill. One book that contains a wide selection of classroom games and activities to reinforce spelling skill is *Selling Spelling to Kids* (Forte & Pangle, 1985).

Study Strategies: Auditory

(Related Section: Auditory Processing)

1. To improve spelling, help the student improve his/her auditory analysis skills. For example, teach him/her to tap out the "rhythm" of a word when counting the number of syllables. Help the student identify which sound in a syllable or a word is heard first, second, etc.

2. To improve spelling, help the student learn to determine the number of syllables that s/he hears in a word and then the number of sounds. Have him/her pronounce the word slowly as s/he makes a mark or pushes out a tile for each sound. As skill improves, have the student write the sounds that s/he hears.

3. Have the student study his/her spelling words using a Language Master. One procedure includes the following steps: (a) the student looks at the word while hearing it pronounced through the earphones, (b) the student looks at the word while hearing it spelled letter by letter, (c) the student repeatedly spells the word aloud with the tape until s/he can write it from memory, (d) the student writes the word from memory three times, checking for accuracy after each attempt.

4. Dictate simple spelling words to the student that s/he can rebuild with magnetic plastic letters or letter tiles. Have the student form the word with the

letters, cover the word, write the letters, and then check for accuracy. Have the student repeat the procedure until the word is spelled correctly (Bradley, 1981).

5. Have the student sort words with common phonic elements and spelling patterns (e.g., beginning or ending letters, double letters, medial vowel sounds, etc.). Have him/her then practice spelling the words in categories.

6. Dictate short words with regular sound–symbol correspondence for the student to spell. Pronounce words slowly so that the student can hear the separate phonemes. Have him/her pronounce each sound as s/he writes the letter or letter combinations.

7. Use color to highlight phonemically regular word parts. For example, when helping the student analyze a word, write the phonically regular parts in green and the irregular parts in red.

8. When studying the spelling patterns of words with the student, use a three-part classification with color coding: (a) predictable (green), (b) unpredictable but frequent (yellow), and (c) unpredictable and rare (red) (Venezky, 1970).

9. Help the student learn to generalize the words that s/he is learning to other words with the same phonemic element. For example, if s/he is learning to spell the word *night*, introduce and have the student practice other common words that share the *ight* spelling pattern.

10. Teach the student how to spell phonetically. Have him/her pronounce a word slowly as s/he writes each sound. Although this strategy will not always produce correct spellings, it will enable the student to use a computerized spelling checker or a poor speller's dictionary when s/he wishes to check the spelling of a word.

11. Teach the student how to pronounce long words in syllable units as s/he writes them.

12. Teach a spelling study strategy that emphasizes the auditory modality. One such strategy is Alternate Pronunciation, in which the student pronounces the word s/he is learning in the way it looks as if it would sound (e.g., *lab o rat ory*) (Ormrod, 1986). (See Appendix.)

13. Use an adaptation of the Simultaneous Oral Spelling method (Bradley, 1981; Gillingham & Stillman, 1973) to have the student practice words. (See Appendix.)

14. Teach the student how to spell common prefixes and suffixes and then to add these common affixes to root words.

Study Strategies: Visual

1. Have the student practice high-frequency "spelling demons," commonly used words that are not phonically regular. Have the student look at the word and then practice writing the word without copying from the model.

2. Use a letter cloze procedure to practice spelling. Give the student an index card that has a word written at the top; underneath it the word is written several times with different letters deleted. Gradually, reduce the number of letters provided in the targeted word. On the last trial, have the student turn over the card and write the entire word from memory. This method can be adapted by omitting specific word parts, such as vowels, consonants, consonant blends, prefixes, or suffixes.

3. Teach the student to form a visual image of a word before s/he attempts to spell it.

4. Have the student trace a word repeatedly with different colored crayons as s/he pronounces the word. Have him/her turn over the card and write the word from memory.

5. To practice spelling with the student, write a word on the chalkboard with a wet sponge. Have him/her try to copy the word before it evaporates from the board.

6. Present a spelling word to the student using a tachistoscope, flash card, or computer. Expose a word for several seconds and ask the student to write the word from memory. Decrease exposure time and increase the length of the word as his/her skill develops.

7. As the student is studying irregularly spelled words, have him/her underline the parts of the word that are not predictable from the pronunciation. Have the student use the following steps for practicing spelling: (a) pronounce the word slowly while looking carefully at each word part, (b) say the letters in sequence, (c) recall how the word looks and say the letters, (d) check recall by looking at the correct spelling, (e) write the word from memory, and (f)

compare the written word with the correct spelling. Repeat these steps until the word is spelled correctly (Horn, 1954).

8. For studying spelling words, teach the student the look-cover-write-check routine. Have the student: (a) look carefully at the word, (b) cover the word, (c) write the word without copying, and (d) check the word against the original. If the student has difficulty writing the word from memory, add in a tracing component.

9. Teach the student the Look-Spell-See-Write study strategy for learning spelling words. (See Appendix.)

10. Provide the student with visual imagery practice to improve his/her spelling skill. A procedure suggested by Radaker (1963) included the following steps: Type a word in the middle of an unlined index card. Have the student examine the letter sequence of the word closely. Have him/her close his/her eyes and try to picture the word in large, glossy, black letters on a white background, such as a theater screen, for as long as 1 minute. If s/he cannot maintain the picture, have him/her imagine the words as being created by large, metallic letters with holes in the top and bottom for fantasy nails. S/he should picture the word nailed securely to the screen. For retention, fantasy paste is applied to the back of the letters and the word is glued to the screen. A fantasy floodlight is then flashed on the word for as long as the student wants to maintain the image.

Expression

(Related Sections: Reading Comprehension, Oral Language)

Further Evaluation

1. Conduct a more intensive evaluation of the student's writing skill. Collect and evaluate at least four samples of classroom writing. Determine appropriate goals and objectives for enhancing writing performance.

2. Use the Written Expression Evaluation Guide to evaluate further the student's writing skill. (See Appendix.)

3. Have the student keep a writing folder that contains samples of his/her work. Conduct frequent evaluations to assess progress and establish new objectives.

4. Have the student develop a writing portfolio or a showcase of his/her best work. Use the writings in the portfolio to measure and monitor his/her growth over the school year, or if possible, several years. Have the student be responsible for selecting the pieces to go in the portfolio. Meet with the student to discuss growth, strengths, and goals. If possible, have the student maintain the portfolio for several years.

General

1. Use the writing process approach with the student for all writing assignments (Flower & Hayes, 1980; Graves, 1983). (See Appendix.)

2. Help the student understand the purpose of each stage of the writing process. Explain to him/her that writing is a recursive activity that usually involves multiple drafts and revisions, prior to publishing.

3. Make sure that the student spends at least 30 minutes daily on writing activities.

4. Before writing, have the student consider the purpose, his/her point of view, and the audience who will be reading his/her paper.

Compensations

1. Adapt all writing assignments to match the student's present level of oral language skill. Adjust criteria accordingly.

2. Reduce the amount of writing that the student is expected to complete, both in the classroom and for homework.

3. Provide the student with sufficient time to complete all writing activities.

4. When a lot of writing is necessary to complete an assignment, allow the student to dictate his/her answers to another student or a parent.

5. Allow the student to take all written examinations orally. If necessary, s/he can go to a quiet room and dictate his/her answers to an aide or into a tape recorder.

Motivation

1. Provide the student with a reward for a previously agreed upon amount of writing. Gradually fade the reinforcement as the student's motivation increases.

2. Have the student write short summaries of books from a lower grade level so that students in the lower-grade class can read a summary to see if they are interested in the book. Have the student attach his/her summaries to the inside jacket covers.

3. Have the student incorporate a variety of writing assignments with his/her artwork. For example, have him/her illustrate the stories that s/he is writing or choose a name and write a brief description of a picture that s/he has drawn.

4. Help the student complete written projects that s/he can be proud of, such as writing and illustrating a book. Provide opportunities for the student to share his/her written work with others. For example, have the student go to another class to read his/her story.

5. Have the student work in a cooperative learning group to write a story or play. Make sure that the student participates in the writing activity. For example, as part of a prewriting activity, s/he could be the secretary who records the ideas generated by the students in his/her group.

6. Have the student engage in meaningful writing activities that will emphasize the communicative, interactive nature of writing, such as writing letters or postcards to friends.

7. Identify the types of writing that the student may be required to perform in a vocational setting. Provide a variety of relevant writing assignments.

8. Have the student engage in practical writing activities that will be required in the future, such as completing job applications or applications for college entrance.

Journal

1. Have the student keep a daily writing journal. When reviewing the journal, write positive, specific comments about the content.

2. Encourage the student to keep a personal diary throughout the year.

3. Encourage the student to keep a journal or diary on all trips and during summer vacation.

4. Permit the student to choose his/her own topics when writing in his/her daily journal. If s/he cannot think of anything to write about, provide him/her with a list of possible topics or have him/her brainstorm with a peer.

5. When writing in his/her journal, have the student date the entries and keep them in chronological order.

6. Set specific time limits for the student or designate the quantity of writing (e.g., two sentences, one paragraph, a page) you expect him/her to complete in his/her daily journal.

7. When the student writes in a journal, tell him/her to write you questions if there are specific topics to which s/he would like a response. When the journal is turned in, ask him/her to turn down the corner of any pages that s/he would like you to read.

8. Ask the student to volunteer to read a journal entry to his/her classmates. Secure his/her agreement before calling on him/her.

9. Have the student select entries from his/her journal that s/he could use to develop into stories.

Grammar/Syntax

1. Do not require the student to participate in grammar exercises, such as memorizing and identifying the parts of speech. Instead, concentrate on methods that will improve the quality of his/her writing, such as providing models, direct feedback, or sentence-combining exercises.

2. Use the Phelps sentence guide program to help the student learn how to write simple sentences (Phelps-Teraski & Phelps, 1980). The emphasis in the first part is on writing sentences that are based on concrete picture images.

3. Use sentence starters to give the student practice in different ways to expand sentences (e.g., "That is the man who _____" or "The movie got exciting when _____"). Provide practice with a variety of sentence patterns. Use this activity to complement teaching specific sentence types.

4. Ask the student to expand orally on a sentence that s/he has written, adding descriptive words and phrases, additional details, or more explicit adjectives. Have the student then rewrite his/her sentence incorporating his/her new expansions.

5. Use a slotting technique (Poteet, 1987) to help the student expand sentences. Take a story that the

student has written and put in blanks where the sentence can be expanded. Have him/her add adjectives, adverbs, phrases, and/or clauses to make the writing more mature.

6. Use sentence-combining exercises to help the student write longer, more complex sentences. Present the student with a set of simple sentences to combine. Begin teaching sentence combining with just two sentences and gradually progress to more complex transformations. Specific patterns may be taught, for example, by asking the student to combine the sentences using the word "who." Use this technique several times a week for 10 to 15 minutes.

7. Teach the student to combine sentences into more complex structures where appropriate. Directly teach transitional words to introduce subordinate clauses and to clarify the meaningful relationship among sentences. A good list of transitional words is Signal Words, words the author uses to tell the reader how to read (e.g., continuation, change of direction, sequence, conclusion, cause/condition/result, comparison/contrast) (Fry, Polk, & Fountoukidis, 1985).

Vocabulary

1. Before the student starts writing a paper, have him/her list all of the words that s/he thinks might be important to the topic.

2. Prior to writing, brainstorm with the student any words or phrases that s/he thinks s/he may want to use in his/her paper. List all the words on the board or a piece of paper. As skill improves, designate specific categories of words, such as action or descriptive words.

3. Help the student increase his/her vocabulary by having him/her work with a peer or a small cooperative learning group to generate as many words as they can think of that are related to a topic they are studying. Encourage the students to be prepared to explain how the words are related to the topic.

4. Help the student eliminate overused or redundant words in his/her writing, such as "good" and "nice," by listing the target words at the top of the paper before s/he begins writing a story. Remind him/her that s/he must think of substitutes for these words. If necessary, provide him/her with possible alternatives to use as replacements.

5. Teach the student how to recognize common, overused words that are present in his/her writing. Have him/her underline any words that s/he believes could be more descriptive. Help him/her brainstorm alternative words that have a more precise meaning. Provide a variety of examples.

6. Use a synonym cloze procedure to help the student increase his/her writing vocabulary. After a draft of a story is complete, underline words that could be more descriptive. Delete each word to be changed and then write it under the line. Have the student or help him/her determine other words that would make the story more interesting.

7. Teach the student how to use a thesaurus to locate more precise vocabulary for his/her papers and themes.

8. Have the student review his/her paper and underline all words for which s/he would like a synonym. Teach him/her how to use a thesaurus or a pocket-sized, computerized spelling checker with a thesaurus to find and select alternative words.

Topic Selection

1. For writing assignments, let the student select topics that are familiar and interesting to him/her.

2. Have the student select a topic of interest. Have him/her discuss the topic with several peers and record any information that they can add to the topic.

3. Use a clustering approach to help the student select a topic to write about. In a 2- to 3-minute period, have him/her brainstorm topics of interest and jot them down in circles on a piece of paper. Have him/her draw lines to connect the circles that contain related ideas (Rico, 1983).

4. Have the student pair up with a peer and select a topic to write about that they are both interested in. Have them work together to collect data and organize the information that they acquire about the topic.

5. Make sure that the student is involved in selecting topics that s/he will be writing about. S/he can be helped to choose topics by: (a) engaging in daily journal writing, (b) using peers to suggest topics, (c) watching teachers write and model how they arrived at their topics, (d) being surrounded by children's literature, and (e) having opportunities

to react through writing to events that occur in the environment (Graves, 1985).

6. Have the student keep a writer's notebook where s/he can record any ideas that s/he may have for future writing topics.

7. Have frequent writing conferences with the student to discuss the topics and the development of ideas for his/her papers.

Background Knowledge

1. Prior to presenting writing assignments, make sure that the student has the background knowledge required to write about the topic. If not, provide the necessary instruction.

2. In the prewriting phase, provide the student with a variety of activities that will involve him/her in thinking about and discussing the topic in detail.

3. Prior to writing, provide experiences that are followed by discussion. Make sure that the student has thoughts to express before s/he begins writing.

4. Use prewriting activities with the student that encourage creative thinking.

5. Use a colorful action picture to elicit oral details from the student. Record his/her thoughts about the picture. Let him/her use these notes to write about the picture.

6. Have the student write about an interesting picture. Before s/he begins, have the student describe all the things s/he sees, relate the picture to his/her own experiences, and tell what seeing the picture makes him/her think about. List his/her responses on a paper. When the student cannot think of anything else, help him/her to categorize the ideas. Once the student's ideas are organized, have him/her write a story about the picture.

7. Before writing, spend time talking with the student about the topic. Elicit his/her ideas and experiences related to the topic. Discuss how s/he will organize these ideas into a paper.

8. Have the student generate and then answer a series of questions that s/he will be able to use to organize the writing assignment. Have the student locate and answer the questions before writing.

9. Explain to the student why it is necessary to gather and organize information prior to writing. Help

him/her understand how this planning stage will help him/her structure the content of future stories and reports.

Story Structure

1. Use a progression from concrete to abstract language to help the student develop his/her writing skills. In the first level, Concrete-Descriptive, help the student write in a simple, descriptive manner about what s/he sees. In the second level, Concrete-Imaginative, help the student learn to infer ideas from the picture or experience; help the student imagine that which is not present and think about possibilities. In the third level, Abstract-Descriptive, place emphasis on the concepts of time and sequence. Help the student develop stories with more detail. In the fourth level, Abstract-Imaginative, guide the student's thinking with open-ended questions that lead him/her to perceive relationships. Help him/her develop stories that have an imaginative setting and a well-organized plot (Myklebust, 1954).

2. Have the student read well-organized stories written by peers.

3. Teach the student simple questions to use when writing stories. For example, write on an index card:
   Who?
   Did What?
   And so?
Add additional questions as the student's skill increases.

4. Teach the student a simple story grammar to help him/her organize stories. Teach him/ her that all stories have a beginning (setting, main characters), a middle (a problem), and an ending (resolution to the problem). Have him/her complete a story chart prior to writing. (See Appendix, Story Chart.)

5. Give the student practice with story structure using a macro-cloze technique. Delete specific information from the story, such as the setting, description of the main characters, or the ending. Help the student reconstruct the missing story part. Have him/her check to make sure that the missing story part is consistent with the other information in the story.

6. Have the student write stories to model the "Choose Your Own Adventure" genre. At appropriate places

in his/her adventure, have him/her stop and write several options that will have different outcomes. Help the student organize the structure and complete the various paths. For example, after s/he has described his/her characters entering a haunted house on the first page, s/he may write:

1a. If you decide to go up the stairs, turn to page ____.

1b. If you decide to go in the dining room, turn to page ____.

After s/he writes the outcome for a choice (which may result in new choices, 2a. and 2b., or an ending), have him/her put a slash through 1a. on the first page to show that it is has been completed. Have him/her identify the choice at the top of a separate page (e.g., 1a. would be the outcome to "If you decide to go up the stairs, turn to page ____"). The page numbers are added after the book is completed and all the various paths are resolved.

7. Have the student answer a series of questions before writing stories. His/her responses will then serve as the framework for the story. (See Appendix, Story Questions.)

Semantic Maps/Outlines

1. When teaching the student text structure strategies, such as semantic mapping, provide sufficient practice with the technique before assigning writing. For example, draw semantic maps on the board when lecturing or have students work in groups to create maps based on the lecture.

2. When using a structured overview or semantic map, have the student verbalize the relationships among the ideas and details before writing.

3. In the instructional program, place an emphasis on prewriting activities, such as brainstorming followed by semantic mapping, so that the student's ideas will be organized prior to beginning a writing assignment.

4. Give the student practice in generating ideas and then organizing these ideas into an outline prior to writing.

5. Use graphic organizers, semantic mapping, and/or structured overviews to help the student organize his/her ideas and clarify the relationships among ideas prior to writing.

Paragraphs

1. Teach the student that a paragraph expresses one main idea and the topic sentence introduces the idea. Details are provided to support the main idea, and final sentences are used to summarize the main idea or provide a transition to a related idea.

2. Teach the student how to write short paragraphs that follow a narrative sequence. Give him/her a series of pictures that illustrate a sequence of events and have the student write a sentence about each card. Show him/her how to use sequence words, such as *first*, *then*, *next*, and *finally*.

3. Teach the student how to write enumerative paragraphs. Have him/her write a topic sentence and several supporting details. Provide him/her with a guide that will help him/her organize the paragraph. (See Appendix, Paragraph Guide.)

4. Teach the student how to write a variety of formula paragraphs including: expository or enumerative, contains the main idea and supporting details; sequential, describes an event in chronological order or in a number of ideas; and compare/contrast, describes similarities and differences. Provide sufficient opportunities to master one type of paragraph before introducing another.

5. Teach the student how to organize expository paragraphs by using statement-pie (Hanau, 1974). The statement is the main idea of the paragraph and the "pie" includes the *p*roof, *i*nformation, and *e*xamples. Model how to write a main idea statement and then develop several related supporting sentences (the pies). Provide systematic practice with multiple examples until the student is ready to use this format to write paragraphs.

6. Use the Power Writing program (Sparks, 1982) to help the student develop expository writing skills. This program starts at mastery of a three-sentence paragraph and progresses to seven-paragraph reports.

Report Writing

1. Help the student identify the subtopics to include in a report. Teach him/her how to skim through reference books to locate pertinent information.

2. Help the student learn to differentiate major topics from minor details as s/he is collecting and

organizing facts for a report. Have him/her list all the information that s/he thinks is important (or provide him/her with a list of information) and then help him/her think of ways to categorize the major and minor points.

3. Have the student use a report guide to organize information prior to writing. (See Appendix, Report Guide.) Have the student list the topic and subtopics across the top of the page and list the reference books that s/he used down the side of the page. For longer reports with more references or more subtopics, have the student tape several sheets of paper together.

4. Teach the student how to organize index cards to gather information for writing a report. Teach him/her to write keywords for the major topics in the upper right-hand corner. Teach him/her how to sort and organize the cards prior to beginning the first draft.

Compositions/Essays

1. Help the student improve expository writing skill by providing assignments that will help him/her develop confidence as a writer. Provide intensive feedback and several opportunities for revision.

2. Teach the student how to organize themes by using Kerrigan's integrated method of teaching composition (Kerrigan, 1979). (See Appendix.)

3. When teaching the student how to write compositions, model the procedure by demonstrating each task while talking aloud. List the steps of the process on the board.

4. Teach the student how to write clear introductions and conclusions for fiction and expository writing.

5. When teaching language and thinking skills in writing, such as using descriptive language, organizing information, or using introductions or conclusions, show the student many examples of the skill on his/her independent reading level.

Note Taking

1. Provide the student with direct instruction in note-taking skills.

2. Have the student arrange with another student, who takes good class notes, to make a copy of his/her notes for each class session. This will allow the student to listen carefully to the lecture and to participate in class discussion. If needed, the student may arrange this through the instructor.

3. Have a student who is a good note-taker provide the student with a carbon copy of the class notes.

4. Teach the student how to take notes that highlight the important points and ideas of a lecture or a chapter in a textbook.

5. Instead of writing complete sentences, teach the student how to write down keywords and phrases that will remind him/her of the important information.

6. Use taped lectures from the student's classes to teach active listening and a note-taking strategy. Play back the lecture and discuss and write down the important points.

7. Teach the student a strategy for active listening and note-taking. One such strategy is to teach verbal cues to attend to, such as *first* or *more important*. Teach the student how to recognize keywords and incorporate them into an outline.

8. Teach the student how to organize his/her class notes into a semantic map.

9. Permit the student to tape-record all class lectures so that s/he may play them back at a slower pace later and take notes.

10. Listen to a lecture with the student. After the lecture, encourage the student to develop and organize his/her notes. Have him/her then compare these notes to your notes. Discuss differences and point out important information that the student has omitted.

11. After the student has taken notes during a lecture, have him/her rewrite the notes in a more organized format, such as an outline or semantic map.

Computers/Typing

1. Help the student become proficient at word processing.

2. Provide opportunities for the student to use good computer programs that are designed for creating and publishing stories.

3. If possible, provide a computer at home with the same word processing system that is used at school.

4. If possible, provide the student with a laptop computer to use in his/her classes for recording notes, taking exams, and writing papers.

5. Have the student learn to touch-type using a programmed typing tutor. If needed, provide rewards for consistent achievement of specific levels of speed and accuracy.

Additional Ideas:

7

MATHEMATICS

General

Further Evaluation

1. Use a math diagnostic test, such as the Key-Math—Revised (Connolly, 1988), to assess in depth the student's understanding and mastery of math concepts and skills.

2. Use diagnostic teaching to evaluate the student's mastery of the prerequisite skills necessary to learn the skills currently presented in the classroom. Plan a program to teach the necessary skills.

Teaching Approaches

1. In developing a math program for the student, involve him/her in determining and setting goals. Provide daily opportunities for self-appraisal.

2. When teaching the student mathematical processes and concepts, do not introduce new skills until the prerequisites are mastered.

3. When introducing new concepts and skills, use modeling and demonstrations. Have the student watch you perform the task as you talk yourself through it and then have him/her perform the task as you talk it through.

4. Supplement the student's basal math textbook with additional examples and practice exercises. Allow the student to move on in the text only when s/he has demonstrated mastery of the current skills.

5. When teaching the student, begin each lesson with a review of the mathematical skills and concepts covered the previous day.

6. Provide the student with weekly and monthly reviews of the skills and concepts that have been covered in class.

7. Immerse the student in an integrative, problem-solving approach to mathematics. Provide opportunities for him/her to work in groups, engage in discussions, and make presentations.

8. Avoid competitive games and drills. Emphasize cooperation among students in mathematics activities.

9. Provide the student with classroom activities that encourage students to express their ideas, such as working in small, cooperative learning groups to solve problems.

Modifications

1. When working with the student on math problems, spread the practice time over short periods. Have the student complete six to eight problems rather than an entire page.

2. Before calling on the student in math class, make sure that s/he will be able to respond successfully to the question. If necessary, provide or review a question with him/her before class begins.

3. When grading the student's papers, give him/her partial credit for parts of problems solved correctly. For example, give some credit for correct reasoning even if the computation is incorrect.

4. Do not penalize the student for errors on math worksheets. If necessary, simply record the number of problems correct. Instead, attempt to determine the reason for the errors and then provide appropriate instruction.

Calculators and Computers

1. Because the student has such difficulty memorizing math facts, provide him/her with a calculator to use in all math activities. Write this recommendation on his/her Individual Education Program (IEP).

2. Provide the student with a calculator to use in all math activities. Help the student's teachers and parents understand how the use of a calculator in the classroom will enhance the student's understanding and mastery of arithmetic.

3. After completing problems, have the student use a calculator to check calculations and then rework any incorrect solutions.

4. Provide opportunities for the student to be a teacher's helper by having him/her check other students' papers with a calculator.

5. Teach the student how to use a calculator to perform the four basic operations.

6. Encourage the student to use a calculator for all problem-solving activities.

7. Provide homework assignments that will help the student improve his/her skill using a calculator. For example, when s/he is assigned 10 problems, have him/her solve the problems and then use a calculator to check for accuracy.

8. Teach the student how to use calculators and computers to enrich and expand his/her understanding of mathematics.

9. Teach the student how to use a calculator to add and subtract negative numbers, to compute with decimals, and to convert fractions into decimal equivalents.

10. Obtain permission for the student to use a calculator on any standardized group-administered achievement test.

11. Based on his/her interest and high aptitude in mathematics, teach the student how to use computers as mathematical tools. For example, teach the student how to use electronic spreadsheets, numerical analysis packages, and/or computer graphics.

12. Teach the student how to use tables, graphs, and spreadsheets to organize and present numerical information.

13. Have the student use computer programs that build problem-solving skills in an applied context.

Homework

1. Before the student takes home math assignments, make sure that s/he understands the directions and process for solving the problems. When necessary, the teacher or a peer tutor should work the first few problems with the student at school.

2. For homework assignments, reduce the number of problems to practice. For example, assign the student two-thirds of the problems or all the odd-numbered problems, rather than an entire page.

3. To encourage flexibility, when assigning practice on a new operation (e.g., multiplication of fractions), incorporate problems involving previously presented operations (e.g., addition and subtraction of fractions) throughout the assignment.

4. Make sure that the student has one or two review problems on each homework assignment.

5. Place a limit on the amount of time the student is to work on math homework. Grade his/her work on a percentage basis, using the number of items s/he has completed as the total number of possible points.

6. Request that the student's parents put a check next to those items completed with their assistance. In this way, the teacher can monitor the types of problems with which the student is having difficulty.

Books and Programs

1. For specific math activities, the teacher is referred to *Today's Mathematics: Seventh Edition* (Heddens, 1991). This comprehensive text explains concepts and methods for teaching elementary school mathematics.

2. For specific suggestions for teaching mathematics to children with learning disabilities, the teacher is referred to *Teaching Mathematics to the Learning Disabled* (Bley & Thornton, 1989), *Developmental Teaching of Mathematics for the Learning Disabled* (Cawley, 1984), or *Cognitive Strategies and Mathematics for the Learning Disabled* (Cawley, 1985).

3. Use a comprehensive instructional program for teaching the student mathematics. One example of a complete elementary math education program is *Math Capsules, Moving with Math,* and *Skill Builders Using Action Math.* This program provides materials for diagnosis and placement, and activities for concept development, problem solving, drill, and daily reviews. Available from: Math Teachers Press, P.O. Box 1191, Minneapolis, MN 55440, (800) 852-2435.

4. Use a program with the student such as *Project MATH* (Cawley, Fitzmaurice, Goodstein, Lepore, Sedlak, & Althaus, 1976) that controls the reading level of the material and provides for individualized instruction. This curriculum is designed for students in preschool to grade 6 or secondary students with learning problems. It consists of six strands: patterns, sets, numbers and operations, geometry, fractions, and measurement.

5. Encourage the principal of the student's school to provide inservice training to the teachers on how to teach mathematics as a way of thinking and to make problem solving the focus of the curriculum. Nationwide inservice training is available from: Marilyn Burns Education Associates, 150 Gate 5 Road, Suite 101, Sausalito, CA 94965, (415) 332-4181.

6. Encourage the student's parents to order the book *Family Math* to help them integrate math activities into home life. This book is available from: Math/Science Network, Lawrence Hall of Science, University of California, Berkeley, CA 94720, (415) 642-1823.

Readiness

General

1. Use concrete objects and manipulatives to teach all new concepts and to extend previously presented concepts.

2. Provide the student with discovery-oriented activities that will promote understanding of mathematical relationships. For example, have him/her describe, sort, compare, or order objects.

3. Provide the student with mathematical puzzles and patterns that will allow him/her to discover varying relationships based on quantity, order, size, and shape.

Classification: Creating Sets

1. Teach all sorting and ordering skills first using familiar objects, then using pictures.

2. Teach the student to order objects by a variety of attributes such as height, width, length, thickness, and weight. Teach the terms for these concepts as part of the activity.

3. Introduce the concept of sets and develop classification ability by teaching the student to sort objects.

4. To teach the concept of sets and develop classification ability, provide sorting activities such as the following. Place pictures cut from magazines in a bag. Put one picture representing each category to be identified on the bottom of each of two or more shoe boxes. Have the student sort the pictures from the bag into the appropriate boxes. Check his/her work in order to evaluate his/her understanding of the concept.

5. Provide the student practice in sorting through multiple objects to find all those that match a given object (e.g., all the balls on the toy shelves). Subsequently, have the student find sets of orally described objects (e.g., all the balls in the room, all the tools that may be used for drawing).

6. Using manipulatives such as Attribute Logic Blocks, Cuisenaire Rods, and flannel boards, guide the student to discover a variety of attributes by which these materials may be sorted. Attributes include color, shape, size, thickness, width, height, and use.

7. To provide practice in classifying and creating sets, create experiments in which the students participate. Examples of sets amenable to experimentation are those objects that float/sink, those that feel heavy/light, and those that can be seen through/those that cannot.

8. Teach the student that the members of a set may or may not contain objects/pictures that have a common attribute. For example, a star, a ball, and a tree may all share membership in a set just because they are described as such.

9. Teach the student that sets in which members do have a common attribute may be named for that attribute. For example, a group of colored objects may be sorted into a red and a green set.

10. Help the student to develop conceptualization of sets at the semi-concrete level by representing physical objects by pictures. When the student clearly understands the representation, introduce new concepts with pictures. Assess comprehension by asking questions about the relationship among objects in the environment.

11. Help the student to develop conceptualization of sets at the semi-abstract level by teaching him/her to represent each member of a set with a tally, such as a popsicle stick. This will encourage him/her to

consider the number properties of sets rather than other characteristics of the objects.

12. To help the student learn that numbers may represent sets, teach the student to place sequential numbers, instead of tallies, beneath each member of a set. Help him/her to understand that the set may now be named by the highest (last) number used.

13. Provide activities to develop the concept of the empty set, the idea that a set may have no members. For example, give four students boxes with three, two, one, and no crayons in them, respectively. Have each student describe the contents of their box, ending with the student who has no crayons. Explain that his/her box contains the empty set. Or, ask questions for which the answer is "none," such as the number of members in the set of zebras in the classroom.

14. Assist the student in comparing sets by their number properties, deciding which set has more, less, or the same as other sets.

One-to-One Correspondence/Counting

1. Teach the student the concept of one-to-one correspondence by having him/her match each member of one set with a member in another set. Help him/her verbalize if one set has the same number as the other set, fewer, or more. Concurrently, teach the associated quantitative terms such as "the same as," "more than," and "less/fewer than."

2. Teach the student the concept of one-to-one correspondence to help develop the conceptual basis for the concepts of addition and subtraction.

3. Provide the student with opportunities to count objects that s/he uses daily such as silverware, books, and shoes. Later, use tokens such as poker chips or beads. Show the student how to separate each item from the group as s/he counts it so that the same item is not counted twice.

4. Teach the student how to use an abacus for counting. Manipulating the beads will help reinforce the concept of one-to-one correspondence and help the student develop an initial understanding of place value.

5. Give the student practice in counting and recognizing cardinal numbers by providing activities such

as counting buttons into numbered compartments of an egg carton.

6. Help the student develop an awareness of how counting is used in everyday life by incorporating counting skills into classroom activities. For example, have the student count the students ordering milk, pass out a certain number of books, or play board games that involve moving a marker according to a number on a chosen card.

7. Teach the student to count to 100 using color coding to help him/her see the repeating pattern of numbers.

8. Use games to reinforce number recognition and counting skills. For example, have the student play dominoes with a peer or parent who will encourage accurate counting with comments such as, "See if you have a domino with three dots just like this one."

9. At home, play games that require counting with the student. Suggestions are board games that require moving a marker a specified number of squares, Cribbage, and card games such as Blackjack or "21."

10. Use a number line to help the student learn to count backwards.

Quantitative Terminology

1. Introduce all new terminology while using concrete objects and manipulatives to teach the concept.

2. Teach math vocabulary in concert with the skill/operation for which it is used. For example, teach *minus*, *subtract from*, and *less than* when using manipulatives to teach the concept of subtraction.

3. While teaching classification skills, use each attribute that the student identifies as a springboard for teaching quantitative terms such as *big*, *small*, *narrow*, *wide*, *tall*, *short*, *thick*, and *thin*. Also teach the terms for comparative concepts such as *big*, *bigger*, and *biggest*.

4. Use manipulatives to teach the student and provide practice with the concepts of *bigger than*, *equal to*, and *smaller than*.

5. Encourage the student to notice and compare attributes of objects in his/her environment. Ask questions such as, "Which is the tallest piece of equipment on the playground? Which is the shortest?"

6. When the student is familiar with the concept of joining two sets to create a third set, introduce the vocabulary of addition (e.g., "Four stars added to three stars is the same as seven stars").

7. When the student is familiar with verbalizing the operation of removing one subset from a set, teach him/her the terms for subtraction.

8. Teach the student that several terms can indicate the same process. For example, *adding*, *plus*, and *and* all mean the operation of addition. Other related terms would include *sum*, *total*, *more than*, and *greater than*.

Matching Pictures and Numerals to Sets

1. Do not introduce numerals to the student until s/he is developmentally ready to use the graphic representations. Make sure that s/he understands one-to-one correspondence by providing appropriate readiness experiences, such as counting objects and matching one set of objects to another.

2. To develop skill in counting and number recognition, show the student a card with a set of similar objects, such as stars or circles. Have him/her count the objects, name the amount, and then choose the number from a set of number cards or tiles.

3. Have the student make two corresponding stacks of cards. Have him/her write numbers on one stack (or provide number tiles) and draw illustrations of corresponding sets on the other stack. For example, s/he would write the number 4 on one card and then draw four apples on the other card. S/he can then play a game of matching the number to its corresponding set card.

4. Use games to reinforce the idea of numbers representing a set and rapid recognition of the number of pictures in a set. For example, play a version of Bingo in which the teacher holds up a card with a set of dots on it and the students cover the corresponding number on their Bingo cards.

5. Use worksheets to reinforce rapid recognition of numbers to match picture sets. For example, have the students choose from three numbers the number corresponding to a set of pictured shapes.

6. As a conceptual basis for addition, using manipulatives or pictures, teach the student how to join two sets so that all members of the first set

and all members of the second set are combined to form a new set. When this concept is mastered, have the students give each of the sets a number (in writing or with number tiles).

7. Use objects or pictures to teach the student that sets may be broken up into a variety of subsets. For example, a set of five objects contains: five subsets of one member each; one subset of two and one subset of three; one subset of four and one subset of one; or one subset of five and one subset of zero.

8. As a conceptual basis for subtraction, use manipulatives or pictures, teach the student that one subset of a set may be removed from the set, leaving the other subset(s).

Number Patterns and Ordinal Numbers

1. Use a number line to help the student develop the idea of what number comes before or after another number.

2. Provide the student with practice in number sequencing. Ask him/her questions, such as: "What number comes just before . . . ?" "What number comes just after . . . ?" If needed, let him/her look at a number line as s/he is answering the questions.

3. Provide practice in recognizing sequential number patterns. For example, write on the board a series of numbers that follow a pattern. At the end of the series, leave several blanks for the student to continue the pattern. Gradually, increase the difficulty of the sequences.

4. Introduce the concept of ordinal numbers by using terms for numbers during activities throughout the day in the classroom. For example, when getting ready to go outside, specify who should line up first, second, and so on.

5. Reinforce the use of ordinal numbers with gross-motor activities such as having a few students stand on a number line on the floor. After each one says his/her cardinal number, tell him/her the corresponding ordinal number (e.g., "Joel is first in line, Desiree is second"). Then, using ordinal numbers instead of names, give each student an instruction (e.g., "Will the second child clap her hands two times?").

Recognizing and Writing Numbers

1. To establish familiarity with the visual image of numerals, provide the student with number puzzles and plastic or wooden numbers to place in templates or sequence.

2. Provide multisensory experiences to help the student learn to form and recognize numerals. For example, have the student form numbers with clay, trace them in wet sand, or cut them out of felt.

3. Teach the student to recognize the cardinal numbers by their names. You may use gross-motor activities to reinforce number recognition by writing the numbers 1 to 10 on a long sheet of butcher paper and having the child count his/her paces, simultaneously stepping on each square and looking at the number. Alternatively, you may use numbers on steps.

4. Do not expect the student to write numerals right away. Have him/her practice matching activities with numeral tiles or cards and plastic numbers. Provide ample exposure to numbers for later writing.

5. Provide the student with many opportunities to form a stable visual image of numbers before s/he is asked to write them. Provide ample play opportunities with materials such as number puzzles, number tiles, and dominoes with dots on one side and the corresponding number on the other.

6. Help the student make sandpaper numbers for tracing. With a brush, spread glue evenly in the shape of a number on a card. Quickly, sprinkle sand or dry colored gelatin over the glue.

7. When teaching the student to write numbers, have him/her first trace the number many times using a texture for the number that is tactually different from the background. Place a mark at the point at which the student should start tracing.

8. Give the student practice in forming letters by writing them in wet sand, shaving cream, or chocolate pudding.

9. Hold the student's hand and help him/her form large numbers. Have the student then trace over the number with his/her finger as s/he says the number.

10. Teach the student to write the numbers up to 100. Highlight the repeating patterns of base 10.

11. When the student reverses numbers on a math worksheet, do not count the answers as incorrect. Instead, provide cues to teach and reinforce the correct orientation of those numbers.

Basic Skills

General

1. Introduce the student to all types of computation by beginning with story problems or practical applications that illustrate the need for the computational skill being presented.

2. To assess the student's conceptual understanding of basic computation, give him/her a worksheet with a few addition, subtraction, multiplication, and division problems. Have him/her work out the problems using concrete objects, such as beans or marbles.

3. When reviewing the four basic operations, explain and demonstrate to the student the relationship between addition and multiplication and between subtraction and division. For example, demonstrate how $8 \div 2 = 4$ means that 2 can be subtracted from 8 exactly 4 times.

4. When reviewing the four basic operations, explain and demonstrate to the student the relationship between addition and subtraction and between multiplication and division. Create examples to demonstrate these principles, such as if $2 + 2 = 4$, then $4 - 2 = 2$, or if $4 \times 3 = 12$, then $12 \div 3 = 4$.

5. Review the concept of zero as used within all the basic mathematical operations. For example, teach the student why one cannot subtract a number from zero (unless using negative numbers), but can add any number to zero. Teach the student why any number multiplied by zero is zero and that zero then becomes the place holder in the answer.

6. Make sure that the student understands that many ways exist to perform most algorithms and solve computation problems.

7. Teach the student to do problems in a variety of ways. S/he might first estimate the answer, calculate the answer on paper, and then check it with a calculator.

8. When reviewing computations with the student, place the emphasis on how s/he solved the problems, rather than on the accuracy of the solutions.

9. Avoid the use of timed math tests with the student. Do not emphasize speed or rapid recall of math facts, but instead accuracy, persistence, and understanding.

10. When providing review, make sure that the student's worksheets contain a mixture of problems rather than just one operation, such as a page of addition and subtraction problems.

11. Use a highly structured, sequential program for teaching and reviewing basic math skills that includes teacher-directed instruction as well as independent review activities. One example is the *Corrective Mathematics Program* (Engelmann & Carnine, 1982), a remedial program designed for grade 3 through adult.

Compensations and Strategies

1. Help the student's teachers (parents) understand that it is not the ability to memorize math facts that is most important, but rather the ability to construct strategies to solve problems.

2. Teach the student how to solve simple addition and subtraction calculations using his/her fingers until s/he has to compute with problems containing sums larger than 10.

3. When the student is working independently on math computations, have him/her use an addition or multiplication facts sheet to solve problems.

4. Teach the student how to use a number line, counting forwards and backwards, to solve addition and subtraction problems.

5. When performing simple addition problems, teach the student how to use a "count on" strategy. For example, to solve $6 + 2$, have him/her say the larger number 6 and then "count on" two more to obtain the answer.

6. In memorizing addition facts, teach the student to recognize patterns that will reduce demands on memory. For example, if s/he knows the "doubles" facts but is stuck on $6 + 7$, s/he can think of it as $6 + 6 + 1$.

7. As the student often makes errors in computation, but understands the basic operations, place dot patterns on numbers (e.g., place four dots on the number 4) to help improve his/her accuracy in addition and subtraction. As proficiency increases, the student may just tap his/her pencil on each number as s/he counts to solve simple addition and subtraction facts.

8. Use a multisensory program, such as Touch Math (Bullock, 1991), to help the student increase computational accuracy. (See Appendix.)

9. To compensate for the student's inability to memorize math facts, teach him/her to use Touch Math and a calculator.

10. Teach the student how to solve any multiplication problem by using repeated addition. Have him/her practice skip counting using a number line.

11. When working with the student on multiplication facts, have him/her prove the answer by using any of the following methods: repeated addition, arranging and rearranging sets, or a number line.

12. Teach the student how to use any of the multiplication facts that s/he already knows to figure out those that s/he does not. For example, s/he may solve $(6 \times 6) + 6$ rather than 6×7.

13. To reduce memory demands, teach the student strategies to use to solve computation problems based on facts s/he already knows. Some examples for multiplication follow: (a) use skip counting and either dots on paper or touch points for multiplication facts, (b) use repeated addition for multiplication by two or three, (c) split one factor in half and add the products (e.g., $4 \times 7 = ?$ but $2 \times 7 = 14$, and $14 + 14 = 28$), or lower one factor by 1, multiply, then add one more set (e.g., $4 \times 7 = ?$ but $3 \times 7 = 21$, and $21 + 7 = 28$).

14. Since the student understands the process of multiplication, but has difficulty memorizing the facts, teach him/her one of the two 9's tricks for memorizing the multiplication facts with the number 9.

 a. Start with any number times 9 (e.g., 6). Take one away from that number $(6 - 1 = 5)$ and it represents the 10's place. Think of what number when added to that number would equal 9 $(5 + ? = 9)$. That number represents the units column. Thus, the answer is 54.

 b. Teach the student to hold his/her two hands up with thumbs facing each other. Have him/her imagine one number on each finger, from one to ten, starting with the little finger on the left. To multiply 6 times 9, count on your fingers from the left until you reach 6. Turn finger 6 (right thumb) down. The number of fingers to the left of this finger (5) represents the 10's column. The number of fingers to the right (4) represents the units column. The answer is 54.

Quantitative Terminology

1. Teach the student the meaning of specific mathematical phrases such as *how much more*, *what is the difference*, and *in all*.

2. Have the student develop a written file of math vocabulary. On a 3 × 5 index card, have him/her write the word, the definition, and make a picture to illustrate meaning. Have the student file the words alphabetically. Provide opportunities for review.

3. Using the student's math textbook or a list of math terminology, identify and then teach specific math vocabulary that s/he needs to know. Provide review, as needed.

Visual Format/Page Organization

1. Make sure worksheets are visually clear with only a few problems on each page.

2. Teach the student to fold the paper in fourths or sixths to have "frames" to outline each problem before copying computation problems onto a sheet of paper. Copy/write only one problem in each frame.

3. When doing computation in school and for homework, have the student use graph paper with squares of one centimeter to keep rows and columns of numbers in order. Show the student how to write only one digit in each square.

4. To avoid mistakes due to poor memory, teach the student to use verbal mediation to aid in accurate copying of problems from text to paper. Teach the student to double up long numbers, rather than say every digit. For example, $5234 + 874$ would be said as "fifty-two thirty-four" (write) "plus eight seventy-four" (write).

5. Do not require the student to copy math problems from a chalkboard or math textbook. Instead, provide all practice problems clearly printed and aligned on worksheets.

6. Teach the student to circle the item number so that s/he does not confuse it with digits in the problem.

7. Use a 5 × 8 index card, a folded piece of paper, or a sticky pad to mask the half of the page on which the student is not working.

8. Teach the student to use a template with a cut-out square made out of poster paper. The square should be large enough so that it will expose one computation problem and block out distracting visual information on the page.

9. Provide worksheets with formats already written for the type or types of problems the student is expected to work. The following is an example of a multiplication format.

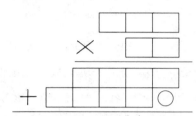

Figure 7–1. Format for Multiplication algorithm.

10. Teach the student how to interpret problems set up horizontally as well as problems set up vertically.

Noting Process Signs

1. Prior to completing a worksheet, have the student color-code the process signs. For example, use green for an addition sign and red for a subtraction sign. Once a color is chosen for a sign, do not change it.

2. Enlarge the operation signs on math worksheets or draw them with heavy lines so that the student is more likely to observe them.

3. Before the student completes a computation problem, have him/her highlight or circle the process sign with a colored marker to draw attention to the operation.

4. Teach the student to look at and say the process sign aloud, before s/he begins to solve a problem.

Procedures for Memorization

1. Do not require the student to memorize facts until his/her understanding of the process is firmly established.

2. Determine exactly what math facts the student knows and which ones s/he still needs to learn. Have the student chart his/her progress as s/he masters new facts.

3. Before teaching math facts, give the student a timed test to see what facts s/he can complete correctly within 2 minutes. Use the assessment results to develop a program for fact learning.

4. Using a test of math facts, identify the facts the student knows from memory, the facts s/he can work out, and the ones s/he cannot solve. Make a chart for him/her to use to help master the unknown facts.

5. Have the student participate in selecting a method that s/he will use to learn his/her facts. After using the approach to study for several days, have the student evaluate whether or not the method seems effective. If not, have him/her select another approach to try.

6. Once the student understands mathematical operations, shift the focus to memorization of facts. Make adequate provisions for overlearning by using games, language masters, tape recorders, computers, and tracing activities.

7. Have a peer or parent provide practice sessions with flash cards so that the student can become automatic with his/her math facts. Have the student practice facts for several minutes daily.

8. Using flash cards that have the answer recorded on the reverse side, have the student practice a few facts daily until mastery is achieved. As new facts are introduced, provide periodic review of the newly mastered facts.

9. Set up a reinforcement program for the student for improving retention of math facts. For example, s/he could earn a sticker or a set number of points for each new fact learned.

10. Do not have the student compete with other students when practicing math facts. Instead, have him/her keep a private performance chart. Draw an analogy to a runner's "Personal Best."

11. Use mnemonic strategies to help the student memorize his/her math facts. For example, based upon his/her interest in football, use NFL Player Flash Cards. These cards have a mathematical equation on the front of the card that corresponds with the jersey number of a football player on the back. Available from: Pacific Trading Cards, 18424 Highway 99, Lynwood, WA 98037, (800) 551-2002.

12. In teaching the student the multiplication tables, begin with the multiples of a table that s/he already knows. For example, begin with the 2's, which are doubles taught in addition. After the 2's are memorized, introduce the 4's, and then the 8's. This technique will help the student determine answers that have not been memorized.

13. Teach particularly difficult multiplication facts by using a rhyme with a picture clue. These may be made by the student or class. Rhymes with associated picture cards are available from Rhyme Times, P.O. Box 28132, San Jose, CA 95159-8132. An example from these cards is "8 × 7 were nifty chicks until they became 56."

14. Use a basic math program with the student, such as MATHFACT (Thornton & Toohey, 1982-1985), that is designed for students with special needs. This individualized program teaches a variety of multisensory organizational strategies to promote rapid recall of addition, subtraction, multiplication, and division facts.

15. Have the student use computer math games that provide immediate feedback to reinforce facts and operations s/he has mastered. Provide time for the student to practice independently.

16. Use a write-say procedure to help the student memorize his/her multiplication facts. Give the student a worksheet of problems with answers. Have him/her cover the row of answers with an index card. Have the student look at the problem, say the answer, and then move the card to check the answer. If the answer is incorrect, have the student look at the problem and answer, cover it with a finger, and then write it from memory several times, checking for accuracy each time.

17. Record a set of number facts on tape at a slow pace, repeating each one twice. Have the student hold a flash card in his/her hand as s/he listens to each fact being said. Encourage the student to repeat the fact aloud with the taped presentation. As an alternate activity, have the student say, then write, each math fact. Present only a few at a time. Provide daily practice for 5 minutes until all facts are mastered.

18. Record a set of multiplication facts, such as the 7's, with answers in a pattern on a piece of paper. Tape-record each fact and leave a pause for the answer. After a problem is stated, have the student repeat the problem and say the answer. Teach the student to use the pause button as needed. Have the student listen to the tape 5 minutes daily until s/he has memorized the facts.

19. Administer daily timed multiplication tests to see how many facts the student can complete within a minute. Record and monitor his/her progress.

20. Use Precision Teaching to help the student memorize his/her math facts. Have the student complete daily timed drill activities where s/he competes against his/her own best score. (See Appendix.)

Algorithms

Teaching Concepts with Manipulatives

1. For any skill or operation, allow the student to use manipulatives as long as necessary. Prematurely shifting him/her to numbers alone may interfere with conceptual mastery.

2. If the student has not acquired the necessary basic number concepts for solving addition and subtraction problems, provide additional practice with manipulatives before requiring him/her to work on the basic facts.

3. Help the student develop and expand his/her mathematical concepts by using visuals and manipulatives. Use real objects (e.g., food, liquid measures, wood for building, money) as well as standard math teaching materials such as Cuisenaire Rods, Base Ten blocks, and Unifix Cubes. A guide for incorporating Unifix cubes into the curriculum is available from Addison-Wesley Publishing Company (Innovative Division), 2725 Sand Hill Road, Menlo Park, CA 94025, (415) 854-0300.

4. Make sure the student understands the concept underlying each new algorithm that is introduced. Use manipulatives, such as Cuisenaire Rods (Davidson, 1969), beans, or money to introduce all new concepts. A variety of resource books for using Cuisenaire Rods and other manipulatives are available from: Cuisenaire Company of America, 12 Church St., Box D, New Rochelle, NY 10802, (800) 237-3142.

5. Use visual aids and manipulatives to illustrate new ideas and extensions of previously learned concepts. Use real objects first (e.g., food, measuring

liquid, wood for building, crayons), then pictures. Later, move to rods, tokens, and other semi-concrete materials.

6. When teaching the student concepts of fractions and decimals, use tangible objects, such as money or food. For example, demonstrate cutting a pizza in pie-shaped pieces.

7. Use manipulatives that are already compartmentalized to teach fractions. For example, an empty egg carton may be used to teach fractions with a denominator of 12.

Teaching Algorithms

1. When the student misses computation problems on a math assignment, perform an error analysis to identify the reasons for the mistakes. Without intervention, the student will continue to make the same systematic errors. Provide remedial teaching as needed.

2. When it is unclear why the student is missing specific computational problems, conduct an oral interview with him/her. Ask him/her to talk through the steps as s/he solves the problems.

3. Use task analysis to help the student master computational algorithms. Identify the algorithm to be learned. List and arrange all the prerequisite skills and the steps needed to perform the algorithm into a logical teaching sequence. Through informal testing, determine exactly which steps the student cannot perform and then teach the steps in sequence.

4. In teaching the student computational algorithms, ensure that s/he understands the underlying concepts so that the procedures and the sequence of steps make sense. For example, one must understand place value to understand regrouping.

5. Provide opportunities for the student to teach the math algorithms and concepts that s/he has recently learned to other students. Have him/her assume the role of instructor and teach the concept using his/her own words.

6. Before introducing decimals, make sure that the student understands fractional concepts so that s/he can see the relationship between the two and acquire an understanding that decimals are an easier and more consistent way to express fractions.

7. Reteach the concept of fractions, including what the numerator and denominator represent, the reason for needing a common denominator, the methods for finding common denominators, the procedures for reducing fractions, and the meaning of improper fractions and mixed numbers.

8. To provide a basis for higher-level math, help the student develop concepts and skills with percents, decimals, fractions, and negative numbers.

Place Value

1. When teaching place value, tell the student a story with pictures to help him/her understand that only 9 of any set may go in one column. An example to illustrate this concept follows:

Once there was a person who moved into a house. Although the landlord had told him/her that no more than 9 people could live in the house, eventually a tenth person moved in. The landlord said, "Ten people cannot live in that house," and s/he evicted all of them. So, they became one family (of 10 people) and moved into an apartment house. The apartment house had room for 9 families just like theirs—10 people each. The population of the apartment house grew until there were 9 families there. Eventually, a tenth family (of 10) moved in and the 10 families formed a community. When the landlord found out, s/he said, "Ten families cannot be in that house," and evicted the whole community (How many families are in that community now? How many people?). The community then moved into an apartment complex where other communities (of 100) lived. But the landlord said, "Only 9 communities can live in this complex." When the tenth community moved in . . .

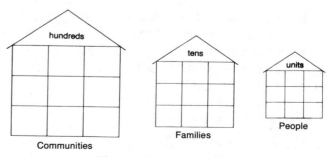

Figure 7-2. Place Value.

2. Use manipulatives such as Unifix Cubes, Snap Cubes, or Base Ten Blocks to teach place value. When the student can "trade in" (regroup) appropriately for the next largest set, teach him/her to use columns on large paper so that s/he may place the blocks/cubes in the proper column and change their places as s/he regroups.

3. Ensure that the student has developed understanding of place value before introducing regrouping (borrowing and carrying).

4. Review the rule of one digit to a column and make sure the student understands and can explain the reason for the rule. Use manipulatives to illustrate this concept.

5. Use manipulatives to teach the student the concept of place value with particular emphasis on the use of zero as a place holder.

Reminders for Algorithm Sequences

1. Use color coding to (a) identify starting and stopping places within a problem, (b) code the units, tens, hundreds, and thousands place, (c) indicate where the final answer should be written, and (d) highlight important features, such as operation signs, the question being asked, or the key information being asked in the problem.

2. Remind the student that reading starts on the left and moves right, whereas the math computations of addition, subtraction, and multiplication start on the right and move left. Make sure that s/he understands how math columns are related to place value.

3. To remind the student to start math problems on the right side, place a green dot or an arrow over the 1's column. Have the student place his/her finger on the dot before beginning the problem.

4. Provide the student with an index card that contains clear verbal explanations of questions to ask him/herself as s/he works math problems. For example, when learning regrouping techniques for subtraction, write the question "Is the top number larger than the bottom number?"

    If yes - subtract

    If no - regroup (borrow)

5. Make flowcharts for the student that illustrate the sequence of steps required for any particular operation that s/he is learning. Have the student keep the flowcharts clipped inside his/her math textbook and/or workbook to refer to whenever necessary.

6. Teach the student memory strategies for performing new math algorithms in the correct sequence. For example, write the following steps for long division on an index card:

    a. ask
    b. multiply
    c. subtract
    d. check
    e. bring down

7. Teach the student to place an "operation mnemonic" for division on the top of his/her math worksheet.

Estimation and Self-Monitoring

1. Make sure that the student becomes proficient in estimating answers to calculations.

2. Help him/her learn to differentiate situations where an exact answer is needed from those where an estimate is more appropriate.

3. Help the student develop self-monitoring skills by estimating answers to math calculations. Have him/her estimate the answer and write it by the side of a problem before s/he calculates the answer.

4. After s/he has learned to estimate, teach the student to ask him/herself, "Does this answer make sense?" after solving a problem.

5. Teach the student to talk through the steps of computation problems as s/he attempts to solve them.

6. Have the student work with a peer or a small group to check each other's answers on an assignment. When they find an answer that is dissimilar, have them review the problem step-by-step to discover the error and then correct the missed problem.

7. Teach the student how to check his/her answers to problems with all types of operations by using the reverse operation. For example, teach the student to check his/her division answers by multiplying the divisor by the quotient to get the dividend.

8. Teach the student how to check for ratio equality by using cross multiplication of terms.

Application

General

1. To promote generalization of math concepts, integrate mathematical activities into other parts of the curriculum.

2. Provide the student with a variety of experiences to increase understanding of how numbers are used in daily activities. Show him/her how these activities relate to pencil-and-paper tasks.

3. Encourage the student to observe the use of mathematics in the surrounding world. Provide careful guided observations in the classroom and home.

4. Help the student increase his/her interest in mathematical activities by emphasizing practical applications and high-interest, problem-solving activities.

5. Before presenting new skills or materials, elicit from the student his/her knowledge regarding related ideas. Explain and demonstrate how the new mathematical concepts are related to what s/he already knows.

6. Use a variety of games and puzzles to help the student build mathematical reasoning skills.

7. Have the student participate in daily problem-solving activities. One good resource is the *Middle Grades Mathematics Project*, five books describing problem-solving activities to use with students in grades 5–9. Available from: Cuisenaire Company of America, 12 Church St., Box D, New Rochelle, NY 10802, (800) 237-3142. Another one is *Problem Solving in Mathematics*, a collection of ideas for grades 4 through 9. Available from: Dale Seymour Publications, P.O. Box 10888, Palo Alto, CA 94303, (800) 872-1100.

Story Problems

1. Provide the student with a mixture of story problems that require different mathematical operations. Have him/her determine what operation(s) is appropriate for each problem.

2. Make sure that all assigned word problems are written at the student's independent reading level.

3. Since the student has difficulty reading the story problems in his/her math textbook, develop taped readings that s/he can listen to as s/he reads along in the book. Teach him/her how to recognize the end of a problem and use the pause button to stop the tape.

4. Have the students work in cooperative groups and read the word problems aloud to each other.

5. Provide the student with oral as well as written practice in solving word problems.

6. Do not teach the student "tricks" for solving math problems, such as identifying cue words (i.e., *how many* or *altogether* means addition). Instead draw attention to understanding the language of the problems.

7. Make sure that when the student is asked to solve story problems, the computation involved is not difficult. This will allow the student to concentrate on understanding the language of the problem.

8. When the student has difficulty with the computation involved in a story problem, have him/her substitute smaller numbers so that s/he can understand the operation(s) involved and then calculate the problem a second time using the original numbers.

9. To ensure that the student understands the different types of story problems that s/he is expected to solve, have him/her solve them first using manipulatives.

10. Be aware of the linguistic complexity of all word problems that the student is expected to answer. Rephrase or rewrite the problems as needed.

11. When asking the student to solve story problems that are presented orally, use concrete objects or visual diagrams to illustrate the problems.

12. When introducing word problems to the student, present concrete situations that s/he will be able to visualize or draw.

13. Have the student draw pictures to illustrate simple story problems.

14. Give the student a set of objects and have him/her create word problems to solve with the manipulatives. Ask the student to create problems that involve a specific operation.

15. Have the student and several peers physically act out word problems. For example, the students

could count up and divide a set of blocks or demonstrate making change for a purchase in a grocery store.

16. Write a simple computation problem on the chalkboard and ask the student to make up several word problems using the computation.

17. Help the student learn to identify extraneous information in word problems. With a marker, have him/her cross out any extraneous information before s/he attempts to solve a problem.

18. Rather than having the student solve the word problems in the math textbook, provide him/her with interesting story problems that incorporate familiar situations.

19. Use high-interest math problems to challenge the student. One example of a book that contains challenging problems is *Math for Smarty Pants* (Burns, 1982), designed for students in grade 3 and up.

20. Develop or have your students develop high-interest story problems for each other. These problems can contain the names of students and describe classroom activities or experiences.

21. Have the student work in a cooperative learning group to write or solve word problems. Provide a variety of activities such as creating problems for a set of objects, writing problems for a given equation, or solving problems written by a peer or another group of students.

22. Give the student word problems in which specific information needed to solve the problem is missing. Have the student identify what is missing, provide the information, and then solve the problem.

23. Have several teams of students create story problems that cannot be solved because information is missing. Have them exchange problems and discuss why they cannot be solved. Have the students then rewrite the problems so they can be solved.

24. Teach the student to recognize the number of steps (operations) involved in a word problem, what they are, and how to sequence them correctly.

25. Teach the student how to interpret what is asked in a math problem as well as how to find the data needed to solve the problem. Several suggestions for how to do this follow:

a. If you use familiar objects to create problems and generate questions, the student's interest level will be higher. Additionally, the student will have the objects to help solve the problem.

b. Combine math and content area learning. For example, use data in reference books to create math problems and teach the student to use the reference books to find the answer. An example would be, "If everybody in the world gave you a penny, approximately how much money would you have?"

c. Provide easy-to-read reference books for each student or cooperative group and challenge them to create math problems using information in the book. Examples of reference books are encyclopedias, atlases, the *Guinness Book of World Records*, or books on the human body.

d. Create problems for the student that require experimentation or that combine experimentation with use of a reference book. Examples would be, "How many tablespoons of liquid equal a cup?" or "If you leave Tucson on foot for Yuma, can you make the trip in less than 1,000,000 steps?"

26. Teach the student how to plan what s/he needs to do to solve a problem. Different techniques, such as the following, may be called for by the type of question asked:

a. Decide what operation(s) to use (e.g., Harry weighed 250 pounds. He weighed 72 more pounds than James. How much did James weigh?)

b. Make a table, graph, or chart of the information provided (e.g., Hansel and Gretel went to the witch's house every day except Sunday. On Mondays and Thursdays, Hansel went twice. On Wednesday, Gretel went in the morning, at noon, and once after Hansel was in bed. Who travelled to the witch's house more times in a month?)

c. Make a drawing of the information provided (e.g., Mehitabel planted a square garden with 12 garlic plants on each side to keep the snails away. How many garlic plants did she plant?)

d. Make inferences and logical deductions (e.g., The Carsons went to Jack-in-the-Bag and spent $20.75 for lunch. An adult meal costs $4.95 and lunch for a child costs $2.95. How many people are in the family? How many of them are children?)

27. Provide the student with an index card that lists several sequenced steps to follow when solving story

problems. A sample flowchart would be: (a) read and reread the problem, (b) draw or mentally picture what is happening, (c) restate what is being asked, (d) choose the operation(s), and (e) compute and check the answer.

28. Teach the student a simple strategy to use for solving story problems. For example, teach him/her to: (a) read the problem, (b) reread the problem to identify what is given (What do I know?) and to decide what is asked for (What do I need to find out?), (c) use objects to solve the problem and identify the operation to use, (d) write the problem, and (e) work the problem (Smith & Alley, 1981). Write the strategy on an index card for easy reference.

29. Teach the student a specific math problem strategy to use for solving story problems. (See Appendix: Math Problem-Solving Strategy.)

Time

1. Teach the student how to read both a digital clock and an analog clock. Have him/her practice setting the hands on the analog clock to match the time on the digital clock.

2. Teach the student how to tell time to the hour, half hour, and quarter hour. Teach him/her the different ways to express these times. For example, 8:30 might be referred to as "eight-thirty," "half-past eight," or "thirty minutes past the hour."

3. Teach the student the meaning of specific vocabulary phrases associated with telling time, such as "almost eleven," "half-past nine," "a quarter after ten," "a little after eight."

Money

1. When teaching the student money concepts, use actual money or realistic facsimiles. Have the student perform problems that involve actual manipulation of the money.

2. Teach the student the value of coins and bills. Provide practice in exchanging coins and bills while maintaining equal value.

3. Provide opportunities for the student to practice making change. Discuss money in relationship to things that the student wishes or needs to purchase. Use a catalog of merchandise for ideas.

4. Provide daily opportunities for the student to increase his/her skill with money. For example, have him/her purchase lunch or budget daily spending.

5. To increase the student's flexibility in making change, provide him/her with practice matching equal value of coins. For example, using real money, ask him/her to show you as many ways as s/he can think of to give someone 50 cents in change. Explain to the student why the combination with the fewest coins is usually returned.

6. Teach the student how to use a cash register. Help him/her increase his/her speed and accuracy in making change.

7. Teach the student the skills needed for money management, such as how to set up a bank account, balance a checkbook, determine interest on a loan, and/or use a credit card.

Calendar

1. In order for the student to develop a better sense of time sequences (days, weeks, months), give him/her a calendar to use to keep track of important events. Cross off each day as part of the daily classroom routine or, if used at home, before bedtime. Mark the end of the month by turning the page. Use a calendar that has a holiday or seasonal picture for each month.

2. Use a yellow highlighter to draw a line separating the weekend days from the weekdays or color the weekend days yellow.

3. Teach the student how to obtain information from a calendar. Make sure that s/he can name the month, day of the week, and the date. As exercises, have him/her count the number of Tuesdays in a month and identify any holidays in the month. Have him/her identify yesterday's date and tomorrow's date.

Life-Skill/Survival Mathematics

1. Identify and teach the student the basic math skills that s/he will need for adult independent living.

2. Encourage the student to enroll in a consumer mathematics course.

3. Provide opportunities for the student to apply math in real situations, such as getting change at

a laundromat, finding the correct bus fare, or determining the cost of clothing on sale.

4. Provide extensive practice in practical application of all new math skills that the student has learned or is learning, both in story problems and real-life (e.g., measuring for cooking, deciding on one shirt over another depending on budget considerations, building a bookshelf).

5. Teach the student the survival math skills that s/he is missing and incorporate them into independent living situations (e.g., balancing a checkbook, determining interest on a car loan, budgeting his/her salary, measuring for cooking).

6. Teach the student to read simple maps, using a highlighter to follow along a route and a different color marker to mark key points along the way. Gradually increase the complexity of the maps.

7. Before the student begins employment, determine the on-the-job demands for mathematical literacy. Make sure that the student is sufficiently prepared to meet these requirements.

8. Devise a variety of real-life situations/simulations in which the type of operation you are teaching is used. Teach the student how to write down computation problems as they arise and use calculators to solve them.

9. Teach the student to estimate length in terms of familiar objects. For example, a regulation baseball bat is 1 meter in length. A notebook is approximately 1 foot in height.

Additional Ideas:

8

KNOWLEDGE/CONTENT AREAS

School
Home

(Related Sections: Oral Language, Reading Comprehension, Written Expression)

School

1. To enhance learning, relate all new concepts to information that the student already knows. Establish and begin instruction at the student's present performance level.

2. Reduce the amount of content presented to the student at any one time. Make sure that s/he has mastered the material before introducing new information.

3. Identify the student's special interests and hobbies. Find ways to use his/her present knowledge to enhance learning in new situations.

4. When introducing new information to the student, use manipulatives or pictures to enhance his/her understanding.

5. Discuss picture situations with the student. Have him/her discuss what is happening in the picture and predict what the outcome will be. Introduce new vocabulary as you discuss the picture.

6. Play the Twenty Questions game with the student to increase background knowledge. The student is allowed to ask 20 questions, that you will answer "yes" or "no," to try to determine something you are thinking of. Use a variety of different classifications. This type of game can also be incorporated into content area learning. For example, say: "I am thinking of a famous explorer. You have 20

questions to guess whom I have chosen." Exchange roles. Model for the student how to move from broad-based questions to more detailed ones. Help him/her learn specific vocabulary related to the topic.

7. Introduce junior encyclopedias to the student as reference material for general information.

8. Have the student bring in current events from the newspaper to discuss.

9. In planning units, incorporate films and videotapes to reinforce textbook content.

10. Use a five-step process to teach the student concepts: (a) decide what concepts and related vocabulary to teach, (b) assess the student's knowledge of the concepts and related vocabulary, (c) use prelearning or prereading activities to facilitate learning, (d) conduct the learning or reading activity, and (e) provide postlearning activities that further reinforce the concepts and information learned (Bos & Vaughn, 1991).

11. Use the Prereading Plan (PReP) strategy (Langer, 1981, 1984), a three-step procedure, to increase the student's background knowledge. In the first step, have the student brainstorm or free associate any keywords or concepts related to the topic that come to mind. In the next step, have the student evaluate his/her responses by answering the question: "What made you think of . . . ?" In the third step, encourage the student to form new questions based on the discussion. (See Appendix.)

12. Before beginning a new unit in any content area class, provide an advance organizer for the student, using Semantic Mapping or Semantic Feature Analysis. (See Appendix.)

13. Before beginning a new unit in any content area class, evaluate and activate the student's prior knowledge of the topic, using Semantic Feature Analysis, the PReP (Prereading Plan) procedure, or Semantic Mapping. If necessary, preteach background knowledge, vocabulary, and key concepts before introducing the unit. (See Appendix.)

14. To increase background knowledge, use thematic units in the classroom. Provide a wide range of experiences around the topic to help the student increase his/her understanding. For example, when studying a specific country, students may prepare a regional dish, learn a folk dance, make change with the currency, and create a topographical map.

15. In science and math classes, do not expect the student to learn any formula by rote. Using familiar concepts and information, teach him/her the general concepts and variables relating to the formula. Then, introduce the formula, provide many examples of its application, and explain why it is applied in that context (Mayer, 1984).

Home

1. At home, encourage your son/daughter to watch educational television programs, such as "3-2-1 Contact," "Sesame Street," "Square One," "Reading Rainbow," "Nova," and "National Geographic."

2. To help your son/daughter increase his/her knowledge of science, social studies, and humanities, rent a wide variety of educationally oriented, interesting videotapes. Sample topics would be: animal habitats, functions of the body, prejudice,

crafts, legends, or conservation. Videotapes can be rented from video stores or borrowed from the public library.

3. Encourage your son/daughter to watch movies on the topics that s/he is studying. If needed, help him/her to locate appropriate videos.

4. Plan field trips for your child where s/he can have direct experiences regarding the information that s/he is studying.

5. In order to increase your child's cultural knowledge, take advantage of the various activities available in the area (e.g., movies, museums, special lectures, ethnic events, and concerts).

6. Provide your son/daughter with varied experiences to expand cultural and world knowledge (e.g., ballet performances, library and museum visits, observances in a variety of religions, visits to historic places). Before going, tell him/her about your trip, the purpose for going, and what s/he can expect to see and do there. Encourage discussion and questions before, during, and after the experience.

7. Encourage home discussions about diverse topics. Talk about school events, current events, and community events.

8. Invest in one or two magazine subscriptions for your son/daughter. Select magazines that will introduce new information about the world and expand his/her current knowledge. The reference librarian at the local library may be able to suggest magazines to review.

Additional Ideas:

9

ATTENTION/ATTENTION DEFICIT DISORDER

(Related Sections: Behavior Management, Social Skills/Self-Esteem, Short-Term Memory)

Because the majority of students with Attention Deficit Disorder (ADD) need behavioral management and intervention, many of the recommendations in the Attention/Attention Deficit Disorder and Behavior Management sections are interrelated. These sections have been separated because, although many of the recommendations in both sections will be appropriate for students with and without ADD, some of the recommendations in the Attention section are only appropriate for students with attentional disorders. Consequently, recommendations most related to the common symptoms of ADD have been included in this section. More general recommendations for behavioral problems are included in the Behavior Management section.

Further Evaluation

1. As the student has noticeable difficulty staying on task, working carefully on mildly challenging work, and sitting reasonably still, consider consulting a developmental pediatrician about the possibility of Attention Deficit Disorder.

2. Have a professional knowledgeable about Attention Deficit Disorder obtain a complete developmental history and profile of current behaviors either to rule out Attention Deficit Disorder as a contributing factor to the student's learning difficulties or to make a further referral to a developmental pediatrician.

3. During the next month, monitor the student's behavior for characteristics of Attention Deficit Disorder. Conduct several formal school observations to gather on-task/off-task data. If a structured behavior management system and high incentives do not produce desired changes, request that the parents schedule an appointment with a pediatrician who has expertise in Attention Deficit Disorder.

4. Meet with the student's parents to further discuss concerns about Attention Deficit Disorder. Refer them to a developmental pediatrician with expertise in Attention Deficit Disorder to investigate this condition, provide education, and establish a treatment plan.

Providing Information

1. Before the beginning of the school year, meet with the student's teacher to explain Attention Deficit Disorder, how this condition is manifested in the student's behavior, the reasons for it, and the situations in which the problem behaviors are most likely to occur. Communicate to the teacher his/her key role as a member of the treatment team and solicit the teacher's cooperation in establishing compensations and interventions as needed.

2. Educate the student's teacher about Attention Deficit Disorder by providing reading material and videotapes. (See Appendix, Attention Deficit Disorder: Informational Resources.)

3. Request that the student's physician contact the teacher to provide additional information and to reinforce that Attention Deficit Disorder is a medical, not a psychological, condition.

4. Copies of some informational articles about Attention Deficit Disorder and a list of recommended readings that include many management suggestions for school and home are attached to this report. Increased understanding of the characteristics associated with this syndrome will help the family understand what to expect and how to handle problems as they arise. (See Appendix, Attention Deficit Disorder: Informational Resources.)

5. Provide information to both the student's teacher and parents regarding the legal rights of children with Attention Deficit Disorder. Section 504 of the Rehabilitation Act of 1973 requires school districts to provide ". . . regular or special education and related services designed to meet individual educational needs of handicapped persons as adequately as the needs of non-handicapped persons are met. . . ." (See Appendix.)

6. For information about joining a support group for parents of children with Attention Deficit Disorder, contact: Attention Deficit Disorder Association, 2620 Ivy Place, Toledo, OH 43613.

Compensations

Environmental

1. Place the student in as small a class as possible.

2. Keep classroom noise at a minimum level.

3. Seat the student away from possible distractions, such as the air conditioner, the window, or a talkative classmate.

4. Seat the student close to the teacher so that the teacher may help him/her to remain on task or to return to task. The proximity of the teacher will help the student stay involved in teacher-directed and interactional activities.

5. To help the student stay on task, the following seating arrangements are recommended. For class discussions or teacher-directed activities, arrange seats in a circle or semicircle. For independent seatwork, unless group cooperation is encouraged, seat children in rows.

6. Require students to keep unnecessary objects off their desks.

Teacher-Directed

General

1. If possible, enlist the school principal's aid in choosing a teacher for the student. Select a patient teacher who is consistent in classroom rules, daily routines, and expectations. The teacher will need to use positive behavior management techniques, to correct without being critical, and to learn about the behavioral characteristics associated with Attention Deficit Disorder.

2. Help the student start his/her day in an organized fashion. For example, if a student typically needs to be reminded to turn in his homework and put his backpack away, you might greet him by saying, "Good morning, Josh. Homework and backpack."

3. Keep informal transitions between activities to a minimum. Provide extra structure during transitions and positive reinforcement if the student is ready for the next activity on time.

4. Allow the student to move in and around his/her seat as long as s/he is not disruptive to others.

Maintaining a Consistent Routine

1. Keep the daily schedule consistent. Routine sets up a structure that allows the student's attention to be directed to the content of the activities.

2. Keep classroom routine consistent from day to day, but vary the tasks and teaching context within

the routine. For example, math might be at 10 a.m. each day, but on one day the class may work on worksheets, the next day the class may play a teacher-directed math game, and on the third day the students may meet in cooperative groups for a math-related experiment.

3. Within the classroom routine, vary types of tasks, shorten work periods, and provide reinforcers.

4. As children with Attention Deficit Disorder often respond poorly to changes in routine, warn the student ahead of time, privately if possible, about any upcoming change and how it will affect him/her.

5. When planning situations that will depart from the normal routine, such as field trips, assemblies, or parties, think ahead to the problems this may cause the student and use preventive techniques to avoid them. For example, on a lengthy bus ride, you may ask the student to act as your helper and sit next to you. On a trip through the planetarium, you could pair the student with a well-behaved student and have them lead the line. Provide frequent positive feedback for good behavior.

Giving Assignments

1. Encourage the student to ask for help on assignments when s/he needs it.

2. Teach the student strategies that will enable him/her to work independently on assignments.

3. Reduce the amount of work the student is required to do during independent assignments so that s/he is more likely to complete his/her work in school.

4. Reduce the amount of work in each area assigned for homework so that the student can complete his/her assignment in approximately the same amount of time other students are expected to spend. Examples of modified assignments are: solving the odd-numbered math problems instead of all the items, studying 10 spelling words instead of 20, writing a half-page report instead of a whole page, and reading a short story instead of a book for a book report.

Modifying Task Characteristics

1. Keep tasks at the student's independent or instructional level. More difficult tasks make it harder for the student to remain on task.

2. Allow the student to work at his/her own pace rather than at a pace set by another person.

3. On easy or repetitive tasks, increase stimulation through the addition of shapes, colors, and textures.

4. Use as many games and interesting, colorful materials as possible to sustain the student's attention and make learning fun.

5. Divide the student's in-class assignments into smaller, more manageable chunks. Give him/her one chunk at a time with instructions to hand each in as it is completed and pick up the next. Each time the student hands in a portion of the work, provide reinforcement for completed work and for time on task. Examples for dividing the work are: placing a piece of paper from a "sticky pad" over the bottom half of a worksheet with instructions for the student to raise his/her hand when s/he reaches the paper; giving the student one worksheet at a time; putting a sticker on the bottom of every two pages of a story.

6. Limit the amount of time that the student is required to work on a difficult task, such as writing. Let him/her help decide the amount of time s/he will spend on a task. Follow a difficult assignment with an enjoyable activity.

7. Alternate teaching contexts. The student may find it easier to attend to task better when involved in cooperative learning groups, guided student discussions, and activities with a high level of teacher–student interaction. Brief periods of independent seatwork may be interspersed with these types of activities.

8. Observe the student's attention span during a variety of teaching contexts and activities (e.g., listening to instructions, working independently, cooperating in group activities, writing, doing math worksheets) and note patterns of behavior specific to the activity. Use the information about contexts/activities in which s/he has most success to help you modify contexts/activities in which s/he has less success.

9. Keep in mind that children with Attention Deficit Disorder are easily frustrated. Sudden behavioral outbursts may signal that a task is too difficult.

Giving Instructions

1. Make it comfortable for the student to ask for clarification and repetition of instructions.

2. Make sure you have the student's attention before speaking to him/her or giving a series of oral instructions.

3. Maintain eye contact with the student when giving him/her oral instructions.

4. Make oral instructions clear and concise. Simplify complex instructions and avoid multiple commands.

5. When giving instructions for an activity, provide enough time for the student to accomplish each step before going on. For example, in a spelling test, after you have asked the student to number the paper, wait until s/he has finished that task before you begin to read the words.

6. During transitions, help the student get organized by using the following procedures: (a) require the class to stay seated and quiet while you give all instructions. Say, "Go ahead" when you have finished; (b) give all instructions in the same order as they are to follow them; and (c) limit the number of instructions.

7. Clearly specify expectations regarding: (a) type of assignment, (b) quality and quantity of work for each assignment, (c) length of time to spend working on each assignment, and (d) specific due dates for the assignment.

Peer-Assisted

1. Within the classroom seating arrangement, surround the student with model students who will help him/her return to task and socialize only at appropriate times.

2. Set up a buddy system whereby a student who sits next to the target student agrees to give him/her an unobtrusive signal when his/her attention wanders.

3. Set up a buddy system by selecting a student who will repeat or explain instructions to the target student whenever s/he needs it. If appropriate, discuss the student's special needs with the buddy.

4. Use peer tutors to assist the student during independent work periods.

Behavioral Interventions

(See also: Behavior Management: Behavioral Interventions)

General

1. Have an educational specialist trained in quantitative observation sit in the student's class periodically to observe his/her behavior. The purposes would be to document changes in behavior and to make suggestions regarding compensations or interventions to improve classroom functioning.

2. When setting up a behavioral intervention for a child with Attention Deficit Disorder, ensure that the adults involved understand that external support for maintaining certain behaviors (e.g., attention to task, reflective work) may continue to be necessary. The final step of teaching the student to self-monitor so that s/he can take over full responsibility for maintaining the behavior has not proven successful for many children with ADD who are not on medication (Abikoff, 1991; Abramowitz & O'Leary, 1991).

3. Use the classroom aide to provide extra feedback to the student for a specific positive behavior that has been targeted for improvement. Examples are praising the student for spending time on task, starting work as soon as directed to do so, getting through a transition efficiently, and putting materials away.

4. When training specific behaviors, often the teacher has to be content with one aspect of a job done well. Adjust expectations and remain focused on the goal. For example, ask yourself, "Which is more important? Writing the correct information on a science quiz or spelling the words correctly?" "Getting the homework done or remembering to write down the assignment independently?"

5. When the student fails at a task or interaction, structure an opportunity for him/her to try again and succeed. This will prevent the student from developing a sense of helplessness and lack of interest and motivation toward school and learning.

6. Try to provide reinforcement in a ratio of nine positive comments to one negative or correcting comment.

7. For both praise and reprimands, keep statements brief.

Monitoring and Reinforcing Behavior

Teacher/Parent

1. Have the teacher complete a checklist at specified intervals to monitor the student's response to medical or behavioral interventions. Three commonly used checklists are the Conners' Teacher Rating Scales (Conners, 1989), The ANSER System (Levine, 1985, 1988), and the ACTeRS (Ullman, Sleator, & Sprague, 1985).

2. The teacher may keep a small chart on his/her desk with the following behaviors of concern delineated: (Specify behaviors, such as the percent of on-task behavior, quality of academic assignments, percent of assignments turned in, completeness of assignments, behavior in class, and social interactions). Each day the teacher should assign a specific number of points in each area based on a 5-point scale. Tally the points and send a report home on a daily or weekly basis.

3. The parents should speak with the student's teacher at least once every 2 weeks and ask specifically about their son's/daughter's activity level, ability to stay on task, level of fatigue, impulsivity, social interactions, the quality and completeness of his/her work, and academic progress.

Teacher/Student

1. Praise specific behaviors in the student that you want to encourage. For example, stop by his/her desk and say quietly, "You're concentrating well on this assignment," or, after the activity, say to the class, "Many of you really stayed focused on this assignment," with a smile at the student so s/he knows s/he is included. This technique serves to make the student aware of the behavior and encourages him/her to continue it and repeat it at a later time.

2. The student needs a strategy to reduce his/her time off task. One possibility is to have an adult (teacher or aide) monitor the student at regular intervals, such as every 10 minutes, and record the percentage of times s/he is on task (e.g., 5 times on task out of 10 times = 50%). The student can chart his/her on-task percentages daily so that s/he may see the improvement.

3. Teach the student how to use an "Attention Tape" (Glynn & Thomas, 1974). Either the student or his/her teacher can make a tape that is completely quiet except for a nonabrasive noise at odd intervals, such as tapping a spoon gently against a glass. The recommended time intervals, in minutes, for a 30-minute tape are: 3, 4, 3, 5, 4, 2, 4, 3, 2. Each time the student hears the sound, s/he asks him/herself, "Am I on task?" If so, s/he places a check on a chart. If not, s/he resumes work. Build in positive reinforcement for increasing the number of checks s/he accumulates within a taped period.

4. Increase the student's attention span in challenging tasks by providing rewards for gradually increasing the amount of time s/he works in a reflective manner. Give frequent positive reinforcement.

Organization of Materials

1. Help the student set up a work space that has a designated place for all materials. Provide daily reinforcement to the student for maintaining the work area in an organized fashion.

2. If possible, provide the student with a second set of books to keep at home. This will reduce the likelihood of him/her losing books, not having the necessary books at school for class work, or not having the necessary books at home for the night's homework.

3. Request that the student's parents provide him/her with the necessary equipment to help him/her organize school materials. This might include a notebook containing separate compartments for each subject, a compartment for homework to be handed in, and an assignment calendar. Also, the student may benefit from a backpack with compartments labeled for what goes in them (e.g., books, glasses, pencils).

4. Use a different color book cover for each subject and label each in marker on the front cover and binding. Alternatively, place a sticker associated with the subject on each cover (e.g., an American flag for social studies, a skeleton for health).

Homework

1. Meet with the student's parents to obtain their cooperation in monitoring homework assignments. Explain to them that although the final goal is for their child to do his/her homework independently, at present, parental supervision and support are required.

2. Request that the parents provide a well-organized and quiet work area for the student at home where a parent is available to help the student remain on task and provide help when needed.

3. Request that the parents designate a specific time each afternoon or evening as homework time. The student should be allowed breaks at predetermined intervals, but not more frequently.

4. In order to teach the student to write down assignments and bring home the proper books, set up a system whereby the student is responsible for writing down his/her homework on an assignment calendar at the same time each day. The teacher checks it for accuracy, legibility, and completeness, corrects it if necessary, and initials it. The teacher may need to help the student remember to put the required book in his/her backpack. At home, the parents check that the student has written down the assignment and has all of the correct books, and provide a reward.

Gradually, fade the teacher assistance and have the student take over more of the responsibility him/herself. Continue rewards at home until the student consistently brings home assignments and the appropriate books.

5. Have the parent sign the assignment calendar when the student has finished his/her homework so that, if the student cannot find the homework, the teacher will know it was completed.

6. Notify the student's parents as far in advance as possible of any major project the student is to do at home, all requirements for the project, and the grading criteria. Students with Attention Deficit Disorder often need a great deal of extra time to create and revise a project.

7. At least once a week, notify the parents of any incomplete or missing assignments.

Noneducational Treatment Considerations

Medication

1. Remind the student privately when it is time to take his/her medication.

2. If the student is on medication, observe him/her carefully throughout the day to determine the time of day that the beneficial effects of the medication appear to be wearing off. Notify the student's parents.

3. If the student is on medication, ask the parents or physician what behavioral changes to expect, what time(s) during the day the student should exhibit optimal behavioral control, and how long the effects of the medication should last. If the student is still displaying off-task behavior, impulsivity, hyperactivity, or disruptive behavior, notify his/her parents.

4. Ask the student's parents about possible negative side effects of the medication the student is taking. Report any observed pattern of these behaviors to the parents.

5. Schedule a conference for (date) to include the student's parents, the teacher(s), and the school psychologist or counselor. If, at that time, the student has not made considerable progress in the behavioral manifestations of Attention Deficit Disorder, consider the use of medication to allow him/her to benefit from the other interventions that have been established.

6. Due to the inconsistency of the student's behavior in the classroom, combined with his/her apparent continued impulsivity and lack of attention, the parents should discuss the adequacy of the student's current medication with his/her doctor.

7. Discuss with the student's pediatrician the possible need for the student to continue taking medication during the summer. This recommendation is made to allow the student to control his/her own behavior, learn from modeled behavior, and minimize possible negative feedback s/he may receive from staff and other children in the summer program. As others may not understand Attention Deficit Disorder, they may not be tolerant of the student's inattention, social insensitivity, overactivity, and impulsivity.

Counseling

1. Parents of children with Attention Deficit Disorder often benefit from training in parenting skills specific to the needs of the child. Encourage the student's parents to seek further education about Attention Deficit Disorder and parenting training from a mental health professional who specializes in this area.

2. Many families of children with Attention Deficit Disorder find family counseling helpful. Often, the goals of counseling are to help set up a consistent behavior management system in the home, help the

child deal with the sense of failure and frustration that often accompanies this condition, and help siblings cope with the child's behavioral differences and need for special attention. Also, counseling can provide support and education for the parents in an often frustrating and puzzling situation, while helping them to develop realistic expectations for their child.

3. Provide counseling to ensure that the student understands the nature of Attention Deficit Disorder, how it affects him/her, and the reason for medication. Counseling also provides an opportunity for the child to discuss his/her feelings about having this condition, ask questions as they arise, and learn how to handle problem situations.

4. The student may benefit from a group for children/adolescents with Attention Deficit Disorder led by a mental health professional with expertise in this area. The focus should be on education about ADD, social relationships, and effective problem solving.

Additional Ideas:

10

BEHAVIOR MANAGEMENT

(Related Sections: Attention, Social Skills/Self-Esteem)

General

1. Post classroom rules in a conspicuous place along with the rewards for positive behavior and consequences for negative behavior.

2. Avoid punitive consequences for misbehavior. Instead, develop a plan that will focus on positive behaviors while systematically attempting to reduce the negative behaviors.

3. Identify the specific behaviors that are interfering with school success. Clearly specify and provide rewards for behaviors that are incompatible with the negative behaviors; clearly specify and provide consequences for the negative behaviors.

4. Choose consequences, both positive and negative, that matter to the student.

5. Before activities in which the student typically has behavioral difficulties, meet with the student privately and review the rules for that particular activity (e.g., recess, school bus, field trip). Then have the student state the rules.

Verbal Reinforcement and Self-Awareness

1. Praise appropriate behaviors frequently and, as far as possible, ignore inappropriate behaviors.

2. Give at least nine positive comments for each correction or criticism. If you would like to monitor your comments, place a piece of masking tape on your desk or sleeve. Make a mark on the left side each time you make a positive comment and a mark on the right for each negative comment.

3. Make every effort to reinforce the student when s/he is behaving appropriately (e.g., verbal comments, smiles, nods, pats on the back). Comment on the specific positive behavior immediately.

4. Praise the student for positive academic behaviors, such as turning in a particularly neat assignment. For example, say: "Amber, this paper is easy to read because you were so careful with your handwriting. It must feel good to hand in such a nice paper."

5. Recognize the student for appropriate social behavior. For example, say: "I think Jackie felt happy when you let her go ahead of you in line" or "We were able to go to the assembly early because you and the others put your books away so quickly."

6. Watch the student carefully during the day for times s/he demonstrates the target behavior (such as talking out a problem). Praise the specific behavior. For example, immediately after s/he handles a problem properly, tell the student, "You told Hank you were angry with him and you stayed calm. That was mature behavior" (rather than, "You did a good job with Hank"). Later, when appropriate, praise the behavior again.

7. Help the student recognize how his/her actions affect others. Immediately after a negative behavior, discuss with the student how others may interpret his/her behavior, the reason for your concern, and a solution. Alternatively, help the student to devise a solution.

Examples:

I know you were just playing, but the rule is, "Keep your hands to yourself." Other students might not realize that you're playing when you push them and they may get angry. Or, they may bump into something and get hurt. How can you remind yourself about not pushing when we come in from recess tomorrow?

I know you're trying to be funny when you yell at the other students to take out their books, but they think you're being bossy. How could you set a good example for the others?

8. Enlist the aid of other students to provide approval when the student exhibits the targeted behavior. So as not to single out the student, all students in a group could choose behaviors they would like to improve. Train all students to reinforce positive behaviors verbally and to ignore negative instances of the behavior.

Correction and Redirection

1. In cooperation with the student, make up a signal, such as a hand signal or a soft touch on the shoulder, that will remind him/her to return to task.

2. Correct the student's negative behavior by reinforcing positive behavior in another student. For example, when the student is looking around, say, "I see that Ginger and Taro are concentrating on their work."

3. State corrections and redirections in a positive, nonhumiliating manner. State what you would like the student to do rather than what you want him/her to stop doing (e.g., "Marlo, we're returning to our desks now to take out our social studies books").

4. When reprimands for inappropriate behavior are necessary, give them immediately and consistently. Stand near the student and obtain eye contact. Be calm and firm.

5. When the student breaks a classroom or school rule, remain calm and state the rule that was broken,

his/her infraction, and the consequence. Avoid arguing with the student.

Behavioral Interventions

Guidelines

The following guidelines are written so that they may be selected for use individually or used as a block.

1. When attempting to eliminate specific problem behaviors systematically, list the positive behaviors that when developed will eliminate the student's negative behaviors. Prioritize those that are of most concern and target one for intervention.

2. Before initiating an intervention, take baseline data to establish the frequency, severity, and/or intensity of the behavior of concern. Within the intervention, establish a method of objectively monitoring progress. Examples are counting the number of times the behavior occurs in a day or the number of intervals that the student has passed through without exhibiting the targeted behavior.

3. Ensure that the student can be successful and earn rewards at the initial level of behavioral criteria.

4. If the student has difficulty succeeding with the contract, reduce the behavioral criteria, shorten time intervals between the rewarding of tokens, or provide different rewards.

5. Ensure that the reward chosen is highly motivating to the student and is not easily available except as a reward.

6. Do not make rewards time-dependent (e.g., taking a trip on a specific day). The student *must* have the ability to earn the reward. The unknown element is *when*, not if, s/he will receive the reward. Do not take points away for negative behavior.

7. Periodically change the reward to maintain interest and motivation.

8. When a behavior appears to have been mastered or eliminated, but external support (e.g., teacher reinforcement and points) is still provided, gradually fade the external support giving the student increased responsibility for monitoring his/her own behavior.

9. Make provisions in advance for departures from the normal routine, such as assemblies, field trips, parties, or substitute teachers.

10. Build in reinforcement for generalization of the positive behaviors to other contexts where the token economy is not used.

11. If a system using only positive consequences does not prove effective, consider incorporating response-cost. In this system, the student loses some portion of the primary reinforcer (e.g., points, tokens) each time s/he displays the negative behavior. If the student begins to lose more than s/he is gaining, reduce the behavioral criteria, shorten time intervals between the rewarding of tokens, or provide more attractive rewards until the student attains consistent success.

12. Combine contingencies in developing a behavioral intervention for the student. Some effective combinations are: (a) praise with increased privileges, and (b) rewards with response-cost.

Token Economy

Increasing Positive Behaviors

1. Meet with the student privately. State your concern about a specific behavior and the reason for your concern. Or, ask the student if s/he recognizes any behaviors s/he would like assistance in changing. Set up a contract with the student, targeting the positive behavior to be developed (e.g., staying on task, keeping hands to self, raising hand before speaking). Agree on a system of awarding points or tokens for each time the student exhibits the target behavior and the reward for which the student can trade his/her points/tokens. Initially, allow the student to trade in the points daily. In some cases, a twice daily trade-in may be necessary. When the student maintains appropriate behavior for a pre-determined interval of time (e.g., 1 or 2 weeks) with this level of external support, increase the intervals between rewards or increase the number of points/tokens needed for a reward. (See Appendix, Contract [Student-Teacher].)

Reducing Negative Behaviors

2. Meet with the student privately. State your concern about a specific behavior and the reason for your concern. Set up a contract with the student, targeting a negative behavior for reduction (e.g., leaving the seat or work area, speaking to other students, discourteous comments). Agree on a number of points or tokens the student will earn for passing a predetermined time period without exhibiting the behavior. Ensure that the time interval initially chosen for not exhibiting the behavior is within the capability of the student. Use a timer and provide tokens for each successful interval. Gradually increase the intervals. (See Appendix, Contract [Student-Teacher].)

Home–School Cooperation

3. Set up a consistent behavior management system between school and home with rewards built into a point system. With the student, establish specific, high-incentive rewards for earning a pre-set number of points. Points for increasing a positive behavior or decreasing a negative behavior are to be awarded by the teacher daily and, at first, traded daily for a reward at home. Later they may be tallied daily, but sent home weekly. Possible reinforcers are praise, tangible items such as money, special privileges, events, or trips. Do not make rewards time-dependent (e.g., taking a trip on a specific day). The student *must* have the ability to earn the reward. The unknown element is *when*, not if, s/he will receive the reward. Do not take points away for negative behavior. Ensure that parents are adequately trained in this system. (See Appendix, Contract [Child-Parent].)

Additional Ideas:

11

SOCIAL SKILLS/SELF-ESTEEM

(Related Sections: Attention, Behavior Management)

Social Skills

Instruction/Training

1. Establish classroom rules for social interactions. Discuss and provide examples of appropriate and inappropriate comments. Make sure that the students understand the importance of respecting others. Post the rules on the wall along with the pre-established consequences.

2. Observe the student's social interactions in a variety of situations. Identify the social skills that s/he should acquire and then prioritize the skills for instruction.

3. Since social skills have been targeted as a specific problem for the student at school and home, provide specific training.

4. Help the student improve social appropriateness by imagining how other people will react to his/her words and behavior. Teach the student to consider another person's possible reaction *before* s/he speaks or acts.

5. Teach the student how to maintain eye contact with a person when speaking. Provide structured situations for practice.

6. Teach the student to notice and interpret facial expressions and body language when s/he is talking to people.

7. Provide the student with practice in rehearsing what s/he will say in a situation before it occurs. For example, if the student wants to join a group of students on the playground, have him/her think of exactly what s/he will say before walking over to the group.

8. Use live demonstrations or films to present the social skills to be learned. Provide opportunities to role-play. After structured practice, give the student constructive feedback.

9. Discuss problematic social situations and brainstorm with the student different ways to resolve the problem. For example, draw a semantic map on the board with the problem in the center. Connect and write each proposed solution in an outside circle. Discuss how different solutions are related to each other and any underlying concepts (e.g., respect).

10. Praise the student for behaviors such as helping, sharing, or saying something nice to another person. Through role modeling, teach him/her how to compliment other people sincerely.

11. Have the student work on a project with a peer who will model positive social interactions.

Activities

1. To help the student become more accepted by other students, tailor some classroom activities to

fit his/her specific strengths. Ask the student's parents to provide a list of the student's specific skills, interests, or areas of knowledge. For example, if you are planning a science project, identify an aspect of the topic in which the student has expertise and could present information or lead a group discussion.

2. Create situations that allow the student to have successful social experiences. For example, select a peer who would like to play a game with the student on the playground during recess.

3. Use highly structured cooperative learning groups to help the student participate in positive social interactions.

4. Encourage the student to join and participate in a school club or organization in which s/he is interested.

5. Encourage the student to participate in well-supervised, mildly competitive activities, such as team sports.

6. Teach the student or ask the physical education teacher to teach the student the rules and skills of a game. Select a game that the student will be able to participate in during recess or after school.

7. Improve the student's social skills by having him/her participate in a team sport with a coach who is aware of the student's behaviors and is interested in providing a *positive* learning experience.

8. Use the student's involvement in athletics to train socially acceptable behavior. If possible, enlist the aid of the physical education teacher. Provide regular feedback to the student about how his/her behavior and actions in physical education or on a team were received. When negative behaviors occur, brainstorm alternative behaviors with the student.

Self-Esteem

General

1. Show the student that you like and approve of him/her by providing frequent positive reinforcements, such as a smile, a hug, a positive comment on a paper, special privileges, or rewards.

2. Watch for situations where the student is doing something correctly or behaving appropriately.

Make a positive comment to the student in front of others regarding the behavior.

3. Assign the student a classroom task that s/he would enjoy, such as watering the plants or collecting homework assignments. Express gratitude after s/he has completed the task.

4. Create opportunities to ask the student what s/he thinks about certain things. Make it apparent that you value his/her opinion.

5. Have the student participate in any decisions that concern him/herself.

6. Use a prescriptive skill-based approach for raising self-esteem in the classroom, such as provided in *How to Raise Student Self-Esteem: Strategies and Techniques for Teachers*. This handbook, directed at grades kindergarten through 6, covers a wide range of topics focusing on developing social, group, individual learner, and goal-setting skills. Each topic is accompanied by "how to" instructions as well as several reproducible worksheets or activities to do with students. Available from: Judy Cooper, Ed.D., 7230 101st St. N., White Bear Lake, MN 55110, (612) 426-9505.

Strengths/Activities

1. Recognize the student's unique talents. When you acknowledge a student's strengths, you provide an opportunity for the other students to do so as well.

2. Help the student become better in whatever s/he already does well. For example, if the student is struggling with reading, but not having difficulty in math, be sure to direct attention to increasing skill in both reading and math.

3. Discuss with the student how all people are unique and have areas in which they excel and areas in which they struggle. Help the student understand his/her own individuality so that s/he is able to make an accurate, noncritical, and honest self-appraisal.

4. Help the student develop his/her strengths. The student should participate in enrichment programs that will enhance his/her abilities in ( ). Two examples might be: (a) an advanced hands-on science program that emphasizes discussion and activity rather than reading and writing or (b) classes or discussion sessions that use questioning strategies designed to encourage and develop critical thinking skills.

5. Capitalize on instructional activities where the student is successful. For example, have the student participate in a cross-age tutoring program in a structured setting where s/he teaches a younger student the skills that s/he has mastered.

6. Have the student teach something s/he knows or a skill s/he knows how to perform to another student or small group of students.

7. Encourage the student to develop his/her skills in specific areas of interest. If s/he does not express interest in anything, help him/her choose a hobby or sport to pursue.

8. Help the student develop specialty areas. Encourage him/her to study topics of interest in depth. Provide opportunities in the classroom for the student to share his/her expertise.

9. Place value in the classroom on nonacademic strengths, such as mechanical or musical abilities. Provide opportunities for the student to demonstrate his/her knowledge or abilities to classmates.

10. Encourage the student to participate in extracurricular and recreational activities in which s/he will be successful. Discuss with the student his/her participation and successes in the activity.

11. Ask that the physical education teacher or parents help the student develop skill in a one-to-one sport, such as tennis or handball. Provide opportunities for the student to play with others.

12. Encourage the student's parents to have their son/daughter be responsible for completing several chores at home. Have them make a chart on which s/he may check tasks as they are completed.

13. Encourage the student to participate in some type of volunteer program, such as at a local hospital or nursing home. Make sure that the expectations of the job are clear to the student.

Assignments

1. Do not assign the student work that is too difficult for him/her to complete independently. If additional instructional support is required, such as a peer tutor or parent volunteer, be sure to provide it. Reinforce the student for the work s/he completes successfully.

2. Provide the student with assignments that s/he is able to complete independently both in level of difficulty and quantity. Provide praise for completion of assignments.

3. Reduce the amount of work the student is required to do during independent seatwork assignments so that s/he completes his/her work successfully in school. Comment upon how diligently the student worked on the assignment.

4. When the student has difficulty with an assignment or project, provide the student with an opportunity to redo the work for a higher grade.

5. Remember that a student will become successful by having successful experiences. Initially, ignore the student's errors and mistakes and praise his/her effort. As effort improves, help the student understand that mistakes are just part of the learning process.

6. Consistently praise the student for sincere effort rather than accomplishment. Increases in effort will result in improvement of the final product.

7. Keep a folder with the student's schoolwork. Occasionally, review past work and discuss with the student his/her own progress and development.

8. As the student's confidence increases, teach him/her strategies for coping with failure. For example, if s/he fails an assignment or a test, brainstorm alternative methods of handling the situation.

Class Discussions

1. When the student provides a correct response in class, make a positive comment. Commenting upon the right responses will increase confidence and, as a result, help the student develop a more positive attitude toward school.

2. When the student is uncertain about answers, encourage risk taking. Even if a response is incorrect, make a positive comment that acknowledges the student's willingness to express ideas.

3. Until his/her confidence increases, when calling on the student in class, only ask him/her questions that you know s/he will be able to answer successfully.

4. Help the student organize his/her thoughts and knowledge about a topic prior to a class discussion. Call on the student when you know s/he will be able to answer a question. If needed, let the student know the question you will ask him/her before class begins.

Additional Ideas:

12

SENSORY IMPAIRMENTS

Hearing

General

1. Obtain a comprehensive hearing evaluation for the student that measures the degree of loss and the individual's level of hearing at various frequencies if the student wears a hearing aid. The evaluation should include unaided and aided hearing levels.

2. In planning the student's educational program, consult with a hearing specialist who can recommend necessary classroom modifications, provide resource help, and identify community resources.

3. Consult with a hearing specialist regarding the type of hearing loss. Realize that one major type of hearing loss (conductive) can be assisted by amplifying sound, whereas another type of hearing loss (sensorineural) may not be helped by amplification since the distortion is also amplified.

4. Maintain contact with resource personnel so that information in classroom lessons can be reviewed in individual therapy.

5. Identify the local, state, and national resources that can help you develop a program for a student with a hearing impairment.

Accommodations

Environmental

1. Provide the student with preferential seating. Place the student near the teacher or major source of instruction. Make sure that the student has his/her better ear toward the teacher.

2. Use seating arrangements that allow the student with a hearing impairment to see other students (e.g., horseshoe, circle). This type of arrangement is particularly important during group activities.

3. Attempt to reduce distracting sounds and minimize background noise by seating the student away from noisy hallways, ventilation ducts, windows near playgrounds, or other obvious noise sources. Use rubber tips on chair legs, unless the room is carpeted, or plant thick shrubbery outside windows that face noisy streets.

4. Attempt to minimize reverberation effects by using carpeting, drapery, acoustical ceiling tile, sound-absorbing bulletin boards, and sound-absorbing room dividers to separate work areas.

Instructional

1. Even though the student's hearing may be improved by use of a hearing aid, it is still not corrected. Provide special classroom adaptations, as needed.

2. Discuss with the specialist ways you can regularly reinforce skills that the student is learning.

3. If the student with a hearing impairment uses sign language, provide opportunities for other students in the classroom to learn this language. You may begin by teaching finger spelling, the hand positions for individual letters of the alphabet, to the entire class. Explain to the students that they will be learning a new communication system.

4. When speaking to the student, use a normal voice, face the individual, and speak slowly. Stand within 2 to 6 feet from him/her.

5. When speaking to the student, paraphrase or reword your statement instead of repeating it to provide clarification. Move to within 18 to 36 inches of the student at his/her eye level.

6. Check the student's comprehension before changing topics. When you are introducing a new subject, give some indication to the student that you are changing the topic. For example, you may write the new topic on the board.

7. Encourage the student to ask questions when s/he does not understand what has been said. Rephrase the information to convey the intended meaning.

8. Check the student's comprehension by asking open-ended questions.

9. For group discussions, develop a system for indicating which student is about to speak so that the student with a hearing impairment does not lose the content of what is said while trying to locate the source of the voice. The teacher may call on a student by name or the student who is to speak may raise his/her hand or stand.

10. Write on the board any keywords, indicators of topic change, and homework assignments.

11. Assign the student a buddy who will help him/her write down the daily assignments.

12. Preteach difficult or important words and concepts. Resource teachers, itinerant teachers of the hearing-impaired, teaching assistants, and parent volunteers can assist in this area.

13. Have the student prepare ahead for topics that will be discussed in class. For example, the student may read the chapter before it is introduced in the class. This will help the student to participate more fully in class discussions.

14. To enhance learning, provide relevant visual stimulation such as movies, books, and pictures to help the student form associations for new learning.

15. Help the student expand his/her vocabulary by providing field trips to a variety of locations.

Technological

1. Remember that the student's hearing aid amplifies all sounds and that at times the student may need to lower the volume.

2. Consult the school's educational audiologist about using assistive listening devices such as personal FM systems and Sound Field Amplification.

3. Ensure that the student's hearing aids and/or FM systems are functioning properly. High malfunction rates are common in systems that are not routinely monitored.

4. Have the school audiologist or speech/language pathologist teach you how to operate a hearing aid or an FM Auditory Trainer. Be able to check to see if the equipment is turned on and switched to the proper setting. Keep spare batteries in your desk and know how to change them.

5. Provide opportunities for the student to use a Language Master in the classroom. Hearing the prerecorded speech as the student looks at words and phrases will increase the student's oral and reading vocabulary.

6. Use films and videotapes with language-controlled captions (subtitles) so that the student will understand the same information that other students are hearing from the soundtrack. A catalogue of captioned, rental-free films is available from Captioned Films for the Deaf, 5000 Park Street North, St. Petersburg, FL 33709-9989 (1-800-237-6213 Voice/TTY). Films and videotapes may be requested in advance for dates throughout the school year.

7. Make sure that the student who cannot use the telephone has access to a teletypewriter system (TTY). This system will enable the student to send and receive typewritten messages over telephone lines.

Vision

General

1. Obtain a complete, clinical vision evaluation, preferably from an ophthalmologist. The evaluation

should provide information on visual acuity, visual fields, use of binocular vision, visual disorders (if any), and prognosis for visual functioning. A complete vision evaluation also requires a functional assessment, which provides specific information on how the student uses his/her vision in typical activities. If additional information is needed, a low vision evaluation can provide suggestions for optical and nonoptical aids and materials to enhance visual functioning.

2. In planning the student's educational program, consult with a vision specialist who can clarify or explain information regarding a student's visual abilities and recommend necessary classroom modifications, provide resource help and appropriate instructional materials, and identify community resources.

3. Consult the vision specialist regarding the student's residual vision. Attempt to reinforce any training being provided in daily activities.

4. Identify the local, state, and national resources that can help you understand the visual problem, develop an appropriate program, and obtain materials for a student with a visual impairment.

Accommodations

Environmental

1. Help the student with a visual impairment learn how to care for his/her own materials in the classroom.

2. Keep classroom supplies and materials in the same place so that the student may locate them easily. These materials should be kept neat, organized, and easily accessible.

3. When doing chalkboard work, make sure that the student is seated so that s/he can see the board. Keep chalkboards clean.

4. Make sure that the illumination in the classroom is appropriate for the student. Make sure that the student does not have to look at direct light or into the glare of direct light on surfaces. Information may have to be raised on a slant board to accommodate individual needs. Small directional lights can be added to these boards to illuminate the work.

5. Help the student with very limited vision learn to move about the classroom environment safely and

independently. If necessary, an orientation and mobility specialist can provide training in this area.

6. Avoid rearranging large pieces of furniture/equipment without first bringing it to the attention of the student.

7. Have the student travel with a peer (sighted guide) to frequently used rooms in the school. Once the student learns to move around the school independently, s/he will no longer need a sighted guide. Sighted guides will be necessary for unfamiliar environments.

Instructional

1. Obtain help from the vision specialist on ways to adapt lessons/materials so that the student can participate.

2. Encourage the student to participate in as many classroom activities as possible. If an activity is inappropriate for the student, arrange an alternative activity.

3. Have the student perform the same types of tasks as other children, such as watering plants, erasing the chalkboard, or collecting lunch money.

4. Adjust written and reading requirements to the student's ability level.

5. Ask the low vision specialist if the use of magnification aids will facilitate reading.

6. Obtain large-print books from local or state libraries, if needed.

7. Provide the student with paper and other materials that are clear, well spaced, and easy to read.

8. Consult the vision specialist to obtain braille texts for the student.

9. Remember that a student using braille or large print will typically read at a rate two or three times slower than the average reader. Be sure to allow him/her sufficient time to complete readings or shorten the assignments.

10. Have the vision specialist make labels and signs in braille to post around the classroom. Explain to the students how braille is another system of communication.

11. Based upon the student's limited vision, s/he may benefit from raised line paper for writing

assignments. This paper will help the student keep his/her printing on the line.

12. Provide the student with black felt-tip markers for writing, if needed. A yellow highlighter can be used by the teacher or student to enhance visual information.

13. Allow the student to have frequent rest periods from near-point visually demanding materials and tasks.

14. When writing on the chalkboard, make large, clear letters. In addition, remember to read any information aloud that you write.

15. In the classroom, provide the student with concrete objects to accompany a lesson and encourage exploration of the environment. Explain relationships between objects and encourage the student to touch and manipulate objects.

16. Provide concrete systematic experiences to help the student master science and social studies concepts. One example of a program designed to teach science content to elementary children with visual impairments is *Science Activities for the Visually Impaired* (Malone, DeLucchi, & Their, 1981). This program includes hands-on activities for conducting a variety of science experiments.

17. Whenever you use visual displays in the classroom, remember to describe the diagrams or illustrations in detail.

18. Provide the student with carbon copies of notes taken by another student.

19. Provide the student with additional time on assignments, as needed.

20. Provide the student with appropriate modifications for testing, ranging from extension of time limits to provision of oral examinations.

21. Work closely with the physical education teacher to develop an appropriate physical education program. Try not to exclude the student from typical activities, unless indicated by the ophthalmologist.

22. Allow the student to record all class lectures on an audio tape.

Technological

1. Teach the student how to use a computer to enhance communication skills. Provide the student with a computer with voice output or, if available, a computer with print and braille output.

2. Provide the student with a large-type typewriter, if needed.

3. Encourage the student to use an abacus to perform basic mathematical calculations when other students are using pencil and paper.

4. Provide the student with a talking calculator to use for math class.

5. Use closed-circuit television that will enlarge printed materials. Realize that reading rate will be slower when print is enlarged.

6. Allow the student to use a tape recorder to record information that s/he wants to use in a paper or report. At a later time, the information can be transferred into print or braille.

7. Ensure that the student has a taped copy of any book that the class is reading. Provide headsets and encourage the student to listen to the book during silent reading time.

8. If needed, provide the student with access to a Kurzweil Reading Machine. This computer reads books aloud at a speed and tone that are controlled by the user.

Additional Ideas:

PART II
FROM THE DIAGNOSTIC REPORT TO BEHAVIORAL OBJECTIVES

BEHAVIORAL OBJECTIVES

Introduction

One outcome of a good evaluation is clear, practical recommendations tailored to the cognitive and academic needs and learning style of the student. Usually, the results of the Woodcock-Johnson Psycho-Educational Battery—Revised lead the evaluator to a statement of major concerns regarding the student's educational needs. It then falls to the special education teacher, the speech/language pathologist, the school psychologist, or the vocational specialist to turn these concerns into long-term goals and behavioral objectives. Well-written recommendations can be easily translated into short-term goals.

Selecting the Long-Term Goal

Using the WJ-R and any supplemental tests, the evaluator has identified major and specific areas of academic or cognitive strengths and deficiencies. A long-term goal, a general statement of need for improvement in a targeted area, should be created for each major area of deficiency identified. If many major areas of deficit have been identified, they should be prioritized before identifying those to translate into long-term goals. Based on results from the WJ-R, three types of long-term goals might be written: goals specifically for a cognitive ability of concern, goals for a cognitive ability within the context of an academic skill, or goals for an academic skill.

An example of a long-term goal for a cognitive ability might be to improve short-term memory. For this goal, the focus of instruction might be on teaching specific memory strategies, such as chunking and using mnemonics. Another goal could be to improve receptive vocabulary, for which a variety of vocabulary objectives would be generated. An example of the second type of long-term goal, more in keeping with task-process training (Kirk & Chalfant, 1984), would be to improve short-term memory within the context of reading comprehension; here, the focus of instruction would be on reading comprehension strategies that aid recall. Another goal of this type would be to increase reading vocabulary with generalization to comprehension of oral language. The third type of long-term goal is the most familiar. Examples include increasing sight vocabulary, improving reading comprehension, improving the ability to solve math word problems, improving written expression, and improving basic writing skills. Other types of long-term goals, which may not come directly from the results of the WJ-R but should come from concerns identified in the diagnostic report or from parents and teachers, might focus on language, behavioral, or higher-level academic skills, such as classroom listening skills, sustained attention to task, organization, time management, and note taking.

Once long-term goals have been identified, the next step is to create a series of short-term goals, a road map for reaching the long-term goal.

Writing the Problem Statement

To produce clearly sequenced short-term goals for each long-term goal, the writer needs to identify more specifically the student's skill level in relation to the long-term goal. This may have already been done in the psychoeducational evaluation, but additional diagnostic teaching or curriculum-based assessment is often necessary for this level of the process. Writing a problem statement is helpful for clarifying what the student can and cannot do within the identified skill area. Some problem statements that were written for the students in our reports were:

a. gives many details after reading three paragraphs of varying content in a grade 4 basal reader, but is unable to state the main idea;

b. knows addition and subtraction math facts and the multiplication tables through 5's, but has difficulty translating related word problems into computation;

c. stays on task when the whole class is quiet and working, but is distracted by any external activity and is unable to redirect himself to task independently.

Writing the Short-Term Goals

At this point, the writer decides what steps are necessary to take the student from where s/he is to the long-term goal. If the recommendations in the diagnostic report have been written as short-term goals, they may be used as guidelines.

For the long-term goal of improving reading comprehension, appropriate short-term goals might be that the student:

a. recognize the main idea, supporting details, and extraneous information within a paragraph;

b. recognize how the details support the main idea (when, where, what, why, etc.);

c. recognize the structural relationship among main ideas in a longer selection; and

d. recognize the overall message of a longer selection in a variety of content areas and literature.

For improving attention to task, the short-term goals might be that the student will:

a. be aware of, take responsibility for, and want to solve that problem;

b. participate in the creation of a behavioral intervention and help to choose reinforcers;

c. move from teacher monitoring of attention to self-monitoring; and

d. move from self-monitoring to appropriate attention without charted monitoring.

Writing the Behavioral Objective

The final step in this process is to translate the selected short-term goals into behavioral objectives. A behavioral objective states exactly what the student is expected to *do* to demonstrate mastery of this particular level of skill. A clear behavioral objective should include:

Behavior the student is expected to demonstrate (e.g., draw a three-level semantic map);

Materials to be used (e.g., history, literature, and math texts);

Grade or skill level (e.g., grade 5);

Number of trials (e.g., one subsection of a chapter in each book);

Criteria of accuracy indicating mastery (not necessarily a percentage);

Date by which the objective is to be met.

Some behavioral objectives might take 1 week to meet, others, 2 months. If it appears that it will require the entire semester to meet the objective, it may be too comprehensive and should be broken into two or more objectives.

Examples of behavioral objectives containing these elements are:

a. Given two teacher-selected paragraphs from each of his grade 6 history, literature, and science textbooks, Joe will paraphrase the main idea, omitting supporting details. Criterion: 5/6 main idea statements. (January 15)

b. Given three types of teacher-written word problems pertaining to measuring elapsed time, in random order (four within a.m., four within p.m., four crossing a.m./p.m.) and based on real-life situations, Maria will show the start time and finish times on a clock face, set the problems up on paper, and solve them with 100% accuracy. (February 1)

c. When observed in three 30-minute sessions of independent seatwork in the regular classroom, over the period of a week, Josh will spontaneously return to task 80% of the times that he goes off task, charting his return each time. The teacher will not provide reminders during the evaluation time. (March 30) (A teacher aide or parent aide can be trained to do this type of observation.)

The point of this specificity is to have a clear sense of where the teacher and student are going and how they will know when they get there. This information should be shared with the student so that s/he also sees where the road is leading and can recognize his/her progress along the way. The short-term goal is a major milepost. The behavioral objective is the criterion by which mastery is measured.

Getting There: Task Analysis

Once the writer has identified the short-term goals and has written clearly stated behavioral objectives, the next, most obvious, question is, "How do we get there?" This is done through task analysis. The teacher breaks down the selected short-term goal into specific steps or subskills that must be attained in order to reach the goal. If a student is able to participate in task analysis, s/he will be more invested in the goal and understand the process more clearly.

In task-analyzing the short-term goal of recognizing the main idea, supporting details, and extraneous information within a paragraph, the teacher might decide that the necessary subskills are as follows:

a. ability to identify the topic sentence in a paragraph;
b. ability to identify and differentiate between sentences or ideas that either support the topic sentence or are extraneous;
c. ability to paraphrase the topic sentence;
d. ability to paraphrase only the supporting details;
e. ability to state the main idea and supporting details of a paragraph in which there is no clear topic sentence.

The particular subskills chosen for each short-term goal will depend in large part on the particular cognitive strengths and weaknesses of the student, as well as the materials and teaching techniques the teacher plans to use. The subskills lead to the short-term goal, just as the short-term goals lead to the long-term goal. Behavioral objectives do not necessarily need to be written for each subskill; in lesson planning, however, many teachers do so. This helps them to recognize when it is time, or when it is too soon, to move a student to the next subskill.

Perspective

In writing the short-term goals, the writer should consider the most *functional* result. Mastery of the short-term goal should include generalization of the skill into the setting in which the student is ultimately expected to use it. This may mean the ability to recognize independently when to use the skill, as well as the ability to use it accurately, to use it within classroom materials, and to use it in the classroom and/or at home. The teacher and parent may work together to decide which of these, or what other criteria, might apply.

Technique

Knowing what teaching technique will be used may help in tailoring the task analysis. For example, the decision to use a patterned language approach to teach sight words will yield different steps to the short-term goal than the use of the Fernald method (Fernald, 1943). An alternative process would be to analyze the task first, consider the child's abilities, and then select the most appropriate technique for each step.

For the objective referred to above, pertaining to main idea and details, a teacher may choose among a variety of techniques. If the student has good language and auditory memory skills, but poor visualization and visual conceptualization ability, the teacher might choose to use highly organized and structured verbal explanations with continuous oral feedback from the student. For a student with a generalized language impairment who has good visual perception and visual conceptualization abilities, the teacher might use visual displays to explain the concept, such as semantic maps and other graphic organizers.

If it seems that it takes much longer than expected to meet the targeted objective, then perhaps the teaching technique or materials need to be altered, or the level of subskill being taught may be too advanced.

Teaching to Multiple Objectives

In any skill area, many short-term goals may be addressed simultaneously, within the same materials. It is helpful to delineate each objective, however, so that progress can be more easily and objectively monitored.

Sample Behavioral Objectives

The following are behavioral objectives, taken from a variety of sources, that are in need of clarification. They have been rewritten to include the appropriate elements.

1. *Original*: Given fractions and mixed numbers, Josephine will add and subtract with and without common denominators with 90% accuracy.

   Rewritten: Given 20 addition problems and 20 subtraction problems, in random order, using proper fractions and mixed numbers with and without common denominators, Josephine will compute each of the two operations with 90% accuracy. (March 21)

2. *Original*: By the end of February, Katherine will be able to show progress in the organization of her writing skills by semantic mapping, organizing, prewriting, proofreading, and editing her material.

   Rewritten: By February 28, given a choice of topics for an expository composition, Katherine will use semantic mapping to write a 2-page rough draft in the following sequence of steps:

   a. brainstorm ideas in writing,
   b. group the ideas and label each group,
   c. use groups of ideas to draw and label a three-level semantic map (with main idea as the first level),
   d. verbalize the relationships among the ideas on the map, and
   e. use the semantic map to write a rough draft.

   Note: The first two steps in this objective were taught previously. The current focus is on using semantic mapping to create a first draft. The skill of proofreading listed in the original objective requires its own objective in that it must be learned in a series of steps and with ample practice before the student can use it effectively in context.

3. *Original*: In nonstructured writing, Yuki will identify run-on sentences and fragments 80% of the time.

   Rewritten: In each of two papers that she has written, Yuki will identify and label 80% of the run-on sentences and fragments. (November 15)

4. *Original*: When relating an experience approximately 5 minutes in length, Michelle will use relevant detail.

   Rewritten: By May 1, in two tape recordings of oral narratives, each approximately 5 minutes in length, Michelle will provide the following information in 80% of the places in which it is or would have been appropriate: clear referent for each pronoun used and sufficient pieces of information.

5. *Original*: Steven will develop functional literacy in the areas of: signs and labels, following directions, forms and applications, reference material, reading newspapers, consumer education.

   Note: *Each* of the above areas requires at least one short-term goal to achieve mastery; consequently, each will require one or more behavioral objectives.

   Rewritten: Steven will identify, read, and state the meaning of the following street signs when shown a picture and when riding in the car: stop, railroad, yield, street narrows to one lane, slippery pavement, one way—do not enter, train crossing. (September 15)

The plan delineated here for writing long- and short-term goals and behavioral objectives should decrease instructional preparation time. During this process, the instructional plan is designed, specific objectives are set in place, and, often, materials and techniques are chosen. Thus the instructional process flows without the harrowing question, "What will I do tomorrow?"

PART III
DIAGNOSTIC REPORTS

DIAGNOSTIC REPORTS

Name	Age	Diagnosis
Opal Parks p. 184	9-11	Deficit in rote, decontextualized visual-auditory associational memory
Gabriel Frazier p. 187	11-0	Deficits in abstract logical reasoning, mental reorganization of symbols, and visual recall
Hee Chan Kim p. 192	11-3	Academic improvement in the areas of reading comprehension, written expression, and calculation; limited or no improvement in basic reading skills, basic writing skills, and math application
Flavio Tapia p. 196	12-2	Deficits in receptive and expressive language; weakness in processing and recall of visual symbols; weakness in functional vision; linguistic/cultural difference
Lisa Goldman p. 220	13-0	Borderline mentally handicapped; relative weakness in oral language; relative strength in lower-level visual processing
Ben Testa p. 226	13-11	Mild hearing impairment with severe academic delay; need for further evaluation
Jon Floyd p. 228	15-6	*Average* to *High Average* verbal skills; *Superior* to *Very Superior* visual skills; weak reading strategies
Billy Jackson p. 233	15-9	Deficits in auditory processing and oral language; weakness in recall of visual symbols; Attention Deficit Disorder
Tiffany Erickson p. 243	16-3	Deficits in auditory processing, auditory short-term memory, and receptive and expressive language

Name	Age	Diagnosis
Rima Harris p. 254	17-10	Deficits in abstract, logical reasoning, rapid processing of visual symbols, and memory for decontextualized information
Max Kresge p. 266	18-9	Inappropriate educational program, emotional problems
Jill Streffer p. 269	20-2	Deficits in delayed recall; poor learning strategies
Hector Alcoser p. 273	26-4	Weaknesses in efficient processing of visual symbols, auditory processing, memory, and vocabulary
Roger Carp p. 277	29	Deficits in auditory and visual memory and processing speed; residual academic delay
Ruth Tanner p. 281	33	Deficit in short-term memory; thought disorder
William Gillette p. 284	56	Deficits in attention, rapid processing of visual symbols, short-term memory, and word retrieval
Robert Steiger p. 287	86	Receptive and expressive aphasia

Introduction

In building a new skill or polishing a frequently used one, a model is often helpful. Rather than "starting from scratch," one may adopt what fits and adapt what does not. The purpose of this section is to provide a variety of sample diagnostic reports that illustrate how the Woodcock-Johnson Psycho-Educational Battery—Revised may be used in psychoeducational assessments.

The diagnostic reports represent real people evaluated by the authors, by their colleagues, and by graduate interns. For the sake of confidentiality, names and identifying information have been changed. The diagnostic reports were chosen to illustrate a wide variety of reasons for referral, client ages and backgrounds, educational and employment situations, and diagnoses. Although many different diagnoses are represented here—from superior cognitive abilities to language impairment with Attention Deficit Disorder and history of severe abuse and neglect—the types of cases are far from exhaustive.

Occasionally, it is appropriate to report a person's race or ethnicity in a diagnostic report, especially when cultural factors might affect the interpretation of the results. Many school districts indicate a student's race or ethnicity by an ethnic code placed with the identifying information. In the following reports, race or ethnic background has been reported only when this information might have some bearing on the interpretation of the test results.

Most of the diagnostic information for these reports was derived from WJ-R assessments, student work samples, and interviews with parents and/or teachers. In instances in which the evaluator thought that test results did not show an existing deficit with sufficient clarity, supplementary or extension testing was conducted using other assessment instruments. Where contributing factors outside the expertise of the evaluator were suspected, such as a language impairment, Attention Deficit Disorder, or clinical depression, a recommendation was made for further investigation by an appropriate professional. In some cases, this investigation was done as a part of the initial assessment process. Although this arrangement is often not possible in a school setting, it is preferable to have all pertinent information before writing the final report so that the data may be integrated. The finding of a learning, language, emotional, or medical problem that might not be clearly demonstrated on the WJ-R, but which negatively impacts school achievement, may alter the final diagnosis. Comprehensive diagnosis of conditions affecting a person's ability to function efficiently in the appropriate setting, such as the school or workplace, makes it possible to write more useful recommendations for enhancing performance.

For the convenience of the reader, descriptions of the cognitive factors, achievement clusters, individual tests, and scores most commonly used are included following this Introduction. Also included is a chart of the verbal labels associated with the Relative Mastery Indexes and with the 68% confidence band for standard scores and percentile ranks (Woodcock & Mather, 1989a, 1989b).

To facilitate locating types of cases in which the reader may have specific interest, each diagnosis has been placed at the top of the first page of each case study. *It is not recommended that a diagnosis be so placed in psychoeducational reports.*

Types of Evaluations

Evaluations may be requested for a variety of reasons, leading to different types of assessments and recommendations. Likewise, the setting in which the evaluation takes place, such as a school, hospital, private clinic, or vocational training center, may dictate the scope and type of testing done. For a child or adult without a previous diagnosis, a full psychoeducational battery may be administered with language, occupational therapy, medical, and psychological evaluations as indicated. Where continued eligibility for special education services is an issue, administration of selected cognitive and academic clusters of the WJ-R, supplemented by informal testing and work samples, might be sufficient. Where evaluation or documentation of progress in academic skills is needed, the evaluator might decide to administer only the WJ-R Tests of Achievement: Standard Battery.

Level of Information

The purpose and setting of an evaluation might also influence the levels of information sought through testing and interpretation, as well as the amount of detail included in the report. A lengthy report with detailed information does not necessarily signal the complexity of the case, although a person with many handicapping conditions and/or an atypical background may certainly warrant more extensive evaluation and a more complex report. In a private setting, more time may be allotted to each case and fuller information written into the report. In the school setting, practicality may dictate less time for testing, error analysis, and writing reports. An advantage of the school setting, however, is the ongoing opportunity for diagnostic teaching and observation.

The setting in which a person is evaluated, as well as the purpose for evaluation, might also influence the level of diagnosis or the manner in which it is worded. In a clinical or private setting, the principal evaluator may diagnose a specific learning disability or some other handicapping condition. In the school setting, the evaluator would be more likely to report that the child met certain criteria for a handicapping condition and make a referral to the multidisciplinary team for the diagnosis.

Types of Scores

Also depending on the purpose of the evaluation and specific information offered within the report, the evaluator might report different types of scores. For example, information concerning the most appropriate level of instructional materials to be used for a variety of tasks would be reported by Instructional Ranges, representing the range of easy to difficult tasks and materials for each skill area. An approximate instructional level is expressed by the Grade Equivalent score. In using the Instructional Range as a guideline, the teacher should exercise caution in matching child with materials. Although the Grade Equivalent score shows a person's developmental standing within the normative sample, it may not directly match the level of performance among peers in a specific educational environment. Considering the variability of schools and individual classes across the nation, a third-grade child could receive a Grade Equivalent score 1 year below his/her actual grade level but be at the same level of instruction as the average third-grader in his/her specific school. Moreover, different materials intended for a certain grade level may vary considerably from each other in the initial level of student skill and knowledge assumed.

The Relative Mastery Index (RMI) is a useful score for approximating a student's accuracy on a task on which his/her peers would score 90%. The RMI does not vary according to the percentile ranks and standard scores. For example, when comparing a second-grade child (GE: 2.9) and a college student (GE: 16.9), both of whom scored in the 5th percentile on the Word Attack test, the child's RMI would be much lower (RMI: 10/90) than the college student's (RMI: 68/90). The difference between the RMIs suggests that, in relation to their peers, the child is much more deficient than the adult in application of phonic and structural analysis skills.

If the evaluation is mainly for purposes of diagnosing a handicapping condition and determining eligibility for special education services, common practice is to use standard scores or percentile ranks, as these scores express a person's relative standing in a group of age- or grade-peers. Some of the diagnostic reports in this section include both standard scores and percentile ranks. Although both types of scores provide the same information, percentile ranks are easier for many people to interpret, whereas standard scores are necessary for intertest comparisons and eligibility decisions.

Some schools or institutions may require Stanine scores, Normal Curve Equivalents, or T-scores, all of which are available from the WJ-R, but are not used in these reports. A fuller description of types of scores is available in the test manuals (Woodcock & Mather, 1989a, 1989b).

Several of the reports in this section include a notation stating, "All test scores are attached to this report," although, in actuality, the reader will not find scores attached. It is common practice for evaluators to attach score pages as a supplement to the information given in the report if they have not included the test scores in the body of the report. For the purposes of this book, however, the Compuscore pages have been attached to only two reports. Students and evaluators who are new to the WJ-R may use these cases for practice in hand scoring and may check their scores against the Compuscore for accuracy.

Recommendations

Reports might also differ in scope and specificity of recommendations. In some reports, whether private or school-based, recommendations might be offered to cover all areas of deficit—cognitive, academic, and behavioral—and include suggestions for enrichment of strengths. Other reports might include recommendations only for areas of deficit seen as critical for immediate intervention. Some reports might suggest specific skills and content area knowledge for remediation, whereas others might include suggestions for specific techniques and materials.

Aptitude–Achievement Discrepancy

The reader may note that some of the children in the reports who were diagnosed as learning disabled do not show a significant aptitude-achievement discrepancy. The lack of an aptitude-achievement discrepancy does not necessarily indicate the absence of a learning disability. Frequently, this discrepancy will not be found, as aptitude is based on the child's performance on related cognitive abilities tests, and it is just this poor performance in some cognitive abilities, relative to others, that indicates the presence of a learning disability. In this case, it would be more appropriate to look for an intracognitive discrepancy. This issue is discussed more thoroughly in Mather and Healey (1990).

Sources of Information

The information in these diagnostic reports was based on many types of data gathered from a variety of sources. Information regarding the home environment; physical, emotional, social, and cognitive development; functioning in the educational setting; previous educational opportunities; results of previous evaluations; and the individual's description of the problem provide a basis for interpreting and judging the validity of the new test data. Additionally, full use of information from formal and informal tests includes consideration of scores, behavior during testing, and analysis of error patterns. In some cases, as with some school reports, this information is collected by different people and integrated at the multidisciplinary conference. Consequently, the diagnostician's report may only present and interpret test results.

Use of Information

Ultimately, the quality and validity of evaluation results for any specific individual depend on the skill of the evaluator in proper choice and administration of tests, in evaluating the validity of individual test scores in light of possible interfering factors (e.g., fatigue, inattention, reluctance to test), in interpreting and integrating test results, in analyzing error patterns, and in discerning the person's strategies and compensations.

Outline

An outline is often helpful in structuring reports, although the nature of each assessment will ultimately determine the information to be included. Figure III-1, adapted from Sattler (1988), may be used as a starting point.

It is hoped that these diagnostic reports will provide guidance to the reader in expanding his/her use of the WJ-R, in writing reports tailored to the purpose of the evaluation, and in using WJ-R results to generate recommendations for enrichment of strengths and remediation of learning and behavioral weaknesses.

GUIDE TO WRITING REPORTS

I. Identifying Information
   a. student's name and date of birth
   b. student's age and grade
   c. examination date(s)
   d. examiner's name
   e. school, parents' names, teacher's name (optional)

II. Reason for Referral
   a. person who referred the student
   b. reason for referral
   c. specific concerns of the referral source

III. Background Information
   a. relevant family history
   b. current family situation
   c. health/developmental history
   d. relevant educational history

IV. Previous Evaluations and Results
   a. relevant medical or psychological
   b. relevant cognitive or achievement
   c. recent vision and hearing

V. Tests Administered
   a. names of tests administered
   b. other assessments used

VI. Behavioral Observations
   a. reactions to assessment
   b. general response style (impulsive to reflective)
   c. activity level
   d. attentional level and consistency
   e. language style
   f. response to success or failure

VII. Cognitive Abilities and/or Achievement
   a. report scores in text or attach at end
   b. interpret and integrate data
   c. consider findings from a variety of sources
   d. separate paragraphs for each cognitive and academic area, such as reading, mathematics
   e. give specific examples to document clinical interpretation

VIII. Summary and Conclusions
   a. briefly summarize results
   b. state implication of results
   c. do not include new information
   d. include statement of diagnosis or refer to multidisciplinary team for consideration of next step

IX. Recommendations
   a. base on both strengths and weaknesses
   b. provide realistic and practical intervention objectives and strategies
   c. suggest any further evaluation needed
   d. involve student, parents, and teachers

Figure III-1.

WOODCOCK-JOHNSON PSYCHO-EDUCATIONAL BATTERY--REVISED
CLUSTER CONSTRUCTION

Adjoining tests, left to right or top to bottom, result in a cluster shown in BOLD type. Broad Cognitive Ability clusters include tests listed.

Cognitive Factors

| Long-Term Retrieval (Glr) |
| Short-Term Memory (Gsm) |
| Processing Speed (Gs) |
| Auditory Processing (Ga) |
| Visual Processing (Gv) |
| Comprehension-Knowledge (Gc) |
| Fluid Reasoning (Gf) |

Broad Cognitive Ability (Std) (Tests 1 - 7)

1	Memory for Names	Glr
2	Memory for Sentences	Gsm
3	Visual Matching	Gs
4	Incomplete Words	Ga
5	Visual Closure	Gv
6	Picture Vocabulary	Gc
7	Analysis-Synthesis	Gf

Broad Cognitive Ability (E Dev) (Tests 1,2,4,5,6)

Broad Cognitive Ability (Ext) (Tests 1 - 14)

8	Visual-Auditory Learning	Glr
9	Memory for Words	Gsm
10	Cross Out	Gs
11	Sound Blending	Ga
12	Picture Recognition	Gv
13	Oral Vocabulary	Gc
14	Concept Formation	Gf

Oral Language

2	Memory for Sentences	Gsm
6	Picture Vocabulary	Gc
13	Oral Vocabulary	Gc
20	Listening Comprehension	Gc
21	Verbal Analogies	Gf / Gc

Oral Language Aptitude

12	Picture Recognition	Gv
14	Concept Formation	Gf
17	Numbers Reversed	Gsm/Gf
18	Sound Patterns	Ga / Gf

Reading Aptitude

2	Memory for Sentences	Gsm
3	Visual Matching	Gs
11	Sound Blending	Ga
13	Oral Vocabulary	Gc

Basic Reading Skills
Reading Comprehension

22	Letter-Word Identification	Gc
23	Passage Comprehension	Gc
31	Word Attack	Ga
32	Reading Vocabulary	

Broad Reading

Mathematics Aptitude

3	Visual Matching	Gs
7	Analysis-Synthesis	Gf
13	Oral Vocabulary	Gc
14	Concept Formation	Gf

Basic Mathematics Skills
Mathematics Reasoning*

24	Calculation	Gq
25	Applied Problems	Gq
33	Quantitative Concepts	Gq
	- - -	

Broad Mathematics

Written Language Aptitude

3	Visual Matching	Gs
8	Visual-Auditory Learning	Glr
11	Sound Blending	Ga
13	Oral Vocabulary	Gc

Basic Writing Skills (P,S,U)*
Written Expression

26	Dictation	(H)*
27	Writing Samples	
34	Proofing	
35	Writing Fluency	Gs

Broad Written Language

Knowledge Aptitude

2	Memory for Sentences	Gsm
5	Visual Closure	Gv
11	Sound Blending	Ga
14	Concept Formation	Gf

Skills

22	Letter-Word Identification	
25	Applied Problems	Gq
26	Dictation	

Broad Knowledge

28	Science	Gc
29	Social Studies	Gc
30	Humanities	Gc

* A Handwriting score may be obtained from Test 27, Writing Samples.   ** Punctuation, Spelling, and Usage scores can be obtained from Tests 26 & 34, Dictation & Proofing.

*** Though not an actual "cluster", Test 25, Applied Problems, is used as the measure of *Mathematics Reasoning* and is used in the computation of discrepancy scores.

TESTS NOT INCLUDED IN ANY CLUSTER

| 15 | Delayed Recall - Memory for Names | Glr | 16 | Delayed Recall - Visual-Auditory Learning | Glr | 19 | Spatial Relations | Gf / Gv |

Prepared by David McPhail, Oklahoma City, OK

WOODCOCK-JOHNSON PSYCHO-EDUCATIONAL BATTERY - REVISED
TESTS OF COGNITIVE ABILITY

BROAD COGNITIVE ABILITY

Broad Cognitive Ability - Early Development : A broad-based measure of intellectual ability appropriate for preschool children or low-functioning individuals at any age. Consists of Tests 1, 2, 4, 5, 6.

Broad Cognitive Ability - Standard Scale : A broad-based measure of intellectual ability appropriate for students at kindergarten level or above. Consists of Tests 1 - 7, of the Standard Battery.

Broad Cognitive Ability - Extended Scale : A broad-based measure of intellectual ability appropriate for students at kindergarten level or above. This score is used if Tests 1 - 14 are administered.

COGNITIVE FACTOR CLUSTERS

Long-Term Retrieval (Glr): Effectiveness in storing and retrieving information by association over extended time periods (Tests 1, 8).

Short-Term Memory (Gsm): Apprehension and use of information within a short period of time (Tests 2, 9).

Processing Speed (Gs): Ability on clerical speed type tasks, particularly under pressure to maintain focused attention (Tests 3, 10).

Auditory Processing (Ga): Analysis and synthesis of auditory patterns and sounds (Tests 4, 11).

Visual Processing (Gv): Perceiving non-linguistic visual patterns, spatial configurations, and visual details (Tests 5, 12).

Comprehension-Knowledge (Gc): Breadth and depth of knowledge and its effective application, including language comprehension (Tests 6, 13).

Fluid Reasoning (Gf): Capability for abstract reasoning in novel situations (Tests 7, 14).

Quantitative Ability (Gq): Ability to comprehend quantitative concepts and relationships, skill in mentally manipulating numerical symbols (Tests 24, 25).

TESTS OF COGNITIVE ABILITY

1 Memory for Names (Glr): Ability to learn associations between unfamiliar auditory and visual stimuli (auditory-visual association).

2 Memory for Sentences (Gsm): Immediate recall of meaningful phrases and sentences presented auditorily.

3 Visual Matching (Gs): Ability to quickly locate and circle two identical numbers in a series.

4 Incomplete Words (Ga): Ability to identify words with missing phonemes (auditory closure).

5 Visual Closure (Gv): Ability to identify pictured objects that have missing parts, are altered by distortion, or have superimposed patterns.

6 Picture Vocabulary (Gc): Ability to name pictured objects.

7 Analysis-Synthesis (Gf): Ability to analyze an incomplete logic puzzle and determine the missing components.

8 Visual-Auditory Learning (Glr): Ability to associate new visual symbols with familiar words and translate the symbols into verbal sentences (visual-auditory association).

9 Memory for Words (Gsm): Ability to repeat lists of unrelated words in correct sequence.

10 Cross Out (Gs): Ability to quickly scan and compare visual information.

11 Sound Blending (Ga): Ability to synthesize auditorily presented syllables and/or phonemes into whole words.

12 Picture Recognition (Gv): Ability to recognize a subset of previously presented pictures within a field of distracting pictures.

13 Oral Vocabulary (Gc): Ability to state antonyms or synonyms for given words.

14 Concept Formation (Gf): Ability to identify rules for concepts when presented with instances and non-instances of the concept.

15 Delayed Recall--Memory for Names (Glr): Ability to recall previously learned auditory-visual associations after 1 to 8 days.

16 Delayed Recall--Visual-Auditory Learning (Glr): Ability to recall names for previously learned visual-auditory associations after 1 to 8 days.

17 Numbers Reversed (Gsm/Gf): Ability to repeat a series of digits in reverse order.

18 Sound Patterns (Ga/Gf): Ability to determine whether or not complex sound patterns differ in pitch, rhythm, or sound content.

19 Spatial Relations (Gf/Gv): Ability to visually determine which component parts are needed to make a given whole shape.

20 Listening Comprehension (Gc): Ability to listen to a short passage and supply a missing final word.

21 Verbal Analogies (Gf/Gc): Ability to complete analogies with words that indicate comprehension.

ORAL LANGUAGE

Oral Language : Broad-based verbal ability. Consists of Tests 2, 6, 13, 20, 21.

Oral Language Aptitude : Non-verbal abilities most related to Oral Language proficiency. Consists of Tests 12, 14, 17, 18.

APTITUDE CLUSTERS

Reading Aptitude : A measure of the student's predicted reading achievement based on a relevant set of cognitive skills. Consists of Tests 2, 3, 11, 13.

Mathematics Aptitude : A measure of the student's predicted mathematics achievement based on a relevant set of cognitive skills. Consists of Tests 3, 7, 13, 14.

Written Language Aptitude : A measure of the student's predicted written language achievement based on a relevant set of cognitive skills. Consists of Tests 3, 8, 11, 13.

Knowledge Aptitude : A measure of the student's predicted general knowledge based on a relevant set of cognitive skills. Consists of Tests 2, 5, 11, 14.

WOODCOCK-JOHNSON PSYCHO-EDUCATIONAL BATTERY - REVISED
TESTS OF ACHIEVEMENT

ACHIEVEMENT CLUSTERS

Broad Reading : A broad measure of reading ability based on letter and word identification and comprehension of brief passages (Tests 22, 23).

Basic Reading Skills : Use of phonic and structural analysis skills in the pronunciation of real words and phonically regular nonsense words (Tests 22, 31).

Reading Comprehension : Comprehension of reading vocabulary and short passages (Tests 23, 32).

Broad Mathematics : Mathematics computational skills and practical problem solving (Tests 24, 25).

Basic Mathematics Skills : Mathematics computational skills and knowledge of mathematical concepts and vocabulary (Tests 24, 33).

Mathematics Reasoning : Skill in analyzing and solving practical problems in mathematics (Test 25).

Broad Written Language : Written production of both single-word responses and sentences (Tests 26, 27).

Basic Writing Skills : Spelling, punctuation, capitalization, and word usage skills evaluated by written responses and proofreading (Tests 26, 34).

Written Expression : Written production of sentences, increasingly complex in form, given specific task demands (Tests 27, 35).

Broad Knowledge : A broad measure of information in various areas including biological and physical sciences, social studies, and humanities (Tests 28, 29, 30).

Skills : A measure of basic academic skills (Tests 22, 25, 26).

TESTS OF ACHIEVEMENT

22 *Letter-Word Identification* : Skill in identifying symbols, letters and words in isolation.

23 *Passage Comprehension* : Skill in identifying a contextually appropriate, missing key word in a short reading passage.

24 *Calculation (Gq)*: Skill in performing mathematical calculations.

25 *Applied Problems (Gq)*: Skill in analyzing and solving practical problems in mathematics.

26 *Dictation* : Skill in writing single-word responses involving spelling, punctuation, capitalization, and word usage.

27 *Writing Samples* : Skill in writing responses that are evaluated with respect to the quality of expression.

28 *Science (Gc)*: Knowledge in the various areas of biological and physical sciences.

29 *Social Studies (Gc)*: Knowledge of history, geography, government, economics, and other aspects of social studies.

30 *Humanities (Gc)*: Knowledge in various areas of art, music, and literature.

31 *Word Attack (Ga)*: Skill in applying phonic and structural analysis to the pronunciation of phonically regular nonsense words.

32 *Reading Vocabulary* : Skill in reading words and supplying appropriate synonyms or antonyms.

33 *Quantitative Concepts (Gq)*: Knowledge of mathematical concepts and vocabulary and analysis of mathematical relationships.

34 *Proofing* : Skill in identifying errors of spelling, punctuation, capitalization, and word usage in short typewritten passages.

35 *Writing Fluency (Gs)*: Skill in formulating and writing simple sentences quickly.

P *Punctuation/Capitalization* : Ability to produce correct forms and detect and correct errors in punctuation and capitalization.

S *Spelling* : Ability to produce correct forms and detect and correct errors in spelling.

U *Usage* : Ability to produce correct forms and detect and correct errors in word usage.

H *Handwriting* : Overall legibility of written production.

Sources: **Woodcock, R.W., & Mather, N.** (1989). WJ-R Tests of Cognitive Ability--Standard and Supplemental Batteries: Examiner's Manual. In R.W. Woodcock & M.B. Johnson, Woodcock-Johnson Psycho-Educational Battery--Revised. Allen, TX: DLM. **Woodcock, R.W., & Mather, N.** (1989). WJ-R Tests of Achievement--Standard and Supplemental Batteries: Examiner's Manual. In R.W. Woodcock & M.B. Johnson, Woodcock-Johnson Psycho-Educational Battery--Revised. Allen, TX: DLM. **Mather, N.** (1991). An instructional guide to the Woodcock-Johnson Psycho-Educational Battery--Revised. Brandon, VT: Clinical Psychology Publishing Company. **Woodcock, R.W.** (1990, Sept.). Theoretical foundations of the WJ-R measures of cognitive ability. Journal of Psychoeducational Assessment, 8, 231-258. Prepared by David McPhail, Oklahoma City, Oklahoma.

WOODCOCK-JOHNSON PSYCHO-EDUCATIONAL BATTERY - REVISED

SCORES AND INTERPRETIVE INFORMATION

LEVEL 1 - QUALITATIVE

Qualitative information is obtained through observation of behavior during test performance and error analysis of responses to test items. Qualitative information, though not a *score*, is the foundation for understanding and interpreting all scores obtained by the subject. Qualitative information can also be viewed as *qualifying* information. Often a description of how a subject obtained a particular score is at least as important as the information provided by the score itself. Qualitative information is the backbone of individualized assessment and should be an integral part of the reporting of test results.

LEVEL 2 - LEVEL OF DEVELOPMENT

Level 2 information is derived directly from the raw score. This information indicates the level of development and is usually transformed to metrics that compare raw scores to age-or grade-level groups.

W Scores

An intermediate score for test interpretation. The W scale provides a common scale of equal-interval measurement that represents both a person's ability and the task difficulty. The W scale for each test is centered on a value of 500, which has been set to approximate the average performance of beginning fifth-grade students. The W score for any cluster is the average W score for the tests included in the cluster.

The W score is also used to plot the Age/Grade Profile which illustrates Developmental Levels on the WJ-R COG and Instructional Ranges on the WJ-R ACH (see Level 3 - Degree of Mastery).

Age Equivalents

An age equivalent (AE) or age score, reflects the subject's performance in terms of the age level in the norming sample at which the median score is the same as the subject's score. If half the eight year, five month old subjects obtained a raw score of 20 or greater, and half the eight year, five month old subjects obtained a raw score of 20 or less, then the raw score of 20 is assigned the age equivalent of eight years, five months (8-5). All subjects, regardless of age, who obtain a raw score of 20 will have an 8-5 age equivalent assigned as their level of development.

Age equivalents are expressed in years and months with a dash (-) as the delimiter. The age scale starts at 2-0 on the early development tests, and 4-0 on the other tests, and extends to the age of peak median performance in the norming sample for each test.

Grade Equivalents

A grade equivalent (GE) or grade score, reflects the subject's performance in terms of the grade level in the norming sample at which the median score is the same as the subject's score. If half the subjects in the sixth month of the third grade obtained a raw score of 20 or greater, and half the subjects in the sixth month of the third grade obtained a raw score of 20 or less, then the raw score of 20 is assigned the grade equivalent of third grade, sixth month (3.6). All subjects, regardless of age, who obtain a raw score of 20 will have a 3.6 grade equivalent assigned as their level of development.

Grade equivalents are expressed in grade and month with a decimal point (.) as the delimiter. The grade scale ranges from K.0 (beginning kindergarten) to 16.9 (finishing college senior).

Extended Age and Grade Score Scales

For subjects whose performance is above or below the established grade or age scale limits, extensions are made possible through the use of superscript numbers. The superscript numbers represent the subject's percentile rank score when compared to the age or grade reference group shown. A grade equivalent of $K.0^{12}$ indicates that the student's score was equal to the 12th percentile of student's entering kindergarten. Similarly, an age score of 33^{87} indicates that the person scored at the 87th percentile for subjects at the peak median level of performance.

(continued)

For Compuscore users, the extended age and grade scores are not represented as superscript numbers, but rather are placed in brackets following the age or grade score. The extended grade score for the 12th percentile rank of student's entering kindergarten is presented as K.0[12].

LEVEL 3 - DEGREE OF MASTERY

Level 3 information indicates the quality of a subject's performance on criterion tasks of given difficulty when compared to an age or grade reference group.

Relative Mastery Index (RMI)

The Relative Mastery Index (RMI), predicts the level of mastery on tasks similar to the ones tested. It reflects the subject's expected percent of mastery for tasks that the comparison group (age or grade) would perform with 90% mastery.

The RMI is recorded with the subject's expected percent of mastery and the comparison group's 90% expected mastery separated by a slash (/). Using an age comparison group, if a subject, age 6-0, obtains an RMI of 50/90, it would indicate that on tasks that the average subject, age 6-0, performs with 90% mastery, this subject only performs with 50% mastery. Interpretation guidlelines, paralleling Informal Reading Inventory criteria, are as follows:

> Independent Level (easy)......96/90
> Instructional Level.................90/90
> Frustration Level (difficult)......75/90

Age/Grade Profiles

The Instructional Range in the WJ-R ACH and the Developmental Level in the WJ-R COG are special applications of the RMI. These bands extend from -10 W score units (easy) to +10 W score units (difficult). These bands display the range between an RMI of 96/90 (easy) to an RMI of 75/90 (difficult). The length of these bands directly reflects the rate of growth. Long bands are associated with a slow rate of growth, whereas short bands reflect rapid growth. In a period of development when growth is rapid, the Developmental Level or Instructional Range band will be quite short, repeating or stepping in a sense, many times. In a period of development when little growth occurs, the Developmental Level or Instructional Range band will be quite wide, stepping only a few times. Examples of the Instructional Range bands for Letter-Word Identification and Word Attack tests are presented below to illustrate this point. The short band for Letter-Word Identification test indicates that growth is rapid during this period of skill development, whereas the long band for Word Attack indicates that growth takes place slowly.

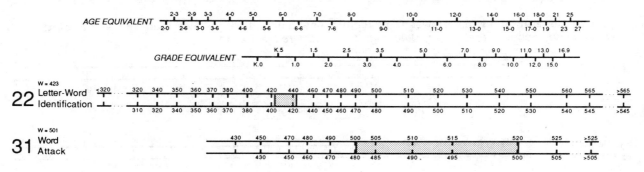

LEVEL 4 - COMPARISON WITH PEERS

Level 4 information indicates the deviation from a reference point when compared to age or grade peers.

Percentile Ranks (PR)

A percentile rank describes a subject's relative standing in a comparison group on a scale of 1 to 99. The subject's percentile rank indicates the percentage of subjects from the comparison group who had scores as low or lower than the subject's score. A subject's percentile rank of 68 indicates that 68% of the comparison group had scores as low or lower than the subject's score.

(continued)

Extended percentile ranks provide scores down to a percentile rank of one-tenth (0.1) and up to a percentile rank of ninety-nine and nine-tenths (99.9). A subject's percentile rank of 0.1 indicates that only 1 in 1000 subjects in a reference group would score as low or lower. A subject's percentile rank of 99.9 indicates that 999 in 1000 subjects in a reference group would score as low or lower.

Standard Scores (SS)

A standard score describes a subject's performance relative to the average performance of the comparison group. It is based on a mean or average score being assigned a value of 100, with a standard deviation, an indication of the variance of scores in the population, assigned a value of 15. The range of standard scores includes 0 to 200 with lower and higher scores expressed as <0 and >200, respectively. Recall that 0 is only a placeholder representing 6.67 standard deviations below the mean. <0 means the obtained score is more than 6.67 standard deviations below the mean, not zero or less than zero ability.

Standard Error of Measurement

The standard error of measurement (SEM) is an estimate of the amount of error attached to an individual's test score, or how much to expect a person's score to vary if he or she were tested on the same test again and again. The WJ-R provides the unique SEM associated with each possible score, rather than average SEMs based on entire samples.

Standard Score/Percentile Rank Profiles

Standard Score/Percentile Rank Profiles are plotted as bands using the Standard Score -1 SEM and the Standard Score +1 SEM. These bands represent the range of scores that contain the subject's true score at a 68% confidence level. To evaluate differences between performances on any two tests or any two clusters, the following guidelines may be used:

1) If the confidence bands overlap, assume that *no significant difference exists*.

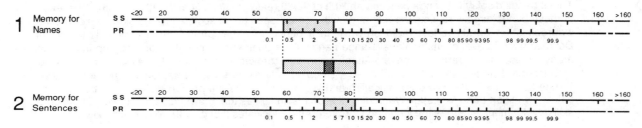

2) If a separation exists between the confidence bands that is less than the width of the wider band, assume that *a possible significant difference exists*.

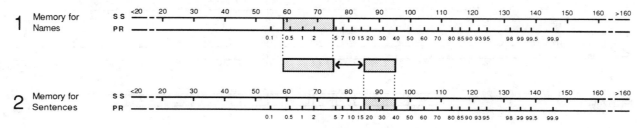

3) If a separation exists between the confidence bands that is greater than the width of the wider band, assume that *a significant difference exists*.

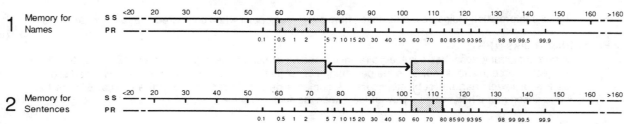

(continued)

These *differences* are only statements of statistical probability. Whether or not the differences in test scores are due to chance provides little information regarding the practical or educational significance of performance differences. The practical implications are more clearly apparent on the Age/Grade Profiles.

Discrepancy Terminology

Actual SS

The subject's obtained standard score on a cognitive or achievement cluster.

Aptitude or "Other" SS

This score is the starting value for deriving the predicted or expected score in computing discrepancies.

For Type 1 discrepancies, Aptitude/Achievement, this score is the standard score obtained for the appropriate Scholastic Aptitude cluster or the Broad Cognitive Ability cluster.

For Type 2 discrepancies, Intra-Cognitive, this score is the average standard score of the other six cognitive factor clusters.

For Type 3 discrepancies, Intra-Achievement, this score is the average standard score of the other three Broad Achievement clusters.

Predicted SS

The predicted standard score (also called the expected standard score) is based on the actual scores of peers with the same Aptitude, or Other, SS.

SS Diff

The Actual SS minus the Predicted SS.

Discrepancy Percentile Rank (PR)

For Type 1, Aptitude/Achievement discrepancies, this score represents the percent of the population that has achievement as low, or lower, compared to predicted achievement based on relevant tests of cognitive ability.

For Type 2, Intra-Cognitive discrepancies, this score represents the percent of the population that has cognitive factor ability as low, or lower, compared to predicted cognitive factor ability.

For Type 3, Intra-Achievement discrepancies, this score represents the percent of the population that has achievement as low, or lower, compared to predicted achievement based on other achievement tests.

SD Diff

The difference between the subject's actual and predicted standard scores in units of the standard error of estimate, the appropriate standard deviation statistic for this application.

Sources: Woodcock, R.W., & Mather, N. (1989). WJ-R Tests of Cognitive Ability -- Standard and Supplemental Batteries: Examiner's Manual. In R.W. Woodcock & M.B. Johnson, Woodcock-Johnson Psycho-Educational Battery--Revised. Allen, TX: DLM.

Mather, N. (1991). An instructional guide to the Woodcock-Johnson Psycho-Educational Battery--Revised. Brandon, VT: Clinical Psychology Publishing Company.

Prepared by Nancy Mather (University of Arizona) and David McPhail (Oklahoma State Department of Education).

Classification of Relative Mastery Index (RMI) Ranges

Relative Mastery Index (RMI)	Cluster Difference Score	Level of Mastery
99/90 to 100/90	+21 and above	Very Advanced
97/90 to 99/90	+11 to +20	Advanced
75/90 to 96/90	-10 to +10	Average
50/90 to 74/90	-20 to -11	Limited
0/90 to 49/90	-21 and below	Very Limited

Note: Adapted from WJ-R Tests of Cognitive Ability: Examiner's Manual (p. 69) by R.W. Woodcock & N. Mather, 1989, Allen, TX: DLM. Copyright 1989 by DLM. Reprinted by permission.

RMI Interpretation Guidelines
Independent Level (Easy)...................96/90
Instructional Level..............................90/90
Frustration Level (Difficult)..................75/90

Classification of Standard Score and Percentile Rank Ranges

Standard Score Range	Percentile Rank Range	WJ-R Classification	Alternate Labels
131 and above	98 to 99.9	Very Superior	Very High, Upper Extreme
121 to 130	92 to 97	Superior	High, Well Above Average
111 to 120	76 to 91	High Average	Above Average, Bright Normal
90 to 110	25 to 75	Average	Normal
80 to 89	9 to 24	Low Average	Below Average, Dull Normal
70 to 79	3 to 8	Low	Borderline, Slow Learner, Poor, Well Below Average
69 and below	0.1 to 2	Very Low	Mentally Deficient, Deficient, Mentally Retarded, Very Poor, Lower Extreme
55 to 69	0.1 to 2	----	Mild Mental Retardation
40 to 54	0.1	----	Moderate Mental Retardation
25 to 39	0.1	----	Severe Mental Retardation
24 and below	0.1	----	Profound Mental Retardation

Note: From WJ-R Tests of Cognitive Ability: Examiner's Manual (p. 72) by R.W. Woodcock & N. Mather, 1989, Allen, TX: DLM. Copyright 1989 by DLM. Reprinted by permission. Prepared by David McPhail, Oklahoma State Department of Education.

Diagnosis: Delay in visual-motor integration

PSYCHOEDUCATIONAL EVALUATION

Student: Rubin Gonzales   Evaluator:

Birthdate: 8/27/87   Parents: Martha and Leon Gonzales

Chronological Age: 4-7   School: Desert Oasis Preschool

Grade: Preschool   Date of Evaluation: 3/14, 3/16/92

Reason for Referral

Rubin was referred for an evaluation by his preschool teacher who was concerned about his slow development of eye-hand coordination and his increasing frustration with drawing and cutting tasks. Mrs. Stevens requested ideas regarding specific classroom interventions to help Rubin develop these skills.

Background Information

Rubin's mother has a Master's degree in Education and is an educational consultant. His father completed a 2-year technical college program and is a woodworker. They are both naturalized United States citizens from Mexico. Rubin and his 11-year-old brother, Miguel, were born in this country. Mr. and Mrs. Gonzales speak both Spanish and standard English at home. They noted that although the boys are comfortable in either language, they attend monolingual English schools and prefer to speak English. Previous language testing indicated that Rubin has a slight preference for English. Mr. and Mrs. Gonzales stated that they place a high value on education and read to Rubin and Miguel nightly. Mrs. Gonzales noted that they have been careful to support but not push Rubin in his interest in academic skills. Rubin started to sound out simple words 2 months ago, can phonetically spell one-syllable words, can read the first of a series of linguistic readers, and enjoys listening to books written for older children. He can count to 40. Rubin has never shown much interest in drawing or coloring, but recently has attempted to cut pictures out of magazines and wants to write the words he can spell orally. He used to ask for help, but more recently he becomes angry and throws the scissors or marker down or rips his paper with them.

Tests Administered

Woodcock-Johnson Psycho-Educational Battery — Revised (WJ-R): Early Development Scale: Cognitive and Achievement (Form A)
Developmental Test of Visual-Motor Integration — Revised (VMI-R)

Behavioral Observations

Testing was accomplished in one 1-hour session and one ½-hour session. Rubin was cooperative throughout testing and did not need a break in either session. He appeared comfortable, stayed on task, and, when necessary, thought before responding. He tried almost every item presented, saying, "I don't know" only on the more difficult ones.

Test Results

The tests of the WJ-R were scored according to age norms. Test results are expressed as Relative Mastery Index (RMI) scores and their verbal labels, comparing him to his age-peers on tasks similar to the ones administered. A complete set of test scores is appended to this report.

Cognitive Abilities

Rubin's standard score on the Broad Cognitive Ability-Early Development Scale, a broad-based measure of intellectual abilities, borders the *Superior* and *Very Superior* ranges. According to test results, Rubin is *Advanced* in his ability to learn and recall picture-word associations. On these types of tasks, Rubin would have approximately 99% accuracy compared to his age-peers' 90% accuracy (RMI: 99/90). Rubin also appears *Advanced* in visual processing of pictorial information (RMI: 97/90), *Advanced* in ability to recall verbal information immediately (RMI: 98/90), and *Very Advanced* in his expressive vocabulary (RMI: 99/90).

In sharp contrast to his other abilities, Rubin's performance in visual-motor skills was *Low/Low Average* in comparison to his age-peers and significantly below his other cognitive abilities. On the VMI-R, a measure of the ability to copy shapes, Rubin scored lower than 87% to 96% of his age-peers (exact percentile not given for age 4-7). His score was similar to that of a child age 3-6. His drawings suggested difficulty with intersecting lines and orientation, but not with direction. Rubin noted that his drawings were different from the models and, after attempting to draw a square, looked at the examiner and said somewhat dispiritedly, "That's how I make it."

Academic Achievement

Rubin's performance on the WJ-R Achievement Battery, with the exception of the Dictation test, was consistent with his cognitive abilities. His performance in the Basic Reading Skills cluster was *Very Advanced* (RMI: 100/90) compared to his age-peers. He sounded out most consonant-vowel-consonant words, displaying proficiency in phonics and sound blending. The Age/Grade Profile indicates that, in reading, early grade 1 instructional materials would be appropriate for Rubin.

Rubin's performance on the Applied Problems test indicated that he is *Advanced* in arithmetic concepts and applications (RMI: 99/90) and that he would benefit from instructional materials for late kindergarten. During the test, using illustrations, Rubin correctly answered subtraction problems such as "If you had 4 apples and you gave 3 away, how many would you have?" He covered up the number of objects to be taken away and counted those left. He was not able to answer similarly presented addition problems. After the test sessions, however, using some pretzels on the table in front of him, Rubin easily answered the same type of addition questions he had just missed. Thus, his RMI might be an underestimation of his math achievement.

Rubin's knowledge of science, social studies, and humanities appears to be *Very Advanced* in comparison to his age-peers (Broad Knowledge cluster, RMI: 100/90). His guesses on missed items indicated some knowledge of the concepts, such as "tool worker" for "mechanic" and "amphibian" for "reptile." The Age/Grade Profile indicates that he could benefit from second-grade instructional materials.

In contrast, consistent with his performance on the VMI-R, Rubin was *Very Limited* in writing skills as measured by the Dictation test (RMI: 0/90). His pencil grip was poor, impeding control. He was unable to stay within the given lines with his pencil. When writing letters, he wrote them in the top margin of the page instead of on the response lines, and, although his intent was clear, he could not form clearly recognizable letters.

Summary and Conclusions

Rubin's general cognitive abilities border the *Superior/Very Superior* ranges with relative strengths in vocabulary and visual/auditory association and retrieval. With the exception of writing, his academic skills are *Very Advanced*. His fine-motor skills are *Very Limited*, impeding the development of writing and art-related skills and causing Rubin frustration.

Recommendations

1. Teach Rubin the proper way to hold a pencil, crayon, or marker. Use a triangular rubber grip or modeling clay around pencils to help him develop a more efficient grip.

2. Provide Rubin with many opportunities for use of his fine-motor skills in activities consistent with his current ability level. Such activities may include simple paper folding; tracing large, simple shapes with bold borders and coloring them; cutting paper across a bold line; and copying large, simple shapes on the chalkboard. A variety of interesting and fun mediums should be used, such as fingerpaints, watercolors, pudding (to lick off his finger after making a shape), and sparkles-on-glue designs. Many activities should also be provided in which the goal is not recognizable figures, but simply free-form designs.

3. Gradually decrease the size of the shapes to be copied or traced as Rubin's success increases and the tasks become easier for him to accomplish. Do not increase the task difficulty until he has mastered the current task.

4. Keep fine-motor activity periods short and intersperse them with activities that are fun, interesting, or active, such as listening to a story, dancing, and playing on the playground.

5. Since Rubin is highly motivated to write words that he is able to read, explain to him how spending time coloring, painting, drawing, and cutting will make it easier for him to learn to write the alphabet.

6. Provide encouragement and praise for increase in skill rather than for quality of product.

7. Emphasize activities and skills in which Rubin excels. Encourage Mr. and Mrs. Gonzales to

participate with him in interesting activities that will stimulate his cognitive development further and increase his general knowledge.

8. Consider an enriched kindergarten program to support Rubin's advanced cognitive and academic skills.

Diagnosis: Developmental delay

PSYCHOEDUCATIONAL EVALUATION

Name: Annie Flowers

Birthdate: 2/10/87

Chronological Age: 4-7

Grade: Preschool

Evaluator:

Parent: Margaret Flowers

Agency: Dept. of Economic Security

Date of Evaluation: 9/6/91

Reason for Referral

Annie was referred for a psychoeducational evaluation by her social worker at the Department of Economic Security. She reported that Annie's preschool teacher felt she was immature and slow in developing pre-academic skills.

Background Information

Margaret Flowers is a single parent who works full-time at night and attends school in the daytime to complete her GED. She reported that all of her children attend day care and that she has very little time to spend with them. Mrs. Flowers is no longer in contact with the children's father.

Annie is a Caucasian child, the sixth of eight siblings. Mrs. Flowers stated that during her pregnancy with Annie she developed gestational diabetes. Annie was delivered by Caesarian section and subsequently had respiratory distress. Mrs. Flowers recalled that Annie attained all of her developmental milestones on the late side of normal and described her as a quiet and complacent child.

Results of vision and hearing tests arranged by DES were normal.

Tests Administered

Woodcock-Johnson Psycho-Educational Battery—Revised (WJ-R): Early Development Scale: Cognitive and Achievement (Form A)

Peabody Picture Vocabulary Test—Revised (PPVT-R)

Informal tasks

Behavioral Observations

Annie is a small child with a hesitant smile. She was cooperative and pleasant throughout the 1½-hour testing session. In general, her attention to tasks diminished as items increased in difficulty. She occasionally initiated conversation during a test by asking a personal question of the examiner, but was easily redirected to the task.

Test Results

The tests of the WJ-R were scored according to age norms. Standard scores are reported as 68% confidence bands. A 68% confidence band is expressed as ±1 standard error of measurement (SS ±1 SEM).

Cognitive Abilities

	SS ±1 SEM	Classi-fication	Age Equiv-alents	RMI
Memory for Names	76-86	L/LA	3-2 to 3-9	73/90
Memory for Sentences	68-78	L	2-11 to 3-4	32/90
Incomplete Words	79-89	LA	2-8 to 3-2	42/90
Visual Closure	78-90	LA	3-3 to 3-8	71/90
Picture Vocabulary	78-92	LA	3-2 to 3-9	63/90
BROAD COGNITIVE ABILITY (EDev)	71-79	L	3-1 to 3-5	58/90
Peabody Picture Vocabulary Test—Revised	76-90		3-7	

Annie's present level of general cognitive development, as measured by the WJ-R standard scores, falls within the *Low* range. She scored in the *Low Average* range in tasks that require memory for visual-verbal associations, auditory and visual closure, and vocabulary. She scored in the *Low* range on a task of auditory memory. Interpretation of the RMIs indicates that when compared to age-peers on similar tasks, Annie's abilities are *Limited* in visual-auditory associations, visual closure, and vocabulary and *Very Limited* in auditory closure and memory. Her performance on the PPVT-R, a test of oral vocabulary comprehension, was consistent with the vocabulary results of the WJ-R. Occasionally, Annie seemed to have some familiarity with a concept being presented or a word requested, but lacked the specific label. For example, she identified a fan as a "cooler," and a wagon as a "dragon."

Academic Achievement

	SS ± 1 SEM	Classi-fication	Age Equiv-alents	RMI
Letter-Word Identification	91-99	A	3-8 to 4-5	79/90
Dictation	73-83	L	3-0 to 3-8	2/90
Applied Problems	82-92	LA	3-4 to 3-10	50/90
Science	84-96	LA/A	3-6 to 4-2	73/90
Social Studies	79-93	LA	3-2 to 4-1	55/90
Humanities	81-93	LA	3-4 to 3-11	66/90
SKILLS	78-84	LA	3-6 to 3-8	32/90
BROAD KNOWLEDGE	81-89	LA	3-6 to 3-11	63/90

Annie's standard score on Letter-Word Identification was in the *Average* range. Her RMI of 79/90 indicates that she is in the lower end of the *Average* range when compared to her age-peers on matching rebuses with pictures and naming uppercase letters. She named A, B, G, and O. On these types of tasks, she would have approximately 79% accuracy as compared to 90% accuracy of her average age-peers.

In contrast, Annie scored in the *Low* range on Dictation. Her RMI of 2/90 indicates that her mastery of form and letter writing is *Very Limited* compared to her average age-peers. The only recognizable letters Annie could write were those in her name. She wrote her name as *enA* and could name none of the letters except *A*. Informally, Annie was asked to copy some geometric forms. She was successful with the circle and the right-slanting oblique line; she had difficulty on the square and the cross, however, in getting her lines to intersect. Annie is right-handed. Although her pencil grip was correct, she seemed to have difficulty planning her strokes correctly.

Annie scored in the *Low Average* range on Applied Problems. Her RMI of 50/90 indicated that her mastery of number concepts is *Limited*. She demonstrated knowledge of one-to-one correspondence in choosing sets of objects to match numbers up to seven. On informal tasks, she was only able to count to 11; she could count objects only up to 8.

Annie's standard score on the Broad Knowledge cluster places her in the *Low Average* range. Based on her RMI of 63/90, Annie's level of general knowledge is *Limited* compared to her average age-peers. She was able to point to all common body parts as they were named, with the exception of

"chest" and "ankle." She identified all primary and several secondary colors correctly.

Summary and Implications

Formal and informal test results indicate that Annie is delayed in the development of cognitive and pre-academic skills. She scored in the *Low Average* range in most cognitive abilities, with a relative weakness in auditory memory. Her pre-academic skills are commensurate with her cognitive abilities, most of which are also in the *Low Average* range, with a relative weakness in fine-motor skills. Annie will require a concerted effort between her mother and the preschool staff to be developmentally ready for kindergarten in 1 year.

Recommendations

General

1. Secure agreement from Annie's current preschool teacher to focus on Annie's development of pre-academic skills. Ask that she write behavioral objectives based on the following recommendations and cooperate with monitoring of Annie's progress by the social worker.

2. If these accommodations are not possible within the structure of Annie's current school, enroll her in a structured preschool program designed to promote pre-academic development.

3. Expose Annie to as wide a variety of experiences as possible with an adult who can explain what is happening, name objects and actions, and answer questions.

4. At school or at home, if possible, encourage Annie to watch "Sesame Street."

Language Development

1. Provide consultation from a speech/language pathologist to Mrs. Flowers and Annie's preschool teacher for specific ways to enhance language development.

2. Play games that focus on the sounds of words. These include rhyming games and songs, thinking of words that start with a particular sound, and counting the "beats" (syllables) of words.

3. Play games that focus on the meaning of words. These include thinking of words that go together,

making collages of pictures that go together and discussing them, and thinking of opposites.

4. Explain words that may not be familiar to Annie as they come up in stories and provide practice using them.

5. Arrange some activities around certain themes that the children are familiar with, such as medical offices, plants, transportation, and various ethnic groups within the class. Teach and reinforce vocabulary for each of the themes.

6. Increase Annie's exposure to literature. Read to Annie and discuss the story with her. Try to build in a basic concept of story grammar.

7. Teach/reinforce positional (e.g., first/last) and directional (e.g., right/left) concepts.

Number Concepts

1. Teach number concepts in the following progression:

   a. Teach the concept of sets (classification) using familiar physical objects that may be sorted in a variety of ways (e.g., size, color, shape, use). Later, introduce manipulatives such as pictures on flannel boards, Attribute Logic Blocks, Cuisenaire Rods, and Snap Cubes.

   b. Use pictures to represent physical objects in sets.

   c. Name sets by the major identifying attribute (e.g., big).

   d. Teach one-to-one correspondence. The child learns to match each element of a set with a counting number to determine the cardinal number of the set (i.e., answers the question, "How many?"). At this point, teach quantitative vocabulary and concepts (e.g., more, less, same). Move from using physical objects to match sets (concrete level), to using pictures (semiconcrete), to using tallies (semiabstract), to identifying cardinal numbers (abstract).

   e. Teach that a cardinal number may be expressed by a numeral.

   f. Teach that a number can be compared with any other number (e.g., bigger than, the same as).

2. Do not expect Annie to write numerals. Provide her with numeral tiles or cards and plastic numbers to use for matching activities. Provide ample exposure to the image of the numbers for later writing.

3. For specific activities, the teacher is referred to *Today's Mathematics: Seventh Edition* (Heddens, 1991).

Reading

1. Provide ample exposure to uppercase letters using games and puzzles. Later, use games and puzzles to match upper- and lowercase letters.

2. Use a simple electronic speller so that Annie can key in a letter and hear the letter name or choose a key, guess the name, and check herself.

3. Teach Annie the alphabet song.

4. When Annie is thoroughly familiar with many of the consonants and vowels, explain to her how the letters are put together to make up words in the reading book and how the words go together to make the story. Reinforce the concept that letters and words are the building blocks of written language.

5. Teach Annie that letters are like animals in that they have both names and sounds. For example, the teacher might show Annie a picture of a lion and say, "His name is lion, but his sound is /roar/." When she understands this concept, teach about letter names and sounds.

Visual-Motor Skills

1. Give Annie lots of practice using utensils in activities that will give her the opportunity to plan and execute a movement using the small muscles of her hand. If necessary, directly teach Annie how to visualize where her pencil, marker, scissors, etc., should be at the end of each stroke or cut.

2. Use activities such as tracing, using templates, and coloring within simple, bold-line drawings before moving on to copying forms and drawing pictures.

3. Provide ample positive reinforcement for effort rather than just for quality of her product.

Diagnosis: Deficits in visual processing and recall, visual-auditory association, and visual-motor integration; questions concerning oral language development and vision

PSYCHOEDUCATIONAL EVALUATION

Name: Angelica Venelli

Birthdate: 2/4/86

Chronological Age: 5-11

Grade: K.4

Evaluator:

Parents: Henry & Cecelia Venelli

School: Cross Elementary

Test Date: 1/18/92

Reason for Referral

Angelica's teacher reports that she appears to be unable to follow directions, retain letter names, and learn number concepts. The teacher requested an evaluation to determine if Angelica qualifies for special education services and for recommendations of how she might teach Angelica more effectively in the classroom.

Background Information and Previous Test Results

This is Angelica's first year at Cross Elementary. Her teacher reports that she is attentive and polite and plays well with the other children. She participates voluntarily in morning circle, but sometimes her comments and questions are tangential to the topic the group is discussing. See the social worker's report for the developmental history.

Tests Administered

Woodcock-Johnson Psycho-Educational Battery— Revised (WJ-R):
    Tests of Cognitive Ability: 1–2, 4–6, 8–9, 12
    Tests of Achievement (Form A): 22, 25–26, 28–30
Developmental Test of Visual-Motor Integration— Revised (VMI-R)
Brigance Diagnostic Comprehensive Inventory of Basic Skills
Brief language sample

Behavioral Observations

Angelica was attentive and cooperative throughout the testing session. She appeared to have difficulty understanding directions for a variety of tasks. During the Visual-Auditory Learning test, she placed her chin on her hand and said, "This is so confusing." Asked about her difficulty learning letters, she stated, "Sometimes they look a little like blobs."

Test Results

The tests of the WJ-R were scored according to age norms. When no difference was found between the two component tests of a factor or cluster, only the factor or cluster score is discussed. Test results are reported as verbal labels for the standard score 68% confidence bands. A complete set of test scores is appended to this report.

Cognitive Abilities

Based on Angelica's Broad Cognitive Ability— Early Development Scale score, her overall cognitive ability is in the *Low Average* range. Discrepancies among the cognitive factors and between individual tests indicated specific cognitive strengths and weaknesses. Angelica demonstrated relative strengths (*Average*) in auditory memory for unrelated words; in auditory processing of sounds, syllables, and words; and in vocabulary.

A discrepancy between scores on the two tests of the Short-Term Memory factor suggests that her ability to remember unrelated words (*Average*) is significantly better than her ability to remember sentences (*Low/Low Average*). When attempting to repeat sentences, she seemed to recall the content, but her syntax was often incorrect. For a brief language sample, Angelica was asked to tell a story about a picture. She used simple sentence constructions almost exclusively. Her few attempts at complex structures resulted in fragmented clauses that were syntactically unrelated to the next sentence.

A significant discrepancy existed also on the WJ-R Visual Processing factor. In pictorial stimuli, her visual closure ability (*Low Average/Average*) was significantly better than her ability to scan an array of pictures and note critical details for later recall (*Low*). Her performance on the Long-Term Retrieval factor (*Very Low*) indicated a significant deficit in retention of associations between visual and verbal stimuli (e.g., pictures and symbols corresponding to names and words).

On the VMI-R, a measure of visual-motor skills, Angelica scored in the *Low* range, significantly below other children her age. She was unable to reproduce a cross, a diagonal line, or a square. Her attempts suggest particular difficulty with intersection of lines and with judging length, which, in turn, suggest a severe delay in visual-motor integration.

Academic Achievement

The Early Development scale of the WJ-R Achievement Battery was administered to determine Angelica's current academic achievement in relation to her age-peers. Her performance on the tests of the Skills cluster reflected serious delays in the skills prerequisite to reading (*Low*), written language (*Very Low*), and math (*Low/Low Average*).

Selected subtests of the Brigance were also administered. In the area of general readiness and prereading skills, Angelica was able to sort objects by color and shape and visually discriminate between like and different shapes and uppercase letters. She recalled all primary and secondary color names and the labels for the circle and triangle. Presented with more shapes, however, she also identified the square as a triangle and could name no others. She recited the alphabet to J and then became confused. She could name only six upper- and four lowercase letters and often confused letter and number names.

Angelica's knowledge of phonics was limited to matching initial consonant sounds and associated pictures for B (ball) and Z (zebra). She could not give any sounds for letters in isolation or identify any sight words.

Angelica printed her first name in uppercase letters, but could write only A and O in isolation.

In math, Angelica counted by rote from 1 to 15, but could only name the numerals 1, 2, and 3 when presented with the printed form. She displayed understanding of one-to-one correspondence for the numbers 1, 2, and 3 only.

Angelica scored in the *Low Average* range in general knowledge. Her fund of information related to the humanities was significantly above her knowledge of science-related information.

Summary

Angelica's current test results suggest strengths in rote auditory memory, auditory processing, and vocabulary. In contrast, Angelica demonstrates significant deficits in processing and recalling visual information, visual-motor integration, and retention of visual-verbal associations. She also appears to have a weakness in processing and using complex syntax which may contribute to her difficulty in auditory memory for connected language and in following instructions. She exhibits serious deficits in all pre-academic skills.

Recommendations

Prior to the multidisciplinary conference, Angelica's hearing should be evaluated and her receptive and expressive language development assessed by the speech/language pathologist.

The possibility of a weakness in visual acuity and/or functional vision (e.g., eye teaming, focusing, tracking) should be discussed with Angelica's parents with a recommendation for an examination.

These findings will be integrated with the findings of the speech/language pathologist, psychologist, and social worker at the multidisciplinary conference. The parents will be requested to provide the results of the vision evaluation. Recommendations for educational placement and remediation will be made at that time.

Diagnosis: Deficit in auditory processing; delay in visual-motor integration; question concerning Attention Deficit Disorder

PSYCHOEDUCATIONAL EVALUATION

Student: Jamie Leone	Evaluator:
Birthdate: 4/2/85	Parents: Jonathan & Joanne Leone
Chronological Age: 6-2	Test Dates: 5/18, 5/19/91
Grade: K.9	

Reason for Referral

Jamie was referred for evaluation by her parents due to the teacher's recommendation that she repeat kindergarten next year. The Leones wanted information concerning the adequacy of her skill development compared to her peers, reasons for her possible delay, and recommendations to help prepare her for first grade.

Background Information

Developmental History

Mr. and Mrs. Leone are both high school graduates. Mr. Leone drives a lumber truck and Mrs. Leone provides child care in her home so that she can be home with her children. Previously, she was a bank teller. Mr. Leone reported no learning problems in school. Mrs. Leone recalled that throughout school, she was unable to concentrate adequately in the classroom and rarely turned in homework assignments. She remembered making a concerted effort to pay attention to what the teacher was saying, but feeling as if "the words just went by, rather than into" her head.

Mrs. Leone reported normal developmental milestones for Jamie. Although Jamie is quite active when she is outside, her activity level is appropriate in the house. Generally, throughout her preschool years, Jamie has been able to sit and play by herself in age-appropriate activities such as putting puzzles together and playing with dolls, but she also has periods when she moves from activity to activity, changing her mind as to what she wants to do shortly after starting. She needs constant redirection to complete any tasks around the house, such as getting ready for bed or cleaning up. She does not enjoy coloring and usually scribbles outside the lines.

The Leones stated that Jamie is quite impulsive and has gotten herself into some dangerous situations. Some incidences this past year included getting stuck in a tree while trying to climb to the roof, drinking a bottle of medicine, and locking herself in the trunk of the car.

In the past month, Jamie has improved in her ability to delay gratification at home and at school no longer demonstrates any difficulty in this area. Jamie's parents describe her as having sudden mood swings, but when she is too excited and is instructed to calm down, she can do so by going to her room for a few minutes. Jamie gets along well with other children; she shares and can take turns.

Educational History

Two weeks into the school year, Jamie was transferred into developmental kindergarten due to "immature attentional skills." No behavioral interventions were attempted prior to the move.

Throughout this year, Mrs. Leone has spoken frequently with Mr. Harris, the present teacher, and stated that he had indicated consistently that Jamie was improving in classroom skills. In a recent conference, however, Mr. Harris noted that Jamie still fidgets, looks around, and daydreams while he is giving instructions. In contrast, he stated that she now usually stays with a task until completion, as compared with approximately 50% on-task behavior at the beginning of the year. She has a tendency to rush through coloring tasks and letter practice. Mr. Harris stated that Jamie does not like using crayon for writing and drawing, but he feels that the children in his class are not ready for pencils.

Previous Evaluations

Results of two hearing screenings over the course of this school year have been normal. Recently, Dr. Elba Ruiz, ophthalmologist, evaluated Jamie. She found that Jamie is moderately farsighted which causes her discomfort and requires extra effort for her to sustain focus at near-point. Dr. Ruiz prescribed glasses.

Behavioral Observations

Jamie was tested in one 2-hour and one 1½-hour session with breaks in which she was active and outside. She wore her glasses throughout testing. She was cooperative and appeared to try her best on each test. She volunteered that the testing was fun but that she didn't like school. On the first day, after approximately 20 minutes of testing, Jamie became increasingly active. For most of the tests on both days, she rocked in her chair so that the legs left the floor. When she wasn't rocking, she was moving her legs and arms. Jamie's activity level was appropriate only during informal writing tasks and diagnostic teaching. Given her level of activity, it is highly unlikely that Jamie could have focused optimally on the tests.

Jamie's behavior on some tests demonstrated lack of familiarity with the tasks, such as using antonyms and synonyms and tracking along a row of symbols rather than across rows. On other tests, Jamie did not scan the stimuli carefully enough to give well-thought-out responses.

Tests Administered

Woodcock-Johnson Psycho-Educational Battery— Revised (WJ-R):
    Cognitive Battery: Tests 1-14, 20
    Achievement Battery (Form A): Tests 22-30
Developmental Test of Visual-Motor Integration— Revised (VMI-R)
Brigance Diagnostic Comprehensive Inventory of Basic Skills: Readiness, Word Analysis, Listening
Diagnostic teaching

Test Results

The tests of the WJ-R were scored according to age norms. When no difference was found between the two component tests of a factor or cluster, only the factor or cluster score is discussed. The Relative Mastery Index (RMI) predicts the student's level of mastery on tasks similar to the ones tested. This mastery level is written as a comparison to the 90% mastery expected for average age- or grade-peers. Because of the built-in comparison on related tasks, the RMI was chosen as the most appropriate score to present in the report. Comparisons are presented using the labels *Very Advanced*, *Advanced*, *Average*, *Limited*, and *Very Limited*. A complete set of test scores and descriptions of the WJ-R tests is appended to this report.

Cognitive Abilities

Based on the results of the Woodcock-Johnson Psycho-Educational Battery—Revised (WJ-R) Broad Cognitive Ability—Extended Scale (BCA), Jamie's overall cognitive abilities fell in the *Average* range (SS: 100, PR: 50) when compared to her age-peers.

Based on the RMIs, in comparison to her age-peers, Jamie's accuracy would be in the *Average* range on tasks requiring rapid processing of small visual symbols/forms, and processing of nonsymbolic visual information, such as pictures. Jamie's performance on the informal tasks of the Brigance reinforced the findings of *Average* visual abilities, including visual recall for symbols.

Jamie would also be expected to be on par with her age-peers in association and retention of visual-verbal information, understanding short discourse, vocabulary knowledge, and abstract reasoning. Jamie's behaviors on the vocabulary tests suggested age-appropriate vocabulary, but lack of familiarity with the concepts of antonyms and synonyms.

Jamie's Short-Term Memory RMI indicates that her ability to recall immediately what she hears is *Advanced*. Based on these findings, Jamie should have no difficulty recalling oral instructions in the classroom. Jamie's strength on this factor represented the only significant strength among cognitive abilities. Of Jamie's age-peers with the same predicted standard score, only 4 out of 100 (PR: 96) would obtain a score as high or higher.

Auditory processing appeared to be a weakness for Jamie (RMI: 43/90). Compared to her age-peers on tasks such as blending sounds and syllables to come up with a whole word, her predicted mastery would be *Very Limited*. The Age/Grade Profile indicated that age-appropriate instructional materials for skill development in auditory blending and closure may be difficult for Jamie. Jamie's instructional level in these skills is beginning kindergarten. Jamie had no difficulty with discrimination between sounds on the Brigance.

On the VMI-R, Jamie scored lower than 89% of her age peers (PR: 11). She used an awkward pencil grip which allowed the pencil to slip and limited wrist mobility. She used the edges of the boxes on the VMI-R as borders for her forms rather than trying to copy the size of the target forms. Jamie noticed the difference between her forms and the target forms but did not attempt to fix them.

Jamie's teacher stated that Jamie's class did not begin to practice drawing shapes and writing letter strokes until the last few weeks of the school year. The children write only with crayons on unlined paper.

Academic Achievement

Basic Concepts

Based on the Brigance, Jamie demonstrated good comprehension of almost all grade-appropriate quantitative, directional, and positional concepts (e.g., least/most, forward/backward, middle/end). She was unsure of right and left on herself.

Reading

Jamie sang the alphabet. When shown printed letters, she named about half of the uppercase and less of the lowercase letters. She was unable to identify initial consonants in spoken words.

According to her RMI of 55/90, Jamie's sight vocabulary is in the *Limited* range in comparison to her age-peers. During a 15-minute diagnostic teaching session, Jamie learned the sounds of *b*, *d*, *s*, and *a*. She was not able to learn to blend these sounds; however, when shown and told a three-letter word, she was able to substitute initial consonants without instruction and "read" the new words. She also had difficulty completing short poems with rhyming words.

Written Language

Jamie's RMI of 84/90 on the Dictation test was in the *Average* range. She was able to write recognizable capital letters, although they were poorly formed. Her performance on informal tasks, however, indicated a further delay in writing skills. She could write only five letters of the alphabet and did not know how to use kindergarten paper with guidelines. Nevertheless, she immediately caught on to a story explaining the height of different letters within the lines. She then wrote her name and copied four words correctly and neatly. Her response to diagnostic teaching suggests that her low performance on visual-motor skills may be at least partially due to lack of instruction and practice in using grade-appropriate paper and pencils in school.

Jamie is left-handed. Although her pencil grip is awkward, she resisted using a plastic pencil grip. Jamie did not steady her paper with her right hand.

When asked to do so, she replied, "We don't do that."

Math

Jamie's RMI of 81/90 on the Applied Problems test placed her in the *Average* range. When problems were presented with pictures, Jamie was able to do simple addition and subtraction but made careless errors. Compared to other children her age, Jamie demonstrated more of a delay on informal tasks. She counted by rote only to 20, counted objects up to 12, read numbers to 10, and showed quantities of objects to match number symbols to 10.

General Knowledge

Jamie's RMI of 93/90 in Broad Knowledge indicated that her fund of information in the areas of science, social studies, and humanities was in the *Average* range.

Summary

Due to Jamie's activity level during testing and intermittently impulsive responses, the following results should be accepted with the caution that they may underestimate her true cognitive abilities and academic achievement.

Test results indicated that Jamie's overall cognitive abilities fall in the *Average* range. When compared to her age-peers on tasks requiring specific cognitive skills, her accuracy would be *Average* in processing visual information, sound discrimination, visual-verbal association and retention, oral language, and reasoning. She demonstrated a significant strength in auditory short-term memory and a significant weakness in auditory processing. She demonstrated a significant delay in visual-motor skills, which may be at least partially due to inadequate practice with age-appropriate writing tasks and tools.

Jamie appears to need instruction at the mid-kindergarten level in reading, writing, and math. She appears to be *Limited* in sight vocabulary. In diagnostic teaching, however, Jamie demonstrated immediate grasp of the writing skills presented, indicating good potential for learning these skills. She also had success with reading word families. On informal tasks, Jamie demonstrated mild delays in number concepts.

Although intermittent attention may be a partial contributing factor to her academic delays, it is also possible that the developmental kindergarten did not meet Jamie's particular needs. The two areas of weakness, auditory processing and visual-motor integration, should not be considered learning disabilities until appropriate interventions have been attempted and Jamie's progress has been evaluated.

Recommendations

For the Parents

1. Ensure that Jamie wears her glasses for all near-point tasks.

2. Provide Jamie with tutoring throughout the summer in the skill areas described below.

3. Provide activities throughout the summer that will help Jamie improve her visual-motor skills, such as drawing, painting, and practicing her letter strokes. Obtain worksheets from the teacher that will allow the parent or tutor to work ahead with Jamie on writing letters.

4. Play more games with Jamie that focus on the sounds of words. Examples include having her complete familiar nursery rhymes with the appropriate rhyming words, singing silly songs, and reading to her from predictable books emphasizing rhyming words, such as those by Dr. Seuss. You may also show Jamie an array of pictures and help her to match those with rhyming names.

5. Have a conference with Jamie's teacher at the beginning of the school year. Share the contents of this report.

   a. Ask the teacher to observe Jamie's attention span during a variety of activity types (e.g., listening to instructions, independent seatwork, small group activities, writing, matching) and note any patterns of behavior. Make arrangements to contact the teacher by phone at the end of each week for the first month.

   b. Request that the teacher correct Jamie and bring her back to task when necessary in a gentle, nonhumiliating manner. A soft touch on the shoulder or making eye contact with a smile are examples. Communicate that it is crucial for Jamie to feel self-confident and successful from the start of the year to overcome her negative feelings about school.

6. If, next year, Jamie has considerable difficulty staying on task, carefully working through mildly challenging work, and sitting reasonably still, as compared to the average student, consult a developmental pediatrician about the possibility of Attention Deficit Disorder.

For the Tutor

1. Obtain a list of academic and behavioral skills expected of the average child entering first grade. Use these to create the teaching objectives for the summer.

2. Increase Jamie's attention span in challenging tasks by providing rewards for gradually increasing the amount of time she works in a reflective manner. Give frequent positive reinforcement.

3. Use graphs and charts and keep samples of previous work so that Jamie can monitor her own progress in all areas of tutoring.

4. Teach and emphasize development of abilities in analyzing and synthesizing the sounds and syllables of words. Research findings indicate that children who enter grade 1 with a solid base in taking apart and blending the sounds and syllables of words learn to read more easily than children who do not.

   Play games that focus on the sounds of words. These include rhyming games and songs, thinking of words that start with a particular sound, and counting the number of words in sentences or syllables in words.

   Provide Jamie with direct instruction in sound blending using the following steps: (a) have Jamie say the word, (b) present the word with prolonged sounds but no break between the sounds and ask Jamie to say the word, (c) present the sounds with a short break between them and ask Jamie to say the word, (d) present the word with a quarter-second, then half-second, then 1-second break between the sounds, with Jamie saying the word after each presentation (Kirk, Kirk, & Minskoff, 1985).

   Train Jamie in auditory closure, first using familiar words with sounds omitted and later using printed words with letters or syllables omitted.

5. Provide practice in using the concepts of antonyms and synonyms.

6. Integrate reading and writing skills so that Jamie learns many of the basic reading skills through writing.

7. Teach Jamie to read the names of and discriminate between upper- and lowercase letters.

8. Teach the sounds of the letters using consistent visual clues, a few letters at a time. Match the letters taught to specific instructional materials.

9. As soon as Jamie has learned several sounds, incorporate practice in blending, pronunciation of common word families, and sound substitution.

10. Use Language Experience, Dolch Popper Words (flash cards), and games such as the Dolch Group Word Teaching game to teach sight words. The Dolch materials are available from DLM, 1 DLM Park, Allen, TX 75002, 800-527-4747.

11. Teach D'Nealian letter formation, the method that is used in her school.

12. Teach Jamie to write on primary paper with a dotted middle line.

13. Teach Jamie to learn the proper heights of the letters by the following story: "All letters start out living on the ground. Some, the short letters, stay there. Other letters stick their heads up into the sky, and still others hang their bottoms into the ocean. If letters who don't belong in the sky stick their heads up there, they might blow away. If letters who don't belong in the ocean hang their bottoms in the ocean, they might drown."

14. Teach Jamie to count to 100 using visuals that make obvious the repeating pattern of numbers. Use color coding.

15. Teach Jamie to match quantities of objects to written numbers up to 25 or above.

16. Teach Jamie to write the numbers up to 100.

17. Teach Jamie the concept of sets and subjects within a number.

18. Teach all math skills and concepts using familiar objects and manipulatives.

19. Provide reinforcement activities for Mrs. Leone to do with Jamie between tutoring sessions to advance her rate of learning and help to ensure that she is ready for first grade next year.

20. Use as many games and interesting, colorful materials as possible to sustain Jamie's attention and make learning fun. Use active learning techniques.

Diagnosis: Deficits in oral language; questions regarding efficiency of functional vision

PSYCHOEDUCATIONAL EVALUATION

Name: Peter Martin
Birthdate: 3/28/84

Chronological Age: 7-4
Grade Placement: 1.9

Evaluator:
Parents: Mildred Temple
George Martin
School: Hooper Elementary
Test Dates: 7/27, 7/29/91

Reason for Referral

Peter was referred for a psychoeducational evaluation by his mother based upon concern regarding low academic performance and a somewhat negative attitude toward school. She wanted to know what factors were affecting Peter's learning and wished to determine an appropriate educational placement for the following school year.

Background Information

Peter's mother described him as "a very sweet boy." He is responsible about completing routine chores without being reminded, but appears to have difficulty understanding a series of instructions for unfamiliar tasks. Ms. Temple stated that she has learned to go over new tasks in simple terms, making sure that Peter understands each step. He can then complete the task without supervision and do a thorough job relative to his age. She noted that Peter enjoys listening to stories only if the book has many pictures and comparatively little text. Ms. Temple also noted that she often has to explain jokes and riddles to him. Peter plays well with his friends in the neighborhood and is generally well-behaved.

The classroom teacher described Peter's performance as below grade level in reading, but average in math. She noted that Peter had difficulty in staying on task and working independently during academic tasks. He tended to talk to other students rather than work and appeared unable to follow or profit from group instruction. His performance, however, improved in small group or one-to-one instruction. He had no problem with attention during tasks involving manipulatives and art.

Previous and Concurrent Evaluations

On 10/8/90 Peter was evaluated at Hooper Elementary School to determine eligibility for special services. On the Wechsler Intelligence Scale for Children — Revised, Peter obtained a Verbal score of 90, a Performance score of 100, and a Full Scale score of 93. He did not show evidence of visual-motor integration problems on the Bender Visual-Motor Gestalt Test. No significant strengths or weaknesses were noted in his profile.

Based upon results of both formal and informal testing, Peter's academic functioning levels were reported as preprimer in reading and mid-first-grade level in math. Peter obtained a percentile score of 14 or a reading age of 6-1 on the Test of Early Reading. At this time, the multidisciplinary team determined that he did not qualify for special services because the test results did not indicate a significant discrepancy between aptitude and achievement.

More recently, an evaluation (6/19/91) was conducted at the University Speech-Language Clinic based upon his mother's concerns regarding delayed speech and language skills. Ms. Temple reported that Peter does not enunciate clearly and sometimes loses track of what he is saying. She also stated that Peter has a history of chronic ear infections.

Pure tone audiometric screening indicated that Peter's hearing sensitivity was adequate, bilaterally, for speech reception. Results from a variety of formal and informal tests to assess communication skills indicated mild difficulties with language comprehension and mild to moderate difficulties with expressive language skills. Peter demonstrated mild difficulties in comprehending linguistic relationships and oral instructions. Expressively, Peter evidenced mild difficulties in grammar and sentence formulation and moderate difficulties in linguistic flexibility, the ability to rephrase and paraphrase statements. Syntactic and pragmatic language skills were described as mildly to moderately impaired. Observations did not support an auditory processing disorder. The speech/language pathologist noted that whenever a language task became too difficult for Peter, his attention flagged or he tried to initiate conversation irrelevant to the task. A recommendation was made for individual articulation and language therapy, two times weekly for 45-minute sessions. Recommendations were also made for classroom compensations for Peter's language deficiencies and ways that the parents and teacher could reinforce the skills presented in language therapy.

Tests Administered

Peter was administered the Woodcock-Johnson Tests of Cognitive Ability—Revised (Tests 1-16, 20, 21), the Woodcock-Johnson Tests of Achievement—Revised, Form A, Standard Battery, and an informal reading inventory. Testing was conducted in two 1½-hour sessions.

Behavioral Observations

Although Peter was cooperative throughout the majority of the testing, he sometimes complained that a test was "getting too hard." At times, his behavior could be described as "pleasantly oppositional." For example, smiling at the examiner, he initially refused to write sentences. As tasks increased in difficulty, his attention diminished. He displayed impulsivity in his test-taking style and he would frequently have to be redirected to the task at hand. He appeared impatient with tasks that required a specified exposure time to a stimulus. For example, when a set of pictures that he was supposed to remember was exposed for 5 seconds, he would glance quickly at the page and then say, "Let's go." Similarly, on listening tasks, he attempted to respond immediately after the first presentation, rather than waiting to hear the stimulus again as directed.

Assessment Results

The tests of the WJ-R were scored according to grade norms. When no difference was found between the two component tests of a factor or cluster, only the factor or cluster score is discussed. Standard scores are reported as obtained scores or as 68% confidence bands. A 68% confidence band is expressed as ±1 standard error of measurement (SS ±1 SEM). A complete set of test scores is appended to this report.

Cognitive Abilities

Peter's Broad Cognitive Ability—Extended Scale score fell within the *Average* range when compared to grade-peers (SS ±1 SEM: 96–100). A significant strength was observed on the Short-Term Memory factor. On this factor, one test requires repetition of sentences, whereas the other requires repetition of strings of unrelated words. When Peter's standard score on Short-Term Memory (SS ±1 SEM: 116–124, *High Average/Superior*) is compared to the average of his scores on the other six cognitive factors, only 1 out of 100 students (PR: 99) with the same predicted score would obtain a score as high or higher.

A relative strength was noted on the Auditory Processing factor (SS ±1 SEM: 103–113, *Average*), which requires the student to pronounce whole words after hearing parts. Peter's Relative Mastery Index (RMI) of 95/90 suggests that he will have 95% success on tasks requiring sound blending and closure, compared with average grade-mates who would have 90% success. This finding suggests good prognosis for learning phonic skills for reading decoding and spelling.

A relative weakness was noted on the Processing Speed factor (SS ±1 SEM: 82–92, *Low Average*), which consists of two timed tests. One test requires locating and circling the two identical numbers in a row of six numbers, whereas the other test requires finding the five drawings that are identical to the first drawing in a row of 20 drawings. Peter skipped lines on both of these tests. When the Processing Speed factor is compared to his average performance on the other six cognitive factors, only 7 out of 100 students (PR: 7) would obtain a score as low or lower.

Peter's overall performance on the Oral Language cluster fell within the *Average* range (SS ±1 SEM: 94–100). Within this cluster, performance on the Memory for Sentences test (SS ±1 SEM: 110–120) was in the *High Average* range, on the Picture Vocabulary (SS ±1 SEM: 93–107) and Oral Vocabulary tests (SS ±1 SEM: 94–106) in the *Average* range, and on the Listening Comprehension (SS ±1 SEM: 76–88) and Verbal Analogies tests (SS ±1 SEM: 81–95) in the *Low Average* range.

All other cognitive abilities were in the *Average* range when compared to his grade-peers'.

Academic Achievement

Reading

Peter's instructional range on the Broad Reading cluster extended from mid-kindergarten (easy) to mid-first (frustration). His RMI of 15/90 on Broad Reading suggests that he will have 15% success on grade-level reading tasks, whereas average grade-mates will have 90% success. He was able to identify

19 letters of the alphabet. He did not use any strategies to help him identify unfamiliar words. He was unable to pronounce simple nonsense words with phonically regular patterns. When attempting to read several short sentences, he commented that they were too hard. On an informal reading inventory, he correctly identified two words from a 20-word list at the primer level and was at the frustration level on a primer passage.

When asked to follow the movement of a pencil eraser with his eyes, difficulties in ocular pursuit were noted. At first he moved his head, instead of moving his eyes. When asked to hold his head still, he was able to follow the target until he reached the midline. Then his eyes jerked upward and he lost the target.

Similar difficulties were noted on tasks involving rapid visual tracking or scanning. On several occasions, he skipped over complete lines of symbols, or would put down his hand or finger to aid in tracking. Peter also had difficulty in tasks involving copying. When asked to copy a sentence, he would lose his place each time his eyes moved from one paper to another.

Written Language

Peter's instructional range on the Broad Written Language cluster extended from beginning first grade (easy) to late first grade (difficult). His RMI of 55/90 indicated that on tasks of letter and word writing, Peter would demonstrate 55% mastery as compared to his average classmate's 90%. Peter was able to write several letters of the alphabet and his name. Peter appears, however, to have difficulty recalling letter orientation. He successfully spelled the word *cat* but the letter *c* was reversed. He reversed both the lowercase and uppercase form of the letter *e*. Additionally, his attempted spellings illustrated limited knowledge of sound–symbol correspondence. For example, he spelled the word "old" as *ooi* and the word "house" as *hais*.

Mathematics

Peter's instructional range on the Broad Mathematics cluster extended from mid-first (easy) to beginning third grade (difficult). His RMI of 95/90 suggests that he will have 95% success on math tasks, whereas average grade-mates will have 90% success. When his Broad Mathematics cluster standard score (SS ± 1 SEM: 109) is compared to his average on the other three achievement areas, only 1 out of 100 students (99%) with the same predicted score would obtain a score as high or higher. He worked slowly, but accurately. He was able to add and subtract one-digit numbers, although he reversed the numeral 6. Peter used excellent strategies to solve problems involving mathematical reasoning. He worked his answers out with pencil and paper, using small circles to perform calculations. After he produced the correct answer, he then insisted on erasing his drawings. His attention improved during the mathematics tests.

Knowledge

Peter's instructional range on the Broad Knowledge cluster extended from mid-kindergarten (easy) to mid-second-grade level (difficult). His RMI of 85/90 suggests that he will have *Average* mastery on tasks requiring content area knowledge.

Aptitude–Achievement Discrepancies

Peter presently has significant discrepancies between his predicted and actual performances in reading and written language. When his Broad Reading cluster standard score of 74 is compared to his predicted reading score of 104, only 2 out of 1,000 students (PR: 0.2) with the same predicted score would obtain a score as low or lower. When the Broad Written Language cluster standard score of 77 is compared to his predicted written language score of 97, only 2 out of 100 students (PR: 2) with the same predicted score would obtain a score as low or lower.

Summary

Peter is a 7-year-old boy who has profited very little from his educational experiences in reading and writing, but is at grade level in mathematics. Several factors appear to have contributed to his lack of academic success. His poor ocular control, apparent weakness in symbol orientation, and slow visual processing have affected his mastery of complex perceptual tasks, such as reading decoding and writing. Additionally, mild impairments in a combination of language skills coupled with a short attention span for linguistic information have further reduced his ability to understand and learn from classroom experiences. Other cognitive abilities, such as short-term auditory memory, auditory processing, retention of visual-auditory associations, vocabulary, and reasoning are strengths that may be capitalized upon for reading and written language remediation.

It is essential that an intensive program of scholastic remediation and intervention for his visual and language problems begin soon to reduce Peter's frustration regarding his lack of learning, to increase his self-esteem, and to resolve attitudinal concerns regarding school.

Recommendations

Educational Programming

Peter presently needs a structured, systematic reading method to help him acquire both reading and writing skills. This program should begin as soon as possible. His parents should consider the following three options:

1. Place Peter in a private school that specializes in teaching children with language and learning disabilities and provides a systematic, structured approach to reading and writing instruction. One recommendation is the Stevens School. The Slingerland method used at this school will capitalize on Peter's strengths (auditory memory and sound blending) and help him compensate for visual weaknesses. The tracing component of the method may also help Peter improve ocular control. The goal would be to return Peter to public school after 2 years.

2. Keep Peter in his present setting, but hire a learning disability specialist with a strong background in remedial methodology in academics and language. Provide one-to-one tutoring for Peter after school at least three times a week for an hour.

3. Have the school review Peter's eligibility for learning disability services because at the present time a significant discrepancy between aptitude and achievement as well as processing deficits (language, processing speed) exist. If Peter is eligible, ensure that he receives intensive remedial help in reading, written language, and oral language.

For the classroom, enlist the school principal's aid in choosing a teacher for Peter. Select a patient teacher who is willing to work with an outside consultant and who is flexible enough to provide Peter with a variety of academic compensations.

Classroom Compensations

1. To improve Peter's language functioning and compensate for his language deficiencies in the classroom, follow the recommendations included in the speech/language pathologist's report.

2. When giving instructions, make eye contact with Peter. Stop by his desk when the class begins working to make sure that he has understood the instructions. Alternatively, seat him next to a "buddy" who may reexplain instructions to Peter when asked.

3. Peter's comprehension, and thus his attention, improve in small group activities and during one-to-one instruction. To maximize comprehension and attention in the classroom, when possible, use cooperative learning groups or peer tutoring.

4. Reduce the amount of reading and writing that Peter is required to do during independent seatwork assignments so that he is more likely to complete his work. Provide verbal reinforcement for completed work. As he becomes more competent in language and visual skills, gradually increase the length of the assignments.

Visual Efficiency

1. Have Peter's vision assessed by a functional optometrist who has expertise in evaluating eye health, acuity, visual tracking, visual accommodation and flexibility, and convergence.

2. When the students are doing seatwork, periodically pass Peter's desk to make sure that he has not inadvertently skipped items. If he has, point out the missed problems.

3. Limit copying activities until skill improves. When Peter has to copy material from the chalkboard, allow him to move to the front of the room.

4. Teach Peter to use verbal mediation when he copies material from the chalkboard or from a book to paper. Have him say each letter, word, or phrase as he copies it from the board to his paper.

Diagnosis: Deficit in short-term memory

PSYCHOEDUCATIONAL EVALUATION

Name: Mark Arnold
Birthdate: 2/6/82

Chronological Age: 8-3

Grade Placement: 1.5

Evaluator:
Parents: Ed and Elba Arnold

School: Fountain Hill

Test Dates: 5/20, 5/21/91

Reason for Referral

Mark was referred by his first-grade teacher, Mr. Lander, who stated that Mark's reading achievement was considerably below his achievement in other academic areas, particularly math and social studies. He noted that Mark's main difficulty was in retaining words and that he did not seem to remember to use the strategies that the class continually practices. Mr. Lander was concerned that Mark was becoming extremely frustrated with reading and was losing motivation to read.

Background Information

Mark attended a full-day kindergarten. His kindergarten teacher observed that Mark was having difficulty learning the alphabet and recommended that he enter a developmental first-grade class. Mark attended developmental first grade and then entered first grade the following year. In first grade, Mark was placed in the Reading Support Program. Although he has been in the program for the entire school year, the support teacher reported that he has made limited progress. All classes in this school use a whole language approach to reading instruction. Results from vision and hearing screenings conducted by the school nurse were normal.

Tests Administered

Mark was administered the Woodcock-Johnson Tests of Cognitive Ability—Revised (Tests 1-14) and the Woodcock-Johnson Tests of Achievement—Revised, Standard Battery. An informal reading inventory was also administered. Testing was conducted in two 1½-hour sessions.

Behavioral Observations

Mark was cooperative and attentive during testing, but became easily discouraged when he did not know an answer. When he was unsure of a response, he would sigh and shake his head. Mark seemed to lack confidence even when he answered questions correctly.

Test Results

The tests of the WJ-R were scored according to age norms. When no difference was found between the two component tests of a factor or cluster, only the factor or cluster score is discussed. Standard scores are reported as obtained scores or as 68% confidence bands. A 68% confidence band is expressed as ±1 standard error of measurement (SEM). A complete set of test scores is appended to this report.

Cognitive Abilities

	SS	SS ±1 SEM	Classi-fication	RMI
BROAD COGNITIVE ABILITY	98	96-100	*Average*	89/90
LONG-TERM RETRIEVAL	98	94-102	*Average*	88/90
SHORT-TERM MEMORY	85	80-90	*Low Aver.*	55/90
PROCESSING SPEED	97	92-102	*Average*	88/90
AUDITORY PROCESSING	97	92-102	*Average*	87/90
VISUAL PROCESSING	104	97-111	*Average*	92/90
COMPREHENSION-KNOWLEDGE	111	107-115	*Average*	95/90
FLUID REASONING	110	107-113	*Average*	96/90

Mark's Broad Cognitive Ability—Extended Scale score fell in the *Average* range. Based on observation of confidence bands, he demonstrated relative strengths in analytical reasoning and vocabulary use and a relative weakness in short-term auditory memory. On the Short-Term Memory factor, his performance was slightly lower on the Memory for Words test (SS ±1 SEM: 74 to 88), which requires repeating a string of unrelated words, than on the Memory for Sentences test (SS ±1 SEM: 87 to 99), which requires repeating sentences. When the Short-Term Memory factor is compared to his average performance on the other six cognitive factors, only 6 out of 100 students with the same predicted standard score (PR: 6) would obtain an actual standard score of 85 or lower.

Academic Achievement

	SS	SS ± 1 SEM	Classification	RMI
BROAD READING	80	77-83	*Low/ Low Aver.*	21/90
BROAD MATHEMATICS	86	82-90	*Low Aver.*	68/90
BROAD WRITTEN LANGUAGE	78	75-81	*Low*	32/90
BROAD KNOWLEDGE	100	96-104	*Average*	90/90

When scores and results of error analysis are considered compared with those of other children his age, Mark demonstrated deficits in reading and basic writing skills. Mark's Broad Reading cluster score was in the *Low/Low Average* range. His Relative Mastery Index (RMI) indicates that on tasks of sight word recognition and comprehension of short cloze passages, Mark is *Very Limited* compared to his age-peers.

On an informal reading inventory, Mark read only 55% of the primer word list accurately. The primer-level passage was at his instructional level for word recognition and at his frustration level for comprehension. Although Mark's word recognition skills improve when he uses context, his word attack skills are so low that he is unable to use context clues successfully. His reading was characterized by a slow rate, repetitions, and hesitations. He appeared to look at the first and last letter of a word and then make a guess. He had to sound out many consonant-vowel-consonant words, such as *bag*, letter by letter, indicating limited recognition of word families. Mark was obviously frustrated with his limited reading skill. Once while trying to identify a word, he slammed his hand down on his chair and said under his breath, "What is that stupid word?"

Mark scored in the *Low* range in Broad Written Language. His RMI indicates that his performance is *Very Limited* when compared to his age-peers. Mark's score on the Writing Samples test was reduced by spelling errors; several of his responses were indecipherable, although he was able to tell the examiner the words he had intended to write. Error analysis suggests that Mark is unfamiliar with sound–symbol correspondence for some consonants, consonant digraphs, and vowel combinations. His spelling contained letter transpositions and omissions suggesting a weakness in word analysis skills.

Although Mark scored in the *Low Average* range in Broad Mathematics, his performance on computation (*Very Low*) was significantly lower than his performance on applications (*High Average*). Error analysis and later informal extension testing indicated that Mark's computation errors were due to inattention to operation signs. He demonstrated knowledge of both arithmetic facts and operations, and solved orally presented problems involving time and money. Thus, math appears to be a strength for Mark.

Mark's performance in Broad Knowledge was in the *Average* range, suggesting that he is acquiring general knowledge from home and school.

Aptitude–Achievement Discrepancy

Mark has significant aptitude–achievement discrepancies in the areas of reading and written language. Out of 100 students with the same Broad Reading Aptitude score as Mark's, only 3 would obtain a standard score of 80 or lower (PR: 3). In Broad Written Language, only 1 out of 100 students with the same predicted standard score would obtain an actual standard score of 74 or lower (PR: 1).

Summary

Mark is a first-grade student who is experiencing considerable difficulty in developing basic reading and spelling skills, despite *Average* background knowledge and *Average* ability in all cognitive areas tested with the exception of auditory short-term memory. In addition, he has made minimal progress in developmental first grade, regular first grade, and remedial reading. He is presently frustrated with his limited reading skills. Test results and error analysis indicate that significant weaknesses in auditory memory for rote information contribute to his academic difficulties. Quite possibly, limited phonics instruction in Mark's school has contributed further to Mark's difficulties.

Recommendations

1. The multidisciplinary team should determine whether Mark qualifies for the learning disabilities program at Fountain Hill Elementary School.

2. Because he has not learned to read easily and has had difficulty acquiring a sight vocabulary, Mark will require direct instruction in sound–symbol correspondence. Use diagnostic teaching to determine whether a phonics method or a word family approach would be the most effective way for building basic reading skills. If he continues to have difficulty with retention of words, use a multisensory approach.

3. Reassure Mark that his reading difficulties are not the result of low abilities, but rather a mismatch between learner and reading method. Before beginning a new reading method, explain to him that you expect he will make rapid progress using this new method.

4. As soon as Mark has made sufficient progress, provide high-interest, low vocabulary books for reading practice.

5. To sustain Mark's interest in books and increase his general information, capitalize on his vocabulary and reasoning abilities. Read to Mark and discuss high-interest books with him.

6. Teach Mark how to analyze words auditorily to include all sounds in the correct sequence. Make a variety of games out of sounding out and distinguishing between real and nonsense words.

7. Integrate the teaching of spelling patterns with the reading method you use. Use writing for reinforcement of reading patterns as well as for spelling.

8. Teach Mark that red-flag words (irregular sound–symbol correspondence) must be memorized as they look rather than as they sound.

9. Set up a strategy to help Mark attend to operation signs in computation problems. Examples are having Mark color-code all signs before beginning a worksheet or giving points for each problem in which Mark has used the correct operation. Explain and demonstrate to Mark why it is important to use the correct operation.

Diagnosis: General cognitive abilities in the *Superior* range

PSYCHOEDUCATIONAL EVALUATION

Student: Jessica Amherst
Birthdate: 3/3/83

Chronological Age: 8-3

Grade: 2.9

Evaluator:
Parents: Lewis and Billie Amherst
School: Northport Elementary
Test Date: 5/19/91

Reason for Referral

Jessica was referred for a brief assessment of cognitive abilities to investigate the need for advanced educational placement.

Background Information

Jessica had chronic ear infections until age 18 months, when tubes were placed in her ears. Her gross- and fine-motor skills developed normally. She spoke in three-word sentences at 14 months. She has always enjoyed school and has consistently been a straight-A student.

Behavioral Observations

Jessica appeared quite comfortable throughout testing. She sat quietly and concentrated on all of the tests. She understood all instructions the first time they were given and never requested repetition of test items.

Tests Administered

Woodcock-Johnson Psycho-Educational Battery—Revised:
Cognitive Battery: Tests 1–14

The tests of the WJ-R were scored according to grade norms. When no difference was found between the two component tests of a factor, only the factor score is discussed. Standard scores and percentile ranks are reported as obtained scores or as 68% confidence bands. A 68% confidence band is expressed as ±1 standard error of measurement (SEM). A complete set of test scores is appended to this report.

Test Results

Based on the results of the Woodcock-Johnson Psycho-Educational Battery—Revised Broad Cognitive Ability score, Jessica's overall cognitive abilities are in the *Superior* range (SS ±1 SEM: 120–126, PR: 94) when compared to her grade-peers.

Jessica scored in the *Very Superior* range in visual skills. In the Processing Speed factor, she scored above 99% of her grade-peers in rapid visual processing of small symbols and forms. On the Visual Processing factor, she scored above 99.9% in noting and recalling details in pictures but in the *Average* range, above 37% of her grade-peers, in identifying familiar objects from pictures that had been partially obscured.

Jessica's performance bordered the *High Average/Superior* ranges on the language-related cognitive factors of Auditory Processing, Short-Term Memory, and Comprehension-Knowledge. These results indicate that Jessica performs above approximately 90% of her grade-peers in the following abilities: synthesizing sounds and syllables into whole words, immediate recall of orally presented information, and vocabulary.

Within the Long-Term Retrieval factor, Jessica's scores were significantly different from each other. Jessica scored in the *High Average* range, above 83% of her grade-peers, on Visual-Auditory Learning, a test that involves learning and retaining word–symbol associations. As this task included "reading" a story composed of these symbols, it is likely that she was aided by the language context. She scored in the *Low Average* range, above 21% of her grade-peers, on the other visual-verbal association test, Memory for Names, which did not have a meaningful context.

Jessica scored in the *Average* range on the Fluid Reasoning factor, above 57% of her grade-peers, in tests of analytical reasoning. This factor is composed of learning tasks that require comprehension of verbal instructions as well as ongoing corrective feedback to solve visually presented problems.

Intracognitive Discrepancies

Based on the current test results, Jessica demonstrates a significant discrepancy in Fluid Reasoning. When Jessica's performance is compared to her grade-peers with the same predicted score, only 4 out of 100 would obtain a score as low as or lower than Jessica's (PR: 4).

Conclusions

Jessica appears to be functioning overall in the *Superior* range of cognitive abilities with a weakness in certain types of analytical reasoning skills. Based on parent report, her academic functioning appears to be commensurate with her overall *Superior* cognitive abilities.

Recommendations

Jessica appears to be doing well in her current placement. Unless she is bored and lacks stimulation, it is probably appropriate for her. The Amhersts might consider speaking with her teacher about including enrichment activities in her regular program.

If a pull-out program, rather than a self-contained program, for gifted children is offered at her school, where a variety of factors, such as academic performance and teacher recommendation, are considered for selection, the Amhersts may request that she be evaluated by the school.

Diagnosis: Deficits in visual perception and recall of visual symbols

PSYCHOEDUCATIONAL EVALUATION

Student: Martin O'Connor   Evaluator:
Birthdate: 9/17/82   Parent: Marshall O'Connor
Chronological Age: 8-7   School: Silver River Elementary
Grade: 2.8   Test Dates: 4/12, 4/13, 4/14, 4/16/91

Reason for Referral

Geraldine Osgood, Martin's teacher, referred Martin for a psychoeducational evaluation due to difficulties with reading, spelling, and memorization of subtraction facts.

Background Information

Martin is an only child. His parents are divorced and he lives with his father. Despite Martin's frequent ear infections until the age of 2, his father reported developmental milestones within normal limits. Martin is currently in good health.

Ms. Osgood described Martin as "a very creative child with a wonderful imagination." She noted that although he seems to be bright and has good language skills, he has difficulty in reading, spelling, and memorizing subtraction facts. He often makes careless computational errors.

Prior to this evaluation, Martin's vision was evaluated by Dr. Daniel Freedman, an ophthalmologist. Dr. Freedman prescribed glasses, which Martin wore throughout the evaluation.

Tests Administered

Woodcock-Johnson Psycho-Educational Battery— Revised (WJ-R):
    Cognitive Battery: Tests 1–21
    Achievement Battery (Form A): Tests 22–31, 33–35
Burns-Roe Informal Reading Inventory (IRI)
Analysis of schoolwork

Behavioral Observations

Martin was seen in four 2½-hour sessions. He appeared to fatigue quickly, especially on the academic tasks, and needed frequent breaks. He was cheerful and interested in the tests. Frequently, when a test was completed, he described in detail the strategy he had used to help himself.

Test Results

The tests of the WJ-R were scored according to grade norms. When no difference was found between the two component tests of a factor or cluster, only the factor or cluster score is discussed. Test results are expressed as verbal labels for the standard score 68% confidence bands and as Relative Mastery Index (RMI) scores. The Relative Mastery Index (RMI) predicts the student's level of mastery on tasks similar to the ones tested. This mastery level is written as a comparison to the 90% mastery expected for average age- or grade-peers. A complete set of test scores and descriptions of the WJ-R tests are appended to this report.

Cognitive Abilities

Martin scored in the *High Average* range on the Broad Cognitive Ability (BCA) score of the Woodcock-Johnson Psycho-Educational Battery— Revised, Extended Scale. His BCA score was composed of scores indicating significant cognitive strengths and weaknesses, limiting the value of the full-scale score for predicting scholastic performance.

Martin scored in the *Superior/Very Superior* range in auditory short-term memory, significantly above the average of his other cognitive factor scores. Among second-grade students with a predicted Short-Term Memory standard score of 110, only 4 out of 100 would have obtained Martin's score of 131 (PR: 96). Martin scored in the *Superior* range on tasks of visual-auditory association and recall. His ability to recall the associations 2 days later was in the *Average* range. He also scored in the *Superior* range in oral language skills. The only language-related test on which he scored relatively low was Verbal Analogies (*Average*), which was the last test of the session. Possibly his performance was impeded by fatigue, as at the end of the test, Martin slumped and said, "I'm tuckered." He performed in the *High Average* range on auditory processing at the sound and word level, on visual processing and recall of pictures, in vocabulary and cultural knowledge, and in using logical reasoning for problem solving. On the latter factor, Fluid Reasoning, Martin scored significantly lower on Analysis-Synthesis (*Average*) than on Concept Formation (*High Average/Superior*). Based on his other scores and excellent reasoning throughout testing, this discrepancy is not considered to be of educational significance.

In sharp contrast, Martin scored at the bottom of the *Low Average* range in rapid processing of visual symbols and forms. Based on the average of the other cognitive factor scores, Martin's predicted Processing Speed standard score was 117. Among second-grade students with the same predicted score, only 2 out of 1,000 would have obtained a score as low as or lower than Martin's score of 81 (PR: 0.2). When attempting to match identical numbers in a row of numbers, Martin tapped each number with his pencil, possibly to compensate for weak visual tracking. Still he made one transposition. His only relatively low memory score was in recalling an orally presented sequence of digits in reverse order. He explained that he had attempted to remember the digits visually, but could not remember the sequence. This was, in fact, his error pattern.

Consequently, it appears that efficient visual processing of symbols, such as letters and numbers, is a significant deficit for Martin and negatively affects visual recall. He is aided by auditory information provided simultaneously with visual symbolic information and may require it for adequate learning. As Martin's handwriting is neat and fluent, visual-motor integration was not formally assessed.

Academic Achievement

Reading

Basic Skills

Based on the results of the WJ-R, Martin's basic reading skills are within the *Average* range when compared with his grade-peers. His Relative Mastery Index (RMI), however, indicated that on word recognition and word analysis tasks on which the average late second-grade student would score 90%, Martin would score approximately 73% and 77%,

respectively. His instructional level in basic reading skills was early to mid-second grade.

On the Burns-Roe Informal Reading Inventory (IRI), Martin's proficiency in reading word lists was consistent with his instructional level on the WJ-R. He had considerably more difficulty, however, in reading words within the context of the longer passages of the IRI. He obtained an instructional level of grade 1 with a reading speed of 60 words per minute. Martin's patterns of errors obviously reflected his difficulty in processing visual symbols. He skipped words and whole lines. He made few attempts at word analysis; he confused visually similar words such as *the/he/she* and transposed and omitted letters in words (e.g., "wall" for *allow*, "accusing" for *causing*, "sweet and" for *wet sand*). His oral reading was dysfluent and was characterized by repetitions and self-corrections.

Comprehension

Martin's comprehension of one- to two-sentence passages was in the *High Average* range. In contrast to his RMIs in basic skills, Martin's RMI for reading comprehension was 97/90. The WJ-R Age/Grade Profile indicated that appropriate instructional materials for reading comprehension would be at the late third-grade level. Again, Martin had more difficulty on the IRI than on the WJ-R. Probably due to the longer passages and the visual aspects of increased text, Martin's instructional level on the Burns-Roe was second grade. Martin used context clues well in trying to maintain meaning, but gave up at frustration level.

On both the WJ-R and the IRI, Martin's performance in reading comprehension was higher than in reading recognition, indicating that he is engaging his strong language and metalinguistic skills. He occasionally answered comprehension questions on a higher cognitive level than expected. For example, he defined a friend as "Someone you can depend on, who won't turn their back on you," rather than, "Someone you play with." Martin's strong performances on the two listening comprehension tests reinforced the indications that visual deficits rather than language or memory problems are inhibiting his progress in reading. On the WJ-R Listening Comprehension test, Martin scored in the *Superior* range with a grade equivalent of mid-sixth grade. On the longer passages of the IRI, his listening comprehension level was fourth grade.

Written Language

Written Expression

Martin scored in the *High Average* range on the Writing Samples test, indicating good ability to express his thoughts in writing. His Writing Samples RMI was 97/90. His responses were organized, imaginative, and syntactically correct. Classroom writing samples were also imaginative, with thoughts well-sequenced and organized around a central idea. (See Figure III-2.) The WJ-R Age/Grade Profile indicated that appropriate instructional materials for written expression would be at the mid-third-grade level.

Basic Skills

Martin's score on the Basic Writing Skills cluster was in the *Average* range, significantly below his score on Writing Samples. Within the Basic Skills cluster, his Spelling score was in the *Low Average* range, significantly lower than his scores on the other basic skills (see below). His Spelling RMI of 63/90 indicated that his spelling was *Limited* compared to his grade-peers'. In all writing tasks, Martin made many phonetic spelling errors, indicating little dependence on visual memory or a confused initial perception of words. For example, in a story he wrote:

I cwd not find the gold it wus grdid be the cening. I bet up the gards and rept dawn the gats. I finle got to the ceing he was umasd he ran uya.

(I could not find the gold. It was guarded by the king. I beat up the guards and ripped down the gates. I finally got to the king. He was amazed. He ran away.)

Within the Basic Writing Skills cluster, Martin scored in the *Average/High Average* range on the skills of Usage and Punctuation/Capitalization, suggesting that he is familiar with these basic writing skills. In his own writing, however, his use of these skills was inconsistent. Appropriate instructional materials for basic writing skills would be at the mid-second-grade level.

Mathematics

Martin scored in the *Average* range, compared to his grade-peers, on the Broad Mathematics cluster, with no significant difference between his scores on the Calculation and Applied Problems tests. Based on these scores, mid-third-grade instructional materials would be appropriate. His RMIs were 88/90 and 87/90, respectively. Again, his visual perception deficit was evident in the types of computation errors he made, such as misreading or perseverating on process signs and forgetting to use digits he had correctly carried over in addition problems. His use of pencil dots in subtraction problems indicated lack of automaticity with subtraction facts.

Later extension testing and Martin's use of strategies demonstrated that he can correctly use addition and subtraction algorithms, understands the concepts, and has good math reasoning. Given computation problems similar to those on the Calculation test, Martin made the same types of errors. When asked to explain each problem, however, he not only caught and corrected his errors, but explained why each was incorrect. When given the problem 13 × 7, he drew 13 circles and put 7 slashes through each, counting as he went. Although his strategy was correct, he came up with the wrong answer. His only errors on the Applied Problems test were in computation.

Knowledge

Martin's response to questions relating to general knowledge placed him in the *High Average* range when compared to his grade-peers. He scored in the *Superior* range in Science and in the *High Average* range in Social Studies and Humanities. These results suggest that Martin is able to pick up information from school and his environment, and, as previously noted, he can retain information over time. His obtained score on the Knowledge cluster was relatively high when compared to his average on the other three achievement clusters.

Aptitude–Achievement Discrepancies

No significant aptitude–achievement discrepancies were found. Martin's score on the Visual Matching test lowered his predicted scores on the Reading, Written Language, and Math Aptitude clusters. As rapid visual processing is necessary for success in reading, written language, and math, Martin would not be predicted to perform well in these areas, as indeed, he did not. Consequently, his academic performance is consistent with his aptitude for reading, written language, and math.

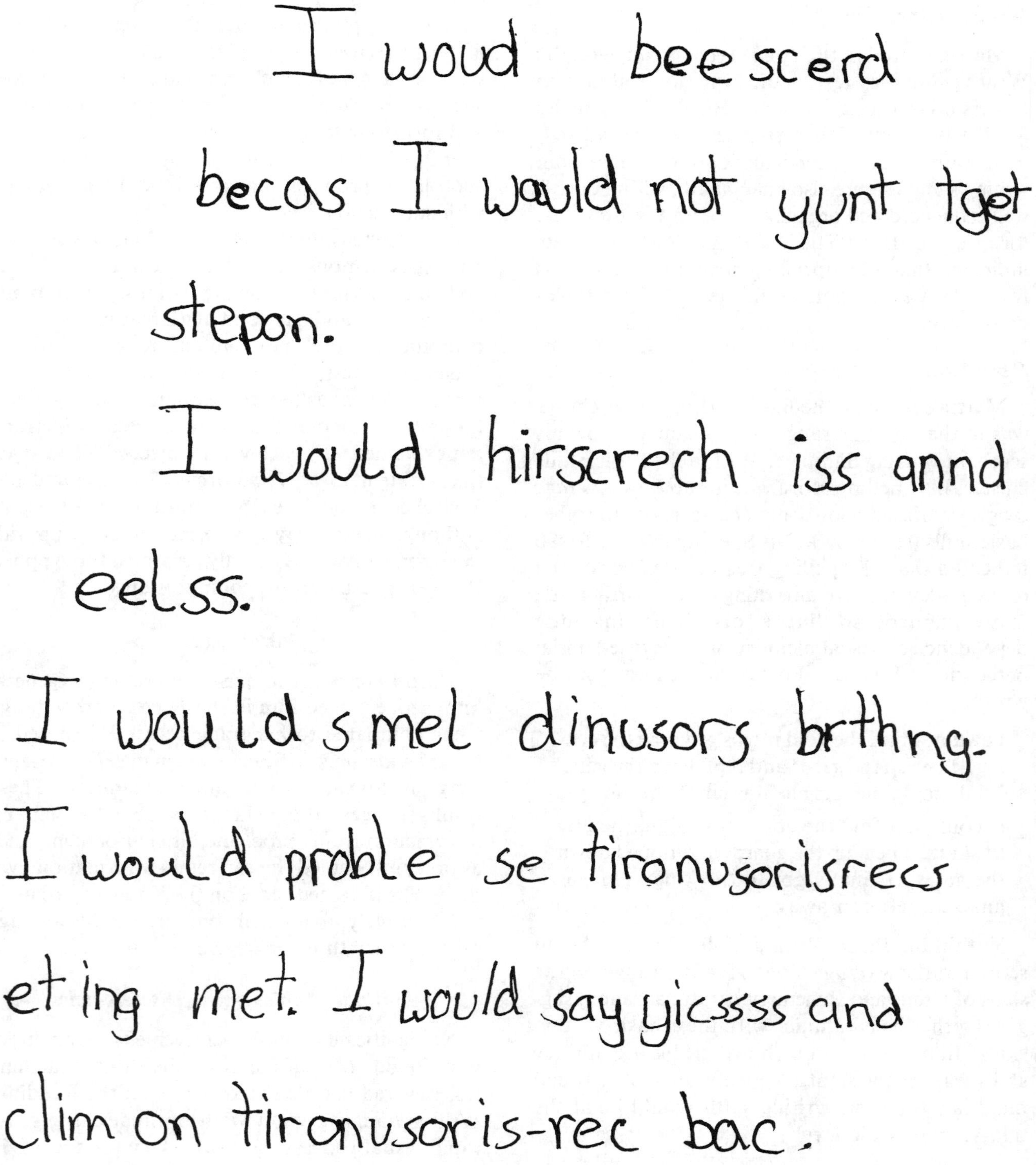

I woud bee scerd becas I would not yunt tget stepon.

I would hirscrech iss annd eelss.

I would smel dinusors brthng. I would proble se tironusorisrecs eting met. I would say yicssss and clim on tironusoris-rec bac.

Figure III-2.   Martin's Writing Sample, Illustrating Strong Language Skills and Weak Visual Recall.

Summary and Conclusions

Martin appears to be a child with at least *High Average* abilities with *Superior* to *Very Superior* oral language and auditory memory skills. His performance in basic academic skills appears to be affected by severe deficits in automatic and fluent processing and recall of visual symbols. Although basic academic skills are generally in the *Average* range, they are significantly lower than would be expected. Martin uses his language, memory, reasoning abilities, and strategies to compensate for his deficits. In academic skills more dependent on his cognitive strengths, such as reading comprehension, written expression, math reasoning, and general knowledge, Martin's skill levels are higher.

Presently, reading decoding and spelling are particularly frustrating to Martin and are not likely to improve significantly without specific remediation. As Martin's deficits do not appear to be secondary to sensory impairments, cultural or language differences, subnormal intelligence, emotional problems, or lack of educational opportunity, he should be referred to the school multidisciplinary team for consideration of special education services in learning disabilities. He should also be considered for services for gifted students.

Recommendations

Home

1. Make sure Martin uses his glasses for all homework.

2. Buy two 8″ × 11″ glass magnifying plates that Martin can use on a book for reading and math if the print is too small for comfort. Keep one at home and one at school.

3. Help Martin maintain his enthusiasm for reading. Enlist the help of the children's librarian at the public library to find books on his reading level with large print. Ask about books for the visually impaired.

4. Due to Martin's tendency toward visual fatigue, try to schedule short periods for reading (5 to 10 minutes) each evening as a pleasurable activity. Take turns reading, switching off paragraphs or pages. To help Martin keep his place (which may not be necessary with large-print books), hold an index card under the line being read. To encourage proper tracking, make a game that either of you can stop reading anywhere after a minimum number of sentences and the other has to know where to start.

5. Invest in one or two magazine subscriptions that would interest Martin. Try to read them with him. Suggestions include: *Ranger Rick*, *3-2-1 Contact*, and *Kid City*. You may review these magazines at a library.

6. To enrich Martin's knowledge base further, encourage him to watch certain educational television programs, such as "Square One," "3-2-1 Contact," and "National Geographic."

7. Speak with Martin's teacher before the beginning of the school year. Explain Martin's strengths, as well as difficulties with visual symbolic tasks. Request that s/he call you at any time with concerns about Martin.

School

Remind Martin to wear his glasses for all near-point visual activities.

Reading

Compensations

1. To maintain motivation and emphasize comprehension in reading, directly reinforce (e.g., verbally, with a smile) Martin's good comprehension of reading material.

2. Allow Martin extra time to complete reading tasks. Provide this in a way that will not be embarrassing.

3. Provide a tape of a book Martin is to read so that he may listen and read simultaneously. (See attached materials on taped books.)

4. Use large-print books.

5. Remind Martin to use his magnifying plate when needed.

6. Provide Martin with a 5″ × 8″ index card with a window the size of one line of print. See if it is easier for him to read through the window or with the card under the line.

7. Ask Martin if he wants to be called on to read aloud in class.

Remediation

1. Teach new phonic elements using a highly structured phonics program, such as the Phonic Remedial

Reading Lessons (Kirk, Kirk, & Minskoff, 1985), The Writing Road to Reading (Spalding & Spalding, 1986), or Angling for Words (Bowen, 1972).

2. For supplemental reinforcement of automatic recognition of new phonic elements, have him practice circling the phonic element in text or on worksheets. Cues and Signals in Reading (Wehrli, 1971) would be useful for this.

3. Have Martin practice writing word families as he learns new phonic elements and affixes.

4. Color-code phonic elements and affixes you are teaching.

5. Teach structural analysis. Keep the letters of the words you are working with relatively large. Gradually decrease size. Make interlocking puzzle pieces that can be combined in many ways, each one printed with a common syllable or affix.

Basic Writing Skills

1. Provide positive feedback to Martin for his good ideas, organization, and sentence structure in his writing.

2. Teach Martin to use verbal mediation more effectively to improve his efficiency and accuracy in copying from texts and the board.

3. For spelling words with which Martin has consistent difficulty, teach a study strategy based in the auditory modality. One such strategy is called Alternate Pronunciation (Ormrod, 1986). For each target word, the student learns a specific, alternate pronunciation that will match the visual image (e.g., lab ō rat ory). An alternative method might be an adaptation of Simultaneous Oral Spelling (Bradley, 1981; Gillingham & Stillman, 1973). (See attached materials describing these methods.)

4. Use a highly structured program with ample reinforcement activities to teach spelling patterns. One such program is Corrective Spelling Through Morphographs (Dixon & Engelman, 1979). An advantage of this program for Martin is the emphasis on teaching meaningful word parts.

5. Since Martin is familiar with the mechanics of writing, but does not apply the skills he knows, teach him a proofreading strategy to help him find and correct his errors. The Error Monitoring Strategy (Schumaker, Deshler, Nolan, Clark, Alley, & Warner, 1981) uses the mnemonic COPS (Capitalization, Overall appearance, Punctuation, Spelling) to remind the student of the steps to use. (See attached description.)

Math

1. To compensate for Martin's difficulty in learning math facts, teach Touch Math (Bullock, 1991) for computation. This program has cues for working in the proper direction built into it. Teach the more advanced skills as soon as he learns the previous ones, even if he moves ahead of his class. He should have no difficulty learning the skip counting (using the posters and verbal drill) or the algorithms necessary for multiplication and division.

2. When Martin is given a page of computation problems, have him go over all of the process signs first in colored marker, using a different color for each operation.

3. Martin will make fewer computation errors if his worksheets have ample space between problems and large-size numerals. Provide worksheets printed like this and teach Martin to copy math problems in the same manner. He can use paper folded into six parts to delineate spaces.

4. Show Martin how to use his magnifying plate over a page of math problems that he has to copy onto another sheet of paper.

5. Teach Martin how to use verbal mediation when he has to copy problems from one page to another or from the chalkboard to his paper.

Diagnosis: Deficit in perception and recall of visual symbols; weakness in memory for auditory information presented outside of a meaningful context

PSYCHOEDUCATIONAL EVALUATION

Name: Sara Mandel

Birthdate: 6/21/83

Chronological Age: 8-9

Grade Placement: 3.5

Evaluator:

Parents: Edward and Rose Mandel

School: Stanton Primary

Test Dates: 3/24, 3/25, 3/26, 3/27/92

Reason for Referral

Sara was referred to the child study team at Stanton Primary School by her classroom teacher, Ms. Everett. Ms. Everett stated that Sara was experiencing academic difficulties in her classroom, especially with reading and writing tasks.

Background Information

A developmental history was completed by Sara's mother. Ms. Mandel noted one complication during pregnancy, abnormal bleeding that required drug interventions. Sara's developmental milestones occurred within normal limits. She has had thorough vision and hearing evaluations. Sara was prescribed glasses for nearsightedness but does not wear them on a consistent basis.

Sara attended kindergarten at Stanton Primary. Her parents enrolled her in first grade at Rosemont Elementary. In February of that school year, Ms. Mandel transferred Sara back to Stanton Primary because she felt that Sara needed a phonics program to learn to read and this type of instruction was provided at Stanton. In second grade, Sara received reading support services as she qualified for the lower quartile reading program.

A variety of interventions have been attempted to address Sara's reading and writing difficulties. She has received extensive help at home from her mother and summer tutoring from a learning disabilities specialist. Her third-grade classroom teacher has placed Sara in a small, homogeneous reading group, has provided reduced spelling lists, and has set up a peer tutor to help Sara when assigned tasks are too difficult for her.

Tests Administered

Sara was administered the Woodcock-Johnson Psycho-Educational Battery—Revised (WJ-R), Tests of Cognitive Ability (1–14), and Tests of Achievement, Form A (22–32, 34–35).

Behavioral Observations

Testing was conducted in four 1-hour sessions. Sara was cooperative and attentive throughout all of the testing sessions. On several occasions, Sara asked the examiner to provide assistance. Sara tended to talk herself through tasks and subvocalized during all of the reading and writing tests.

Test Results

The tests of the WJ-R were scored according to grade norms. When no difference was found between the two component tests of a factor or cluster, only the factor or cluster score is discussed. Percentile ranks are reported as 68% confidence bands. A 68% confidence band is expressed as ± 1 standard error of measurement (SEM). A complete set of test scores is appended to this report. (See Figure III-3.)

Cognitive Abilities

Sara's overall cognitive performance fell in the *Average* range (PR ± 1 SEM: 55-70). Significant discrepancies were noted among the factors. A significant strength was noted in Visual Processing (PR ± 1 SEM: 98-99.9, *Very Superior*), her capability to perceive and think with nonsymbolic visual patterns. Only 1 out of 1,000 students (PR: 99.9) with the same predicted score as Sara's would obtain a score as high or higher. A relative strength was noted in Fluid Reasoning (PR ± 1 SEM: 68–81, *Average/High Average*), her capability to see patterns and use logical reasoning. In contrast, a significant weakness was noted in Processing Speed (PR ± 1 SEM: 10–32, *Low Average*), her ability to scan and process visual symbols quickly. Only 6% of students with the same predicted score would obtain a score as low as or lower than Sara's (PR: 6).

Discrepancies were also noted between the tests within each of the two memory factors. On the component tests of the Long-Term Retrieval factor, Sara scored significantly higher on Visual-Auditory Learning (PR ± 1 SEM: 87–96, *Superior*), a test that requires the student to retain visual-auditory associations within a language context, than on Memory for Names (PR ± 1 SEM: 10–23, *Low Average*), a test that requires the student to retain novel, unrelated, auditory-visual associations. On the two tests of the Short-Term Memory factor, Sara scored higher on Memory for Sentences (PR ± 1 SEM: 77–94, *High Average*), a test that requires the student to repeat back sentences, than on Memory for Words (PR ± 1 SEM: 23–58, *Average*), a test that requires the student to repeat back a string of unrelated words. These discrepancies between the tests within these two factors suggest that a significant difference exists between Sara's strong ability to recall visual or auditory information presented in a meaningful context versus her weaker ability to recall visual or auditory information presented in a decontextualized format.

Difficulty with tasks requiring rote learning was also apparent in Sara's responses to certain tests. The Picture Recognition test requires a subject to identify a subset of previously presented pictures within a field of distracting pictures. Each picture is identified on the response page with a letter of the alphabet. On several items, Sara had to point to a picture because she could not recall the letter name. Sara scored in the *Average* range on the factors of Auditory Processing (PR ± 1 SEM: 25–50) and Comprehension-Knowledge (PR ± 1 SEM: 30–55).

Achievement

Reading

Sara scored in the *Low Average* range in Basic Reading (PR ± 1 SEM: 13–23) when compared to grade-peers. When her Broad Reading score is compared to her average performance in the other three achievement clusters, only 4 out of 100 students (PR: 4) would obtain a score as low as or lower than hers. Sara's Relative Mastery Index (RMI) on Basic Reading Skills (53/90) suggests that she would have 53% success on word identification tasks when her average grade-mates are having 90% success. Sara had the most difficulty with the Letter-Word Identification test (RMI: 24/90). When she encountered unfamiliar words, she stated: "I've never

seen these words before. How would I know how to say them?" Sara was able to produce initial consonant sounds and knew when an initial consonant was silent. Her word substitutions suggest that she guessed words based on whole-word configurations.

Based on the results of the Reading Comprehension cluster score (PR ± 1 SEM: 42–58), Sara's ability to comprehend reading material falls in the *Average* range. Her RMI of 90/90 indicates that she will have the same success in understanding grade-level reading material as her average classmates. On the Passage Comprehension test (RMI: 93/90), Sara was successful in using syntactic and semantic clues to supply a missing word in a brief passage. Her Reading Vocabulary RMI was 85/90.

Written Language

Based on the Broad Written Language cluster, Sara is functioning in the *Low/Low Average* range when compared to peers (PR ± 1 SEM: 7–14). When her Broad Written Language score is compared to her average performance in the other three achievement clusters, only 2 out of 1,000 students (PR: 0.2) would obtain a score as low as or lower than hers. Sara had greater difficulty on tasks involving basic writing skills (RMI: 39/90) than on tests involving written expression (RMI: 81/90).

In analyzing Sara's responses, her abilities to express an idea in a structured writing task and to write simple sentence patterns quickly are significantly higher than her skills in spelling, punctuation, and capitalization. Although Sara's handwriting is quite legible, she has numerous *b/d* reversals. When she was writing a word containing the letter *b* or *d*, she occasionally erased the letter and tried to self-correct. For example, she changed *dirb* to *birb* (bird). Several of Sara's attempted spellings have poor sound–symbol correspondence. Two pages from the Writing Samples test are attached to illustrate her performance. (See Figure III-4.)

Mathematics

Test results indicate that Sara is functioning in the *Superior* range on the Broad Mathematics cluster (PR ± 1 SEM: 91–97). When her performance on the Broad Mathematics cluster is compared to her average performance in the other achievement areas, 2 out of 1,000 students (PR: 99.8) would obtain a standard score as high or higher. Sara's RMI of 97/90 suggests that she would demonstrate 97%

mastery compared to her average grade-mates' 90% mastery on similar tasks.

Knowledge

Sara scored in the *Average* to *High Average* range on the Broad Knowledge cluster (PR ±1 SEM: 68–84). Sara's Science RMI of 97/90 and Social Studies RMI of 96/90 were higher than her Humanities RMI of 91/90. This suggests that Sara will be functioning at the independent level on classroom tasks requiring knowledge of science and social studies and at the instructional level on tasks requiring knowledge of literature, art, and music.

Aptitude–Achievement Discrepancy

Sara has a significant discrepancy between her predicted performance in Written Language and her actual performance. Only 4% of third-grade students with the same Written Language Aptitude score as Sara's would obtain a standard score as low as or lower than Sara's on the Broad Written Language Achievement cluster.

Conclusions and Implications

Sara demonstrates a significant intracognitive deficit in Processing Speed. Within the factors of Long-Term Retrieval and Short-Term Memory, discrepancies existed between the tests. Sara was able to recall visual or auditory information presented in a meaningful context, but had difficulty recalling visual or auditory information presented in a decontextualized format. Sara had an aptitude–achievement discrepancy between her predicted and actual performance in written language. Based on the average of her other Achievement cluster scores, Sara is functioning significantly below predicted performance in Broad Reading and Written Language. In contrast, her performance in mathematics is *Superior*.

Generally, Sara's performances on cognitive and academic tests involving the higher-order cognitive abilities of problem solving, language comprehension, and acquired knowledge were higher than her performances on tests involving automatic cognitive processes and rote memory. In addition, Sara's difficulties learning the letters of the alphabet, developing a sight vocabulary for reading, revisualizing words for spelling, and recalling the orientation of *b* and *d* suggest a weakness in visual memory

for orthographic information and in memory for auditory information outside of a meaningful context.

Recommendations

The multidisciplinary team should review Sara's performance on this test and others to determine whether Sara qualifies for learning disability services. More extensive informal assessment or diagnostic teaching will help determine the most appropriate instructional reading methods to use with Sara. Several recommendations are made for strategies in basic reading and writing skills that may be used by the classroom teacher, parents, learning disability specialist, or an educational therapist.

Memory

1. For tasks requiring memorization, provide as much meaning as possible. Help Sara develop meaningful associations to enhance memory. Make sure that she understands information she must remember.

2. Teach Sara specific memory strategies and how to recognize which strategy may be most useful in a variety of situations. Examples of memory strategies include: verbal rehearsal, chunking, making ridiculous visual images composed of items that one has to remember, and mnemonics.

Reading

1. Teach Sara phonic skills by using a highly structured program. Examples include the Phonic Remedial Reading Drills (Kirk, Kirk, & Minskoff, 1985), the Spalding method (Spalding & Spalding, 1986), Angling for Words (Bowen, 1972), Reading Mastery (Engelmann et al., 1983-1984), and Corrective Reading (Engelmann et al., 1988).

2. Teach sight words from one of the lists of most frequently used words in reading material such as 1,000 Instant Words (Fry, Polk, & Fountoukidis, 1985).

3. Emphasize sound–symbol associations when teaching Sara reading and provide intensive training in structural analysis. Ensure that Sara overlearns these skills so that she begins to see unfamiliar words as a sequence of familiar word parts. The Glass-Analysis Method for Decoding Only (Glass, 1973,

1976) may be used to help Sara develop an automatic response to common visual and auditory clusters.

4. Provide activities for Sara to help her see herself as an accomplished, fluent reader. As examples, have Sara be a cross-age tutor for a first-grade student who is having difficulty learning to read or include Sara in Readers' Theater productions. Cast Sara in a major role so that she has numerous lines to practice and read aloud. Provide her help in learning them.

Spelling

1. Do not penalize Sara for poor spelling on rough drafts. Instead, help Sara analyze and correct her mistakes as needed.

2. Use a modified Fernald method with Sara to practice spelling words. Select the words to study from her writing and from word patterns being studied when using Glass-Analysis. Write each word in large letters on a 5″ × 8″ index card. Have her trace the word several times as she pronounces the word. Have her turn over the index card and write the word from memory on a separate piece of paper. Have Sara continue studying a word until she can write the word correctly from memory three times.

3. Have Sara file the spelling words that she has studied in a word box or an alphabetized spelling notebook. Provide opportunities for review and extended practice.

4. When time permits, have a peer help Sara study and review her spelling words.

Proofreading

1. Teach Sara a strategy to help her check her papers for *b/d* reversals. For example, teach her how to form the letters in different ways. The letter *d* may be formed like a cursive *a* with a line that goes up. Or, Sara can make a capital *B* at the top of her paper, erase the top, and check to see that all her letter *b*s are pointing to the right and all of her letter *d*s are pointing to the left.

2. When Sara is editing a rough draft, provide extra time so that she may proofread her paper for *b/d* reversals.

Name _Sara Mandel_   Grade _3.5_   Date of Test _3 - 23 - 91_

School _Stanton_   Date of Birth _6 - 21 - 82_

Teacher _Ms. Everett_   Chronological Age _8 - 9 - 2_

Examiner _____ Norms based on: Age _____ Grade _3.5_

WOODCOCK-JOHNSON PSYCHO-EDUCATIONAL BATTERY - REVISED
TESTS OF COGNITIVE ABILITY - STANDARD & SUPPLEMENTAL

Test / CLUSTER	Factors	Age Equivalent	Grade Equivalent	Relative Mastery Index	Standard Scores SS	Standard Scores Range	Percentile Ranks PR	Percentile Ranks Range
1 Memory for Names	Glr	5-11	K.5	77 /90	85	81-89	15	10-23
8 Visual-Auditory Learning	Glr	25	14.6	97 /90	122	117-127	93	87-96
LONG-TERM RETRIEVAL	Glr	9-4	4.0	91 /90	102	98-106	56	45-66
15 Del. Rec.-Mem.for Names	Glr			/90				
16 Del. Rec.-Vis.-Aud. Lrng.	Glr			/90				
2 Memory for Sentences	Gsm	14-0	8.2	98 /90	117	111-123	87	77-94
9 Memory for Words	Gsm	7-7	2.3	82 /90	96	89-103	38	23-58
SHORT-TERM MEMORY	Gsm	9-8	4.5	93 /90	105	100-110	63	50-75
17 Numbers Reversed	Gsm,Gf			/90				
3 Visual Matching	Gs	8-3	2.8	81 /90	92	85-99	30	16-47
10 Cross Out	Gs	7-5	2.1	77 /90	84	76-92	14	5-30
PROCESSING SPEED	Gs	8-0	2.6	79 /90	87	81-93	19	10-32
4 Incomplete Words	Ga	7-6	2.4	85 /90	94	86-102	35	18-55
11 Sound Blending	Ga	7-11	2.4	84 /90	96	91-101	39	27-53
AUDITORY PROCESSING	Ga	7-8	2.3	85 /90	95	90-100	37	25-50
18 Sound Patterns	Ga, Gf			/90				
5 Visual Closure	Gv	29	16.9	99 /90	139	131-147	99.6	98-99.9
12 Picture Recognition	Gv	22	15.5	98 /90	131	124-138	98	95-99.5
VISUAL PROCESSING	Gv	29	16.8	98 /90	134	132-146	99.5	98-99.9
6 Picture Vocabulary	Gc	8-5	2.9	85 /90	96	90-102	38	25-55
13 Oral Vocabulary	Gc	9-0	3.7	92 /90	103	97-109	58	42-73
COMPREHEN.-KNOWLEDGE	Gc	8-8	3.3	88 /90	97	92-100	43	30-55
20 Listening Comprehension	Gc			/90				
7 Analysis-Synthesis	Gf	8-8	3.4	90 /90	100	95-105	50	37-63
14 Concept Formation	Gf	12-1	7.2	98 /90	117	113-121	88	81-92
FLUID REASONING	Gf	10-5	5.0	95 /90	110	107-113	74	68-81
19 Spatial Relations	Gf, Gv			/90				
21 Verbal Analogies	Gf, Gc			/90				
READING APTITUDE				91 /90	102	99-105	55	47-63
MATHEMATICS APTITUDE				92 /90	104	101-107	59	53-68
WRITTEN LANGUAGE APTITUDE				90 /90	100	97-103	50	42-58
KNOWLEDGE APTITUDE				97 /90	121	118-124	92	88-95
ORAL LANGUAGE APTITUDE				/90				
ORAL LANGUAGE				/90				
BROAD COGNITIVE ABILITY(E Dev)				/90				
BROAD COGNITIVE ABILITY(Std)				/90				
BROAD COGNITIVE ABILITY(Ext)		9-4	4.0	92 /90	105	102-103	62	55-70

DMc C0G2

Prepared by: David McPhail, Oklahoma City, Oklahoma.

(continued)

Figure III-3. Sara's Scores on the WJ-R Cognitive and Achievement Batteries.

TESTS OF ACHIEVEMENT - STANDARD & SUPPLEMENTAL   Form __A__

Test / CLUSTER	Factors	Age Equivalent	Grade Equivalent	Relative Mastery Index	Standard Scores SS	Standard Scores Range	Percentile Ranks PR	Percentile Ranks Range
READING								
22 Letter-Word Identification		7-7	2.0	29 /90	79	75-83	8	5-13
23 Passage Comprehension		9-5	3.9	93 /90	105	100-110	63	50-75
31 Word Attack	Ga	8-0	2.4	75 /90	93	89-97	33	23-42
32 Reading Vocabulary		8-8	3.1	85 /90	96	92-100	40	30-50
BROAD READING		8-2	2.7	71 /90	90	87-93	25	19-32
BASIC READING SKILLS		7-8	2.1	53 /90	86	83-89	17	13-23
READING COMPREHENSION		9-0	3.5	90 /90	100	97-103	50	42-58
MATHEMATICS								
24 Calculation	Gq	9-8	4.3	96 /90	118	113-123	88	81-94
25 Applied Problems	Gq	10-9	5.4	98 /90	122	117-127	93	87-96
33 Quantitative Concepts	Gq	8-0	2.5	66 /90	85	79-91	16	8-27
*BROAD MATHEMATICS**	*Gq*	10-1	4.7	97 /90	124	120-128	95	91-97
BASIC MATHEMATICS SKILLS	Gq	8-9	3.3	88 /90	98	94-102	44	34-55
MATHEMATICS REASONING	Gq	Not an actual "cluster". The Applied Problems test measures Mathematics Reasoning.						

*Also for use as a cognitive factor.

Test / CLUSTER	Factors	Age Equivalent	Grade Equivalent	Relative Mastery Index	Standard Scores SS	Standard Scores Range	Percentile Ranks PR	Percentile Ranks Range
WRITTEN LANGUAGE								
26 Dictation		7-0	1.5	21 /90	68	63-73	2	1-4
27 Writing Samples		7-9	2.6	81 /90	93	89-97	33	23-42
34 Proofing		7-9	2.3	58 /90	86	81-91	18	10-27
35 Writing Fluency	Gs	8-2	2.6	79 /90	89	80-98	24	9-45
P Punctuation/Capitalization		7-2	1.7	29 /90	75	69-81	4	2-10
S Spelling		7-6	2.0	42 /90	80	75-85	9	5-16
U Usage		6-9	1.2	16 /90	77	71-83	7	3-13
H Handwriting				/90				
BROAD WRITTEN LANGUAGE		7-5	1.8	53 /90	81	78-84	10	7-14
BASIC WRITING SKILLS		7-4	1.8	39 /90	76	72-80	5	3-9
WRITTEN EXPRESSION		8-0	2.6	81 /90	89	85-93	22	16-32
KNOWLEDGE								
28 Science	Gc	10-8	5.2	97 /90	118	111-125	88	77-95
29 Social Studies	Gc	10-2	4.8	96 /90	115	108-122	84	70-93
30 Humanities	Gc	9-2	3.7	91 /90	101	95-107	54	37-68
BROAD KNOWLEDGE	Gc	9-11	4.6	95 /90	111	107-115	78	68-84

INTRA-COGNITIVE DISCREPANCIES

COGNITIVE FACTOR CLUSTER	PR	SD DIFF
LONG-TERM RETRIEVAL	31	-0.51
SHORT-TERM MEMORY	50	0.00
PROCESSING SPEED	6	-1.54
AUDITORY PROCESSING	14	-1.10
VISUAL PROCESSING	99.9	+3.08
COMPREHENSION-KNOWLEDGE	13	-1.12
FLUID REASONING	66	+0.42

INTRA-ACHIEVEMENT DISCREPANCIES

BROAD ACHIEVEMENT CLUSTER	PR	SD DIFF
BROAD READING (R)	4	-1.74
BROAD MATHEMATICS (M)	99.8	+2.84
BROAD WRITTEN LANGUAGE (W)	0.3	-2.78
BROAD KNOWLEDGE (K)	89	+1.31

APTITUDE/ACHIEVEMENT DISCREPANCIES

BASED ON: BCA _____ APTITUDE _X_

ACHIEVEMENT CLUSTER	PR	SD DIFF
BROAD READING	14	-1.08
BASIC READING SKILLS		
READING COMPREHENSION		
BROAD MATHEMATICS	98	+1.96
BASIC MATHEMATICS SKILLS		
MATHEMATICS REASONING		
BROAD WRITTEN LANGUAGE	4	-1.70
BASIC WRITING SKILLS		
WRITTEN EXPRESSION		
BROAD KNOWLEDGE	39	-0.28

Prepared by: David McPhail, Oklahoma City, Oklahoma.

Figure III-3. *(continued)*

TEST 27

Writing Samples (cont.)

6.

The birb is sing.

7.

These is a kine.

8.

The birb is bone.

9.

These is a cow.

10.

in the closet

The belt is not in the closet.

(continued)

Figure III–4. Examples of Sara's Responses on the Writing Samples Test.

Writing Samples (cont.)

11.

The boy got a airplan.

12.

The sill is hloing a boll on his hos.

13.

and

The boy and grill is thoing a boll to esh uther.

14.

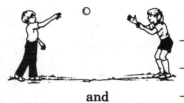

They both lite up.

15.

because

The boy hot his lag because he fell.

Figure III–4. *(continued)*

Diagnosis: Possible Attention Deficit Disorder

PSYCHOEDUCATIONAL EVALUATION

Student: Thomas Stevens   Evaluator:
Birthdate: 4/5/82   Guardians: Jack and
                             Joanne Tunner
Chronological Age: 9-4   School: Gunderson
                             Elementary
Grade: 3.9   Test Dates: 8/17,
                             8/18/91

Reason for Referral

Due to concerns about Thomas's behavior in the classroom, his teacher requested a brief evaluation of Thomas's learning skills to supplement the psychological evaluation completed in April by Blake Ansell, Ph.D., school psychologist.

Background Information

Thomas, a 9-year-old Caucasian boy, just finishing third grade, has a traumatic history of abuse and neglect. Since removal from their parents' home 4 years ago, Thomas and his older brother have lived with their aunt and uncle. The Tunners have no records of the boys' developmental milestones, but do not recall any delays. The social worker's report concerning Thomas's behavior at home states that he requires a high degree of supervision to ensure the safety of household items. When Thomas does homework, Mrs. Tunner sits with him to keep him on task and to monitor his accuracy.

In previous classroom observation reports, Dr. Ansell indicated that Thomas exhibited sporadic distractibility and impulsivity, but noted that Mrs. Weintraub's classroom management system and teaching techniques appear to be appropriate for him. Nevertheless, throughout this year and in previous school years, Thomas has received unsatisfactory ratings in following oral and written instructions, organizing time and materials, considering the rights of others, and assuming responsibility for his actions. Mrs. Weintraub stated that he frequently blurts out comments unrelated to the task, comments that occasionally "border on the bizarre."

Previous Evaluations

In April, at the request of the school's child study team, Dr. Ansell conducted a psychological evaluation. Dr. Ansell noted that Thomas was highly impulsive throughout testing, impeding careful thought. Results of the Wechsler Intelligence Scale for Children—Revised (WISC-R) indicated that Thomas is functioning in the *Superior* range (PR: 93) on verbal and nonverbal tasks with a possible deficiency in the area of short-term auditory memory or attention. In contrast, he noted that Thomas was able to retell orally presented passages. Visual-motor skills were within normal limits. Dr. Ansell concluded that Thomas evidences symptoms consistent with Attention Deficit Disorder and recommended behavior management techniques. Dr. Ansell also noted a concern about the possibility of Post-Traumatic Stress Disorder.

Behavior During Testing

Thomas entered the test situation easily. During the assessment, he was very aware of the evaluator's actions. He asked, "Are you timing me?" "Are you writing down my answers?" He often wanted to know if he was correct. Consistent with his behavior in previous testing, Thomas was very impulsive and responded too quickly throughout the tests, ignoring the evaluator's frequent reminders to slow down. He continually touched the test easel, attempting to look back or turn the pages himself, even immediately after responding affirmatively to a request that he not do so. Midway through a test Thomas had been told he had 3 minutes to complete, he stopped working to take off his glasses and to request that the evaluator turn off the fan.

Thomas was quite cooperative throughout the first session and clearly enjoyed the opportunity to earn stickers. During the next session, which involved academics, he became easily frustrated and wanted to quit when presented with the more difficult items on each test. His most extreme reaction was on the writing tests. When asked to write a variety of sentences, Thomas became so anxious and frustrated that testing was discontinued until he was more relaxed.

Method of Evaluation

As a brief screening of Thomas's cognitive and academic skills was requested to supplement the

WISC-R, only the Standard Batteries of the Woodcock-Johnson Psycho-Educational Battery—Revised (Achievement: Form A) were administered. Thomas was asked to write a composition, and a writing sample from school was analyzed.

Test Results

The tests of the WJ-R were scored according to grade norms. Standard scores and percentile ranks are expressed as obtained scores or as 68% confidence bands. A 68% confidence band is written as ±1 standard error of measurement (±1 SEM). A complete set of test scores is appended to this report. (See Figure III-5.)

Cognitive Skills

Results of the WJ-R Broad Cognitive Ability—Standard Scale indicated that Thomas was functioning in the *High Average* range, somewhat lower than his full scale score on the WISC-R. Thomas evidenced a strength in visually related tasks on the WJ-R, which is consistent with his performance on the WISC-R. His scores on these tests spanned the *High Average* and *Superior* ranges with all confidence bands overlapping. These scores suggest strengths in visual processing, speed of processing, visual-auditory association, and logical reasoning.

Thomas's scores were significantly lower on those tasks requiring auditory short-term memory and sustained attention. His scores bordered the *Low Average/Average* ranges on tests of automatic auditory processing and immediate recall of sentences. This finding is consistent with the relative weakness found in auditory attention/memory on the WISC-R. Based on the WJ-R and the WISC-R, Thomas's expressive vocabulary is in the *Average/High Average* range.

Academic Achievement

Based on the WJ-R Broad Reading cluster, Thomas is functioning in the *Superior* range in reading when compared to his grade-peers. His abilities in word recognition and comprehension of short passages were equally high. On these tests, Thomas read and responded very quickly.

Thomas also scored in the *Superior* range on the Broad Math cluster, again with equally high performance in computation and application of skills.

He had difficulty with two-digit multiplication and the long division algorithm, but showed good reasoning and use of classroom learning in attempting to subtract repeatedly to solve the long division problems. On the Applied Problems test, he sometimes read ahead of the examiner and made errors in mental calculation when he could have used paper and pencil.

Thomas's performance at the lower limits of *Average* on the Broad Written Language cluster represented his only intra-achievement discrepancy. Of third-grade students whose predicted Broad Written Language cluster score was 122, only 1 out of 1,000 (PR: 0.1) would obtain an actual score as low as or lower than Thomas's score of 92. Thomas scored equally low on both tests and evidenced more anxiety and frustration on these tests than on any of the others in the entire test battery. Thomas became frustrated when he requested help and was told that the evaluator could not provide it. He rushed through his responses on the Writing Samples test. Analysis of his responses demonstrated lack of full use of the verbal or pictorial prompt.

Error patterns were analyzed on the two WJ-R writing tests and two paragraph-long compositions. On all formal and informal writing samples, Thomas had errors in spelling, capitalization, and usage, and his sentences lacked detail. Both compositions were organized, yet differed widely in use of complex sentence structure, fluency of expression, and handwriting. Since the composition written as part of the assessment was superior in all ways to the one done for class homework, it may represent one of his better efforts.

Thomas scored in the *High Average* range on the WJ-R Broad Knowledge cluster. Test scores, however, indicate *Average* knowledge of Social Studies and Humanities with a *Superior* level of information in Science.

Summary and Conclusions

Based on current and previous testing, Thomas possesses *High Average* overall cognitive abilities, but his cognitive functioning is profoundly affected by attentional deficits and impulsivity. *Low* scores in the areas of auditory short-term memory and processing are not supported by observations of Thomas's behavior. Mrs. Tunner and Mrs. Weintraub both report that he can often repeat their instructions verbatim, even when he has not followed them. Thomas appears to have memory capability when he attends sufficiently to process the given information adequately. Likewise, Thomas's excellent word recognition and phonetic spelling contradict his low score on the auditory processing test. Considering this information, Thomas is not considered to be learning disabled, although his learning is negatively affected by impulsivity and lack of focused, sustained attention. Thomas appears to attend to and thus process information better visually than auditorily; the addition of visual cues to verbal information improves his performance significantly.

Thomas scored in the *Superior* range in reading, math, and science knowledge, and in the *Average* range in social studies and humanities. Test results indicate a significant deficit in written language achievement, although informal testing demonstrated great inconsistency from sample to sample. The myriad skills requiring simultaneous flow and integration in written expression may necessitate more focused attention than Thomas is presently able to sustain.

Recommendations

1. To help Thomas improve his writing skills, arrange for him to attend the school Learning Lab for training in the process writing approach. Monitor his progress closely.

2. If possible, provide a computer at home with the same word processing system used at school. This should make writing more enjoyable for Thomas and help him to improve weak skills. An additional benefit might be an increase in self-esteem when he is able to write his papers on a computer.

3. Mrs. Weintraub should list writing skill deficiencies of most concern. Areas of skill deficit noted in this assessment include: incomplete responses, responses not related to the question, short and simple sentences, paucity of ideas, lack of detail, inconsistent handwriting quality, poor spelling, and errors in usage and capitalization. Together, she and Thomas should target the skill of most concern, and write a contract in which he receives daily rewards for successive improvement. At first, it may be necessary to reward Thomas twice a day and keep a reminder card taped to his desk. Help him to make and fill out a progress chart.

4. Meet with Thomas's aunt and uncle to discuss further the concerns about Attention Deficit Disorder. Refer them to a developmental pediatrician with expertise in ADD to investigate this concern and, if necessary, to provide education and appropriate treatment. Suggest that Thomas's aunt and uncle also discuss with the pediatrician the need for further evaluation of Post-Traumatic Stress Disorder as a contributing factor to Thomas's behavioral problems.

Name _Thomas Stevens_   Grade _3.9_   Date of Test _91 - 8 - 18_

School _Gunderson Elementary_   Date of Birth _82 - 4 - 5_

Teacher _____   Chronological Age ___ - ___ - ___

Examiner _____   Norms based on: Age _9-4_   Grade _3.9_

WOODCOCK-JOHNSON PSYCHO-EDUCATIONAL BATTERY - REVISED
TESTS OF COGNITIVE ABILITY

Test / CLUSTER	Factors	Age Equivalent	Grade Equivalent	Relative Mastery Index	Standard Scores SS	Range	Percentile Ranks PR	Range
STANDARD BATTERY								
1 Memory for Names	Glr	22^{59}	16.9^{56}	96 /90	115	111 – 119	84	77 - 90
2 Memory for Sentences	Gsm	7-9	2.3	77 /90	91	85 - 97	28	16 - 42
3 Visual Matching	Gs	10-3	4.8	95 /90	111	104 - 118	78	61 - 88
4 Incomplete Words	Ga	7-6	2.4	84 /90	92	84 - 100	30	14 - 50
5 Visual Closure	Gv	15-3	8.8	97 /90	120	112 - 128	90	79 - 97
6 Picture Vocabulary	Gc	10-4	4.9	94 /90	107	101 - 113	68	53 - 81
7 Analysis-Synthesis	Gf	13-1	8.1	97 /90	118	113 - 123	89	81 - 94
BROAD COGNITIVE ABILITY(Std)		10-4	5.2	94 /90	112	108 - 116	78	70 - 86
ACHIEVEMENT TESTS - STANDARD FORM _A_								
22 Letter-Word Identification		12-0	6.7	99 /90	124	120 - 128	95	91 - 97
23 Passage Comprehension		12-0	6.9	98 /90	122	117 - 127	93	87 - 96
24 Calculation	Gq	10-4	5.0	97 /90	121	116 - 126	92	86 - 96
25 Applied Problems	Gq	11-8	6.3	98 /90	124	119 - 129	94	90 - 97
26 Dictation		8-6	3.1	77 /90	91	86 - 96	27	18 - 39
27 Writing Samples		8-5	3.0	82 /90	94	90 - 98	34	25 - 45
28 Science	Gc	13-4	8.1	99 /90	129	122 - 136	98	93 - 99
29 Social Studies	Gc	10-2	4.8	95 /90	108	101 - 115	71	53 - 84
30 Humanities	Gc	9-2	3.7	89 /90	99	93 - 105	47	32 - 63
BROAD & EARLY DEVELOPMENT CLUSTERS								
BROAD READING		12-2	6.7	99 /90	126	122 - 130	96	93 - 98
BROAD MATHEMATICS		10-8	5.3	98 /90	126	122 - 130	96	93 - 98
BROAD WRITTEN LANGUAGE		8-7	3.2	81 /90	92	89 - 95	92	23 - 37
BROAD KNOWLEDGE		10-6	5.1	96 /90	113	109 - 117	113	73 - 87
SKILLS (E DEV)				/90				

INTRA-ACHIEVEMENT DISCREPANCIES

CLUSTER	Percentile Rank	S D Diff
BROAD READING	95	1.63
BROAD MATHEMATICS	95	1.67
BROAD WRITTEN LANGUAGE	0.1	-3.09
BROAD KNOWLEDGE	50	0.00

Prepared by: David McPhail, Oklahoma City, Oklahoma.

Figure III-5. Thomas's Scores on the WJ-R Cognitive and Achievement Standard Batteries.

Diagnosis: Deficits in auditory processing and visual-auditory association

PSYCHOEDUCATIONAL EVALUATION

Name: Christopher Banes Evaluator:
Birthdate: 11/21/82 Parent: Ms. Helen Banes
Chronological Age: 9-4 School: Highcrest Elementary
Grade Placement: 3.7 Test Dates: 3/20, 3/24/92

Reason for Referral

Chris Banes, a third-grade student at Highcrest Elementary School, was referred for an evaluation by his mother. Ms. Banes stated that although Chris receives special education services, he is still having considerable difficulty in developing both reading and spelling skills. She requested a more extensive evaluation of her son's learning abilities to determine why he is not progressing. In addition, Chris is due for his annual review for special education placement.

Background Information

Chris's mother was first contacted regarding her son's reading problems by his first-grade teacher. At that time he was placed in a special "Chapter 1" reading program. By second grade, Chris was discontinued in the program as he had improved his scores on the Iowa Test of Basic Skills and no longer met the criteria for the program. By mid-second grade, Ms. Banes, concerned by Chris's lack of improvement in reading and spelling, requested a school evaluation. Chris was evaluated by a multidisciplinary team and was determined to be eligible for learning disability services. At the present time, Chris receives special education services on a one-to-one basis, twice weekly for one-half hour in a resource room and twice weekly for one-half hour with a language arts specialist. The Woodcock-Johnson Psycho-Educational Battery—Revised (WJ-R) was administered to obtain further information regarding Chris's processing abilities, present levels of academic performance, and educational needs.

Tests Administered

Chris was administered the Woodcock-Johnson Tests of Cognitive Ability—Revised (Tests 1-14) and the Woodcock-Johnson Tests of Achievement—Revised, Form B (Tests 22-35).

Behavioral Observations

The WJ-R was administered in two sessions, each lasting approximately 2 hours. In the first session, Chris was cooperative and attentive to the tasks. He was quiet and tended to give short responses. In the second session, Chris asked several times when the testing would be over and, in general, seemed to lack persistence. If an answer was not immediately apparent to him, he responded with "I don't know." Upon further prompting, he would often produce the correct response.

Assessment Results

The tests of the WJ-R were scored according to grade norms. When no difference was found between the two component tests of a factor or cluster, only the factor or cluster score is discussed. Standard scores are expressed in 68% confidence bands, written as ±1 standard error of measurement (±1 SEM). A complete set of test scores is appended to this report.

Cognitive Abilities

Chris's overall cognitive performance fell in the *Low Average* to *Average* range (SS ±1 SEM: 86-92). All factor scores fell within the *Average* range except Processing Speed, Auditory Processing, and Long-Term Retrieval. A significant strength was noted in Processing Speed (SS ±1 SEM: 109-121), the ability to perform automatic cognitive tasks quickly. When Processing Speed was compared to his performance on the other six cognitive factors, only 3% of students with a predicted standard score of 90 would obtain an actual standard score of 115 or higher.

In contrast, a significant weakness was noted in Auditory Processing (SS ±1 SEM: 68-78), the ability to synthesize language sounds and patterns. When Auditory Processing was compared to his performance on the other six cognitive factors, only 3% of students with a predicted score of 96 would obtain a standard score of 73 or lower.

Chris's *Low Average* score on the Long-Term Retrieval factor (SS ± 1 SEM: 78–86) suggests a relative weakness in making and retaining associations between symbols or pictures and verbal labels.

Achievement

Chris's performances on the Broad Mathematics (SS ± 1 SEM: 88–96) and Knowledge (SS ± 1 SEM: 87–95) clusters fell within the *Low Average* to *Average* range. In contrast, his performance on the Broad Reading (SS ± 1 SEM: 76–82) and Written Language (SS ± 1 SEM: 74–80) clusters fell in the *Low* range.

Reading

Chris's reading level ranges from mid-first- (easy) to mid-second-grade level (difficult). Weaknesses were noted in identifying sight vocabulary and applying phonic and structural analysis skills. His knowledge of sound–symbol correspondence was extremely low. Chris correctly identified all initial consonant sounds, but had difficulty with medial vowels and ending consonants. When attempting to pronounce words, he either transposed the phonemes, ignored them, or mispronounced the sounds. Specific examples from the Letter-Word Identification test were: "for" for *from*, "ocean" for *once*, "soil" for *social*, and "barge" for *bought*. On several words, Chris commented that he didn't know how to pronounce them. Similar difficulties were observed on the Word Attack test. On several items, Chris added phonemes to the nonsense words. For example, he pronounced *ib* as "ible," *pawk* as "pailk," and *chur* as "chilt."

Written Language

A probable difference existed between Chris's performances in Basic Writing Skills (SS ± 1 SEM: 70–78) and Written Expression (SS ± 1 SEM: 81–89). Error analysis revealed that his performance on the Writing Samples test would have been higher, but several of his responses were deemed undecipherable because of poor spelling. Chris's instructional range for basic writing skills spans beginning first- (easy) to beginning second-grade level (difficult).

Developmentally, Chris's spelling errors were at the semiphonetic to phonetic stage. Error analysis of the Dictation and Writing Samples tests revealed errors consistent with his error patterns in reading.

These included difficulty with consonant blends, final consonants, and medial vowels. Reversals and transpositions were also noted. For example, he wrote *falt* for *flat*, *god* for *dog*, and *doy* for *boy*. Chris did not appear to know that every syllable must contain a vowel. He wrote *skding* for *skating* and *shrpe* for *sharp*. Some of his spellings were characterized by substitutions and insertions: *giley* for *girl* and *geging* for *digging*.

When producing sentences on the Writing Samples test, Chris did not begin sentences with capital letters and was inconsistent with use of ending punctuation. On occasion, he wrote a capital *B* in the middle of a word. When asked why he wrote capital *B*s in the middle of words, Chris responded that he could never remember in which direction the lower-case *b* goes. Two pages from the Writing Samples test are attached to this report to illustrate his performance. (See Figure III-6.)

On the Proofing test, Chris demonstrated good spelling awareness. He correctly identified several misspelled words but did not know how to correct them.

Mathematics

Chris's performance on both the Basic Mathematics (SS ± 1 SEM: 90–98) and Mathematics Reasoning (SS ± 1 SEM: 88–98) clusters fell within the *Average* range. He commented that math was his favorite subject in school. Presently, Chris has not memorized his multiplication facts and was unable to produce the correct solutions to simple problems, such as 3×3. He did, however, successfully use a counting strategy on the Applied Problems test to solve problems. For example, to multiply 20×12, he listed twelve 20s and then added them. Although Chris appears to understand the concept of multiplication, his classroom performance will be affected when time is a factor or when computation involves larger numbers.

Knowledge

Chris's performance on the Knowledge cluster fell within the *Average* range (SS ± 1 SEM: 87–95). His highest performance was on the Social Studies test (SS ± 1 SEM: 94–108).

Summary

Chris is a third-grade student with a significant weakness in auditory processing and a relative weakness in forming and retrieving visual-auditory associations. Presumably, these weaknesses have interfered with his ability to learn sound–symbol associations, blend sounds into words for reading, and analyze words into sounds for spelling.

Recommendations

General

1. Given the difficulty that Chris is having in memorizing math facts, learning letter orientation, and recalling the spelling of common words, the possibility of a weakness in visual memory should be investigated in diagnostic teaching.

2. Chris should continue receiving one-to-one instruction. The learning disabilities teacher and the language arts teacher should ensure that they are using the same methods and mutually reinforcing the skills presented in each program. After a 3-month period, evaluate Chris's progress.

3. All materials in Chris's classroom should be matched to his present performance levels.

Basic Reading Skills

1. Provide Chris with instructional materials at the beginning second-grade level.

2. Provide Chris with explicit instruction in basic word recognition and word attack skills. Administer an informal phonics inventory to determine exactly which sounds Chris knows and which ones he needs to learn. Use an analytic phonics approach, such as word families, rather than a synthetic approach.

3. Teach Chris how to blend a series of sounds together to pronounce a word.

4. Build upon Chris's reading skills by providing him with high-interest reading materials at his independent reading level (mid-first grade).

Basic Writing Skills

1. Provide Chris with instructional materials at a mid-first-grade level.

2. In the classroom, do not penalize Chris for poor spelling on rough drafts or when taking in-class tests, such as in Social Studies. If Chris's written responses are undecipherable, ask him to tell you the answers orally and grade him accordingly. Help Chris discover the need for correct spelling and punctuation in communicating ideas. When evaluating his first drafts, emphasize his ideas. Provide assistance with correcting spelling errors on his final draft.

3. Teach Chris how to use a spelling study strategy that emphasizes pronouncing a word while writing the sounds. Focus on consonants, consonant blends and digraphs, and vowel sound–symbol associations. Encourage Chris to listen carefully to the sequence of sounds when spelling words.

4. Have Chris develop an individualized spelling list where he selects misspelled words from his writing to study. Have him practice and be tested on a few words daily instead of having a weekly spelling test. Provide frequent review.

5. When Chris is studying spelling lists, use a color-coding system to differentiate among words with regular sound–symbol correspondence, such as the word *cat* (highlight in green), words with semiregular patterns, such as the word *night* (highlight in yellow), and words with irregular spelling patterns, such as the word *once* (highlight in red). For studying red-flag words, teach Chris how to use a visually based spelling strategy, such as Look, Spell, See, Write. An outline of this technique is attached.

6. Review basic capitalization and punctuation rules with Chris. Provide him with an index card to use when editing that reminds him to check that each sentence begins with a capital letter and has appropriate ending punctuation.

Mathematics

1. To improve performance in basic math skills, develop a program to help Chris memorize his multiplication facts. Begin by identifying the facts Chris already knows and those he needs to learn. Chart his progress so that Chris is able to see exactly which facts he has learned and which facts are left.

2. Teach Chris how to use any of the multiplication facts that he knows to figure out those that he does not. For example, if he does not know 6×7, he may think $6 \times 6 + 6$.

3. Do not let performance in basic math skills inhibit progress in problem solving and application. Allow Chris to use a calculator or multiplication facts table as long as necessary.

TEST 27

Writing Samples (cont.)

6.

this is a dog skding.

7.

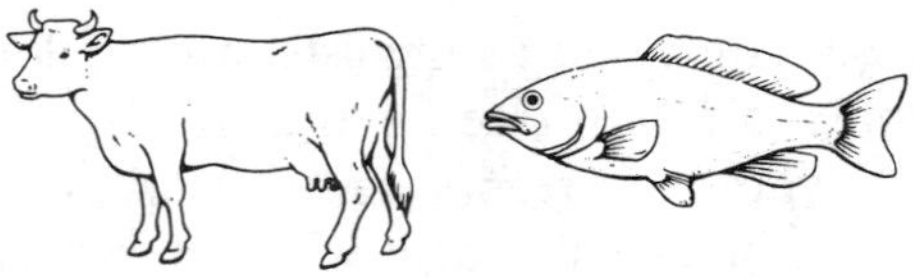

this is a fihe

8.

this giloy is sweeging

9.

under the bed

he is looking of is shoos under the bed

10.

the god is geging a how.

(continued)

Figure III–6. Examples of Chris's Responses on the Writing Samples Test.

TEST 27

Writing Samples (cont.)

11.

the Ball is in the Box.

12.

the tire is falt.

13.

but

the sead But wate

14.

go to my dab, play footBall and wache TV.

15.

(1) They drove off in Elaine's truck.   (2) thay got in the truck and drove off.

(3) "We're being followed," Jeff said.

Figure III-6. *(continued)*

Diagnosis: Educable mentally handicapped

PSYCHOEDUCATIONAL EVALUATION

Name: Tanya Lewis
Birthdate: 2/7/81

Evaluator:
Parents: Abel &
Letitia Lewis

Chronological Age: 9-9

School: Borgstrom
Elementary

Grade: 4.3

Test date: 12/2,
12/5/91

Reason for Referral

Tanya was referred for evaluation to determine eligibility for special education and to identify appropriate educational services. She recently transferred to Holton Unified School District from Phoenix where she had been receiving services for the Educable Mentally Handicapped.

Background Information and Previous Test Results

See H.U.S.D. files and social worker's current report.

Tests Administered

Woodcock-Johnson Psycho-Educational Battery—
Revised (WJ-R):
Cognitive Battery: Tests 1–14
Achievement Battery (Form A): Tests 22–30
Developmental Test of Visual-Motor Integration—
Revised (VMI-R)

Behavioral Observations

Tanya, a Caucasian girl, was friendly and enthusiastic. She appeared to enjoy the evaluation. On the majority of the cognitive tests, she appeared confident of her responses, and commented several times, "I'm doing good, huh?" On the achievement tests, she seemed more aware of her limitations and was somewhat distractible. On visual sequential tasks, such as Visual-Auditory Learning, she lost her place unless the examiner pointed to the items.

Test Results

The tests of the WJ-R were scored according to age norms. When no difference was found between the two component tests of a factor or cluster, only the factor or cluster score is discussed. Tanya's performance is expressed as verbal labels for the Standard Score 68% confidence bands. A complete set of test scores is appended to this report.

Cognitive Abilities

On the Tests of Cognitive Ability, Tanya's overall score is in the *Very Low* range. Her percentile score indicates that she scored lower in overall cognitive abilities than 999 of 1,000 children her age (PR: 0.1). Significant scatter of both factor and individual test scores indicates strengths and weaknesses among her cognitive abilities.

Tanya demonstrated significant strengths on the Visual Processing and Long-Term Retrieval factors. On the Visual Processing factor, Tanya's higher score in Visual Closure (*Average* range) suggests good ability to perceive patterns in pictorial visual stimuli. Tanya's relative strength in Long-Term Retrieval (*Low/Low Average* range) indicates ability to store and retrieve visual-verbal associations.

Tanya's other cognitive factor scores are in the *Very Low* range, indicating severe difficulty with immediate recall of verbal information, recognizing patterns in auditory stimuli, scanning and noting critical details in visual stimuli, learning and retaining vocabulary, and abstract reasoning.

Academic Achievement

On the Tests of Achievement, Tanya scored in the *Very Low* range in all academic skills and in the *Low* range in general knowledge of factual information. On the reading tests, Tanya correctly identified all of the letters presented and could read some of the simpler words. She demonstrated good knowledge of initial consonant sounds. In the comprehension test, she tried to sound out almost every word, apparently without any attempt to use context clues.

Even within the *Very Low* range, Tanya was significantly weaker in written language and mathematics than in reading. In written language, Tanya attempted to spell words from their initial sounds only, then appeared to put down letters randomly. In math, Tanya used her fingers for all computation problems. She was only able to solve addition problems with sums of 10 or less. In math application, she could only solve concrete problems requiring no mental calculation. For example, in beginning addition problems, Tanya could not count in objects that were not pictured. She did not know coin values and could not tell time to the hour.

No error patterns were noted within her knowledge of content area information.

The VMI-R was administered to assess her visual-motor integration. Her standard score of 64 is indicative of significant problems in this skill. Her drawings were executed impulsively with numerous distortions. Additionally, when writing, she demonstrated weak pencil control.

When Tanya's aptitude and achievement, as measured by the WJ-R, are compared in the four academic areas assessed, her achievement in written language and mathematics is significantly below her predicted scores.

Summary

Tanya's overall cognitive abilities are in the *Very Low* range compared to her age-peers. She has relative strengths in recalling visual-verbal associations and in visual closure. All other cognitive areas were below 99.9% of children her age. In general, Tanya's performance improves when tasks are presented in a concrete manner, with pictures and, presumably, with manipulatives. She has considerable difficulty with making inferences and with abstract thinking. Tanya's visual-motor skills are also significantly weak. All academic skills are in the *Very Low* range, except for general knowledge, which is in the *Low* range.

This information will be integrated with the findings of the speech/language pathologist, psychologist, and social worker at the multidisciplinary conference. Recommendations for educational placement and remediation will be made at that time.

Diagnosis: Deficits in auditory processing, visual-spatial perception, visual memory, simultaneous visual-auditory reception, and visual-motor integration; Attention Deficit Disorder

PSYCHOEDUCATIONAL EVALUATION

Name: Jesse Weiss
Birthdate: 10/9/81

Chronological Age: 9-11

Grade: 3.9

Evaluator:
Parents: Aaron and Martha Weiss
School: Clear Springs Elementary
Test Dates: 9/11, 9/12, 9/13, 9/14/91

Reason for Referral

Jesse's third-grade teacher, Mr. Nielson, referred Jesse for a psychoeducational evaluation because his classroom work is not commensurate with his effort or apparent ability level. Mr. Nielson reports that Jesse has been unable to memorize arithmetic facts, becomes frustrated with written work, and usually forgets instructions. He often confuses right and left and is slow in copying from the board. Mr. Nielson inquired about the possibility of learning disabilities and Attention Deficit Disorder.

Background Information

Mrs. Weiss reported that Jesse reached most developmental milestones within normal limits, but was advanced in language development and somewhat delayed in fine-motor skills. He had recurrent ear infections.

Jesse was placed in a learning disabilities resource program at the end of grade 1 for help with listening, sight-word retention, and handwriting. His Performance scale score on the WISC-R was almost 3 standard deviations below his Verbal scale of 120. The scatter of subtest scores displayed a profile that is sometimes associated with problems in attention and concentration. By the end of grade 2, Jesse had caught up with the slowest reading group in his class and was dropped from the learning disabilities program.

Presently, Jesse is completing third grade. He has maintained average grades throughout most of the year. Mr. Nielson has a highly interactive teaching style; he uses cooperative learning and creative activities, such as having the students write and produce a puppet show related to a history unit. Mr. Nielson noted that Jesse has difficulty paying attention when he has to listen to direct instruction rather than participate in a group activity and that he has a great deal of difficulty retaining instructions. He appears to "drift off" during independent seatwork, but spontaneously "wakes up."

Mrs. Weiss reported that Jesse is quite distractible and disorganized at home, especially when getting ready for school and during homework; he needs much help and supervision. Both parents and Mr. Nielson see Jesse as having strong language ability and being skillful in entertaining others.

Mr. Nielson also noted that although Jesse is well-liked and has a good sense of humor, he does not appear to read social situations well and has a tendency to get into arguments with peers.

Previous and Concurrent Evaluations

Jesse's hearing was tested at school and found to be within normal limits.

Dr. Kate Forrester, ophthalmologist, evaluated Jesse's visual functioning in May 1991. She found that Jesse has mild difficulty sustaining visual focus at near point with a tendency to turn one or the other eye in. He also has mild difficulty converging the images of both eyes into one clear image and efficiently moving his eyes along a line of print. Dr. Forrester prescribed glasses. Jesse stated that the glasses make reading somewhat easier and that reading no longer gives him headaches.

As part of the current evaluation, the WISC-R was also administered. Again, results indicated a 2+ standard deviation split with *High Average* verbal abilities and *Low Average* visual, nonverbal abilities. The profile was almost exactly the same as the previous one. Again, directional confusion and a high level of impulsivity were noted.

Based on Jesse's behavioral history and WISC-R profile, it was suggested that the Weisses consult a developmental pediatrician. Dr. Gabriel Dalby diagnosed Attention Deficit Disorder as a contributing factor to Jesse's difficulties at school and home but did not think that medication was warranted at this time.

During a classroom observation, Jesse was on task 65% of the time while writing a short story and 90% while making a pattern for a patchwork quilt by tracing around geometric forms. It was noted that Jesse's handwriting was immature and that he was unable to trace around the forms on a piece of paper.

Tests Administered

Wechsler Intelligence Scale for Children — Revised (WISC-R)
Woodcock-Johnson Psycho-Educational Battery — Revised (WJ-R):
    Cognitive Battery: Tests 1–14, 17, 19–21
    Achievement Battery (Form A): Tests 22–31, 34–35
Developmental Test of Visual-Motor Integration - Revised (VMI-R)
Slingerland Screening Tests for Children with Language Disabilities: Subtest #4 Form C
Analytical Reading Inventory (ARI)
Brigance Diagnostic Comprehensive Inventory of Basic Skills: Map skills, oral and written syllabication
Taped language sample

Behavioral Observations

Jesse was consistently cooperative during testing. Rapport was easily established and he was eager to earn as many stickers as possible for completing tests.

On cognitive tests, Jesse was not obviously impulsive but did not self-monitor. When asked about his attention, he stated, "Sometimes I think about other things." During the academic tasks, however, Jesse obviously rushed, making numerous errors. During the informal reading inventory, he read exceedingly quickly. Although he was reminded to slow down twice, he was unable to maintain a slower pace.

Test Results

The tests of the WJ-R were scored according to grade norms. When no difference was found between the two component tests of a factor or cluster, only the factor or cluster score is discussed. Verbal labels have been used to express standard score 68% confidence bands. A complete set of test scores is appended to this report.

Cognitive Abilities

According to the results of the WJ-R Broad Cognitive Ability and the WISC-R Full Scale, Jesse is functioning within the *Average* range of cognitive abilities. As the WISC-R scale scores were significantly discrepant from each other, the Full Scale score is not a valid predictor of general cognitive ability or scholastic performance. On the WJ-R all scores were closer to the *Average* range. Due to Jesse's impulsivity and inattention during testing, many of his scores may underestimate his cognitive abilities.

Visual-Spatial Orientation

Formal and informal test results indicate that Jesse does not have a strong directional-spatial sense. He was slow in showing right and left on himself and was unable to consistently tell right and left on the examiner. Directional confusion was also noted on the WISC-R as he twice tried to arrange a sequence of pictures from right to left.

On the Brigance, Jesse was able to find places on a simplified map, but misjudged distances and had difficulty judging his direction given a starting point and destination. On another informal test, he had considerable difficulty identifying reversed letters/numbers and finding the reversed word in a sentence. When asked to check his work, he identified about half of his correct responses as incorrect and about half of his incorrect responses as correct.

Visual Processing Speed/Discrimination

Scores on tests of rapid processing of visual symbols and ability to note visual detail in pictures were all in the *Average* range. On both tests of the WJ-R Processing Speed factor, Jesse was exceedingly tense and broke his pencil point within the first 30 seconds. On the Slingerland test, when asked to choose one among four graphically similar words to match a target word, he made three errors, but self-corrected two. Patterns indicating discrimination problems were not evident in Jesse's oral reading. It appears that Jesse might be outgrowing weaknesses in visual discrimination and rapid visual processing of symbols; strong indications of current problems in these areas were not evident.

Visual-Motor Integration

Jesse is right-handed and uses a normal pencil grip. His handwriting and drawing indicate serious deficits in his ability to coordinate the movements of his hand with a mental image. His performance on the VMI-R placed him between the *Low* and *Very Low* ranges when compared to his age-peers. His method of copying the forms indicated lack of spatial planning and self-monitoring in that he spent little time looking at a form before attempting to draw it, made errors indicating that he could not adequately plan where to direct his pencil, and did not appear to notice that his forms were considerably different from the target forms. His poor performance on Coding (WISC-R) may also be due to slow visual-motor coordination and/or deficiencies in binocular coordination.

Visual Memory

Informal test results indicate a deficiency in visual recall for letters and numbers. Jesse was unable to recall the left-right orientation of many letters/numbers and still reverses *b/d* and *p/q* in his writing. His phonetic spelling indicates that he relies on auditory analysis rather than visual memory. His use of different spellings for the same word within one written passage also supports the hypothesis of difficulty recalling visual images of words. Jesse's *Low/Low Average* performance on the WISC-R Coding subtest also adds support to this hypothesis, as success on this test requires the ability to learn and revisualize symbols rapidly.

Auditory Processing

Jesse's auditory processing abilities at the sound and word level appear strong for analysis and deficient for synthesis. In informal assessment, he was easily able to count the syllables in one- to five-syllable words and say the syllables separately. His spelling indicates the ability to analyze a word sequentially into its component sounds.

In contrast, Jesse scored in the *Low* range in blending sounds and syllables together to come up with a familiar word, with and without sounds omitted. The only significant WJ-R intracognitive discrepancy was found in Auditory Processing. Only 2% of Jesse's grade-peers with a predicted standard score of 102 would obtain a score as low as or lower than 77.

Short-Term Memory and Long-Term Retrieval

Jesse scored within the *Average* range on the WJ-R Short-Term Memory factor. The Relative Mastery Indexes (RMI) indicate that on tasks such as repeating sentences of increasing length and complexity, Jesse's accuracy would be *Average* compared to his grade-peers'; however, on tasks such as repeating pieces of information that are not inherently meaningful (e.g., unrelated words, numbers), Jesse's accuracy would be *Limited*. It appears that the context of language aids Jesse in auditory memory.

Jesse also scored in the *Average* range on tasks requiring him to associate verbal with visual information, retaining and using it over a period of approximately 5 minutes.

Average performance on tests of sentence memory and long-term retrieval suggests that the problem with Jesse's forgetting instructions in class may be attentionally related rather than due to a memory deficit. This is reinforced by Mr. Nielson's observation that when Jesse has "forgotten" recent instructions, he can often recall them when questioned.

Simultaneous Auditory-Visual Reception

Jesse's behavior on the WJ-R Fluid Reasoning tests and the Visual-Auditory Learning test suggests that Jesse has difficulty processing information when verbal instructions or explanations are paired with a visual stimulus. While listening to the instructions for these tests, rather than looking at the test easel, he either looked at the examiner or into space. When directed to look, or when the evaluator stopped talking, he quickly glanced at the easel and away again. When asked why he did this, he said it made it easier to understand the instructions. Although Jesse scored in the *Average* to *High Average* range on these tests, he appeared to learn the tasks by doing them. Later, Mrs. Weiss noted similar behavior at home when she has explained diagrams in a book, discussed the use of a kitchen appliance, or read Jesse stories accompanied by pictures. This difficulty processing auditory and visual information simultaneously may impede Jesse's ability to process information adequately in school. An example might be a lecture, accompanied by a poster, on the functions of parts of a plant.

Oral Language

According to formal and informal tests, Jesse's understanding and use of oral language is strong. His scores on vocabulary tests (WJ-R, WISC-R) varied from the *Average* to *High Average* ranges. On the Analytical Reading Inventory, in graded passages read to him, he could define words and infer word meanings from context up to the grade 6 passage. At this level also, Jesse was able to respond accurately to detail and inference questions. This performance suggests that he should be able to understand information presented in language appropriate for grade 6 in an instructional setting; barring decoding difficulties, he should be able to comprehend grade 6 reading material.

After listening to the graded passages, Jesse had difficulty above the grade 2 level with retellings, organizing the information and providing sufficient detail, although he was able to express the main idea. Thus, it appears that Jesse may have difficulty recalling, organizing, and expressing ideas and details that he has just heard. These skills are important for summarizing lectures and text, taking notes, and writing reports. Both Mrs. Weiss and Mr. Nielson have stated that Jesse has difficulty organizing information for report writing. As with his difficulty following instructions, this may be attentionally related.

Jesse's taped language samples included a story and a movie retelling. In contrast to retelling orally presented information, his movie retellings displayed good organization of ideas and details, including orienting/introductory statements and conclusions. His narrative was of at least appropriate length and was imaginative. It had the quality of a legend and included subplots and the resolution of three inter-related problems. His characters were well-introduced and their relationship was clear. Jesse's sentence structure was at least age-appropriate and included complex sentences with relative and subordinate clauses.

Reasoning/Problem Solving

On the WJ-R Fluid Reasoning tests, Jesse scored in the *Average* to *High Average* range when using visual information and verbal instructions to solve novel puzzles. The first task involves solving algebraic-like equations using colored squares; the second task involves generating a rule that correctly accounts for the separation of two sets of forms. Both tasks require logical and categorical thinking. Jesse had great difficulty understanding the verbal instructions when they were initially presented and focused on the visual stimuli only in brief

glances. Between sets of instructions, given feedback on his correct and incorrect responses, he appeared to learn the tasks by doing them. If Jesse's understanding of the instructions was compromised by his attempt to avoid visual-auditory overloading, it is possible that his reasoning ability is underestimated on these tests.

It appears that attentional factors such as impulsivity, inability to process certain kinds of visual and auditory information simultaneously, and possibly fatigue interfere with Jesse's logical thinking process and ability to learn problem-solving techniques. Thus, his performance on these tests may underestimate his inherent reasoning ability, but probably reflects his current functioning level.

Academic Achievement

Reading

Test Results. Based on the results of the WJ-R Broad Reading cluster, Jesse's overall reading ability borders the *Low Average* to *Average* range. His scores were similar on the WJ-R tests of Word Attack (using phonics and structural analysis to sound out unfamiliar words), Letter-Word Identification (naming letters and pronouncing words), and Passage Comprehension (reading one- to two-sentence passages and identifying the missing word). His performance levels on the Analytical Reading Inventory (ARI) were similar.

Patterns/Behaviors. Analysis of error patterns indicates that Jesse is a "whole word guesser." He depends on his sight vocabulary, guessing from the gestalt of a word and making minimal use of phonic clues and structural analysis. Extension testing suggests that this strategy is based on habit and impulsivity. On a list of grade 3 sight words, Jesse improved from 60% to 90% when prompted to look at the words carefully. Given a list of 26 one- to three-syllable words, he divided 24 into reasonable syllables and pronounced 23 correctly. His performance is affected, however, by his limited knowledge of phonics, especially vowel digraphs and diphthongs, r-controlled vowels, and long vowel patterns. Based on his Relative Mastery Index (RMI), Jesse's accuracy with word attack skills would be approximately 58% compared to his grade-peers' 90%, indicating *Limited* mastery.

Jesse rushes when reading and is unable to maintain a reasonably slow pace even with much reminding. He does little self-monitoring, often misreads punctuation, and makes word substitutions that make little sense within the context. Twice he skipped a whole line without noticing it.

Jesse's RMI on the Passage Comprehension test was 75/90, at the lower limits of the *Average* range. On the ARI, Jesse scored at the grade 3 instructional level when responding to questions regarding the passages, but as with the listening comprehension task, he had considerable difficulty retelling the passages without guidance. His retelling indicated poor unaided recall and misinterpretation of details. Jesse's comprehension errors consistently appeared to be related to decoding errors.

The WJ-R Age/Grade Profile indicates that appropriate instructional materials for teaching Jesse word attack skills would be early grade 2, and for sight vocabulary and reading comprehension, early grade 3.

Written Language

Jesse's ability to express his ideas in writing borders the *Low Average* and *Average* ranges; basic writing skills vary from *Low Average* to *Average*. Findings are based on the results of the WJ-R Written Language tests and a variety of school writing samples.

Basic Skills. When printing, Jesse's visual-motor and spatial planning problems appear to interfere with his ability to form letters accurately and neatly, stay on the line, and keep appropriate spacing between letters and words. Jesse noted that his hand gets tired and he cannot make his letters neat, even when he writes slowly. For most people, writing is an automatic skill, requiring no conscious energy. For Jesse, however, the very act of putting letters on paper is difficult. He broke his pencil point two or three times on each of the writing tests.

Based on his score in the *Average* range on the WJ-R Proofing test, Jesse appears familiar with capitalization and punctuation rules. He often does not use them, however, possibly due to his attentional problems as well as the extra effort required in the act of writing.

Reflecting his poor visual recall, Jesse's written spelling is phonetic and inconsistent, even when spelling common words (e.g., *apel/apple*). On the Proofing test, he did not identify any of the spelling errors; on the Dictation test, the majority of his errors

were in spelling. When Jesse proofreads, he looks only for spelling errors but does not recognize them.

Written Expression. Jesse uses age-appropriate vocabulary and adequately complex sentence structure in his writing. His stories were well-organized with a clear introduction and setting, sequential events, and, in the one story that was finished, a well-constructed ending. His writing fluency was in the *Average* range. He appears to have no difficulty generating ideas. A sample of Jesse's writing is attached. (See Figure III-7.)

Arithmetic

Computation. Jesse's performance on the Calculation test was in the *Low Average* range, significantly below his *High Average* score on Applied Problems. It appeared that his computation errors were due to impulsivity and perseveration as well as lack of skill. He used the wrong operation on three problems because he did not notice the change in sign from previous problems. He changed from subtraction to addition in the middle of one problem. He frequently added in multiplication problems. He knows only the multiplication tables from 0 to 2, could not multiply two digits by one digit, and was unable to do the simplest division problem. He worked rapidly and did not check his answers.

Application. Jesse scored in the *High Average* range in Applied Problems. He was able to count money, read an analog clock to the hour, and read a thermometer. He could interpret and solve one-step, but not two-step, addition and subtraction problems. He appropriately ignored extraneous information. He had difficulty setting up multiplication problems and was unable to interpret a division problem. He did not use pencil and paper, but performed calculations mentally.

General Knowledge

Based on the knowledge and information tests of the WJ-R and WISC-R, Jesse appears to be functioning in the *Average* range. He demonstrated a relative strength in science knowledge.

Summary

Cognitive Abilities

Two cognitive batteries indicated global intellectual functioning in the *Average* range. On both tests,

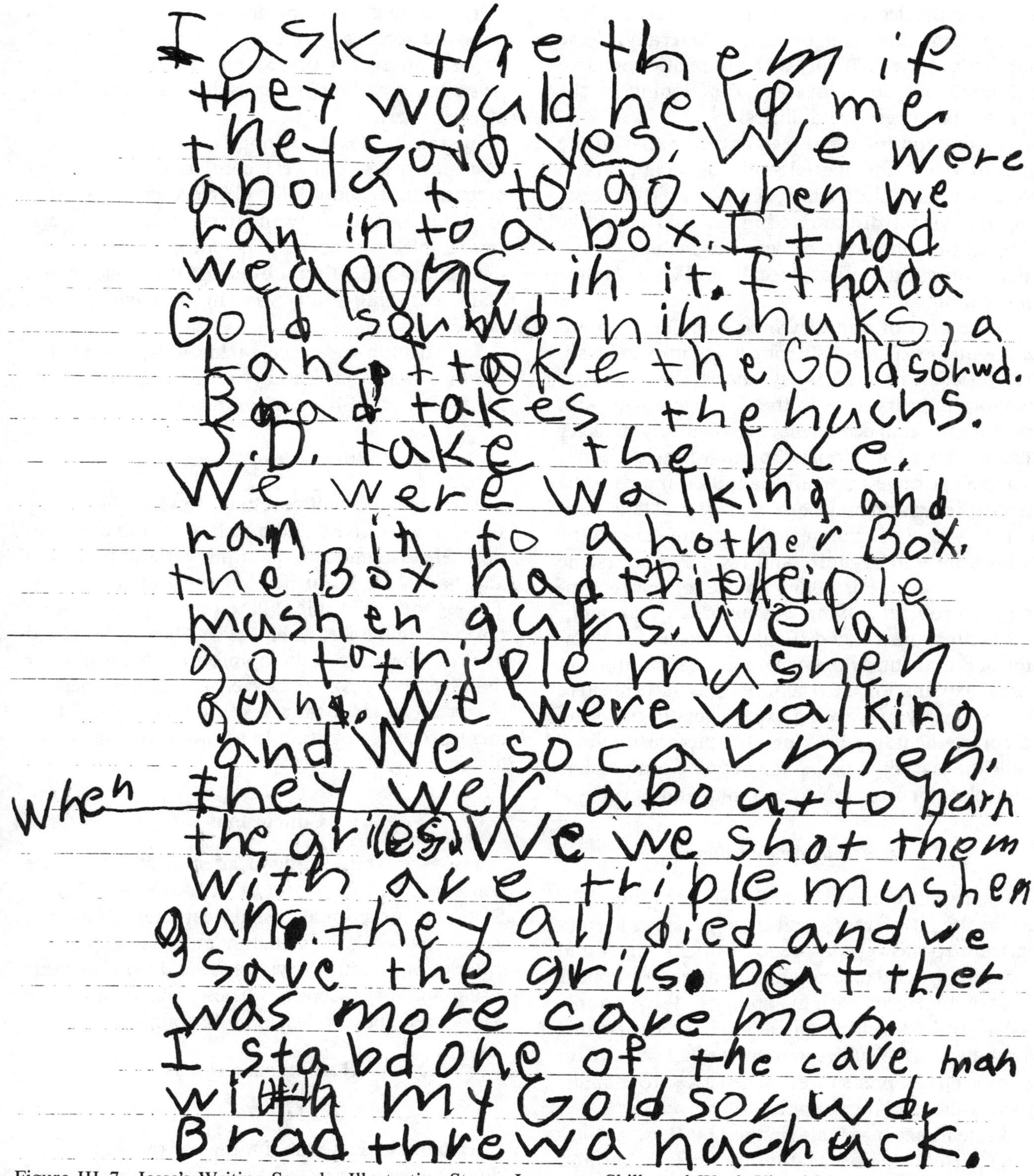

I ask the them if
they would help me
they said yes. We were
about to go when we
ran into a box. I thad
weapons in it. it had a
Gold sowwd ninchuks, a
fanct it oke the Gold sorwd.
Brad takes the huchs.
J.D. take the fae.
We were walking and
ran in to a hother Box.
the Box had triple triple
mushen guns. We all
go to triple mushen
guns. We were walking
and We so cavmen.
When they wer abou to barn
the griles. We we shot them
with are triple mushen
guns. they all died and we
save the grils. but ther
was more cave man.
I stabd one of the cave man
with my Gold sorwd.
Brad threw a nuchack.

Figure III-7. Jesse's Writing Sample, Illustrating Strong Language Skills and Weak Visual-Motor and Visual Recall Skills.

significant strengths and weaknesses were noted, as well as the detrimental effects of impulsivity and intermittent attention to task. Generally, Jesse appears to have difficulty with automatic cognitive processes but above-average functioning in the higher-level cognitive abilities.

Formal and informal tests indicate that in the area of visual and spatial skills, Jesse appears to have adequate ability in speed of visual processing and visual discrimination. Visual cognitive abilities that appear to be deficient include visual-spatial orientation, visual recall, and visual-motor integration.

In the area of auditory processing at the word and sound level, Jesse is strong in auditory analysis, but deficient in auditory synthesis. His auditory memory appears to be in the *Average* range, with memory for connected language relatively stronger than memory for unrelated pieces of information.

Jesse's strongest cognitive abilities appear to be in comprehension and expression of oral language. The only area of relative difficulty appeared to be in his ability to organize and restate discourse he had just heard. His ability to use logical reasoning for problem solving was an area of strength.

Jesse demonstrated difficulty focusing his attention simultaneously on visual pictorial stimuli and verbal explanation/instruction. This may interfere with a variety of learning experiences in the years to come, including looking at a picture/diagram while the teacher is explaining how the components interrelate or learning to use maps and graphs.

Academic Achievement

Test results indicate that all Jesse's reading skills border the *Low Average* and *Average* ranges in comparison to his grade-peers. Deficits in sound blending, in visual recall, and in attention appear to have interfered with his ability to learn phonic skills and develop an adequate sight-word vocabulary. Difficulties in basic reading skills affect his reading comprehension. When asked to examine a word closely, his decoding improves.

Written Language is also in the *Low/Low Average* range. Deficits in visual-motor integration and spatial planning appear to contribute to poorly formed letters and result in labored handwriting. The extra effort that goes into the act of writing appears to detract from Jesse's use of the basic

writing skills with which he is familiar. His difficulty retaining visual images of words results in his phonetic spelling. On the WJ-R, Jesse's Written Expression scores placed him in the *Low/Low Average* range, but stories written at school were at least average.

In math, Jesse demonstrates a significant discrepancy between weak computation and strong practical application skills. Careless errors appeared to be due to impulsivity and perseveration although Jesse also clearly lacks grade-appropriate arithmetic facts and skills. His math-related information and math reasoning ability were in the *High Average* range.

Jesse demonstrates general knowledge within the *Average* range, indicating that he is acquiring information from his environment.

Behaviors of Concern

Throughout cognitive testing, Jesse showed subtle signs of impulsivity and a lack of sustained attention. He responded to questions without reflection and had a casual attitude toward certain tasks. Throughout academic skill testing, Jesse was more obviously impulsive, rushing even when he was asked to slow down. It is the opinion of this evaluator that these behaviors negatively affected his performance on many of the tasks throughout the assessment process, resulting in an underestimation of his abilities.

Conclusions

Jesse's cognitive and academic strengths are depressed by the effects of his Attention Deficit Disorder. Additionally, significant deficits exist in visual-spatial skills, visual memory, visual-motor integration, auditory synthesis, and simultaneous visual-auditory reception. These deficits should be considered specific learning disabilities.

Recommendations

General

1. Explain to Jesse the findings of this report, including what is going to be done to help him. Begin by discussing his strengths.

2. Given Jesse's high level of impulsivity on the academic portions of this assessment battery and

difficulty retaining instructions in the classroom, closely follow his behavior and academic progress for the first month of the coming school year. If problems continue to exist, consult Dr. Dalby about a trial of medication.

3. Remind Jesse to use his glasses for reading and other near-point work.

4. Consistently praise Jesse (and other students) for sincere effort rather than just accomplishment. This will ensure continued effort resulting in accomplishment.

5. Meet with Jesse's teacher before the beginning of the school year to share the results of this evaluation. Provide the teacher with reading material explaining ADD. Also, make sure that the teacher understands Jesse's difficulty taking in information auditorily and visually at the same time.

Behavioral

Attached are suggestions for teaching the child with attentional and behavioral problems in the classroom. Please view these suggestions as a menu from which to choose one or two strategies as appropriate. Target reducing impulsivity and increasing reflectivity as priorities.

Simultaneous Visual-Auditory Integration

1. Minimize Jesse's difficulty when explaining pictorial or graphic material. Give short chunks of information with pauses in between to allow Jesse a chance to look at the visual stimuli.

2. Improve simultaneous reception of information by providing a structured program.
    a. Make Jesse aware of the purpose of this instruction.
    b. Begin with simple auditory instructions and pictorial information. Start with 30 seconds of information and gradually increase until Jesse can handle 5 minutes of instruction.
    c. When Jesse can sustain both visual and auditory attention for 5 minutes, begin to raise the level of complexity of the oral instructions and then to increase the complexity of the visual stimuli. Do not increase the complexity of both simultaneously.
    d. Be aware that spatially oriented instructions may pose an added difficulty for Jesse.

3. Obtain feedback from the classroom teacher as to Jesse's application of these skills in classroom work.

Reading Decoding

Context Clues

Reinforce Jesse for using context clues to help him identify unfamiliar words. Capitalize on this strategy while teaching other methods of word recognition.

Phonics and Structural Analysis

1. Teach the phonic elements that Jesse is missing, particularly the vowel digraphs and diphthongs, r-controlled vowels, and when to use the long sound of a vowel. Also teach common prefixes and suffixes.

2. Teach new patterns using Jesse's own reading vocabulary as a basis for introducing phonic patterns, word families, and common word parts (boat → float). Provide for overlearning.

3. Try placing each phonic element inside a picture that will cue the sound. Examples are oa in the hull of a boat, aw with the w incorporated into a saw blade. These can be made into flash cards.

4. If Jesse still has difficulty learning the association between phonic elements and symbols, include saying the sound while tracing or writing in sand, possibly with eyes closed.

5. Provide practice in recognizing each phonic element or word part in passages.

6. Reinforce Jesse for his current ability to structurally analyze words. Teach him to recognize consistently the more common word patterns. To help him pronounce words, have him make pencil slashes between word parts, first in words in lists, then in sentences, and finally in passages, combining the meaning of the sentence with seeing the word in parts. Reinforce how accuracy in word identification provides more meaning than guessing at words.

Directional Errors

Use stories to remind Jesse which way b, d, p, and q face. For example, a b looks like a bat and ball, but the bat has to come first. If you want to play baseball, *first* you have to have a bat.

Reading Comprehension

1. Teach Jesse to slow down and monitor his reading for meaning. You might set up a system in which he earns a reward if every word in his reading makes sense in the context, even if it is incorrect. The reinforcement could be increased if Jesse stops to sound out a difficult word.

2. Teach Jesse to restate the main idea of a well-structured paragraph and then to give related details. Increase the amount of text and level of content as appropriate.

3. In order to aid Jesse's comprehension of oral and written stories, teach him the framework (story grammar) that most stories share. Thus, Jesse can look for and identify common components, providing organization of ideas and details for himself. Two techniques are STORE the Story and answering a set of story questions. (See attached material for descriptions of these techniques.)

4. Set up activities that will encourage Jesse to read for meaning, interactively, attempting to recall prior knowledge, predicting what will happen, and making judgments about the accuracy of his prediction as he reads. Some such activities are the Directed Reading–Thinking Activity or study guides to prompt Jesse to think and question at certain preselected points as he reads.

5. Teach Jesse how to organize the content of non-fiction reading materials through the use of semantic maps (webbing). The same skill will be useful for writing reports and compositions.

Written Language

Format

1. Demonstrate to Jesse how a paper looks when it is well-organized so he can see the result of using margins, indenting, and correctly placing information.

2. Use paper with margins on both sides or help Jesse draw highly noticeable margins. Use paper with a clear middle guideline and have Jesse write every other line.

Handwriting

1. Reteach D'Nealian cursive writing. Cursive writing minimizes spatial and directional confusion.

a. Although Jesse has already learned how to make the letters, provide specific instruction in the formation as well as the direction of each stroke. Observe him while he practices to ensure correct letter formation.

b. Teach letters with similar formations in groups, such as the loop letters above the line, the hump letters, or the fishhook letters that have their bottoms in the water.

c. Directly teach Jesse how to connect one letter to another fluently, adapting for the different types of connecting strokes (e.g., *a* - tail on the ground, *b* - bridge).

d. Teach handwriting first out of context, then in words, then in dictation. When writing appears to be automatic and fluent, have Jesse write from his own taped dictation of a story.

Computer Skills

1. Provide a touch-typing program for Jesse to use with his home computer.

2. Make sure Jesse learns the word processing system (with a spelling checker program) for his home computer so that he can edit ideas easily. Whenever feasible, allow Jesse to use a computer for writing reports and compositions.

3. Provide Jesse with a pocket-sized, computerized speller. When he enters a phonetic spelling of a word, the correct spelling will appear.

Spelling

1. Do not make spelling a concern within the writing process. Make it part of editing so that spelling does not interfere with expression.

2. Choose spelling words from lists such as those that are attached to this report. One is composed of words most used in students' writing; the other has words most often misspelled.

3. Have Jesse select some of his spelling words from the list or from his writing.

4. Provide two to three new spelling words a day, with continuous reinforcement, rather than one long list at the beginning of the week.

5. Teach Jesse to color-code words by type: Green-flag words are spelled as they sound; yellow-flag words can be spelled more than one way; red-flag words are irregular.

6. Teach Jesse only the most common spelling rules, such as "*i* before *e* except after *c*" and "drop *y* at the end of a word and add *ies* to make the plural."

7. Use diagnostic teaching to establish the most effective spelling study strategy for Jesse. Two are suggested:

a. Adapt a study strategy such as Look-Spell-See-Write to incorporate tracing over a large (2″) cursive model of the word written on rough paper and separated into syllables. Ensure that he can write the word without a model five times in a row and again at the end of the session. Provide frequent reinforcement.

b. Use Alternate Pronunciation, a spelling method that focuses on pronouncing the word the way it is spelled (e.g., *Wed nes day*) rather than the way it is commonly pronounced.

8. Provide for transfer of learning by giving practice using the spelling words in written assignments.

Proofreading

1. Teach Jesse a specific strategy for proofreading his papers. One such strategy is the Error Monitoring strategy, developed at the University of Kansas, which has the acronym COPS - Capitalization, Overall appearance (which includes sentence structure), Punctuation, Spelling. (A description of this strategy is attached.)

2. Teach Jesse how to recognize in his own writing the spelling words he has studied so that he is able to correct them.

Math

1. Teach Jesse to talk through computation and story problems *before* he tries to solve them in order to encourage him to slow down and reflect.

2. Teach Jesse to use Touch Math for multiplication and division computation as skip counting might be easier for him to learn than memorizing all of the facts.

3. Teach Jesse a specific strategy for interpreting and setting up two-step word problems.

4. Make sure worksheets are visually clear with only a few problems (computation or verbal) on each page. Provide ample work space. If necessary, provide Jesse with large-square graph paper to help keep digits in the appropriate columns.

Instructions

1. Secure Jesse's attention before giving him oral instructions. If possible, limit your instructions to two or three steps. When you are finished, get feedback from Jesse or a variety of children including Jesse (e.g., call on Jesse first as he is more likely to recall the first instruction: "Jesse, what was the first thing you are to do? That's right, put your math books away. Mary, what is the second thing you are to do?").

2. Teach Jesse to use verbal rehearsal and visualization for holding instructions in memory. Teach Jesse to visualize what he is going to do *before* he begins.

3. Make it easy for Jesse to ask another child or the teacher when he has missed or forgets part of the instructions.

4. When Jesse has to remember to do something independently, such as give a note to his mother from the teacher or vice versa, place a colored rubber band on his wrist as a reminder. Remind him to remove it as soon as the task is completed.

Test Taking

1. When possible, allow Jesse to take content area exams (social studies, health) orally, unless his writing skills are being assessed. Alternatively, set aside a time to meet with him after a written test to make sure that he did not abbreviate his answers due to the constraints of writing them.

2. When possible, allow Jesse to take untimed tests.

Diagnosis: Deficit in rote associational memory

PSYCHOEDUCATIONAL EVALUATION

Name: Opal Parks
Birthdate: 10/18/81

Chronological Age: 9-11

Grade: 4.2

Evaluator:
Parent: Shulameth Parks
School: Harlan County Elementary
Test date: 3/13, 3/15, 3/17/92

Reason for Referral

Opal was referred for an evaluation by her classroom teacher because she continues to have severe difficulty with reading and written language.

Background Information

Opal has been in Harlan County Elementary since kindergarten and has received services for students with learning disabilities since first grade. In the second semester of second grade, she received a full cognitive and academic evaluation. At that time, continuance of special education services was not recommended.

Tests Administered

Woodcock-Johnson Psycho-Educational Battery — Revised (WJ-R):
    Tests of Cognitive Ability: Tests 1–16, 20–21
    Tests of Achievement (Form A): Tests 22–31, 34
Developmental Test of Visual-Motor Integration — Revised (VMI-R)

Behavioral Observations

Opal was cooperative throughout testing. She easily engaged in spontaneous conversation and interacted in a positive, polite manner. At times, Opal was visually distractible. When receiving instructions for a task, her gaze tended to wander from the visual stimulus. During the controlled learning tasks, she appeared to learn from her involvement in the task rather than from listening to the instructions.

Test Results

The tests of the WJ-R were scored according to grade norms. When no difference was found between the two component tests of a factor or cluster, only the factor or cluster score is discussed. Percentile ranks are reported as 68% confidence bands. A 68% confidence band is expressed as ± 1 standard error of measurement (SEM). A complete set of test scores is appended to this report.

Cognitive Abilities

The WJ-R Tests of Cognitive Ability were administered to assess Opal's processing strengths and weaknesses. Her Broad Cognitive Ability score indicated overall cognitive abilities in the *Average* range (PR ± 1 SEM: 55–70). Comparison of Opal's scores on the seven cognitive factors indicated no significant intracognitive strengths or weaknesses. Within the two auditory factors, however, significant differences were found between the individual tests. Within the Short-Term Memory factor, Opal demonstrated a significant strength in recalling unrelated words (PR ± 1 SEM: 93–99), in the *Superior/Very Superior* range, although her ability to recall sentences was in the *Average* range (PR ± 1 SEM: 32–63). In the Auditory Processing factor, Opal's ability in auditory closure was a significant strength (PR ± 1 SEM: 86–98), in the *High Average/Superior* range, whereas her ability to blend sounds and syllables to make a word was *Low Average* (PR ± 1 SEM: 12–30). The higher test scores may indicate splinter strengths or may suggest a specific strength in more automatic auditory processing abilities. Nevertheless, considered together, these scores indicate at least average ability for Opal to process auditory information at the word and sound level and to hold it in working memory.

Average scores in the other cognitive factors indicated adequate abilities in processing non-symbolic visual information, rapid scanning and processing of symbolic visual information, processing language, and abstract reasoning.

Opal's test behavior on the one remaining cognitive factor indicates a deficiency that is not reflected in her factor score. Although she scored in the *Average* range on the Long-Term Retrieval factor, the strategy she used on the Memory for Names test indicated that she did not learn the visual-verbal associations. Instead, on each page, she covered those "creatures" she had already named and guessed from those that were left. On the Delayed Recall - Memory for Names test, however, the page is turned after each item, disallowing that strategy. Immediately, Opal exclaimed, "You're not supposed to be turning the pages. Tell me another one on this page and I can figure it out." Her score on this test was in the *Very Low* range (PR ± 1 SEM: 0.1–0.5). On the Visual-Auditory Learning - Delayed Recall test, Opal was able to recall labels for only the rebuses that had some visual similarity to the concept they represented, giving her a score in the *Low Average* to *Average* range (PR ± 1 SEM: 19–42). A deficiency in the ability to make an visual-auditory match for verbal labels and visual stimuli that are not inherently related could affect the ability to learn phonics, sight words, and math facts.

On the VMI-R, Opal scored in the *Average* range when compared to her age-peers. She is right-handed and used a satisfactory pencil grip.

Academic Achievement

Opal's performance on the WJ-R Achievement Battery in reading ability fell in the *Very Low* range (PR ± 1 SEM: 0.5–2), written language skills in the *Low* range (PR ± 1 SEM: 5–12), math in the *Superior/Very Superior* range (PR ± 1 SEM: 96–99), and general knowledge in the *Low Average* to *Average* range (PR ± 1 SEM: 19–37).

Within the Broad Reading cluster, Opal's instructional level for sight vocabulary was at the mid-first grade-level. Error analysis indicated serious weaknesses in basic phonics knowledge, such as consonant blends and digraphs, and short and long vowel sounds. The Passage Comprehension test was difficult for Opal due to her low basic skills. Her Relative Mastery Index of 9/90 indicates that on similar reading tasks, in which the average fourth-grade student would attain 90% accuracy, Opal would attain approximately 9% accuracy.

On the Broad Written Language cluster, Opal demonstrated significant weaknesses in spelling, punctuation, and capitalization. Her score on Basic Writing Skills was in the *Low/Low Average* range (PR ± 1 SEM: 5–14). Her contextual writing abilities were relatively higher (PR ± 1 SEM: 13–27), in the *Low Average* range. Analysis of her written responses indicated satisfactory content, but some difficulties with sentence structure, in addition to the writing mechanics. She frequently asked if she could dictate her response to the examiner. The discrepancy between her performances on the two levels of skills are observed in her RMI of 37/90 for the Dictation test versus her RMI of 68/90 for the Writing Samples test.

Math was Opal's strength. When her obtained math standard score is compared to the average of her other academic cluster scores, only 1 in 1,000 of her grade-peers (PR: 0.1) with her same predicted score would obtain her actual score of 130. She solved addition and subtraction problems with regrouping and demonstrated knowledge of the concepts and operations of multiplication and division. It appears that she has not learned her math facts as she used her fingers for all calculations and skip counted for multiplication and division. Her Broad Math RMI was 98/90.

Opal's score and responses on the WJ-R Broad Knowledge cluster reflected satisfactory recall of general factual information. Her RMI was 79/90.

Summary

Opal's current test results indicate average overall cognitive abilities when compared to her grade-peers'. Although statistically she demonstrates no significant intracognitive discrepancies, her test behaviors and one score strongly suggest a severe deficit in long-term recall of visual-auditory associations when the association itself is not inherently meaningful. Although she devised a strategy to increase accurate responses on the test, it is not a strategy that could be used to improve academic skills. Academically, Opal exhibits significant deficits in basic reading and writing skills, and in automaticity of math facts. Her math reasoning ability, however, is excellent. Opal demonstrated math achievement significantly above her other academic areas.

Results of the WJ-R indicate a significant aptitude–achievement discrepancy in reading. Of fourth-grade students who obtained the same Broad Reading Aptitude score as Opal's, only 1 in 1,000 (PR: 0.1) would obtain a Broad Reading Achievement score as low as or lower than hers.

Recommendations

Recommendations for appropriate educational placement and remediation will be made in conjunction with the school psychologist and speech/language pathologist at the multidisciplinary conference.

Diagnosis: Deficits in abstract logical reasoning, mental reorganization of symbols, and visual recall

PSYCHOEDUCATIONAL EVALUATION

Student: Gabriel Frazier

Birthdate: 5/18/80

Chronological Age: 11-0

Grade: 5.9

Evaluator:

Parents: Lillian & Marco Frazier

School: Mission Heights Elementary

Test Dates: 5/15, 5/16/91

Reason for Referral

Gabriel was referred for a psychoeducational evaluation by his teacher, Paula Harrison, due to his history of difficulty with math and spelling. She questioned the possibility of learning disabilities and requested suggestions for teaching mathematics and spelling that would be more effective than her current techniques.

Background Information

Gabe lives with his mother, father, and 14-year-old brother. Mr. and Mrs. Frazier recalled that Gabe attained most developmental milestones within the normal range, and spoke in whole sentences at age 2½. The Fraziers reported that Gabe has always had difficulty learning math. Despite their concerted efforts to help him, he just seemed unable to learn math facts. Math homework has always been a source of frustration for Gabe and, ultimately, a source of conflict at homework time. In third and fourth grades, Gabe attended small-group remedial math classes. This year, the Fraziers hired a doctoral student in special education to work with Gabe twice a week on math and spelling. Over the year, Mrs. Harrison and Ms. Nsubuga, his educational therapist, taught Gabe many compensations and provided him with a great deal of supplementary instruction in math.

Previous and Concurrent Evaluations

In January 1991, the school psychologist, Tony LeSeuer, administered the Wechsler Intelligence Scale for Children - Revised (WISC-R). Gabe scored in the *High Average* range with no discrepancies between the Verbal and Performance scales and no significant subtest scatter.

Also in January, the Fraziers had Gabe's vision evaluated by Dr. Anne Fratkin, ophthalmologist. Dr. Fratkin reported that Gabe had normal visual health, acuity, and ocular functioning.

Behavioral Observations

Gabe was tested in two 2-hour sessions. Because he was familiar with the evaluator, rapport was readily established. Gabe was cooperative and friendly throughout testing. He concentrated well and worked steadily. On cognitive tasks, he often self-monitored. He appeared to fatigue more easily on the second day, when most of the academic tests were administered.

Tests Administered

Woodcock-Johnson Psycho-Educational Battery—Revised (WJ-R):

Cognitive Battery: Tests 1–17, 19–21

Achievement Battery (Form A): Tests 22–30

Slingerland Screening Tests for Identifying Children with Specific Language Disability, Form D: Tests 1, 3–5

Writing sample

Analysis of schoolwork

Test Results

The tests of the WJ-R were scored according to grade norms. When no difference was found between the two component tests of a factor or cluster, only the factor or cluster score is discussed. Standard scores and percentile ranks are reported as obtained scores or as 68% confidence bands. A 68% confidence band is expressed as ± 1 standard error of measurement (SEM). A complete set of test scores is appended to this report.

Cognitive Abilities

Based on the results of the Woodcock-Johnson Psycho-Educational Battery—Revised (WJ-R) Broad Cognitive Ability—Extended Scale (BCA), Gabe appears to have general cognitive abilities in the *Average* range (SS: 102, PR ± 1 SEM: 47–63) when compared to his grade-peers. This single, full-scale score masks significant discrepancies among the seven cognitive factors measured by this test battery.

Strengths

Gabe scored in the *Average* range on the WJ-R Processing Speed factor, indicating *Average* ability in rapid visual processing of small symbols/forms, such as letters and numbers, and in processing and noting details in nonsymbolic visual information, such as pictures. He scored in the *Superior* range on the Spatial Relations test indicating good reasoning using such visual abilities as visualizing a mirror image, judging size, and perceiving a gestalt.

Gabe's score in the *Superior* range on the Auditory Processing factor indicates strong ability to synthesize auditory information at the sound and word level. Based on his ability to spell words phonetically, auditory analysis of words is also strong.

Gabe scored in the *Average/High Average* range on tests of short-term memory of sentences and unrelated words. He performed in the *Average* range on tasks requiring him to integrate verbal with visual information and recall it over a period of approximately 10 minutes and then, again, 24 hours later. Gabe's scores on the Oral Language cluster of the WJ-R indicated that he is functioning in the *Average* range in overall oral language abilities.

Weaknesses

Gabe's phonetic spelling errors and variable spelling of the same word suggest the possibility of a visual-symbolic recall deficit. Informal testing supported the existence of a weakness in short-term recall of letter sequences. On the Slingerland, although Gabe easily matched the two like words among distractors (Test 4), he made numerous errors recognizing, among distractors, words he had just been shown and writing words and numbers he had just been shown. Prior to this evaluation, Ms. Nsubuga stated that Gabe has not been able to retain the spelling of words he has studied using a visually oriented study strategy. When she taught him to sing the spellings of some state names, he had no difficulty retaining them. In contrast, he has been unable to learn to match homophones to their spellings according to their meaning (e.g., *weather/ whether*; *too/to/two*).

Gabe's score on a test requiring the restatement of a sequence of digits in reverse order was significantly lower than his score on the language-based short-term memory tests. Gabe stated that he attempted to visualize the numbers and read them back, but that he could not picture them.

Gabe's Fluid Reasoning score in the *Low/Low Average* range represents a significant deficit in logical, abstract reasoning using complex patterns and verbal instructions. These types of abilities are also required in mathematical reasoning. Gabe was not able to use corrective feedback on either of the two controlled-learning tasks to improve his understanding of the task or the pattern of his errors. He had difficulty in perceiving how the visual layout of a problem displayed the relationship among the elements and in discerning the factor(s) that distinguished one group of colored shapes from another. Gabe also had considerable difficulty understanding the instructions on the Visual Matching test, a much simpler task. Despite initial practice in circling matching numbers within rows of numbers, when given more than one row, he ignored the lines between the rows and tried to match numbers across the rows. Finally, after considerable repetition of the instructions and queries on the trial items, he understood the task. Thus, on this and the Fluid Reasoning tests, he demonstrated obvious spatial confusion, evidently unable to see the whole picture or the relationships among the elements.

Gabe's Relative Mastery Index (RMI) score of 50/90 on the Fluid Reasoning factor indicates that on tasks similar to the reasoning tests, Gabe would attain 50% accuracy compared with his average grade-peers' 90%, placing his performance in the *Limited* range.

Learning Strategies

Gabe used strategies sporadically to aid him in task performance. He created clues to connect specific visual characteristics of a picture with the verbal label (e.g., "Squeeg's wheels squeak") and used verbal mediation and rehearsal on auditory tests. The addition of a linguistic context appeared to facilitate his ability to associate and retain visual and auditory information.

Intracognitive Discrepancies

Based on the results of the WJ-R, Gabe has a significant strength in Auditory Processing and a significant deficit in Fluid Reasoning. Of Gabe's grade-peers whose predicted Auditory Processing standard scores were identical to his, only 5% would obtain a score as high or higher (PR: 95). Of those with the same predicted Fluid Reasoning score, only 1% would obtain a score as low or lower (PR: 1).

Academic Achievement

Strengths

Gabe scored in the *High Average* range on overall reading skills with no significant difference in performance between the skills of sight-word identification and comprehension of brief passages.

Gabe performed in the *Average/High Average* range on the Writing Samples test. This performance and error analysis of a story Gabe had written in class indicated strengths in language-based written expression skills such as sentence structure and sequence of ideas. His story was imaginative and included a complete story grammar—setting, problem, sequence of events, resolution, and ending.

Gabe demonstrated knowledge of factual information in science and social studies in the *Average* range and knowledge of humanities in the *Low Average* range. His errors indicated lack of familiarity with art and music.

Weaknesses

Gabe's *Low/Low Average* performance on the Dictation test was significantly below his *Average/High Average* performance on the Writing Samples test. Error analysis of these tests and the story noted above indicated particular difficulty in spelling. As noted previously, his spelling is both phonetic and inconsistent. He also demonstrated weaknesses in application of punctuation and capitalization rules.

On both tests of the Broad Math cluster, Gabe scored in the middle of the *Average* range for his grade-peers in the WJ-R normative sample. Results from error analysis and Gabe's test behaviors, however, suggested that he is not functioning up to the level of his classmates. Gabe counted on his fingers for addition and subtraction problems and used skip counting for multiplication, indicating that he has not learned math facts to an automatic level. He did not know the operation for two-digit multiplication and did not attempt division problems with two-digit divisors. When he reached fractions, he exclaimed, "Oh, no! Not fractions!" Gabe did not understand the concept of common denominators and could not reduce fractions. He was unable to translate two-step word problems into computation.

In contrast, Gabe's teacher reported that from November through the end of the year, her class had learned multiplication and division by two-digit numbers, all operations using fractions with common denominators, and addition and subtraction of fractions with unlike denominators. She noted that only Gabe and one or two other students had not mastered these skills.

Intra-Achievement Discrepancies

Gabe demonstrated a significant strength in reading and significant deficit in written language. Of Gabe's grade-peers whose predicted standard scores were identical to his, only 1% would obtain a score as high as or higher than his actual standard score of 115 in Broad Reading. In Broad Written Language, only 3% of students whose predicted standard scores were identical to Gabe's would obtain a Broad Written Language standard score of 87. The largest contributing factor to his low score in Broad Written Language was spelling errors; his written expression score was in the high end of the *Average* range.

Conclusion

The cognitive weaknesses identified in this evaluation are some of the abilities necessary for mathematical learning and reasoning. Accordingly, Gabe's significant level of difficulty in visual recall, mental reorganization of symbols, and abstract, logical reasoning using visual stimuli should be considered major contributing factors to a math disability. Additionally, the weakness in visual recall appears to be impeding his ability to retain spelling words and math facts.

Recommendations

Math

General

1. More information concerning strengths and weaknesses in math subskills would be helpful in developing a remediation program. Consider administering the *KeyMath—Revised: A Diagnostic Inventory of Essential Mathematics*.

2. When giving instructions or teaching a math skill:
   a. provide well-organized, step-by-step information;

b. use visual aids. Directly point out each element in the visual stimuli and explain its function (e.g., each part of a division problem);

c. unless attempting to highlight a concept by teaching the same skill in alternative patterns, do not vary the procedure for doing a specific operation. If you teach alternative patterns, allow Gabe to stick with the one he knows;

d. expect Gabe to need more information, multiple explanations, and possibly compensatory techniques for learning any new skill/procedure.

3. Teach Gabe how to plan what he needs to do to solve the problem. Different techniques may be called for by the type of question asked.

a. Decide which operation(s) to use;

b. Make a table, graph, or chart of the information provided;

c. Make a drawing of the information provided;

4. Teach Gabe how to talk himself through math problems.

5. When grading papers, give partial credit for parts of problems solved correctly. For example, give some credit for correct reasoning even if the computation is incorrect.

6. After completing problems, have Gabe use a calculator to check his computation and then rework any incorrect solutions.

7. Math worksheets with many problems to a page will be visually confusing for Gabe. Try to keep worksheets visually clear with only a few problems on each page.

8. If Gabe needs to copy problems from the text, teach him the following techniques:

a. Before copying computation problems onto a sheet of paper, fold the paper in fourths or sixths to have "frames" to outline each problem. Copy/write only one problem in a frame.

b. Circle the item number so Gabe does not confuse it with digits in the problem.

9. Have Gabe use computer math games that provide immediate feedback and allow him to practice independently.

10. Before Gabe takes home math assignments, make sure that he understands the directions and process for solving the problems. When necessary,

the teacher or a peer tutor should work the first few problems with Gabe at school.

11. After Gabe has learned a math skill well, provide an opportunity for him to teach the skill to a younger child or a classmate who is having difficulty.

Concepts

1. Use visual aids and manipulatives to illustrate new ideas and extensions of previously learned concepts. Use real objects first (e.g., food, measuring liquid, wood for building, crayons), moving to rods, tokens, and other semiconcrete materials later. A variety of manipulatives and manuals for their use are available from: Cuisenaire Company of America, 12 Church St., Box D, New Rochelle, NY 10802, (800) 237-3142.

2. Make sure Gabe understands the concept underlying each new algorithm that is introduced by having him demonstrate the algorithm with manipulatives.

Computation

1. Use task analysis to help Gabe master computational algorithms. Identify the algorithm to be learned. List all the prerequisite skills and the steps needed to perform the algorithm in a logical teaching sequence. Determine what steps Gabe cannot perform through informal testing and then teach the steps in sequence.

2. When it is unclear why Gabe is missing specific computational problems, conduct an oral interview with him. Ask him to talk through the steps as he solves the problems.

3. Use a multisensory program, such as Touch Math (Bullock, 1991), to help Gabe increase his computational accuracy.

4. Reteach the concept of fractions, including what the numerator and denominator represent, the reason for needing a common denominator, the methods for finding common denominators, the procedures for reducing fractions, and the meaning of improper fractions and mixed numbers.

Word Problems

1. Do not teach Gabe "tricks" for solving math problems, such as identifying cue words (e.g., *altogether* means *to add*). Instead draw attention to understanding how the language of the problem describes the situation.

2. When Gabe has difficulty with the computation involved in a story problem, have him substitute smaller numbers so that he can understand the operation(s) involved and then calculate the problem a second time using the original numbers.

3. To ensure that Gabe understands all of the types of story problems he is expected to solve, have him solve them first using manipulatives or have him draw a picture to represent the situation.

4. Provide Gabe with an index card that lists several sequenced steps to follow when solving story problems. A sample flowchart would be: (a) read and reread the problem, (b) draw or mentally picture what is happening, (c) restate what is being asked, (d) choose the operation(s), and (e) compute and check the answer.

Reasoning

1. To help Gabe reason with numbers, teach him strategies to figure out information based on what he already knows. Some examples for multiplication facts are:

    a. Split one factor in half and add the products.
    Example: $4 \times 7 = ?$ $2 \times 7 = 14$ and
               $14 + 14 = 28$
    b. Lower one factor by 1, multiply, then add one more set.
    Example: $4 \times 7 = ?$ $3 \times 7 = 21$ and
               $21 + 7 = 28$

2. Combine math and content area learning. For example, you could use data in reference books to create math problems and teach Gabe to use the reference books to find the answer. An example would be, "If everybody in the world gave you a penny, approximately how much money would you have?"

3. Create problems for Gabe that require experimenting or that combine experimenting with use of a reference book. Examples would be, "How many tablespoons of liquid equal a cup?" and "If you leave Tucson on foot for Yuma, can you make the trip in less than 1,000,000 steps?"

4. Give Gabe word problems where specific information needed to solve the problem is missing. Have Gabe identify and provide the missing information and then solve the problem.

5. Provide extensive practice in practical application of all new math skills that Gabe has learned or is learning, both in story problems and real life (e.g., measuring for cooking, deciding on one shirt over another depending on budget considerations, building a bookshelf).

6. When working with higher-level math reasoning problems, allow Gabe to use a calculator. This should facilitate his attention to the reasoning process.

Basic Writing Skills

1. For spelling, teach a study strategy based in the auditory modality, such as Simultaneous Oral Spelling.

2. At intervals throughout the week, give Gabe three or four spelling words to learn rather than giving all of them in one day. Limit Gabe's spelling words to approximately 12 per week.

3. Review punctuation and capitalization rules, ensuring that Gabe has mastered one skill before introducing another.

Results: Academic improvement in the areas of reading comprehension, written expression, and calculation. Limited or no improvement in basic reading skills, basic writing skills, and math application.

Name: Hee Chan Kim

Birthdate: 7/25/80

Chronological Age: 11-3

Grade: 5.2

Evaluator:

Parents: Eun Hee & Jae Kwan Kim

School: Rose Miller Elementary

Test Dates: 10/27, 11/8/91

Reason for Referral

Hee was referred for academic testing to assess his progress in the special education program and the appropriateness of his current IEP.

Background Information

Hee Chan is in a fifth-grade class and has been attending the resource program for students with learning disabilities three times per week for the past year. He is receiving remediation in the areas of reading, written language, and math. In reading, specific objectives entailed building reading decoding and comprehension skills. Included in the objectives is a home-based reading plan in which Hee Chan's mother reads with him for 20 minutes nightly. In written language, his objectives focused on improving cursive handwriting, spelling, punctuation, and capitalization. In math, objectives included memorizing addition, subtraction, and multiplication facts, improving computation of multiple-digit addition and subtraction problems, learning operations for one- and two-digit multiplication problems, and solving word problems. More extensive background information is included in the initial evaluation report dated 11/90.

Tests Administered

Hee was administered the Woodcock-Johnson Psycho-Educational Battery—Revised, Tests of Achievement, Form A (22–30, 34). He was also administered the Analytical Reading Inventory (ARI). Two classroom writing samples were used for analysis.

Academic Achievement

The tests of the WJ-R were scored according to grade norms. Hee's performance is reported in terms of percentile rank confidence bands, relative mastery indexes, and grade equivalents. A 68% confidence band is expressed as ± 1 standard error of measurement (SEM).

Reading

Date: 11/90

Test	PR ±1 SEM	RMI	Grade Equivalent
Letter-Word Identification	7-18	39/90	2.6
Passage Comprehension	3-12	32/90	2.2

Date: 11/91

Cluster/Test	PR ±1 SEM	RMI	Grade Equivalent
Letter-Word Identification	4-12	27/90	2.8
Passage Comprehension	32-63	89/90	5.1

Woodcock-Johnson—Revised/Analytic Reading Inventory
(Date: 11/91)

	Word Recognition WJ-R 11/90	Word Recognition ARI 11/91		Reading Comprehension WJ-R 11/90	Reading Comprehension ARI 11/91	Listening Comprehension ARI 11/91	Listening Comprehension ARI 11/91
Easy	—	2.5	1	—	4.0	1	—
GE	2.6	2.8	2	2.2	5.1	2-3	3-4
Difficult	—	3.5	3	—	7.5	4	5

Basic Skills

Based on the WJ-R and the ARI, Hee Chan has not made progress in phonetic and structural analysis. His RMI indicates that he is still *Very Limited* on these types of tasks when compared to his grade-peers. When reading words in isolation and in context, his instructional level is still mid- to late second grade.

He continues to attempt to read words as wholes, often guessing at a word based on the first and last letters or letter combinations. Examples of his miscues are: "beacher" for *bachelor*, "shed" for *shined*, "fingers" for *fierce*, and "from" for *of*. He demonstrated a tendency to omit word endings and, as the passages became more difficult (grade 4), to omit punctuation, indicating that he does not consistently attend to syntactic cues.

Hee Chan used word analysis skills more successfully on the shorter passages of the WJ-R than on the longer passages of the ARI. He read the passages of the ARI quickly, appearing to focus more on overall meaning than on details. His higher listening comprehension (grade 3 to 4) than reading comprehension levels (grade 2 to 3) suggest that his miscues are interfering with comprehension.

Comprehension

Based on the WJ-R Passage Comprehension test, Hee Chan has made significant improvement in the area of reading comprehension. Considering his RMIs, his performance improved from *Very Limited* to *Average* on comprehension of brief cloze passages. On this test, he used context clues in reading to the end of the sentence before responding and in self-correcting words that did not make sense within the context. Hee Chan had considerable difficulty when reading aloud the longer passages of the ARI. He did not use context clues and his reading was dysfluent. Thus, on brief passages, similar to those on the WJ-R, Hee Chan's instructional level for reading comprehension is early fifth grade, but on longer passages, similar to a section in a textbook, particularly if Hee Chan has to read aloud, his instructional level is mid-second grade.

Hee Chan's retellings of the passages on the ARI were short, but generally complete in that they included the main characters, the setting, the plot, and how the story ended. The questions that Hee Chan had difficulty answering were related to his decoding errors.

Written Language

Date: 11/90

Test	PR ±1 SEM	RMI	Grade Equivalent
Dictation	1-5	27/90	1.8
Writing Samples	3-8	39/90	1.6

Date: 11/91

Test	PR ±1 SEM	RMI	Grade Equivalent
Dictation	1-4	21/90	2.2
Writing Samples	5-16	61/90	2.4

Basic Skills

According to the results of the WJ-R Dictation test and analysis of his writing samples, Hee Chan has not made significant progress in basic skills. His RMIs indicate that his performance remains *Very Limited* compared to his grade-peers. The change in his instructional level from late first to early second grade does not constitute a significant improvement. Error analysis of his tests and writing samples, however, shows some specific gains in punctuation and capitalization, but not in spelling.

Currently, Hee Chan continues to spell many words phonetically, but has difficulty with all vowel patterns. He uses capital letters for the first word in every sentence and *I*; he ended each sentence with a period. Although limited, this use of capitalization and punctuation represents improvement in that his writing samples in the last assessment included no punctuation and erratic use of capitals. His handwriting is sloppy but legible with generally adequate letter formation. Spacing between words is appropriate, but within a word, letters are positioned from above to below the line. Nevertheless, his handwriting has improved substantially since last year.

Written Expression

Based on his WJ-R Writing Samples RMI, Hee Chan's performance on written expression tasks has improved from the *Very Limited* range to the *Limited* range. His instructional level has increased from mid-first to mid-second grade. The changes noted in the Writing Samples test and in his spontaneous writing are that currently Hee Chan includes all parts of a story grammar, uses some description, and does not omit important words.

Mathematics

Date: 11/90

Cluster/Test	PR ±1 SEM	RMI	Grade Equivalent
BROAD MATHEMATICS	19-37	81/90	3.6
Calculation	9-25	71/90	3.3
Applied Problems	32-58	88/90	4.0

Date: 11/91

Cluster/Test	PR ±1 SEM	RMI	Grade Equivalent
BROAD MATHEMATICS	18-34	79/90	4.2
Calculation	18-39	79/90	4.5
Applied Problems	18-45	77/90	4.0

Basic Skills

The WJ-R Calculation test results indicate that Hee Chan's basic math skills have improved from early third- to mid-fourth-grade level in the past year. The minimal increase in his RMI, however, indicates that compared to his grade-peers, he is still functioning at the bottom of the *Average* range on tasks requiring computational accuracy.

Item analysis and test behaviors indicate that Hee Chan now knows addition and subtraction facts to an automatic level and can solve multiple-digit addition and subtraction problems with regrouping. He understands the concept of multiplication as repeated addition, but does not know many multiplication facts. Hee Chan's numerals are often poorly formed and his columns are not aligned.

Applied Problems

Test results indicate no increase in Hee Chan's instructional level in application of math knowledge. His RMI indicates that he will have moderate difficulty on story problems when compared to his grade-peers.

When solving story problems, Hee Chan ignored extraneous information and in several instances talked himself through solutions to come up with the correct answer. Still, Hee Chan appears to have difficulty translating word problems into computation.

Summary

Comparisons of recent test results and classroom work to those of a year ago indicate improvement in some areas of academic functioning and little improvement in others.

In reading, overall, Hee Chan is still *Very Limited* on tasks requiring phonic and structural analysis skills, but is better able to use the skills he does have in short passages. He has shown significant improvement in reading comprehension and, presently, his RMI is in the *Average* range. Again,

he is more proficient in comprehending short passages. On longer passages he does not use word analysis skills or context clues and his decoding errors diminish comprehension.

In written language, Hee Chan has made progress in handwriting and in use of specific punctuation and capitalization skills, but his accuracy on these tasks is still *Very Limited*. His written expression is now in the *Limited* range, representing inclusion of a more complete story grammar and fewer omissions of important words.

In math, in basic skills and application, Hee Chan is between the *Limited* and *Average* ranges. He has improved in addition and subtraction but has not shown improvement in multiplication facts or operations. In applications, he has shown no improvement in translating word problems into computation.

Recommendations

Based on the current findings, Hee Chan's IEP for this school year should reflect the following changes.

Reading

1. Continue with instruction in phonics and structural analysis with a change in technique. For example, a method might be tailored to include increased structure in presentation of phonic elements, adding a tracing component, and reinforcement with writing words that include the new phonic element.

2. Include specific objectives for:
   a. the use of context clues in longer passages
   b. stating the main idea
   c. drawing conclusions
   d. increasing fluency
   e. activating prior knowledge before reading
   f. teaching compensations for visual distractibility (e.g., using an index card under the line he is reading).

Writing

1. Continue teaching punctuation and capitalization rules systematically and reinforce with frequent writing practice.

2. Change the technique currently being used for teaching spelling. Use diagnostic teaching to present Hee Chan with a variety of spelling study strategies and decide with him which one works the best for long-term retention.

3. Integrate the teaching of spelling patterns with the basic reading skills being presented. Emphasize vowel patterns and memorizing the visual patterns of words.

4. Include an objective for increased description and content in written expression.

Math

1. Continue the objectives for teaching multiplication facts and operations.

2. Include an objective for teaching division as the inverse operation of multiplication.

3. Include an objective for translating word problems into computation.

Diagnosis: Deficits in receptive and expressive language; weakness in processing and recall of visual symbols; weakness in functional vision; linguistic/cultural difference

PSYCHOEDUCATIONAL EVALUATION

Name: Flavio Tapia

Birthdate: 11/18/79

Chronological Age: 12-2

Grade: 6.5

Evaluator:

Foster Parents: Cecelia & Martin Lopez

School: Carlton Middle School

Test Dates: 1/5, 1/6/91

Reason for Referral

Flavio was referred for a full psychoeducational assessment by his social worker, Ms. Linda Able, due to his continued difficulty in all areas of academics and ongoing behavioral difficulties in specific classes. Ms. Able requested recommendations to aid Flavio in his educational progress.

Method of Evaluation

Due to the complexity of Flavio's case, this evaluation was conducted by a multidisciplinary team, including assessments by a functional optometrist, a bilingual/bicultural psychologist, a bilingual speech/language pathologist, and a learning disabilities specialist. A behavioral specialist did a classroom observation. The findings of these professionals are integrated in this report. With the exception of informal probes in Spanish to confirm language dominance, all tests were administered in English. In addition to formal testing, this evaluator conducted structured interviews with Flavio's foster mother and his past and current teachers.

Background Information

Details of Flavio's social-emotional background are in his file at the referring agency. Most pertinent to this evaluation are his school history and bilingual language development.

Flavio is a handsome young man of Yaqui descent. Since the age of 6, he has been in the foster home of Martin and Cecelia Lopez. The identified culture of this home is Yaqui. The foster care agency files indicate that Flavio's biological mother abused drugs and drank heavily during her pregnancy and that Flavio may have eaten lead-based paint as a toddler.

Between the ages of 2 and 6, Flavio was moved frequently between his biological mother's home and foster homes. Flavio's placements varied in language usage from monolingual Spanish to monolingual English. The Lopezes speak both Spanish and English in their home, to each other and to the children. Mrs. Lopez stated that once Flavio started kindergarten, he refused to speak Spanish. Currently she believes that he understands some basic Spanish, but could not follow or participate in a conversation. Mrs. Lopez stated that Flavio has difficulty expressing himself in an organized fashion and often gives insufficient information. When she asks clarifying questions, he says, "Oh, forget it."

Flavio started school in a monolingual English kindergarten class before he was proficient in either language. He was provided English language instruction for three 20-minute sessions per week for kindergarten only. In second grade, Flavio was transferred to a private school due to his slow progress in reading. He made little progress in the phonics-based program and felt culturally alienated, so he was transferred to his home school for fourth grade. Flavio has always struggled with reading and writing, but is relatively strong in math computation. He is quite interested in science and social studies.

Flavio has an inconsistent history of behavior in school. Teachers have complained about inattention to task and unfinished work. These behaviors have been noted during academic tasks from first grade until mid-fourth grade when Flavio was transferred to a new teacher. This teacher and his fifth-grade teacher reported that although Flavio liked to joke and socialize, his behavior was appropriate, and his lack of attention to seatwork was usually related to task difficulty. When he received guidance, he went back to work. These teachers used cooperative teaching and whole group discussions, and paired Flavio with good students for independent seatwork.

This year, Flavio's behavior is appropriate in his morning classes, the content areas and math, although he does not complete all assignments. In his afternoon classes, reading and English, he is often off task, but not disruptive. Flavio complained that he cannot do the work in these classes and that he is embarrassed to ask for help "for such stupid stuff." A recent classroom observation concurred with the teachers' reports. Flavio was on task 89% in his morning classes and 58% in his afternoon classes. In both classes, Flavio sustained attention to task best when he had an active role in a cooperative group effort. It appears that Flavio's attention is at least partially dependent on the teaching approach, teacher personality, and task demands.

Mrs. Lopez reported that at home Flavio is responsible and thoughtful. Occasionally he does extra chores to surprise her. Flavio gets ready for school independently each morning, does not daydream, is popular with his friends, and excels in team sports.

In January 1989, Flavio's vision was assessed by Dr. Morris Jampol, functional optometrist. Results indicated mild farsightedness with some inefficiencies in eye tracking, focusing stability at near-point, and changing focus between near-point and far-point. His visual acuity was 20/20; no problems were found in eye-teaming skills. Testing also indicated a weakness in visual memory. Dr. Jampol prescribed reading glasses.

Behavior During Testing

All evaluators reported that Flavio was cooperative, attentive, and physically calm during testing. Even when obviously fatigued, he was willing to continue. Two short breaks were given in each of the testing sessions. Flavio did not initiate conversation, but appropriately engaged in conversation when it was elicited. He wore his glasses throughout testing.

Tests Administered

Flavio's linguistic and cultural differences should be taken into consideration when interpreting the results of the assessment. All scores reported should be interpreted with caution and considered as indicators of intra-individual skill strengths or weaknesses.

The tests of the WJ-R were scored according to grade norms. When no difference was found between the two component tests of a factor or cluster, only the factor or cluster score is discussed.

Standard scores and percentile ranks are expressed as obtained scores or as 68% confidence bands. A 68% confidence band is written as ±1 standard error of measurement (±1 SEM). A complete set of test scores and profiles is appended to this report. (See Figures III-10 and III-11.)

Administered by Anne Compton, Ph.D.

Woodcock-Johnson Psycho-Educational Battery—Revised:
    Achievement (Form A): Tests 22–31, 33
Analytical Reading Inventory: Reading recognition, reading comprehension, listening comprehension
Paragraphs for dictation
Written language sample
ANSER System questionnaire for parents and teachers

Administered by Irene Romero, Ph.D.

Wechsler Intelligence Scale for Children—Revised (WISC-R)
Woodcock-Johnson Psycho-Educational Battery—Revised:
    Cognitive Battery: Tests 1–14, 17, 19–21
Bender Visual-Motor Gestalt Test: Koppitz Scoring System

Administered by Sharon Kwang-Olafssen, M.S., M.A., SLP/CCC

Clinical Evaluation of Language Fundamentals - Revised (CELF-R)
Test of Language Competence - Expanded
Spontaneous language sample

Test Results: Cognitive Skills

Global Intelligence

Results of the WJ-R Cognitive Battery indicated a significant discrepancy between Flavio's *Average* to *High Average* scores in visual, nonverbal cognitive abilities and *Low* to *Low Average* scores in language processing abilities. His WISC-R Performance scale score of 112 and Verbal scale score of 77 were consistent with these findings. Thus, one overall score such as the WJ-R Broad Cognitive Ability score or the WISC-R Full Scale score give a misleading representation of his cognitive abilities.

Visual Skills

All of Flavio's scores on the visual tests of the WJ-R and the WISC-R were in the *Average* to *Superior* ranges, indicating that he can easily process, interpret, and organize symbolic and nonsymbolic visual information, such as letters and numbers, pictures and designs.

Informal test results and error pattern analysis indicate that Flavio has difficulty revisualizing the directional orientation of letters and their sequence in words. On an informal test, Flavio could not identify many of the letters, numbers, and words that were written backwards. He attempted to trace many of the items on the table, but often could not remember the correct orientation. His spelling suggests an attempt to use visual recall, albeit unsuccessfully (e.g., *apple* for *ape*, *ang* for *and*, *gril* for *girl*, and *onboby* for *nobody*).

Additionally, Flavio's weaknesses in visual tracking and focusing stability, diagnosed by Dr. Jampol, combined with his minimal development of phonic skills (see Reading), may contribute to his lack of attention to critical details in words, reducing his ability to store them accurately for later recall.

Neat, fluent handwriting, an error score of 1 on the Bender Visual-Motor Gestalt test (PR $\pm$ 1 SEM: 50-60), and *High Average* performance on the WISC-R Coding test indicate good visual-fine motor integration.

Visual-Auditory Association and Retrieval

Flavio scored in the *Average* range on tasks requiring him to associate verbal labels (names, words) with pictures and symbols and retrieve them over a period of approximately 10 minutes. Thus, Flavio appears able to form and retain associations between auditory and visual information.

Short-Term Auditory Memory

On all tests, Flavio scored at the lower end of the *Average* range on auditory memory tasks that did not require processing of connected language. In contrast, his scores on two sentence imitation tasks placed him between the *Very Low* and *Low* ranges when compared to his age- and grade-peers. Error analysis on these tasks indicated that much of Flavio's difficulty in storing and recalling purely auditory information may be attributed to a weakness in processing certain types of sentence constructions. (See Oral Language.)

Auditory Processing

Test results and analysis of error patterns indicate that Flavio is deficient in synthesizing separate sounds and syllables into words and analyzing words into the correct sequence of sounds. He scored in the *Low* range on the WJ-R Auditory Processing factor, despite remedial reading classes and individual tutoring focusing on these skills.

Oral Language

Semantics

Flavio scored generally in the *Low* and *Low Average* range on all tests of receptive and expressive vocabulary. On informal testing of comprehension of language in context, he did not know the meanings of such words as "dawn," "colt," "unknown," "determination," or "antibiotics." On the WISC-R Similarities test, he was unfamiliar with some of the vocabulary and often didn't know words specific enough to label the concept he was trying to describe.

Formal and informal test results also indicated that Flavio has specific difficulty comprehending and using vocabulary for spatial, temporal, comparative, and exclusionary concepts.

Syntax

In testing and language samples, Flavio understood and used coordinating conjunctions, prepositional phrases, and simple relative and conditional clauses. He typically used active declarative statements. Ms. Kwang-Olafssen noted that "Flavio was most successful when he used his preferred strategies of formulating strings of simple sentences connected by simple coordinating and subordinating conjunctions." He was unable to understand and use the following sentence constructions: passive voice, all but simple subordinate clauses, clauses indicating direction, complex forms of negation such as exclusion, qualifiers, and complex sentences with multiple clauses.

Semantic/Syntactic Relationships

Flavio's deficits in understanding complex sentences that incorporate the concepts and/or sentence constructions described above are likely to impede his ability to understand and remember verbal instructions in the classroom, lectures, and textbooks. In testing, Flavio was unable to follow three-step commands.

Longer Discourse

Formal and informal tests indicate that Flavio is aided by the amount of information and the framework provided by longer discourse (100 to 200 words). He scored in the *Low Average* range on comprehension of one- to two-sentence passages, but at the lower limit of the *Average* range when responding to longer discourse. His retelling of the longer passages indicated that he had grasped much of the content as well as the sequence of events. As the passages increased in difficulty, he was still able to relate the most important events. Response analysis suggested that his comprehension of discourse was impeded by his deficits in understanding complex syntax and the words for certain concepts (see above), in vocabulary knowledge, in background knowledge, and in making inferences. Thus, although he grasped much of the overall content, he missed many key relationships among the details.

Pragmatics

Flavio appeared to enjoy storytelling and relating experiences, making use of facial expressions and gestures. He also maintained eye contact, stayed on the topic, and initiated conversation. When cued by questions, Flavio spontaneously slowed his pace and included clarifying phrases in his narrative.

Flavio had difficulty in understanding and using idiomatic and metaphoric expressions. In his narratives and retellings, he did not clearly indicate referents for pronouns, left out key details, and often did not provide orienting statements when he began to speak or concluding statements when he finished. These omissions had the effect of leaving his listener somewhat confused as to the content of his message.

Reasoning/Problem Solving

Flavio appears to have reasoning skills in the *Average* range, although receptive and expressive language difficulties impaired his performance on some tasks. On the two out of five tasks on which he scored below the *Average* range, his error patterns

indicated difficulty either understanding the complexity of the verbal instructions or lack of adequate vocabulary to formulate his responses.

On the two controlled learning tasks of the WJ-R (Analysis–Synthesis, Concept Formation), in which the subject is given feedback on the correctness of his responses, Flavio scored in the *Low Average* and *Average* ranges. Both tasks require logical reasoning to solve visually presented puzzles using verbal instructions. On the first task, Flavio had difficulty only when the task became more complicated and abstract, with concomitant complexity in the instructions. On the second task, Flavio again had difficulty understanding the task demands, but was better able to use the corrective feedback.

Based on his *Average* score on the WJ-R Verbal Analogies test and his responses to the listening and reading comprehension tests (see Oral Language and Reading), Flavio appears to be able to use verbal information for reasoning if he processes it correctly. Although he scored at the lower limit of the *Low Average* range on the WISC-R Similarities subtest, another verbal reasoning task, his responses suggested that he often had the concept, but lacked the vocabulary to formulate the correct responses.

Reflecting his visual strengths, on a relatively language-free, visual reasoning task (Spatial Relations), he scored in the *Superior* range.

Learning Strategies

Flavio used both verbal rehearsal and verbal mediation to aid his performance of tasks. He appropriately asked questions for clarification of task requirements.

Test Results: Academic

Reading

Basic Skills

The WJ-R Basic Reading Skills cluster places Flavio's abilities to identify sight words and to use phonic and structural analysis skills in decoding unfamiliar words in the *Low* range (PR: 3). His Relative Mastery Index (RMI) of 25/90 indicates that on tasks of basic reading skills on which other sixth-grade students would score 90%, Flavio would score approximately 25%, indicating that his skills are *Very Limited*.

The Analytical Reading Inventory (ARI) was administered for more information regarding error patterns. An Independent reading level was not obtained. His highest instructional level for word recognition in context was grade 3 and out of context, grade 2, indicating that he is making use of context clues. Error analysis indicated that Flavio recognizes the number of syllables in a word. Most of his phonic errors were on pronunciation of vowels, vowel combinations, and word endings. He appeared to depend on sight recognition, often not analyzing a word carefully enough to distinguish it from graphically similar words (e.g., "hand" for *head*, "forth" for *forty*). On difficult words, he appeared to guess based on the first three letters, but occasionally made an attempt at all parts (e.g., *petrifies* for *particles*).

Both the WJ-R Age/Grade Profile and the ARI results indicated that appropriate instructional materials for basic reading skills would be at late grade 1 level for phonics and early third-grade level skills for word identification.

Comprehension

The WJ-R Passage Comprehension test placed Flavio's ability to comprehend text in the *Low/Low Average* range (PR: 9), consistent with his basic skills. His RMI was 45/90, *Very Limited* compared to his grade-peers. On the passages of the ARI, his independent reading level was grade 3 and Instructional reading level, grade 4. His decoding problems clearly interfered with comprehension. Moreover, content area text for which Flavio had little background knowledge was more difficult for him to comprehend than literature. Throughout, he tried hard and did grasp much of the content. In contrast to his retellings of orally presented stories, his retellings of text included good orienting and concluding statements and well-sequenced details. His retellings deteriorated concomitant with increased passage difficulty and poorer decoding.

Written Language

A significant discrepancy was found between Flavio's aptitude and achievement on the WJ-R Broad Written Language cluster. Only 2% of his grade peers with a predicted standard score of 88 would obtain Flavio's score of 66. No significant intra-achievement discrepancies were found, but Broad Written Language was an area of relative weakness.

According to the WJ-R Broad Writing cluster, Flavio's basic writing skills are in the *Very Low* range (PR: 1). His RMI was 15/90 which is considered *Very Limited*. His score on Writing Samples was somewhat higher, in the *Low/Low Average* range (PR: 10), with an RMI of 68/90, indicating *Limited* proficiency.

Error analysis of test responses and a writing sample provided the following information.

Basic Skills

Flavio's handwriting is neat; his letters are formed correctly and are well-spaced. He is inconsistent in his use of capital letters and arbitrary in his use of punctuation. He does not use clear sentence boundaries.

Flavio's spelling suggested reliance on both auditory processing and visual recall with limited success. Auditory errors included sounds mis-sequenced, added, or omitted and incorrect vowels (e.g., *sharet* for *searched*, *scenule* for *certainly*). Visual errors included letter reversals, inversions, and transpositions, graphically similar word substitutions, and phonetic spelling of common words (e.g., *anamle* for *animal*, *ski* for *sky*, and *cot* for *coat*).

Flavio's weakness in processing and recalling complex sentences appeared to interfere with his ability to write from dictation. He omitted and substituted many words, sometimes losing the sentence meaning. He needed much repetition.

Written Expression

Flavio's use of vocabulary was immature and lacking in description. He had subject-verb agreement errors and occasionally omitted small words and word endings. As in his oral language, Flavio created long sentences out of strings of simple sentences joined by coordinating conjunctions. Occasionally, he incorporated simple relative clauses. Examples of his responses to the WJ-R Writing Samples test and his written story are attached. (See Figures III-8 and III-9.)

Organization

Apparently, Flavio is aware of the major elements in a story grammar. Given a picture as a prompt, he first wrote a simple description. Then, when asked to write a "real story," he did so. Although he did not spend any time planning his story, it was well-organized in the framework of an embedded causal chain, including most relevant parts (setting, problem, resolution, ending). He provided good orienting and concluding statements and a clear, connected sequence of events. Although the content was not well-developed and lacked richness of description, Flavio demonstrated a sophisticated use of irony in that his main character, an ape, misunderstood the harmless intentions of a group of people and, in trying to protect himself, brought about the situation he had feared.

Writing Fluency

The ideas for Flavio's story appeared to come easily. He wrote 15 words per minute.

Math

Test results from the WJ-R Broad Mathematics cluster indicated that Flavio's overall math ability is in the *Low Average* range (PR: 20), with equivalent scores in Calculation and Applied Problems. His RMI was 73/90, at the top of the *Limited* range. His performance on Quantitative Concepts gave him an RMI of 34/90, indicating *Very Limited* proficiency.

Error analysis provided the following information. Flavio was not automatic on arithmetic facts. He counted on his fingers and either skip-counted or added repeatedly when multiplying. His lack of automaticity with math facts interfered with his ability to add the values of coins efficiently. He was able to divide only with a one-digit divisor. He appeared unfamiliar with decimals except in the context of money. In response to the evaluator's comment about fractions, Flavio responded, "Fractions! What's that?" He was not able to tell what one-half would be when shown a picture of four objects. He was also unfamiliar with percents and was missing math-related information such as the number of weeks/months in 1 year. In one-step story problems, Flavio appropriately ignored extraneous information. He was unable to interpret any two-step problems, even if the computation required was within his ability.

According to the WJ-R Age/Grade Profile, appropriate materials in computation and practical problems would be at the late-fourth- to mid-fifth-grade level. Early fourth-grade materials would be appropriate for math concepts.

Knowledge

According to the WJ-R, Flavio's general knowledge appears to be in the *Low/Low Average*

range (PR: 7) compared to his grade-peers. Based on his RMIs, his knowledge of Science (RMI 73/90) and Social Studies (RMI 50/90) was *Limited*; his knowledge of humanities (RMI 25/90) was *Very Limited*. Flavio's level of achievement in content areas probably reflects the interference of his language deficits in processing and retaining new information, his limited ability to learn through reading, and his cultural and linguistic differences from other children in the normative sample.

Summary

Flavio is a 12-year-old foster child of Yaqui descent. His foster parents speak both English and Spanish at home. Flavio was immersed in English before he had adequately developed language concepts in Spanish and was never provided adequate instruction in either language. He has always had difficulty in learning academic skills. Inattention in the classroom appears to be related to teaching style, teacher personality, and task demands.

Cognitive Abilities

Cognitive testing indicated that Flavio has a significant discrepancy between his strong visual, nonverbal abilities and his weak language abilities. Flavio performed in the *Average* and *High Average* ranges in all visual and visual-motor skills tested. The only exception to his visual strengths was an apparent deficiency in visual memory for symbols.

Flavio scored in the *Very Low/Low* range in auditory short-term memory for sentences but in the *Low Average* range for words and numbers. Error analysis indicated that a deficit in language processing might strongly contribute to the apparent memory deficit. Flavio also scored in the *Low* range in auditory processing of words and sounds.

Flavio's difficulties in the area of oral language appear to stem from both a deficit in primary language processing as well as severely inadequate opportunities to develop first or second language skills. Significant weaknesses in oral language include vocabulary knowledge, complex sentences using a variety of clause-types and concepts, figurative language, and awareness of the listener's communication needs. These weaknesses critically affect Flavio's ability to understand fully classroom lectures and instruction, oral directions, textual information, and social conversation. They also impair his ability to express his thoughts clearly.

Flavio appears to have reasoning in the *Average* range, although complex oral instructions may negatively affect his understanding of a task. He can reason using verbal information if the vocabulary and sentence structure are simple enough for him to process. His performance on relatively language-free, visual reasoning tasks was *High Average* to *Superior*. Flavio used learning strategies and asked questions when appropriate.

Academic Achievement

According to test results, Flavio's basic reading skills are in the *Low* range and comprehension skills in the *Low/Low Average* range in comparison to grade-peers. His deficits in auditory processing, visual recall, and visual tracking/focusing, combined with a different phonemic/linguistic base, appear to have interfered with all aspects of decoding, preventing him from benefiting from phonics instruction. Thus, he tends to rely on his sight vocabulary. His instructional level for word analysis is late grade 1 and for sight vocabulary, early grade 3. His instructional level for reading comprehension is grade 4. His poor decoding and deficit in language comprehension appear to interfere with his reading comprehension.

Flavio scored in the *Very Low* range in basic writing skills and *Low/Low Average* in written expression. He had difficulty in all mechanics. His oral language deficits are reflected in his written expression in immature vocabulary and syntax.

Flavio's math skills, in the *Low Average* range, appear to be a relative strength, with lower scores in math concepts. Error analysis indicated limited recall of math facts and ability to handle computation up through simple division of whole numbers. His instructional level is approximately late grade 4.

Consistent with his language processing deficit and linguistic/cultural difference, Flavio's general knowledge appears to be in the *Low* range.

Conclusions

Flavio is a child with many average to above-average cognitive abilities whose educational development has been negatively affected by a combination of a language processing disorder, premature immersion in English, inadequate instruction in English, inappropriate educational techniques, and a linguistic/cultural difference. Flavio's current communication skills place him at severe risk for academic and subsequent vocational failure. All involved professionals agree that his language disorder constitutes a severe learning disability and is not secondary to other contributing factors.

Recommendations

For the Parents and Social Worker

1. Provide tutoring at least three times per week by an educational therapist who has training in language disorders, with consultation from a speech/language pathologist.

2. Have a conference with Flavio's teachers at the beginning of the school year to discuss the findings of this report. Make a copy available for them to read.

3. In order to provide Flavio with an increased foundation of general information on which to build, rent videotapes or borrow them from the public library on a wide range of topics. Examples include: documentaries on a variety of cultures; the "National Geographic" series; the "Nova" series; "Fairy Tale Theater"; documentaries on dance, music, and art; movies based on classic books; and docudramas on historic events.

4. Invest in one or two magazine subscriptions for Flavio according to his interest and reading ability. One suggestion is *Zillions*, the *Consumers' Reports* for children.

For the Educational Specialist

General

1. Gradually teach Flavio about his strengths and weaknesses. Help him to predict situations that might present problems for him and how to plan compensations in advance.

2. Encourage the Lopezes to obtain the videotapes recommended above. Use them as starting points for reading or writing activities.

Oral Language

1. Directly work on vocabulary development:
   a. Take vocabulary from words presented in Flavio's content area texts and literature.

b. Teach Flavio the vocabulary necessary to create subordinate clauses in complex sentences (transition words). Specific needs include spatial, temporal, comparative, exclusionary, and directional concepts. Teach him how to use connecting words such as, *consequently*, *although*, and *while*. (See attached materials on cohesive devices.)

c. Make sure that Flavio learns how to pronounce and spell new words correctly.

2. When Flavio understands the meaning of a transition word, teach him to comprehend complex sentences using that word. Then provide ample practice in creating complex sentences using the word.

3. Teach words in categories. For example, teach a group of words denoting spatial concepts, making sure that Flavio understands the common factor (space).

4. Create an awareness of the need to provide a clear referent for every pronoun used.

5. Increase Flavio's awareness of his language behaviors and progress by audiotaping or videotaping him before and while you are working on a skill.

6. Use visual aids, such as pictures or graphs, to illustrate new skills and concepts. Overteach and make sure Flavio understands the concept before removing the visual aids. Continue working with the same skill or concept using the printed form on Flavio's independent reading level as a model for explanation. When Flavio can read and understand the new skill/concept, have him practice writing examples.

Reading

1. Teach decoding skills and structural analysis by presenting common word parts and families. Build a word part bank with word families on each card. Do not use a phonics approach.

2. For all decoding skills taught, use writing and the computer for drill and practice. Make sure that Flavio is fairly adept at a skill before he practices it independently.

3. Use the suggestions under oral language to teach and reinforce reading skills at the vocabulary and sentence level.

4. Help Flavio learn to paraphrase complex sentences to ensure he has understood the sentence and to build linguistic flexibility.

5. Reinforce Flavio's attempts to use context clues. (See attached material on context clues.)

6. Teach Flavio to state the main idea and supporting details of a paragraph, and to recognize extraneous information.

7. Teach Flavio how to survey a chapter or section of a chapter before reading it to develop a mental framework for the information. Have him write all the chapter questions on a notecard to refer to as he reads the chapter.

Written Language

1. Use the word families taught for reading to introduce new spelling words.

2. For more difficult spelling words, teach Flavio to study using the Look-Spell-See-Write strategy. (See attached outline.)

3. Teach Flavio to recognize sentence boundaries so that he will know where to end a sentence.

4. Teach all writing mechanics in a consistent, sequential manner, a few at a time. Provide a great amount of practice. Use strategies to aid in remembering the rules for punctuation. For example, help Flavio develop a mnemonic strategy.

5. To help Flavio with planning and organization, teach him the writing process approach (i.e., brainstorming, categorizing, mapping, verbalizing relationships among ideas and details, drafting, editing, and revising).

6. Teach Flavio an adaptation of the Error Monitoring strategy, using the mnemonic SH! COPS! (Sentences complete, Handwriting, Capitalization, Overall appearance, Punctuation, Spelling). (See attached material on Error Monitoring.)

7. Teach Flavio touch-typing. When he is proficient, introduce a word processing program with a spelling checker. Using a word processor will make writing more enjoyable and revising easier.

8. Provide Flavio with a pocket-sized, electronic speller.

Math

1. Teach Touch Math (Bullock, 1991) for computation of the basic operations. Overteach it so that it is absolutely automatic.

2. Teach Flavio how to count, trade, and change money.

3. Teach Flavio basic fraction concepts using manipulatives, such as Cuisenaire Rods. Also use real objects such as fruit, a dozen eggs, and a yard-stick. Then introduce decimals.

4. Teach Flavio to translate two-step word problems into computation.

5. In order to teach word problems, engage Flavio in a short project that requires computation. When the need for computation arises, teach him to state the question that has to be answered to solve the problem.

6. Assign computer math games for homework/fun between sessions.

For the Teachers

1. Be aware of the complexity of the instructions you give and paraphrase whenever possible into simpler sentences.

2. Give Flavio as much time as he needs to respond to a question. If he hesitates, do not assume that he does not know the answer.

3. When possible, allow Flavio to take untimed tests.

4. After a test, give Flavio an opportunity to tell you the answers. He may have the information, but be unable to express it adequately in writing.

5. Flavio will learn best and remain involved with activities that are taught through cooperative learning groups and whole group discussion with active student participation, interspersed with short periods of lecture or instruction.

6. Be aware that Flavio may need extra instructions for a task after the class has begun to work and extra help with the task periodically throughout. Stop by his desk or assign a peer tutor to check in with him.

7. Use visual aids that clearly illustrate and accompany the verbal information that Flavio is expected to learn. Be aware that he may not benefit from purely auditory activities.

8. Encourage Flavio to ask questions in class when he has not understood something. Provide positive reinforcement when he asks for clarification.

Scores

Administered by Irene Romero, Ph.D.

Wechsler Intelligence Scale for Children — Revised
Subtests

Information	7	Picture Completion	12
Similarities	6	Picture Arrangement	12
Arithmetic	7	Block Design	10
Vocabulary	4	Object Assembly	12
Comprehension	7	Coding	13
(Digit Span)	6		
Verbal scale	77	*Performance scale*	112

Woodcock-Johnson Psycho-Educational Battery — Revised: Cognitive Battery
See attached Compuscore

Bender Visual-Motor Gestalt Test: Koppitz Scoring System
   1 error   50-60 percentile

Administered by Anne Compton, Ph.D.

Woodcock-Johnson Psycho-Educational Battery — Revised: Achievement Battery (Form A)
See attached Compuscore

Analytical Reading Inventory:

Grade Level	Word Lists	Contextual Recognition	Reading Comprehension	Listening Comprehension
1	Inst	Inst	Ind	
2	Inst	Inst	Ind	
3	F	Inst	Ind	
4		Inst/F	Inst	Ind
4 (Science)		F	Inst/F	
5		F	F	F
6				Inst
7				Inst/F

Administered by Sharon Kwang-Olafssen M.S., M.A., SLP/CCC

Clinical Evaluation of Language Fundamentals — Revised		Test of Language Competence — Expanded	
Subtests		Subtests	
Word Classes	8	Ambiguous Sentences	4
Semantic Relationships	5	Making Inferences	7
Listening to Paragraphs	9		
Oral Directions	6		
Recalling Sentences	3		

TEST 27

Writing Samples (cont.)

11.

the boy is opening his box.

12.

The sel is playing with a boll.

13.

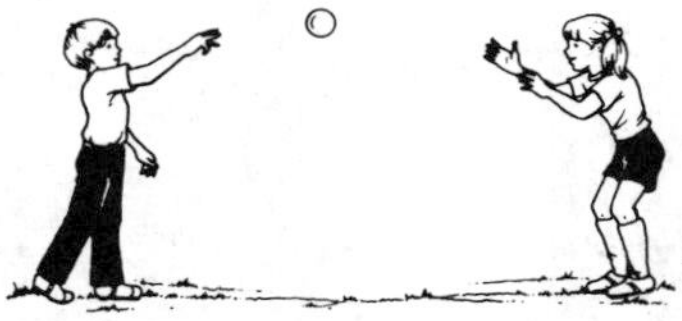

and

The boy and grils are through ball to each other.

14.

both can light up and are worm.

15.

because

the boy and girl are run up a" he" said that with can do not but he can because his lage is broken

Figure III–8. Examples of Flavio's Responses on the Writing Samples Test.

<u>First attempt</u>

The monkey is trying to break the rock for it can hit the house to kill the people because the people want to kill him that why he want to kill the people in the house

<u>Asked to write a "real" story</u>

Once day some people want to sky on top a mountains that onboby want befor, "Because they," said that a big appe was up there live in a cave but the people did not know that the appe was up there, So they where walking up the mountin and the people was singing and the appe here's the people singing and then the appe went out side and sew that people, Where come to kill him but the people where not going to kill they were going to sky on top the mountrou. Than he ~~the~~ went back into the cave to wite for tham and the appe sew the people with fire stick in there hend to bran him up, And then eat him for lunch when the people sew the appe tring to break the rock to kill tham the people ran down as fast as they can but they where only 2 guys. When the 2 guys when in to the house they toled what they sew everboby came to kill the appe and when they did kill the appe they had him for lunch.

Figure III-9. Flavio's Writing Sample Illustrating Good Story Grammar but Poor Language and Visual Recall Skills.

```
              COMPUSCORE FOR THE WJ-R 3.0
                      11:11 am
                Norms Based on Grade
=====================================================================
Name: Flavio Tapia                 ID:                    Page: 1
=====================================================================

Sex: M                          School/Agency: Carlton Middle
Examiner:                       Teacher/Dept:
Testing Date: 01/06/1992        City:                    State:
Birth Date: 11/18/1979          Adult Subjects
Age:  12 years  2 months          Education:
Grade Placement: 6.5              Occupation:
Years Retained: 0               Other Info:
Years Skipped: 0                  Glasses: No              Used: No
Years of Schooling:  6.5          Hearing Aid: No          Used: No

---------------------------------------------------------------------
```

Test Name	Raw Score	W		Age Equiv.	Grade Equiv.	RMI			SS	PR
1. Memory for Names	63-C	506		22[55]	14.2	94/90			107	68
			(E)	8-10	3.2		-1	SEM	103	58
			(D)	22[82]	16.9[84]		+1	SEM	111	77
2. Memory for Sentences	37	474		5-4	K.3	23/90			73	4
			(E)	4-6	K.0[36]		-1	SEM	67	1
			(D)	7-0	1.7		+1	SEM	79	8
3. Visual Matching	43	509		11-8	6.1	88/90			98	44
			(E)	10-3	4.8		-1	SEM	91	27
			(D)	13-10	8.6		+1	SEM	105	63
4. Incomplete Words	23	489		6-7	1.3	68/90			78	7
			(E)	5-6	K.3		-1	SEM	69	2
			(D)	9-11	4.6		+1	SEM	87	19
5. Visual Closure	37	513		24	16.9[55]	96/90			116	86
			(E)	11-8	6.2		-1	SEM	107	68
			(D)	29[83]	16.9[89]		+1	SEM	125	95
6. Picture Vocabulary	30	490		8-5	2.9	53/90			80	9
			(E)	7-0	1.7		-1	SEM	74	4
			(D)	10-1	4.7		+1	SEM	86	18
7. Analysis-Synthesis	18-F	488		7-10	2.5	58/90			83	13
			(E)	6-9	1.4		-1	SEM	77	6
			(D)	9-9	4.4		+1	SEM	89	23
BROAD COGNITIVE ABILITY (E Dev)	---	494		8-8	3.1	75/90			81	11
			(E)	6-6	1.2		-1	SEM	77	6
			(D)	11-9	6.3		+1	SEM	85	16
BROAD COGNITIVE ABILITY (Std)	---	496		9-4	3.9	77/90			81	11
			(E)	7-6	2.1		-1	SEM	77	6
			(D)	12-2	6.7		+1	SEM	85	16

Figure III-10. Flavio's Compuscore.   *(continued)*

===
Name: Flavio Tapia   ID: Page: 2
===

Test Name	Raw Score	W		Age Equiv.	Grade Equiv.	RMI			SS	PR
8. Visual-Auditory Learning	12-K	502		14-4	9.2	92/90			104	60
			(E)	7-7	2.1		-1	SEM	98	45
			(D)	25[77]	16.9[71]		+1	SEM	110	75
9. Memory for Words	16	495		9-2	3.8	77/90			94	33
			(E)	7-4	2.0		-1	SEM	86	18
			(D)	12-2	6.8		+1	SEM	102	55
10. Cross Out	26	517		15-4	10.2	97/90			121	92
			(E)	12-1	6.7		-1	SEM	113	81
			(D)	25[82]	16.9[64]		+1	SEM	129	97
11. Sound Blending	20	487		7-5	1.7	58/90			85	15
			(E)	6-4	1.0		-1	SEM	78	7
			(D)	9-3	3.9		+1	SEM	92	30
12. Picture Recognition	21	512		22	15.5	96/90			118	89
			(E)	11-0	5.5		-1	SEM	111	77
			(D)	30[79]	16.9[85]		+1	SEM	125	95
13. Oral Vocabulary	15	481		7-9	2.5	32/90			73	4
			(E)	6-9	1.5		-1	SEM	67	1
			(D)	9-0	3.7		+1	SEM	79	8
14. Concept Formation	21-O	502		10-7	5.0	84/90			96	40
			(E)	8-8	3.3		-1	SEM	92	30
			(D)	14-4	9.2		+1	SEM	100	50
LONG-TERM RETRIEVAL (Glr)	---	504		17-3	11.0	93/90			107	68
			(E)	7-11	2.6		-1	SEM	103	58
			(D)	24[78]	16.9[75]		+1	SEM	111	77
SHORT-TERM MEMORY (Gsm)	---	484		7-1	1.7	50/90			81	10
			(E)	5-6	K.3		-1	SEM	75	5
			(D)	8-9	3.4		+1	SEM	87	19
PROCESSING SPEED (Gs)	---	513		12-11	7.4	94/90			109	72
			(E)	10-11	5.4		-1	SEM	103	58
			(D)	18-7	11.5		+1	SEM	115	84
AUDITORY PROCESSING (Ga)	---	488		7-1	1.6	63/90			76	5
			(E)	5-11	K.7		-1	SEM	70	2
			(D)	9-5	4.1		+1	SEM	82	12
VISUAL PROCESSING (Gv)	---	512		21	14.9	96/90			120	91
			(E)	11-0	5.6		-1	SEM	113	81
			(D)	29[86]	16.9[89]		+1	SEM	127	96

Figure III–10. *(continued)*

```
========================================================================
Name: Flavio Tapia                    ID:                        Page: 3
========================================================================
```

Test Name	Raw Score	W		Age Equiv.	Grade Equiv.	RMI			SS	PR
COMPREHENSION- KNOWLEDGE (Gc)	---	486		8-1	2.8	45/90			77	6
			(E)	6-11	1.6		-1	SEM	73	4
			(D)	9-6	4.2		+1	SEM	81	10
FLUID REASONING (Gf)	---	495		9-2	3.7	73/90			90	24
			(E)	7-8	2.3		-1	SEM	86	18
			(D)	11-5	6.1		+1	SEM	94	34
BROAD COGNITIVE ABILITY (Ext)	---	498		9-9	4.4	81/90			85	17
			(E)	7-9	2.4		-1	SEM	82	12
			(D)	13-1	7.6		+1	SEM	88	21
READING APTITUDE	---	488		-----	-----	53/90			72	3
			(E)	-----	-----		-1	SEM	69	2
			(D)	-----	-----		+1	SEM	75	5
MATHEMATICS APTITUDE	---	495		-----	-----	68/90			83	12
			(E)	-----	-----		-1	SEM	80	9
			(D)	-----	-----		+1	SEM	86	18
WRITTEN LANGUAGE APTITUDE	---	495		-----	-----	73/90			82	12
			(E)	-----	-----		-1	SEM	79	8
			(D)	-----	-----		+1	SEM	85	16
KNOWLEDGE APTITUDE	---	494		-----	-----	73/90			84	14
			(E)	-----	-----		-1	SEM	81	10
			(D)	-----	-----		+1	SEM	87	19
17. Numbers Reversed	11	495		9-7	4.3	71/90			90	25
			(E)	8-1	2.8		-1	SEM	83	13
			(D)	11-6	6.0		+1	SEM	97	42
19. Spatial Relations	25	517		23	14.9	98/90			122	93
			(E)	14-6	9.3		-1	SEM	115	84
			(D)	30[78]	16.9[72]		+1	SEM	129	97
20. Listening Comprehension	23	490		8-7	3.1	61/90			84	14
			(E)	7-0	1.6		-1	SEM	76	5
			(D)	10-8	4.9		+1	SEM	92	30
21. Verbal Analogies	15	504		11-0	5.6	85/90			97	41
			(E)	9-1	3.8		-1	SEM	91	27
			(D)	14-0	8.6		+1	SEM	103	58
ORAL LANGUAGE	---	488		8-2	2.8	53/90			76	5
			(E)	6-10	1.5		-1	SEM	72	3
			(D)	9-10	4.4		+1	SEM	80	9

Figure III-10. *(continued)*

```
===================================================================================
Name: Flavio Tapia                    ID:                          Page: 4
===================================================================================
```

Test Name	Raw Score	W		Age Equiv.	Grade Equiv.	RMI			SS	PR

```
===================================================================================
                  Form A was used to obtain Achievement Scores
===================================================================================
```

Test Name	Raw Score	W		Age Equiv.	Grade Equiv.	RMI			SS	PR
22. Letter-Word Identification	35	479		8-8	3.3	25/90			79	8
			(E)	8-2	2.7		-1	SEM	74	4
			(D)	9-3	4.1		+1	SEM	84	14
23. Passage Comprehension	18	484		8-10	3.3	45/90			80	9
			(E)	8-1	2.6		-1	SEM	74	4
			(D)	9-10	4.4		+1	SEM	86	18
24. Calculation	23	503		10-9	5.4	71/90			89	22
			(E)	9-11	4.6		-1	SEM	84	14
			(D)	11-9	6.3		+1	SEM	94	34
25. Applied Problems	33	499		10-4	4.9	75/90			91	28
			(E)	9-3	3.6		-1	SEM	85	16
			(D)	11-11	6.5		+1	SEM	97	42
26. Dictation	23	472		8-0	2.5	15/90			66	1
			(E)	7-5	1.8		-1	SEM	60	0.4
			(D)	8-7	3.2		+1	SEM	72	3
27. Writing Samples	22-V	492		8-8	3.3	68/90			81	10
			(E)	7-6	2.2		-1	SEM	75	5
			(D)	10-10	5.6		+1	SEM	87	19
28. Science	25	498		9-10	4.5	73/90			88	22
			(E)	8-6	3.2		-1	SEM	81	10
			(D)	11-10	6.4		+1	SEM	95	37
29. Social Studies	19	490		9-1	3.7	50/90			83	13
			(E)	7-11	2.4		-1	SEM	77	6
			(D)	10-5	5.1		+1	SEM	89	23
30. Humanities	19	478		6-8	1.3	25/90			70	2
			(E)	5-3	K.2		-1	SEM	64	1
			(D)	8-0	2.6		+1	SEM	76	5
BROAD READING	---	482		8-9	3.4	34/90			76	6
			(E)	8-2	2.7		-1	SEM	72	3
			(D)	9-8	4.3		+1	SEM	80	9
BROAD MATH (Gq)	---	501		10-7	5.2	73/90			87	20
			(E)	9-7	4.1		-1	SEM	83	13
			(D)	11-9	6.4		+1	SEM	91	27

Figure III-10. *(continued)*

```
===============================================================================
Name: Flavio Tapia                    ID:                          Page: 5
===============================================================================
```

```
-------------------------------------------------------------------------------
                   Raw              Age      Grade
Test Name        Score    W      Equiv.    Equiv.      RMI              SS   PR
-------------------------------------------------------------------------------
```

Test Name	Raw Score	W		Age Equiv.	Grade Equiv.	RMI			SS	PR
BROAD WRITTEN LANGUAGE	---	482		8-2	2.8	39/90			66	1
			(E)	7-6	1.9		-1	SEM	61	0.5
			(D)	9-3	3.9		+1	SEM	71	3
BROAD KNOWLEDGE (E Dev)	---	489		8-7	3.2	50/90			78	7
			(E)	7-4	1.9		-1	SEM	74	4
			(D)	10-1	4.7		+1	SEM	82	12
SKILLS (E Dev)	---	483		8-9	3.4	34/90			74	4
			(E)	8-1	2.6		-1	SEM	70	2
			(D)	9-8	4.4		+1	SEM	78	7
31. Word Attack	6	472		7-5	1.9	21/90			68	2
			(E)	6-10	1.5		-1	SEM	63	1
			(D)	8-1	2.5		+1	SEM	73	4
33. Quantitative Concepts	28	488		9-4	4.0	34/90			78	7
			(E)	8-8	3.2		-1	SEM	71	3
			(D)	10-3	4.9		+1	SEM	85	16
BASIC READING SKILLS	---	476		8-2	2.7	25/90			73	3
			(E)	7-8	2.0		-1	SEM	69	2
			(D)	8-9	3.5		+1	SEM	77	6
BASIC MATH SKILLS	---	496		10-2	4.8	55/90			80	9
			(E)	9-4	3.9		-1	SEM	75	5
			(D)	11-1	5.7		+1	SEM	85	16
MATHEMATICS REASONING	Use scores from Test 25: Applied Problems									

Figure III-10. *(continued)*

```
================================================================================
Name: Flavio Tapia                    ID:                        Page: 6
================================================================================
```

Intra-Cognitive Discrepancies

```
================================================================================
```

	ACTUAL SS	OTHER SS	PREDICTED SS	SS DIFF	PR	SD DIFF
Long-Term Retrieval (Glr)	107	92	89	18	94	1.53
Short-Term Memory (Gsm)	81	96	96	-15	12	-1.15
Processing Speed (Gs)	109	92	93	16	88	1.18
Auditory Processing (Ga)	76	97	97	-21	6	-1.54
Visual Processing (Gv)	120	90	91	29	98	2.13
Comprehension-Knowledge (Gc)	77	97	96	-19	5	-1.61
Fluid Reasoning (Gf)	90	95	93	-3	40	-0.24

Aptitude/Achievement Discrepancies
(Based on Scholastic Aptitude with ACH Broad Clusters)

```
================================================================================
```

	ACTUAL ACH SS	APTITUDE SS	PREDICTED SS	SS DIFF	PR	SD DIFF
Oral Language	---	---	---	----	-----	------
Broad Reading	76	72	79	-3	39	-0.28
Broad Mathematics (Gq)	87	83	88	-1	46	-0.09
Broad Written Language	66	82	88	-22	2	-1.96
Broad Knowledge	78	84	90	-12	15	-1.02

Intra-Achievement Discrepancies

```
================================================================================
```

	ACTUAL SS	OTHER SS	PREDICTED SS	SS DIFF	PR	SD DIFF
Broad Reading (R)	76	77	76	0	50	0.00
Broad Mathematics (M)	87	73	75	12	88	1.18
Broad Written Language (W)	66	80	80	-14	7	-1.44
Broad Knowledge (K)	78	76	77	1	54	0.10

Figure III-10. *(continued)*

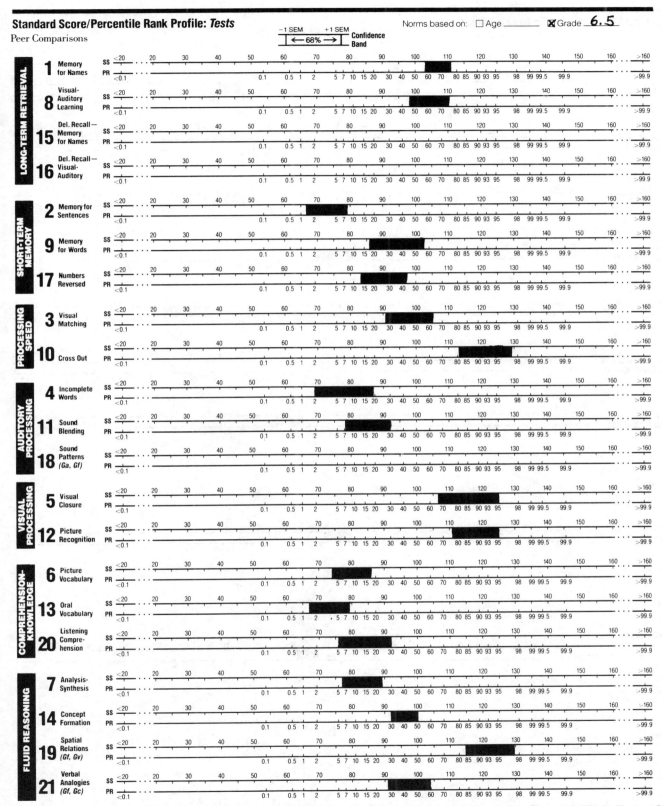

Figure III–11. Flavio's WJ-R Tests of Cognitive Ability Standard Score/Percentile Rank Profiles and WJ-R Tests of Achievement Standard Score/Percentile Rank and Age/Grade Profiles. *(continued)*

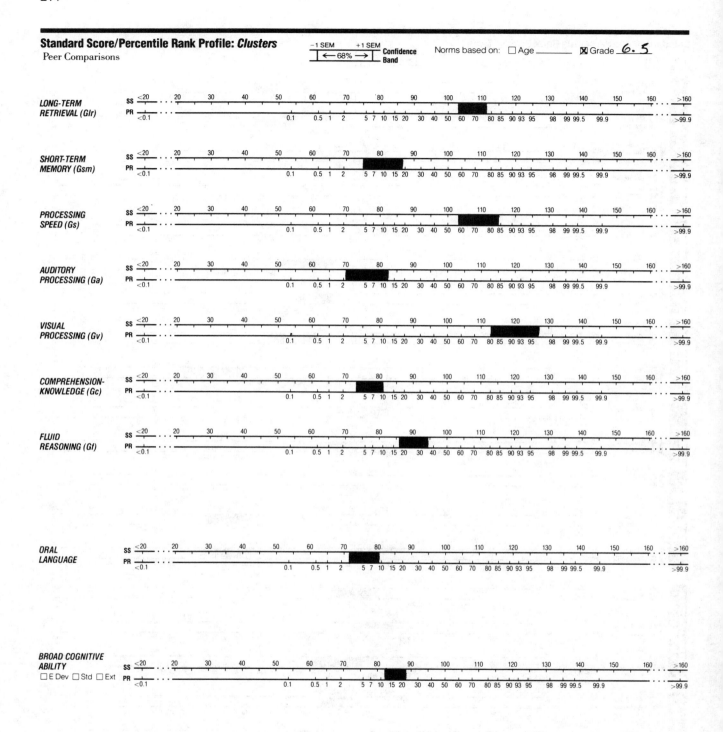

Figure III-11. *(continued)*

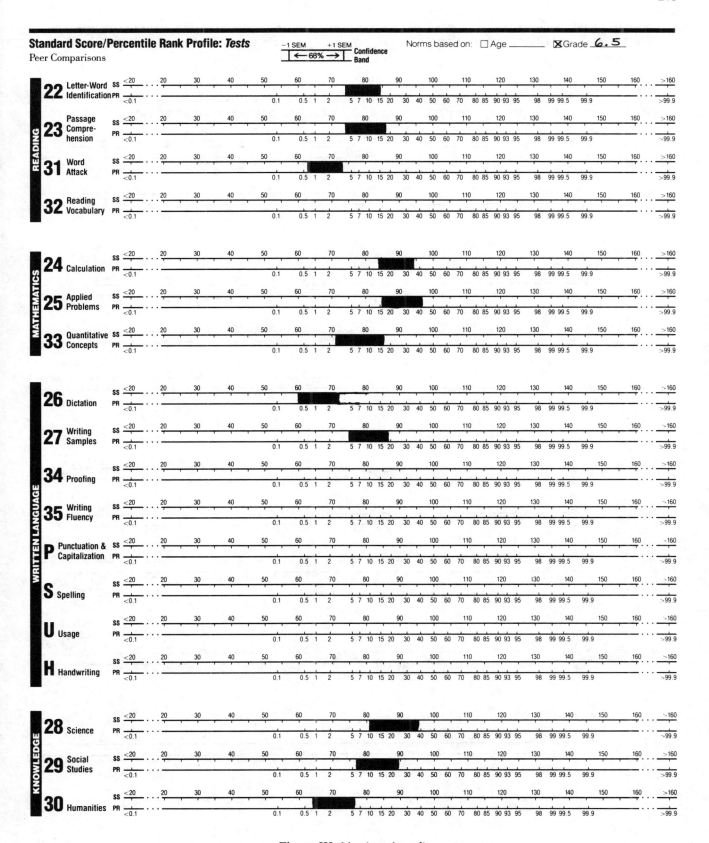

Figure III-11. *(continued)*

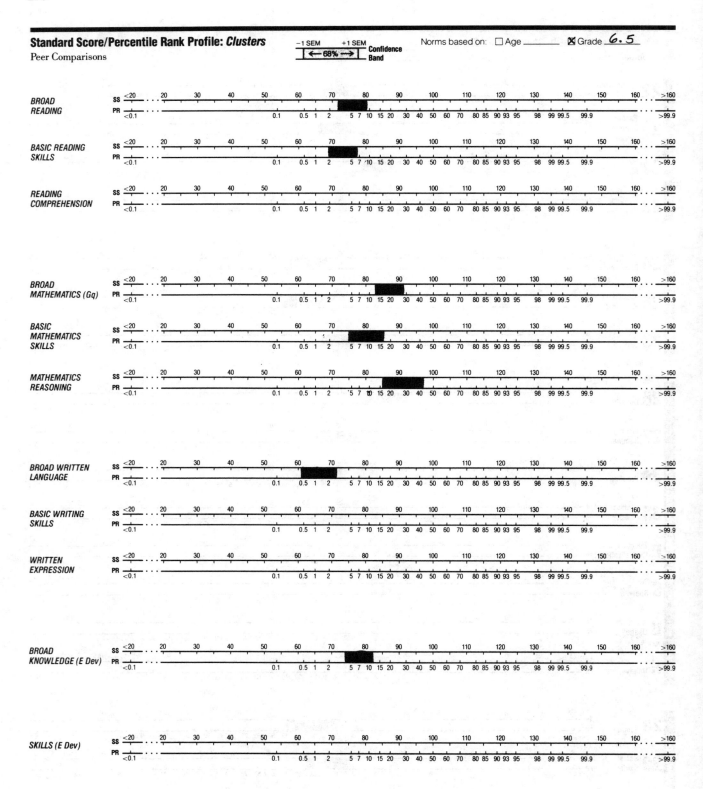

Figure III-11. *(continued)*

WOODCOCK-JOHNSON

Richard W. Woodcock
M. Bonner Johnson

FORM A

Tests of Achievement

WJ-R

STANDARD & SUPPLEMENTAL BATTERIES

TEST RECORD

Name __Flavio Tapia__ ID _____ Sex: ☒M ☐F Examiner _____

Grade Placement __6.5__ Years Retained __0__ Years Skipped __0__ Years of Schooling __6.5__

School/ Agency __Carlton Middle__ Teacher/ Department _____ City/ State _____

Adult Subjects: Education _____ Occupation _____

Other Information _____

	Year	Month	Day
Testing Date:	92	1	6
Birth Date: −	79	11	18
Difference:			
Age:	12 − 2	·	

(Round to whole months)

Does the subject have glasses? ☐ Yes ☒ No   Were they used during testing? ☐ Yes ☒ No
Does the subject have a hearing aid? ☐ Yes ☒ No   Was it used during testing? ☐ Yes ☒ No

---

Age/Grade Profile: *Tests*
Developmental Levels

RMIs based on ☐ Age _____ ☒ Grade __6.5__

EASY ← → DIFFICULT **Instructional Range**

Scores

Test	W	RMI	
22 Letter-Word Identification	479	25 /90	Other
23 Passage Comprehension	484	45 /90	Other
31 Word Attack	472	21 /90	Other
32 Reading Vocabulary		/90	Other
24 Calculation	503	71 /90	Other
25 Applied Problems	499	75 /90	Other
33 Quantitative Concepts	488	34 /90	Other

READING

MATHEMATICS

Do these test results provide a fair representation of the subject's present functioning? ☒ Yes ☐ No

If not, what is the reason for questioning the results? _____

DLM Teaching Resources

One DLM Park • Allen, Texas 75002

Figure III–11. *(continued)*

Age/Grade Profile: Tests *(Continued)*
Developmental Levels

RMIs based on ☐ Age _____ ☒ Grade *6.5*

EASY ← → DIFFICULT
Instructional Range

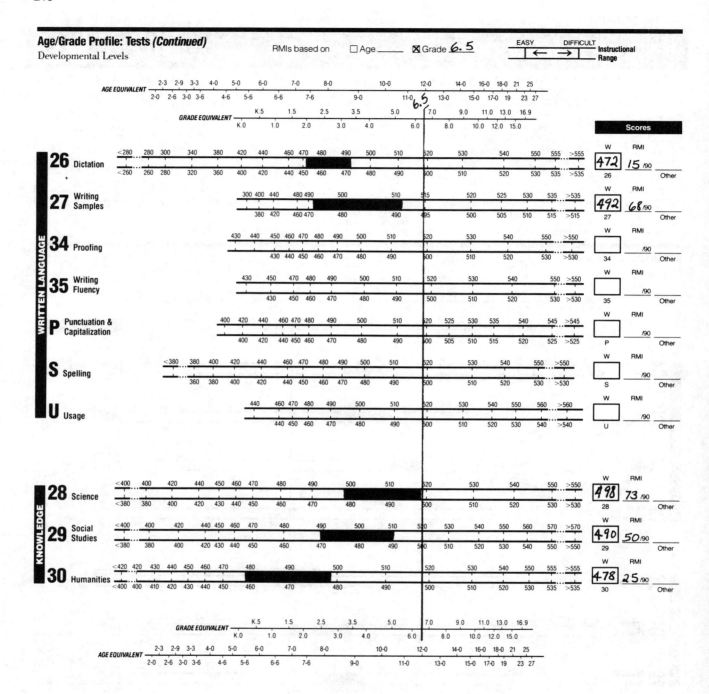

Figure III–11. *(continued)*

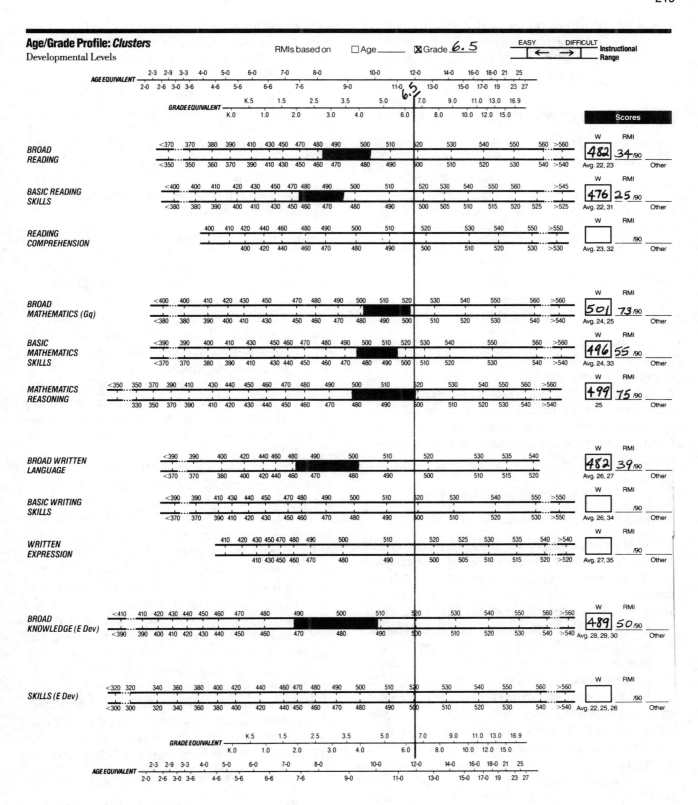

Figure III–11. *(continued)*

Diagnosis: Borderline mentally handicapped; relative weakness in oral language; relative strength in lower-level visual processing

PSYCHOEDUCATIONAL EVALUATION

Name: Lisa Goldman
Birthdate: 9/7/78

Evaluator:
Foster Parents: George & Andrea Goldman

Chronological Age: 13-0

School: Palo Verde Elementary

Grade: 7.1

Test Dates: 9/15, 9/16, 9/17/91

Reason for Referral

Lisa was referred for testing by her school counselor, David Forrest, because she does not appear to be making academic or social progress in her current special education placement for children with emotional disturbances. Mr. Forrest requested more specific information about her cognitive abilities and recommendations for increased academic success.

Background Information

Home

Lisa is a 13-year-old female of Hispanic and Anglo descent. She and her 10-year-old sister were adopted by Mr. and Mrs. Goldman 5 years ago. Mr. Forrest described the home environment as stable, secure, and loving. The Department of Economic Security's records report that Lisa's mother used crack cocaine and drank alcohol heavily throughout both of her pregnancies and that Lisa was subjected to severe physical and emotional abuse and neglect until she and her sister were removed from the home 7 years ago. Lisa has subtle facial characteristics that suggest Fetal Alcohol Syndrome. No information is available regarding her attainment of developmental milestones.

The Goldmans provide excellent guidance to the girls in terms of social and adaptive behavior and have revised their expectations to their perceptions of the girls' abilities. They stated that when talking to Lisa, they must face her, limit the number of instructions given, and get verbal feedback from her. They described her as "visually astute." She is able to learn day-to-day activities, such as how to do the laundry, but has difficulty making decisions, such as sequencing the steps of the process or handling different types of clothing. She is very thorough in the jobs she has learned and this makes her slow. Additionally, she is neat and organized.

The Goldmans stated that Lisa has a particularly poor vocabulary. They noted that Lisa is also becoming aware that she does not understand most of what she hears and is beginning to express her frustration.

School

Due to the school's cutoff date for enrollment, Lisa turned 6 shortly after she began kindergarten. Consequently, she has always been one of the oldest children in her class. Until this year, Lisa has been in a self-contained class for the Emotionally Handicapped at Monroe School. This placement was originally made because Lisa paid little attention to task, evidenced severe social withdrawal, and often hid under her desk making odd noises or singing to herself. She has never received language therapy and was mainstreamed last year into a sixth-grade class for reading.

In a recent conference, both of Lisa's teachers from last year noted that Lisa is missing many of the concepts with which other children her age are familiar and that she appears to be significantly deficient in the amount of words she understands and can use. She was recently placed in a third-grade class for social studies, as an aide, because she could read so few of the words in her already-adapted classroom text and understood almost none of the content. The third-grade teacher teaches Lisa the words and concepts associated with the current unit so that Lisa can learn them herself as well as help the younger children. Sometimes, however, the children end up explaining the concepts to Lisa.

Both teachers have noted that Lisa is more able to pay attention to task when the task is appropriate for her level of skill and that she no longer demonstrates her previous strange behaviors. She is still shy, but not excessively so.

Previous and Concurrent Evaluations

Within the past 2 months, Lisa has been examined by her pediatrician and ophthalmologist. Her hearing was found to be within normal limits and her glasses prescription is appropriate.

Subsequent to this evaluation but prior to the writing of this report, Lisa was evaluated by the speech/language pathologist and was found to have significant language deficits in both comprehension and expression. Those findings are integrated into the body of this report.

In January 1991, Lisa was administered the Wechsler Intelligence Scale for Children - Revised. She obtained a Verbal scale score of 67, a Performance scale score of 74, and a full scale score of 69, placing her just below the range of borderline mental retardation. Due to indications of a low level of general cognitive abilities, an adaptive behavior scale, the Scales of Independent Behavior (SIB), was administered to the Goldmans.

Tests Administered

Woodcock-Johnson Psycho-Educational Battery — Revised (WJ-R):
    Cognitive Battery: Tests 1–14, 20–21
      Achievement Battery (Form A): Tests 22–30
Analytical Reading Inventory (ARI)
Scales of Independent Behavior (SIB)

Behavioral Observations

Lisa was cooperative during testing and concentrated well on every task. She appeared to care about her performance. She worked hard and tried to think through every difficult question, which increased the length of the test sessions. She was able to stay totally on task for one 3-hour session and two 2-hour sessions with short breaks.

Test Results

The tests of the WJ-R were scored according to grade norms. When no difference was found between the two component tests of a factor or cluster, only the factor or cluster score is discussed. Verbal labels are used to express standard score 68% confidence bands. A complete set of test scores is appended to this report.

Cognitive Abilities

According to the WJ-R results, Lisa's overall cognitive functioning is in the *Very Low/Low* range, or between mild and borderline mental retardation,

with some specific cognitive strengths. A test of adaptive behavior confirmed a generalized low level of functioning (see below).

Lisa demonstrates *Average* ability in processing pictorial information and *Low Average* ability in rapid processing of visual symbols. Her ability to associate verbal labels with visual cues and retrieve the associations later was in the *Low Average* range. These results clearly indicate that the visual channel is a critical learning modality for Lisa and that any new information she is expected to learn and remember should be introduced visually.

In contrast, Lisa evidenced considerable difficulty on the higher-level reasoning tasks which are presented visually along with oral instructions. She scored in the *Low* range and despite many errors and continuous corrective feedback, persisted in a simple strategy until each test was discontinued. These results suggest that Lisa is not able to use her relatively strong visual processing skills for higher-level reasoning.

In processing and producing linguistic information at all levels, word to discourse, Lisa's scores varied from the *Very Low* to the *Low* range. She has great difficulty with phonological processing at the word level, interfering with learning correct pronunciations of words and decoding skills for reading and spelling. Her fund of vocabulary, from concrete to abstract, is severely limited, impeding her ability to learn new words and information. She can understand and use a low level of complex sentence structures, but does not understand the transition words that signal specific linguistic relationships between clauses and between sentences (e.g., *if/then, except, while*). Lisa understands the "wh" question words, but not relative clauses introduced by them. She has difficulty processing and remembering sentences of more than eight words, and her comprehension of spoken language is literal. Her ability to make inferences appears to be restricted, at least in part, by her lack of experience and general knowledge. Pragmatically, Lisa inappropriately presupposes listener knowledge of her topic and uses unclear pronoun referents, but has some strong conversational skills, such as turn taking and conversation break down and repair. In discourse, Lisa can generate ideas, but needs cues to help her with organization and separation of critical from trivial details. Formal and informal test results also indicate that Lisa has difficulty using verbal information for reasoning and problem solving.

Lisa demonstrates a significant intracognitive discrepancy in Comprehension-Knowledge, which reflects vocabulary and cultural knowledge. Only 4% of students with the same predicted Comprehension-Knowledge standard score of 80 would have obtained a score as low as or lower than Lisa's score of 61. Lisa demonstrates a significant strength in Visual Processing. Only 5% of students with her predicted score of 79 would have obtained a Visual Processing score as high as or higher than her score of 100.

Academic Achievement

Generally, Lisa scored in the *Very Low/Low* range in reading, math, and written language. Her general knowledge was in the *Very Low* range.

Lisa's reading deficits reflect her language weaknesses in the subskills of word attack, word recognition, vocabulary knowledge, comprehension of complex sentence structure and linguistic relationships, recall of facts, using prior knowledge, and making inferences. Lisa's reading instructional level is between Primer and grade 1. She performed significantly higher on the Passage Comprehension test than on the Listening Comprehension test, again demonstrating her advantage when she can use the visual modality. An important factor here is that when reading, Lisa has control over how fast she takes in the information, but when listening, she must process information at the speaker's pace.

Based on the WJ-R, Lisa's ability to express her ideas in writing, *Low Average* when compared to her grade-peers, is significantly higher than her knowledge and use of basic writing skills, which are in the *Very Low* range. Her written composition, although quite immature in all aspects, was better organized and more fluent than her oral language. This difference may be due to the amount of time she has to organize her ideas on paper and her ability to self-monitor and revise, so that the reader sees only the final product. Still, she is very slow at putting ideas on paper (three words per minute), and her final product reflects the same language deficits that affect reading.

Lisa's math achievement is in the *Low* range. She can add and subtract with regrouping and can compute one-digit by two-digit multiplication problems with factors below six. She was able to apply these skills to the problems presented with illustrations,

but not to printed word problems. She had difficulty with some basic math vocabulary, such as "how much more."

Lisa's general knowledge is significantly below her other achievement scores. This discrepancy may be understood in terms of her deprived background and significant language and reasoning deficits. As well, lack of background knowledge restricts her ability to learn from reading and spoken language at home and in the classroom.

No intra-achievement discrepancies were found. The only aptitude–achievement discrepancy was in the area of Broad Knowledge. Only 2% of seventh-grade students with a Broad Knowledge Aptitude score identical to Lisa's score of 84 would obtain a Broad Knowledge Achievement score as low as or lower than her score of 62.

Adaptive Behavior

The Scales of Independent Behavior were administered to Mr. and Mrs. Goldman. The purposes were to substantiate the diagnosis of mild to borderline mental retardation, to obtain information about Lisa's ability to function in nonacademic areas of life, and to establish and prioritize a list of skills necessary for functional independence in adult life, specific to Lisa's needs. A separate report was generated which includes a prioritized list of skills needing development based on the results from the 14 subscales of the four clusters. Only the results of the four major clusters and the Broad Independence cluster are reported here.

When compared to a broad sample of children her age, Lisa is seriously deficient in the four major areas measured. Except in Personal Living Skills (Percentile Rank: 4), Lisa is in the lower 1% of her age-peers in development of functional living skills. In Motor Skills, both gross and fine, Lisa's functioning is equivalent to that of an 8-year-old child. She appears to have most difficulty in Social and Communication Skills; her greatest deficiency is in the area of language comprehension, in which her functioning level is equivalent to that of a 2-year-old child. Lisa's most variable area is Community Living Skills, with her greatest needs in understanding the value of money and using money. In Personal Living Skills, Lisa functions generally like a 10-year-old, with her greatest need in learning to dress herself.

Conclusions

Lisa has general cognitive abilities in the upper level of the mild mentally retarded range. Even compared with this level of cognitive functioning, she has a significant language impairment and is significantly delayed in all areas of functional living skills. *Low Average* to *Average* visual processing skills provide a critical channel for learning. Lisa demonstrates high motivation in that she appears to be using all of her cognitive abilities in attempting academic tasks, has devised numerous strategies to help herself, and is persistent.

Recommendations

General

1. Schedule a multidisciplinary meeting to discuss the appropriateness of Lisa's current placement in the class for children with emotional disturbances. Another placement would be better suited to her needs at this time.

2. Provide Lisa language therapy with a speech/language pathologist for a minimum of 1 hour daily.

3. The speech/language pathologist should have ongoing communication with Lisa's teachers concerning:

   a. the current focus of therapy and ways to integrate this into classroom work to reinforce newly acquired language skills;

   b. the current unit or skill being presented in class and any modifications in teaching techniques or style of presentation that will allow Lisa to process the information adequately; and

   c. lack of adequate social language or social language that Lisa appears to misinterpret or use inappropriately.

4. It would be beneficial for Lisa's parents and all professionals involved with Lisa to discuss which of the following recommendations will best fit into each of their programs, how others might be included, and ways in which they could assist each other. As much as possible, the following recommendations should be used in all teaching situations throughout Lisa's day.

Teaching Approaches

1. Integrate oral language, reading, and writing for all language skills taught. The flow of presentation of any new skill or concept should move from pictorial to print (reading/writing) and oral language (listening/speaking). For example, when teaching cause/effect terms, use pictures that clearly depict the relationship, offer many printed sentences that denote the relationship, and have Lisa incorporate the terms into her writing and into oral comprehension and expression.

2. When possible, involve Lisa in any task or skill tactile-kinesthetically or experientially.

3. Be aware that Lisa's ability to benefit from any activity that is purely auditory, such as round-robin reading, is extremely limited.

4. Never assume prior knowledge or previous experience of words or information you are using to teach new concepts.

5. When teaching or speaking to Lisa, face her, pause between phrases for processing time, limit sentence or clause length to approximately 7 or 8 words, use simple vocabulary, and give Lisa an opportunity to request repetition or clarification.

6. Wait as long as necessary for Lisa to organize her thoughts and formulate her response after raising her hand or being called on. Alert Lisa that she will be given any time she needs or that she may say "I pass" if she does not know the answer.

7. Encourage Lisa to ask for clarification when she does not understand a question, instructions, tasks, or procedures.

8. Try to provide Lisa with 5 to 9 positive comments for each corrective or critical comment.

Integrated Reading, Writing, Oral Language Skills

Semantics

1. Focus on increasing vocabulary comprehension and expression. At home, the book *Animalia* (Base, 1986) might provide a source of great enjoyment while Lisa learns to name the objects and activities in the detailed pictures. Each page represents a letter; all of the pictures on the page begin with that letter.

2. Teach Lisa to comprehend and use such linguistic relationships as temporal, spatial, cause/effect, analogous, and comparative. Lisa must learn the terms indicating these concepts and how they affect meaning in phrases, simple sentences, and eventually in more complex sentences.

Syntax

1. Using terms denoting simple linguistic relationships, teach Lisa to understand, and subsequently use, complex sentences, beginning with sentences composed of only two clauses, main and subordinate.

2. Once Lisa is comfortable with the basic level of a complex sentence, teach her to understand and use sentences containing relative clauses (i.e., clauses embedded in a sentence that begin with the words *who, what, where, that*).

Organization

1. Teach Lisa how to sequence her ideas mentally so that she can state them in an organized fashion. For example, before she speaks, have her think to herself, "What is the beginning, the middle, the end?"

2. Teach Lisa story grammar to help her follow and tell a story.

3. Teach Lisa to comprehend the sequence of instructions, the terms used to denote sequence, and a strategy to remember more than two steps.

4. Teach Lisa some different ways that information might be organized and draw a visual pattern for that type of organization. For example, contrast might be depicted as a divided square with a general heading, subheadings for each side, and blocks for categories down the side (See Figure III-12a); description might be depicted as a tree with smaller branches coming off each major limb (See Figure III-12b); and cause/effect might be depicted as a circle or number of circles with an arrow leading to another circle (See Figure III-12c); chronological sequence might be depicted as a timeline.

Subsequently, teach Lisa to recognize these patterns in reading material and in orally presented information and to use these patterns to organize information for writing.

5. Teach Lisa how to give sequential instructions, including sufficient detail, concerning any task she knows how to do (e.g., cooking, getting to her house, working the VCR). Practice should always be based on tasks that she might actually have to explain.

Pragmatics

1. Teach Lisa to be aware of what information her listener could be expected to have. Teach her to explain the people and places she includes in her narratives.

Instructions

1. Get Lisa's attention before talking to her or giving any instructions (to her or to the class).

2. When giving instructions, use brief simple statements that are sequenced in the order of the tasks. Train Lisa to use verbal rehearsal for information or instructions that she has to remember for only a short time. Initially, give no more than two. When she can routinely complete all the tasks without reminders, increase the instructions to three.

3. If verbal rehearsal is not effective, teach Lisa to count the number of tasks/instructions, say the number aloud, and repeat the instructions as she "anchors" each to a finger. "Anchoring" is done by touching a finger while naming the task and visualizing its completion.

4. Teach Lisa to write lists of things she has to do or remember.

Reading

Basic Skills

1. Teach Lisa word attack skills through the use of word families. Capitalize on Lisa's strong visual memory to use well-established sight words as a basis for introducing phonic patterns, families, and common word parts. Provide sufficient practice so that

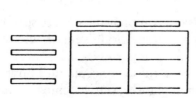

Figure III–12a. Contrast.

Figure III–12b. Description.

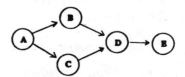

Figure III–12c. Cause-Effect.

she can automatically generalize these patterns to new words (e.g., boat → float).

2. When phonics training must be used, provide pictorial clues to help Lisa remember the sounds of any phonic elements or rules (e.g., a cup with a handle representing the *c*, and *a, o, u* in the cup to show when to use the hard *c* sound).

3. When selecting new sight words, be aware as to whether or not they are in Lisa's oral vocabulary. If not, either teach the words as new vocabulary or omit them.

Comprehension

1. Use reading materials that Lisa can easily relate to her own life and ask her guiding questions to encourage discussion.

2. Directly teach Lisa to create mental images of what she reads.

3. Teach Lisa to restate the main idea of a well-organized paragraph on a primer level and then to give related details.

4. Teach Lisa specific strategies to use when she has not understood what she has read (e.g., use context clues, reread, ask someone).

Math

1. Emphasize the meaning of math by using visuals and manipulatives to illustrate new ideas and extensions of previously learned concepts. Use real things (e.g., food, liquid measures, wood for building, money) as well as standard math teaching materials such as Cuisenaire Rods, Powers of Ten blocks, and Unifix Cubes.

2. Provide substantial practice in practical application of any new arithmetic skill Lisa is learning, both in story problems and real-life use (e.g., measuring for cooking, deciding how much to hem a dress, deciding to purchase one dress over another depending on budget considerations).

3. Teach the meaning of specific math terminology such as "how much more," "what is the difference," or "in all."

4. Be aware of the linguistic complexity of word problems that Lisa is expected to answer. You may have to simplify them.

5. In order for Lisa to develop a better sense of calendar time (days, weeks, months), give her a calendar and have her parents help her to use it to keep track of important events. She should cross off each day before bedtime and mark the end of each week. The end of the month is marked by turning the page. Use a calendar that has a holiday or seasonal picture for each month.

Problem Solving

1. Teach Lisa a problem-solving strategy. Overteach it and provide enormous amounts of practice in a variety of situations. Emphasize the need to evaluate the effectiveness of the solution and change when needed. Provide encouragement and praise for careful thinking and good reasoning.

2. Teachers and parents can learn the problem-solving strategy that Lisa learns. Use it when you are with her, especially to solve everyday problems where an immediate outcome can be seen. Verbalize the steps as you do so.

Results: Mild hearing impairment with severe academic delay; need for further evaluation

EDUCATIONAL EVALUATION

Name: Ben Testa
Birthdate: 7/10/77

Chronological Age: 13-11

Grade: 7.9

Evaluator:
Grandmother: Mrs. Rachel Cloud
School: Liberty Middle School
Test Date: 5/29/91

Reason for Referral

Ben was referred for an academic evaluation by his grandmother, Mrs. Rachel Cloud, who was concerned about Ben's poor school grades. Ben has just failed seventh grade and retention has been recommended. Mrs. Cloud requested an estimate of present academic performance and an opinion regarding the advantages and disadvantages of retention for Ben.

Background Information

Mrs. Cloud reported that Ben had chronic otitis media severe enough to prevent him from hearing most speech sounds until the age of 2. Tubes were placed in his ears, and shortly after that he began speaking single words. His speech remained delayed until he began kindergarten at which time Mrs. Cloud felt his speech was comparable to his peers'. Currently, she noted, Ben is a quiet child but appears to be able to make himself understood when he wants. She further noted that he does not appear to listen very well.

Since fourth grade, Ben has attended a different school each year. The exception was fifth grade, which he repeated at the same school. This past year, in Liberty Middle School, he failed most of his courses, thus prompting the recommendation for retention. Mrs. Cloud commented that Ben gave up on school this year and turned in no homework assignments. In turn, his teachers gave up on him. Mrs. Cloud is concerned that repeating seventh grade will not solve the problem and only contribute further to Ben's low self-esteem and dislike of school.

Previous Evaluations

In the interview prior to testing, Mrs. Cloud stated that Ben continues to have fluid in his ears. She recalled his doctor saying that Ben had a "30% hearing loss" but that tubes were not warranted. Due to the concern about the effect of a hearing loss on test results, the examiner requested an audiological evaluation on Ben and medical follow-up, if prescribed, before initiating the educational evaluation. Results of the hearing test indicated an average 25 decibel loss bilaterally in the range of speech sounds.

Tests Administered

Ben was administered the Woodcock-Johnson Psycho-Educational Battery—Revised, Standard Achievement Battery, Form A. In addition, the examiner also listened to Ben read a short series of graded passages. Testing was conducted in one 1-hour session. The WJ-R was scored according to age-norms. Scores and descriptions of the tests are attached.

Behavioral Observations

Ben was cooperative and pleasant throughout the testing session. Frequently, he showed a puzzled expression, indicating that he did not understand the test questions. He needed to have several questions repeated two or three times before he was able to respond. When test items were repeated, his performance improved. On several occasions, Ben did not seem to sustain his best effort. For example, on the Writing Samples test, he commented that his hand was tired from writing and then began to write short, incomplete sentences. At times, he appeared to be distracted, and on three occasions, he asked questions unrelated to the task and had to be redirected.

Achievement Test Results

In general, test scores indicate that Ben is achieving considerably below grade level in all academic areas tested. Ben's academic deficiencies are of particular concern when his Relative Mastery Indexes are considered. On tasks similar to those of the Reading, Written Language, Math, and Knowledge clusters, Ben's accuracy would range from 45% to 63% compared to 90% accuracy for average students of his age.

In reading and spelling, Ben had particular difficulty on medial vowel sounds, vowel combinations, consonant blends, and plurals. On some items of the Passage Comprehension test, he read the item, shrugged his shoulders, and guessed. Many of Ben's responses indicated that he did not understand the concepts or vocabulary involved in the question. Ben's limited mastery of mathematical operations and applications was also apparent in his responses. For example, when asked to solve the long division problem 126 divided by 42, Ben pointed to the 2 in 42 and asked if he was supposed to divide 126 by the 2.

Recommendations

Because Ben is significantly below grade level in all academic areas, retention is not an appropriate option, as it would not solve the problem. Instructional materials at a seventh-grade level will be too difficult for Ben. Appropriate instructional materials for Ben in reading and math would be early fifth-grade level; in written language, mid-third-grade level; and in general knowledge, mid-fourth-grade level. Additionally, another retention would further damage his self-esteem. Instead, Mrs. Cloud should request help from district personnel to find an appropriate educational placement for Ben in a program that is designed to accommodate students at diverse performance levels and in which hands-on and visual activities are well-integrated. One possibility would be a magnet school. Additionally, in order to plan the most effective educational program, the following recommendations are offered.

1. Request that a full psychoeducational evaluation be conducted either by school personnel or a private agency. This evaluation should include a thorough assessment of cognitive abilities and receptive and expressive language abilities.

2. A professional knowledgeable about Attention Deficit Disorder should obtain a complete developmental history and profile of current behaviors either to rule out ADD as a contributing factor to Ben's learning difficulties or to make a further referral to a developmental pediatrician. Care must be taken not to confuse the pervasive effects of a hearing loss and possible receptive language impairment with ADD.

3. Based on the evaluation, request a conference to discuss any special education services for which Ben might be eligible, including compensations in the classroom for his hearing loss.

4. If Ben is not eligible for special education, Mrs. Cloud may wish to hire a learning disabilities specialist to tutor Ben.

5. Mrs. Cloud should familiarize herself and Ben with compensations for hearing-impaired children that can be used easily in the regular classroom. At the beginning of each school year, she and Ben should meet with his teachers and share with them compensations that will help Ben to be successful in their classrooms. A list of recommendations is attached to this report.

Ben's instructional needs must be addressed immediately to ensure that he does not quit trying and that he progresses academically. With a highly structured teaching situation and with appropriate activities and materials modified to his performance levels, he should make progress, gain self-confidence, and renew his interest in learning. Ben's progress should be monitored closely by his grandmother and his school in the following year.

Diagnosis: *Average* to *High Average* verbal skills; *Superior* to *Very Superior* visual skills; weak reading strategies

PSYCHOEDUCATIONAL EVALUATION

Student: Jon Floyd

Birthdate: 10/22/75

Chronological Age: 15-6

Grade: 10.5

Evaluator:

Parents: Barbara & Roger Floyd

School: Steel Hills High School

Test Dates: 4/27, 5/1/91

Reason for Referral

Jon was referred for testing by the school child study team due to difficulty in reading comprehension and written expression. As classroom interventions had not been successful, the team questioned the possibility of learning disabilities.

Background Information

Jon, a 15-year-old Caucasian male, has changed schools frequently due to his parents' military service. Results of vision and hearing screenings were within normal limits. His developmental history is unremarkable. Jon earned above-average grades until sixth grade, but below-average to failing grades in junior high school when he had significant behavioral problems. During this period, his parents were getting a divorce. On standardized academic tests, he has consistently scored in the *Average* to *Superior* ranges. A previous administration of the Wechsler Intelligence Scale for Children - Revised indicated *High Average* verbal skills and *Superior* to *Very Superior* visual, nonverbal skills. His current therapist described his memory as "good times three." Jon is earning Ds in English and History, and As in Computer-Aided Drafting and Algebra.

Early in ninth grade, Jon was diagnosed as clinically depressed and placed in a residential treatment center where he made good behavioral and emotional progress. He returned to public school at the beginning of this year. Recently, on a questionnaire filled out by Jon's teachers, no problems were noted in attentional areas. Four teachers wrote positive comments regarding his courtesy, cooperation, and class participation. The only behavior of concern was isolation from peers.

Behavioral Observations

Jon was cooperative throughout testing. On some tests he worked rapidly, sometimes impeding accuracy. He maintained a somewhat casual attitude on the cognitive and academic tests. During one test session, Jon complained that he had daily headaches after school. When his mother was notified of this complaint and pursued it, he denied it.

Tests Administered

Woodcock-Johnson Psycho-Educational Battery— Revised (WJ-R):

Tests of Cognitive Ability: 1–14, 17, 19–21

Tests of Achievement (Form A): 22–30

Watson-Glaser Critical Thinking Appraisal (Watson-Glaser)

Burns-Roe Informal Reading Inventory

School writing sample

Test Results

The tests of the WJ-R were scored according to grade norms. When no difference was found between the two component tests of a factor or cluster, only the factor or cluster score is discussed. Standard scores and percentile ranks are reported as obtained scores or as 68% confidence bands. A 68% confidence band is expressed as ± 1 standard error of measurement (SEM).

Cognitive Abilities

WJ-R	SS	PR ± 1 SEM	Classi-fication	RMI
BROAD COGNITIVE ABILITY	122	90-95	HA/S	96/90

Jon's score on the WJ-R Broad Cognitive Ability factor indicates that his general cognitive abilities border the *High Average/Superior* ranges.

WJ-R	SS	PR ± 1 SEM	Classi-fication	RMI
PROCESSING SPEED	127	92-99	S	98/90
VISUAL PROCESSING	131	95-99.5	S/VS	97/90
Spatial Relations	138	98-99.8	VS	99/90

Jon's performance on the Visual Processing factor is in the *Superior* range; on the Processing Speed factor, it borders the *Superior/Very Superior* ranges.

No significant differences were found among the component tests. The tests comprising these factors require the ability to match numbers and forms rapidly, to identify partly obscured pictures, and to recall pictures previously seen. Additionally, Jon scored in the *Very Superior* range on the Spatial Relations test, mentally manipulating puzzle pieces to match a target design. Jon's performance on these tests indicates particular strengths in efficient visual processing and spatial reasoning using nonverbal stimuli.

WJ-R	SS	PR ±1 SEM	Classi-fication	RMI
LONG-TERM RETRIEVAL	115	77-90	HA	96/90

Jon scored in the *High Average* range on tasks of visual-auditory association and recall. These tasks required Jon to associate orally presented names with pictures and words with symbols, recalling them over a period of approximately 5 minutes.

WJ-R	SS	PR ±1 SEM	Classi-fication	RMI
AUDITORY PROCESSING	114	70-91	HA	95/90

Jon scored in the *High Average* range on auditory processing of sounds and words. These tasks required the synthesis of orally presented sounds and syllables into familiar words.

WJ-R	SS	PR ±1 SEM	Classi-fication	RMI
SHORT-TERM MEMORY	98	32-58	A	87/90
Memory for Sentences	105	47-77	A	93/90
Memory for Words	94	19-53	A	77/90
Numbers Reversed	117	79-93	HA	98/90

Jon scored in the *Average* range on the Short-Term Memory factor. The Relative Mastery Index (77/90) indicated that on tasks requiring immediate recall of unrelated words, Jon would have approximately 77% mastery in comparison to his average grade-peers' 90%. Due to the influence of the Memory for Words test, this factor score was significantly lower than the mean of Jon's other cognitive abilities factors. Apparently, recalling verbal information that is not inherently meaningful is relatively difficult for Jon. Conversely, Jon's score on the Numbers Reversed test, repeating a series

of digits in reverse order, was in the *High Average* range. Jon described using a verbal rehearsal strategy rather than a visualization strategy to aid in this task.

WJ-R	SS	PR ±1 SEM	Classi-fication	RMI
ORAL LANGUAGE	113	75-86	HA	95/90

Jon performed in the *High Average* range in general oral language skills although most of the component test scores were in the *Average* range. He was able to provide antonyms and synonyms for given words, name pictures of objects, and fill in the missing word for increasingly complex, orally presented passages of one to two sentences. On the latter test, some of his error responses suggested good comprehension but inaccurate choice of words (e.g., "carrier" for "compartment"). Jon scored in the *High Average* range on the Verbal Analogies test, suggesting good ability to discern the relationships among verbal concepts.

WJ-R	SS	PR ±1 SEM	Classi-fication	RMI
FLUID REASONING	122	88-96	S	98/90
Verbal Analogies	117	79-93	HA	98/90
Watson-Glaser Critical Thinking Appraisal		45	A	

Test results indicate that Jon's critical and abstract reasoning skills vary from the *Average* to *Superior* ranges, but that problem solving involving visual stimuli may be easier for him than verbal problem solving. Jon scored in the *Superior* range on the WJ-R Fluid Reasoning factor. This factor is composed of learning tasks that require the use of verbal instructions as well as ongoing corrective feedback to solve visually presented problems. These types of problems require the ability to see patterns; to think logically; and to generate, prove, and disprove alternate hypotheses.

On the Watson-Glaser Critical Thinking Appraisal, Jon scored in the 45th percentile using the tenth-grade norms. This multiple-choice test, which is completed independently, requires careful reading and has no pictures or graphs. It assesses the ability to make inferences, recognize assumptions, make deductions, evaluate the validity of generalizations and conclusions, and evaluate the strength and relevancy of certain arguments to a given issue. Although administration guidelines recommend the allowance of 40 minutes, Jon finished in 27 minutes.

Learning Strategies

With the exception of the use of verbal rehearsal on Numbers Reversed, Jon did not obviously employ any learning strategies to aid in task performance.

Academic Achievement

WJ-R	SS	PR ± 1 SEM	Classi- fication	RMI
BROAD READING	97	32-53	A	85/90
Letter-Word Identification	101	39-66	A	91/90
Passage Comprehension	94	21-50	A	81/90

Burns-Roe Informal Reading Inventory

Reading Level Word Recognition		Reading Comprehension			
		1st Trial	WPM	2nd Trial	WPM
Grade 8	100%	55%	188	80%	389
Grade 9	100%	65%	178	70%	355

Based on the results of the WJ-R, Jon's basic reading skills and comprehension skills are within the *Average* range when compared to his grade-peers'. The WJ-R Passage Comprehension test is structured so that Jon was required to read a one-to two-sentence passage silently and provide the missing word. The RMI indicated that on tasks similar to this one, Jon would score 81% to his average classmate's 90%. Based on this assessment, appropriate instructional materials would be at the early eighth-grade level.

On the Burns-Roe, Jon was tested on the grade 8 and 9 passages, each approximately 200 words in length. He made no word recognition errors, but on both passages, his comprehension was at *Frustration* level. Because he had read the passages orally, he was asked to reread the passages silently and more slowly. Although he more than doubled his reading rate, he brought his comprehension of the grade 8 passage (but not the grade 9 passage) up to the *Instructional* level.

On both reading tests, Jon appeared to read too quickly and superficially, without focused intent to gain meaning. He used no strategies or self-monitoring. He grasped the main idea and the structure of both passages, but missed or misinterpreted many details, consequently making poor inferences.

WJ-R	SS	PR ± 1 SEM	Classi- fication	RMI
BROAD MATH	127	94-98	S	99/90

Jon's Broad Math score, in the *Superior* range, was significantly higher than the mean of his other achievement cluster scores. Among the tenth-grade students with a predicted score of 98, only 2 out of 1,000 (PR: 99.8) would have obtained his score of 127. On Calculation, he was correct on every item he tried. His only errors on Applied Problems were in areas of math he had not studied. His carefulness on these tests was in sharp contrast to his behavior on the reading tests.

WJ-R	SS	PR ± 1 SEM	Classi- fication	RMI
BROAD WRITTEN LANGUAGE	98	32-58	A	88/90

Jon scored in the *Average* range on basic writing skills. A school writing sample was also used for analysis. Error analysis of the Dictation test indicated some difficulty with irregular plurals and phonetic spelling of unfamiliar words. Appropriate instructional materials for basic writing skills would be on a late grade 8 level.

Jon's ability to express his ideas in writing also appears to be in the *Average* range. On the Writing Samples test, he was asked to write one good sentence to fill different task requirements for each item. Jon's sentences were generally adequate when compared to his grade-peers', but occasionally he did not grasp instructional details which would have led him to write a better sentence. As with the reading tests, he appeared somewhat casual in his approach. An informal writing sample was organized around a central theme and included appropriately complex sentences. His ideas were good, but undeveloped, as though he were writing without preplanning his key points. He used no paragraph separations.

WJ-R	SS	PR ± 1 SEM	Classi- fication	RMI
BROAD KNOWLEDGE	100	39-61	A	90/90

Results of the Broad Knowledge cluster placed Jon's level of factual information in the *Average* range when compared to his grade-peers'. He made errors, however, on some of the developmentally lower items. No significant discrepancies were found among the Science, Social Studies, and Humanities tests. On the Humanities test, he missed all of the questions specific to music. In general, these results suggest that Jon is able to acquire and retain information from his environment.

Aptitude–Achievement Discrepancies

Test results indicate that Jon's academic achievement is not commensurate with his predicted achievement in any academic area except math. Reading and Written Language were significantly below his predicted scores based on his cognitive abilities. Among tenth-grade students, in Reading, only 5% with Jon's predicted standard score of 113 would obtain his score of 97; in Written Language, only 5% of Jon's grade-peers with his predicted score of 115 would obtain his score of 98; in Knowledge, only 11% with a predicted score of 113 would have obtained his score of 100.

Summary and Conclusions

Jon has generally *Average* to *High Average* cognitive abilities in language processing and using language for reasoning. These abilities seem to be enhanced by the use of visual information. His abilities in processing information and reasoning using visual stimuli appear to be in the *Superior* to *Very Superior* ranges. Short-term auditory memory, Jon's lowest cognitive ability, appears to be a relative weakness, but only in the area of recalling unrelated pieces of information. This presumed weakness does not seem to have affected his ability to learn basic skills in any academic area.

Jon's academic abilities appeared to be generally in the *Average* range, except for math, which was in the *Superior* range. Specific reading deficiencies were found in superficial reading without awareness of appropriate reading rate or use of comprehension strategies; specific written language deficiencies were found in higher-level organization and support of key ideas, and paragraph shift.

Aptitude–achievement discrepancies indicate that Jon is not academically achieving commensurate with his cognitive abilities except in math skills. Jon does appear to have the aptitude for school achievement and does not exhibit the processing deficit(s) often seen in a child with learning disabilities. A variety of factors may have interfered with his ability to benefit from the instruction offered in school, including frequent school changes and emotional and behavioral problems.

Recommendations

For the Parents

1. Explain to Jon the findings of this evaluation.

2. Jon demonstrated strengths in the cognitive abilities underlying his areas of stated interest, computer-aided drafting and programming high-resolution animation. Mathematics is another area of strength. Enrichment courses related to computer technology and/or math should be made available.

3. With the help of a vocational counselor, guide Jon in career exploration focusing on careers that capitalize on strengths in visual and visual-spatial abilities, and mathematics.

4. If Jon's parents decide to provide summer tutoring, attempt to borrow the school texts that Jon will be using next year so that they may be used to teach reading and writing strategies.

5. Find out what courses Jon will be taking next year and the materials he will be using. Help him learn the skills and strategies suggested using those or similar materials. If possible, obtain a syllabus for each course.

For the Language Arts Lab or Tutor

Reading Comprehension

1. Explain to Jon the difference between active and passive reading. Create periodic lessons that will demonstrate to Jon the difference in comprehension that active reading will make. For example, have him read a section of text and take a test on it. Then, when he has learned one of the strategies suggested (e.g., Surveying, mental movies, Reciprocal Questioning, setting a purpose for reading), test him again on the same section.

2. Teach Jon to alter his reading rate according to his purpose. Content area text should be read at a considerably slower pace than pleasure reading.

3. Teach Jon to recognize and use a variety of context cues within the text. Examples include: direct explanation; explanation through example; synonym

or restatement; summary; comparison or contrast; words in a series; and inference. (See attached materials on context clues.)

4. Teach Jon to set a purpose for reading by turning chapter subheadings into questions, writing them, and then reading to find the answers. Also have him write the questions at the end of the subsection or chapter on a card and note when he has found the answer as he reads through the text.

5. Teach Jon to recognize when a question cannot be answered based solely on the information given in the reading selection. Teach him to use his prior knowledge as well as the information given in the text to make inferences.

6. Teach Jon to use semantic mapping to clarify the key ideas and supporting details in a selection and the structure by which they are interrelated. After Jon reads the selection, he may: (a) brainstorm everything that he can remember, categorize this information, and depict the organization of this information in a semantic map; or (b) use the headings and subheadings in the chapter to create a preliminary map and fill in the critical details from the text. This map may then be used as a study guide for tests.

Written Expression

1. Help Jon to understand that writing is an activity that usually requires multiple drafts and revisions. Use the writing process approach with Jon for all writing assignments. This includes several stages: (a) prewriting, such as brainstorming ideas to write about and details to include, (b) outlining or mapping the paper, (c) writing the first draft, (d) revising for ideas, clarity, organization, and (e) editing.

2. Clearly demonstrate to Jon the connection between finding the organizational structure in a well-written passage and creating a framework for written assignments.

3. Teach Jon to write a variety of paragraph structures: *enumerative* contains the main idea and supporting details; *sequential* describes an event in chronological order or in a number of ideas; and *comparison/contrast* describes similarities and differences. Provide sufficient opportunities to master one type of paragraph before introducing another. This may be integrated with his learning to recognize the same type of structures in his reading.

4. Encourage computer-assisted writing by providing incentives for Jon to learn touch-typing proficiently. Then teach him revision skills within his word processing program. This includes revising sentences for better structure and semantic explicitness, reorganizing paragraphs, and moving large pieces of text from one area to another.

Proofreading

1. Teach Jon a specific strategy for proofreading and editing his papers. One strategy is the Error Monitoring strategy, which uses the mnemonic COPS (Capitalization, Overall appearance, Punctuation, Spelling). (See attached materials describing this strategy.)

2. When proofreading, encourage Jon to read his paper aloud. This will help him hear sentences that can be improved.

3. Have a brief revision conference with Jon before he attempts to edit and revise a paper. Discuss any parts that need correction and ask him to come up with ideas for improvement.

Diagnosis: Deficits in auditory processing and oral language; weakness in recall of visual symbols; Attention Deficit Disorder

PSYCHOEDUCATIONAL EVALUATION

Name: Billy Jackson   Evaluator:
Birthdate: 10/24/75   Parent: Maura Jackson
Chronological Age: 15-9   School: Lovell High School
Grade: 10.9   Test Dates: 7/9, 7/10, 7/11, 7/12/91

Reason for Referral

Billy was referred by his mother for a full psychoeducational evaluation due to concerns about longstanding difficulty with all academic subjects and behavior problems. She requested a diagnosis and recommendations for ameliorating the academic and behavioral problems.

Background Information

Billy, a 15-year-old male, lives with his mother, a single parent, and 13-year-old brother, Thomas. Mrs. Jackson described their home life as consistent and stable. The boys have a set homework time every night, and Mrs. Jackson checks Billy's work to make sure it is complete and acceptable. Billy and Thomas both study karate.

Billy was born prematurely, weighed 3 lbs. 12 oz., and remained in the hospital for 2 months. Due to his history of behavioral problems, Billy changed schools frequently. He was diagnosed as learning disabled in grade 1. His special education designation was changed to emotionally handicapped in grade 2 and then, in grade 8, changed back to learning disabled. He is currently classified as learning disabled and has been mainstreamed out of special education classes into classes for students needing extra academic support.

Throughout Billy's school history, teachers and psychologists have reported problems with self-control, attention, impulsivity, and distractibility, but good response to individual attention. Reports from his teachers early this year indicated that during class, he quickly forgot skills that he appeared to have learned and that, during instruction, he sometimes seemed to be listening but missed much of what was said. Billy was also reported to have poor social skills, often bothering other students verbally and physically, making comments in particularly poor taste, and blaming others for his own behavior. It is important to note, however, that in Physical Education and in a science class with a strong hands-on component, Billy's behavior was appropriate and his cooperation good. The Science teacher found that checking in with Billy every 3 to 4 minutes helped him to stay on task.

In February 1991, based on his behavioral history, Billy was referred to Dr. George Sentari, was diagnosed as having Attention Deficit Disorder, and was placed on imipramine. Family and individual therapy was initiated with Dr. Constance Swanson for education concerning ADD and training in parenting skills. According to teacher reports, all aspects of his behavior in school improved dramatically and remained acceptable through the end of the year. Presently, Billy states that he does not feel the need to seek attention as he used to. He is still having considerable difficulty, however, with academic skills and organization of his work.

Previous and Concurrent Evaluations

In January 1991, Billy's vision was evaluated by Dr. David Feinstein. Results indicated that Billy was farsighted with a mild astigmatism, and glasses were prescribed. Other aspects of visual functioning were good. Also in January, Billy's hearing was evaluated with results within the normal range. As noted above, in February of 1991 Billy was diagnosed as having ADD, for which he is currently taking imipramine with good results.

During this evaluation, Nancy Holloway, M.S., SLP-CCC, evaluated a taped language sample to assess the need for a language evaluation. Some concerns were noted and are discussed in the body of this report. It was suggested that a full evaluation would be appropriate at the end of the school year, after Billy had time to benefit from the new medication.

Behavior During Testing

Billy was interviewed and tested in four 3-hour sessions. Working with Billy was enjoyable as he maintained a good attitude and sense of humor even when the tests were difficult for him. Billy often asked if his answer was correct or wanted to know the correct answer. Contrary to his previous impulsive behavior, Billy was remarkably reflective during testing. He followed directions well and never "jumped the gun" when responding to questions or being presented with tasks. He reflected on his own responses and would change his response if he was not satisfied. Throughout, he asked appropriate questions (e.g., "Can I use more than one sentence?"). A notable characteristic of Billy's style of response was his sustained effort at reasoning through any problem or task that was not immediately obvious to him.

During testing, Billy's attention to task was excellent, with few exceptions. He had most difficulty sustaining focused attention when listening to orally presented passages. During breaks, when conversing with the evaluator, he tended to ramble to whatever topic seemed to interest him at the time, seemingly unaware of the pragmatic rule for topic maintenance.

Because of the nondistracting environment of the test setting, as well as Billy's excellent cooperation and effort, his current performance is probably optimal and may be better than that which he displays day to day in school and on homework. It is considered to be a valid representation of his current ability, given high motivation and minimal distractions.

Tests Administered

Woodcock-Johnson Psycho-Educational Battery— Revised:
   Cognitive Battery: Tests 7–14, 19–21
   Achievement Battery (Form A): Tests 22–31, 34–35
Analytical Reading Inventory (Reading & Listening)
Writing sample
Oral language sample

Test Results

The tests of the WJ-R were scored according to grade norms. When no difference was found between the two component tests of a factor or cluster, only the factor or cluster score is discussed. Standard scores and percentile ranks are expressed as obtained scores or as 68% confidence bands. A 68% confidence band is written as ± 1 standard error of measurement (± 1 SEM). A complete set of test scores is appended to this report.

Cognitive Abilities

Global Intelligence

According to the results of the Woodcock-Johnson Broad Cognitive Ability—Extended Scale (SS ± 1 SEM: 81–87), Billy is generally functioning in the *Low Average* range, which is higher than his current functioning in school. His scores ranged from *Low Average* to *High Average*. Billy consistently performed better on academic tasks that involved reasoning than on tasks that involved basic skills or factual knowledge.

Visual Skills

Based on the WJ-R, Billy appears to function in the *High Average* range on visual processing of pictorial information (Visual Processing, SS ± 1 SEM: 106–120) and in the *Average/High Average* range in visual reasoning (Spatial Relations, SS ± 1 SEM: 104–116). In contrast, Billy's *Low Average* score on the Processing Speed factor (SS ± 1 SEM: 80–92) suggests the possibility of a relative weakness in rapid perception of visual symbols. The possibility of a relative weakness in this skill or in visual memory for symbols is reinforced by his attempts at phonetic spelling ("agene"/*again*), inability to recall the correct spelling of words that should be quite familiar ("I'am"/*I'm*, "canned"/*can't*), and dysfluent reading. As Billy's handwriting appears fluent and quite legible, visual-motor integration was not formally tested.

Visual-Auditory Association and Recall

Billy appears to have *Average* ability to learn and retain certain types of visual-auditory associations. He consciously used verbal rehearsal as a memory aid, especially when he was corrected, according to standardized procedure, for an error. Providing visual and auditory information simultaneously appears to help Billy.

Auditory Processing and Memory

Although his test scores range from *Low Average* to *Average*, Billy does appear to have some minor difficulty with auditory processing at the sound and word level. When attempting to blend sounds and syllables into words, he substituted and missequenced them. Additionally, his spelling indicates problems discriminating among similar sounds ("on tail"/*until*, "dill"/*deal*, "canned"/*can't*).

Tests indicate that Billy's ability to recall immediately what he has just heard appears to be in the *Low Average* range. Thus, in school and at home, Billy should be able to remember most instructions given, if he processes them accurately. In testing, Billy was able to recall instructions.

Oral Language

Word Retrieval. Throughout testing, Billy demonstrated intermittent problems both with whole-word retrieval and with retrieving sounds and syllables within certain words. Difficulties were noted when he was asked to label pictures, identify printed words, and tell or retell stories. Examples were: "Alphabet squares. Three-dimensional squares. I played with them at day care" for *blocks*; "cupburnder" for *cupboard*; "car-like-thing" for *luggage cart*.

Vocabulary. On the Analytical Reading Inventory (ARI), Billy demonstrated inconsistent ability to understand the vocabulary in spoken discourse appropriate to grade 8. The WJ-R Comprehension-Knowledge factor (SS ± 1 SEM: 78-86) and language samples indicate that Billy's expressive vocabulary is in the *Low Average* range and is further hampered by a word-retrieval problem of moderate severity.

Sentence Level. Billy scored in the *Average* range in the ability to discern meaningful relationships among words (Verbal Analogies) and in the *High Average* range in understanding two-sentence passages presented orally (Listening Comprehension). On the ARI, adapted to listening comprehension, however, he clearly had difficulty processing information presented in long and complex sentence structures, interfering with his general comprehension. Analysis of Billy's language samples indicated that his attempts at expressing complex sentences were awkward and his use of transitional words between clauses or sentences was sometimes incorrect.

Discourse Level. Performance in listening comprehension on the ARI indicated that Billy was best able to benefit from instruction in longer discourse, such as a lecture, if the language was geared toward grades 6 or 7. He was unable to grasp adequately the overall structure of the passages. He often understood the main idea but misinterpreted important details or misunderstood the connections between them. When his literal comprehension was accurate, however, so were his inferences, further substantiating good reasoning ability. Billy's language samples reflected the above pattern of language comprehension. He did not provide a structure for the ideas he was trying to express and depended instead on stringing details together. His pronoun referents were often unclear.

Summary. These results indicate that Billy's vocabulary is somewhat limited; moreover, he has difficulty accessing some words he does know. He has difficulty understanding and using complex sentence structures with multiple clauses and does not easily grasp an overall structure for longer discourse such as a lecture. He does, however, exhibit average ability to use language for reasoning.

Reasoning

Based on the WJ-R Fluid Reasoning factor, Billy's abstract reasoning skills appear to be in the *Low Average* range. This factor is composed of learning tasks that require the use of verbal instructions as well as ongoing corrective feedback to solve visually presented problems. These types of problems require the ability to see patterns; think logically; and to generate, prove, and disprove alternative hypotheses. Billy had no difficulty understanding the instructions, talked himself through most of the problems, and continuously attempted to use the corrective feedback given to understand his error (e.g., "How is this happening?" "How did it get to be yellow?"). He appeared to have difficulty with mentally combining elements/attributes as part of the solution, but his errors were not based on too simplistic a strategy; he seemed to understand the strategy, but could not always implement it.

Billy appeared to have more facility in using language for reasoning, as exhibited by his performance in the *Average* range on Verbal Analogies. Again, he talked himself through many of the problems. Sometimes, however, despite good reasoning, he gave the wrong answer. Later, when using analogies from another source, he talked through initially incorrect responses and corrected them.

Thus, although Billy scored in the *Low Average* range on two out of three reasoning tests, his effort at problem solving and the attempted strategies indicate good potential for improving reasoning ability. His current functioning may be more a reflection of lack of training and practice rather than limited ability.

Learning Strategies

Billy used a verbal rehearsal strategy to help him learn information he was to memorize. Additionally, he talked himself through many items on the reasoning tests, even though this strategy did not always help him. Billy appears to recognize when to apply a strategy as an aid to learning.

Academic Achievement

Reading

Behaviors. Billy both self-monitored and made an effort to sound out unrecognized words in an attempt to maintain meaning and syntactic integrity. This enhanced his success in decoding and comprehension. When the words and content became too difficult, however, his word substitutions did not always make sense.

Decoding. Compared to his grade-peers, Billy's performance on Letter-Word Identification was in the *Low* range (SS $\pm$ 1 SEM: 70–80) and on Word Attack in the *Very Low* range (SS $\pm$ 1 SEM: 62–74). Instructional levels for Billy in these skills were at the mid-fourth- and mid-second-grade levels, respectively. His RMIs indicate that on tasks requiring word recognition and word analysis, Billy would score approximately 9% and 27%, respectively, compared to his classmates' 90%.

Billy depended on his sight vocabulary. He attempted syllabication and structural analysis, but did not have adequate skills. He displayed limited familiarity with more advanced word endings (e.g., *-cian, -tious*). Generally, he was lacking in phonic skills, especially regarding vowels and diphthongs. His reading fluency was inconsistent, even within a paragraph.

Billy's deficits in auditory processing and word retrieval presented obvious interferences to his word analysis and word recognition. Intermittently, the verbal labels for familiar words came slowly, sometimes incorrectly, and sometimes not at all. The following are examples: Billy carefully sounded out *arithmetic*, then blended it as "athermetic"; he pronounced *navigator* as "negrivator"; he could not come up with any verbal label for *consequence*, although he stated its meaning. In each case, he recognized his error or difficulty and stated that he did, indeed, know the word, but could not recall it just then. When words he had missed were presented at a later time, Billy was often able to pronounce them. Occasionally, Billy looked at a word he had read previously without difficulty (e.g., *sink*), did not recognize it, and attempted, unsuccessfully, to sound it out.

Comprehension. Results of the Passage Comprehension test indicate that compared to his grade-peers, Billy's reading comprehension was in the *Low Average* range (SS $\pm$ 1 SEM: 82-94). Appropriate instructional materials should be on the late grade 6 level.

Possibly due to good reasoning skills and a consistent effort to make sense out of what he was reading, Billy's reading comprehension was consistently higher than his basic reading skills. Also, his performance on the Listening Comprehension test (RMI: 96/90) was significantly above his performance on the Passage Comprehension test (RMI: 68/90), indicating that his decoding problems are a significant factor limiting comprehension. On the longer passages of the ARI, Billy's instructional reading comprehension level ranged from the listening comprehension level found on the oral administration of the ARI (grade 6) to above it (grade 8). This suggests that having the text in front of him helps Billy to process longer discourse by allowing him to take in information at his own pace. The information in lengthy spoken discourse may go by too quickly for adequate processing.

Billy's specific weaknesses in reading comprehension reflected those identified in his oral language comprehension. Areas of need included interpreting complex sentences with multiple clauses, vocabulary development, grasping the overall framework of the passage, noting how details relate to the overall structure and to each other, increasing background information, activating prior knowledge, and understanding that it is critical to read for the meaning that the author intends before adding a personal interpretation.

Written Language

Writing appears to be the area of greatest academic difficulty for Billy. As with reading, Billy's writing performance reflected his patterns of strengths and weaknesses in oral language. A significant discrepancy existed between his ability to express his ideas at the sentence level (Writing Samples, RMI: 68/90) and his weaker mechanics (Dictation, RMI: 6/90). Thus, again, test results suggest that Billy performs better in academic skills involving reasoning than in the more basic fact/memory areas. A variety of written language samples provided for a more in-depth analysis of Billy's writing skills.

Basic Skills. Both in formal tests and written compositions, Billy made consistent errors in spelling, punctuation, capitalization, and usage. He appeared unaware of sentence boundaries, as he often used commas in place of periods, creating run-on sentences. The only punctuation marks he used properly were question marks. His usage errors were in the areas of comparatives, irregular plurals, and possessives. Billy's spelling reflected problems with phonics, revisualization, and auditory discrimination. As noted previously, sometimes his errors were surprising because of the high frequency of the word in text. His Instructional level for basic skills was early grade 4; for usage, mid-grade 3.

Syntax. As in his oral narratives, Billy's written sentence construction was often awkward. Also, he omitted syntactically necessary words, had run-ons and fragments, and confused word sequence when writing quickly (e.g., *This big is ball round*).

Organization. In writing, Billy appears dependent on sequential organization; this works adequately for more concrete topics, but not for expository writing or the higher level of content or critical thinking expected in high school. A narrative based on an experience was organized chronologically and had good introductory and concluding sentences. An essay on a more abstract topic, selected by Billy, did maintain one idea (life is tough) but was stream-of-consciousness with no support for any specific points.

Content. The level of content of Billy's writing was not what would be expected of a high school junior. His essay presented poorly expressed and nonspecific ideas that needed substantial development. Billy omitted words critical to meaning and used pronouns with unclear referents. Infrequently, word retrieval problems were evident in nonmeaningful word substitutions (e.g., "mad" for *make*, "smile" for *shallower*). As noted above, Billy's communication of his message was limited because of a lack of clear, meaningful connections among his ideas.

On the experiential composition he wrote in school, however, his message was clear and included a fairly explicit description of his feelings along with the events. Using a relatively concrete topic appears to help Billy formulate and express his ideas clearly.

Fluency. On the Writing Fluency test, Billy's RMI was 23/90. In his essay, Billy's speed was 3 words per minute; he appeared to write almost letter by letter. As his handwriting does not indicate visual-motor problems, his slow pace may be attributed to difficulty formulating his ideas in writing.

Proofreading/Revision. Billy has a great deal of difficulty with editing, probably due to weak basic skills. His RMI on the Proofing test, which required him to find errors in typewritten passages, was 55/90. He attempted to proofread his own writing, but found very few errors. His proofreading was most effective when he read aloud a typed version of his paper.

Math

Basic Skills. Billy scored in the *Low/Low Average* range on the Calculation test (SS ± 1 SEM: 75–85), compared to grade-peers. His RMI was 37/90. Appropriate instructional materials would be at the mid-grade 6 level. Error pattern analysis indicated that Billy knows the basic arithmetic operations and facts with the exception of multiplication of decimal numbers and division using a 2-digit divisor. On the division problems, he attempted a short-cut strategy that didn't work. On items for which he couldn't use the strategy, he divided correctly. In fractions, Billy could add and subtract fractions with like denominators, but could not do any other operations using fractions. He appears to be missing some factual information concerning measurement of length, time, and weight.

Although Billy was careful, he worked too many of the math problems in his head, contributing to computation errors.

Applications. Again, Billy was relatively more successful on the test involving reasoning, Applied Problems, than on the test involving more basic skills, Calculation. He scored in the *Average* range on the Applied Problems test (SS ± 1 SEM: 89–97). His RMI was 77/90. His instructional level was at approximately mid-grade 8 level. Billy used good reasoning on all word problems, even when he didn't have the basic information necessary. He was able to interpret the word problems, ignore extraneous information, and recognize important details. He consistently monitored his responses and sometimes corrected a previous answer.

General Knowledge

According to the WJ-R Broad Knowledge cluster, Billy's fund of general information was in the *Low* range (SS ± 1 SEM: 70–78) compared to grade-peers. This deficit is consistent with his continuously disrupted family and school placements, severe attentional and behavioral problems, and language/learning disabilities. His RMI for Social Studies was 39/90, for Humanities 37/90, and for Science, 10/90. It appears that Billy has missed opportunities for acquiring basic information in the content areas.

Summary

Cognitive Skills

Based on current test results, Billy's general cognitive ability is in the *Low Average* range. He has strengths in visual processing of pictorial information, but a relative weakness in rapid processing of symbolic information such as letters. Billy has a weakness in auditory processing at the sound and word level. In the language area, Billy appears to have problems in receptive and expressive vocabulary, syntax, and organization of verbal information. Thus, he often misses or misinterprets details. Billy uses reasoning successfully as an aid to comprehension and, with correct information, can make inferences. Although short-term auditory memory appears to be in the *Low Average* range, Billy has specific deficits in retrieval of words and sounds within words, which appears to interfere with recall of visual-auditory associations in academic

skills, such as phonics and sight words. Although test scores place Billy's abstract reasoning ability in the *Low Average* range, test behaviors suggest good potential for development of these skills. Billy's consistent uses of reasoning and verbal rehearsal were his major learning strategies.

Academic Achievement

Based on test results, Billy's instructional reading levels are mid-grade 2 for word attack, mid-grade 4 for sight words, and late grade 6 for comprehension. Intermittent problems in word and sound retrieval and problems in auditory processing interfere with decoding skills. Weaknesses in decoding and oral language skills appear to contribute to problems in reading comprehension. Use of context clues helps him to maintain comprehension considerably above his ability to use basic skills.

Written Language appears to be Billy's most difficult academic area. He had difficulty with all writing subskills. Test results place his instructional levels in basic skills at early grade 4, and in expressing his ideas in sentences at early grade 5. Billy does not purposefully organize the ideas in his writing. Thus, his ideas follow a sequence of events or stream of consciousness, more representative of an oral style of language than literate. Reflecting his oral language deficits, his vocabulary is limited and his sentence structure awkward or incorrect. His fluency is exceedingly slow, substantiating difficulty with formulation of ideas in words. His editing skills are ineffective.

Billy's instructional level for math computation is approximately mid-grade 6 and for word problems, late grade 8. Billy's knowledge of basic math facts and operations is adequate, but he has difficulty with rational numbers and more advanced operations. Application of math skills was limited only by basic skills and factual information.

Consistent with his background, attentional problems, and language/learning disabilities, Billy's level of general knowledge is seriously deficient. Instructional levels for science, humanities, and social studies range from mid-grade 2 to early grade 6.

Conclusions

Based on Billy's performance and behaviors during testing, his potential for school success appears higher than his current performance levels. Due to frequent disruptions in school placements, as well as attentional and behavioral problems, Billy has had limited opportunities to develop and consistently practice many of the skills necessary for academic success. Thus his cognitive development is seen as delayed with good potential for development if Billy is cooperative and motivated, and receives appropriate educational therapy. Nevertheless, Billy's deficits in the areas of oral language and auditory retrieval appear to constitute specific learning disabilities that have significantly interfered with development of academic skills and will require special education techniques for remediation. Although Billy's background complicates his history, his specific learning disabilities do not appear to be secondary to subnormal intelligence, sensory impairments, primary emotional problems, or educational or environmental deprivation.

Recommendations

For the Parent

1. Near the end of the next school year, request a full speech-language evaluation from the school, Speech and Hearing Department of the local university, or private agency.

2. If possible, make a word processor (with a spell checker) and printer available to Billy and provide for his learning typing. Proficient word processing skills will greatly facilitate his ability to organize and revise his writing assignments and reduce frustration.

3. To increase Billy's knowledge in the areas of science, social studies, and humanities, provide a *wide* variety of educational videotapes. Examples are: "Nova," "National Geographic," historic documentaries and docudramas, and films on other cultures.

4. To encourage reading, invest in a magazine subscription for Billy according to his interests.

5. Continue counseling with Dr. Swanson to ensure that Billy understands the nature of ADD, how it affects him, and the reason for medication. Just as important is the provision of an outlet for him to discuss his feelings about having this condition, to ask questions as they arise, and to learn to handle problem situations.

6. For information about joining a support group for parents of children with ADD, contact: Attention Deficit Disorder Association, 2620 Ivy Place, Toledo, OH 43613.

For the Classroom Teachers

General

1. Remind Billy to wear his glasses in the classroom.

2. Consider that Billy will be most successful with teachers who teach in a well-organized manner and who make clear their expectations concerning classroom behavior, quality and quantity of work for each assignment, the approximate amount of time the students are expected to spend on each assignment, and the due date (with periodic reminders).

3. Billy will understand and retain all types of information best if verbal information is presented in association with visual stimuli such as pictures, charts, graphs, semantic maps, and videotapes.

4. Make sure you have Billy's attention before speaking to him or giving him a series of oral instructions.

5. When teaching or speaking to Billy, pause briefly between sentences for processing time. Be aware that he may have difficulty when you speak in long and complex sentences.

6. When you call on Billy, even if he has raised his hand, wait as long as necessary for him to organize his thoughts and formulate his response.

7. Reduce reading and writing assignments. When this is not possible, allow Billy extra time to complete them.

8. If Billy is comfortable with this recommendation, arrange with another student, one who takes excellent notes, to give him a copy of class notes for each session. This will allow Billy to listen carefully to the lecture and to participate in discussion.

Behavior

1. To help Billy sustain attention to task or lecture, seat him close to you and make frequent eye contact. This should not be seen as punitive, but as a team effort to help him benefit from the information provided in class.

2. Billy will find it easier to stay on task in classes that have a strong element of teacher-student interaction, cooperative learning, and/or hands-on learning.

3. Praise specific behaviors in Billy that you want to encourage. For example, stop by his desk and say quietly, "You're concentrating well on this assignment," or after the activity, say to the class, "Many of you really stayed focused on this assignment," with a smile at Billy so he knows he is included. An important aspect of this technique is to provide ample reinforcement of the positive behavior both as a reminder for it to continue during that period and for its repetition at later times.

For the Educational Specialist

Oral Language

1. As Billy's word retrieval problem limits his ability to articulate his thoughts orally and in writing and to read aloud, consider strategies to help him compensate for this problem a priority. Some suggested strategies are:

    a. Teach Billy to visualize the object or the spelling of the word to prompt recall of the verbal label.

    b. Teach Billy to think of a category for the target word and mentally list associated objects to try and prompt recall. For example, if he is trying to retrieve the word "thief," he could list "crook," "robber," and "bad guy."

    c. Teach Billy to visualize a different context for the word and mentally describe it with a sentence. Example: For "blocks," Billy would think, "Children build with _____."

    d. To facilitate word retrieval, encourage Billy to try to recall and say the first sound of the word.

3. Emphasize vocabulary development, especially multiple meanings of words, within the contexts of academic work and conversation. Correct mispronunciations by teaching Billy the correct spelling of a word.

4. Focus on building receptive and expressive vocabulary skills through vocabulary games (e.g., based on any unfamiliar words Billy finds in his reading or hears during the day).

5. Teach Billy to use a thesaurus for writing.

6. Teach Billy pragmatic language skills (i.e., the rules of language in a social context) by using a

combination of modeling, direct teaching, and videotaping so that Billy can observe himself. Particular areas of concern include:

    a. maintaining the topic of conversation and responding specifically to what his conversation partner has said;

    b. organizing the content of his message;

    c. using clear referents for pronouns.

Listening/Note Taking

1. Teach Billy a strategy for active listening and note taking. One such strategy includes teaching the verbal cues that signal important ideas (e.g., *first, more important, to summarize*), how to recognize the key words within the ideas, and how to incorporate the key words into an outline. Use taped lectures from Billy's classes for teaching and practice.

2. Teach Billy to monitor his understanding of what the teacher is saying and question for clarity. One method of promoting active listening is to present mock lectures in which certain information doesn't make sense. Challenge Billy to identify those statements and ask questions about them. Present mock lectures that gradually approximate those he will hear in the classroom.

3. Encourage Billy to ask questions whenever he does not understand the instructions the teacher has given. It may be necessary to train this as described above.

Basic Reading Skills

1. Teach phonics, syllabication, and structural analysis through a highly structured and sequential program that highlights the visual aspect of the word parts and reinforces a strong association with their corresponding sounds. One such method is the Glass-Analysis Method for Decoding Only. (See attached material for a description of this method.)

2. Emphasize the visual aspect of reading/spelling words to compensate for possible slow visual processing of symbols or difficulty with visual recall of symbol sequences. For example, have Billy color-code or highlight word parts or affixes that you are teaching.

3. Provide an index card for Billy to use under the line he is reading.

Reading Comprehension

1. Provide Billy with taped copies of his textbooks and assigned trade books. (See attached page for ordering information.)

2. Directly teach Billy to create mental images (a movie) of what he reads.

3. Teach Billy cues to discern the meaningful connection among sentences and the kind of information each sentence provides (e.g., who, what, where, when, why, how).

4. Teach Billy to grasp the type of organization inherent in paragraphs (e.g., comparison/contrast, sequential, cause/effect).

5. Teach Billy to check and reinforce his comprehension of text, paragraph by paragraph, by paraphrasing the main idea and at least two supporting details orally or in writing. Have him include a statement describing the relationship among main ideas.

6. In nonfiction materials, teach Billy to use main ideas and details to draw a semantic map of the structure and content of the material.

7. When working with text ordered chronologically/sequentially, such as history or some literature, teach Billy to place events on a timeline to help him visualize the temporal and possibly the cause/effect relationships.

Written Language

1. When teaching language and thinking skills in writing, such as the use of descriptive language, organization of information, and using introductions or conclusions, show Billy many examples of the skill in text on his independent reading level.

2. Teach Billy to combine sentences into more complex structures where appropriate. Directly teach transitional words to introduce subordinate clauses and to clarify the meaningful relationship among sentences.

3. Teach process writing. Include the steps of brainstorming, clustering, creating a semantic map, verbalizing the relationship among the ideas in the map, writing the rough draft, and editing and revising. (See attached material for a description of the Writing Process Approach.)

4. Teach Billy a proofreading strategy. The Error Monitoring strategy uses the mnemonic COPS (Capitalization, Overall appearance, Punctuation, Spelling) to remind students of the steps to use. (See attached material for a description of the Error Monitoring strategy.)

5. Teach Billy to proofread aloud to listen for sentence structure and inclusion of all words and necessary pieces of information.

Spelling

Spelling is not considered a priority at this time because of the immediacy of Billy's other learning needs.

1. Provide Billy with a pocket-sized, computerized spelling checker and thesaurus.

2. Teach spelling using the most common spelling patterns or use a highly structured and meaningful approach such as Spelling with Morphographs. Reinforce with writing.

3. For specific words, use diagnostic teaching to ascertain an effective spelling study method for Billy (e.g., Look-Spell-See-Write, Alternate Pronunciation) and teach him to use it. Make sure that the strategy includes multiple writing of the word without copying from a model. Take spelling words from common errors in Billy's own writing or from a list of words frequently used in writing.

Math

1. Reteach multiplication of decimals, ensuring that Billy understands the meaning of the zero as a place holder.

2. Reteach long division, including the use of multiple-digit divisors.

3. Reteach the concept of fractions, including what the numerator and denominator represent, the reason for needing a common denominator, how to find it and change the numerator accordingly, and how to change improper fractions into mixed numbers.

4. Introduce the concepts of negative numbers and solution of simple algebraic equations. Provide support and reinforcement for skills taught in Billy's pre-algebra class.

Reasoning/Problem Solving

1. Throughout all tasks and activities, encourage and directly teach the process of using logical reasoning for problem solving. Use all possible situations

to make Billy aware of when he has reasoned through a problem successfully. Guide him when the process breaks down.

2. Directly teach Billy how to solve problems. Many problem-solving strategies exist that are generalizable to a variety of situations. Most include the following steps: decide what the problem is and what you would like the outcome to be; brainstorm possible solutions; consider which solutions are feasible; consider the positive and the negative outcomes of each possible solution; choose that which seems best; try it; and determine if it works. If it does not work, modify it or choose a different solution. Provide practice in a variety of situations. Involve Billy's mother in reinforcing the use of this strategy at home.

Organization and Time Management

1. Teach Billy to keep a daily calendar. Provide reinforcement for writing down all scheduled appointments and for keeping these appointments.

2. When beginning homework, teach Billy to review all of the assignments, estimate the time each will take, and prioritize them.

3. For long-term assignments, teach Billy to break them into stages and write deadlines for the completion of each stage on his calendar. Set aside a certain amount of time nightly or weekly to work on them. Include ample time for revising.

Diagnosis: Deficits in auditory processing, auditory short-term memory, and receptive and expressive language

PSYCHOEDUCATIONAL EVALUATION

Student: Tiffany Erickson   Evaluator:
Birthdate: 11/13/75   Parents: Alta and
                            Maxwell Erickson
Chronological Age: 16-3   School: Sundale
                            High School
Grade: 9.8   Test Dates: 2/3,
                            2/4, 2/5, 2/6/92

Reason for Referral

Tiffany was referred for testing by her parents to determine the nature and extent of her learning difficulties. They also requested specific recommendations to help Tiffany become more successful in school.

Background Information

School

Tiffany was retained in kindergarten and has been receiving special education help since then. She is currently in ninth grade at Sundale High School in the support program for students with learning disabilities. She receives language services for vocabulary building one-half hour per week. She is in Adaptive Education classes for English, science, and math and is in regular classes for world history and physical education. She is passing her special education classes with Cs but failing her history class. In a recent conference, her history teacher reported that she does not ask questions or volunteer answers. She is on task, appears to be interested in her work, and turns in all assignments. Her assignments are complete but not correct.

Home

Tiffany's developmental milestones were reported as unremarkable except for a delay in language development. She had a few ear infections. Tiffany has a brother, 25, who is blind, and two sisters, Rosemarie, age 12, and Becca, age 8. Her mother described Tiffany as responsible about chores, but unmotivated to do schoolwork unless Mrs. Erickson

sits with her. She described Tiffany as having the desire to learn but not the skills or the discipline to apply herself. Tiffany likes Mrs. Erickson to read her world history textbook to her and discuss it, but her own reading is slow with poor comprehension.

When asked about Tiffany's language skills, Mrs. Erickson stated Tiffany can handle casual conversation, but has difficulty communicating more complex concepts and uses vocabulary appropriate for a much younger child. She sometimes omits or missequences syllables or sounds in complex words.

Tiffany reported that she has difficulty following instructions and that she cannot understand the "long sentences" and many of the words that her teachers and peers use. She forgets the meaning of new words and often has difficulty pronouncing them.

Tiffany expressed great difficulty and frustration in putting her thoughts into words. She has difficulty describing events, but finds it almost impossible to express her feelings: "I have what I want to say in my brain—all the words—but when I go to say it, it comes out wrong." It is clear that anxiety exacerbates her expressive difficulties, as she noted that she can speak easily only to her mother. She is especially upset by her inability to participate in conversations with her peers and cried when she discussed this.

Concerning academic skills, Tiffany stated that she cannot sound out many words and cannot learn a new sight word until it has been pronounced for her many times. Sometimes she can sound out the syllables, but then she has trouble putting them back together. Tiffany stated that she cannot outline or write reports because she cannot paraphrase what she has read nor can she separate key ideas from supporting details.

Tiffany sees herself as dependent on the help of others: "I always have to have help wherever I go." She is concerned that she is "stupid" and is frustrated by her inability to understand many words, to express her thoughts, and to succeed in school. She expressed a strong desire "to know how to do the work, how to learn better," but feels that she needs someone who can explain it better than her teachers can. Tiffany also expressed a strong desire for counseling.

Previous and Concurrent Evaluations

Tiffany has been evaluated every 3 years by the school multidisciplinary team as required by federal law. She has been diagnosed as having an auditory processing deficit and specific difficulties in vocabulary.

As part of this evaluation, Tiffany was referred to Ann-Marie Nutter, speech/language pathologist, M.S., SLP-CCC, for evaluation of language skills. Results are incorporated herein.

Behavior During Testing

Tiffany was seen in four sessions for 2 hours each. Tiffany cried while discussing her difficulty in expressing herself and in learning and stated, "I feel dumb." After considerable discussion, the test session was rescheduled for the next day. Subsequently, Tiffany was very cooperative and demonstrated excellent attention and effort. She attempted every item presented and finally had to be told that it was permissible to say "I don't know" when she really didn't know the answer.

Tests Administered

Woodcock-Johnson Psycho-Educational Battery—
    Revised (WJ-R):
        Cognitive Battery: Tests 1–21
        Achievement Battery (Form A): Tests 22–32, 34
Analytical Reading Inventory (ARI)
    (reading and listening comprehension)
Informal reading/listening comprehension test from
    Tiffany's world history text
Written and oral language samples

Test Results

The tests of the WJ-R were scored according to age and grade norms. Comparison of age and grade norms on each test, factor, and cluster showed little difference in scores. Age scores are reported here. When no difference was found between the two component tests of a factor or cluster, only the factor or cluster score is discussed. Standard scores are expressed as obtained scores or as 68% confidence bands. A 68% confidence band is written as ±1 standard error of measurement (±1 SEM).

Cognitive Abilities

Global Intelligence

According to the results of the WJ-R Broad Cognitive Ability - Extended Scale (BCA), Tiffany's overall cognitive abilities are in the *Low Average* range (SS ±1 SEM: 81–85) when compared to her age-peers'. The BCA score is composed of significantly discrepant test scores indicating strengths and weaknesses in cognitive skills that cannot be accounted for by normal variability alone. Accordingly, the BCA score is not a valid predictor of Tiffany's scholastic achievement in all areas.

Reasoning/Problem Solving

	SS	SS ±1 SEM	Classi-fication	RMI	Func-tioning Level
FLUID REASONING	92	88-96	A	77/90	*Average*
(Spatial Relations)	97	91-103	A	87/90	*Average*
(Verbal Analogies)	91	86-96	LA/A	71/90	*Limited*

Tiffany scored near the lower limit of the *Average* range on all reasoning tasks, indicating normal ability to use reasoning for problem solving. Problem-solving skills were assessed in terms of visual-spatial problems, problems with visual stimuli and verbal instructions, and verbal analogies. Based on her Relative Mastery Indexes, Tiffany would best be able to compete with her age-peers on reasoning tasks that are visual and relatively language free. On tasks such as mentally reorganizing the pieces of a design, Tiffany would have 87% mastery similar to the average 16-year-old's 90% (RMI: 87/90). She would be less successful on tests that have a stronger language component.

Visual Skills

	SS	SS ±1 SEM	Classi-fication	RMI	Func-tioning Level
VISUAL PROCESSING	123	117-129	S	96/90	*Average*
PROCESSING SPEED	96	90-102	A	87/90	*Average*

According to her performance on the WJ-R, Tiffany's ability to mentally interpret and recall pictorial information is in the *Superior* range. No significant differences were found between her ability to identify a partially obscured object and to use visual details to aid her in selecting from an array those objects she had been shown previously. Tiffany's performance was significantly lower, although within the *Average* range, on the factor measuring speed of visual processing of small symbols and forms.

Visual-Motor Integration

Tiffany is seen as having average ability in integrating visual and fine-motor skills. Her handwriting is at least adequate in neatness and fluency. Consequently, no formal measures of visual-motor skills were administered.

Auditory Processing

	SS	SS ± 1 SEM	Classi-fication	RMI	Func-tioning Level
AUDITORY PROCESSING	71	66-76	VL/L	39/90	Very Limited
(Sound Patterns)	72	66-78	VL/L	39/90	Very Limited

Tiffany's abilities to recognize patterns of sounds in individual words and to blend sounds and syllables into familiar words are uniformly in the *Very Low/Low* range. Her RMI of 39/90 indicates that in these types of skills, Tiffany is *Very Limited* compared to her age-peers. Deficits at this level of auditory processing might interfere with adequate development of phonics skills for reading and spelling. Misperception of sounds in individual words is likely to interfere with accurate pronunciation of words as well as with comprehension of longer discourse. Tiffany demonstrates all of these problems.

Memory: Visual and Auditory

	SS	SS ± 1 SEM	Classi-fication	RMI	Func-tioning Level
LONG-TERM RETRIEVAL	103	100-106	A	92/90	Average
SHORT-TERM MEMORY	77	72-82	L	27/90	Very Limited
(Numbers Reversed)	91	86-96	LA/A	73/90	Limited

Based on the WJ-R memory tests, it appears that in order for Tiffany to learn and recall information successfully, the information must be presented both visually and verbally. Her ability to retain visual-auditory associations was well within the *Average* range, as was her ability to recall the associations 2 days later. Moreover, her retention of visual-auditory associations is significantly higher than her ability to remember verbal information alone. This is clearly demonstrated by a comparison between her Long-Term Retrieval RMI of 92/90, indicating that her mastery of similar visual-auditory tasks would be *Average* when compared to other 16-year-olds', and her Short-Term Memory RMI of 27/90, indicating that her ability to recall auditory information is *Very Limited*. For example, she is far more likely to understand and remember information that has been presented in a movie or on a well-organized chart than that which has been presented in a lecture or text.

Oral Language

For the purposes of brevity and organization, the results of this evaluation and the language evaluation are combined. This evaluation included tests of the WJ-R, an informal listening comprehension test, and language samples. Scores from the speech/language pathologist's evaluation may be found in her report. Results of both evaluations were consistent.

Vocabulary

	SS	SS ± 1 SEM	Classi-fication	RMI	Func-tioning Level
COMPREHENSION-KNOWLEDGE	78	75-81	L	39/90	Very Limited

Test results and language samples indicate that, compared to age-peers, Tiffany is in the *Low* range in the variety and sophistication of words she understands and can use. Poor receptive vocabulary suggests that she will not understand many of the words used by her teachers to explain new concepts and that much of what is taught in class will not be understood unless accompanied by a visual aid that clearly depicts the concept. Tiffany's limited vocabulary also restricts her ability to express her ideas and possibly to clarify her ideas even in her own thoughts.

Language samples indicated that a deficit in word retrieval complicates Tiffany's limited vocabulary. When speaking, she often cannot recall a word that she knows, so that the word she finally selects is less specific or inaccurate. An example is her description of a historic change from matrilineal rule: "And then they decided t'let them have certain parts of the higherness but they're gonna take some of it away from them and the guy has some charge too." In class, her teacher and classmates might assume that she does not know what she is talking about when, in actuality, she has a clear idea in mind.

Sentence Structure

Tiffany appears to understand complex sentence structure, but may not understand the meaning of the connecting words between clauses (e.g., *although, nevertheless*). When speaking, however, Tiffany has such difficulty constructing her own sentences that it is often difficult to understand what she is trying to say. When asked if she knew what "toll" meant, she explained, "That he rather have his money that they for — for them to use his land that has a road and river on it so that he rather have his money for they use it." She often uses nonparallel clauses, misuses relative clauses and connective words, and omits words.

Level of Abstractness

Tiffany does not understand abstract language. This includes concepts that are not concrete (e.g., "government," "trade") and figurative language (e.g., "no laughing matter," "a change was called for").

Integrated Content

	SS SS ±1 SEM	Classi-fication	RMI	Func-tioning Level
ORAL LANGUAGE (Listening	81 78-84	L/LA	53/90	*Limited*
Comprehension)	98 91-105	A	88/90	*Average*

Analytical Reading Inventory (ARI):
  Listening Instructional Level: grades 4–5

Based on the WJ-R results, Tiffany's overall language ability falls in the *Low Average* range or is *Limited*, based on the RMI. When required to integrate all aspects of language, she appears to function better with a limited amount of information and in a more structured task. She performed in the *Average* range when asked to listen to one- to two-sentence passages and fill in the last word. In contrast, when she listened to longer passages that were read to her (ARI), simulating a lecture or story that might be presented in a class, her comprehension level was in the grade 4 to 5 range, well below her

grade level. The longer passages increase the demand on the ability to process, organize, and recall information and make inferences. Generally, Tiffany missed or misinterpreted details, often as a result of misunderstood vocabulary or concepts, and made inaccurate inferences.

Self-Awareness

Tiffany is aware of her language comprehension deficits and her inability to express herself clearly. Her self-monitoring is both a help and a hindrance. As she listens to her own speech and recognizes her lack of clarity, she attempts to clarify what she is saying, sometimes managing to do so. Her self-awareness also improves her prognosis for remediation. In contrast, her awareness of her linguistic difficulties increases her frustration and diminishes her self-esteem.

Pragmatics

Tiffany uses language well according to the social context. She takes turns, recognizes when she or her listener does not understand, attempts to clarify or asks a question, and speaks in a manner appropriate to the social status of her listener.

Intracognitive Discrepancies

The WJ-R Intra-Cognitive Discrepancies scores indicate that Tiffany has a significant strength in processing nonsymbolic visual information and a probable strength in retention of visual-auditory associations. A person's predicted score on the cognitive factors is the average of his/her other cognitive factor scores. Of 16-year-olds with a predicted Visual Processing standard score of 87, only 0.2% (PR: 99.8) would obtain a standard score as high as or higher than Tiffany's score of 125. Of her age-peers with the same predicted Long-Term Retrieval score of 87, only 9% (PR: 91) would have obtained a score as high as or higher than Tiffany's score of 103.

In contrast, Tiffany has a significant deficit in auditory processing of words and sounds and a probable deficit in auditory short-term memory. Of her age-peers with a predicted Auditory Processing score of 95, only 2% (PR: 2) would have obtained a score as low as or lower than her score of 69. Of her age-peers with a predicted Short-Term Memory score of 95, only 8% (PR: 8) would have obtained a score as low as or lower than her score of 77.

Academic Achievement

Reading

	SS	SS ±1 SEM	RMI	Func-tioning Level	Grade Equiv-alent
BROAD READING	81	73-84	37/90	*Very Limited*	Mid 4
Word Identification	77	73-81	10/90	*Very Limited*	Mid 4
Passage Comprehension	91	86-96	73/90	*Limited*	Early 2
Word Attack	70	65-75	21/90	*Very Limited*	Early 2
Reading Vocabulary	90	86-94	71/90	*Limited*	Mid 7
BASIC READING SKILLS	73	70-76	15/90	*Very Limited*	Early 3
READING COM-PREHENSION	90	86-94	71/90	*Limited*	Early 3

	Word Identification WJ-R	ARI	Passage Compre-hension WJ-R	ARI	Word Attack WJ-R	Reading Vocab-ulary WJ-R
Easy	Mid-3	—	Early 5	—	Mid-1	Mid-5
Grade Equivalent	Mid-4	4-5	Mid-7	4-5	Early 2	Late 7
Difficult	Late 5	6	Mid-10	6	Early 3	Mid-10

Based on the WJ-R Broad Reading cluster, Tiffany's overall reading achievement is in the *Low Average* range. When compared to age-peers who would achieve 90% accuracy on similar tasks, Tiffany's RMI scores indicate that she would achieve 10% accuracy (*Very Limited*) on sight-word recognition, 21% (*Very Limited*) on the use of phonics and structural analysis to sound out unfamiliar words, and 73% accuracy (*Limited*) on comprehension of one- to two-sentence passages.

Basic Skills. For more information concerning reading, the Analytical Reading Inventory (ARI) was administered. Both the WJ-R and the ARI indicated that appropriate instructional materials for sight-word recognition would be at the mid-grade 4 level. On the ARI, Tiffany carefully attempted to sound out words with which she was unfamiliar, but she obviously lacked basic phonics and structural analysis skills. Her auditory processing and recall problems may have contributed to errors in phonic and structural analysis (e.g., "problem"/ *program*, "situation"/*association*), oral mispronunciations (e.g. "emeny"/*enemy*), and pronouncing a word differently each time she saw it. Her word retrieval problem appeared to interfere with her ability to retrieve the verbal label for words that she had previously read with no difficulty. Her reading fluency was poor at every passage level.

Reading Comprehension. On the ARI, no discrepancies existed between Tiffany's decoding skill and her comprehension, placing ability to comprehend long passages, with guidance, at mid-grade 4 to mid-grade 5. Consistent with the results of the WJ-R and ARI tests of listening comprehension, Tiffany performed considerably better on the brief passages (one or two sentences) of the WJ-R Passage Comprehension test than on the longer passages of the ARI (approximately 200 words). Again, this discrepancy is probably due to the difference in task demands. The added language load of the ARI, in addition to the interference from Tiffany's poor decoding skills and weak sight vocabulary, make processing longer passages a considerably more difficult task.

Within her instructional level, Tiffany consistently tried to monitor her reading. She seemed to understand generally the main idea of each passage but was unable to state it with enough clarity to reflect full comprehension. Much of the vocabulary (e.g., *hoax, plunged*) was unfamiliar to her. Consistent with her errors in listening comprehension, she missed some key details, made inaccurate inferences, and could not put the information into a cohesive framework.

Based on the Fry Readability Scale (Fry, 1978), Tiffany's world history text has a readability level of grade 14. Tiffany needed sentence-by-sentence guidance to understand a passage, including being guided to or given the definitions of many words. She was unable to outline the passage because although she knew to write down the subheadings, she was unable to find and paraphrase key ideas.

Tiffany gives the impression of an active reader who uses all her skills to make sense of the passage. She is greatly hampered, both in reading decoding and in comprehension, by her auditory processing and oral language deficits.

Written Language

	SS	SS ±1 SEM	RMI	Functioning Level	Grade Equivalent
BROAD WRITTEN LANGUAGE	83	78-88	58/90	*Limited*	Mid 5
Writing Samples	89	84-94	77/90	*Average*	Late 5
Dictation	78	73-83	34/90	*Very Limited*	Early 5
Proofing	93	88-98	75/90	*Average*	Late 7
BASIC WRITING SKILLS	85	81-89	55/90	*Limited*	Early 6

Reflecting her language deficits, Tiffany's writing is immature in all aspects. Scores on the WJ-R Broad Written Language cluster indicate that Tiffany is functioning in the *Low Average* range when compared to her age-peers. Basic writing skills were assessed through the WJ-R Dictation and Proofing tests and two informal writing samples. Expression of ideas was assessed by the Writing Samples test and the informal writing samples.

Basic Skills. Tiffany's Dictation RMI of 34/90 indicates that her mastery of the mechanics of writing is *Very Limited* compared to her age-peers. In contrast, based on her Proofing RMI of 75/90, it appears that Tiffany is familiar with the rules of writing mechanics, but is more proficient at proofreading than recalling the elements on demand. Error analysis revealed no strong patterns in any one skill, but a variety of errors in punctuation, capitalization, spelling, and usage. Spelling errors were often not phonetic ("gargage"/*garage*, "aperching"/*approaching*), but did show evidence of visual recall of spelling patterns (e.g., "spair"/*spare*).

Written Expression. Tiffany's RMI of 77/90 for the Writing Samples test indicates that on tasks in which she is asked to write individual sentences according to specific task demands, her performance would be at the lower limit of *Average* compared to her age-peers'. The quality of her compositions was considerably poorer than her performance on the Writing Samples test. Error analysis of all written work provided the following information. Tiffany's vocabulary was immature. Her sentence structure consisted mainly of simple and compound sentences, some run-on. Occasionally, she used a complex sentence with an embedded clause, but awkwardly. She appeared unaware of story grammar as her narratives were sequentially organized by events with no plot or problem to be resolved. She did not use paragraphs. The only cohesive device used was "then," and she was unable to use temporal conjunctions (e.g., *before*) to state events in a different order than they happened. The content of her papers was concrete, with no discussion of thoughts about the events, and no point made.

Math

	SS	SS ±1 SEM	RMI	Functioning Level	Grade Equivalent
BROAD MATHEMATICS	85	82-88	47/90	*Very Limited*	Early 6

Tiffany's performance on the WJ-R Mathematics cluster was in the *Low Average* range with no discrepancy between tests. Her RMI of 47/90 indicated that her mastery of similar types of computation and practical applications of math knowledge would be approximately 47% (*Very Limited*) compared to the average 16-year-old's 90% mastery.

Error pattern analysis of computation abilities indicates that Tiffany can perform all of the basic operations when dealing with whole numbers, but has difficulty with multiplication and division using decimals. She can add and subtract fractions with common denominators, but cannot deal with different denominators, improper fractions, or mixed numbers. She made errors using percents and counting elapsed time and was unfamiliar with averaging. She did not attempt problems involving simple algebraic equations, negative numbers, or multiplication or division of fractions. Tiffany's performance on Applied Problems was negatively affected by computation errors and difficulty translating word problems into computation. She had specific difficulties in deciding the correct operation to use, including all steps, and eliminating extraneous information. Tiffany was unable to read numbers with decimals in them correctly. For example, she read $480.00 as "four thousand, eight hundred dollars."

Clearly, Tiffany needs to learn math skills and concepts starting from the meaning of and relationship among basic fractions, decimals, and percents. She needs specific emphasis on understanding word problems and application of computation skills to practical situations. An appropriate instructional level at which to start math remediation would be early grade 6.

General Knowledge

	SS	SS ±1 SEM	RMI	Func-tioning Level	Grade Equiv-alent
BROAD KNOWLEDGE	77	74-80	29/90	*Very Limited*	Mid 4

According to the WJ-R, Tiffany performs in the *Low* range on general world knowledge with no discrepancies among her scores on the Science, Social Studies, and Humanities tests. It is likely that her language disorder and its concomitant effect on reading ability have interfered with her ability to learn and retain information to which she was exposed both at home and at school.

Aptitude–Achievement and Intra-Achievement Discrepancies

No significant discrepancies were found between Tiffany's aptitude for each of the achievement areas and her obtained scores on the achievement clusters. As well, when each academic cluster score was compared to the average of the other three academic cluster scores no intra-achievement discrepancies were found.

The lack of a significant aptitude–achievement discrepancy may be explained by the need for adequate language-related cognitive skills for success in academics. Tiffany's weak abilities in auditory memory, auditory processing, and oral language indicate low aptitude for academic success and therefore validly predict her academic difficulties.

Summary

Cognitive Abilities

Based on the current test results, Tiffany's *Low Average* Broad Cognitive Ability score masks significant cognitive strengths and weaknesses. Significant strengths were demonstrated in processing and interpreting pictorial information, in noting visual details, and in reasoning with visual patterns. She scored in the *Average* range in rapid processing of small visual symbols. She demonstrated strengths in learning and recalling information presented in a visual or simultaneous visual and verbal manner. Visual-motor coordination appeared to be adequate. Reasoning/problem-solving abilities were also in the *Average* range.

Tiffany demonstrated significant deficits in comprehension and expression of oral language. Results of the WJ-R, informal tests, and a speech/language evaluation provided the following information. Formal tests indicate that Tiffany's general language abilities border the *Low/Low Average* ranges. Compared to her age-peers, her vocabulary knowledge and ability to recall auditory information are in the *Low* range. Her abilities in auditory processing at the sound/word level bordered the *Very Low/Low* ranges. Formal and informal language tests supported these findings and identified additional processing deficits in understanding abstract concepts, figurative language, and the connecting words relating clauses in complex sentences. Additional expressive deficits were identified in word retrieval, word pronunciation, sentence structure and organization, and use of abstract language.

Tiffany's awareness of her language deficits has negative effects in increasing her frustration and lowering her self-esteem. It has positive effects in allowing her to clarify her statements and in good prognosis for remediation.

Academic Achievement

Generally, Tiffany shows *Low* to *Low Average* performance in all areas of academics tested. In reading, she is functioning instructionally at approximately the mid-grade 4 to mid-grade 5 level with weaknesses parallel, and probably secondary to, those demonstrated in oral language comprehension. Poor auditory processing interferes with decoding in word pronunciation, phonics, and structural analysis skills. Basic skill deficits and higher-level language deficits impair vocabulary comprehension, comprehension of main ideas and supporting details, formation of inferences based on accurate information, and retention of information.

In writing, Tiffany is also functioning approximately on a grade 5 level with limited proficiency in basic skills and immature content, vocabulary, sentence structure, and organization.

In math, Tiffany functions at a mid-grade 6 level in computation and late-grade 5 level in word problems. She is relatively comfortable with the basic operations using whole numbers but needs review and reteaching for all other skills. She has particular difficulty with interpreting word problems.

In knowledge, Tiffany functions in a range between grade 3 to 5, depending on the academic area. Her language disorder has undoubtedly interfered with her learning and retention of general world knowledge and culturally based knowledge.

Conclusions

Based on test results and error pattern analysis, Tiffany has significant discrepancies between her strong visual processing and reasoning abilities and her moderate to severe deficits in auditory processing, auditory memory, and oral language. Current test results are consistent with all information provided by interview respondents, including Tiffany. Tiffany's language/learning disabilities do not appear to have been caused primarily by subnormal intelligence, sensory impairments, medical factors, emotional disturbance, or environmental or educational deprivation. Tiffany requires immediate intervention with appropriate special education techniques to succeed academically.

Recommendations

For the Parents

1. If possible, engage an educational therapist skilled in teaching learning strategies and self-advocacy for adolescents with learning disabilities and language disorders. Self-advocacy requires that Tiffany understand her language learning strengths and weaknesses, accept her learning disabilities matter-of-factly, know what compensations she needs in the classroom, and know how to request them.

2. Provide a copy of this report to the school multidisciplinary committee and request a meeting to revise Tiffany's IEP according to these recommendations. Design a program that will integrate language and academic remediation.

3. To help Tiffany increase her knowledge of science, social studies, and humanities, rent a wide variety of educationally oriented, but interesting videotapes. These could range from animal habitats, to body functions and health, to crafts, to legends, to conservation. Include documentaries and

docudramas. Check your public library and look in the education, documentary and children's sections of video stores.

4. Invest in at least one magazine subscription for Tiffany according to her interests.

For the Teachers

1. Provide Tiffany with textbooks and adapted classroom materials that are commensurate with her current performance levels.

2. Present new information and concepts visually or with visual information that clearly illustrates the accompanying verbal information. Be aware that Tiffany may only understand and retain pieces of any verbal activity.

3. Use strategies for activating prior knowledge before assigning reading on a new topic. (See attached material on PReP and Semantic Feature Analysis.)

4. Give Tiffany as much extra time as she needs to organize her thoughts and formulate her response after she raises her hand or is called on to answer a question. Do not assume that she does not know the answer. Privately, alert Tiffany that she will be given time or that she may say "I pass" if she does not know the answer.

5. When teaching or speaking to Tiffany, pause between phrases for processing time. Give Tiffany an opportunity to request repetition or clarification.

6. Allow Tiffany to take untimed tests.

7. Encourage Tiffany to ask questions whenever she does not understand the instructions or how to do a task.

For the Speech/Language Pathologist and/or Educational Therapist

General

1. Teach Tiffany self-advocacy so that she can meet with teachers at the beginning of next year to alert them to her strengths and weaknesses and to request specific compensations to help her succeed in their classrooms.

2. If possible, work with Tiffany's school counselor to choose teachers who emphasize visual teaching materials over lectures and who are well-organized both in class structure and in lecture style.

3. Document Tiffany's proficiency in a skill before and during instruction in such a way that she is aware of her progress. Use charts, graphs, or stars, but make sure that Tiffany is aware of what she is learning, why it is important, what she has accomplished, and how her learning relates to the long-term goal.

Oral Language

General

1. Teach Tiffany to create a visual image of what she hears and reads so that she can provide for herself visual input to supplement verbal information.

2. Use reading and writing as models and reinforcement of oral language skills.

3. Directly teach Tiffany to generalize the language skills described below to reading comprehension and written expression.

Pronunciation

1. Use printed words to demonstrate the correct pronunciation of words Tiffany often mispronounces.

Vocabulary

1. Build awareness of terms denoting linguistic relationships (e.g., temporal, spatial, cause/effect, analogous, exceptions, comparison/contrast) in text and in oral language to help clarify relationships among events, objects, and people. Use examples from social studies, science, and literature.

2. Directly work on development of vocabulary in reading, writing, and oral discussion. Ensure that oral vocabulary continues to develop and that new words are pronounced and used correctly.

3. Teach dual meanings. For example, the word *prompt* can mean *on time* or a *cue*.

4. One way to foster vocabulary development at home is to use the book *Animalia* by Graeme Base (Base, 1986). *Animalia* might provide a source of enjoyment while Tiffany learns to name the objects and activities in the detailed pictures. Each page represents a letter, and all the pictures on the page begin with that letter. This may also give Tiffany a visual cue to use later when she is trying to retrieve one of these words from memory.

5. Teach Tiffany how to use a thesaurus for writing.

6. Provide Tiffany with practice using vocabulary words orally, in reading, and in writing.

Listening/Language Comprehension

1. Teach Tiffany to monitor her understanding of her teachers' lectures and question for clarity. Have her tape some of her teachers' lectures. Go through them with her, helping her to recognize when a question would have been appropriate.

2. Evaluate further Tiffany's ability to use prior knowledge and experience to interpret oral or textual information. Attend to the types of cohesive devices she can interpret and her ability to infer information within as well as across sentences. (See attached material on cohesive devices.)

3. Use techniques to activate prior knowledge before introducing new concepts, reading material, or oral information. Directly teach Tiffany the necessity of using her own prior knowledge and experience to help understand the information. (See attached descriptions of PReP and Semantic Feature Analysis.)

Language Expression

1. Using diagnostic teaching, further evaluate the extent to which problems in word retrieval and/or complex sentence structure interfere with Tiffany's ability to formulate well-constructed sentences.

2. Teach oral formulation of complex syntax using printed sentences as a model for explanation and examples, and generalizing this skill into oral and written form.

3. To help her organize her thoughts before beginning to speak, teach Tiffany to think in terms of "What is the beginning? Middle? End?"

4. To facilitate writing and speaking in a more literate style, teach Tiffany to differentiate between oral and literate language. A sequence of activities requiring increasing skill may include: (a) dividing pairs of sentences into categories of style (oral and literate), (b) labeling a given sentence as oral or literate in style, (c) rewriting sentences from oral to literate style based on previous practice in complex sentence structures and cohesive devices, and (d) rewriting passages in a variety of styles (e.g., letter to a close friend, news article) (Wallach & Miller, 1988). As much as possible, include practice using Tiffany's language.

Example:

Oral: This one guy goes scraping salt on-onto the road everyday and he's been scared of him - then he met him in the church - he was nice and everything.

Literate: The boy's been scared of a man who scraped salt onto the street every day, but when he met the man in church, the man was nice.

Language Comprehension and Expression

1. Teach a strategy to help Tiffany understand narrative structure and to organize and elaborate her own narratives. One example is STORE the Story, which stands for Setting, Time, Order of events, Resolution, Ending (Schlegel & Bos, 1986). An alternative is the use of "reporter questions" (e.g., who, what, where, when, why, how). Ensure that any strategy that Tiffany learns for narrative organization is generalized to writing.

2. Teach Tiffany the differences between narrative and expository styles. As a basis for discussion, give her a paragraph written in narrative style and another written in expository style, but with similar information. Discuss with Tiffany the stylistic differences.

3. Teach Tiffany different ways expository information might be organized and draw a visual pattern to illustrate that type of organization. For example, contrast might be depicted as a divided square with two subheadings and blocks down the side for categories (see Figure III-13a); description might be depicted as a tree with smaller branches coming off each major limb (see Figure III-13b); and cause/effect might be depicted as a circle or number of circles with an arrow leading to another circle (see Figure III-13c); chronological sequence might be depicted as a timeline.

Subsequently, teach Tiffany to recognize these patterns in reading material and orally presented information and to use these patterns to organize information for writing.

4. Provide extensive oral practice with sentence-combining exercises. Present Tiffany with several clauses or short sentences and have her generate as many sentence patterns as she can by using a variety of connecting words. As an alternative activity, provide Tiffany with a specific word or words to use in joining several clauses or sentences.

5. Teach Tiffany to interpret and use cohesive devices in oral and written language. Cohesive devices include the categories of referential, lexical, conjunction, substitution, and ellipsis. (See attached material on cohesive devices.)

6. Teach Tiffany to understand and use figurative language such as metaphors (e.g., "The teacher watched him with an eagle eye"), similes (e.g., "The teacher watched him like a hawk"), idioms (e.g., "He threw away a wonderful opportunity"), and proverbs (e.g., "Necessity is the mother of invention").

Reading

Decoding

Teach phonics, syllabication, and structural analysis through a highly structured and sequential program of word families. To capitalize on Tiffany's visual strengths, use well-established reading vocabulary as a basis for introducing patterns. Provide enough practice so that she can automatically generalize these patterns to new words (e.g., *boat* → *float*). An alternative to the word families approach is to teach common clusters of letters using a program such as the Glass-Analysis Method of Decoding Only (Glass, 1973, 1976). (See attached description.)

Comprehension

1. Teach Tiffany strategies for using context clues to help her decipher the meaning of unknown words.

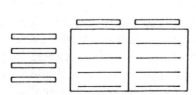

Figure III–13a. Contrast.

Figure III–13b. Description.

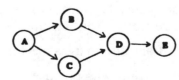

Figure III–13c. Cause-Effect.

These include recognizing appositives, definitions given in the text, and comparisons or contrasting information. (See attached material on context clues.)

2. Directly teach Tiffany to predict coming events and reactions to events in text and to judge her accuracy.

3. Teach Tiffany to restate the main idea of a well-organized paragraph, and to recognize related details and tangential information on a grade 3 reading level in a variety of content areas. Gradually increase the reading level and level of abstractness of the concepts.

4. Teach Tiffany to establish a framework for fiction and nonfiction materials through the use of semantic mapping. See the recommendation on teaching expository structures under Oral Language. Other techniques that might be of benefit are study guides and surveying.

Writing

Mechanics

1. Teach capitalization and punctuation rules, one at a time, with practice for each one in a variety of situations (e.g., completing worksheets, finding an example of the rule in reading, writing sentences and paragraphs).

2. Teach recognition of sentence boundaries. Teach other skills as problems appear in her writing assignments.

Spelling

1. Teach Tiffany how to listen for the syllables and sounds in words so that her spelling will be phonetic. Then, she may use a pocket-sized, electronic speller to find the correct spelling.

2. Use diagnostic teaching to ascertain an effective spelling study strategy for Tiffany and teach her to use it independently. Make sure that any strategy chosen requires multiple writing of the word without copying it from a model.

Written Expression

1. Teach the organizational strategies discussed under Oral Language. These may be taught in listening, speaking, reading, and writing skills simultaneously. For example, teach semantic mapping to help Tiffany organize her ideas and clarify the relationships among them before writing an assignment. Teach her to use this strategy as the basis for giving a short oral report as well, first based on what she has written, later developing into mental organization.

2. When teaching language and thinking skills in writing, such as descriptive language, organization of information, or development of introductions and conclusions, show Tiffany many examples of writing on her independent reading level as models of what is expected.

3. If the family has a computer, teach Tiffany to become proficient on a word processing program. This will improve her ability to organize and express her thoughts on paper. A spelling checker would be a useful addition to the program.

Note Taking

1. Have Tiffany tape-record lectures for review at home. Use the tape to teach Tiffany listening skills and how to take notes. One method might be to teach Tiffany to organize the material as a semantic map or graphic organizer.

2. While Tiffany is learning how to take notes for herself, arrange for another student to make her a copy of the notes for each class session. This will allow Tiffany to listen carefully to the lecture and to participate in class discussion. The speech/language pathologist, special education teacher, or educational therapist may help Tiffany arrange this.

Math

1. Teach fractions, percents, decimals, and conversion.

2. Specifically teach strategies for translating word problems into computation. Teach Tiffany to visualize what is happening in the problem.

3. Teach all math skills using independent living skills: checkbook balancing, interest on a car loan, budgeting her salary, measuring for cooking, adjusting a recipe, map skills (e.g., rate $\times$ time = distance).

Memory

Teach Tiffany specific memory strategies and how to recognize which strategy might be most useful in a variety of situations. Strategies include verbal rehearsal, chunking, a variety of ways to organize information, making ridiculous visual images composed of items one has to remember, and mnemonics. Teach memory strategies within the context for which each might be used.

Diagnosis: Deficits in abstract, logical reasoning, rapid processing of visual symbols, and memory for decontextualized information

PSYCHOEDUCATIONAL EVALUATION

Name: Rima Harris
Birthdate: 12/2/73

Evaluator:
Parent: Coretta & William Harris

Chronological Age: 17-10

School: Santa Rita High School

Grade: 12-0

Test Dates: 9/19, 9/23/91

Reason for Referral

Mr. and Dr. Harris requested that Rima be evaluated to help them understand why she has had such a difficult time in math courses. They questioned the possibility of a learning disability that will qualify her for modified entrance requirements to the state university and enrollment into the university program for students with learning disabilities.

Background Information and Previous Test Results

Rima is a young Black woman who is poised and articulate. Rima's mother is a neurologist at University Medical Center and Mr. Harris is a small-business owner. Both have family histories of learning problems. Rima passed all developmental milestones within normal limits.

In grade 1, Rima was enrolled in a French immersion class. At the end of that year, her family moved to Ohio and she was retained because she could not read English and was delayed in her knowledge of math facts. Rima quickly caught up in reading and has had no problems since. Conversely, math has been consistently difficult for her; Rima recalls being the last in her class to learn to count to 100 and to memorize the multiplication tables.

Currently, Rima is beginning her senior year in a private religious school. Last year, her chemistry teacher stated that Rima had particular difficulty with the math involved in chemistry, in flexibility in solving problems, in memorization of facts, in understanding of abstract concepts, and in ability to analyze information. Rima failed Geometry once, withdrew during her second attempt, and recently passed the course in summer school with a grade of D. Rima stated that in math and the math-related sciences, she memorizes formulas and patterns but cannot follow the logic, so that when the application changes, she cannot figure out how to solve the problems. She pointed out that math is different from other subject areas because it builds on itself. When she begins to lose the logic or does not learn certain facts, she becomes lost as new topics are introduced. She thinks that her difficulties with chemistry and biology were largely related to their mathematical aspects (e.g., formulas, genetic probabilities, equations).

Rima acknowledged that tests in all academic areas exhaust her due to high stress related to her performance. She noted that if she sees one question that she cannot answer, her anxiety interferes with her performance on the entire test.

Tests Administered

Woodcock-Johnson Psycho-Educational Battery— Revised (WJ-R):
  Tests of Cognitive Ability: 1–17, 19–21
  Tests of Achievement (Form A): 22–30, 33
School writing samples

Behavioral Observations

During testing, Rima was consistently personable, cooperative, and attentive. During breaks, however, she sat stiffly on the edge of an easy chair "waiting for the next onslaught." Midway through one session, Rima fabricated a credible story about having to leave, and did so, when she learned that the next section of tests was on math. With her mother's insistence, another session was scheduled.

Test Results

The tests of the WJ-R were scored according to grade norms. When no difference was found between the two component tests of a factor or cluster, only the factor or cluster score is discussed. The Compuscore printout and the Standard Score/Percentile Rank Profiles are appended to this report. (See Figures III-14 and III-15.)

Cognitive Abilities

Based on the WJ-R results, Rima's overall cognitive abilities are in the *Average* range. Significant discrepancies exist, however, among cognitive abilities. Consequently, the Full Scale score should not be used as a predictor of scholastic achievement.

Visual Processing and Speed

Rima performed in the *Low Average* range on the Processing Speed factor, composed of tests measuring speed of processing visual symbols, such as numbers and small forms. She scored in the *Average* range on the Visual Processing factor, measuring processing and retention of nonsymbolic information such as pictures. The separation of confidence bands between these two factors suggested a probable difference. This discrepancy suggests that although Rima may have adequate ability to organize what she sees on a perceptual level, she requires more time than average to do so. Unless adequate time is provided, she may have difficulty processing new information of a primarily visual symbolic nature. Based on the average of her other cognitive factor scores, processing speed is an area of significant deficit.

Auditory Processing and Oral Language

Test results indicate that Rima's auditory processing abilities are in the *High Average* range. Rima's performance on a variety of language-related tests indicates that her overall ability in oral language is in the *Superior* range. Orally and in writing, Rima uses language effectively to convey her ideas.

Memory

Significant discrepancies existed among the tests within the Short-Term Memory factor. Rima scored in the *Superior* range in repeating sentences verbatim, the most linguistically meaningful of the short-term memory tasks presented. She scored in the *Low Average* to *Average* range in recalling sequences of unrelated words and in restating series of digits in reverse order.

On tests of association and retrieval of visual-verbal associations over a 5- to 10-minute period, Rima scored in the *Average* to *High Average* range, but when asked to recall this information 4 days later, her performance dropped significantly, to the *Low Average/Average* range.

The implication of these test results is that Rima's ability to store and recall information that is not tied to meaningful language is significantly lower than her ability to store and recall information that is linguistically meaningful.

Reasoning

Based on the results of the WJ-R Fluid Reasoning factor, Rima performed in the *Low Average* range when presented with novel problems. Discerning the abstract patterns in these visual puzzles requires logical reasoning, the ability to comprehend verbal instructions, and the ability to use corrective feedback to generate new strategies as the problems become more complex and abstract. Rima profited minimally from the instructions and corrections. She gave up easily. Rima's standard score on Fluid Reasoning was significantly below the average of her other cognitive abilities, representing a significant cognitive deficit.

In contrast, Rima's score on the Verbal Analogies test, an indicator of language-based reasoning, was in the *High Average* to *Superior* range. Rima appears to have difficulty with visual reasoning tasks, but not necessarily with problem-solving tasks that are linguistically based.

Quantitative Ability

Quantitative ability, a broad, but distinct area of intelligence, reflects competence in comprehending quantitative concepts and relationships and in manipulating numerical symbols. The mathematical problem-solving process makes use of reasoning to discern visual patterns, to understand abstract relations, and to follow the logic of linear patterns as well as the logic involved in integrating multiple components of a problem. It is, however, uniquely logical-mathematical knowledge that is necessary for deciding which of previously learned facts, algorithms, methods, and theorems would be useful in solving a specific problem, as well as for applying the mathematical information accurately.

The WJ-R measures this cognitive ability as mathematical achievement in the areas of computation, application, and concepts. Rima's performance in the Broad Math cluster was in the *Low Average* range with no significant discrepancies among the individual tests. Broad Math was a significant deficit among the achievement clusters and, when placed on the Standard Score/Percentile Rank Profile, was in the same range as the two deficient cognitive factors, Processing Speed and Fluid Reasoning.

Academic Achievement

Reading

The results of the WJ-R Broad Reading cluster indicate that Rima's reading ability is in the *Superior* to *Very Superior* range. This score represents a significant strength among her other achievement scores and is significantly above her predicted reading success as measured by the cognitive tests most related to reading achievement.

Written Language

Results of the WJ-R Written Language cluster indicate that Rima's overall written language skills are in the *High Average* to *Superior* range. Basic skills were relatively lower than written expression skills, with most errors in spelling. Rima's ability to articulate a thought in writing was in the *Very Superior* range. Among the achievement clusters, written language was a significant strength and was significantly above her written language aptitude as measured by the cognitive tests most related to achievement in written language.

A writing sample provided for a more in-depth analysis of written expression. Rima's ideas were well-sequenced, had clear transitions, and were clearly organized around a central theme. She made good use of examples, details, and description to add interest. Some editing and revision would improve her writing, as she used some immature wording, made minor usage and punctuation errors, and had many run-on sentences.

Mathematics

Rima scored in the *Low Average* to *Average* range in Broad Mathematics. Her score on the Calculation test was in the *Low Average* range, her score on Applied Problems near the lower limit of the *Average* range, and her score on Quantitative Concepts in the *Low Average* to *Average* range. Analysis of her errors on these tests indicated that Rima has difficulty with problems involving division with three-digit divisors, fractions, percents, conversion of fractions to percents, place value with decimal numbers, negative numbers, and two- and three-dimensional measurement. She also appears to be missing some

basic math information such as the number of weeks in a year and the differences in time zones.

Rima's math achievement was significantly lower than predicted based on the average of her other achievement cluster scores. The Aptitude-Achievement Discrepancies scores indicated no discrepancy between her cognitive aptitude for math and her math achievement, as both were in the *Low Average* to *Average* range.

Knowledge

Results of the Broad Knowledge cluster indicate that Rima's general knowledge of science, social studies, and humanities is in the *Average* range with a relative weakness in science. This cluster score is significantly below the average of her other achievement scores, representing a significant academic weakness. No discrepancy was found between her aptitude and achievement on the Broad Knowledge cluster.

Summary

Test results indicate that Rima's general cognitive abilities are in the *Average* range with significant discrepancies between her strong linguistic abilities and her weaker visual and abstract reasoning abilities. Rima's cognitive strengths lie in her *Superior* ability in oral language, linguistic reasoning, and in memory for linguistically meaningful information. Her ability to store and retrieve information that was not embedded in a strong linguistic context was in the *Average* range, but was significantly lower after a delay of 4 days. These results suggest that Rima would have difficulty with long-term retrieval of information that initially was not fully meaningful to her.

Rima's significant deficits in three cognitive areas might interact to interfere with ease of learning mathematics and related sciences. Math is highly visual and spatial; Rima appears to have significant difficulty with abstract reasoning using visual patterns. Comprehension of mathematical patterns and numerical problems also requires adequate visual processing of symbols. As Rima's processing of visual symbols appears to be slower than average, when learning new math skills, she might not have enough time to process the current information before the teacher moves on, continually leaving Rima behind. Rima also appears to have an intrinsic weakness in quantitative thinking. The interactive effect of these weaknesses appears to be a specific math disability.

Rima's self-description and behavior during testing suggest that she has developed a level of math anxiety that is further contributing to her math difficulties.

Conclusions

Based on the findings of this report, Rima should be eligible for modified entrance requirements to the state university and should be eligible for the university program for students with learning disabilities.

A multidisciplinary conference has been scheduled at Santa Rita High School to consider Rima's eligibility for Special Education services for math remediation and support.

```
                  COMPUSCORE FOR THE WJ-R 3.0
                          11:28 am
                    Norms Based on Grade
===============================================================
Name: Rima Harris              ID:                    Page: 1
===============================================================

Sex: F                         School/Agency: Santa Rita
Examiner:                      Teacher/Dept:
Testing Date: 09/19/1991       City:                  State:
Birth Date: 12/02/1973         Adult Subjects
Age:  17 years 10 months         Education:
Grade Placement: 12.0            Occupation:
Years Retained: 1              Other Info:
Years Skipped: 0               Glasses: No            Used: No
Years of Schooling: 13.0       Hearing Aid: No        Used: No
```

Test Name	Raw Score	W		Age Equiv.	Grade Equiv.	RMI			SS	PR
1. Memory for	67-C	512		22[73]	16.9[71]	95/90			108	70
Names			(E)	12-3	7.0		-1	SEM	104	61
			(D)	22[91]	16.9[95]		+1	SEM	112	79
2. Memory for	54	534		29[85]	16.9[89]	98/90			122	93
Sentences			(E)	29[59]	16.9[56]		-1	SEM	116	86
			(D)	29[96]	16.9[98]		+1	SEM	128	97
3. Visual	47	518		13-8	8.3	73/90			90	24
Matching			(E)	11-7	6.0		-1	SEM	82	12
			(D)	19	11.7		+1	SEM	98	45
4. Incomplete	33	514		30[70]	16.9[70]	96/90			117	88
Words			(E)	14-7	8.7		-1	SEM	109	73
			(D)	30[95]	16.9[96]		+1	SEM	125	95
5. Visual	38	517		29[60]	16.9[69]	95/90			114	82
Closure			(E)	15-1	8.6		-1	SEM	105	63
			(D)	29[92]	16.9[96]		+1	SEM	123	94
6. Picture	44	537		22	14.4	96/90			113	80
Vocabulary			(E)	17-5	11.7		-1	SEM	108	70
			(D)	35	16.9[64]		+1	SEM	118	88
7. Analysis-	23-F	502		10-10	5.5	68/90			88	22
Synthesis			(E)	8-4	3.0		-1	SEM	82	12
			(D)	15-0	10.0		+1	SEM	94	34
BROAD COGNITIVE	---	523		32[71]	16.9[72]	96/90			122	93
ABILITY (E Dev)			(E)	18-3	11.9		-1	SEM	118	88
			(D)	32[96]	16.9[99]		+1	SEM	126	96
BROAD COGNITIVE	---	519		24	14.7	93/90			107	69
ABILITY (Std)			(E)	13-6	8.1		-1	SEM	103	58
			(D)	32[88]	16.9[90]		+1	SEM	111	77

(continued)

Figure III-14. Rima's Compuscore.

```
================================================================
Name: Rima Harris                ID:                    Page: 2
================================================================
```

```
------------------------------------------------------------------------
```

Test Name	Raw Score	W		Age Equiv.	Grade Equiv.	RMI			SS	PR
8. Visual-Auditory Learning	6-K	510		25[71]	16.9[64]	95/90			109	72
			(E)	12-2	6.7		-1	SEM	104	61
			(D)	25[93]	16.9[90]		+1	SEM	114	82
9. Memory for Words	17	504		11-10	6.6	73/90			93	32
			(E)	9-0	3.7		-1	SEM	86	18
			(D)	17-1	11.3		+1	SEM	100	50
10. Cross Out	22	507		12-1	6.7	71/90			82	12
			(E)	9-10	4.5		-1	SEM	75	5
			(D)	15-4	10.2		+1	SEM	89	23
11. Sound Blending	27	516		26[60]	16.8	94/90			107	67
			(E)	12-10	8.0		-1	SEM	100	50
			(D)	26[85]	16.9[76]		+1	SEM	114	82
12. Picture Recognition	19	508		14-8	8.8	88/90			97	43
			(E)	9-3	3.9		-1	SEM	90	25
			(D)	30[66]	16.9[71]		+1	SEM	104	61
13. Oral Vocabulary	32	538		20	13.8	95/90			108	70
			(E)	16-6	10.9		-1	SEM	103	58
			(D)	34[50]	16.9[51]		+1	SEM	113	81
14. Concept Formation	20-O	500		10-2	4.6	61/90			88	20
			(E)	8-4	3.0		-1	SEM	84	14
			(D)	12-10	8.2		+1	SEM	92	30
LONG-TERM RETRIEVAL (Glr)	---	511		24[70]	16.9[65]	95/90			110	75
			(E)	12-4	6.9		-1	SEM	106	66
			(D)	24[90]	16.9[92]		+1	SEM	114	82
SHORT-TERM MEMORY (Gsm)	---	519		28[53]	14.6	93/90			104	61
			(E)	14-0	8.3		-1	SEM	99	47
			(D)	28[76]	16.9[69]		+1	SEM	109	73
PROCESSING SPEED (Gs)	---	512		12-9	7.2	71/90			83	13
			(E)	10-8	5.3		-1	SEM	77	6
			(D)	17-5	11.0		+1	SEM	89	23
AUDITORY PROCESSING (Ga)	---	515		28[64]	16.9[62]	95/90			113	81
			(E)	13-3	8.1		-1	SEM	107	68
			(D)	28[91]	16.9[91]		+1	SEM	119	90
VISUAL PROCESSING (Gv)	---	512		21	14.9	92/90			105	63
			(E)	11-0	5.6		-1	SEM	98	45
			(D)	29[86]	16.9[89]		+1	SEM	112	79

Figure III-14. *(continued)*.

```
=================================================================
Name: Rima Harris                ID:                    Page: 3
=================================================================
```

```
-----------------------------------------------------------------
```

Test Name	Raw Score	W		Age Equiv.	Grade Equiv.	RMI			SS	PR
COMPREHENSION-	---	538		21	14.3	96/90			112	78
KNOWLEDGE (Gc)			(E)	17-0	11.4		-1	SEM	108	70
			(D)	36[51]	16.9[58]		+1	SEM	116	86
FLUID	---	501		10-5	5.0	63/90			86	17
REASONING (Gf)			(E)	8-5	3.1		-1	SEM	82	12
			(D)	13-10	9.1		+1	SEM	90	25
BROAD COGNITIVE	---	516		18-8	12.3	91/90			102	56
ABILITY (Ext)			(E)	12-3	6.8		-1	SEM	99	47
			(D)	29[73]	16.9[78]		+1	SEM	105	63
READING APTITUDE	---	526		-----	-----	93/90			107	68
			(E)	-----	-----		-1	SEM	104	61
			(D)	-----	-----		+1	SEM	110	75
MATHEMATICS	---	514		-----	-----	77/90			89	23
APTITUDE			(E)	-----	-----		-1	SEM	86	18
			(D)	-----	-----		+1	SEM	92	30
WRITTEN LANGUAGE	---	520		-----	-----	91/90			102	56
APTITUDE			(E)	-----	-----		-1	SEM	99	47
			(D)	-----	-----		+1	SEM	105	63
KNOWLEDGE	---	517		-----	-----	93/90			108	69
APTITUDE			(E)	-----	-----		-1	SEM	105	63
			(D)	-----	-----		+1	SEM	111	77
15. Del. Recall-	20-4	497		7-10	2.9	82/90			92	31
Mem. for Names			(E)	4-2	K.0[43]		-1	SEM	88	21
			(D)	20[62]	16.9[55]		+1	SEM	96	39
16. Del. Recall-	20-3	493		4-0[37]	K.0[26]	77/90			89	22
V-A Learning			(E)	4-0[3]	K.0[1]		-1	SEM	84	14
			(D)	15-7[59]	16.9[54]		+1	SEM	94	34
17. Numbers	13	507		12-2	6.7	63/90			88	22
Reversed			(E)	9-10	4.5		-1	SEM	83	13
			(D)	15-8	10.1		+1	SEM	93	32
19. Spatial	21	507		14-6	9.3	84/90			95	36
Relations			(E)	9-6	3.9		-1	SEM	89	23
			(D)	23	14.9		+1	SEM	101	53
20. Listening	32	531		29[62]	16.9[56]	97/90			120	90
Comprehension			(E)	19-2	13.0		-1	SEM	113	81
			(D)	29[88]	16.9[83]		+1	SEM	127	96

Figure III-14. *(continued)*.

```
==============================================================================
Name: Rima Harris                    ID:                         Page: 4
==============================================================================


------------------------------------------------------------------------------
                  Raw          Age        Grade
Test Name         Score   W     Equiv.     Equiv.    RMI            SS    PR
------------------------------------------------------------------------------
21. Verbal        29     541        30[76]   16.9[72]  98/90          119   90
    Analogies                 (E) 25         14.7              -1 SEM  114   82
                              (D) 30[94]     16.9[95]          +1 SEM  124   95

ORAL LANGUAGE     ---    536        34[52]   16.9[50]  97/90          121   92
                              (E) 18-11      12.9              -1 SEM  118   88
                              (D) 34[82]     16.9[86]          +1 SEM  124   95


==============================================================================
              Form A was used to obtain Achievement Scores
==============================================================================

22. Letter-Word   55     557        32[70]   16.9[70]  99/90          124   95
    Identification            (E) 26         16.2              -1 SEM  120   91
                              (D) 32[80]     16.9[80]          +1 SEM  128   97

23. Passage       39     545        30[88]   16.9[77]  99/90          132   98
    Comprehension             (E) 30[56]     16.9[52]          -1 SEM  127   96
                              (D) 30[98]     16.9[93]          +1 SEM  137   99

24. Calculation   30     523        12-11     7.3     50/90           84   15
                              (E) 11-9        6.3              -1 SEM   80    9
                              (D) 14-7        9.3              +1 SEM   88   21

25. Applied       42     525        15-3     10.1     81/90           95   36
    Problems                  (E) 13-0        7.6              -1 SEM   91   27
                              (D) 18-11      12.8              +1 SEM   99   47

26. Dictation     49     540        30[66]   16.9[54]  97/90          113   81
                              (E) 19         12.4              -1 SEM  107   68
                              (D) 30[88]     16.9[86]          +1 SEM  119   90

27. Writing       24-Y   530        26[92]   16.9[92]  98/90          132   98
    Samples                   (E) 26[58]     15.6              -1 SEM  127   96
                              (D) 26[99]     16.9[99]          +1 SEM  137   99

28. Science       29     514        13-4      8.1     73/90           91   28
                              (E) 11-0        5.6              -1 SEM   85   16
                              (D) 17-4       11.6              +1 SEM   97   42

29. Social Studies 37    543        20       13.8     95/90          109   73
                              (E) 16-9       11.2              -1 SEM  104   61
                              (D) 37[68]     16.9[52]          +1 SEM  114   82

30. Humanities    38     531        20       13.4     93/90          105   63
                              (E) 15-6       10.2              -1 SEM  100   50
                              (D) 32[62]     16.3              +1 SEM  110   75
```

Figure III-14. *(continued).*

```
================================================================================
Name: Rima Harris                      ID:                           Page: 5
================================================================================
```

Test Name	Raw Score	W		Age Equiv.	Grade Equiv.	RMI			SS	PR
BROAD READING	---	551		32[71]	16.9[87]	99/90			129	98
			(E)	28	16.7		-1	SEM	125	95
			(D)	32[91]	16.9[99]		+1	SEM	133	99
BROAD MATH (Gq)	---	524		13-10	8.5	66/90			89	23
			(E)	12-2	6.6		-1	SEM	86	18
			(D)	16-10	11.0		+1	SEM	92	30
BROAD WRITTEN LANGUAGE	---	535		32[76]	16.9[77]	97/90			120	91
			(E)	23	13.0		-1	SEM	115	84
			(D)	32[94]	16.9[99]		+1	SEM	125	95
BROAD KNOWLEDGE (E Dev)	---	529		17-9	11.9	90/90			100	50
			(E)	14-2	9.0		-1	SEM	97	42
			(D)	32[50]	15.3		+1	SEM	103	58
SKILLS (E Dev)	---	541		26	14.9	96/90			111	76
			(E)	17-3	11.5		-1	SEM	108	70
			(D)	30[71]	16.9[74]		+1	SEM	114	82
33. Quantitative Concepts	37	527		13-10	8.6	71/90			91	28
			(E)	12-4	6.9		-1	SEM	85	16
			(D)	18-1	11.4		+1	SEM	97	42
BASIC MATH SKILLS	---	525		13-4	7.9	61/90			88	20
			(E)	12-0	6.6		-1	SEM	84	14
			(D)	15-7	10.2		+1	SEM	92	30
MATHEMATICS REASONING	Use scores from Test 25: Applied Problems									

Figure III-14. *(continued)*.

```
================================================================================
Name: Rima Harris                    ID:                              Page: 6
================================================================================
```

Intra-Cognitive Discrepancies
```
================================================================================
```

	ACTUAL SS	OTHER SS	PREDICTED SS	SS DIFF	PR	SD DIFF
Long-Term Retrieval (Glr)	110	100	100	10	79	0.81
Short-Term Memory (Gsm)	104	102	102	2	56	0.15
Processing Speed (Gs)	83	105	104	-21	6	-1.54
Auditory Processing (Ga)	113	100	100	13	86	1.10
Visual Processing (Gv)	105	101	101	4	62	0.31
Comprehension-Knowledge (Gc)	112	100	100	12	86	1.07
Fluid Reasoning (Gf)	86	104	105	-19	5	-1.61

Aptitude/Achievement Discrepancies
(Based on Scholastic Aptitude with ACH Broad Clusters)
```
================================================================================
```

	ACTUAL ACH SS	APTITUDE SS	PREDICTED SS	SS DIFF	PR	SD DIFF
Oral Language	---	---	---	----	-----	------
Broad Reading	129	107	105	24	99	2.47
Broad Mathematics (Gq)	89	89	92	-3	39	-0.28
Broad Written Language	120	102	101	19	97	1.86
Broad Knowledge	100	108	105	-5	32	-0.47

Intra-Achievement Discrepancies
```
================================================================================
```

	ACTUAL SS	OTHER SS	PREDICTED SS	SS DIFF	PR	SD DIFF
Broad Reading (R)	129	103	103	26	99.6	2.68
Broad Mathematics (M)	89	116	115	-26	1	-2.43
Broad Written Language (W)	120	106	106	14	94	1.52
Broad Knowledge (K)	100	113	114	-14	6	-1.59

Figure III–14. *(continued)*.

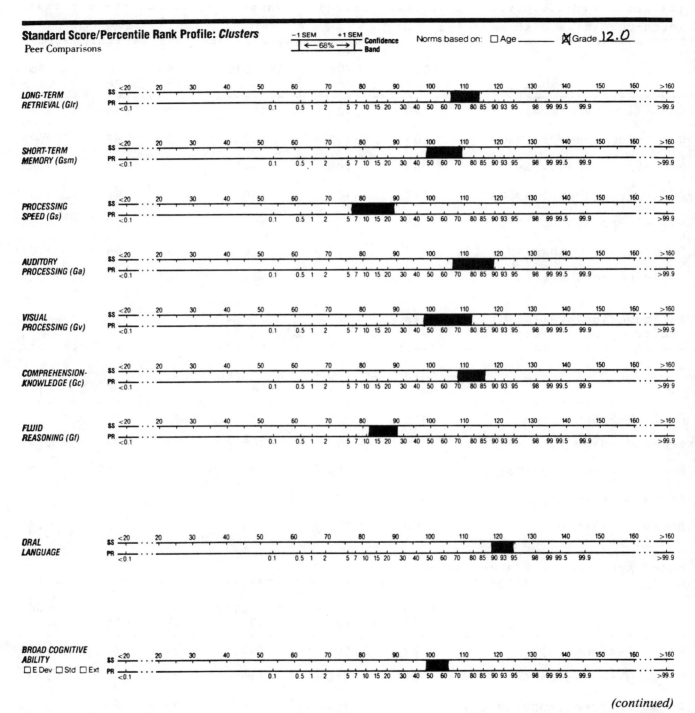

Figure III–15. Rima's WJ-R Tests of Cognitive Ability and Tests of Achievement Standard Score/Percentile Rank Profiles for Clusters.

(continued)

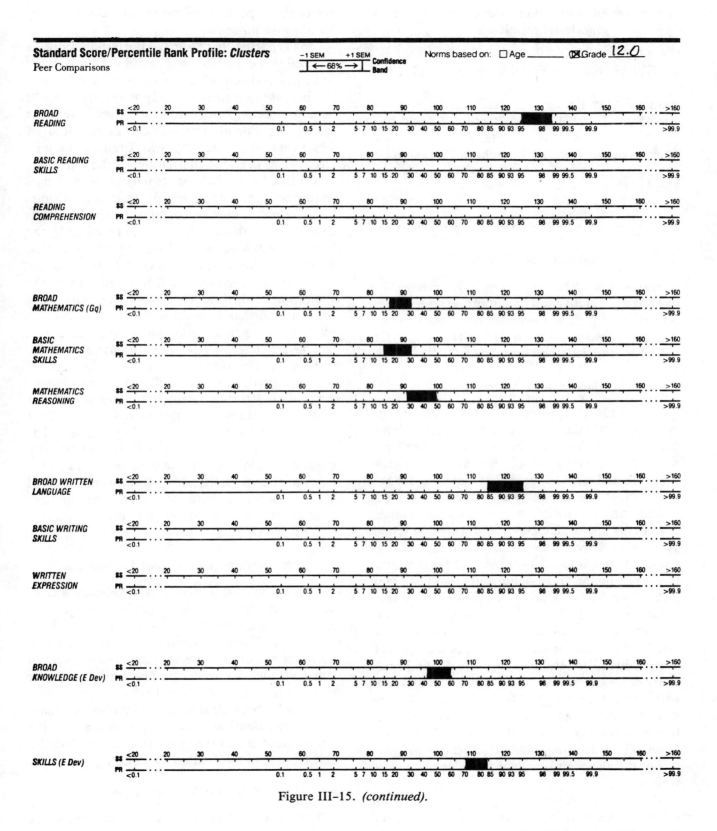

Figure III-15. *(continued)*.

Diagnosis: Inappropriate educational program, emotional problems

PSYCHOEDUCATIONAL EVALUATION

Student: Max Kresge	Evaluator:
Birthdate: 7/30/73	Parents: Lucille & Hal Kresge
Chronological Age: 18-9	School: Southern Ohio University
Grade: 13.8	Test Dates: 4/20, 4/21/92

Reason for Referral

Max was referred for testing by his mother due to his lack of motivation in school and poor grades. She asked if he has a learning disability or other cognitively based problem that might be interfering with scholastic performance.

Background Information

Mrs. Kresge reported that Max reached his developmental milestones on the early side of normal and had no difficulties with behavior or academic skills in elementary school. She did note that he often seemed sad and somewhat insecure. He had a few close friends but was never in the social mainstream. When Max was entering seventh grade, his parents divorced. Sometime during that school year, Max began using marijuana and cutting school. Throughout the next 5 years, Max continued to use marijuana and alcohol and periodically ran away from home. During this time, Max earned grades of B and C when he was attending school regularly and grades of D and F when he was cutting. In his junior and senior years of high school, Max attended counseling intermittently and spent 6 weeks in a residential program for adolescents with substance abuse problems. Subsequently, he stopped running away from home but continued to use marijuana. During these years, Max maintained a B to C average, and despite earlier irregular school attendance and continued drug use, graduated with his class.

Mrs. Kresge reported that Max has a gift for acting, assuming different types of characters, and duplicating accents and dialects. He can caricature personality types and real people with extraordinary insight and humor.

Max reported that shortly after graduation, he stopped using marijuana, but did not know what to do next. He enrolled in Southern Ohio University because he wanted to study acting and thought he had to be in college to do so. Currently, he is taking the liberal arts curriculum required of freshmen at that university, with Drama as his only elective. Max stated that Drama is the only class in which he has any interest. He enjoys the challenges of this class, but would like his teacher to critique his work more often and in more depth. Max feels that the other theater students are annoyed by the intensity with which he involves himself in his roles. He is maintaining an A average in Drama, but his other grades range from a C in English to a D in Biology and Algebra. He states that math is hard for him and that he dislikes "struggling with it." He feels that he asks more questions in class than the other students, and that this irritates them. Generally, in his other courses, he thinks he could get better grades if he were willing to apply himself. He studies infrequently and states that he does not know how. He never writes more than one draft of an English paper. Max also stated that he has no real friends and feels that he does not fit in with the other freshmen. He claimed he would rather be alone than to befriend "shallow people." Asked if he reads for pleasure, Max stated that he likes to read oriental philosophy and plays by contemporary playwrights.

Previous and Concurrent Evaluations

Max has had one psychological evaluation, administered when he was in eighth grade. His scores on the Verbal and Performance scales of the Wechsler Intelligence Scale for Children - Revised were in the lower end of the *Superior* range and in the *High Average* range, respectively. The Arithmetic score was one standard deviation below the average of the other Verbal scale subtests. Otherwise, no subtest scatter was identified. The diagnosis made by the psychologist at that time was Adjustment Disorder and Oppositional/Defiant Disorder.

Behavioral Observations

Testing took place in two 2-hour sessions. Max was pleasant and readily answered all questions about his background. He offered information about his feelings and social relationships with surprising candor. His affect suggested a sense of hopelessness regarding his ability to succeed in school.

Throughout testing, Max appeared quite anxious. He initiated conversations only during breaks and gave up easily on most of the items he found challenging. More often than not, he shook his head or shrugged his shoulders rather than try to reason through or guess at an item. When encouraged to do so, he frequently responded, "I don't know how to do it." In contrast, Max visibly relaxed during the Writing Samples test and appeared to take pleasure in writing the most creative responses he could. Asked about this change, Max replied, "I can *always* think of the right words."

Tests Administered

Max was administered the Woodcock-Johnson Psycho-Educational Battery—Revised, Cognitive Tests (1–14, 20) and Achievement Tests: Form A (22–30). Two writing samples were also analyzed.

Test Results

The tests of the WJ-R were scored according to grade norms. When no difference was found between the two component tests of a factor or cluster, only the factor or cluster score is discussed. A complete set of test scores is appended to this report.

Cognitive Abilities

Based on the results of the Woodcock-Johnson Psycho-Educational Battery—Revised (WJ-R) Broad Cognitive Ability (BCA) factor, Max appears to have general cognitive abilities in the *Average/High Average* range (BCA Percentile Rank: 72) when compared to his grade-peers. Significant discrepancies were found among the seven cognitive factors, but not between the individual tests within each factor.

Max scored in the *Average* range in the following cognitive areas: the ability to recall words and sentences immediately after hearing them (Short-Term Memory, PR: 53), the ability to form associations between visual and verbal information and recall them later (Long-Term Retrieval, PR: 50), the ability to process visual symbols rapidly (Processing Speed, PR: 38), and the ability to use logical

reasoning to solve visually presented "puzzles" according to verbal instructions (Fluid Reasoning, PR: 50). On the tests of the Fluid Reasoning factor, despite his *Average* score, Max appeared inflexible in his strategies. He was slow to grasp the verbal instructions and initially, despite instructions to the contrary, Max assumed he had to memorize the key. He asked many questions that could not be answered within standardized procedures and finally protested, "How can I figure it out if you don't tell me the rule?"

Max scored in the *High Average* range in interpreting and recalling pictorial information (Visual Processing, PR: 82) and in vocabulary knowledge (Comprehension-Knowledge, PR: 75). Max's ability to understand one- to two-sentence, orally presented passages was also in the *High Average* range (Listening Comprehension, PR: 78). Max scored in the *Superior* to *Very Superior* range in the ability to synthesize separate sounds into a familiar word (Auditory Processing, PR: 97). The Auditory Processing factor represents a significant strength for Max. Of college freshmen with the same predicted Auditory Processing standard score of 102, only 2% would obtain a score as high as or higher than Max's actual score of 129.

Academic Achievement

Reading

Max scored in the *Very Superior* range on the Letter-Word Identification test (PR: 98), significantly higher than his *Average/High Average* score on the Passage Comprehension test (PR: 75). On the latter test, Max did not appear to read carefully and occasionally missed critical details. The WJ-R Age/Grade Profile indicates that Max should have no difficulty reading grade-appropriate texts. More likely, Max's stated lack of study techniques frustrates what efforts he does expend to learn textual and lecture material.

Written Language

In addition to the WJ-R Written Language tests, two writing samples—a movie review and a short story—were used to analyze Max's writing skills. As noted above, Max enjoyed the Writing Samples test and scored in the *Very Superior* range (PR: 99). His ideas were original, clearly expressed, and well-organized. His choice of words was specific and descriptive. The style of his movie review, however, indicated a need for training in literate versus oral (conversational) writing. Max's knowledge of basic writing skills, as measured by the Dictation test, was in the *Low Average* range (PR: 19), significantly below his performance in written expression. In all writing tests and samples, Max made errors in spelling and formation of irregular plurals.

Math

Max scored in the lower end of the *Average* range on both math tests, Calculation (PR: 33) and Applied Problems (PR: 30). Max's performance indicated that he knows the math facts to an automatic level and understands the basic operations using whole numbers, decimals, and fractions. He was not able to convert a mixed number into an improper fraction and did not attempt any algebraic equations, although he is currently in an algebra course. He made some apparently careless errors, such as misreading process signs. Once, he carried a number within a multiplication problem and forgot to add it in. Max had no difficulty translating story problems into computation as long as he understood the concepts underlying the required computation.

General Knowledge

Max scored in the *Low Average/Average* range in the Broad Knowledge cluster (PR: 23), representing a significant weakness in general factual knowledge. Out of college freshmen with the same predicted standard score of 107, only 3% would obtain a score as low as or lower than Max's actual standard score of 89.

Summary and Conclusions

Based on the WJ-R, Max's cognitive abilities range from *Average* to *Superior/Very Superior*. He demonstrated specific strengths in language and auditory processing skills. It is possible that his high level of anxiety contributed to his apparent inflexibility of reasoning and his tendency to give up on challenging items, thus underestimating his actual level of cognitive abilities.

Max's anxiety also appeared to impair the care with which he approached certain reading and math items and his willingness to work through difficult items. Test results indicate that Max has strengths in reading and written expression; he has relative weaknesses in certain math operations, writing mechanics, and literate writing style. By his own report, Max lacks study strategies. His significant weakness in general knowledge may be related to his history of sporadic school attendance and his narrow focus of reading materials.

Based on the current testing, Max appears to have the cognitive abilities to succeed in college, but would need tutorial support or remedial coursework to improve some areas of academic weakness. More important is that Max appears to have chosen college for lack of another option, erroneously believing that it was the only way to study acting. It is recommended that Max reevaluate his decision to pursue a college career, perhaps with the help of a vocational specialist or college counselor. Instead, he may choose to apply to a reputable acting school and obtain professional guidance in pursuing a career in acting. Regardless of his choice, Max's tendencies to give up on a task when he feels inadequate and to blame others for interpersonal problems are likely to interfere with his ability to attain his goals. He might consider working with a mental health professional to understand and change these behavioral patterns.

Diagnosis: Deficit in delayed recall; poor learning
   strategies

PSYCHOEDUCATIONAL EVALUATION

Name: Jill Streffer   School: Lanyard
                        Community College

Birthdate: 9/10/71   Grade: Sophomore
Chronological Age: 20-2 Test Dates: 1/12,
                        1/15, 1/16/92

Reason for Referral

Jill was referred by her college counselor, Myra
Coltner, for a psychoeducational evaluation in order
to identify the nature and extent of Jill's learning
disabilities and to obtain recommendations to help
her succeed in college. Ms. Coltner requested specific
advice about how she could help Jill achieve her
professional goals.

Background Information

In an interview, Jill recalled difficulty with school
subjects since the third grade. She also reported
anxiety and self-esteem problems throughout school.
She noted that she had difficulty learning to read
and that even after decoding became less of a
problem, she had difficulty remembering what she
had read. She stated that she had trouble remembering the steps in math problems and that she often
became confused midway through a problem. She
described her difficulty keeping several ideas in her
mind simultaneously and noted that it was difficult
for her to read lengthy chapters in textbooks or to
follow a lecture if the professor talked too long or
changed topics frequently. She also commented that
she really does not know how to prepare for exams.

Throughout school, Jill has received learning
disability services in both self-contained and resource
rooms. During her sophomore year in high school,
Jill did well and was dropped from her special education classes. Her grades went down in her junior
year, despite tutoring, and she was re-enrolled in
special education. She continued in the special
education program until graduation.

Jill is currently a sophomore at Lanyard Community College, a 2-year college known for its
technical training programs. For the first semester
Jill received tutorial services through Lanyard's
learning disability program, but stopped attending
at the beginning of the second semester because she
felt that she no longer needed support services.
Although Jill completed her freshman year with a
2.5 grade point average, for the past three semesters
she has either received low grades, failed classes,
or withdrawn from classes. During these three
semesters, she has completed only three courses,
9 credit hours, with passing grades.

Presently, Jill is between semesters and working
full-time at a pet shop. She has helped with animal
care at the city zoo for the past 2 years on a volunteer
basis, and states that she wants to complete a degree
in zoology so that she can become a zookeeper. She
is aware of the courses that are required for this
career and currently wishes to complete the prerequisites. She also noted that she loves to draw
intricate scenes with desert animals. Jill commented
that she is bored with her job at the pet store, and
plans to resume full-time study in the upcoming
Spring semester.

Tests Administered

Jill was administered the Woodcock-Johnson
Psycho-Educational Battery—Revised (WJ-R), Tests
of Cognitive Ability (1–16, 19) and Tests of Achievement, Form A (22–31). Additionally, an informal
assessment of study skills was conducted. Testing
was conducted in three 3-hour sessions.

Behavioral Observations

When initially discussing the testing, Jill stated
that she had always been "test phobic." She had
been tested many times throughout school and,
rather than benefit from the results, she felt that
they were used to reaffirm that she was "dumb."

During testing Jill was cooperative and pleasant
and attempted to answer all questions asked. She
conversed easily during breaks but during the testing
seemed somewhat tense and removed.

Test Results

The tests of the WJ-R were scored according to
grade norms so that Jill's abilities might be compared to her peers at college. When no difference
was found between the two component tests of a
factor or cluster, only the factor or cluster score
is discussed. For the purposes of this report,

standard scores and percentile ranks are expressed as obtained scores. A complete set of test scores is appended to this report.

Cognitive Abilities

Based upon the WJ-R Broad Cognitive Ability—Extended Scale score (SS: 90, PR: 25), Jill appears to be functioning in the *Low Average/Average* range when compared to her grade-peers.

Jill demonstrated particular strengths on the factors of Long-Term Retrieval and Visual Processing, but discrepancies between tests within those factors warrant explanation. Jill scored in the *High Average* range on the Long-Term Retrieval factor (SS: 115, PR: 84), but her scores on the two Delayed Recall (DR) tests administered 2 days later were in the *Low Average* range (DR Memory for Names, SS: 87, PR: 20; DR Visual-Auditory Learning, SS: 82, PR: 12). Although Jill was able to store and retrieve the visual-auditory associations over approximately 10 minutes, her ability to retrieve that information a few days later was significantly lower. After she had completed the two Delayed Recall tests, Jill commented: "That's my problem. I remember what we did, but nothing seems to stick." Thus, although Jill appears to have a significant strength in initially recalling visual-auditory associations, her ability to retain that information over a period of more than a day is more consistent with her other cognitive abilities. Nevertheless, her initial strength in this area may have implications for teaching.

Within the Visual Processing factor, a significant discrepancy existed between the two test scores. Based on the Picture Recognition test, Jill appears particularly adept at noting and retaining visual details in pictures (SS: 126: PR: 96). Her artwork indicates that she can then reproduce an image in great detail. Her *Low Average/Average* score on the Visual Closure test, however, was consistent with her other cognitive abilities. Her performance on the Spatial Relations test (SS: 100, PR: 50) was in the *Average* range.

On the Standard Score/Percentile Rank Profile, the 68% confidence bands for the remaining six cognitive factors overlap, indicating no significant differences. Consequently, Jill appears to be functioning in the *Low Average* and *Low Average/Average* ranges in the cognitive areas of short-term auditory memory, auditory processing of sounds and syllables in words, vocabulary knowledge, general language comprehension and reasoning, speed of processing visual symbolic information, and abstract, logical reasoning.

Academic Achievement

Reading

Based on the WJ-R Broad Reading cluster, Jill's overall achievement was in the *Low Average/Average* range (SS: 89, PR: 23). No significant differences existed among the tests of word recognition, decoding nonsense words (phonics and structural analysis), and comprehending short passages. When Jill did not immediately recognize a word, she tended to give up rather than attempt to pronounce it. When encouraged, she used a strategy of "whole word guessing." Her errors suggested a lack of phonic and structural analysis skills. On the Passage Comprehension test, Jill showed awareness of sentence structure and grammar, but did not appear to consider critical details carefully. Occasionally, she requested the meaning of a word.

Written Language

Scores on the WJ-R Broad Written Language cluster (SS: 78, PR: 7) indicate that Jill is functioning in the *Low* range when compared to grade-peers. She appeared to have difficulty both on a conceptual level and on the level of basic skills. On the more difficult items of the Writing Samples test, Jill seemed to misunderstand the task demands or misinterpret the wording of the item itself. Also, on several items, she wrote incomplete sentences; on others, she wrote two or three sentences without proper punctuation, so that only a part of her response could be scored. In addition to her difficulty with awareness of sentence boundaries, she made a variety of errors in spelling, punctuation, and capitalization.

Mathematics

Jill's performance on the WJ-R Mathematics cluster was in the *Low Average* range (SS: 87, PR: 20) with no discrepancy between tests. Error pattern analysis of computation skills indicates that Jill can perform all of the basic operations involving whole numbers and decimals. Additionally, she can add and subtract fractions with common denominators.

She made errors in multiplying and dividing fractions, converting fractions to percentages, calculating averages, adding and subtracting negative numbers, and solving algebraic equations. Jill made errors in translating word problems more complicated than one step into computation and stated, "I never was any good at word problems." She lacked factual measurement information such as the number of inches in a yard and weeks in a year.

Knowledge

Jill obtained scores in the *Low* range on general knowledge (Broad Knowledge: SS: 75, PR: 5) with no discrepancies among the tests of Science, Social Studies, and Humanities. On the Humanities test, Jill commented that she used to know the answers to a lot of the questions but could not remember them.

Study Strategies

To assess Jill's study strategies informally, she was asked to read a chapter of a text that she had previously used in a history course, study it as though for a test, and take notes on a simulated lecture. Jill opened the book directly to the first page of the assigned chapter and began reading the text without looking at the unit or chapter headings. When she had turned the page, she was unable to tell either the title of the chapter or what it might be about. When she had completed the chapter, she was able to give many details, but could not relate them in a coherent framework or recall the key ideas of the chapter. When asked to study the chapter, she said she would just read it over again or read over her notes. During the simulated lecture, the examiner noted that Jill attempted to write everything, rather than key ideas. When asked about this method, she said that she usually gives up on taking notes about halfway through the class period. She stated that at one time she had taped class lectures, but then didn't have time to listen to them.

Discrepancies

No significant discrepancies were noted among the cognitive factors or among the achievement clusters. Jill appears to have significant aptitude-achievement discrepancies in Written Language and Broad Knowledge.

Summary

Results of the WJ-R indicate that Jill's overall cognitive abilities are in the *Low Average* range. Jill demonstrated a strength in learning visual-auditory associations and retaining them over a few minutes but not over longer periods of time. She also appears to have strengths in noting and retaining details in pictures and in visual reasoning. All other cognitive abilities appear to be in the *Low Average* range or bordering the *Low Average* and *Average* ranges.

Jill's *Low Average* reading and math skills appear to be consistent with her cognitive abilities, but her achievement in written language and general knowledge is significantly lower than expected. Although *Low Average* cognitive abilities might require Jill to work harder than many of her classmates to progress normally in school, her ineffective reading-study strategies and note-taking skills probably account for some of the difficulty she is having in learning and retaining her coursework. Moreover, given a hypothetical range within which she could be expected to perform academically, Jill's tendency to give up when challenged might move her achievement toward the lower rather than the higher end of that range.

No specific processing deficits were found on the WJ-R; however, due to the pervasive nature and sometimes subtle effects of a language disorder, it is possible that Jill's difficulties in following a lecture, reading comprehension, written expression, and math word problems are, at least, in part due to a language-learning disability.

Recommendations

For the Counselor

1. Help Jill contact a certified speech/language pathologist with expertise in evaluating young adults to arrange a complete evaluation of her receptive and expressive language skills.

2. Obtain a commitment from Jill that she wishes to receive additional support with her college courses. Investigate the possibility of hiring a tutor with expertise in teaching study strategies, note taking, and organizational skills.

3. Review with Jill the courses that she will be required to take in the next few years to complete

a degree in zoology. Develop a master plan and a realistic timeline so that Jill can see exactly what she needs to accomplish.

4. Suggest that Jill invest one semester in improving her learning skills by enrolling in remedial courses that focus on reading comprehension, expository writing, study strategies, and organizational skills. She should limit her coursework that semester only to these courses. If she has a tutor, the tutor should work with her on developing and refining these skills in material that is directly applicable to the academic courses she will take subsequently in her zoology program.

5. Meet with Jill periodically to discuss how her program is progressing. Review with her what she has accomplished and what she has left to complete.

For the Tutor

1. Whenever possible, obtain the syllabus for each course prior to the beginning of the semester. Use the required course readings to help Jill develop study strategies.

2. Teach Jill time-management skills. For example, when notified of a term paper or project, help Jill break it into stages and write deadlines for the completion of each stage on a calendar. Teach Jill to set aside a certain amount of time daily or weekly to work on the project.

3. Teach Jill to monitor her understanding of what the lecturer is saying and to question for clarity. If she wishes to ask a question but does not want to interrupt class, teach her to write down the question and ask the instructor after class or during office hours.

4. Teach specific prereading strategies to help Jill develop a mental framework for the information she is about to read. For example, teach Jill to survey the chapter before reading and turn the subheadings into specific questions to answer as she reads.

5. Teach Jill to recognize the type of structure used to organize the key ideas in paragraphs or sections of her text. Some examples are enumerative, problem/solution, comparison/contrast, and cause/effect.

6. Teach Jill to develop an expectation to understand what she reads and, concomitantly, teach her how to monitor her comprehension. Demonstrate how to read interactively. Show Jill how to recall related prior knowledge, to predict what will happen, and to make judgments regarding the accuracy of the prediction. Teach her to monitor her comprehension by stopping periodically as she reads and asking herself if she understands the meaning.

For nonfiction text, two strategies that have been demonstrated to be effective are paraphrasing the main idea and supporting details of a paragraph after reading it and reading for the purpose of answering questions about the main ideas in a passage.

7. Teach Jill how to use specific prewriting strategies to organize information prior to writing. For example, she may benefit from semantic mapping or more structured outlining techniques.

8. Have Jill use a tape recorder to tape lectures for review. Use the tape to teach Jill how to take notes on class lectures. Given Jill's visual strengths, try teaching Jill to organize the material as a semantic map.

9. Teach Jill specific test-taking strategies, such as reading over the entire test before starting it, outlining the answers to essay questions, and reading all multiple-choice answers with the stem sentence before choosing a response. Test-taking strategies should help Jill to perform better on tests both by allowing her to demonstrate her knowledge and by alleviating the anxiety that may be affecting her performance.

10. Review with Jill a variety of mnemonic strategies that she may use to memorize information for examinations. Provide practice in applying the strategies with the knowledge and information that she is expected to learn for her courses.

11. Review with Jill the math skills that she is missing and incorporate them into survival math for independent living (e.g., checkbook balancing, calculating interest on a car loan, budgeting her salary, measuring for cooking). Provide practice in practical application of any new math skill.

12. If and when Jill enrolls in a math class, provide tutoring for her by introducing the curriculum a little ahead of the teacher. Plan sufficient time to teach concepts and build in repetition and reinforcement that the teacher may not provide.

Diagnosis: Weaknesses in efficient processing of visual symbols, auditory processing and memory, and vocabulary

PSYCHOEDUCATIONAL EVALUATION

Name: Hector Alcoser
Birthdate: 3/11/64

Chronological Age: 26-4

Evaluator:
School: Alamo Community College
Test Dates: 7/1, 7/2, 7/15, 7/16/91

Reason for Referral

Mr. Alcoser referred himself to the Learning Lab at Alamo Community College for a psychoeducational evaluation. He hoped that the evaluation would identify his specific learning strengths and weaknesses to assist him in the selection of college courses and to guide him in vocational planning. As Mr. Alcoser was also considering transferring to a 4-year college program, he wanted an estimate of his current levels of academic performance. Mr. Alcoser also wished to determine if he would be eligible for tutorial services at the community college.

Background Information

Hector Alcoser, a Hispanic male, is completing his fifth semester at Alamo Community College. During an interview, he provided the following history. Mr. Alcoser stuttered until approximately third grade and recalls avoiding situations in the classroom in which he would have to speak. He received speech therapy at school and, sometime around fourth grade, his stuttering stopped. Mr. Alcoser also recalled that in the first through third grades he had great difficulty learning to read, spell, and memorize math facts. He was retained at the end of third grade, which he remembers as socially debilitating. The school retained him again in sixth grade, but Mr. Alcoser refused to go to school until he was placed in seventh grade, 3 weeks into the school year. Mr. Alcoser remembers studying after school and on weekends to prove he could do the work and, after making the honor roll for three consecutive quarters, he lost his motivation

to study and his grades declined. In the eighth grade, he was bussed out of his Hispanic/Black neighborhood to a school on the East side due to a new school district policy of desegregation. By ninth grade, he was "ditching school every other day." Mr. Alcoser dropped out of high school midway through his third year in ninth grade.

Mr. Alcoser eventually entered night school and finished his General Equivalency Diploma. He attended a vocational school for carpentry and welding and became a construction worker. In 1984, because of alcohol problems and trouble with the law, he was arrested and placed on probation. In 1987, he was convicted of armed robbery and sentenced to three years in prison. While in prison, he completed 48 Alamo Community College credit hours. The majority of courses were in electronics and computers.

Since his release in August of 1990, Mr. Alcoser has been attending Alamo Community College full-time on a grant. Presently, he has completed 54 credits out of an attempted 89 and has a 2.52 grade point average. Mr. Alcoser has been successful in computer and electronics courses, but has had difficulty with classes that require a lot of reading and writing, such as English literature, philosophy, and history. Mr. Alcoser stated that his reading has always been slow and, in the type of books he wants to read, there appear to be many words he does not understand. He is not interested in reading for pleasure, but is frustrated at not being able to read easily for information.

Tests Administered

Mr. Alcoser was administered the Woodcock-Johnson Tests of Cognitive Ability—Revised (Tests 1–21) and the Woodcock-Johnson Tests of Achievement—Revised, Form B (Tests 22–35). Testing was completed in four sessions, each session lasting about 1½ hours.

Behavioral Observations

Mr. Alcoser was motivated and attentive throughout the four test sessions. He commented that it was important to him to know how he was doing. On many of the tests, Mr. Alcoser seemed to consider his answers for a long time before responding. When trying to learn information, he used a variety of strategies such as verbal rehearsal and tracing with his finger on the table. During the Broad Knowledge tests, he talked about the concepts in question to prompt recall of specific information. This strategy was often successful. Generally, Mr. Alcoser was persistent and resourceful. He informed the examiner that he was "a crummy speller" and since he had never learned his math facts, he relied on a calculator for all computations. On several tests, Mr. Alcoser asked the examiner to repeat the instructions.

Assessment Results

The tests of the WJ-R were scored according to age norms. When no difference was found between the two component tests of a factor or cluster, only the factor or cluster score is discussed. Standard scores are expressed as 68% confidence bands. A 68% confidence band is written as the standard score ± 1 standard error of measurement (SS ± 1 SEM). A complete set of test scores is appended to this report.

Cognitive Abilities

Mr. Alcoser's overall performance on the Broad Cognitive Ability—Extended Scale fell in the *Average* range (SS ± 1 SEM: 94–98). Discrepancies, however, were noted among his scores.

Based on the WJ-R results, Mr. Alcoser has particular strengths in the lower cognitive process of perceiving and retaining critical details in pictures and in the higher cognitive process of abstract, logical reasoning using verbal information and visual patterns. He scored in the *Superior* range in the Fluid Reasoning factor (SS ± 1 SEM: 119–125) and the Spatial Relations test (SS ± 1 SEM: 119–131), and in the *High Average* to *Superior* range in the Visual Processing factor (SS ± 1 SEM: 111–123).

Based on the results of the Oral Language cluster, Mr. Alcoser's oral language skills appear to be in the *Average* range (SS ± 1 SEM: 96–102), but with probable discrepancies among the component skills. Within this cluster, Mr. Alcoser demonstrated relative strengths in verbal reasoning and comprehension. His scores on the tests of Listening Comprehension and Verbal Analogies were in the *Average/High Average* range (SS ± 1 SEM: 105–117) and *High Average* range (SS ± 1 SEM: 110–118), respectively. In contrast, within the Oral Language cluster, he demonstrated relative weaknesses in his

vocabulary knowledge and his ability to recall orally presented sentences. His score on the Comprehension-Knowledge factor was in the *Low Average* range (SS ± 1 SEM: 79–87) as was his score on the Memory for Sentences test (SS ± 1 SEM: 80–94).

A relative weakness was also noted in his ability to comprehend patterns fluently among auditory stimuli at the word and sound level, as measured by the Auditory Processing factor (SS ± 1 SEM: 84–94). This ability is an important factor in early learning of reading and spelling. Mr. Alcoser scored in the *Low* range on the Memory for Words test (SS ± 1 SEM: 68–82), relatively lower than his score on Memory for Sentences.

Mr. Alcoser scored in the *Low Average* range on the Processing Speed factor (SS ± 1 SEM: 81–93), indicating a relative weakness in fluent, accurate processing of visual symbols. Mr. Alcoser tracked along the lines of numbers and forms with his pencil and self-corrected his only two errors.

The Long-Term Retrieval factor measures the ability to establish and retrieve associations between visual and auditory stimuli. Mr. Alcoser scored in the *High Average* range (SS ± 1 SEM: 111–119) on the Visual-Auditory Learning test, a test in which words are given for unfamiliar symbols and the symbols are then "read" in the context of a story; he scored in the *Low Average* range (SS ± 1 SEM: 82–90) on Memory for Names, a test requiring forming associations between drawings of "space creatures" and their names. The significant discrepancy between Mr. Alcoser's scores on the two tests suggests that he was considerably aided by a meaningful linguistic context. He did not use any strategies to aid him in associating the names of the space creatures with their visual features. When Mr. Alcoser was administered the Delayed Recall tests 2 days later, he scored in the *Low Average* range in both tests. This represented a significant drop in performance from his previous score on Visual-Auditory Learning. When he was presented with a list of the symbols from this test and was asked to give the associated words, he asked, "How am I supposed to remember these out of context?"

Intracognitive Discrepancies

Mr. Alcoser demonstrated significant strengths in the factors of Fluid Reasoning and Visual

Processing. Of 26-year-olds with the same predicted standard scores in Fluid Reasoning and Visual Processing, only 1% and 5%, respectively, would obtain a score as high as or higher than Mr. Alcoser's.

Academic Achievement

Reading

Although Mr. Alcoser's Broad Reading score was in the *Average* range, he obtained a relatively higher score on the Reading Comprehension cluster (SS ± 1 SEM: 93–101) than on the Basic Reading Skills cluster (SS ± 1 SEM: 86–94). On both the Letter-Word Identification and Word Attack tests, he had difficulty pronouncing multisyllabic words. He tended to insert or omit medial sounds. He tried pronouncing the words in several different ways. On the Word Attack test, he made several of the nonsense words into real words. For example, he pronounced *cimp* as "chimp" and *cythe* as "kite."

Written Language

Mr. Alcoser's only significant intra-achievement discrepancy was in the area of written language. Of 26-year-olds with the same predicted Broad Reading score, only 3% would obtain a score as low as or lower than Mr. Alcoser's.

Although Mr. Alcoser scored in the *Average* range on the Writing Samples test, indicating that he can express his ideas in writing, he had particular difficulty with basic writing skills. His lowest writing score was on the Dictation test (SS ± 1 SEM: 66–76). His Relative Mastery Index of 9/90 suggests that on tasks involving basic writing skills, Mr. Alcoser would have only 9% success whereas average people of his age would have 90% success. Although Mr. Alcoser's spelling errors were generally phonetically correct, he omitted letters in many words, confused vowels, and misspelled common words (e.g., *wemen* for *woman*, *vary* for *very*, *lauge* for *laugh*). On the Proofing test, Mr. Alcoser's poor spelling contributed to the majority of his errors. He assumed that most of the items had a spelling error and proceeded to misspell several correctly spelled words.

Usage errors were also apparent in Mr. Alcoser's writing. Occasionally, he wrote singular forms of verbs when the plural form was needed, used present verb tense when past tense was needed, and omitted the endings of plural nouns.

Mathematics

Mr. Alcoser's Basic Mathematics Skills cluster was in the *Low Average* range (SS ± 1 SEM: 85–91), whereas Mathematics Reasoning was in the *Average* range (SS ± 1 SEM: 94–102). When working on the Calculation test, Mr. Alcoser commented that he did not know all his math facts and could do better if he could use a calculator. Mr. Alcoser made some computation errors on both tests of the Broad Mathematics cluster, but appeared to understand the concepts underlying all of the basic operations. He demonstrated difficulty with operations at and above the level of rational numbers.

Knowledge

Mr. Alcoser scored in the *Average* range on the Broad Knowledge cluster. His score on the Science test (SS ± 1 SEM: 98–110) was significantly higher than his score on the Humanities test (SS ± 1 SEM: 80–90). His score on the Social Studies test was in the *Average* range (SS ± 1 SEM: 89–99).

Summary and Interpretation

Although not always significant, Mr. Alcoser's consistent performance discrepancies between certain cognitive factors and between individual tests within factors lead to the following conclusions. Mr. Alcoser appears to have significant strengths in processing nonsymbolic visual patterns and in abstract, logical reasoning using visual patterns. He has relative strengths in verbal reasoning and comprehension of oral language. Mr. Alcoser appears to have relative weaknesses in fluent, accurate perception of visual symbols and in memory of auditory information and visual-auditory associations outside of a meaningful linguistic context. The combination of these weaknesses would certainly account for the level of difficulty Mr. Alcoser had learning to read, spell, and memorize math facts. It appears continued weaknesses in basic skills interfere with Mr. Alcoser's performance at the more conceptual levels of academic skills. Currently, mild difficulty in efficient perception of visual symbols may also contribute to Mr. Alcoser's slow reading pace.

Additionally, Mr. Alcoser's level of vocabulary knowledge is a relative weakness. Lack of age-expected vocabulary may be attributed to Mr. Alcoser's interrupted education and infrequent reading. Additionally, his difficulty with learning and remembering auditory information out of context may have interfered with his ability to benefit from many of the vocabulary activities presented in school.

Recommendations

In preparation for his transfer to a 4-year college, Mr. Alcoser would benefit from tutorial services at the Alamo Community College Learning Lab. The main focus of instruction would be to help Mr. Alcoser improve his word identification, reading vocabulary, and reading rate, as well as to train him in the use of reading study strategies. Before beginning services, obtain a commitment from Mr. Alcoser that he wants to improve his reading skill and is willing to devote study time to this endeavor. Mr. Alcoser should also consider enrolling in remedial reading, writing, mathematics, and study skills courses at Alamo. The following specific recommendations may help Mr. Alcoser improve his reading and writing skills:

Reading

1. Teach Mr. Alcoser structural analysis skills. Focus on common root words, prefixes, and suffixes. If he requires additional help in word attack, use a program that teaches automatic recognition of common word parts, such as Glass-Analysis for Decoding Only (Glass, 1973, 1976). An outline of this method is attached.

2. Teach Mr. Alcoser SQ3R (Survey, Question, Read, Recite, Review) as a reading study strategy. An outline of this method is attached. Adapt this method, however, to include writing the answers to the questions formed from headings and subheadings, as well as any questions provided at the end of the chapter. To help Mr. Alcoser understand the organization of the chapter, emphasize the Survey step.

Written Language

1. Have Mr. Alcoser enroll in a class to develop keyboarding skills and to learn to use a word processing program with a spelling checker.

2. Encourage Mr. Alcoser to buy a pocket-sized, computerized spelling checker with thesaurus and teach him how to use it.

3. Provide Mr. Alcoser with a list of high-frequency words for spelling that he can master independently. Encourage Mr. Alcoser to devote 5 minutes daily to spelling common words.

4. Teach Mr. Alcoser a spelling study method that he can use independently, such as an adaptation of Simultaneous Oral Spelling. (See attached.)

5. Teach Mr. Alcoser how to improve his expository writing. Teach him how to plan a paper, organize his ideas, and gather and incorporate additional information.

6. Help Mr. Alcoser develop a proofreading checklist that is composed of a list of the most frequent usage errors he makes in his writing, such as errors involving word endings, verb tense, and possessive pronouns. Have him read his papers aloud, paying careful attention to what he has written.

Vocational

Mr. Alcoser has high aptitude for tasks requiring reasoning and visual planning and organization. Examples of fields that would require these aptitudes include engineering, computers, electronics, or design. Many jobs in these fields also require good math skills. Mr. Alcoser should request the help of a vocational counselor at Alamo Community College. Career interest and aptitude inventories, combined with the results of this assessment, should allow a vocational counselor to guide Mr. Alcoser in his exploration of vocational options. As Mr. Alcoser narrows his focus on a career, he should take courses toward that goal. Additionally, he should find out what math skills are required in that type of work and enroll in remedial and then regular math courses appropriate to his chosen field of study.

Diagnosis: Deficits in auditory and visual memory processing speed; residual academic delay

PSYCHOEDUCATIONAL EVALUATION

Name: Roger Carp

Birthdate: 3/29/62

Chronological Age: 29

Evaluator:

School: Glen State University

Test Dates: 5/1, 5/4, 5/7, 5/8/91

Reason for Referral

Roger referred himself for a psychoeducational evaluation to gain a better understanding of his strengths and weaknesses in learning and to find out if he has a learning disability. He also requested recommendations to help him perform more successfully in his college courses.

Background Information

Roger is in his second year at Glen State University. He is interested in studying psychology, but is having difficulty keeping up with the assigned work in his undergraduate courses. Dr. Austin Brown, a professor in the Department of Psychology, suggested to Roger that his difficulties may be due to a specific learning disability and suggested an evaluation.

Roger attended elementary school in the early '70s. He had trouble learning to read in elementary school, but special services were either not available or not offered. He remembered being isolated from the rest of the class because he could not keep up in reading and writing. He recalled being ridiculed for his poor reading performance and stated that one teacher made him stand in the corner of the classroom during reading time. Roger stated that he did not learn to read until he dropped out of high school in his junior year. When asked how he learned, he said that he obtained children's books and forced himself to read them. When he was less embarrassed about his reading level, he sought tutoring in an adult literacy program. The tutor had him "trace words on paper," which Roger felt helped him "learn to sound words out."

After quitting school, Roger worked as a custodian at a local hospital for 10 years. At this time,

he decided that he wanted to pursue another occupation and that if he was going "to get anywhere," he would have to complete college. At age 26, he enrolled in Sono Community College. Although he passed all of his courses and graduated from the 2-year program, Roger stated that every course was a struggle, and on several occasions, he failed major exams.

Tests Administered

The Woodcock-Johnson Psycho-Educational Battery—Revised, Tests of Cognitive Ability (Tests 1-16), and the Woodcock-Johnson Psycho-Educational Battery—Revised, Tests of Achievement, Form A (Tests 22-32, 34), were administered.

Behavioral Observations

Testing was conducted in four 1-hour sessions. Roger was cooperative and maintained attention throughout the testing sessions. He did not engage in spontaneous conversation and answered most questions with one- or two-word responses. On two occasions, when he was asked questions that he could not answer, he stated that he thought he should know the answer, and that he felt "really dumb."

Assessment Results

The tests of the WJ-R were scored according to age norms. When no difference was found between the two component tests of a factor or cluster, only the factor or cluster score is discussed. Standard scores and percentile ranks are reported as 68% confidence bands. A 68% confidence band is expressed as ±1 standard error of measurement (SEM). A complete set of test scores is appended to this report.

Cognitive Abilities

Roger's performance on the Broad Cognitive Ability—Extended Scale (BCA) fell in the *Low Average* to *Average* range (SS ±1 SEM: 87-93). Although no significant intracognitive discrepancies were noted among the cognitive factors, Roger obtained deficient mastery levels on several of the tests. His Relative Mastery Index (RMI) of 39/90 on the Visual Matching test suggests that his speed of processing visual symbols is *Very Limited*. On tasks requiring rapid scanning and discrimination of visual symbols, Roger would demonstrate 39%

mastery, whereas average individuals of his age would attain 90% mastery. His RMI of 45/90 on the Memory for Words test suggests that he is *Very Limited* in immediate recall of unrelated words or sounds, and his RMI of 55/90 on the Incomplete Words test suggests that Roger is *Limited* in auditory closure, or the identification of a familiar word from hearing it with sounds omitted. The Incomplete Words test is one of the two tests in the Auditory Processing factor, an indicator of a person's ability to synthesize unrelated sounds into a word, a skill necessary for beginning reading. Roger scored in the *Average* range on the other test in the factor, Sound Blending, requiring the integration of isolated sounds into a word. His strategy, however, was noteworthy. As Roger heard each sound, he repeated it to himself until the next sound was given. He then continued to blend and rehearse larger and larger portions of the word until all parts had been given. Roger's use of this strategy suggests that sound blending is not an automatic process for him.

Roger's limited mastery on tasks that require short-term memory and automatic processing of sounds and symbols are likely to have contributed to his difficulty acquiring basic skills in reading and writing. In contrast, Roger's levels of mastery on tasks requiring oral language and reasoning abilities were *Average* for his age-peers.

Academic Achievement

Reading

Roger's score on the Broad Reading cluster (SS ± 1 SEM: 78–86) was in the *Low Average* range with no difference in performance between the two tests. Instructional materials written at the sixth-grade reading level would be easy for Roger and materials at the tenth-grade level would be difficult. His instructional reading level is approximately late seventh grade. When asked if he was able to read his college textbooks, he answered that he could read the books, but that he never had enough time to get through all the material.

Roger's difficulties on tasks involving visual memory and auditory processing were apparent on both the Letter-Word Identification test and the Word Attack test. He had difficulty pronouncing vowel sounds in real words and phonically regular nonsense words (e.g., "bonties"/*bounties*, "zop"/*zoop*, "lost"/*loast*) and missequenced sounds in multisyllabic words. His RMI of 37/90 on the WJ-R Basic Skills cluster suggests that Roger is *Very Limited* in his sight vocabulary and ability to sound out unfamiliar words.

Roger's weakness in basic reading skills clearly interfered with his comprehension of short passages on the Passage Comprehension test. Twice, he asked for the pronunciation of a word but, after the first time, reminded himself, "Right, you can't tell me." His score on the Listening Comprehension test, a similar task except for its oral, rather than written, presentation, was in the middle of the *Average* range, with an RMI of 90/90.

Written Language

Roger's lowest area of achievement was in written language. His score on the Broad Written Language cluster (SS ± 1 SEM: 72–80) was in the *Low* range. Significant discrepancies existed between his *Low* performance in writing mechanics (Basic Writing Skills, SS ± 1 SEM: 70–78) and his *Low Average/Average* performance in written expression (Writing Samples, SS ± 1 SEM: 85–93).

Basic Skills. In all writing tasks, he made numerous errors in spelling (RMI: 11/90), punctuation and capitalization (RMI: 12/90), and usage (RMI: 13/90). Again weaknesses in visual memory and auditory processing were evident. Roger transposed letters when spelling common words (e.g., *gril/girl*, *childern/children*) and misspelled words that he could have copied from the test response sheet (e.g., *dispit/despite*). On several of the items, Roger omitted critical words, making it difficult to interpret his responses; he also omitted verb endings. Roger wrote all letter *b*s as capitals. When asked why he only wrote capital *b*s, he commented that it was a strategy he had developed in elementary school to help him discriminate between the letters *b* and *d*.

Written Expression. Roger's Writing Samples RMI of 76/90 suggests that his ability to articulate specific ideas in written sentences is *Average* for his age-peers, although at the lower limits of this range. Roger's responses were somewhat lacking in detail and he had difficulty writing a sentence that would integrate two given ideas.

According to the results of the WJ-R, Roger appears to be achieving significantly below his aptitude in written language. Based on his performance on the cognitive tests that best predict achievement in Broad Written Language, only 5 out of 100 26-year-olds (PR: 5%) with the same predicted standard score as Roger's would obtain an actual score as low as or lower than his.

Mathematics

Roger's score on the Broad Mathematics cluster was in the *Average* range (SS ± 1 SEM: 94–100). His RMIs on the tests of Calculation and Applied Problems were 82/90 and 87/90, respectively. Instructional materials at the eleventh-grade level would be appropriate for Roger except for his recall of math facts. Before he began the Calculation tests, Roger mentioned that although math was one of his better subjects, he had difficulty with basic facts. This was evident in his performance of the four basic operations. Although he understood the operations, he used touchpoints for computation, tapping out a number with his pencil as he added or subtracted. He was able to solve problems using rational numbers and basic algebraic equations. He had no difficulty with word problems as long as they did not surpass his knowledge of the computation involved.

Knowledge

Although Roger's scores on the Knowledge cluster fell in the *Low Average* range (SS ± 1 SEM: 81–97), his scores on the Science (SS ± 1 SEM: 83–95) and Social Studies tests (SS ± 1 SEM: 87–97) were relatively higher than his score on the Humanities test (SS ± 1 SEM: 72–82). Roger expressed a concern that he could not answer more questions on the Humanities test. Most of his errors were in the areas of art and music.

Summary

Although standard score comparisons would not support a finding of a learning disability as defined by a significant intracognitive discrepancy, Roger does demonstrate a significant aptitude–achievement discrepancy in the area of written language. Moreover, consideration of the Relative Mastery Indexes suggests that Roger lacks mastery in some of the lower cognitive processing skills thought to underlie learning of basic skills in reading, writing, and math. Roger appears to have developed compensations and strategies that allow him to perform at least within the *Low Average* range. Clinically, however, it is apparent that as a child Roger had deficits in short-term memory for information that is not inherently meaningful, as well as in visual memory and in processing of symbols and sounds, and that these problems persist. Despite his tutoring and years of community college and university study, Roger still makes errors indicative of these processing problems. Roger's deficits in reading decoding, writing mechanics, and math facts appear to be interfering with his ability to benefit from his courses and learn from his texts in an efficient manner. Based on the mastery scores and clinical evidence, Roger appears to have specific learning disabilities in the lower-level cognitive processes and should be eligible for special services for students with learning disabilities at Glen State University.

Recommendations

1. Apply to the REACH program, the college's program for students with learning disabilities. As part of the intake service, REACH personnel will conduct a more extensive evaluation to determine the level of support you require and design appropriate interventions. They will also help you select appropriate courses.

2. Enroll in a course or courses that are designed to teach reading, writing, and study skills. This type of course may be taken for college credit and is offered each semester through the REACH program.

3. Request a tutor from the REACH program to help you learn more effective phonic and structural analysis skills for reading and to provide additional support in learning the skills presented in your skills classes.

4. Once you are certified as eligible for learning disability services, you may order taped books through the Foundation for the Blind. See attached information sheet for sources. Taped versions of many of the required college textbooks are also available at the campus library. Listening to your textbooks will help you complete the required reading more quickly. Reading along with the tape may also help develop your reading speed.

5. In April or May, plan your classes for September. Meet with each teacher to obtain reading lists for your classes so that you may do some advance reading in the summer. If possible, obtain tutoring

from an educational therapist and use these materials to learn reading study strategies, organizational techniques for writing, and math concepts.

6. Before your classes begin, inform your college professors that you work slowly on reading and writing tasks and may require additional time on exams. Request also that you not be penalized for poor spelling on in-class essays and exams.

7. Learn to use a pocket-sized, computerized spelling checker to edit your work or a spelling checker on a word processing program.

8. Learn strategies that will help you improve your proofreading skill. For example, read a paper aloud slowly and carefully to ensure that you have included all of the words that you intended. If necessary, find someone who will help you edit and revise your papers.

9. If you decide not to enroll in the REACH program, you may wish to hire an educational therapist who specializes in higher education. Locate a person who is able to teach you a variety of learning and study strategies and can provide tutorial assistance with the reading and writing requirements of any of your courses. A list of qualified educational therapists is available through the REACH program.

Diagnosis: Deficit in short-term memory, thought disorder

PSYCHOEDUCATIONAL EVALUATION

Name: Ruth Tanner   Evaluator:
Birthdate: 4/21/57   Test Dates: 7/10,
                                        7/15/91

Chronological Age: 33

Reason for Referral

Ruth was referred by a friend, Margaret Kaplan, for a psychoeducational evaluation. Ms. Kaplan had suggested to Ruth that she may have specific learning problems that were affecting her ability to adjust to change and maintain employment. Margaret volunteered to sponsor a private evaluation. Ruth agreed to testing but commented to the examiner that she was unsure of what she could gain from the testing results. She noted that she would like to "get her life going."

Background Information

Ruth is a high school graduate; she stated that her grades had been "kind of average." She is single, lives alone, and was one of eight children. She described her upbringing as abusive, characterized by beatings by her father and an aloof and uncaring mother. She stated that her mother was hospitalized a few times for a nervous condition and that she witnessed several of her mother's suicide attempts. Ruth is currently living independently 2,000 miles away from her family but says that she still feels the emotional scars of her childhood.

Ruth reported that she has been hospitalized several times for anxiety, and was diagnosed 6 years ago as having a thought disorder. Since that time, she had been taking Navane, Prozac, and Artane to control her thoughts and to help her sleep. Recently, Ruth lost her job at a convenience store because of inconsistent performance. As a result of being laid off, Ruth's health insurance expired and she could no longer afford to see her psychiatrist, Dr. Allen Thomas. Two weeks prior to testing, she discontinued the medications.

She stated that she did not like the mental health center she was referred to and had stopped taking her medication because it was too expensive. Ruth commented that since she discontinued the medications, she has been unable to sleep more than a few interrupted hours a night, but that she has not noticed any changes in mood or behavior. Ruth said that in her free time she liked to write poetry and short stories.

Tests Administered

Ruth was administered the Woodcock-Johnson Tests of Cognitive Ability—Revised (Tests 1–14) and the Woodcock-Johnson Tests of Achievement—Revised, Form A, Standard Battery (Tests 22–30). Testing was conducted in three 1½-hour sessions.

Behavioral Observations

Ruth was cooperative throughout the sessions. When she was asked a question that she was unsure of, she would laugh and shrug her shoulders. She responded positively to encouragement and upon prompting would reengage her effort.

Ruth appeared to have a tremor in her right hand. She shook her leg and tapped her foot throughout the sessions. During the last testing session, Ruth confided to the examiner her difficult circumstances growing up. After she began talking about this topic, she had difficulty refocusing her attention; but after a short break, she was able to do so.

Assessment Results

The tests of the WJ-R were scored according to age norms. When no difference was found between the two component tests of a factor or cluster, only the factor or cluster score is discussed. Percentile ranks are expressed as the 68% confidence band around the obtained score. A 68% confidence band is written as Percentile Rank ± 1 Standard Error of Measurement (PR ± 1 SEM). A complete set of test scores is appended to this report.

Ruth's performance on the Woodcock-Johnson Psycho-Educational Battery—Revised must be interpreted with caution and with consideration of her present condition. She has recently discontinued psychoactive medication without the advice of a physician and, as a result, has not been sleeping normally. Her low performance on tasks requiring short-term and associational memory and sustained attention may be affected by her psychological condition, her use or discontinuance of psychoactive medication, and/or her lack of sleep.

Cognitive Abilities

Ruth's overall cognitive performance fell in the *Low* range (PR ± 1 SEM: 4–7). Her score on the Short-Term Memory factor, a measure of immediate auditory recall, was in the *Very Low* range (PR ± 1 SEM: 0.1–2) and her score on the Long-Term Retrieval factor, a measure of the ability to form and retrieve associations between visual and auditory information, was in the *Low* range (PR ± 1 SEM: 2–5). In contrast, Ruth's score on the Comprehension-Knowledge factor, a measure of vocabulary and background knowledge, fell in the *Average* range (PR ± 1 SEM: 35–49). This type of discrepancy between performance on tasks that require formerly assimilated data and tasks that are dependent on recent memory may be attributed to the effects of psychoactive medication. Such findings have been noted in testing chronically mentally ill individuals with the Wechsler Adult Intelligence Scale - Revised and the Wechsler Memory Scales (Everett, Laplante, & Thomas 1989; Nelson et al., 1990; Piedmont, Sokolove, & Fleming, 1989). These authors note a decrease in short-term memory and retrieval as a result of daily use of major tranquilizers for 5 years or longer.

Ruth scored in the *Low* range in the Fluid Reasoning factor (PR ± 1 SEM: 4–8), indicating that she is having difficulty with abstract, logical thinking in novel situations. All of Ruth's other cognitive factor scores were in the *Low Average* range.

Academic Achievement

Ruth scored in the *Low Average* range on the Broad Reading, Broad Mathematics, and Broad Written Language clusters. Her performance on the Broad Knowledge cluster (PR ± 1 SEM: 38–45) was in the *Average* range.

Reading

On the reading tests, a significant difference existed between Ruth's *Low Average/Average* performance on Letter-Word Identification (PR ± 1 SEM: 21–39) and her *Very Low/Low* performance on Passage Comprehension (PR ± 1 SEM: 1–5). An unusual response pattern was noted on Passage Comprehension. Despite the difficulty level of the question, Ruth made errors on every third or fourth item until they became consistently too difficult. Her ability to sustain concentration seemed to fluctuate.

Written Language

Similarly, on the writing tests, a significant difference existed between her *Low Average/Average* score on Dictation (PR ± 1 SEM: 19–30), a measure of writing mechanics tested out of context, and her *Very Low* score on Writing Samples (PR ± 1 SEM: 1–3), a measure of the ability to write individual sentences according to specific task demands. In general, Ruth's sentences on Writing Samples were concrete and unembellished. These results were surprising, given her statement that she loved to write. On occasion, she failed to respond to the requirements of the task. For example, when asked to write a sentence describing what a snake looks like, she wrote: *A snake moves back and forth.* When asked to write her name, she asked whether it would be acceptable to write someone else's name.

Mathematics

No difference existed between performance on the Calculation and Applied Problems tests. Ruth demonstrated skill in the basic operations using whole numbers, but had difficulty with problems involving fractions and decimals. She commented that she really liked working with numbers, as long as she could remember what to do. Again, a sporadic error pattern was noted. On the Applied Problems test, she missed easier questions and then answered more difficult questions correctly.

Knowledge

Ruth's highest scores were on the Knowledge tests. Her *Average* score on the Humanities test (PR ± 1 SEM: 32–50) was significantly higher than her *Low* score on the Science test (PR ± 1 SEM: 2–12). She scored in the *Low Average* range on the Social Studies test.

Summary

Although Ruth's overall cognitive abilities fell in the *Low* range on this administration of the WJ-R, her current psychological condition, residual effects of her medications, the effect of discontinuing medications, her lack of sleep, or any combination of these factors may have affected her performance on these tests. Consequently, it is difficult to judge the validity of these results for the purpose of generalizing them into her daily functioning. Nevertheless, the factors that may have interfered with her test performance in the areas of short-term and associational memory and logical reasoning may also affect her ability to remember what she hears, learn new information in her job, and solve unexpected problems. The fluctuation of attention noted on the achievement tests would also interfere with her job performance, intermittently and unpredictably, causing her to make mistakes or forget to take care of responsibilities. Due to the lack of stability of Ruth's condition, it is impossible to discern how longstanding her present cognitive deficits are or whether they will continue to affect her job performance in the future. Ruth's other cognitive factor and achievement cluster scores in the *Low Average* and *Average* ranges suggest the potential for higher cognitive functioning than she is currently demonstrating.

Recommendations

To profit from any interventions, Ruth must first address her present psychological condition.

1. Ruth should contact Dr. Thomas and resume appropriate psychiatric treatment. If the cost of returning to therapy with Dr. Thomas is prohibitive, Ruth should ask him to recommend a specific psychiatrist at the mental health center. Dr. Thomas should review Ruth's case with the new psychiatrist prior to treatment so that the transition is successful.

2. At least 6 months after treatment has been resumed, Ruth may wish to be reevaluated. Results may demonstrate improved cognitive functioning and help in further delineating the presence of specific learning impairments that may affect job performance.

3. Once stabilized in treatment, Ruth may be eligible for Department of Vocational Rehabilitation services. Through these services, Ruth will obtain assistance in developing skills and pursuing appropriate schooling or employment.

4. Ruth expressed interest in basic math and in writing. Conceivably, these skills may be used in a vocational setting. For example, Ruth may be interested in pursuing bookkeeping or basic accounting or being trained in word processing for a secretarial position.

5. To improve self-esteem and help her develop confidence, Ruth should join a support group with others in similar situations. Information regarding appropriate counseling groups can be obtained from HOPE, a local organization designed to help adults come to terms with traumatic childhoods and become successful in independent living.

References

Everett, J., LaPlante, L., & Thomas, J. (1989). The selective attention deficit in schizophrenia. *Journal of Nervous and Mental Disorders, 177*, 735-738.

Nelson, H. E., Pantelis, C., Carruthers, K., Speller, J., Baxendale, S., & Barnes, T. R. (1990). Cognitive functioning and symptomatology in chronic schizophrenia. *Psychological Medicine, 20*, 357-365.

Piedmont, R. L., Sokolove, R. L., & Fleming, M. Z. (1989). Discriminating psychotic and affective disorders using the WAIS-R. *Journal of Personality Assessment, 53*, 739-748.

Diagnosis: Deficits in attention, rapid processing of visual symbols, short-term memory, and word retrieval

PSYCHOEDUCATIONAL EVALUATION

Client: William Gillette   Evaluator:
Birthdate: 5/7/35   Chronological Age:
             56
Admission Date:
11/27/90   Test Dates: 9/15/91

Reason for Referral

Approximately 10 months after a left thrombotic stroke, Mr. Gillette was referred by his neurologist, Dr. Lydia Montego, for evaluation of general cognitive abilities with particular questions concerning concentration and short-term memory. Results of this assessment have been requested by the company that insures Mr. Gillette for disability benefits.

Background Information

During the night of November 27, 1990, Mr. Gillette, a 56-year-old man, was admitted to Massachusetts General Hospital with paralysis of the right side. A computerized axial tomography scan indicated a left pontine level cerebral vascular infarc. Paralysis of the right upper and lower extremities was total, with lesser paralysis of the larynx and posterior portion of the tongue. Subsequent to his stroke, Mr. Gillette has experienced lower-extremity muscle spasms during sleep and a chronic sleep disorder that allows him approximately 3 hours per night of interrupted sleep. Mr. Gillette currently is taking 30 mg. of benzodiazepine to induce sleep and one tablet daily of Sinemet to reduce muscle spasms.

Subsequent to his stroke, Mr. Gillette had 6 weeks of speech therapy, physical therapy, and cognitive therapy for attentional and memory problems. Currently, he reports relatively minor physical residuals. He has minor paralysis of the posterior portion of the tongue, but with effort, he can speak clearly. He experiences a weakness in the right extremities, causing him to limp and to write with some impairment of control and speed. He reports reduced right-hand accuracy in typing on the computer.

Mr. Gillette has been employed by a large metropolitan newspaper with responsibility for writing daily editorials and reporting on foreign political affairs. Mr. Gillette has master's degrees in Journalism and Political Affairs. He has won several writing awards and is a respected member of the journalism community. Since his stroke, he reports that concentration and memory problems have interfered with his ability to analyze and organize information, and to write his editorials and stories in a sufficiently coherent manner. Currently, Mr. Gillette is on disability leave.

Mr. Gillette reported that as a child, until the third grade, he had difficulty learning to read and required tutoring. Since then, he has been a slow reader and, although he reads voluminous material on foreign political affairs, he does not read for pleasure. He recalls that as a child he had some initial difficulty with penmanship, but that expressing his thoughts in writing has always come easily. The use of a typewriter and, subsequently, a word processor for writing increased his writing efficiency substantially.

Behavioral Observations

Mr. Gillette was tested in one 3-hour session. During testing, he joked about the specific tasks and about his difficulty in responding. Testing was slow because Mr. Gillette often began conversations between tests. Frequently, he began commenting on the type of difficulty he had with the task and then began discussing related topics until the evaluator brought him back to the test. Mr. Gillette's expression of his thoughts was always coherent and highly articulate, but his tendency to move from topic to topic suggested some tangential thinking. On some tests, he appeared to grasp the task only after a few initial items had been presented. To accommodate Mr. Gillette's weakness in his right hand, at his request he was permitted to line out, rather than circle, his responses on the Processing Speed tests.

Tests Administered

Woodcock-Johnson Psycho-Educational Battery—
    Revised (WJ-R):
        Cognitive Battery: Tests 1–14, 20–21

The tests of the WJ-R were scored according to age norms. When no difference was found between the two component tests of a factor or cluster, only the factor or cluster score is discussed. Verbal labels (e.g., *Average, Superior*) are used to express 68% confidence bands around the obtained score. A complete set of test scores is appended to this report.

Test Results

Mr. Gillette demonstrated strengths in the cognitive areas of visual-auditory association and retrieval, listening comprehension for short passages, and verbal reasoning, with scores in the *Superior* to *Very Superior* ranges. The visual-auditory association tasks required association of verbal with visual information and recall of the associations over a period of approximately 10 minutes. Mr. Gillette appeared to be significantly aided by the language context of one of the tests in which the client "reads" a story composed of rebus-like symbols. Mr. Gillette's score was significantly lower when he was required to memorize names for drawings of "space creatures." Based on these tests, Mr. Gillette appears to have strengths in processing contextual language and learning new information within contextual language.

In the vocabulary tasks, Mr. Gillette was asked to supply words in response to visual and auditory stimuli. He scored in the *Average* range on recalling labels for pictures, frequently describing the function of an item or giving a number of synonyms for a less specific term (e.g., "engraving, carving, etching" for *epitaph*). He scored in the *High Average* range, indicating significantly less difficulty, when asked to give synonyms and antonyms for orally presented words.

Mr. Gillette scored significantly lower, in the middle of the *Low Average* range, in the more automatic cognitive skills of rapid processing of visual symbols and auditory short-term memory. In the processing speed tests, observation indicated that Mr. Gillette's slow responses were due to inefficient visual scanning rather than slow motor response. When asked to recall sentences verbatim, Mr. Gillette spoke quickly and in a monotone. On the more advanced items, he evidenced frustration that he was not able to recall more than the first clause and a few subsequent details of the target sentences.

Mr. Gillette scored in the *High Average* range in visual processing of nonsymbolic visual information, such as pictures, and in synthesizing discrete

sounds of a word to come up with the whole word. In the Visual Closure test, however, when asked to identify distorted or partially obscured pictures of objects, Mr. Gillette occasionally described the function of the object correctly, but could not recall the correct word (e.g., "A toy - a clown pops out of a box," "You stand on it to reach something. I have one in the garage").

Mr. Gillette also scored in the *High Average* range on the Fluid Reasoning factor, but evidenced some problems in sustaining focused attention. The component tests require the use of verbal instructions as well as ongoing corrective feedback to solve visually presented problems. These types of problems require the ability to see patterns, to think logically, and to generate, prove, and disprove alternative hypotheses. On both tests, Mr. Gillette thought aloud, thus facilitating error analysis. On one test, Analysis-Synthesis, when the task became more complex, Mr. Gillette asked for the entire set of instructions to be repeated. When his initial strategy did not work, he appeared to try again, but in approximately 70% of these situations, gave up part of the way through the solution. On the Concept Formation test, he was unable to remain focused on the difference between two sets of figures and intermittently described the wrong set. At one point, he shook his head with a smile and said, "I have a tendency to answer why these are *out* of the box."

Conclusions

Based on the current testing, Mr. Gillette appears to have significant strengths in processing language in context and retrieving information learned within a language context. *High Average* scores on the cognitive factors of Auditory Processing (blending sounds), Visual Processing (pictorial stimuli), Comprehension-Knowledge (vocabulary), and Fluid Reasoning (abstract, logical reasoning) also indicate strengths in these areas. Nevertheless, individual test scores and patterns of behaviors indicate specific weaknesses. Mr. Gillette demonstrates a mild to moderate deficit in word retrieval when asked to recall verbal labels for pictures, a problem that is not obvious in the flow of casual conversation. Additionally, Mr. Gillette's frequent conversational departure from the test process and obvious difficulty sustaining focus during the Fluid Reasoning tests reinforce his complaint of inadequate concentration.

The significant discrepancy between Mr. Gillette's performance on language tasks and his performance on tasks requiring auditory short-term memory and processing speed indicates deficits in both of the latter areas. Intracognitive discrepancies indicate that in the cognitive factors of Processing Speed and Short-Term Memory, age-peers with the same predicted scores would obtain standard scores as low as or lower than Mr. Gillette's only 1% and 3% of the time, respectively.

Thus, it appears that Mr. Gillette is currently experiencing deficits in attentional abilities, auditory short-term memory, word retrieval, and rapid processing of visual symbols. Given his profession for the past 30 years as a political analyst and writer, Mr. Gillette's deficits in attention, short-term memory, and word retrieval appear to be directly related to his recent stroke.

Diagnosis: Receptive and expressive aphasia

PSYCHOEDUCATIONAL EVALUATION

Name: Robert E. Steiger,   Evaluator:
    Ph.D.
Date of Admission: Birthdate: 10/01/04
    8/7/91
Test Dates: 8/13, 8/14,   Chronological Age:
    8/15/91   86
Referring Physician:
    Dr. Katrina Foster

Reason for Referral

Dr. Robert E. Steiger was referred for a psycho-educational evaluation by Dr. Katrina Foster, his neurologist at William Roth Hospital. The purposes of this evaluation were to identify present cognitive and linguistic strengths and limitations and to make general recommendations for further evaluations and treatment.

Background Information

Dr. Steiger was a philosophy professor for 45 years at several major universities. During these years, he was a prolific writer and speaker who was highly respected in his field. He published over 200 articles and monographs, wrote seven books, and was a keynote speaker at both national and international conferences. He received many awards for outstanding contributions to his field. In 1980, Dr. Steiger retired from his university position and became a Professor Emeritus. During this 11-year period, he continued to publish, speak, and teach university courses.

On the evening of August 7, 1991, at the age of 86, Dr. Steiger had a massive coronary stroke affecting both receptive and expressive language, indicating involvement in both Broca's and Wernicke's areas. Additionally, the stroke affected kinesthetic and tactual reception on the right side of the body, resulting in right facial droop and poor control and use of the right hand, arm, and leg. Further evaluation indicated paralysis of his right upper extremity, as well as marked weakness of the lower extremity. A computerized axial tomography (CT) scan ruled out the possibility of intercranial bleeding. Pertinent medical history indicated a history of hypertension which has been treated and no prior history of cerebrovascular dysfunction.

Tests Administered

Woodcock-Johnson Psycho-Educational Battery—
    Revised:
        Tests of Cognitive Ability: 1-14, 19
        Tests of Achievement (Form A): 22-30, 31, 33

Behavioral Observations

Testing was conducted in 1-hour sessions on three consecutive days. Dr. Steiger was cooperative and alert throughout the evaluations. At times, however, he became extremely frustrated with his inability to respond to questions. On occasion, when he could not understand test instructions or a specific question after several repetitions, he would rub the left side of his head and say, "Bad for me. Nothing comes for me." Although the patient has marked receptive and expressive aphasia, he was able to express anger and swear articulately. He wrote with his left hand.

Test Results

The tests of the WJ-R were scored according to age norms. When no difference was found between the two component tests of a factor or cluster, only the factor or cluster score is discussed. Standard scores (SS) and percentile ranks (PR) are reported as obtained scores or as 68% confidence bands. A 68% confidence band is expressed as ± 1 standard error of measurement (SEM). A complete set of test scores is appended to this report.

Cognitive Abilities

In general Dr. Steiger's performances on all of the cognitive tests were affected by difficulty with both receptive and expressive language. His lowest scores were on tasks involving memory (Short-Term Memory and Long-Term Retrieval, PR: 2) and vocabulary and acquired knowledge (Comprehension Knowledge, PR: 2).

Dr. Steiger's highest performances were on tests with visual stimuli and minimal language requirements (Fluid Reasoning, PR: 47; Processing Speed, PR: 23). When his performance on the Fluid Reasoning factor (Actual SS: 99) is compared to his average performance on the other six cognitive factors, only 2 out of 1,000 individuals of his age would obtain a score as high or higher (Discrepancy PR: 99.8). He also obtained a relatively high score on the Spatial Relations test, which requires the subject to match shapes visually (PR: 34). This test is a measure of both reasoning and visual processing.

Dr. Steiger's performance on several tests with visual stimuli was affected by his difficulties in receptive and expressive language. The Picture Recognition test requires identification of a set of previously seen pictures. When asked to identify either one, two, three, or four pictures, Dr. Steiger would point to an incorrect number of pictures. On the Memory for Names test, which requires the pairing of auditory and visual information, Dr. Steiger was unable to form the associations. He did, however, demonstrate visual retention of the "space creatures" who had been introduced. Although he did not identify the space creatures correctly by name, as additional space creatures were introduced he was able to point to all of those he had seen previously.

On several test questions requiring verbal responses, Dr. Steiger would make gestures that demonstrated he knew the meaning of a word or the function of the word, but could not produce a verbal label. On several items of the Visual Closure test, he appeared to recognize an object but was unable to retrieve the label. When asked to identify a stethoscope on the Picture Vocabulary test, he pantomimed using this instrument to listen to a heart. On other occasions, after he had identified an object, he would perseverate with the same response on a later question. As examples, on the Visual Closure test, he identified the picture of a cat as "scissors" and then the picture of a duck as "scissors." On the Humanities test, he correctly pointed to the picture of a newspaper and then, several items later, identified the paint brushes as "newspaper."

To accommodate difficulties with word retrieval and attention, certain test modifications were made. On the Analysis-Synthesis test, which requires color naming, Dr. Steiger was unable to identify correctly and consistently the color names of the squares. For example, he pointed to the red square and said "blue." To eliminate this language requirement, four colored squares were placed on cards and Dr. Steiger was asked to respond by pointing to the color needed to solve the problem. On both the Picture Recognition and Spatial Relations tests, Dr. Steiger pointed to the pictures or shapes needed to answer the problem, rather than identifying them by the associated letter. On tests where several items were present on a page, Dr. Steiger would look at one problem and then another as he was listening to the accompanying instructions. To enhance attention to the problem being presented, a card was used to block out the other items on the page.

Academic Achievement

Similar to his performance on the cognitive tests, Dr. Steiger's performance was higher on achievement tests containing visual stimuli and lower on tests requiring receptive and expressive language skills.

Reading

Scores on all reading tests fell between the 3rd and 5th percentile. On the Letter-Word Identification test, Dr. Steiger identified the letter S as a "c" and the letter z as a "j." The words identified correctly seemed to be known by sight. He pronounced "knew," "because," and "whole" correctly, but pronounced "as" as "has" and "about" as "a boy." He did not appear to use phonics to aid in word identification. On the Word Attack test, he tried to find meaning or make the nonsense words into real words. He pronounced the nonsense word *nat* as "ton," and then running his finger over the word from left to right said, "not." Recognizing the visual configuration, he pronounced the nonsense word *dright* as "right." On the Passage Comprehension test, he was able to match short phrases to pictures, but was unable to identify the missing word in sentences.

Written Language

On the Dictation test (PR: 1), Dr. Steiger was able to imitate motor patterns, trace and copy a letter, and form the letter *o*. Although he wrote several letters and words, they were not the correct ones. When asked to spell the word "six," he wrote the word *dog*. Performance was slightly higher on the Writing Samples test (PR: 6), where visual prompts are provided for each item. He was able to write his name and the words *kitten*, *apple*, *dog*, *old hat*, and *cow* successfully.

Mathematics

Presently, mathematics is a strength for Dr. Steiger. When his actual Broad Mathematics standard score (SS: 83) is compared to his average standard score in the other three achievement areas, only 4 out of 1,000 individuals of his age with the same predicted score would obtain a score as high or higher (Discrepancy PR: 99.6). Although his highest score was on the Calculation test (PR: 24), Dr. Steiger was unable to complete the Sample items. When asked to make the numeral 1, he made a zero; when asked to make the numeral 3, he wrote a backwards letter *c*. He proceeded to solve the next ten simple addition and subtraction problems correctly, which included making the numerals 1 and 3. He also successfully added fractions. He performed all of the multiplication problems as addition problems.

Knowledge

Dr. Steiger's performance on the Humanities test (PR: 11) was significantly higher than his performances on the Science (PR: 0.1) and Social Studies tests (PR: 1). On the Humanities test, he successfully completed all of the nursery rhymes. After listening to a rhyme, he produced the answers immediately. Identification of the missing word appeared to be at the automatic level of processing, rather than at a level requiring language comprehension. Dr. Steiger's responses indicated general dysfluency with an occasional automatic fluent phrase.

Recommendations

1. Based upon prior history, Dr. Steiger is an excellent candidate for a comprehensive rehabilitation effort. When the patient is medically stable, he should be transferred to the Rehabilitation Unit. The goal will be to help Dr. Steiger attain the level of self care and independence consistent with home discharge.

2. Refer Dr. Steiger to the speech/language pathologist for a more comprehensive assessment and development of a treatment plan.

3. Refer Dr. Steiger to the physical/occupational therapist for assessment in activities of daily living and for development of treatment, as indicated.

4. Incorporate the visual modality whenever possible in instructional and social situations.

5. To enhance language comprehension, keep supportive visual information simple and clear. For example, when discussing a person with Dr. Steiger, write the person's name in bold letters on a slip of paper for him to see.

6. Be sure to secure Dr. Steiger's attention before providing directions, asking questions, or shifting topics. When needed, prior to speaking, cue Dr. Steiger by placing a hand on his shoulder, calling his name, or establishing eye contact.

7. To enhance language comprehension, speak slowly and clearly to Dr. Steiger. Present only one concept or topic at a time. Paraphrase any information you are presenting when it is unclear.

8. To bypass difficulty with visual-verbal associations, use a multisensory technique, such as the Fernald method for teaching reading and writing skills.

9. Select appropriate computer software for reinforcement of words and word families taught. Use programs that provide graphics to reinforce vocabulary.

10. Provide opportunities for leisure activities that Dr. Steiger is able to participate in and enjoys, such as backgammon, poker, and bridge.

11. After his discharge from the Rehabilitation Unit, continue to follow Dr. Steiger's progress from the rehabilitation perspective.

Test References

Beery, K. E. (1989). *Administration, scoring, and teaching manual for the Developmental Test of Visual-Motor Integration* (3rd rev. ed.). Cleveland: Modern Curriculum Press.

Bender, L. (1938). A Visual Motor Gestalt Test and its clinical use. *American Orthopsychiatric Association Research Monograph, 3.*

Brigance, A. H. (1983). *Brigance Diagnostic Comprehensive Inventory of Basic Skills.* N. Billerica, MA: Curriculum Associates.

Bruininks, R. H., Woodcock, R. W., Weatherman, R. F., & Hill, B. K. (1984). *Scales of Independent Behavior.* Allen, TX: DLM.

Burns, P. C., & Roe, B. D. (1989). *Burns/Roe Informal Reading Inventory* (3rd ed.). Boston: Houghton Mifflin.

Connolly, A. J. (1988). *KeyMath—Revised: A Diagnostic Inventory of Essential Mathematics.* Circle Pines, MN: American Guidance Service.

Dunn, L. M., & Dunn, L. M. (1981). *Peabody Picture Vocabulary Test—Revised.* Circle Pines, MN: American Guidance Service.

Koppitz, E. M. (1964). *The Bender-Gestalt Test for young children* (Vol. 1). New York: Grune & Stratton.

Koppitz, E. M. (1975). *The Bender-Gestalt Test for young children* (Vol. 2). New York: Grune & Stratton.

Levine, M. D. (1985). *The ANSER System: School Questionnaire for Developmental, Behavioral, and Health Assessment of the Elementary School Student.* Cambridge: Educators Publishing Service.

Levine, M. D. (1988). *The ANSER System: School Questionnaire for Developmental, Behavioral, and Health Assessment of the Secondary School Student.* Cambridge: Educators Publishing Service.

Semel, E., Wiig, E., & Secord, W. (1987). *Clinical Evaluation of Language Fundamentals—Revised.* San Antonio: The Psychological Corporation.

Slingerland, B. H. (1970). *Slingerland Screening Tests for Identifying Children with Specific Language Disability* (rev. ed.). Cambridge, MA: Educators Publishing Service.

Watson, G., & Glaser, E. (1980). *Watson-Glaser Critical Thinking Appraisal: 1980 Edition.* San Antonio: The Psychological Corporation.

Wechsler, D. (1974). *Wechsler Intelligence Scale for Children—Revised.* San Antonio: The Psychological Corporation.

Wechsler, D. (1981). *Wechsler Adult Intelligence Scale—Revised.* San Antonio: The Psychological Corporation.

Wechsler, D. (1987). *Wechsler Memory Scale—Revised.* San Antonio: The Psychological Corporation.

Wiig, E., & Secord, W. (1989). *Test of Language Competence: Expanded Edition.* San Antonio: The Psychological Corporation.

Woods, M. L., & Moe, A. J. (1989). *Analytical Reading Inventory* (4th ed.). Columbus, OH: Merrill.

PART IV

APPENDIX:
TECHNIQUES AND INTERVENTIONS

APPENDIX

Introduction

Diagnostic reports usually include recommendations that address the educational and behavioral concerns observed in the evaluation. Individuals implementing the recommendations may not, however, be familiar with the suggested methods or techniques. Since writing descriptions of methodology is time-consuming, the authors have attempted to provide supplemental information for evaluators such as might be attached to reports.

The Appendix includes summaries of some of the techniques and interventions referred to in the Recommendations section. Several forms, such as charts, graphs, and contracts, are provided to facilitate use of these methods. The Appendix also includes a variety of supplemental information, ranging from types of context clues, to where to obtain taped books, to how to select a teacher for a student with attentional difficulties. As with other sections of this book, the purpose of this section is to expedite the writing of comprehensive, practical reports.

Alternate Pronunciation for Spelling

Purpose

The purpose of this spelling strategy is to enable phonetic spellers, weak in visual memory, to recall the correct spelling of a word although the letters may not carry their most common sounds or may be silent.

Introduction

The student using Alternate Pronunciation learns two pronunciations of words that s/he is having difficulty recalling visually. One pronunciation is how the word is spoken. The other—invented— pronunciation is how the word is written. The second pronunciation is memorized solely for the purpose of spelling. Each student may devise a different pronunciation for the same word, depending on the pronunciation s/he thinks will give the best clue to the actual spelling.

Steps

1. Break the word up into parts in such a way that any letters that may be difficult to visualize will be pronounced.

Examples	Actual Spelling	Spoken Pronunciation	Alternate Pronunciation
	laboratory	lab ru to ry	lab o rat ory
	fluorescent	flor es int	flu or es cent
	ache	ake	a chee
	probably	prob lee	pro bab lee
		(for some students)	

2. Memorize the alternate pronunciation.

3. Write the word according to the alternate pronunciation without looking at the model. Check the spelling.

4. If correct, repeat Step 3 two to four times more, depending on the severity of the student's revisualization deficit.

5. If incorrect, devise a new pronunciation that will help the student correct the error.

Adapted from:

Ormrod, J. E. (1986). A learning strategy for phonetic spellers. *Academic Therapy*, *22*, 195-198.

Attention Deficit Disorder: Classroom Suggestions

Many children with Attention Deficit Disorder (ADD) require some special compensations and interventions to function optimally in a regular classroom. Often it is helpful for the parent to have a conference at the end of the school year with the principal and the child's current teacher in order to select a teacher for the next year. The following suggestions may be used as guidelines in choosing a classroom environment or teacher for the child with ADD. Remember, no guidelines are appropriate for every child. Tailor the following for the needs of individual children.

Organization

A student with ADD is typically disorganized. Without specific training, s/he does not have the ability to look ahead, plan for contingencies, gather appropriate materials, prioritize and sequence the steps to a task, keep track of work, etc. All parts of the student's day, tasks, and events might seem equally important. Therefore, success depends on organization from an external source.

The teacher for this type of student must be well organized. Examples include having a well-planned day; providing clear, sequenced instructions; creating a classroom management system (rules, reinforcement, consequences) that is easy for the student to understand; establishing efficient methods of handing out and collecting assignments and materials; and teaching the student organizational skills, directly and by modeling (e.g., having appropriate materials, getting homework home and back, analyzing and prioritizing the steps in a task, time management).

Structure and Consistency

Because of difficulty with organization, the student with ADD typically has difficulty structuring the day. Often, s/he does not adapt well to change (teacher, schedule, rules) and his/her security and ability to operate successfully within a system depend on a thorough familiarity with it. Consequently, the student requires consistency and structure for optimal performance.

The student will benefit from having the same type of activities at the same time every day, although this does not mean a structure so rigid as to be boring. For example, homework/assignments may be given at the same time and in the same way each day, and the order and approximate amount of time spent on subjects may be consistent. Within a consistent structure, however, the teacher may vary teaching approaches.

Participatory Learning

The student with ADD has difficulty maintaining sufficient focus of attention for the necessary length of time to any one task unless it is highly stimulating and engaging. The types of tasks meeting these criteria are unique to the individual. Attention is easily drawn to a different, perhaps less important, stimulus. Accordingly, the student is likely to stay with tasks that require active participation, such as cooperative small group work in which the student has an active role, or a reading activity in which the students read small portions of text and make predictions rather than reading the whole story with discussion following.

Attention Span

The most debilitating impediment to learning for the child with ADD is an inability to sustain focused attention to a task that is not intrinsically engaging. Consequently, this child may find it easier to remain involved in tasks if the type of activity changes throughout the day and seating arrangements vary.

Flexibility

As the success of a child with ADD may depend on compensations for difficulties as well as interventions to train more effective learning and behavioral patterns, the teacher needs to be somewhat flexible in expectations of amount and quality of work and level of individual responsibility. The student may need a reduced amount of work in certain subjects, positive reinforcement for quality of work that is less than expected of other students, and frequent reminders for tasks that others handle independently.

Positive Reinforcement

The student with ADD typically does not learn from negative consequences because often the error or misbehavior was not deliberate. Between the impulse to act and the action itself, the child does not have that moment, available to others, in which to consider the correction or punishment experienced the last time. Although the child with ADD experiences criticism and negative consequences far in excess of that which other children receive, the effects are short-term in changing behavior. The effects in reinforcing low self-esteem, however, are long-term. Concomitantly, the child with ADD receives far less praise and encouragement than other children because the comparable successes are few. Frequent and specific positive reinforcement (e.g., praise for a specific behavior, stickers, points, notes home) is far more likely to encourage long-term behavioral changes as well as to heal seriously damaged self-esteem.

Behavioral Interventions

Many of the unacceptable and inefficient social and learning behaviors demonstrated by the child with ADD are not primary characteristics of the Attention Deficit Disorder. They are often secondary to inattention to social cues, lack of appropriate social habits, or inability to control impulsive behavior. Consequently, medication will not completely alleviate the individual's social and learning problems. Medication may, however, make it possible for the individual to benefit from positive behavioral interventions aimed at changing specific behaviors. The teacher may help by targeting and prioritizing specific behaviors that the person needs to develop and implementing a positive, structured intervention. Interventions may need to last throughout the year as some behaviors are developed and new ones are targeted for change.

Working with an Outside Consultant

Sometimes an educational consultant or physician will need to be in contact with the teacher to follow the child's progress in school, to evaluate the adequacy of the dosage of medication, to determine the need for outside tutoring, to offer help in designing behavioral interventions, and to offer suggestions for relatively simple compensations, such as preferential seating. The student with ADD may fare best with a teacher who is open to this type of support.

Attention Deficit Disorder: Informational Resources

Books and Publications

For Professionals

Barkley, R. A. (1990). *Attention deficit hyperactivity disorder: A handbook for diagnosis and treatment.* New York: Guilford Press.

Copeland, E. D., & Love, V. L. (1990). *Attention without tension: A teacher's handbook on attention disorders (ADHD and ADD).* Atlanta: 3 C's of Childhood.

Goldstein, S., & Goldstein, M. (1990). *Managing attention disorders in children.* New York: John Wiley & Sons.

Jones, C. B. (1991). *A sourcebook for managing attention disorders: For early childhood professionals.* Tucson, AZ: Communication Skill Builders.

For Parents and Professionals

Challenge, Newsletter of the Attention Deficit Disorder Association, 2620 Ivy Place, Toledo, OH 43613

Copeland, E. D. (1991). *Medications for attention disorders (ADHD/ADD) and related medical problems (Tourette's syndrome, sleep apnea, seizure disorders): A comprehensive handbook.* Atlanta: SPI Press.

Copeland, E. D., & Love, V. L. (1991). *Attention, please! A comprehensive guide for successfully parenting children with attention disorders and hyperactivity.* Atlanta: SPI Press.

Ingersoll, B. (1988). *Your hyperactive child: A parent's guide to coping with attention deficit disorder.* New York: Doubleday.

Parker, H. C. (1988). *The ADD hyperactivity workbook for parents, teachers and kids.* Plantation, FL: Impact Publications.

Wender, P. H. (1987). *The hyperactive child, adolescent, and adult: Attention deficit disorder through the lifespan.* Oxford: Oxford University Press.

For Children

Levine, M. D. (1990). *Keeping a head in school.* Cambridge: Educators Publishing Service. (For students in middle school and up).

Moss, D. (1989). *Shelly, the hyperactive turtle.* Rockville, MD: Woodbine House. (For young children.)

Quinn, P. O., & Stern, J. M. (1991). *Putting on the brakes.* New York: Magination. (For children ages 8–13.)

Videotapes

The School's Role in ADD (1990).
Copeland, E. D., P.O. Box 12389, Atlanta, GA 30355-2389
Phone: 404-256-0903

Why Won't My Child Pay Attention? (1989).

Educating the Inattentive Child (1990).
Goldstein, S., & Goldstein, M.
The Neurology, Learning and Behavior Center
230 South 500 East, Suite #100,
Salt Lake City, UT 84102-2015
Phone: 801-532-1484

All About Attention Deficit Disorder Parts 1 & 2 (1990).
Phelan, T. W.
Child Management, Inc.,
800 Roosevelt Road,
Glen Ellyn, IL 60137-9973
Phone: 800-442-4453

Attention Deficit Disorder: Legal Rights

Two major laws protect the right of students with handicaps to a free appropriate education at public expense. The two laws are the Individuals with Disabilities Education Act (IDEA) and Section 504 of the Rehabilitation Act of 1973.

Under IDEA, formerly the Education of the Handicapped Act (Public Law 94-142), children with specified handicaps are eligible for special education and related services. Related services are defined as the services necessary to allow the child to benefit from special education and may include such services as transportation, counseling, or occupational therapy. The handicapping conditions identified in this law are mental retardation, hearing impairment, visual impairment, speech impairment, serious emotional disturbance, orthopedic impairment, other health impairment, deaf-blind, multi-handicapped, specific learning disability, brain injury, and autism. For children with these handicapping conditions, the parents and school personnel jointly write an Individualized Educational Plan (IEP) specifying the educational goals and objectives of the child's specialized instruction, criteria by which his/her progress is to be evaluated, and the amount of time that the child will receive special services. Although Attention Deficit Disorder is not specifically listed in IDEA, the law has been interpreted so that if a child is considered eligible for services under this law, any handicapping condition, including ADD, that interferes with the child's learning must be addressed when services are designated. For example, if a child were diagnosed as having a learning disability, s/he would qualify for services under IDEA. If the child also had been diagnosed as ADD, and needed special services to help him/her develop more effective work habits and learn to follow classroom rules, goals and objectives for these needs also would be written into the IEP. Some states have been serving children with ADD by qualifying them as "other health impaired." If a parent feels that his/her child qualifies for special educational services under IDEA, s/he should request an evaluation. If, after the school has completed its evaluation, the parent disagrees with the findings concerning his/her child's handicapping condition or with the placement options considered appropriate by the school, the parent may follow a set of procedures that are specified in the guidelines for IDEA.

Section 504 of the Rehabilitation Act of 1973 is a civil rights act protecting individuals with handicaps. Under this law, the definition of handicap is broader than under IDEA, and includes any person who has a physical or mental impairment that substantially limits one or more major life activities, such as speaking, walking, working, or learning. As Section 504 prohibits any recipient of federal funds from discriminating against individuals with handicaps, it requires school districts to provide ". . . regular or special education and related services designed to meet individual educational needs of handicapped persons as adequately as the needs of non-handicapped persons are met . . ." (Rehabilitation Act, 1973). To these ends, a plan must also be written for the student designated as handicapped under Section 504, although the information to be included is not specified as it is under IDEA. Failing to provide appropriate educational and related services that will allow the individual with a handicap to benefit from his/her education to the same extent as a nonhandicapped individual is considered discrimination for which the school district could lose all federal funds. The regulations for Section 504 require each school district to develop a set of procedures that parents can follow to ensure that their child receives the level of education to which s/he is entitled under the law. Using these procedures, parents may challenge decisions that the school might have made in regard to the evaluation, designation of handicapping condition, educational placement of the child, and the provision of an appropriate educational program. Each school district must appoint a compliance officer, a person who is not directly involved in the education of children with handicaps, to become knowledgeable about Section 504 and to be available to provide information about the rights of children with handicaps under this law.

Public agencies, called protection and advocacy agencies, have been established in each state to provide information and referrals to individuals with handicaps regarding their legal rights and how to rectify a situation that may violate these rights. Some of these agencies also provide advocacy services. The protection and advocacy agency in each state may be located by calling or writing to the National Association of Protection and Advocacy Systems,

900 Second Street, N.E., Suite 211, Washington, DC 20002 (202-408-9514; TDD: 202-408-9521).

Parents, individuals with handicaps, or teachers who want to file a complaint under IDEA may also directly contact the State Department of Education. Parents or individuals with handicaps who want to file a complaint under Section 504 should contact their Regional Office of Civil Rights of the United States Department of Education.

Sources:

Education for all Handicapped Children Act (1975), 34 C.F.R. 300.1-300.754 (1977).

Individuals with Disabilities Education Act (1990), 20 U.S.C. 1400-1485.

Rehabilitation Act of 1973, 29 U.S.C. 794.

Rehabilitation Act of 1973, 34 C.F.R. 104.1-104.39 (1977).

Cloze Procedure

The cloze technique may be used for informal assessment or as an instructional strategy. This strategy may be used to help students increase their efficiency in language processing and in using context clues. Typically, in this procedure, every *n*th word is deleted and replaced with a blank of uniform length. The number of words deleted is based upon the level of conceptual difficulty of the material and the competency of the reader. The following three-phase teaching procedure may be used as a basic framework to implement the cloze technique:

Phase 1: Presentation and Preparation

The teacher uses prereading activities, such as developing a purpose for reading, to motivate the student and build background information. The teacher then provides short practice sessions where s/he works with the student, modeling how the exercises are completed. Only use materials that are at the student's independent reading level.

Phase 2: Preview and Completion

The student reads the passage three times. During the first reading the student gains an overview of the material and fills in the blanks mentally. In the second reading, the student fills in all of the blanks. For the third reading, the student checks to see if the responses make sense. During the second and third readings, students may work in pairs or small groups.

Phase 3: Follow-up

The most important step is the follow-up conference where the teacher discusses with the student(s) their choices, reviews other acceptable alternatives, and asks the student(s) to explain why they chose a particular response. At this point the teacher may point out specific context clues that are found around the blank and assist in word selection. As a final step, student(s) may compare their responses with the original.

Adaptations

Many adaptations of this procedure may be used depending upon the purpose of the instruction. The following applications were field tested by Thomas (1978).

1. *Context/Content Clues*

The teacher deletes the specific terms that complete the key ideas in the passage. The reader then focuses on these essential elements. This adaptation is particularly appropriate for content-area material.

Example:
The largest state in the United States is _____.

2. *Process Strategies/Combined Clues*

The teacher provides different graphophonic clues to help the student identify the word, such as the initial consonant, several letters, or the ending of the word.

Example:
The little girl loved to ride her b_____.

3. *Specific Phonic Elements*

The teacher selects specific phonic elements to delete from words, such as consonant blends or digraphs or short vowel sounds. This adaptation requires the student to use context clues as well as phonic skills and may be used to reinforce specific phonic elements that the student is learning.

Example:
The b__g d__g r__n to the house.

4. *Specific Morphemic Elements*

The teacher deletes root words, prefixes, or suffixes. If necessary, the specific elements to use can be listed for the student.

Example:
The ____school teach____ was sing_____ her favorite song__.

5. *Relationships: Function Words*

The teacher deletes function words from various types of syntactic structures, such as prepositions, articles, conjunctions, or auxiliary verbs. The teacher may decide to delete a particular part of speech. The purpose is to help the student attend to language features.

Example:
Sally _____ leaving _____ school ____ the morning.

6. *Relationships: Pronouns and Pronoun Referents*

The teacher deletes pronouns, selected pronoun referents, or both.

Example:
In many ways, _____ had treated _____ kindly.

7. *Relationships: Organizational Patterns*

The teacher deletes the keywords and phrases that signal the organizational pattern of a passage, such as the words *first*, *next*, or *finally*. This variation can also be used with words signaling time order, such as *before, after*, or *when*; words signaling a comparison/contrast organizational pattern, such as *however*, *but*, *as well as*, or *yet*; or words signaling a cause/effect organizational pattern, such as *because*, *therefore*, or *consequently*.

Example:
When you start any project, _____ plan the steps and _____ decide what materials you will need.

Adapted from:

Thomas, K. (1978). Instructional applications of the cloze technique. *Reading World*, *18*, 1-12.

Cohesive Devices: Activities

These activities teach students how to interpret and use referential and lexical cohesive devices in oral and written language.

Activity #1

Steps

1. Provide the students with a passage in which names and words are repeated rather than being replaced by pronouns, demonstrative articles, or other words, thus reducing the need for inference (e.g., Peter went into the forest. Peter had never been in the forest before).

2. Show the students how the sentence may be rewritten using whatever cohesive device is being taught (e.g., Peter went into the forest. *He* had never been there before).

3. Provide direct instruction on the meanings of specific devices. For example, create a pronoun chart with categories for gender and number of people. Using pictures, if necessary, teach the students to whom each of the pronouns refers.

4. Provide the students with sentence pairs in which cohesive devices (e.g., pronouns) in the second sentence provide the meaningful tie with the first sentence. Underline the cohesive devices.

5. Ask students to replace the cohesive devices with the words they represent.

6. Expand the exercise to include longer passages and have the students answer questions regarding interpretation of the cohesive devices.

7. Have the students find and interpret the cohesive devices in passages from their textbooks.

Activity #2

Repeat Steps 1 through 3 above. For Steps 4 and 5, however, provide the students with sentences and passages with redundant words and ask the students to replace them with cohesive devices.

Adapted from:

Baumann, J. (1986). Teaching third-grade students to comprehend anaphoric relationships: The application of a direct instruction model. *Reading Research Quarterly, 21,* 70-90.

Activity #3

Steps

1. Provide students with ambiguous sentences in which the referents for the cohesive devices are unclear.

Example:

    He threw it to her—hard—and then ran like crazy.

2. Guide a discussion as to why the lack of clarity is a problem. Have the students add sentences before and after the given sentence that will help to clarify the ambiguous sentence.

Example:

    The gunman spotted his accomplice, Mazie, as he stepped out of the bank door, holding the sack of money under his arm. He threw it to her—hard—and then ran like crazy. Mazie nonchalantly blended into the crowd and walked into a Fifth Avenue department store.

    (Note that the target sentence could also have referred to a baseball game.)

Adapted from:

Wallach, G. P., & Miller, L. (1988). *Language intervention and academic success.* Boston: Little, Brown and Company.

Cohesive Devices: Types

Reference

Cohesion is formed by a word (or words) that refers to information, found elsewhere in the text, that is necessary for comprehension of the statement. The *exact* identity of the referent is stated elsewhere.

Pronominal: *Hansel* took some bread crumbs. *He* put them in his pocket.
Demonstrative: Their parents took them to the *forest* and left them *there*.

Lexical

Textual cohesion between one word and another is created by repetition of the word or use of a synonym, a superordinate word, a more general word, or an associated word.

Same word: The *darkness* of night came swiftly. The children were afraid of the *darkness*.
Synonym: Hansel and Gretel huddled together to wait for *daybreak*. Oh, when would *dawn* come?
Superordinate word: *Mice and raccoons* snuffled closer to investigate the intruders. The *animals* were curious.
General word: Finally, the tired children snuggled down in the *leaves and pine needles* that composed the forest *bed* and went to sleep.
Associated word: As the *dawn* broke, *sunlight* filled the forest.

Conjunction

A semantic relation that expresses how a clause or statement is related in meaning to a previous clause or statement and is signaled by a specific connecting word or phrase. A variety of types of semantic relations, with examples of words that typically signal each, follow.

Additive: and, also, in addition
Amplification: furthermore, moreover
Adversative: but, however, in contrast, nevertheless
Causal: if/then, because, due to, as a result
Conclusion: therefore, accordingly, consequently
Temporal: after, meanwhile, whenever, previously
Sequence: first, second, then, lastly, finally
Spatial: next to, between, in front of, adjacent to
Continuative: after all, again, finally, another
Likeness: likewise, similarly
Example: for example, as an illustration
Restatement: in other words, that is, in summary
Exception: except, barring, beside, excluding

Substitution

A word is substituted for the referent that is not identical in meaning or carries some differentiation, but performs the same structural function.

Nominal: The witch wanted a bigger *pot*. She ordered Gretel to go and get *one*.
Clausal: Could Gretel *save Hansel*? She thought *so*.

Ellipsis

A word, phrase, or clause is left unsaid, but is understood.

Verbal: "Are you coming?" called the witch. "I am (coming)," answered Gretel.
Nominal: Gretel looked for a sharp tool, but she knew she would take whatever (tool) she could find.
Clausal: I know I can kill the witch. I'm sure I can (kill the witch).

Adapted from:

Wallach, G. P., & Miller, L. (1988). *Language intervention and academic success*. Boston: Little, Brown and Company.

Context Clues

Introduction

The use of context clues to derive the meaning of new words from text is the most effective way for students to increase vocabulary independently. Furthermore, it frees students from overreliance on looking up words in the dictionary, a method that is cumbersome and interrupts the flow of meaning in reading.

Purpose

The following explanation of context clues is provided as a guide for the teacher in introducing context clues to their students. Teaching context clues within a variety of activities, such as the Directed Vocabulary Thinking Activity (Cunningham, 1979), will facilitate learning and retention of the clues.

1. *Direct Explanation*

a. Appositive: The writer provides the definition, as an appositive, immediately following the word it defines.

Example:
An *environmentalist*, a person devoted to protecting the ecological balance of the earth, opposes the destruction of vast tracts of rain forest.

b. That is: The phrase *that is* alerts the reader to an explanation for the word preceding it.

Example:
The *descrambler*—that is, the device for decoding scrambled messages—did not prove to be an effective tool for the Axis powers, as the Allied messages were being sent in the Navaho language.

c. Placed at a distance from the word to be explained.

Example:
Life on the *kibbutz* was hard, but rewarding. They had awaited this life of communal living on a collective farm.

2. *Experience Clue*

The use of past experience to infer the meaning of a word from the situation depicted in the text.

Example:
Arriving home to find his rare and most precious classical records shattered on the floor *infuriated* Mr. Witherspoon beyond reason.

3. *Mood or Tone:*

The reader finds the clue to the unknown word's meaning in the general mood or tone of the passage.

Example:
The small *disheartened* group trudged slowly through the sultry, dusty, streets, burdened with the tiny casket.

4. *Explanation Through Example*

The reader may find an example of the meaning of the unfamiliar word in the same or the next sentence.

Example:
An undiagnosed learning disability may have serious emotional *ramifications*. An adolescent who has consistently tried, but has had difficulty learning, may assume that "good grades" are beyond him and drop out of school as soon as age and the law permit.

Example:
Eyes sparkling, doing little dance steps through the crowded market, and flashing her smile at the vendors and patrons alike, Jillian was surprised by her own *vivacity*.

5. *Summary*

The unknown word sums up the situation described in the passage. The word may be placed either before or after the situation.

Example:
Through the beveled panes of the leaded glass windows, the sunlight splintered into kaleidoscopic hues. The effect was *prismatic*.

6. *Synonym or Restatement*

The reader must infer the relationship between the word and a previously stated idea.

Example:
The exercises to improve his binocular coordination were time consuming. He had to admit, however, that the *orthoptics* were helping.

7. *Comparison or Contrast*

A comparison clue allows the reader to infer a similarity between the new word and another idea in the sentence or passage.

Example:

The sweet and gentle tones of the cello drifted through the halls of the building like the *mellifluous* tones of an angel.

The meaning of the new word is clearly meant to be dissimilar from another word or idea.

Example:

Almost to a fault, Maura was conscientious and meticulous about her obligations; Brandon, on the other hand, was as *unreliable* as the weather in Dublin.

8. *Familiar Expression or Language Experience*

This type of clue is rather like a restatement/synonym, except that the clue words are idioms or everyday expressions.

Example:

As the eye of the hurricane passed, it rained buckets. The *torrent* seemed to hit the ground in waves.

9. *Words in Series*

The reader can glean some idea of the meaning of a strange word if it is listed in a series of others.

Example:

Her dress was in shockingly poor fashion. Flowers of pink, purple, red, and *puce* fought with each other against a yellow background.

10. *Inference*

Many types of context clues share characteristics with the inference clue.

Example:

He was a short, wiry, aggressive little boy who had a propensity for fighting. Who would have expected a *pugilist* in such a little package?

Comment

To evaluate a student's ability to use a variety of context clues, the teacher may construct a test with all 10 types of clues. Make sure that all words except the new vocabulary are at the student's independent reading level.

Source:

Thomas, E. L., & Robinson, H. A. (1972). *Improving reading in every class: A sourcebook for teachers*. Boston: Allyn and Bacon.

CONTRACT (Child-Parent)

Name: _____

Behavior to develop: _____

_____

_____

_____

To help myself I will: _____

_____

_____

_____

My parent will help by: _____

_____

_____

_____

Agreement: _____

_____

_____

_____

_____ points earn _____

Signed: _____   _____
                Child   Parent

CONTRACT (Student-Teacher)

Name: _____

Behavior to develop: _____
_____
_____
_____

To help myself I will: _____
_____
_____
_____

My teacher will help by: _____
_____
_____
_____

Agreement: _____
_____
_____
_____

_____ points earn _____

Signed: _____   _____
              Student   Teacher

Directed Reading-Thinking Activity

The purpose of the Directed Reading-Thinking Activity (DRTA) is to improve reading comprehension by promoting critical thinking in the reading process. Students are expected to learn to set a purpose for reading, read to prove or disprove a hypothesis, and evaluate the accuracy of their hypotheses based on the textual information. Students' active involvement in the reading process improves comprehension and retention of information. Other expected outcomes include increased ability to make logical predictions and support decisions based on given information.

DRTA may be used individually or in groups of 8 to 10 students. It is appropriate as a developmental reading activity or for students who have adequate decoding ability but below-average comprehension. DRTA was originally developed for use with basal readers; initial teaching of the activity is done with literature, but may be adapted later to content area material as the students gain familiarity with the process.

Preparation

Choose a high-interest reading selection and divide it into parts. The first part includes just the title and possibly an introductory picture. The last part includes the final portion of the reading selection. The remainder of the selection may be divided into two or three segments. The segments are selected on the basis of events in the story rather than number of pages.

Procedure

1. Direct the students to the title of the selection and introductory picture (if there is one) and ask the following questions:

    a. Based on the title (and picture), what do you think this story will be about?
    b. What do you think might happen in this story?
    c. Why?

Lead a discussion wherein students state and give reasons for their predictions. Each student's prediction forms the basis for further reading.

2. Direct the students to read to a predetermined point for the purpose of verifying or disproving their predictions. Have the students close their books and ask questions to help them evaluate their predictions:

    a. Were you correct? (Partially correct? Incorrect?)
    b. What will happen now?

Require students to provide support from the text (e.g., by reading relevant sentences) in discussing the accuracy of their previous predictions.

3. Encourage the students to use evidence given by other students to make or refine their subsequent predictions.

Note

As students repeat the predict–read–evaluate cycle, their diverse hypotheses should tend to converge.

Guidelines

1. All students must have instructional reading levels that permit adequate decoding of the material.

2. The teacher's role in DRTA is as a facilitator, helping students to clarify and refine their responses and asking students open-ended questions.

3. The teacher must maintain neutrality in responding to students' statements.

4. To keep the momentum, the teacher should not paraphrase student responses, but should encourage students to state their predictions and explanations clearly and in a sufficiently loud voice for the group to hear.

Modifications

1. Slow readers may be paired up with a partner who will read the selection aloud.

2. All students may be divided into teams of two, read to each other, and discuss predictions prior to whole-group discussion.

3. To develop listening/thinking skills, this procedure may be conducted orally, with the teacher reading the selection to the class or telling a story.

4. DRTA may be individualized for one-to-one teaching of reading-thinking skills. In this case, the teacher may provide more questions to help the student clarify and support his/her predictions.

Sources:

Stauffer, R. G. (1969). *Directing reading maturity as a cognitive process.* New York: Harper & Row.

Tierney, R. J., Readence, J. E., & Dishner, E. K. (1985). *Reading strategies and practices: A compendium* (2nd ed.). Boston: Allyn and Bacon.

Directed Vocabulary Thinking Activity

This procedure may be used to introduce a unit on the use of context clues or to introduce keywords before reading. The purpose is to build awareness of how one can use context to infer the meaning of unknown words.

Preparation

1. Choose a few keywords from the selection that are likely to be unfamiliar to the student(s).

2. List the words.

3. Write a sentence for each word. Each sentence should incorporate the use of one of the types of context clues that will be included in the unit (e.g., direct explanation, contrast, synonym, restatement).

Procedure

1. Write the words without definitions on the board or on paper. Have the student(s) guess definitions. Either the teacher or a student may record the guesses.

2. Show the words within the sentences. Have the student(s) guess definitions and record them.

3. For each word, have the student(s) discuss how other words in the sentence helped him/her to come up with the new definitions.

4. Look up each word in the dictionary or provide a paraphrased definition appropriate to the student's language level.

Source:

Cunningham, P. M. (1979). Teaching vocabulary in the content areas. *NASSP Bulletin*, *613*(424), 112-116.

Error Monitoring Strategy (COPS)

Error Monitoring (Schumaker et al., 1981) is a strategy used to help students develop proofreading skills and incorporate the basic writing skills they have learned.

Pretest

1. Give the student a list of expository writing topics from which to choose. Ask him/her to write at least six lines. Allow at least 20 minutes.

2. Ask the student to read the composition, circle the errors, and correct them.

3. Ask the student to rewrite the composition, corrected.

4. Repeat Steps 1–3 in the next session with a new topic.

5. If the student has identified less than 80% of the errors, teach the Error Monitoring Strategy.

Introducing Error Monitoring to the Student

1. Explain to the student that if s/he is able to identify the errors in compositions, his/her papers will be better and his/her grades will improve.

2. Show the student the percentage of errors s/he identified and the percentage s/he did not identify.

3. Explain that you can teach him/her a strategy that will help with proofreading. Make sure s/he understands why proofreading is necessary. Check for understanding.

4. Obtain a commitment from the student to learn the strategy.

5. Describe the steps in the strategy.

Modeling the Steps in the Strategy

1. Have available a short composition, written on every other line, with a variety of errors in capitalization, punctuation, paragraph indentations, margins, spelling, and sentence construction.

2. Using the cue card, model the steps and think aloud.

Steps in the Error Monitoring Strategy

1. Write a draft of a composition on every other line.

2. Write COPS on the top of the page.

3. Read through the composition once for each type of error you are trying to locate. Use a colored pencil. When you have checked the entire composition for a specific type of error, check off the cue letter on the top of the page.

Cue	Error	Correction
C =	CAPITALS	Write over error.
O =	OVERALL APPEARANCE	
	Fragments & Run-ons	Line out and write new sentence above.
	Paragraph indent	→
	Margins	Write lines down the side of page.
	Note marks, rips	
P =	PUNCTUATION	Circle each incorrect/omitted mark.
S =	SPELLING	Write SP above word.

4. Optional: Ask someone to double-check your paper.

5. Look up spelling words; ask for help with corrections.

6. Recopy composition neatly. Use every line.

7. Reread and proofread.

Guided Practice

For practice, use copies of a variety of prepared handwritten passages, on which the student just marks and corrects the errors.

1. Have the student memorize COPS, the type of error each letter represents, and the proofing mark. If needed, provide a cue card.

2. Have the student practice the Error Monitoring Strategy on passages starting at the student's independent reading level, moving up to more advanced levels. Mastery at each level is 80%.

Independent Practice

When the student has attained 80% mastery on passages slightly higher than his/her own writing level, have him/her use COPS on his/her own writing. At this point, include Step 8: Reread and Proofread.

Posttest and Commitment to Generalize

1. When the student is familiar with the procedure and is using it well in his/her own writing, give a posttest similar to the pretest.

2. With the student, compare the posttest with the pretest. Ask the student to tell you what s/he has learned and its usefulness.

3. Explain the importance of generalization and obtain the student's commitment to use the strategy in the classroom and at home.

4. Give the student a cue card tailored to remind him/her of the basic skills s/he has already learned. This will vary according to the student's skill level.

Generalization

1. Talk with the student's regular classroom teachers. Ask them to remind the student to use Error Monitoring and, if needed, to provide him/her with a cue card.

2. Possibly, offer to teach Error Monitoring to the whole class or to the teacher.

3. Collect the student's writing from other classes to see if s/he is using the strategy and provide incentives.

CUE CARD

C =	CAPITALS	FIRST WORD IN EACH SENTENCE
		NAMES OF PEOPLE & PLACES
		DATES
O =	OVERALL APPEARANCE	FRAGMENTS OR RUN-ON SENTENCES
		PARAGRAPH INDENTATION
		MARGINS
		MARKS, RIPS
P =	PUNCTUATION	ENDS OF SENTENCES MARKED
		COMMAS
S =	SPELLING	CORRECT

Adaptation

For students who need to have skills more clearly delineated, you may use the acronym SH! COPS!

Cue	Error	Correction
S =	SENTENCE	Line out and write new sentence above it.
H =	HANDWRITING	Underline poorly written words.
C =	CAPITALS	Write over error.

Cue	Error	Correction
O =	OVERALL APPEARANCE	
	Paragraph indent	→
	Margins	Write lines down the side of page.
	Note marks, rips	
P =	PUNCTUATION	Circle each incorrect/ omitted mark.
S =	SPELLING	Write SP above word.

CUE CARD: SH! COPS!

S =	SENTENCES	FRAGMENTS & RUN-ONS
H =	HANDWRITING	NEAT
C =	CAPITALS	FIRST WORD IN EACH SENTENCE
		NAMES OF PEOPLE & PLACES
		DATES
O =	OVERALL APPEARANCE	PARAGRAPH INDENTATION
		MARGINS
		MARKS, RIPS
P =	PUNCTUATION	ENDS OF SENTENCES MARKED
		COMMAS
S =	SPELLING	CORRECT

Comments

Self-monitoring is the ultimate objective for each of the basic writing skills the student may learn. The teacher should not, however, wait until the student has mastered basic writing skills to teach this strategy. If the student has learned Error Monitoring, s/he will use it as s/he learns the basic skills.

Sources:

Schumaker, J. B., Deshler, D. D., Alley, G. R., Warner, M. M., Clark, F .L., & Nolan, S. (1982). Error monitoring: A learning strategy for improving adolescent performance. In W. M. Cruickshank & J. Lerner (Eds.), *Best of ACLD: Vol. 3* (pp. 170-182). Syracuse, NY: Syracuse University Press.

Schumaker, J. B., Deshler, D. D., Nolan, S., Clark, F. L., Alley, G. R., & Warner, M. M. (1981). *Error monitoring: A learning strategy for improving academic performance of LD adolescents* (Research Report No. 32). Lawrence, KS: University of Kansas Institute for Research in Learning Disabilities.

Adaptation by author.

Fernald Method for Reading Instruction

Purpose

To improve recognition and memory of words and to facilitate greater fluency and comprehension in reading.

Rationale

The Fernald Method provides instruction in a systematic multisensory way, in which visual, auditory, kinesthetic, and tactile channels (VAKT) are used simultaneously by the learner. The association of sensory and perceptual cues in this multisensory approach reinforces visualization, visual-auditory associations, and improves memory for words and word parts.

Type of Student

The Fernald Method is appropriate for students who have failed to learn to read through other instructional methods due to possible problems in visual perception, visual-verbal association, auditory memory, attention deficits, or visual-motor skills. Individual or small group instruction is necessary.

Procedure

The Fernald Method consists of four stages through which the student progresses as reading proficiency increases.

Stage I

1. *Solicit the student's interest and involvement.* Tell the student that you will be showing him/her a new way to learn words. Explain that while the method may require concentration and effort, it has been successful with other students who have problems remembering words.

2. *Select a word to learn.* Have the student select a word which s/he cannot read but would like to learn. Discuss the meaning of the word.

3. *Write the word.* Sitting beside the student, have him/her watch and listen while you: (a) say the word, (b) use a crayon to write the word in large print in manuscript or cursive (depending upon what is used by the student) on a 5" × 8" index card, and (c) say the word again as you smoothly run your finger underneath the word.

4. *Model* word tracing for the student. Ask him/her to "watch what I do and listen to what I say." Use the following steps: (a) say the word; (b) trace the word using one or two fingers, saying each part of the word as you trace it; (c) say the word again while moving the tracing fingers underneath the word in a fluent motion; and (d) have the student practice tracing and saying the word until the process is completed correctly.

5. *Trace the word until learned.* Have the student continue tracing and saying the word until the student is sure he/she can write the word from memory.

6. *Write the word from memory.* When the student feels s/he is ready, remove the model and have the student write the word from memory saying the word as s/he writes it. If at any point the student makes an error, stop him/her immediately, cover the error, model the tracing procedure again, and have the student continue tracing.

7. *File the word.* After the word has been written correctly by the student three times without the model, have the student file it in his/her word bank alphabetically.

8. *Type the word.* Within 24 hours, each word learned is typed and read by the student to help establish the link between written and typed words.

As soon as a student has discovered that he/she can write words, begin story writing. The student selects a topic. When the student encounters a word that s/he cannot spell, the tracing process is repeated. Stories are typed within 24 hours so that the student has an opportunity to read newly learned words within context.

Important points. During stage one instruction, observe the following cautions:

–Finger contact is important in tracing.
–After tracing, the student should always write the word without looking at the model to avoid breaking it up into meaningless units.
–The word should always be written as a unit from the beginning. In case of interruption, cover and remove the error and start over from the beginning.
–Words should always be used in context to provide meaning.
–The student must say each part of the word to him/herself as s/he traces it and writes it.

Stage II

During Stage II the student no longer needs to trace words to learn them. The student learns a word by looking at it, saying it, and writing it. The teacher writes requested words saying each part of the word as it is written while the student listens and watches. The student looks at the word, saying it over as s/he looks at it, and then writes it without looking at the copy. As in Stage I, words to be learned are obtained from words the student requests as s/he writes stories. Learned words continue to be filed. Stories increase in length.

Stage III

By Stage III the student learns directly from the printed word without having it written. S/he simply looks at the word and pronounces it before writing it. At this stage the student wants to read books and other more difficult material. Have the student choose books and tell the student any unknown words. After reading, have the student review and write the new words.

Stage IV

At this stage, the student recognizes known words in print and also begins to notice similarity of unknown to known words. S/he begins to recognize many new words without being told what they are. Provide enough assistance at Stage IV so that reading proceeds smoothly.

One helpful technique at this stage is to have the student glance over a paragraph and underline any unknown words before reading. Tell the student the words and have him/her write the words. Do not have the student sound out unknown words. Phonics instruction is unnecessary with this method.

Sources:

Cotterell, G. C. (1973). The Fernald auditory-kinaesthetic technique. In A. W. Franklin & S. Naidoo (Eds.), *Assessment and teaching of dyslexic children* (pp. 97-100). London: Richard Madley.

Fernald, G. (1943). *Remedial techniques in basic school subjects.* New York: McGraw-Hill.

Mather, N. (1985). *The Fernald kinesthetic method revisited.* Unpublished manuscript, University of Arizona, Department of Special Education and Rehabilitation, Tucson.

Fernald Method for Spelling Instruction

This spelling method is appropriate for students who have difficulty retaining spelling words. Words are selected that the student uses frequently in his/her writing.

Procedure

1. The word to be learned is written on the chalkboard or on paper by the teacher.

2. The word is pronounced clearly and distinctly by the teacher. The student pronounces the word with emphasis on correct pronunciation. The student looks at the word while pronouncing it.

3. Time is allowed for the student to study the word to develop an image of it. Depending upon the learning style of the student, different senses are emphasized. A student who learns visually tries to picture the word; a student who learns auditorily says the word; and the student who learns kinesthetically traces the word with his/her finger. The student studies the word until the correct form is fixed in his/her mind.

4. When the student indicates that s/he is sure of the word, the word is erased or removed and written from memory.

5. The paper is turned over and the word is written a second time from memory.

In daily writing, any misspelled words are marked out entirely and the correct form is written in its place. When a student asks how to spell a word, the teacher writes the word, while pronouncing it. Students are encouraged to make their own dictionaries from words they have learned or words that are especially difficult for them.

Source:

Fernald, G. (1943). *Remedial techniques in basic school subjects.* New York: McGraw-Hill.

Glass-Analysis for Decoding Only

Individual words are presented to the student on flash cards. The student is asked to look at the whole word. Parts of the word are never covered up, nor are structural units presented alone. The teacher trains only letter clusters that can be generalized. Words for practice may be selected from the student's reading material. The method may be used for one or two 15-minute sessions daily.

This method is appropriate for students who need assistance in developing decoding skill.

Steps

Five general steps for presenting each word are followed:

1. *Identify the whole word.*

For example, present the word *carpenter* on an index card and say: "This word is 'carpenter.'"

2. *Pronounce a sound in the word and ask the student to name the letter or letters that make that sound.*

Say: "In the word 'carpenter,' what letters make the 'ar' sound? What letters make the 'pen' sound?," etc.

3. *Ask for the sound that certain letters or letter combinations make.*

Say: "What sound does e/r make? What sound does the t/e/r make?," etc.

4. *Take away letters (auditorily, not visually) and ask for the remaining sound.*

Say: "In the word 'carpenter,' if I took off the c/a/r/, what sounds would be left?," etc.

5. *Identify the whole word.*

Sources:

Glass, G. G. (1973). *Teaching decoding as separate from reading.* New York: Adelphi University.

Glass, G. G. (1976). *Glass-Analysis for decoding only teacher guide.* Garden City, NY: Easier to Learn.

Inference: Deciding the Types

The purpose of this activity is to help students understand the types of inference that can be made within and across sentences. (See Inference: Types.)

Steps

1. Give students sentences or short passages that require a specific type of inference. The complexity of the sentences or passage and inference will depend on the students' language level.

Example:

As she strapped her pack on, she looked out over the clouds and felt the grip of fear in her belly. She had never before jumped from such a height.

2. Point out the keywords that give clues to the inference by underlining them within the text and possibly listing them underneath. The number and explicitness of clues should reflect the age and language ability of the students.

Example:

strapped, pack, over the clouds, jumped, height

3. Have the students guess the word that would make explicit the inference in the sentence or passage and the type of inference required.

Example:

The pack is a parachute. Inference type: instrument.

In this case, one could add other inferences, such as:

Location: Airplane.

Agent: Pilot

Problem-solution: The plane has engine trouble, so the pilot is bailing out.

Additional Activities

1. Give the students sentences or passages and have them pick out the keywords themselves before deciding the type of inference required.

2. Give students a passage one sentence at a time and discuss how the interpretation may change depending on the amount and type of information given.

Example:

We discovered a pit.

We came across a pit while we were exploring a wilderness area.

It looked as though it had been there for a long time.

After finishing the fruit, some litterbug must have thrown it on the ground.

Object: the stone or pit of a fruit (as opposed to a tar pit)

Keywords: finishing, fruit, litterbug, thrown, ground (Johnson & von Hoff Johnson, 1986, p. 625).

Sources:

Johnson, D. D., & von Hoff Johnson, B. (1986). Highlighting vocabulary in inferential comprehension. *Journal of Reading, 29*, 622-625.

Wallach, G. P., & Miller, L. (1988). *Language intervention and academic success.* Boston: Little, Brown and Company.

Inference: Getting the Idea

Before teaching specific types of inferencing skills, such as recognizing the type of inference that must be made (e.g., agent, cause/effect) or interpreting specific cohesive devices (e.g., lexical, conjunction), help the students understand that they must actively *construct* comprehension by applying prior knowledge to the oral or printed information presented. The purpose of the suggested activities is to bring to a conscious level the application of prior knowledge to written and oral language. These exercises should follow activities for activating prior knowledge; some incorporate this step. Since these activities require discussion, they are best done in small groups.

Activity #1

The purpose of this activity is to provide students practice in relating their own experiences to those in the given reading/listening material.

Steps

1. Select a significant aspect of the story/material in which the students might have had experience. Guide a discussion of their experiences (e.g., a time they were frightened).

2. Provide some information about the story, relevant to their discussion.

3. Ask a question requiring inference (e.g., "In this story, a young man is going to apply for a job and he is frightened. Why do you think he is frightened?"). List the students' answers on the board.

4. Help the students combine their answers into more general ideas.

5. Have the students read or listen to the story and discuss the accuracy of their ideas.

6. Have the students write their answers to inference questions about the story and discuss their answers.

Adapted from:

Hansen, J., & Pearson, P. D. (1983). An instructional study: Improving the inferential comprehension of good and poor fourth-graders. *Journal of Educational Psychology*, *75*, 821-829.

Wallach, G. P., & Miller, L. (1988). *Language intervention and academic success*. Boston: Little, Brown and Company.

Activity #2

The purpose of this activity is to help students understand how much of their comprehension of reading material is based on their assumption of information not given in the text, as well as to highlight the constructive nature of comprehension.

Steps

1. Select a paragraph that could have differing interpretations depending on prior beliefs about the situation. It is best if the paragraph can be taken from the students' instructional materials. An example of such a paragraph comes from Bransford and Johnson (1973):

> The man stood before the mirror and combed his hair. He checked his face carefully for any places he might have missed shaving and then put on the conservative tie he had decided to wear. At breakfast, he studied the newspaper carefully and, over coffee, discussed the possibility of buying a new washing machine with his wife. Then he made several phone calls. As he was leaving the house he thought about the fact that his children would probably want to go to that private camp again this summer. When the car didn't start he got out, slammed the door, and walked down to the bus stop in a very angry mood. Now he would be late. (p. 415)

2. Divide students into two groups. Both are given the same printed paragraphs with identical inferential comprehension questions, but each group has a different title for the paragraph, such as "The Unemployed Man" and "The Stock Broker." The students read or listen to the teacher read the paragraph.

3. Have students answer the questions according to the title they have been given. Suggested questions included:
   a. Where is the man going?
   b. What section of the newspaper is he reading?
   c. What might he do about the washing machine?
   d. What might he do about his children wanting to go to camp?
   e. What are some of the things he is concerned about?

4. Have the students discuss the different types of inferences they made and the reasons they made them.

5. Have the students rewrite the paragraphs adding explicit information based on the titles and their answers.

Adapted from:

Bransford, J. D., & Johnson, M. (1973). Considerations of some problems in comprehension. In W. Chase (Ed.), *Visual information processing* (pp. 383-438). New York: Academic Press.

Wallach, G. P., & Lee, A. D. (1982). So you want to know what to do with language-disabled children above the age of six. In K. G. Butler & G. P. Wallach (Eds.), *Language disorders and learning disabilities* (pp. 99-113). Rockville, MD: Aspen.

Inference: Types

1. *Location Inferences* (deciding place)
Example:
Standing at the edge, she could see the clouds below her. Where is she?

2. *Agent* (deciding occupation or role)
Example:
Jessie pulled up hard on the stick, trying to right the plane after the turbulence. What is Jessie's job?

3. *Time* (deciding when an event occurred)
Example:
The glow on the dusky horizon would soon to turn the sky red. What time of the day is this?

4. *Action* (deciding activity)
Example:
With a watchful eye, Mr. Mitford made sure that the students at their desks kept their eyes on their own papers. What was Mr. Mitford doing? What were the children doing?

5. *Instrument* (deciding tool or device)
Example:
Noting that the man had his finger on the trigger, the bank teller handed over all of the money. What was the man holding?

6. *Category* (deciding suprastructure)
Example:
Zinnias, begonias, and roses spilled over the garden wall to mingle with the pansies and sweet William growing in wild profusion. What type of garden was this?

7. *Object* (deciding the thing spoken about)
Example:
Twisting and arching the gleaming, silver hose of his body, the denizen of the deep fought the line all the way into the boat. What was caught?

8. *Cause-Effect* (deciding the cause for a happening or a result of a happening)
Example:
As thunder crashed overhead and water ran in sheets down the walls of the mud house, the family feared that soon the thatched roof would fall in. What would cause the roof to fall in?

9. *Problem-Solution* (deciding about a problem situation or its solution)
Example:
Jillian wanted desperately to stay at the party, but had been forbidden to be in the house unless Mark's parents were present. How will Jillian solve this problem?

10. *Feelings-Attitudes* (deciding how characters will act/react or why they act/react in a certain way)
Example:
As she looked through her veil, she was surprised to see tears glittering in Brian's eyes above the now familiar smile. What was Brian feeling?

Adapted from:

Johnson, D. D., & von Hoff Johnson, B. (1986). Highlighting vocabulary in inferential comprehension. *Journal of Reading, 29,* 623.

Instant Words*

First Hundred

Words 1-25	*Words 26-50*	*Words 51-75*	*Words 76-100*
the	or	will	number
of	one	up	no
and	had	other	way
a	by	about	could
to	word	out	people
in	but	many	my
is	not	then	than
you	what	them	first
that	all	these	water
it	were	so	been
he	we	some	call
was	when	her	who
for	your	would	oil
on	can	make	now
are	said	like	find
as	there	him	long
with	use	into	down
his	an	time	day
they	each	has	did
I	which	look	get
at	she	two	come
be	do	more	made
this	how	write	may
have	their	go	part
from	if	see	over

Common suffixes: *-s, -ing, -ed*

*The first 100 words make up 50% of all written material. The 300 words make up 65% of all written materials.

Note: From "The New Instant Word List" by E. B. Fry, 1980, *The Reading Teacher, 34,* pp. 286–288. Copyright 1980 by Edward B. Fry. Reprinted by permission.

Instant Words*

Second Hundred

Words 101-125	*Words 126-150*	*Words 150-175*	*Words 176-200*
new	great	put	kind
sound	where	end	hand
take	help	does	picture
only	through	another	again
little	much	well	change
work	before	large	off
know	line	must	play
place	right	big	spell
year	too	even	air
live	mean	such	away
me	old	because	animal
back	any	turn	house
give	same	here	point
most	tell	why	page
very	boy	ask	letter
after	follow	went	mother
thing	came	men	answer
our	want	read	found
just	show	need	study
name	also	land	still
good	around	different	learn
sentence	form	home	should
man	three	us	America
think	small	move	world
say	set	try	high

Common suffixes: *-s, -ing, -ed, -er, -ly, -est*

*The first 100 words make up 50% of all written material. The 300 words make up 65% of all written materials.

Note: From "The New Instant Word List" by E. B. Fry, 1980, *The Reading Teacher, 34,* pp. 286–288. Copyright 1980 by Edward B. Fry. Reprinted by permission.

Instant Words*

Third Hundred

Words 201-225	*Words 226-250*	*Words 251-275*	*Words 276-300*
every	left	until	idea
near	don't	children	enough
add	few	side	eat
food	while	feet	face
between	along	car	watch
own	might	mile	far
below	close	night	Indian
country	something	walk	real
plant	seem	white	almost
last	next	sea	let
school	hard	began	above
father	open	grow	girl
keep	example	took	sometimes
tree	begin	river	mountain
never	life	four	cut
start	always	carry	young
city	those	state	talk
earth	both	once	soon
eye	paper	book	list
light	together	hear	song
thought	got	stop	leave
head	group	without	family
under	often	second	body
story	run	late	music
saw	important	miss	color

Common suffixes: *-s, -ing, -ed, -er, -ly, -est*

*The first 100 words make up 50% of all written material. The 300 words make up 65% of all written materials.

Note: From "The New Instant Word List" by E. B. Fry, 1980, *The Reading Teacher, 34,* pp. 286–288. Copyright 1980 by Edward B. Fry. Reprinted by permission.

Kerrigan's Integrated Method of Teaching Composition

This method takes the writer step-by-step through the process of theme organization and the actual writing of the composition.

Steps

1. Write a short, simple declarative sentence that makes one statement.

2. Write three sentences about the sentence in Step 1 that are clearly and directly about the whole of that sentence, not just something in it. These three sentences will then become the topic sentences for the paragraphs.

3. Write four or five sentences about each of the three sentences in Step 2.

4. Make the material in the four or five sentences in Step 3 as concrete and specific as possible. Go into detail and give examples. Do not introduce new ideas into the paragraph.

5. In the first sentence of the second paragraph and every paragraph following, insert a clear reference to the idea in the preceding paragraph.

6. Try to make sure that every sentence in your theme is connected with, and makes a clear reference to, the preceding sentence. Use explicit references, such as the same word in a sentence, an antonym or synonym of the word, a pronoun, or a connective (e.g., *for example, however, but*).

Example:

Step 1: I dislike winter.

Step 2: I dislike cold weather.

I dislike wearing the heavy winter clothing that winter requires.

I dislike the colds that I always get in the winter.

Steps 3 + 4:

I dislike cold weather. It makes me shiver. I hate to slide and slip on the ice on the streets and sidewalks. I hate to have cold feet, so I always wear two pairs of socks.

I dislike, however, wearing the heavy winter clothing that winter requires. I have to wear earmuffs or a hat. I have to wear boots. I have to wear a heavy coat. When it's really cold I have to wear long underwear. If I don't wear heavy clothing, I usually get sick.

I dislike the colds that I always get in the winter. I catch at least two colds a winter. My nose gets stuffed up and I cough all night. I have to take medicine that makes me sleepy. I miss school for several days.

Source:

Kerrigan, W. J. (1979). *Writing to the point: Six basic steps* (2nd ed.). New York: Harcourt Brace Jovanovich.

K - W - L - S Strategy Sheet

Topic: _____

K - Know	W - Want to find out	L - Learned	S - Still Need to Learn

Adapted from:

Ogle, D.M. (1986). K-W-L: A teaching model that develops active reading of expository text. _Reading Teacher_, _39_, 564-570.

Language Experience Approach for Sight Words: Modified

The purpose of using the Language Experience Approach to teach sight words is to emphasize the concept that reading is communication—or talk written down. For a student who is just learning to read, especially one who is experiencing difficulty, the reading material must be meaningful and provide some intrinsic motivation. Additionally, the reading material must be at or below the student's level of oral language. This adaptation of the Language Experience Approach provides allowances for specific difficulties of the individual and places emphasis on what the student *can* do.

Procedure

Day 1

1. The teacher explains that the student will learn to read by using his/her own stories.

2. The student dictates an experience to the teacher. It may be necessary for the teacher to provide an experience and have the student tell about it afterward. The teacher writes the student's words exactly as spoken, but notes errors (e.g., usage) for later remediation.

3. The teacher selects part of the story to work with, depending on the amount the student can master. S/he reads the story to the student and asks for any corrections or changes.

4. The teacher reads the story to the student and then does choral reading until the student can read it independently.

5. The teacher types the story and makes a copy.

Day 2

1. The teacher provides practice in reading the typed version of the story. S/he uses choral reading and has the student read the story to others.

2. The teacher has the student read the story silently, underlining the known words.

3. The teacher has the student read the story to him/her, noting errors on the teacher's copy.

4. The teacher types the words on cards.

Day 3

1. The student practices reading the story, as in Step 1 of Day 2.

2. The teacher has the student match word cards to the individual words in the typed story.

3. The teacher sequences the words as in the story and has the student read the word cards to him/her, recording the correct words.

Day 4

1. The student repeats the procedures of practice reading and matching word cards to the story.

2. The teacher places the cards in random order and has the student read them. The teacher makes a list of the correct words.

Day 5

1. The teacher has the student read the cards in random order.

2. Using only the correct words, the student files the word cards alphabetically in a word box.

3. The teacher reads the story, has the student illustrate it, and includes it in an ongoing book of the student's language experience stories.

The student continues to review the sight words using a variety of activities (see Word Bank Activities), while starting work on a new story.

Adapted from:

Bos, C. S., & Vaughn, S. (1991). *Strategies for teaching students with learning and behavior problems* (2nd ed.). Boston: Allyn and Bacon.

Look-Spell-See-Write

Purpose

To highlight the visual image of a word for spelling.

Preparation

The word to be learned is neatly printed or written in cursive on a piece of paper or index card for the student. The word must be one the student can read easily.

1. LOOK: The student looks at the word and reads it aloud.

2. SPELL: The student says each letter of the word aloud.

3. SEE: The student looks carefully at the word, trying to "take a picture" of it, then closes his/her eyes and tries to see it.

4. WRITE: The student turns the model over, writes the word from memory, and then checks it against the model for accuracy. If the response is correct, s/he repeats this step twice more. If the response is incorrect, s/he goes back to LOOK (Step 1).

Note

The student must write the word correctly three times *consecutively* before s/he has completed study of the word.

As an added support, the model word might be written in parts for the student to study. In this case, the student would pause between parts when reading the letters aloud in the SPELL step.

Math Problem-Solving Strategy

This eight-step learning strategy was designed to teach adolescents a procedure for solving story problems. The steps of the strategy may be adjusted or modified depending upon the learner's characteristics.

Steps

1. *Read the problem aloud.* Have a teacher help you identify any unknown words.

2. *Paraphrase the problem aloud.* Reread the problem, identify the question that is asked, and summarize the information that will be important for solving the problem.

3. *Visualize.* Draw a picture of the problem or visualize the situation and tell what it is about.

4. *State the problem.* Underline the most important information in the problem and then complete the sentences: "What I know is . . . ," "What I want to find out is . . ."

5. *Hypothesize.* Complete the sentence: "If . . . , then . . ." For example, "If 7 people each want to buy 20 tickets, then I need to multiply to determine the number of tickets." For multistep problems, think through the series of steps and write the operation signs in the order they will be used.

6. *Estimate.* Write an estimate of the answer.

7. *Calculate.* Calculate the answer and label it (e.g., 140 tickets).

8. *Self-check.* Review the problem, check the computation, and ask if the answer makes sense.

Adapted from:

Montague, M., & Bos, C. S. (1986). The effect of cognitive strategy training on verbal math problem solving performance of learning disabled adolescents. *Journal of Learning Disabilities, 19,* 26-33.

Neurological Impress Method

The goal of this method is to establish fluent reading patterns. The method is used 10 to 15 minutes daily for a period of from 8 to 12 instructional hours. Heckelman (1966) noted that the method is ineffective if the student has not made some progress after 4 hours of total instruction. The method works effectively with a student whose listening comprehension is higher than his/her word recognition skill.

Steps

1. The teacher selects high-interest reading materials that are slightly below the student's grade level.

2. The teacher and student sit side-by-side with the student slightly in front of the teacher.

3. The teacher and student read material in unison. In beginning sessions, the teacher reads in a louder voice and at a slightly faster pace than the student. The teacher and student may reread initial lines or paragraphs until a normal, fluid reading pattern is established. The student is encouraged to forget about mistakes.

4. While reading, the teacher moves his/her finger under the words. Later, as skill develops, the student may track the line of print with his/her finger.

5. By the end of eight 15-minute sessions, the teacher increases the difficulty level of the material. At this time, materials at the student's frustration level may be used.

Sources:

Heckelman, R. G. (1966). Using the neurological impress reading technique. *Academic Therapy*, *1*, 235-239.

Heckelman, R. G. (1986). N.I.M. revisited. *Academic Therapy*, *21*, 411-420.

PARAGRAPH GUIDE

Topic Sentence: _____

_____

_____

Supporting Details:

1. _____

_____

_____

2. _____

_____

_____

3. _____

_____

_____

4. _____

_____

_____

Concluding or Transition Sentence: _____

_____

_____

_____

Phonics Check-off Chart

Consonants		Short Vowels		Initial Consonant Blends 2		3		Consonant Digraphs		Final Consonant Blends		Long Vowel Sounds	
b		ă		bl		scr		ch		ck		ai	
c		ȧ		br		spl		ch(k)		ng		ay	
d		ĕ		cl		spr		ph		nk		ea	
f		ĭ		cr		str		sh		tch		ee	
g		ŏ		dr		squ		th		mp		ey	
h		ŭ		dw		thr		t̶h̶		nd		oa	
j		y̆		fl		chr		wh		nt		oe	
k				fr		sch				ct		ow	
l				gl						ft		ue	
m				gr						pt		vcᶒ	
n				pl						xt		a	
p				pr						nch		e	
r				st						mpt		i	
s				sc						lth		o	
t				sl						fth		ū	
v				sm						lfth		u(o͞o)	
w				sn									
x				sp									
y				sw									
z				tr									
qu				tw									
s(z)													
soft c													
soft g													

(continued)

V	=	vowel
C	=	consonant

Phonics Check-off Chart (continued)

Vowel Diphthongs and Digraphs		Initial Silent Letters		Final Silent Letters		Word Patterns		Word Endings					
au		kn		dge		ar		le		al		cient	
aw		gn		stle		er		ly		el		ture	
ea(ĕ)		wr		scle		ir		ed(id)		able		tual	
ea(ā)		gh		mb		or		ed(d)		ation		tuate	
ei(ā)		h		mn		ur		ed(t)		er		ic	
ei(ē)		pn		bt		igh		s		ery		ity	
ey(ā)		ps		gh		eigh		s(z)		ar		ism	
eu(ōō)		rh		pt		ear		(c)le		ary		ent	
ew(ōō)		pt		lf		ind		less		or		ence	
ew(ū)				lv		old		ness		ory		ency	
ie(ē)				lk		wa		ful		tia		ant	
ie(ī)						qua		ing		tial		ance	
oi						quar		y		tian		ancy	
oy						wor		tion		tious		ia	
ōō						al		sion(sh)		tient		ial	
ŏŏ						tu		sion(zh)		sia(sh)		ian	
ou(ow)								ous		sia(zh)		ious	
ou(ōō)								ive		sial(sh)		fȳ	
ou(ō)								ile		sial(zh)			
ou(ŭ)								ice		sian(sh)			
ow								ace		sian(zh)			
ui(ōō)								ite		sient(sh)			
ui(ĭ)								ate		sient(zh)			
								ine(in)		cial			
								ine(een)		cian			
								ain(in)		cious			
										ceous			

Precision Teaching

Precision teaching is a measurement procedure that may be adapted for use with a variety of instructional materials. The instructor determines the skills for instruction, identifies the instructional goal, takes baseline measures, teaches the skill, and charts and evaluates the student's performance. This procedure is particularly appropriate for skills requiring accuracy, fluency, and maintenance, such as memorization of math facts or rapid recognition of sight words.

Steps

Use the following steps:

1. Select the behavior for change, such as memorizing multiplication facts. The behavior must be observable, repeatable, and able to occur at least 10 times during the timed period.

2. Decide how the skill will be presented (input) and how performance will be demonstrated (output). Examples of learning channels include seeing, hearing, writing, saying, thinking, etc. A worksheet of multiplication facts would have a *visual* input with a *written* output.

3. Define the goal necessary to demonstrate mastery. The goal may be determined by assessing three children who are performing the skill adequately and taking their average scores. For example, the goal on a multiplication worksheet may be to write 70 digits within a minute.

4. Design a diagnostic probe to sample a student's performance on the skill. Include more problems than can be completed in the time period. If the skill involves an oral output, a follow-along sheet is developed with spaces to score the items.

5. Determine how to score the probe. For example, on a multiplication worksheet, the number of correct digits written could be counted, as an alternative to counting the number of correctly solved problems.

The instructor may tally both the number of correct responses (c = correct) and the number of error responses (x = incorrect) on the same chart. Do not count incomplete problems as errors.

6. Administer the diagnostic probe to the student for a specified time period, usually 1 to 2 minutes, for 3 to 5 days, to establish a baseline. Draw a vertical line on the chart after the baseline data.

7. Analyze the student's performance. Determine if the skill level is appropriate. If not, go back to an easier skill. If so, continue with the skill and begin instruction.

8. Identify the student's learning stage. If the student is in the acquisition phase, the count correct is gradually increasing; for the fluency stage, the number correct is two times greater than the number of errors; and in the maintenance stage, the predetermined goal has been met.

9. Record the student's daily performance and graph the results on an equal-interval chart or a semilogarithmic chart where the vertical axis is scaled with proportional distances between numbers.

10. Select an appropriate intervention based on the student's learning stage. Examples for the acquisition stage include prompting, cueing, modeling, and demonstrating; for the fluency stage, drill activities and reinforcers; for the maintenance stage, practical opportunities to apply the skill.

11. Administer the probe daily or at least three times weekly and chart the results. Use the same probe until the goal is met.

12. Analyze and evaluate the charting of the student's learning patterns frequently to determine whether instructional changes should be made. Draw a vertical line on the chart any time a change in intervention is made.

Adapted from:

Algozzine, B. (1990). *Problem behavior management*. Rockville, MD: Aspen.

Name: _____

Precision Teaching Graph

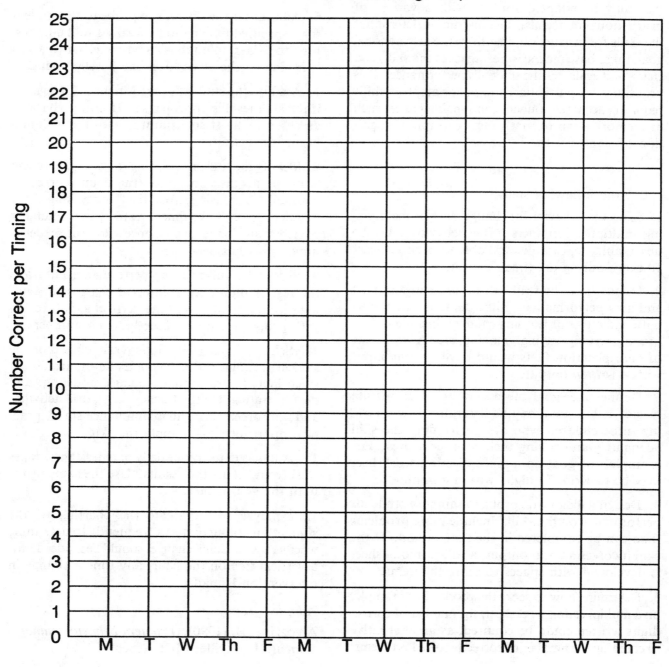

Number Correct per Timing

0 1 2 3 4 5 6 7 8 9 10 11 12 13 14 15 16 17 18 19 20 21 22 23 24 25

M T W Th F M T W Th F M T W Th F

One-Minute Timings

Name: _____

Precision Teaching Graph

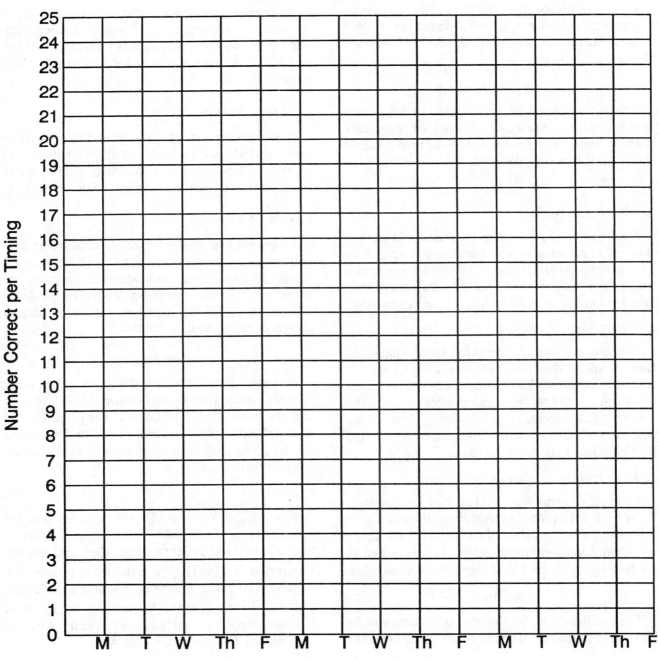

Two-Minute Timings

PReP: Prereading Plan

Purpose

PReP is a prelearning group activity for assessing students' background knowledge on a topic before starting a new unit or reading selection (Langer, 1981).

Preparation

The teacher reviews the material to be taught and selects a word, phrase, or picture that represents the key concept to be presented. S/he then presents the stimulus to the students.

Steps

1. Initial Association

The teacher asks the students to tell anything they think of in association with the stimulus and writes all responses on the board. The teacher may place a student's name next to his/her comments to facilitate later evaluation of each student's prior knowledge.

2. Reflections

The teacher asks the students to explain what made them think of the responses they gave in Step 1. In this step, the students consciously connect their prior knowledge to the concept presented by the teacher and elaborate their knowledge through the responses of other students. The teacher encourages participation from each student.

3. Reformation of Knowledge

After all students have shared their associations, the teacher asks them to think about the discussion and tell any new ideas about the topic. This step allows for elaboration and modification of ideas as well as the association of new knowledge to prior knowledge.

Evaluation

The teacher evaluates the level of students' prior knowledge to find out whether or not further concept building is needed prior to reading or teaching the unit.

1. Much Knowledge

Responses reflecting knowledge of superordinate concepts for the topic (e.g., "type of geographical region" for *desert*) or related to the topic, definitions, and analogies indicate knowledge adequate for good comprehension.

2. Some Knowledge

Responses concerning examples and characteristics indicate that comprehension may be adequate but should be supported with activities to strengthen the association between new and prior knowledge.

3. Little Knowledge

Responses based on word associations rather than concept associations (e.g., affixes, rhymes) or on unrelated experiences indicate that instructional activities are required to enrich students' knowledge of the superordinate concept before reading is assigned or the unit is taught.

Comments

Although PReP was not designed with a post-learning component, Bos and Vaughn (1991) suggest that the initial PReP list be reviewed after the unit is completed to allow students to add to and modify the list, bringing to a conscious level the newly learned information.

Sources:

Bos, C. S., & Vaughn, S. (1991). *Strategies for teaching students with learning and behavior problems* (2nd ed.). Boston: Allyn and Bacon.

Langer, J. A. (1981). From theory to practice: A prereading plan. *Journal of Reading, 25,* 152-156.

Langer, J. A. (1984). Examining background knowledge and text comprehension. *Reading Research Quarterly, 19,* 468-481.

Presenting Technique

The Presenting Technique is a prereading method designed to provide a foundation for the reading process. This method may be effective for children with language impairments or for English as a Second Language students.

Steps

To begin, a simple story is selected.

1. The student sits across from the teacher. The teacher reads aloud a short paragraph or two from a story three times as the student watches the teacher's face.

2. The teacher paraphrases the story using vocabulary that will be understood by the student.

3. The teacher rereads the original passage.

4. Using cueing, the teacher has the student retell as much of the story as s/he can remember.

5. The teacher reads a short phrase or sentence and has the student repeat back the material. The length is determined by the ability of the student to repeat back the words.

After this procedure, the teacher may read short phrases or sentences with the student in unison. Once skill is gained with this technique, the teacher may use the Neurological Impress Method, reading the entire story with the student in unison.

Source:

Heckelman, R. G. (1986). N.I.M. revisited. *Academic Therapy*, *21*, 411-420.

Reciprocal Teaching

Reciprocal Teaching was designed for middle school students with adequate reading decoding but depressed comprehension skills. The focus of this technique is on developing critical thinking skills through the medium of reading. The student learns to set a purpose for reading, read for meaning, and self-monitor comprehension.

The specific skills the student learns through this process are generating questions, summarizing, requesting clarification, and predicting upcoming information. Through the questioning and summarizing, the teacher is able to judge the student's ability to extract key information from text. The clarifying step allows the teacher to evaluate the student's comprehension. The predicting step prompts the student to activate current information as a link with incoming information.

Steps

1. The teacher explains the procedure to the student and models the steps. Subsequently, the teacher and student alternate in the leader role.

2. The teacher and the student read a segment of text.

3. The person in the role of leader asks questions similar to those s/he would expect to find on a test.

4. The leader summarizes the content of the segment of text.

5. The leader brings up any difficult parts of the text or material s/he did not understand. These are discussed with the partner.

6. The leader makes a prediction as to the content of the next segment of text.

7. Both readers read the next segment and repeat the process with the other partner taking the lead.

Guidelines

1. Although the teacher models the skills that the students need to use within this procedure, often the teacher may need to prompt and instruct the student in asking questions about key ideas rather than details, reporting key ideas in the summary, and recognizing what was difficult about the passage. The teacher also may need to modify parts of the task until the student can function effectively in the leader role.

2. The teacher always provides instruction concerning questioning, summarizing, clarifying, and predicting within the context of the Reciprocal Teaching process.

3. The teacher must provide feedback consistently on the student's progress in performing the role of the leader.

4. Reciprocal Teaching is often taught in 30-minute sessions.

Modifications

1. Reciprocal Teaching may be applied to content area materials.

2. Reciprocal Teaching may be used as a listening-thinking activity if the teacher reads the material to the student. When presented orally, this technique may be used for younger students and students with reading decoding or language comprehension problems.

Sources:

Palincsar, A. S., & Brown, A. L. (1984). Reciprocal teaching of comprehension-fostering and comprehension-monitoring activities. *Cognition and Instruction, 1,* 117-175.

Palincsar, A. S., & Brown, A. L. (1986). Interactive teaching to promote independent learning from text. *Reading Teacher, 39,* 771-777.

Repeated Readings

The repeated readings technique may be used to improve fluency in reading by increasing accuracy and rate. A graph or chart is used to provide visual reinforcement.

This technique may be appropriate for students who read slowly despite adequate word recognition, are unmotivated, or have listening comprehension ability higher than reading comprehension ability.

Procedure

1. Select a passage of from 50 to 150 words from a book that is at the student's instructional reading level.

2. The student reads the selection orally while the teacher times the reading and counts the number of words that are pronounced incorrectly. The teacher may provide assistance with unknown words as needed.

3. The student's reading time and the number of words pronounced incorrectly are recorded on a chart.

4. The student looks over the selection, rereads it, and practices words that caused difficulty in the initial reading.

5. The teacher and student set goals for both reading speed and accuracy. Or, as an alternative, the teacher and student may decide on a certain number of times the passage will be reread.

6. The student repeatedly practices reading the selection, charting progress after each trial. When the predetermined goal is reached, a new selection may be used and the procedure is repeated.

Sources:

Neill, K. (1979). Turn kids on with repeated reading. *Teaching Exceptional Children, 12,* 63-64.

Samuels, S. J. (1979). The method of repeated readings. *Reading Teacher, 32,* 403-408.

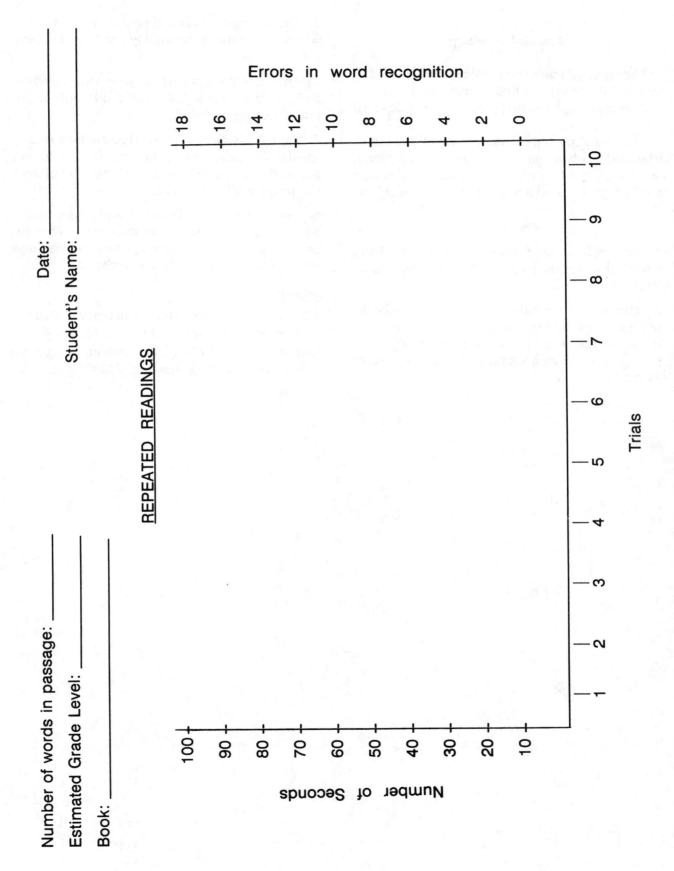

Number of words in passage: _____

Estimated Grade Level: _____

Book: _____

REPEATED READINGS

Date: _____

Student's Name: _____

Errors in word recognition

18 16 14 12 10 8 6 4 2 0

10 9 8 7 6 5 4 3 2 1

Trials

100 90 80 70 60 50 40 30 20 10

Number of Seconds

REPORT CHART

Name: _____

Title: _____

Introduction: _____

_____

Subtopics:

#1 _____

#2 _____

#3 _____

_____

Details: _____

Details: _____

Details: _____

_____

_____

_____

_____

_____

Conclusion: _____

_____

REPORT GUIDE

Name: _____

Topic:

Subtopics:

References I Used

ReQuest Procedure

The purposes of this Reciprocal Questioning procedure are to help students set their own goals for reading and to teach students to raise questions independently.

Before beginning, the teacher and student discuss a purpose for reading the selection. The teacher models questioning behavior and provides direct feedback to the student regarding his/her questions. Questions may require factual recall, recognition, evaluation, and critical thinking. As the procedure is continued, the teacher asks questions that will help the student integrate and evaluate prior sentences.

Steps

1. Both the teacher and the student read the first sentence of a passage silently.

2. The student and teacher alternate asking questions. The teacher closes his/her book and the student asks the teacher as many questions as s/he can think of about the sentence and what it means.

3. The student closes his/her book and the teacher asks as many questions as s/he can think of to enhance the student's understanding. The teacher models good questioning behavior. In addition to asking detail questions about the passage, the teacher can ask questions that require the student to relate his/her own experiences to information in the passage.

4. The process is continued sentence by sentence until the student can provide a reasonable prediction of what is going to happen in the rest of the selection. At this point, the teacher says, "Finish the selection to see if you were correct."

5. After the student has completed the passage, discuss whether the purpose raised initially was the best one for the selection.

Sources:

Manzo, A. V. (1969). The ReQuest procedure. *Journal of Reading, 13*, 123-126.

Manzo, A. V. (1985). Expansion modules for the ReQuest, CAT, GRP, and REAP reading/study procedures. *Journal of Reading, 28*, 498-502.

ReQuest Procedure (Modified)

The purpose of this modified ReQuest procedure is to help students develop verbal reasoning skills and build active reading skills. This approach is appropriate for older students with more advanced reading skills.

Preparation

Choose a literature selection at the student's independent reading level that is short enough that it can be finished by the end of the teaching session. Prepare comprehension questions pertaining to the literature selection or use questions provided in the teacher's manual or text. Include a mixture of literal, inferential, and evaluative questions.

Steps

1. Read the first two paragraphs of the selection with the student using the following procedure: (a) teacher and student read the first sentence silently; (b) student asks the teacher as many questions as s/he can think of about the first sentence and the teacher answers each; (c) teacher asks as many questions as possible pertaining to the first sentence and the student answers or tells why a question cannot be answered. If the question can be answered, the teacher provides the answer. Proceed sentence by sentence through two paragraphs.

2. After two paragraphs have been read, the student asks a question pertaining to the outcome of the story or chapter. The teacher or student writes the question.

3. The teacher and student finish reading the selection silently, and the student answers the outcome question.

4. The student answers the comprehension questions orally (to the teacher or on tape) or in writing. The type of response is the student's choice.

5. The teacher tells the student what his/her overall accuracy and accuracy by level of question results are. Results are recorded on a chart.

6. The student rereads parts of the selection to correct the incorrect responses. The missed questions are answered orally.

When the student consistently reaches 80% accuracy on the comprehension questions, raise the readability of the materials to the instructional level.

Adapted from:

Alley, G. R., & Hori, K. O. (1981). *Effects of teaching a questioning strategy on reading comprehension of learning disabled adolescents* (Report No. 52). Lawrence, KS: Institute for Research in Learning Disabilities, University of Kansas.

Manzo, A. V. (1969). The ReQuest procedure. *Journal of Reading, 13,* 123-126.

Semantic Feature Analysis: Concepts

Purpose

Semantic Feature Analysis is a prelearning activity designed to activate students' prior knowledge of a topic, introduce and organize the key concepts and vocabulary, and help the students relate new information to familiar information. This approach was designed for use with adolescents in content area classes.

Steps

A. *Preparation: Developing the Relationship Chart*

1. Having chosen a topic for study, the teacher reads the material to be introduced to the class and identifies the most important concepts.

2. The teacher chooses vocabulary that will be necessary for the students to know in order to understand the key concepts. The teacher then omits the vocabulary that the students are likely to know already.

3. The teacher now develops a relationship chart — a grid with the key concepts written across the top and the key vocabulary listed down the side. A code is placed on the top of the page:

    + = positive relationship
    − = negative relationship
    0 = no relationship
    ? = unsure, need more information

(See Figure A–1, Semantic Feature Analysis Chart, "Consumer Credit.")

Each student receives a copy of the relationship chart and the teacher uses an overhead projector for the model chart.

B. *Introducing the Concepts and Vocabulary*

1. The teacher introduces the main topic and encourages discussion concerning students' knowledge of and experience with the topic. For example, in a consumer education class, the teacher might introduce a unit on credit. Students then would discuss what they know about credit.

2. The teacher introduces the key concepts across the top of the relationship chart, encouraging discussion and predictions on how each concept relates to the main topic. If students are unable to generate adequate definitions, the teacher explains the key concepts to them.

3. The teacher introduces the key vocabulary, encouraging discussion and predictions as to how

NAME: _____
DATE: _____

CONSUMER CREDIT

RELATIONSHIP CHART

+ = positive relation
− = negative relation
0 = unrelated
? = unsure

	Definition of credit	How to get credit	Advantages of credit	Disadvantages of credit	Consumer protection	Business protection
payment terms	+	0	+	+	+	+
Truth-in-Lending Law	0	?	0	?	+	0
balance (of a debt)	?	+	?	0	0	+
credit risk	0	+	?	+	0	+
credit reporting bureau	0	+	+	?	−	+
Fair Credit Reporting Act (1971)	?	?	?	?	?	0
Equal Credit Opportunity Act (1974)	0	+	?	0	?	0
credit record	0	+	?	+	0	+
starter account	+	+	0	0	+	+
credit rating	0	+	?	?	?	+
finance charges (interest)	+	+	−	+	?	+
consumer	+	0	+	0	+	0

Figure A–1.

each word relates to the main concept. Again, discussion is guided so that the teacher helps the students generate the definitions of the words or tells them the definition.

C. *Predicting Relationships*

1. Starting with the first word in the vocabulary list, the teacher guides discussion and tries to gain consensus regarding the relationship between the vocabulary and each of the key concepts. The students may decide that the relationship between the two is positive or negative, or that no relationship exists between the two. If the class does not have sufficient knowledge of a vocabulary/concept pair to make a good prediction, a question mark is placed in the box. Students are always required to provide support for their decisions.

2. When all of the vocabulary–concept relationships have been discussed, the students read the

assignment with the intention of verifying their predictions, changing incorrect predictions, and finding information to help them fill in the boxes with question marks.

3. After reading, the teacher and students review the chart, confirming correct responses and changing responses where necessary.

Comments

Research with adolescents with learning disabilities has demonstrated that Semantic Feature Analysis is more effective than traditional vocabulary study strategies for learning of new vocabulary and conceptual comprehension of text.

Sources:

Anders, P. L., & Bos, C. S. (1986). Semantic feature analysis: An interactive strategy for vocabulary and text comprehension. *Journal of Reading, 29,* 610-616.

Bos, C. S., Anders, P. L., Filip, D., & Jaffe, L. E. (1989). The effects of an interactive instructional strategy for enhancing reading comprehension and content area learning for students with learning disabilities. *Journal of Learning Disabilities, 22,* 384-390.

Johnson, D. D., & Pearson, P. D. (1984). *Teaching reading vocabulary* (2nd ed.). New York: Holt, Rinehart, and Winston.

Semantic Feature Analysis: Vocabulary

The purpose of this activity is to guide students in analyzing the meanings of specific words while integrating the meanings of new words into their vocabularies. When introducing this activity, use categories that are concrete and within the experience of the students. Later, progress to less familiar or more abstract categories.

Steps

1. Select a category that relates to a topic to be studied or a reading selection. Select key words related to the topic.

2. Make a chart with a topic heading at the top, key words listed down the side, and columns across the page. Head some of the columns with terms that represent features shared by some of the words.

Example:

Transportation in History

	wheels	engine	computer
horses	−	−	−
carriages	+	−	−
bicycle	+	−	−
car	+	+	+
train	+	+	+
airplane	+	+	+

3. Have the students place a plus or minus sign in each column across from each word, depending on whether or not the word has the feature heading the column. A question mark may be used if the student cannot guess at the relationship.

4. Have the students discuss each word, why they chose a plus or minus, and how the word is similar to or different from the other words on the list.

5. Provide the planned lesson (e.g., lecture, reading, video).

6. Based on the information in the lesson, have the students change the signs in the matrix or fill in those that had been left blank.

7. Guide a discussion about the relationship between the words and features. During the discussion, use a class chart shown on an overhead projector or drawn on the board, and fill in the signs that have attained group consensus.

Optional Steps

The following steps may be included after Steps 3 or 7:

1. Have the students add words to the list that fit the category.

2. Have the students add shared features in the empty columns.

3. Have the students complete the matrix with pluses and minuses.

Modification

When students become familiar with this activity, they may use a 10-point scale, rather than pluses or minuses, to indicate the degree of relationship between words and features (Johnson & Pearson, 1984).

Adapted from:

Johnson, D. D., & Pearson, P. D. (1984). *Teaching reading vocabulary* (2nd ed.). New York: Holt, Rinehart, and Winston.

Semantic Maps: Designing

Introduction

The design of a semantic map can take as many forms as the imagination can generate. All should, however, represent the organizational pattern of the text, lecture, or composition represented. On the following pages, a variety of semantic maps are presented.

Concepts may be described in three levels. Superordinate concepts are those ideas that are most inclusive and abstract; subordinate concepts are the most narrow or concrete ideas; coordinate concepts connect the two levels (Bos & Vaughn, 1991).

Superordinate concepts might be compared with the overall concept for a chapter in a book, the coordinate concepts with the section titles, and the subordinate concepts with the section subheadings. The next level of information is referred to as details.

Constructing Semantic Maps

The method of constructing a semantic map will depend on how well-organized a student's concepts are, initially, regarding the topic at hand. If s/he has knowledge of the major categories, but needs to fill out the information, s/he may use the Concept-Based model. A student who has little grasp of overall concepts, but many details, would use the Detail-Based model; a student with a good grasp of the structure may use the Pattern-Based model.

A. Concept-Based Semantic Maps

If using this type of construction, the student already has the superordinate concept, the coordinate concepts, and perhaps some of the subordinate concepts. This situation would occur when: (a) the student is using the headings and subheadings in a well-organized text; (b) s/he is preparing to write or take notes about a topic with which s/he is sufficiently familiar to generate major categories; or (c) the teacher has provided an advance organizer for a lecture, including the major concepts to be covered.

1. The student writes a label for the superordinate concept, placing it on the page where other information can be written around it. The student then draws a shape (e.g., circle, square) around the label and lines extending from it. The number of lines corresponds to the number of coordinate concepts identified. (See Figure A-2.)

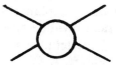

Figure A–2.

2. Next, a shape is drawn at the end of each line and key words for the coordinate concepts are written in. (See Figure A-3.)

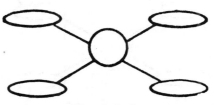

Figure A–3.

3. The student considers the subordinate concepts s/he has and decides which ones relate to which coordinate concepts. Alternatively, s/he may group the subordinate concepts by similarities and then look to see if the given coordinate concepts provide adequate headings (category labels) for each of the groups. If so, outlines and labels for the subordinate concepts should be attached by lines to the appropriate coordinate concepts. If a group of subordinate concepts does not match any of the coordinate concepts, a new coordinate concept may be created and labeled. (See Figure A-4.)

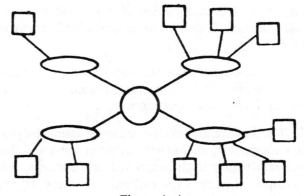

Figure A–4.

4. At this point, any other information to be added to the map (e.g., details remembered, given in the text, or collected in the student's research) should be attached to the appropriate subordinate concept. These details should be outlined and labeled by

key words. If any of the details require the addition of descriptive or explanatory information, another level of detail will be attached by lines to the previous level of detail with which they are associated. (See Figure A-5).

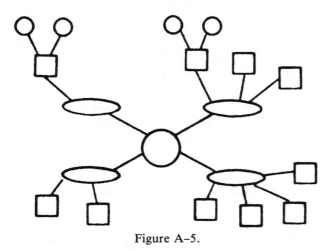

Figure A–5.

The map is then completed and may be used as a study guide or as the basis for writing.

B. *Detail-Based*

The student is able to brainstorm many details concerning a topic about which s/he has read or about which s/he wants to write, but has not conceptualized an organizational pattern to tie them together.

1. The student writes down the superordinate concept for textual information s/he has read, a lecture s/he has heard, or a composition s/he is going to write.

2. The student brainstorms and writes down any details (subordinate concepts) s/he can remember or has included in written notes.

3. The student groups the separate details by putting together those that are similar in some way that will relate them to the superordinate concept. For example, if the superordinate concept is the Southwest and the details include hot climate, Navaho, sandy soil, javelina, Pima, scarcity of water, prairie dogs, and Tohono O'Odham, the details would be grouped as follows:

hot climate	Navaho	javelina
sandy soil	Pima	prairie dogs
scarcity of water	Tohono O'Odham	

Details may be grouped by listing them and then giving the same number to all those sharing the relevant characteristic (coordinate concept). Or, the list may be cut apart into separate strips of paper and grouped.

4. The student then labels the coordinate concept that delineates the relationship among the subordinate concepts.

5. Having started at the level of the narrowest concepts, a level of concepts may be needed between the coordinate concepts and the superordinate concept. Another higher level of coordinate concepts may be obtained by grouping the lower coordinate concepts in the same manner as the subordinate concepts were grouped and labeled in Steps 3 and 4. Alternatively, one of the groups of subordinate concepts may be subsumed under another group. For example, the student may decide that desert animals should be subsumed under desert along with other concepts such as desert plants. Figure A-6 presents a semantic map and subsequent rough draft of a composition about a sailing trip written by a fourth-grade student with learning disabilities.

C. *Pattern-Based*

If the student has clearly conceptualized the organizational pattern for the reading material, lecture, or written piece s/he is planning, s/he may start by drawing a format for the map, labeling the parts as s/he embellishes or adds to the design. Figures A-7 and A-8 illustrate this approach showing maps of an autobiography and a literary comparison between two stories from the *Canterbury Tales*. Figure A-9 provides an illustration of several uses of semantic mapping.

Adapted from:

Bos, C. S., & Vaughn, S. (1991). *Strategies for teaching students with learning and behavior problems* (2nd ed.). Boston: Allyn and Bacon.

Buckley, M. H., & Boyle, O. (1981). *Mapping the writing journey*. Berkeley: University of California Berkeley/Bay Area Writing Project, Curriculum Publication No. 15.

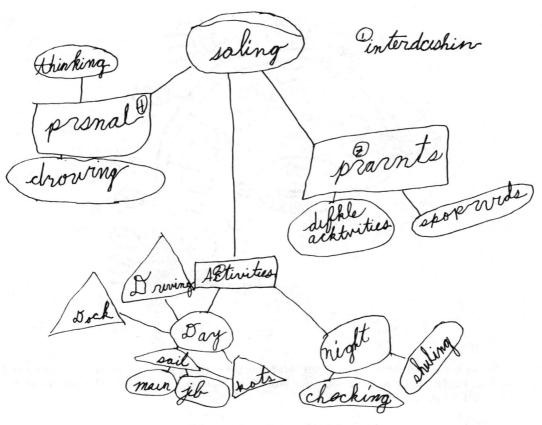

First Draft: Sailing

I went to Seatle Washingtion. My brothers live there. I
sailed becuse I wonted to go and my dad wanted to go. The places
I went to were mansinda, Port tonwson, Grisn bay, Pnter Islind,
Vicktorea, Vancover Islind, Pnter Islind, Susia, Bling Ham,
Everit.
    Sailing a baat is a lot of fun but it's hard. I drive the
boat. driving is fun. You get to ame the boat but yau have to
be ded ackerit.
    It's hard to dock the boat. You have to get lines and tie
speshl knots. I like to jump off the boat to the dock. I love
to do a good job. I love to get off the boat to the dock. I
like to dock the boat.
    A knot is inportent because it's inporten for the boat. A
knot called the steavidor and a crazy eight knot is inporten
becuse it holds the rope from slipping through a hole. The quare
knot is used in holding two ropes together. a clovhich is
inportent because it holds the buppers in place.
    The sails are hard to put up but they look neet. The sails
are hard to put up becuase it's hard to pull the rope whthout
fulling off the boat. ther are two kinds of sail three sizes.
the big jib is neet but the little jib isn't. The mine sail is
prity.
    The night is diferen you have to moter. You need check the
boat. like chick if you'd put a light on the bow polput. shuting
the boat mean to put little slits of wood in a hach.

Figure A–6. Map and First Draft of a Composition Written by a Fourth-Grade Boy with Learning Disabilities.

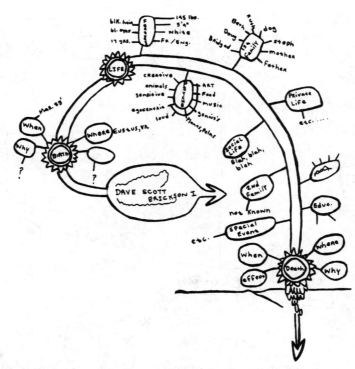

Figure A-7. Map for an Autobiography. *Note.* From "Mapping the Writing Journey" by M. H. Buckley and O. Boyle, 1981, Bay Area Writing Project, Curriculum Publication No. 15, p. 18. Copyright 1981 by The Regents of the University of California. Reprinted by permission.

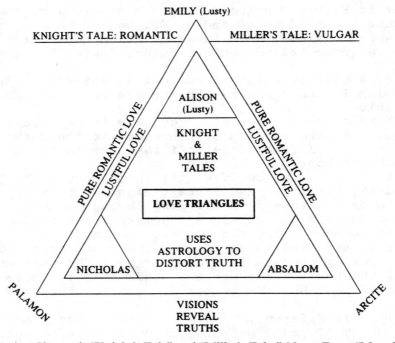

Figure A-8. Map comparing Chaucer's "Knight's Tale" and "Miller's Tale." *Note.* From "Mapping the Writing Journey" by M. H. Buckley and O. Boyle, 1981, Bay Area Writing Project, Curriculum Publication No. 15, p. 31. Copyright 1981 by the Regents of the University of California. Reprinted by permission.

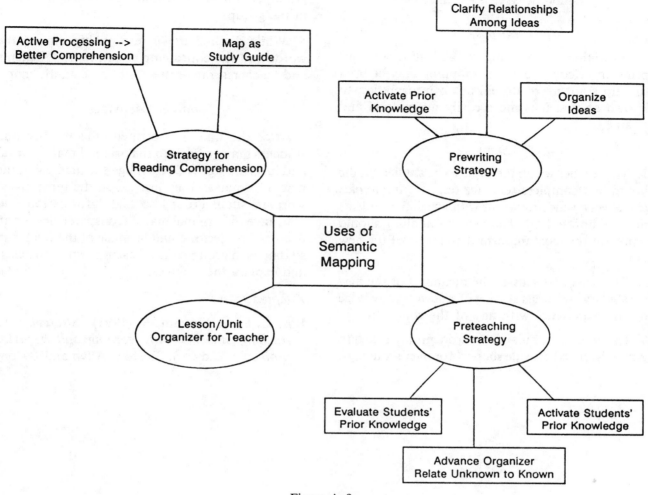

Figure A–9.

Semantic Maps: Evaluating/Activating Prior Knowledge

Purpose

The teacher may use semantic mapping to activate and evaluate the prior knowledge of the students regarding the topic to be studied.

Steps

1. The teacher writes the major concept to be studied (superordinate concept) on the board.

2. The teacher elicits from the students all words and phrases they associate with the topic, making sure that everyone participates. All student responses are listed on the board.

3. The teacher asks the students which words/phrases go together in some way. Students must explain their rationale for the groupings they suggest. The words/phrases are then grouped as suggested.

4. Students are asked to label the groups. These labels become the coordinate concepts associating the details (subordinate concepts) with the superordinate concept.

5. As the students suggest groupings and labels, the teacher generates a semantic map.

6. Based on the students' responses to the mapping activity, the teacher decides whether or not preteaching of concepts and related vocabulary is necessary before presenting the unit or assigning the reading.

Semantic Maps: Organizers

Purpose

In addition to evaluating and activating students' prior knowledge, semantic mapping may be used to help students relate unknown information to known so that it is more easily understood and retained.

Steps

1. The teacher writes the topic to be studied on the board in a complete sentence (e.g., *Life abounds in the desert*) and any words with which the students may be unfamiliar. The new vocabulary should represent the most important concepts of the new unit.

2. The teacher discusses the meanings of the new vocabulary and elicits sharing of students' knowledge of and experience with any of the concepts.

3. Using the vocabulary, the students are asked to group them and provide support for their groupings.

4. Students are asked to provide a label for each group, describing the relationship among the words in the group.

5. While discussing the relationship among the words and the coordinate concepts, the students and teacher arrange them into a semantic map.

Follow-up Activities

After the unit is presented, the teacher and students may go back to the original map and: (a) add information and rearrange the map using the new information they learned in the unit; or (b) work in small groups to add information and rearrange the original map. Transparencies for an overhead projector could be made of the final map so that each group could present them to the class and explain the changes.

Adapted from:

Bos, C. S., & Vaughn, S. (1991). *Strategies for teaching students with learning and behavior problems* (2nd ed.). Boston: Allyn and Bacon.

Sentence Comprehension: Analysis of Sentence Forms

Activity #1

This activity may be used to familiarize the student with a variety of sentence structures (e.g., embedded relative clauses, complex with conjunctive/adjunctive ties) and to form a basis for practice and use in oral language.

Steps

1. Provide the student with a complex sentence representing the structure to be analyzed, and four phrases, some that contain the information in the sentence and some that do not.
    Example:
    The dolphins that were caught in the tuna net struggled to reach the surface.
       a. dolphins were caught in the net
       b. tuna were caught in the net
       c. dolphins struggled to reach the surface
       d. the tuna net was on the surface

2. Have the student choose which information is included in the target sentence and defend his/her choices.

Modifications

1. For discussion purposes, include an inference statement in the multiple-choice phrases.

2. Ask the student to segment the sentence and tell the pieces of information without choices (i.e., "Who did what?").

3. When the student is ready, present sentences orally, in context, and have the student interpret their meanings.

Note

Move the student from simpler to more complex sentence structures, such as:

1. One noun with an embedded relative clause (e.g., *The girl who played catcher had a strong arm*).

2. Two nouns with an embedded relative clause (e.g., *The girl who played catcher argued with the umpire*).

3. Two nouns with an embedded relative clause and possibly confusing word order (e.g., *The girl who played catcher was removed from the game by the umpire*).

Activity #2

This activity may also be used to familiarize students with a variety of sentence constructions (e.g., embedded relative clauses, conjunctive/adjunctive ties) and to form a basis for practice and use in oral language.

The teacher needs two sets of picture sequences for each target sentence and a variety of complex sentences that correspond to the type of sentence structure to be learned.

Steps

1. Present a complex sentence in oral or written form, depending on the developmental level of the student, along with the two sequences of pictures.
    Example: adjoining - because
       Because his friends were outside, David decided to go out to play.

    The two picture sequences would show:
       a. friends outside
          David looking out window
          David outside
       b. David outside
          friends outside
          David inside
    Example: relative clause
       The eagle that flew over the hawk grabbed the rabbit.

    The two picture sequences would show:
       a. eagle flying over hawk
          eagle grabbing rabbit
       b. eagle flying over hawk
          hawk grabbing rabbit

2. Ask the student to show which picture sequence matches the target sentence.

Modifications

For students with more advanced language abilities, the task may be changed so that the student is asked to select one of two sentences to match a given set of pictures.
    Example:
       The eagle that flew over the hawk grabbed the rabbit.
       The eagle flew over the hawk that grabbed the rabbit.
    Picture sequence:
       eagle flying over hawk   eagle grabbing rabbit

Note

Increase the level of structural complexity in a planned sequence. Provide oral practice in contextualized situations before decontextualized situations.

Adapted from:

Wallach, G. P., & Miller, L. (1988). *Language intervention and academic success*. Boston: Little, Brown and Company.

Sentence Comprehension: Order of Events

The purpose of these activities is to provide practice in using conjoining and adjoining conjunctions to interpret the order in which events happen in a sentence regardless of the order of mention (e.g., *Before you come into the house, take off your muddy shoes* rather than *Take off your muddy shoes before you come into the house*).

Activity #1

Steps

1. Provide a sentence (written or spoken) and unsequenced pictures or printed phrases that represent the events in the sentence.

2. Have the student assemble the pictures or phrases to represent the sequence of events described in the sentence.

3. Have the student explain the reasons for his/her choices.

4. Have the student make up other sentences in the same pattern.

Guidelines

1. First, use probable event sequences; second, use event sequences out of probable order; finally, use event sequences that are reversible.
   Examples:
   a. When he fell off his bike, the boy broke his arm.
   b. The boy broke his arm when he fell off his bike.
   c. The boy fell off his bike when he hit a rock. (This sentence is reversible, as *When the boy fell off his bike, he hit a rock* would also make sense.)

2. As far as possible, use vocabulary and/or sentences from the student's curriculum materials.

3. Combine oral and written work.

4. Use pictures for younger children or those with lower language levels. Use written sentences and phrases for older students who have adequate reading ability.

Modifications

1. In oral sentences, use vocal stress to emphasize key words; in written sentences, color-code key words.

2. Color-code the agent of the action.

3. Provide a short story so that the student has a larger context in which to interpret the sentence.

Activity #2

Steps

1. Provide one connecting word or phrase and a variety of clauses. Help the student combine them into complex sentences.

2. Provide a variety of previously studied connecting words or phrases. Also supply a variety of clauses. Help the student combine the clauses and connecting words/phrases into many complex sentences.

3. Provide complex sentences in which the connecting words/phrases are incorrect or the order of events is incorrect. Ask the student to correct the sentences (e.g., *The car had a flat tire because we couldn't drive it*).

Guidelines

When asking students to correct sentences, be aware that:

1. Content changes occur at earlier developmental levels (e.g., *The car had a flat tire because it ran over glass*).

2. Connective changes occur at all developmental levels (e.g., *The car had a flat tire and so we couldn't drive it*).

3. Clausal changes occur at later developmental levels (e.g., *We couldn't drive the car because it had a flat tire*).

Source:

Wallach, G. P., & Miller, L. (1988). *Language intervention and academic success*. Boston: Little, Brown and Company.

Sight Word Association Procedure (SWAP)

The SWAP procedure is a supplemental activity for teaching sight vocabulary to the automatic level. Responses are charted on a record sheet. (See sample on next page.)

Steps

1. Write 5 to 10 words on index cards. Discuss the meaning of the words with the student.

2. Present each word for 5 seconds and say the word twice.

3. Shuffle the cards and ask the student to identify the words.

4. Supply the correct response if an error is made or if the student doesn't respond in 5 seconds.

5. Repeat Step 2.

Continue until the student easily identifies all words. To ensure retention, review the words for several days. As words are learned, they may be filed in a word box.

This procedure may be adapted by using flash cards with a word and picture on one side and only the word on the other side.

Source:

Bos, C. S., & Vaughn, S. (1991). *Strategies for teaching students with learning and behavior problems* (2nd ed.). Boston: Allyn and Bacon.

Simultaneous Oral Spelling (SOS)

This method is an adaptation of the SOS procedure described by Gillingham and Stillman (1973). In this adaptation, the student immediately begins with familiar words from his/her own vocabulary, even if sound–symbol associations are not known.

Steps

1. The student proposes a word that s/he wants to learn.

2. The word is written for the student or made with plastic script letters.

3. The student pronounces the word and says the letter names.

4. The student covers the word as soon as s/he thinks s/he can write the word from memory, saying the alphabetic name of each letter of the word as it is written.

5. The student says the word and checks to see that it is written correctly. The student repeats Steps 2–5 twice more.

6. The student practices the word in this way for 6 consecutive days.

Adapted from:

Bradley, L. (1981). The organization of motor patterns for spelling: An effective remedial strategy for backward spellers. *Developmental Medicine and Child Neurology*, *23*, 83-91.

Gillingham, A., & Stillman, B. W. (1973). *Remedial training for children with specific disability in reading, spelling, and penmanship.* Cambridge, MA: Educators Publishing Service.

SWAP Record Sheet

Sight Words	Trials					Retention		
	1	2	3	4	5	1	2	3

Adapted from:

Bos, C.S., & Vaughn, S. (1991). <u>Strategies for teaching students with learning and behavior problems</u> (2nd ed.). Boston: Allyn and Bacon.

Spelling Flow List

The purpose of using a spelling flow list is to provide systematic instruction and review to promote mastery of spelling words. The spelling list changes as the student learns each word.

Steps

1. Identify three to six words that the student uses in his/her writing to practice.

2. List the words on the spelling flow list form.

3. Have the student study the words and then test the student on the words.

4. Mark each correctly spelled word with a "C" and each incorrectly spelled word with a check.

5. Provide daily testing and practice with the words.

6. When a word is spelled correctly 3 days in a row, cross it off the list and add a new word.

7. Provide periodic review as needed.

Mastered words can be filed alphabetically into a word bank. Provide periodic review of words to ensure retention.

Adapted from:

McCoy, K. M., & Prehm, H. J. (1987). *Teaching mainstreamed students: Methods and techniques.* Denver: Love.

Name _____

Spelling Flow List

Study Words	M	T	W	T	F	M	T	W	T	F	M	T	W	T	F

C = Correct
✓ = Incorrect

Spelling Stories

The purpose of this activity is to provide reinforcement of spelling skills within the context of stories. The game may be used to practice words from a spelling list, an individualized spelling list, or a high-frequency list. Write the words to be practiced on index cards or on strips of tagboard.

Steps

1. Pair students together to play the game. Provide students with a pencil and sheet of lined paper. Place the stack of word cards between them.

2. The first student draws a word card and then writes a sentence to begin the story that uses the word. When the student writes the spelling word, s/he looks at the word, turns over the card, and attempts to write the word from memory on a piece of paper. The spelling is then checked and the procedure continued until the word is written correctly. The student reads his/her sentence aloud.

3. The second student draws a word card and writes the next sentence in the story writing his/her spelling word from memory. The second student then reads the two sentences.

4. The players continue to draw word cards and write and read the sentences until all cards are used and the story is completed.

5. As a final step, the students may want to edit their stories, illustrate them, and/or read them aloud to the class.

Adapted from:

Forte, I., & Pangle, M. A. (1985). *Selling spelling to kids: Motivating games and activities to reinforce spelling skills*. Nashville, TN: Incentive Publications.

SQ3R

The Survey, Question, Read, Recite, Review (SQ3R) study procedure provides students with a systematic, efficient strategy that promotes independent study skills. The method may be most appropriate for students in grade 4 and above who are studying content chapters in textbooks.

Steps

1. Survey

Skim or preview the chapter to gain a general understanding of the chapter. Read introductory paragraphs, all headings, captions, graphs, and summary paragraphs. Attempt to determine what the chapter is about and the kind of information that the author is presenting. Depending upon the reader's skill and the length and complexity of the chapter, the student spends from 5 to 15 minutes on this step.

2. Question

Locate each boldface heading in the chapter and turn it into a question. This step provides more detailed study of the chapter and provides a purpose for reading the material.

3. Read

As soon as the questions are formulated, read to locate the answers. Begin with the first subtopic and find the answer. Move then to the next step of the procedure.

4. Recite

Pause and review the answer to the question. Paraphrase the answer to the question. Outline or underline the important material or write brief notes in a notebook for later review and study. Repeat Steps 2–4 with each question from the chapter.

5. Review

After completing the final subtopic of the chapter, rehearse the major points in the reading for about 5 minutes. Read each heading in the chapter and attempt to recall the major points. To aid in retention, review the material again at a later time.

Adapted from:

Robinson, F. P. (1970). *Effective study* (5th ed.). New York: Harper & Row.

Tierney, R. J., Readence, J. E., & Dishner, E. K. (1985). *Reading strategies and practices: A compendium* (2nd ed.). Boston: Allyn and Bacon.

STORE the Story

Purpose

The purposes of this strategy are to improve comprehension, retrieval, and retelling of fiction or non-fiction stories by identifying consistent components, as well as to improve writing of stories by providing a story frame.

Description

STORE is an acronym for:
S = Setting (Who? What? Where? When?)
T = Trouble (What is the trouble or problem?)
O = Order of events (What happens?)
R = Resolution (What is done to solve the problem?)
E = End (How does the story end?)

Teaching the Strategy

A. *Introduce the Cue STORE*

1. The teacher discusses the meaning of the verb "to store" (save, hold, keep for a while, put away).

2. The teacher discusses the purpose: To help understand and remember (store) any story the students read by recognizing and recalling each part.

3. The teacher explains the parts of a story: Every story has a beginning, middle, and end. Every story also has a SETTING, TROUBLE, ORDER OF EVENTS, RESOLUTION, and ENDING.

B. *Demonstration/Modeling*

1. The teacher reads a short story aloud to the class.

2. Using the STORE frame written on the board, the teacher fills in the parts of the story.

C. *Guided Practice*

1. The students generalize understanding of parts of a story by recalling fairy tales and identifying the parts labeled by STORE.

2. The teacher reads a short story aloud while students follow along in their books.

3. The students direct the teacher in filling in the STORE cue sheet on an overhead projector.

4. The students take turns telling the story using the cue sheet as a guide.

D. *Independent Practice*

1. Each student reads a short story at his/her independent reading level, filling in the cue sheet as s/he reads.

2. Each student has a chance to retell his/her story to the group using the cue sheet as a guide.

3. Further practice in reading, filling in the cue sheet, and retelling the stories is given on subsequent days.

Using STORE for Writing

A. *Demonstration/Modeling*

1. The teacher models the prewriting stage of the Writing Process Approach by thinking aloud the steps of topic selection and brainstorming of ideas. As the teacher brainstorms ideas for his/her story, s/he fills in the STORE cue sheet, crossing out ideas and adding others until s/he is satisfied.

2. The teacher reads over his/her cue sheet to make sure that all parts of the story make sense and fit in relation to other parts.

3. The teacher models the writing stage of the Writing Process Approach, and, subsequently, revising, editing, and rewriting. The teacher explains how the use of STORE ensures continuity of the story line.

Note

These steps may be modeled on different days to fit in with the classroom schedule and the students' attention spans. If the class is already involved in the Writing Process Approach, the teacher may model the steps of using STORE for writing each day for part of the writing session.

B. *Guided Practice*

The teacher guides the students to create a group story using the STORE format.

C. *Independent Practice*

The students create their own stories.

D. *Adaptations for Extra Support and Fading of Support*

1. The teacher may provide picture cards to aid in generating story ideas.

2. The teacher may provide the Setting, Trouble, and some Events. The student adds some Events and finishes the story.

3. The teacher provides the Setting or the Trouble and the student generates the other parts.

Source:

Schlegel, M., & Bos, C. S. (1986). *STORE the story: Fiction/fantasy reading comprehension and writing strategy.* Unpublished manuscript, University of Arizona, Department of Special Education and Rehabilitation, Tucson.

STORE the Story

Name: _____

Date: _____

Working Title: _____

SETTING
   Who _____

   What _____

   Where _____

   When _____

TROUBLE _____

_____

ORDER OF ACTION
  1. _____

  2. _____

  3. _____

  4. _____

  5. _____

RESOLUTION
  1. _____

  2. _____

  3. _____

  4. _____

  5. _____

ENDING _____

_____

STORY CHART

Setting: (Where?) _____

_____

_____

Main Characters: (Who?)

    #1: _____

        Describe: _____

_____

    #2: _____

        Describe: _____

_____

    Other Characters: _____

_____

Problem: (What Happened?) _____

_____

_____

Attempts to Solve Problem:

    First: _____

_____

    Then: _____

_____

Ending: (How problem was solved.) _____

_____

_____

STORY CLOZE

At the beginning of the story, _____

_____

_____

_____

_____

A problem starts when _____

_____

_____

_____

_____ tries to solve the problem by

_____

_____

_____

At the end of the story, _____

_____

_____

_____

Adapted from:

Fowler, G.L. (1982). Developing comprehension skills with primary and remedial readers through the use of story frames. Reading Teacher, 36, 176-179.

STORY QUESTIONS

1. Where does your story take place? _____

_____

_____

_____

2. Who are the main characters and what are they like? _____

_____

_____

_____

3. What happens to them? _____

_____

_____

_____

4. What do they do about it? _____

_____

_____

_____

5. What happens at the end of the story? _____

_____

_____

_____

_____

Study Guides

Introduction

Study guides may be adapted and used for a variety of purposes. A study guide may be used to focus attention on key concepts in text, increase ability to process textual information at higher cognitive levels, heighten awareness of how content might be organized, and assist with evaluation of prior knowledge or information learned.

Preparation

When preparing a study guide, read the material carefully, decide the purpose of the study guide, and identify the key concepts. The method of construction will depend on the type of study guide selected. Several types of study guides have been identified in the literature regarding content area reading. Those described most often concern levels of comprehension, organizational patterns, and specific concepts. Or, the teacher may use a combination of these types.

Levels of Comprehension

A three-level study guide has questions that involve literal, interpretive, and applied comprehension. Depending on how information is presented in the text, any given question may require different levels of cognitive processing. Herber (1978) identified the following three levels of comprehension: (a) literal comprehension involves identifying factual material and knowing what the author said, (b) interpretive comprehension involves inferring relationships among the details and knowing what the author meant, and (c) applied comprehension involves developing generalizations that extend beyond the assigned material.

A single question cannot be considered as requiring a certain level of comprehension. To decide the comprehension level of a question, the teacher has to consider how the information is stated in the text and the level of cognitive processing necessary for the reader to come up with an acceptable answer (Pearson & Johnson, 1978). Even a question such as, "How might local endeavors toward recycling eventually help global conservation?" would be a literal question if this information is directly stated in the text.

A study guide may include open-ended, true-false, or fill-in-the-blank items. Matching items are not recommended as the separation on the page of two related concepts interferes with easy use of the guide for studying.

The three-level study guide is relatively easy to individualize according to students' abilities. For a fairly homogeneous class, the teacher may decide to prepare questions pertinent to the key concepts at only one level of comprehension. Alternatively, the teacher may decide to mix levels of questions. When adapting the study guide for learners at different cognitive levels or reading ability, the teacher may assign certain items to certain students, matching the level of comprehension required to the student's current ability level or scaffolding a student to the next level. For extra assistance, the teacher may write the page number where the answer may be found next to the question. For learners functioning at a lower reading level, the teacher may use the same study guide with adapted materials.

Organizational Patterns

Study guides may be designed to heighten students' awareness of text organization to facilitate comprehension. Some of the more common text patterns used include: main idea/details, cause/effect, comparison/contrast, and order of events. For example, a study guide emphasizing comparison/contrast might ask the students questions about similarities and differences between World War II and the Vietnam War. For a model of cause/effect, the teacher might list specific events down one side of the page with the heading "Cause" and leave blank the other side of the page with the heading "Effect."

Specific Concepts

A teacher may use the content of text to provide practice with a specific concept; the study guide is the medium. For example, a teacher who is trying to teach his/her class the concept of categorization could list words or phrases pertaining to a chapter of text and direct the student to list them in the most appropriate given category. Categories from the Civil War might include: reasons for the war, immediate outcome of the war, long-term outcomes, results nobody had expected, and effect on the economy of the South. A concept guide designed to teach context clues might name and describe three types, with the requirement that, as the student reads, s/he fill in examples of each of the context clues.

Combination Guide

Study guides may be constructed as a combination of the three types described. For example, a teacher may copy a section of text and write questions and notations about key points, structure, or a specific concept in the margin next to the related information. Or, rather than copying the passage, s/he might write questions/notations on a piece of paper that is held next to the text while the student is reading.

Activities

Reading study guides may be completed by students independently, in pairs, or in cooperative groups. Class discussion should follow completion of the study guide to reinforce the purpose of the study guide and to ensure that everyone understands the correct responses.

Cautions

Using a study guide or the same format of a study guide too frequently may become boring for students.

Do not grade study guides. Use them diagnostically, for example, to see if a student can discern essential information from text. Ask the student why s/he answered as s/he did.

Use the study guide as one activity within many in introducing or working with new information. Do not rely on it alone to introduce a new topic or section of text.

Source:

Herber, H. L. (1978). *Teaching reading in content areas* (2nd ed.). Englewood Cliffs, NJ: Prentice-Hall.

Study Guides: Examples

Three-Level Study Guide

All students are to complete questions 1–5.

Mark each of these statements: T for True or F for False.

_____ 1. Count Camillo di Cavour became the first King of Italy.

_____ 2. Garibaldi and his army won the battle in Sicily because the enemy ran out of bullets.

_____ 3. The country called Italy did not exist in the year 1880.

_____ 4. Garibaldi's victorious army was well-trained and well-equipped.

_____ 5. After 3 weeks of fighting, Italy was free.

Of the questions below, answer only those you were assigned. Please answer in complete sentences on notebook paper so that you can use your answers later as a study guide.

** 6. In 1834, Garibaldi escaped from Italy under sentence of death. Why do you think he had been sentenced to die?

** 7. List three words or phrases that describe Garibaldi.

*** 8. This chapter is entitled, "The Fight for Italy." What would another good title be?

** 9. For what reason was an army sent to capture Rome and central Italy even before Garibaldi reached there?

*** 10. Do you think that fighting a war is the best way for people to gain freedom? If so, explain your reason.

** 11. Count di Cavour and Garibaldi were very different men who often clashed with each other. Describe one important way in which they were different and one important way in which they were alike.

*** 12. Today, Garibaldi is considered a great hero throughout the world; Count di Cavour's name is hardly known, although he was also very important in Italy's struggle for independence. What is one good reason for the difference in their fame?

Note

All of the true/false questions are literal. On questions 6–12, those with two stars are interpretive and those with three stars are application.

Organizational Pattern: Chronology

Number the sentences below according to the order in which they occurred in the chapter.

_____ In 1854, Garibaldi left the United States to go back to Italy.

_____ Although the Italians made several attempts to revolt, they failed each time.

_____ The Sardinian King was made King of Italy.

_____ Garibaldi's army forced the Austrians to retreat.

_____ Much of Italy was under the control of foreign kings.

_____ The Sicilians fought alongside of Garibaldi and his men.

Study guides were based on information from:

Johnson, W., Peck, I., Plotkin, F., & Richardson, W. (1976). *The modern world*. New York: Scholastic Book Services.

Taped Books

Taped books are available from *Recording for the Blind* (RFB), a national, nonprofit organization that provides textbooks for individuals unable to read standard print because of a visual, physical, or perceptual disability. The 75,000 master-tape library has educational books that range from upper-elementary to postgraduate level. If a book is unavailable, an individual may request that it be recorded. If deemed to fit within the scope of the collection, the book will be recorded. Over 30 recording studios are operated around the country. To register as a borrower or volunteer as reader, write or call:

Recording for the Blind
The Anne T. Macdonald Center
20 Roszel Road
Princeton, NJ 08540
(800) 221-4792

A wide selection of unabridged audio books is also available from either *Books on Tape* or *Recorded Books*. Selections include best-sellers, classics, history, biographies, and science fiction. Books may be rented for a month and then returned by mail. Prices vary according to the length of the books. Books may be ordered from:

Books on Tape
P.O. Box 7900
Newport Beach, CA 92658
(800) 626-3333

Recorded Books
Box 409
Charlotte Hall, MD 20622
(800) 638-1304

Public libraries also provide a selection of recorded books for loan.

Touch Math™

Touch Math (Bullock, 1991) is a multisensory program used to introduce basic arithmetic and improve basic computational skills. It is an effective alternative for students who have difficulty memorizing math facts. This supplemental program is used in conjunction with the existing math program in kindergarten through fourth grade or with special education students at all levels. Students are taught to perform the four basic operations by touching a pencil to the Touchpoints designated by large dark circles on each of the numbers 1–9. Figures A-10 and A-11 illustrate the Touchpoints and the addition process. The student is taught systematically to eliminate steps as they are no longer needed.

Introduction of skills within each computation area progresses step-by-step from simple to more complex stages. Students are taught to verbalize the simple procedures to reinforce the sequence they follow. For example, in Step 1 addition, the student begins by touching and counting all of the Touchpoints. In Step 2, the student names the larger number and touches points of the smaller number, point by point, while counting on. The student also learns to verbalize the procedure: "I touch the larger number, say its name and continue counting." For subtraction, the student touches the top number, says its name, and counts backwards. For multiplication and division, the student uses sequence counting. The student is taught strategies for both short and long division.

A variety of reproducible masters, workbooks, posters, and games are available for teaching this Touchpoint approach. A videotape and sample program materials can be ordered from the publisher:

Innovative Learning Concepts, Inc.
6760 Corporate Drive
Colorado Springs, CO 80919-1999
(800) 888-9191

Figure A–10 shows the Touchpoint placement for Touch Math numbers. Students learn basic computation by touching and counting Touchpoints in a regular pattern sequence.

Figure A–11 shows examples of the steps involved in the Touch Math addition process.

Note: From *Touch Math: The Touchpoint Approach for Teaching Basic Math Computation* (4th ed.), Revised and Enlarged. By permission of J. Bullock and Innovative Learning Concepts. Copyright 1984, 1986, by Innovative Learning Concepts, Inc., Colorado Springs. All rights reserved. Touch Math™ and Touchpoint™ are trademarks of Innovative Learning Concepts, Inc.

Vocabulary: Activating Awareness

The purpose of this activity is to bring to a conscious level a student's awareness of his/her familiarity with key vocabulary relevant to an upcoming topic of study.

Steps

1. Provide a chart with key vocabulary from an upcoming topic of study listed down the side and three categories of knowledge across the top: *Can Define, Have Seen/Heard Before, Don't Know*.

2. Have the student rate him/herself on each word. Rating may be done before and after a prestudy activity, such as Exclusive Brainstorming (described below), and after the topic has been presented in class.

3. Have the student use the words s/he knows to guess what the topic is about and tell how the words led him/her to that decision.

Source:

Blachowicz, C. L. (1986). Making connections: Alternatives to the vocabulary notebook. *Journal of Reading, 29*, 643-649.

Vocabulary: Exclusive Brainstorming

The purpose of this activity is to associate new vocabulary to known concepts and to raise metalinguistic awareness of the words students know, words they do not know, and the degree of their familiarity. This activity may be done individually or in small or large groups.

Steps

1. Tell the student(s) something about the topic to be studied or reading selection and lists of preselected words.
   Example:
   a. Topic: The stockmarket crash of 1929
      investments   market   crisis
      corporations   stockholders   depression
   b. Topic: Dolphins: Mammals of the sea
      lungs   mammals   land
      gills   fish   manatee

2. Ask the student(s) to decide which words are likely to be included in the topic information and which words are not. Have the student(s) explain the rationale for each decision.

3. As the inclusion and exclusion of each word are discussed, the meaning of the word is also discussed. Encourage the student(s) to request the meanings of unfamiliar words.

Source:

Blachowicz, C. L. (1986). Making connections: Alternatives to the vocabulary notebook. *Journal of Reading, 29*, 643-649.

Word Bank Activities

Once a student has developed a word bank, provide a variety of activities to practice words and increase reading vocabulary. Examples of activities follow:

1. Alphabetize words.

2. For each card, think of other words in the same family and write them on the back of the card.

3. Make up individual cards for each member of a word family, mix up all the cards, and sort them by family.

4. Choose a word, write a list of words that would fit in its family, and check them against the words on the back of the card.

5. Find a variety of ways to categorize the cards (e.g., long versus short words, antonyms and synonyms, words sharing the same affixes, spelling patterns).

6. Put as many words as possible together to form a silly sentence. Write the sentence and add in any extra words that are necessary for it to make sense.

7. Make cards for each new vocabulary word learned and use them in sentences.

8. Teach the student how to use a flash method to teach another student to read his/her sight words.

9. Have two students team up, initial their own word cards, and then mix them together. Place all of the cards face down on the table. Each player selects a card, turns it over, and tries to pronounce it. If s/he pronounces it, s/he keeps it. If not, the other person tells him/her the word (if s/he can) and it goes into a second pile. Any words missed by both students are held aside to be restudied.

Writing Process Approach: Group

The writing process approach is based on an interactive model that is composed of overlapping and recursive stages (Bos, 1988; Flower & Hayes, 1980; Graves, 1983). Although improving basic skills is recognized as one aspect of the process, the emphasis is on communicating the message. Involvement in the process fosters recognition that good writing requires extensive time for planning, composing, and revising, while diminishing the view of writing as an activity to be finished "before the end of the period."

The writing process approach consists of three general stages—prewriting, writing, and postwriting—each with a number of steps.

Prewriting

Selecting a Topic

The teacher gives the students clues for generating writing topics (e.g., family, experiences, reading), but the students select their own topics from the lists they generate. Generating a topic list includes individual brainstorming and sharing ideas with others for additional topics. As each student thinks of new topics, s/he adds them to an ongoing topic list in his/her file.

Planning

The planning step of the writing process may be as informal as thinking out what the writer wants to say before composing a first draft or may incorporate strategies for facilitating the planning process. In the planning process, the students consider the purpose for the composition, as well as the intended audience. Some strategies often used in this stage are brainstorming and clustering ideas, to include a structured overview, such as a Semantic Map or story frame.

Writing

From the ideas the students have organized in the previous step, they write their first draft of their stories or reports. Students are encouraged not to be concerned about handwriting, spelling, or other basic skills in this step to promote full attention to ideas.

Post-Writing

Revising and Editing

In revision, the students focus on the clarity of their message, and the language/thinking skills expressed in their writing, such as organization of ideas and specificity of vocabulary. In editing, the students proofread for and correct errors in spelling, punctuation, capitalization, and usage.

In revising and editing, the teacher may introduce a variety of strategies for helping the students develop independence. Some of these are: peer editing, using a thesaurus or electronic spelling checker/thesaurus, learning to use and read proofreading symbols, learning an editing strategy such as Error Monitoring (see Error Monitoring Strategy), and using a revision guide (see Written Expression Evaluation Guide).

Author's Chair

When students feel they have completed their papers or stories, they read them to the assembled group for comments, questions, and suggestions. Students may then choose to revise again, publish the story, or go on to another writing project. This sharing gives worth and value to the entire process (Bos & Vaughn, 1991).

Publication

When a piece is completed, students may wish to type it or have it typed, illustrate it, and create a cover for it. Subsequently, it may be placed in the classroom, school newspaper, or library for others to read.

Key Features of the Process Approach to Writing

Many features of the writing process approach enhance student interest and excitement. Further, all skills are taught within a purposeful context, making this approach particularly suitable for learners with special needs.

Opportunity for Sustained Writing

The students work in the writing process for at least 30 to 40 minutes daily so that writing becomes as familiar a classroom activity as reading or math. As well, an extended amount of time is necessary to develop good writing skills within a meaningful context.

Teacher Conference

During every stage of the writing process, students have frequent, brief, individual conferences with the teacher. The teacher asks questions to highlight strengths or guide attention to weaknesses in specific areas. For example, s/he may guide certain students to focus on elaborating ideas, modifying organizational structures, or editing basic skills. During the drafting stage, a student may confer and revise several times before feeling satisfied with the final product. During this time, the teacher also may note skills that require more instruction, allowing him/her to group students for specific skill lessons and to incorporate practice activities into the daily writing plan.

Topic Choice

Students' selection of their own topics enhances both interest in writing and ownership of the piece. As students become familiar with the process, more teacher-directed projects may be incorporated.

Writing Community

A classroom conducive to the process approach is arranged to foster collaboration among students and progressive independence from the teacher. Materials should be easily accessible; students should become sufficiently familiar with the process to begin work independently, move on to the next step when appropriate, and seek help when necessary. As students develop areas of expertise (e.g., thinking up ideas, writing mystery stories, spelling), they become resources for their peers. The teacher and students establish an ongoing process of questioning, suggesting, and supporting. An outcome of these factors is an atmosphere of trust and security.

Teacher Modeling

Throughout the writing process, the teacher also writes and shares his/her writing with the students. For instruction, the teacher models and thinks aloud each step of the process before guiding the students through it—first as a group and then individually.

Recursive Process

Anywhere in the process, the students may drop back to an earlier step. For example, in the writing stage, students may realize that they do not have enough information on the topic and drop back to researching it; or, students may realize during brainstorming or drafting that they are not interested in their topics and select new ones.

Sense of Audience

Through conferencing, sharing with peers, author's chair, and publication, students develop the sense that they are writing for an audience— that their writing is to be read and understood by other people.

Taking Control

Helped by peers and guided by the teacher, students take control of and monitor their own progress, often creating or adapting strategies to further enhance their learning.

Sources:

Bos, C. S. (1988). Process-oriented writing: Instructional implications for mildly handicapped students. *Exceptional Children, 54,* 521-527.

Bos, C. S., & Vaughn, S. (1991). *Strategies for teaching students with learning and behavior problems* (2nd ed.). Boston: Allyn and Bacon.

Flower, L., & Hayes, J. R. (1980). Writing as problem solving. *Visible Language, 14,* 388-399.

Graves, D. H. (1983). *Writing: Teachers and children at work.* Exeter, NH: Heinemann Educational Books.

Schlegel, M. (1986, October). *Remediation of written language: Group teaching techniques.* Workshop presented at Arizona Association for Children with Learning Disabilities, Phoenix, AZ.

Vallecorsa, A. L., Ledford, R. R., & Parness, G. G. (1991). Strategies for teaching composition skills to students with learning disabilities. *Teaching Exceptional Children, 23,* 52-55.

Writing Process Approach: Individualized

Purpose

This adaptation of the Writing Process Approach may be used in one-to-one or small group remediation.

Introduction

Tell the student that you are going to teach him/her a new method of writing that has several steps, but will make writing more enjoyable and less overwhelming. Explain to him/her that good writers never complete a paper or story for publication in just one draft and that this new method might require several drafts to complete a paper.

Steps

A. *Prewriting*

1. Selecting a topic
   a. Provide the student with a broad topic on which to write. Within the broad topic assigned, the student brainstorms and lists as many ideas for subtopics as possible.
   b. The student crosses out those subtopics that hold the least interest for him/her and prioritizes the rest.
   c. The student selects the top choice as the topic and makes up a working title (subject to change). The title should work as a main idea statement for the paper.

2. Conducting research

   If necessary, the student researches the topic, taking notes on paper, notecards, or sticky pads.

3. Generating idea statements
   a. The student dictates to the teacher or writes on paper or cards everything about the topic s/he knows or can remember from reading. The student writes only *one idea to a line or card*.
   b. The student cuts the paper between the statements or sorts the cards so that s/he has a pile of separate ideas on the topic.

4. Organizing the idea statements
   a. The teacher asks the student, "How can you group these so that the ideas that are similar in some way are together?" The student then goes through the ideas and groups the pieces of paper. The teacher helps only as much as necessary. At this point, sequential organization within groups is not a concern.
   b. The student organizes the ideas within each group according to the information present. Some may be organized sequentially, others as statement and support, and others as comparison/contrast. The strips of paper are arranged one above the other on the table.

5. Generating main idea statements
   a. The teacher chooses one group and asks the student why s/he put those ideas together. From the student's response, the teacher helps him/her to make a general statement that encompasses the ideas. The teacher or student writes the general statement down and places it at the top of the stack.
   b. All idea groups are titled in the same manner. If one statement in the stack serves as a main idea already, it may be placed at the top.

6. Adding and reorganizing information
   a. The student is encouraged to write and add related ideas to any of the groups.
   b. The student reviews the ideas within each group. S/he is encouraged to move ideas among the groups if any seem to fit better under some other heading.

7. Designing the semantic map

   Using the main idea statements as a guide, the student designs a semantic map depicting the relationship among the main idea statements. The overall topic is the first level, the main idea statements are the second level, and the details are the third level. When drawing the map, however, it may become obvious that one or more of the main idea statements works better as a third-level statement placed as an offshoot of one of the second-level statements.

8. Explaining the relationships and adding to the map
   a. When the map is drawn, the student explains to the teacher why s/he placed the main ideas where s/he did, explaining the relationships among them. Any changes in design or levels are done at this point.

b. The more detailed ideas are now placed in the semantic map associated with their main idea statements.

c. Again, the student explains to the teacher how the information interrelates in the map.

B. *Writing*

1. Using the information in the semantic map, the student writes a first draft of the body of his/her paper. Each second level of the map becomes a paragraph. The idea statement at this level provides the main idea.

2. The student then writes an introduction and a conclusion.

C. *Revising/Editing*

1. The student reads through the paper, making revisions in organization, sentence structure, vocabulary.

2. The student writes transitional sentences where needed to facilitate the connection between paragraphs.

3. The student rewrites the paper with revisions, reads it again for further revision, and writes another draft.

4. When the student and teacher are satisfied with the paper, it is edited for errors in mechanics, such as spelling, punctuation, and capitalization.

D. *Final Copy or Publishing*

A final copy of the paper is written and handed in or published.

Note

Because several drafts of a paper are usually necessary, if a word processor is available, encourage the student to learn to use it. Use of a word processor will facilitate revision and editing.

Adapted from:

Buckley, M. H., & Boyle, O. (1981). *Mapping the writing journey.* Berkeley: University of California Berkeley/Bay Area Writing Project, Curriculum Publication No. 15.

Graves, D. H. (1983). *Writing: Teachers and children at work.* Exeter, NH: Heinemann Educational Books.

Pearson, P. D., & Johnson, D. D. (1978). *Teaching reading comprehension.* New York: Holt, Rinehart and Winston.

Written Expression Evaluation Guide (Student)

Basic Skills

	Check if OK	Need Help With
Visual Format		
Margins	_____	_____
Indented paragraphs	_____	_____
Handwriting		
Neat handwriting	_____	_____
Correct spacing	_____	_____
Spelling	_____	_____
Punctuation	_____	_____
Capitalization	_____	_____

Written Expression

Vocabulary		
Specific words	_____	_____
Descriptive words	_____	_____
Grammar		
Subject-verb agreement	_____	_____
Consistent verb tense	_____	_____
Irregular verbs and plurals	_____	_____
Sentence structure		
Complete sentences	_____	_____
Variety of types	_____	_____
Parallel structure	_____	_____
Structural organization: Paragraphs		
Main idea/details	_____	_____
Separates paragraphs	_____	_____
Varied paragraph development	_____	_____
Structural organization: Whole paper		
All paragraphs relate to theme	_____	_____
Introduction	_____	_____
Conclusion	_____	_____
Style		
Consistent style	_____	_____
Consistent point of view	_____	_____

Mather, N., & Jaffe, L. E. (1992). *Woodcock-Johnson Psycho-Education Battery—Revised: Recommendations and Reports.* Brandon, VT: Clinical Psychology Publishing Company.

Written Expression Evaluation Guide (Teacher)

S = Strong
A = Adequate
N = Needs Improvement

Basic Skills

	S, A, N	Areas of Need
Visual Format		
Uses margins	_____	_____
Indents paragraphs	_____	_____
Handwriting		
Forms letters correctly	_____	_____
Places words on the line	_____	_____
Uses correct spacing	_____	_____
Spelling		
Uses graphophonic correspondence	_____	_____
Uses morphological generalizations	_____	_____
Uses correct number of syllables	_____	_____
Punctuation		
Uses punctuation in appropriate places	_____	_____
Uses correct punctuation marks	_____	_____
Capitalization		
Discriminates between upper/ lowercase letters	_____	_____
Uses capitalization rules	_____	_____

Written Expression

	S, A, N	Areas of Need
Vocabulary		
Uses age-appropriate words	_____	_____
Uses words specific to meaning	_____	_____
Uses descriptive words	_____	_____
Uses imaginative words	_____	_____
Grammar		
Has subject-verb agreement	_____	_____
Uses appropriate/consistent verb tense	_____	_____
Uses irregular verbs and plurals correctly	_____	_____
Sentence structure		
Writes complete sentences	_____	_____
Varies sentence types	_____	_____
Uses parallel clauses	_____	_____
Uses embeddings, relative clauses	_____	_____

Written Expression Evaluation Guide (Teacher)

S = Strong
A = Adequate
N = Needs Improvement

Written Expression (continued)

	S, A, N	Areas of Need
Structural organization		
Includes main idea/details	_____	_____
Separates paragraphs	_____	_____
Varies types of paragraph development	_____	_____
Relates all paragraphs to theme	_____	_____
Includes clear introduction	_____	_____
Includes clear conclusion	_____	_____
Content and maturity of ideas		
Chooses age-appropriate topics	_____	_____
Chooses imaginative topics	_____	_____
Uses abstract ideas	_____	_____
Generates ideas fluently	_____	_____
Style and sense of audience		
Uses emotion/irony/humor, etc.	_____	_____
Maintains consistent point of view	_____	_____
Revising/Editing		
Proofreads without reminding	_____	_____
Revises content	_____	_____
Edits for errors in mechanics	_____	_____

Mather, N., & Jaffe, L. E. (1992). *Woodcock-Johnson Psycho-Educational Battery—Revised: Recommendations and Reports.* Brandon, VT: Clinical Psychology Publishing Company.

REFERENCES

A road map to transition for young adults with severe disabilities. (1990). San Jose, CA: Santa Clara County Office of Education.

Abikoff, H. (1991). Cognitive training in ADHD children: Less to it than meets the eye. *Journal of Learning Disabilities, 24,* 205-209.

Abramowitz. A. J., & O'Leary, S. G. (1991). Behavioral interventions for the classroom: Implications for students with ADHD. *School Psychology Review, 20,* 220-234.

Algozzine, B. (1990). *Problem behavior management.* Rockville, MD: Aspen.

Alley, G. R., & Hori, K. O. (1981). *Effects of teaching a questioning strategy on reading comprehension of learning disabled adolescents* (Report No. 52). Lawrence, KS: Institute for Research in Learning Disabilities, University of Kansas.

Anders, P. L., & Bos, C. S. (1986). Semantic feature analysis: An interactive strategy for vocabulary and text comprehension. *Journal of Reading, 29,* 610-616.

Barkley, R. A. (1990). *Attention deficit hyperactivity disorder: A handbook for diagnosis and treatment.* New York: Guilford Press.

Base, G. (1986). *Animalia.* New York: Harry N. Abrams.

Baumann, J. (1986). Teaching third-grade students to comprehend anaphoric relationships: The application of a direct instruction model. *Reading Research Quarterly, 21,* 70-90.

Bellanca, J., & Fogarty, R. (1986). *Catch them thinking: A handbook of classroom strategies.* Palatine, IL: IRI Group.

Blachowicz, C. (1986). Making connections: Alternatives to the vocabulary notebook. *Journal of Reading, 29,* 643-649.

Bley, N. S., & Thornton, C. A. (1989). *Teaching mathematics to the learning disabled* (2nd ed.). Rockville, MD: Aspen.

Boehm, A. E. (1986). *Boehm Test of Basic Concepts — Revised.* San Antonio: The Psychological Corporation.

Bos, C. S. (1988). Process-oriented writing: Instructional implications for mildly handicapped students. *Exceptional Children, 54,* 521-527.

Bos, C. S., Anders, P. L., Filip, D., & Jaffe, L. E. (1989). The effects of an interactive instructional strategy for enhancing reading comprehension and content area learning for students with learning disabilities. *Journal of Learning Disabilities, 22,* 384-390.

Bos, C. S., & Vaughn, S. (1991). *Strategies for teaching students with learning and behavior problems* (2nd ed.). Boston: Allyn and Bacon.

Bowen, C. (1972). *Angling for words: A study book for language training.* Novato, CA: Academic Therapy.

Bradley, L. (1981). The organization of motor patterns for spelling: An effective remedial strategy for backward spellers. *Developmental Medicine and Child Neurology, 23,* 83-91.

Bransford, J. D., & Johnson, M. (1973). Considerations of some problems in comprehension. In W. Chase (Ed.), *Visual information processing* (pp. 383-438). New York: Academic Press.

Brigance, A. H. (1991). *Brigance Diagnostic Inventory of Early Development*. North Billerica, MA: Curriculum Associates.

Brown, A. L., & Day, J. D. (1983). *Macrorules for summarizing text: The development of expertise* (Tech. Rep. No. 270). Urbana-Champaign: University of Illinois.

Buckley, M. H., & Boyle, O. (1981). *Mapping the writing journey*. Berkeley: University of California Berkeley/Bay Area Writing Project, Curriculum Publication No. 15.

Bullock, J. K. (1991). *Touch math series* (4th ed.). Colorado Springs, CO: Innovative Learning Concepts.

Burns, M. (1982). *Math for smarty pants*. Boston: Little, Brown.

Carnine, D., & Kinder, D. (1985). Teaching low-performing students to apply generative and schema strategies to narrative and expository material. *Remedial and Special Education*, 6(1), 20-29.

Cawley, J. F., Fitzmaurice, A. M., Goodstein, H. A., Lepore, A. V., Sedlak, R., & Althaus, V. (1976). *Project MATH*. Tulsa, OK: Educational Development.

Cawley, J. F. (Ed.). (1984). *Developmental teaching of mathematics for the learning disabled*. Rockville, MD: Aspen.

Cawley, J. F. (1985). *Cognitive strategies and mathematics for the learning disabled*. Rockville, MD: Aspen.

Childs, S. B., & Childs, R. S. (1973). *The Childs spelling system: The rules*. Cambridge, MA: Educators Publishing Service.

Conners, C. K., (1989). *Conners' Teacher Rating Scales*. Toronto: Multi-Health Systems.

Connolly, A. J. (1988). *KeyMath—Revised: A Diagnostic Inventory of Essential Mathematics*. Circle Pines, MN: American Guidance Service.

Copeland, E. D. (1991). *Medications for attention disorders (ADHD/ADD) and related medical problems (Tourette's Syndrome, sleep apnea, seizure disorders): A comprehensive handbook*. Atlanta: SPI Press.

Copeland, E. D., & Love, V. L. (1990). *Attention without tension: A teacher's handbook on attention disorders (ADHD and ADD)*. Atlanta: 3 C's of Childhood.

Copeland, E. D., & Love, V. L. (1991). *Attention please! A comprehensive guide for successfully parenting children with attention disorders and hyperactivity*. Atlanta: SPI Press.

Cotterell, G. C. (1973). The Fernald auditory-kinaesthetic technique. In A. W. Franklin & S. Naidoo (Eds.), *Assessment and teaching of dyslexic children* (pp. 97-100). London: Richard Madley.

Cunningham, P. M. (1979). Teaching vocabulary in the content areas. *NASSP Bulletin*, 613(424), 112-116.

Davidson, J. (1969). *Using the Cuisenaire rods*. New Rochelle, NY: Cuisenaire.

Devine, T. G. (1986). *Teaching reading comprehension: From theory to practice*. Boston: Allyn and Bacon.

Dixon, R., & Engelmann, S. (1979). *Corrective spelling through morphographs*. Chicago: Science Research Associates.

Dolch, E. W. (1939). *A manual for remedial reading*. Champaign, IL: Garrard Press.

Education for all Handicapped Children Act (1975), 34 C.F.R. 300.1-300.754 (1977).

Engelmann, S., Bruner, E. C., Hanner, S., Osborn, J., Osborn, S., & Zoref, L. (1983-1984). *Reading mastery*. Chicago: Science Research Associates.

Engelmann, S., & Carnine, D. (1982). *Corrective mathematics program*. Chicago: Science Research Associates.

Engelmann, S., Johnson, G., Hanner, S., Carnine, D., Meyers, L., Osborn, S., Haddox, P., Becker, W., Osborn, J., & Becker, J. (1988). *Corrective reading*. Chicago: Science Research Associates.

Everett, J., LaPlante, L., & Thomas, J. (1989). The selective attention deficit in schizophrenia. *Journal of Nervous and Mental Disorders*, 177, 735-738.

Fernald, G. (1943). *Remedial techniques in basic school subjects*. New York: McGraw-Hill.

Flower, L., & Hayes, J. R. (1980). Writing as problem solving. *Visible Language*, 14, 388-399.

Forte, I., & Pangle, M. A. (1985). *Selling spelling to kids: Motivating games and activities to reinforce spelling skills*. Nashville, TN: Incentive Publications.

Fowler, G. L. (1982). Developing comprehension skills with primary and remedial readers through the use of story frames. *Reading Teacher*, 36, 176-179.

Fry, E. B. (1978). *Fry Readibility Scale (Extended)*. Providence, RI: Jamestown Publishers.

Fry, E. B. (1980). The new instant word list. *Reading Teacher, 34*, 284-289.

Fry, E., Polk, J., & Fountoukidis, D. (1985). *The new reading teacher's book of lists* (2nd ed.). Englewood Cliffs, NJ: Prentice-Hall.

Gillingham, A., & Stillman, B. W. (1973). *Remedial training for children with specific disability in reading, spelling, and penmanship*. Cambridge, MA: Educators Publishing Service.

Glass, G. G. (1973). *Teaching decoding as separate from reading*. New York: Adelphi University.

Glass, G. G. (1976). *Glass-Analysis for decoding only teacher guide*. Garden City, NY: Easier to Learn.

Glynn, E. L., & Thomas, J. D. (1974). Effect of cueing on self-control of classroom behavior. *Journal of Applied Behavior Analysis, 7*, 299-306.

Goldstein, S., & Goldstein, M. (1990). *Managing attention disorders in children*. New York: John Wiley & Sons.

Graham, K. G., & Robinson, H. A. (1984). *Study skills handbook: A guide for all teachers*. Newark, DE: International Reading Association.

Graves, D. H. (1983). *Writing: Teachers and children at work*. Exeter, NH: Heinemann Educational Books.

Graves, D. H. (1985). All children can write. *Learning Disabilities Focus, 1*(1), 36-43.

Gurney, D., Gersten, R., Dimino, J., & Carnine, D. (1990). Story grammar: Effective literature instruction for high school students with learning disabilities. *Journal of Learning Disabilities, 23*, 335-342, 348.

Hanau, L. (1974). *The study game: How to play and win with statement-pie*. New York: Barnes & Noble.

Hanover, S. (1983). Handwriting comes naturally? *Academic Therapy, 18*, 407-412.

Hansen, J., & Pearson, P. D. (1983). An instructional study: Improving the inferential comprehension of good and poor fourth-graders. *Journal of Educational Psychology, 75*, 821- 829.

Heckelman, R. G. (1966). Using the neurological impress reading technique. *Academic Therapy, 1*, 235-239.

Heckelman, R. G. (1986). N.I.M. revisited. *Academic Therapy, 21*, 411-420.

Heddens, J. W. (1991). *Today's mathematics: Concepts and methods in elementary school mathematics* (7th ed.). Riverside, NJ: Macmillan.

Herber, H. L. (1978). *Teaching reading in content areas* (2nd ed.). Englewood Cliffs, NJ: Prentice-Hall.

Herold, M. (1982). *You can have a near-perfect memory*. Chicago: Contemporary Books.

Horn, E. (1954). *Teaching spelling*. Washington, DC: American Educational Research Association.

Hoskisson, K. (1975). Successive approximation and beginning reading. *Elementary School Journal, 75*, 443-451.

Individuals with Disabilities Education Act (1990), 20 U.S.C. 1400-1485.

Ingersoll, B. (1988). *Your hyperactive child: A parent's guide to coping with attention deficit disorder*. New York: Doubleday.

Johnson, D. D., & Pearson, P. D. (1984). *Teaching reading vocabulary* (2nd ed.). New York: Holt, Rinehart, and Winston.

Johnson, D. D., & von Hoff Johnson, B. (1986). Highlighting vocabulary in inferential comprehension. *Journal of Reading, 29*, 622-625.

Johnson, W., Peck, I., Plotkin, F., & Richardson, W. (1976). *The modern world*. New York: Scholastic Book Services.

Jones, C. B. (1991). *A sourcebook for managing attention disorders: For early childhood professionals*. Tucson, AZ: Communication Skill Builders.

Kerrigan, W. J. (1979). *Writing to the point: Six basic steps* (2nd ed.). New York: Harcourt Brace Jovanovich.

Kirk, S. A., & Chalfant, J. C. (1984). *Academic and developmental learning disabilities*. Denver: Love.

Kirk, S. A., Kirk, W. D., & Minskoff, E. H. (1985). *Phonic remedial reading lessons*. Novato, CA: Academic Therapy.

Kratoville, B. L. (1989). *Word tracking: High frequency words*. Novato, CA: Academic Therapy.

Kucera, H., & Francis, W. N. (1967). *Comparative analysis of present day American English*. Providence, RI: Brown University Press.

Langer, J. A. (1981). From theory to practice: A prereading plan. *Journal of Reading, 25*, 152-156.

Langer, J. A. (1984). Examining background knowledge and text comprehension. *Reading Research Quarterly, 19*, 468-481.

Lenz, B. K., Schumaker, J. B., Deshler, D. D., & Beals, V. L. (1984). *The word identification strategy* (Learning Strategies Curriculum). Lawrence: University of Kansas.

Letter Tracking. (1975). Novato, CA: Academic Therapy.

Levine, M. D. (1985). *The ANSER System: School Questionnaire for Developmental, Behavioral, and Health Assessment of the Elementary School Student.* Cambridge: Educators Publishing Service.

Levine, M. D. (1988). *The ANSER System: School Questionnaire for Developmental, Behavioral, and Health Assessment of the Secondary School Student.* Cambridge: Educators Publishing Service.

Levine, M. D. (1990). *Keeping a head in school.* Cambridge: Educators Publishing Service.

Lindamood, C. H., & Lindamood, P. C. (1975). *Auditory discrimination in depth* (rev. ed.). Allen, TX: DLM.

Lorayne, H., & Lucas, J. (1974). *The memory book.* New York: Ballantine Books.

Malone, L., DeLucchi, L., & Their, H. (1981). *Science activities for the visually impaired: SAVI leadership trainer's manual.* Berkeley, CA: Center for Multisensory Learning, University of California.

Manzo, A. V. (1969). The ReQuest procedure. *Journal of Reading, 13*, 123-126.

Manzo, A. V. (1985). Expansion modules for the ReQuest, CAT, GRP, and REAP reading/study procedures. *Journal of Reading, 28*, 498-502.

Mastropieri, M. A. (1988). Using the keyboard (sic) method. *Teaching Exceptional Children, 20*(2), 4-8.

Mather, N. (1985). *The Fernald kinesthetic method revisited.* Unpublished manuscript, University of Arizona, Department of Special Education and Rehabilitation, Tucson.

Mather, N. (1991). *An instructional guide to the Woodcock-Johnson Psycho-Educational Battery—Revised.* Brandon, VT: Clinical Psychology Publishing Company.

Mather, N., & Healey, W. C. (1990). Deposing aptitude-achievement discrepancy as the imperial criterion for learning disabilities. *Learning Disabilities: A Multidisciplinary Journal, 1*, 40-48.

Mayer, R. E. (1984). What have we learned about increasing the meaningfulness of science prose? *Science Education, 67*, 223-237.

McCoy, K. M., & Prehm, H. J. (1987). *Teaching mainstreamed students: Methods and techniques.* Denver: Love.

Montague, M., & Bos, C. S. (1986). The effect of cognitive strategy training on verbal math problem solving performance of learning disabled adolescents. *Journal of Learning Disabilities, 19*, 26-33.

Moss, D. (1989). *Shelly, the hyperactive turtle.* Rockville, MD: Woodbine House.

Myklebust, H. (1954). *Auditory disorders in children: A manual for differential diagnosis.* New York: Grune & Stratton.

Neill, K. (1979). Turn kids on with repeated reading. *Teaching Exceptional Children, 12*, 63-64.

Nelson, D. L., & Archer, C. S. (1972). The first-letter mnemonic. *Journal of Educational Psychology, 63*, 482-486.

Nelson, H. E., Pantelis, C., Carruthers, K., Speller, J., Baxendale, S., & Barnes, T. R. (1990). Cognitive functioning and symptomatology in chronic schizophrenia. *Psychological Medicine, 20*, 357-365.

Nolan, S., Alley, G. R., & Clark, F. L. (1980). *Self-questioning strategy.* Lawrence, KS: University of Kansas, Institute for Research in Learning Disability.

Ogle, D. M. (1986). K-W-L: A teaching model that develops active reading of expository text. *Reading Teacher, 39*, 564-570.

Ormrod, J. E. (1986). A learning strategy for phonetic spellers. *Academic Therapy, 22*, 195-198.

Palincsar, A. S., & Brown, A. L. (1984). Reciprocal teaching of comprehension-fostering and comprehension-monitoring activities. *Cognition and Instruction, 1*, 117-175.

Palincsar, A. S., & Brown, A. L. (1986). Interactive teaching to promote independent learning from text. *Reading Teacher, 39*, 771-777.

Parker, H. C. (1988). *The ADD hyperactivity workbook for parents, teachers and kids*. Plantation, FL: Impact Publications.

Pearson, P. D., & Johnson, D. D. (1978). *Teaching reading comprehension*. New York: Holt, Rinehart, and Winston.

Peters, M. L. (1979). Paragraphs for dictation. *Diagnostic and remedial spelling manual*. London: Macmillan Education.

Phelps-Teraski, D., & Phelps, T. (1980). *Teaching written expression: The Phelps sentence guide program*. Novato, CA: Academic Therapy.

Piedmont, R. L., Sokolove, R. L., & Fleming, M. Z. (1989). Discriminating psychotic and affective disorders using the WAIS-R. *Journal of Personality Assessment, 53*, 739-748.

Polloway, E., Patton, J., & Cohen, S. (1981). Written language for mildly handicapped students. *Focus on Exceptional Children, 14*(3), 1-16.

Poteet, J. A. (1987). Written expression. In J. S. Choate, T. Z. Bennett, B. E. Enright, L. J. Miller, J. A. Poteet, & T. A. Rakes (Eds.), *Assessing and programming basic curriculum skills* (pp. 147-176). Boston: Allyn and Bacon.

Quinn, P. O., & Stern, J. M. (1991). *Putting on the brakes*. New York: Magination.

Radaker, L. D. (1963). The effect of visual imagery upon spelling performance. *Journal of Educational Research, 56*, 370-372.

Rak, E. T. (1984). *The spell of words: Teacher's manual*. Cambridge, MA: Educators Publishing Service.

Rehabilitation Act of 1973, 29 U.S.C. 794.

Rehabilitation Act of 1973, 34 C.F.R. 104.1-104.39 (1977).

Rico, G. L. (1983). *Writing the natural way*. Boston: Houghton Mifflin.

Robinson, F. P. (1970). *Effective study* (5th ed.). New York: Harper & Row.

Robinson, H. A., Andresen, O., Hittleman, D. R., Patterson, O., & Paulsen, L. (1978). *Strategies for reading: Long selections*. Boston: Allyn and Bacon.

Samuels, S. J. (1979). The method of repeated readings. *Reading Teacher, 32*, 403-408.

Sattler, J. M. (1988). *Assessment of children* (3rd ed.). San Diego: Author.

Schiever, S. W. (1991). *A comprehensive approach to teaching thinking*. Boston: Allyn and Bacon.

Schlegel, M. (1986, October). *Remediation of written language: Group teaching techniques*. Workshop presented at the Arizona Association for Children with Learning Disabilities, Phoenix, AZ.

Schlegel, M., & Bos, C. S. (1986). *STORE the story: Fiction/fantasy reading comprehension and writing strategy*. Unpublished manuscript, University of Arizona, Department of Special Education and Rehabilitation, Tucson.

Schumaker, J. B., Denton, P. H., & Deshler, D. D. (1984). *The paraphrasing strategy (Learning Strategies Curriculum)*. Lawrence, KS: University of Kansas.

Schumaker, J. B., Deshler, D. D., Alley, G. R., Warner, M. M., Clark, F. L., & Nolan, S. (1982). Error monitoring: A learning strategy for improving adolescent performance. In W. M. Cruickshank & J. Lerner (Eds.), *Best of ACLD: Vol. 3* (pp. 170-182). Syracuse, NY: Syracuse University Press.

Schumaker, J. B., Deshler, D. D., Nolan, S., Clark, F. L., Alley, G. R., & Warner, M. M. (1981). *Error monitoring: A learning strategy for improving academic performance of LD adolescents* (Research Report No. 32). Lawrence, KS: University of Kansas Institute for Research in Learning Disabilities.

Slater, W. H., Graves, M. F., & Piche, G. L. (1984, April). *The effects of structural organizers on ninth-grade students' comprehension and recall of four patterns of expository text*. Paper presented at the American Educational Research Association Convention, New Orleans.

Slingerland, B. H. (1971). *A multisensory approach to language arts for specific language disability children: A guide for primary teachers*. Cambridge, MA: Educators Publishing Service.

Smith, E. M., & Alley, G. R. (1981). *The effect of teaching sixth graders with learning difficulties a strategy for solving verbal math problems* (Research Report No. 39). Lawrence, KS: Institute for Research in Learning Disabilities.

Spalding, R. B., & Spalding, W. T. (1986). *The writing road to reading* (3rd ed.). New York: William Morrow.

Spargo, E. (Ed.). (1989). *Timed readings in literature.* Providence, RI: Jamestown.

Sparks, J. E. (1982). *Write for power.* Los Angeles: Communication Associates.

Stauffer, R. G. (1969). *Directing reading maturity as a cognitive process.* New York: Harper & Row.

Thomas, C. C., Englert, C. S., & Morsink, C. (1984). Modifying the classroom program in language. In C. V. Morsink (Ed.), *Teaching special needs students in regular classrooms* (pp. 239-276). Boston: Little, Brown and Company.

Thomas, E. L., & Robinson, H. A. (1972). *Improving reading in every class: A sourcebook for teachers.* Boston: Allyn and Bacon.

Thomas, K. (1978). Instructional applications of the cloze technique. *Reading World, 18,* 1-12.

Thornton, C. A., & Toohey, M. A. (1982-1985). *MATHFACT: An alternative program for children with special needs.* Brisbane, Australia: Queensland Division of Special Education.

Thurber, D. N. (1984). *D'Nealian manuscript: A continuous stroke approach to handwriting.* Novato, CA: Academic Therapy.

Thurber, D. N. (1988). The D'Nealian pencil grip. *Communication Outlook, 9*(4), 11.

Tierney, R. J., Readence, J. E., & Dishner, E. K. (1985). *Reading strategies and practices: A compendium* (2nd ed.). Boston: Allyn and Bacon.

Topping, K. (1987). Paired reading: A powerful technique for parent use. *Reading Teacher, 40,* 608-609.

Udall, A. J., & Daniels, J. E. (1991). *Creating the thoughtful classroom: Strategies to promote student thinking.* Tucson, AZ: Zephyr Press.

Ullman, R. K., Sleator, E. K., & Sprague, R. K. (1985). *ADD-H: Comprehensive Teacher's Rating Scale.* Champaign, IL: MetriTech.

Vallecorsa, A. L., Ledford, R. R., & Parness, G. G. (1991). Strategies for teaching composition skills to students with learning disabilities. *Teaching Exceptional Children, 23,* 52-55.

Venezky, R. L. (1970). Linguistics and spelling. In A. H. Marckwardt (Ed.), *Linguistics in school programs: The sixty-ninth yearbook of the National Society for the Study of Education* (pp. 264-274). Chicago: University of Chicago Press.

Wallach, G. P., & Lee, A. D. (1982). So you want to know what to do with language-disabled children above the age of six. In K. G. Butler & G. P. Wallach (Eds.), *Language disorders and learning disabilities* (pp. 99-113). Rockville, MD: Aspen.

Wallach, G. P., & Miller, L. (1988). *Language intervention and academic success.* Boston: Little, Brown and Company.

Wehrli, K. (1971). *Cues and signals in reading, I-IV.* Novato, CA: Academic Therapy.

Wender, P.H. (1987). *The hyperactive child, adolescent, and adult: Attention deficit disorder through the lifespan.* Oxford: Oxford University Press.

Wiig, E. H., & Secord, W. (1988). *Test of Language Competence—Expanded Edition.* San Antonio: The Psychological Corporation.

Wong, B. Y. L. (1985). Potential means of enhancing content skills acquisition in learning disabled adolescents. *Focus on Exceptional Children, 17*(5), 1-8.

Wong, B. Y. L., & Jones, W. (1982). Increasing metacomprehension in learning disabled and normally achieving students through self-questioning training. *Learning Disability Quarterly, 5,* 228-240.

Woodcock, R. W., & Johnson, M. B. (1989). *Woodcock-Johnson Psycho-Educational Battery— Revised.* Allen, TX: DLM.

Woodcock, R. W., & Mather, N. (1989a). WJ-R Tests of Cognitive Ability—Standard and Supplemental Batteries: Examiner's Manual. In R. W. Woodcock & M. B. Johnson, *Woodcock-Johnson Psycho-Educational Battery—Revised.* Allen, TX: DLM.

Woodcock, R. W., & Mather, N. (1989b). WJ-R Tests of Achievement—Standard and Supplemental Batteries: Examiner's Manual. In R. W. Woodcock & M. B. Johnson, *Woodcock-Johnson Psycho-Educational Battery—Revised.* Allen, TX: DLM.